D1518263

The Japanese Civil Service and
Economic Development

The Japanese Civil Service and Economic Development

Catalysts of Change

Edited by

HYUNG-KI KIM
MICHIO MURAMATSU
T. J. PEMPEL
AND KOZO YAMAMURA

CLARENDON PRESS · OXFORD
1995

Oxford University Press, Walton Street, Oxford OX2 6DP

Oxford New York
Athens Auckland Bangkok Bombay
Calcutta Cape Town Dar es Salaam Delhi
Florence Hong Kong Istanbul Karachi
Kuala Lumpur Madras Madrid Melbourne
Mexico City Nairobi Paris Singapore
Taipei Tokyo Toronto
and associated companies in
Berlin Ibadan

Oxford is a trade mark of Oxford University Press

Published in the United States
by Oxford University Press Inc., New York

Editorial Organization © Hyung-Ki Kim, Michio Muramatsu,
T. J. Pempel, and Kozo Yamamura 1995

All rights reserved. No part of this publication may be reproduced,
stored in a retrieval system, or transmitted, in any form or by any means,
without the prior permission in writing of Oxford University Press.
Within the UK, exceptions are allowed in respect of any fair dealing for the
purpose of research or private study, or criticism or review, as permitted
under the Copyright, Designs and Patents Act, 1988, or in the case of
reprographic reproduction in accordance with the terms of the licences
issued by the Copyright Licensing Agency. Enquiries concerning
reproduction outside these terms and in other countries should be
sent to the Rights Department, Oxford University Press,
at the address above

British Library Cataloguing-in-Publication Data
Data available

Library of Congress Cataloging in Publication Data
The Japanese civil service and economic development: catalysts of
change/edited by Hyung-Ki Kim . . . [et al.].
Includes bibliographical references.
1. Civil service—Japan. 2. Japan—Economic policy—1945–
3. Civil service. I. Kim, Hyung-Ki, 1936–
JQ1646.J35 1995   95-3096   354.520082—dc20

ISBN 0–19–828938–3

1 3 5 7 9 10 8 6 4 2

Typeset by Best-set Typesetter Ltd., Hong Kong
Printed in Great Britain on
acid-free paper by
Bookcraft Ltd., Midsomer Norton, Avon

DEC 1 3 1995

FOREWORD

The decade of the 1980s represents a watershed in economic policy-making worldwide. Most countries, rich and poor, have taken liberalizing measures to create markets that are more efficient, or, as in many of the centrally planned economies, to create markets for the first time.

Governments have often proven to be inefficient in managing economies, and their roles are being challenged, changed, and, often, diminished. Many countries are now in a period of transition, struggling to implement these economically liberalizing measures which are intellectually rooted in what some economists have called the 'neoclassical resurgence'. This school of thought affirms the efficacy of market-determined prices in allocating economic resources. Exceptions to the rule apply to those goods and services for which no markets exist, or where their markets have severe imperfections. In these cases, other arrangements must be made.

In the late 1980s and early 1990s, economic liberalization has had an important influence on institutional development. For example, financial systems and their associated legal and regulatory frameworks must be created to support economic reforms. In the process, existing institutions, in which many people have vested interests, must be dismantled or modified; people must be trained to create and sustain the new institutions; and long-standing preconceptions must be reshaped. Out of this transitional turmoil emerges an important and challenging role for government institution-building activities. In response to this challenge, the World Bank has begun to support institutional development efforts, and civil service reform in particular, in both the developing and transitional economies.

The Japanese Civil Service and Economic Development: Catalysts of Change examines Japan's experience in this regard, and analyses the influence of public institutions and public management on the evolution of the Japanese economy. The study was prepared in the belief that Japan's remarkable economic and political transformation to a modern economy holds some important lessons for developing and transitional economies and for international financing institutions. The book analyses the evolution of Japan's civil service and the Japanese approach to the kinds of issues commonly faced by the civil service in developing and transforming economies—notably those related to structure, size, composition, orientation, function, and instruments for policy implementation. The central purpose is to provide the policy-makers of such economies with some insight into possible methods of reducing the many costs associated with

economic and political transactions. The study also includes a comparative analysis that draws on the experiences of Western European and
other countries with a view to informing decision-makers in the developing and transitional economies as they approach the restructuring of their
own civil services.

The Japanese experience with managing development has intrigued
policy-makers worldwide. In an attempt to understand these successes
the government of Japan established a Human Resources Development
Trust Fund at the World Bank which finances a *Program for the Study of the
Japanese Development Management Experience.* The Program is managed by
the Economic Development Institute of the World Bank.

As part of this program the lessons learned from the Japanese experience are published and offered to policy-makers from developing and
transitional economies to judge the relevance to their own current situations. The views expressed in this book, however, including any findings,
interpretations and conclusions, are entirely those of the authors and
should not be attributed in any manner to the World Bank, to its affiliated
organizations, or to members of its board of Executive Directors or the
countries they represent.

Michael Bruno
Vice President, Development Economics and Chief Economist
The World Bank

CONTENTS

LIST OF FIGURES

LIST OF TABLES

LIST OF CONTRIBUTORS

KENGO AKIZUKI

Kengo Akizuki is Associate Professor of Public Administration at Kyoto University, Faculty of Law. His research interests cover local politics-administration, intergovernmental relations, and bureaucratic behavior. His articles include 'Non Routine Policymaking and Intergovernmental Relations' (*Kyoto Law Review*, Vol. 123 [1988]), 'Interests, Institution, Ideology' (*Kyoto Law Review*, Vol. 131 [1992]), 'Airports as Public Business' (*Nenpo Gyosei Kenkyu*, Vol. 23 [1993]).

JOHN O. HALEY

John Haley is Garvey, Schubert & Barer Professor of Law and Professor of International Studies at the University of Washington, where he has taught Japanese law since 1974. Mr. Haley holds degrees from Princeton University, Yale Law School, and the University of Washington. He has lived in Japan for over six years beginning in 1964 as a teaching assistant at the International Christian University in Tokyo under the auspices of Princeton-in-Asia. In 1971–72 he was a Senior Fulbright Research Scholar at Kyoto University, from 1972–74 with the law firm of Blakemore & Mitsuki, in 1984 a Visiting Professor of Law, Kobe University, and most recently in 1992–93 Fulbright Lecturer at Tohoku University. In 1980–81 he was an Alexander von Humboldt Research Scholar at Freiburg University. He has also served as a Visiting Professor at the Harvard Law School, Monash University in Melbourne, Australia, and Tübingen University in Germany. In addition to his book entitled *Authority without Power: Law and the Japanese Paradox*, by Oxford University Press, he is coauthor with John Henry Merryman and David S. Clark of *The Civil Law Tradition: Europe, Latin America and East Asia* (forthcoming Michie). He has also authored numerous articles on Japanese law and was editor-in-chief of *Law in Japan: An Annual* for over a decade. He is currently working on a book entitled *The Spirit of Japanese Law* for a University of Georgia Press series edited by Professor Alan Watson.

PETER A. HALL

Peter A. Hall is Professor of Government and Senior Research Associate at the Center for European Studies of Harvard University. His books include: *Governing the Economy: The Politics of State Intervention in Britain and France* (New York: Oxford University Press, 1986), *The Political Power of*

xvi *List of Contributors*

Economic Ideas: Keynesianism across Nations (Princeton: Princeton University Press, 1989), and *Developments in French Politics* (with H. Machin and J. Hayward; London: Macmillan, 1991). He is also the author of many articles on public policymaking and comparative political economy with a special emphasis on Western Europe.

TAKENORI INOKI

Takenori Inoki is Professor of Labor Economics at Osaka University (Osaka, Japan). His published works include *Aspects of German Peasant Emigration to the United States 1815–1914* (New York: Arno Press, 1981), *Skill Formation in Japan and Southeast Asia* (coauthored, Tokyo: University of Tokyo Press, 1990), and *Economic Thought* (in Japanese) (Tokyo: Iwanamishoten, 1987). He is one of the editors and authors of an eight-volume series, *Japanese Economic History*, recently published by Iwanamishoten. Currently, he is writing a book on the structure and functioning of the labor market in Japan.

MITSUTOSHI ITO

Mitsutoshi Ito is Professor of Policy Science for College at Ritsumeikan University. He is coauthor (with Michio Muramatsu) of *Chiho gi-in no kenkyu* (The Study of Local Councillors) (Tokyo: Nihon Keizai Shinbunsha, 1986), (with M. Muramatsu and Yutaka Tsujinaka) of *Sengo Nihon no atsuryoku dantai* (Pressure groups in post-war Japan) (Tokyo: Toyo Keizai Shinposha, 1986), and *Nihon no seiji* (Politics in Japan) (Tokyo: Yuhikaku, 1992). His current research focuses on the National Diet, local governments, and public policies in contemporary Japan as compared with other countries.

HYUNG-KI KIM

Hyung-Ki Kim is Chief of the Studies Division at the World Bank's Economic Development Institute (EDI). Before joining the World Bank he was with the Korean government holding such posts as Senior Policy Analyst in the President's Economic and Scientific Council, Director General of Policy Planning and Development in the Ministry of Science and Technology, and Vice Minister of Education. He has also served on the boards of many public entities and managed several public institutions including the School Rehabilitation Fund, the International Education Institute, and the Korea Science and Engineering Foundation. Mr. Kim was educated at Seoul National University, George Washington University, and Columbia University. He taught at Seoul National in the fields of mineral and energy economics and public policy. He was also a fellow at Harvard University's Center for International Affairs. He recently coedited, with

Masahiko Aoki, *Corporate Governance in Transitional Economies: Insider Control and Role of Banks* (1995).

TOSHIYA KITAYAMA

Toshiya Kitayama is Associate Professor in the School of Law at Kwansei Gakuin University where he teaches local government, central–local relations, and political economy of Japan. Mr Kitayama's articles in English include 'The Politics of State-Sanctioned Cartelization: The Case of the National Industrial Recovery Act,' Masters thesis, Dewey Library, Massachusetts Institute of Technology (1989) and 'Institutionalizing the Politics of Productivity in Japan: The Comparative and Historical Perspective,' *Kwansei Gakuin Law Review*, Vol. 13 (1991). He is currently working on a study of Japanese regional political economy from the perspective of technological development.

YUTAKA KOSAI

Yutaka Kosai is the President of the Japan Center for Economic Research. He earned his BA (economics, 1958) from the University of Tokyo and MA (economics, 1967) from Stanford University. From 1958–73, he served in the Planning Bureau, Economic Planning Agency (EPA); Enterprise Bureau, Ministry of International Trade and Industry; and Research Bureau, EPA. His previous posts in the EPA include Director of the Office of Research on the System of National Accounts (1973–6), Director of the Industrial Economic Affairs Division (1976–8), and Director of the Price Coordination Division (1978–80). Mr. Kosai was a Professor at the Tokyo Institute of Technology from 1981 until assuming his present position in 1987. His publications include: *The Contemporary Japanese Economy* (1984) and *The Era of High-Speed Growth* (1986). He was awarded the Suntory Gakugeisho in 1981, the Nikkei Keizai Tosho Bunkasho in 1982, and the Ohira in 1994.

IKUO KUME

Ikuo Kume earned his Ph.D. from Cornell University (government, 1994), and is Professor on the Faculty of Law at Kobe University. Kume's current research interest focuses on labor politics in postwar Japan. His dissertation is entitled 'Disparaged Success: Labor Politics in Postwar Japan.'

MASARU MABUCHI

Masaru Mabuchi is Associate Professor of the Faculty of Law at Osaka City University. He is the author of *The Political Economy of the Treasury Control* (Tokyo: Chuokoron-sha, 1994), which analyzes the role of the

Japanese financial ministry in the postwar era in terms of 'new institutionalism.' He is also the author of 'Deregulation and Legalization of Financial Policy' in Gary D. Allinson and Yasunori Sone, eds., *Political Dynamics in Contemporary Japan* (Ithaca and London: Cornell University Press, 1993) and the coauthor of 'Introducing a New Tax' in Samuel Kernell, ed., *Parallel Politics* (Washington: The Brookings Institution, 1991).

YOSHIRO MIWA

Yoshiro Miwa is Professor of Economics at the University of Tokyo, where he teaches industrial organization. His books include: *The Economic Analysis of Antimonopoly Law* (in Japanese) (Tokyo: Nihon Keizai Shimbunsha, 1982), *Firms and Industrial Organization in Japan* (in Japanese) (Tokyo: The University of Tokyo Press, 1990) (a new book with the same title in English based on this volume is forthcoming in 1995 from Macmillan, London), and *Financial Administration Reform* (in Japanese) (Tokyo: Nihon Keizai Shimbunsha, 1993). He is one of the coeditors of three books (all in Japanese and from the University of Tokyo Press, Tokyo): *Japanese Small Business* (with M. Tsuchiya, 1989), *Stock- and Land-Prices in Japan* (with K. G. Nishimura, 1990), and *Japanese Distribution Systems* (with K. G. Nishimura, 1991).

MICHIO MURAMATSU

Michio Muramatsu is Dean of the Faculty of Law at Kyoto University, and Chairman of the Japanese Political Science Association (*Nihon Seiji Gakkai*). His first book is entitled *Postwar Bureaucracy in Japan* (Tokyo: Toyokeizai Shinposha). His most recent book is on Japanese public administration and bureaucracy explaining the civil service system and personnel administration in postwar Japan. His works extend to pressure groups, local government, etc. He published numerous articles in English on Japanese politics including 'The Bureaucrats and Politicians in Policy Making: The Case of Japan,' *American Political Science Review*, Vol. 78, No. 1 (March 1984); 'The Conservative Policy Line and the Development of Patterned Pluralism', in Y. Yasukichi and K. Yamamura, ed., *Political Economy in Japan* (Stanford: Stanford University Press, 1987), both co-authored by Ellis Krauss.

YUKIO NOGUCHI

Yukio Noguchi is Professor of Economics at Hitotsubashi University, Tokyo, Japan. His recent English publications include 'Tax Reform Debates in Japan,' in M. J. Boskin and C. E. McLure, Jr., eds., *World Tax*

Reform: Case Studies of Developed and Developing Countries (San Francisco: Institute for Contemporary Studies, 1990); 'Budget Policy making in Japan,' in S. Kernell, ed., *Parallel Politics: Economic Policy Making in Japan and the United States* (Washington: The Brookings Institution, 1991); 'Population Aging, Social Security and Tax Reform,' in Anne Krueger and Takatoshi Ito, eds., *NBER East Asia Seminar in Economics and Politics of Tax Reform* (Chicago: University of Chicago Press, 1992); 'Land Problems and Policies in Japan: Structural Aspects,' in John Haley and Kozo Yamamura, eds., *Land Issues in Japan: A Policy Failure?* (Seattle: The Society for Japanese Studies, 1992); 'The Changing Japanese Economy and the Need for a Fundamental Shift in the Tax System,' *American Economic Review, Papers and Proceedings* (May 1992).

T. J. PEMPEL

T. J. Pempel is Glen B. and Cleone Orr Hawkins Professor of Political Science and Chairman of Asian Studies at the University of Wisconsin, Madison. He received his BA, MA, and Ph.D. degrees from Columbia University. From 1972 until 1991 he was on the faculty at Cornell University, and from 1980 to 1985 he was also Director of Cornell's East Asia Program. From 1991 to 1993 he was Professor of Political Science, Adjunct Professor of Business, and Director of the Center for Comparative Politics at the University of Colorado, Boulder. He has received research grants from the Fulbright Commission, the National Endowment for the Humanities, the Japan Foundation, and the National Science Foundation, among others. Most of his research has concentrated on Japanese politics and economics. He is the author of eight books and several dozen articles, including 'Corporatism Without Labor: The Japanese Anomoly?', 'The Unbundling of Japan, Inc.', *Policy and Politics in Japan: Creative Conservatism*, and most recently an edited volume entitled *Uncommon Democracies: The One Party Dominant Regimes*. He is currently finishing a book entitled *Regime Shift: The Changing Character of Japan's Political Economy*.

BERNARD S. SILBERMAN

Bernard S. Silberman is Professor of Political Science at the University of Chicago. His work has been primarily concerned with the development of the Japanese civil service in the period 1868–1945. In this area, he is the author of *Ministers of Modernization: Elite Mobility in the Meiji Restoration: 1868–73* (Tucson: University of Arizona Press, 1964), and editor along with H. D. Harootunian of *Modern Japanese Leadership: Transition and Change* (Tucson: University of Arizona Press, 1966), and *Japan in Crisis: Essays on Taisho Democracy* (Princeton: Princeton University Press, 1974).

More recently he has been working on the comparative aspects of state bureaucratic development which led to the publication of *Cages of Reason: The Rise of the Rational State in France, Japan, the United States, and Great Britain* (Chicago: University of Chicago Press, 1993). His current research focuses on the emergence of the rational organization in the private sphere and the role of the state in this process in Japan, France, Germany, the United States, and Great Britain.

Judith Thornton

Judith Thornton is a Professor of Economics at the University of Washington. Her research focuses on the economy of Russia and its energy sector. She currently serves as Director of the Russian Far East Economy Project at the University of Washington and as president of the Association for Comparative Economic Studies. Recent articles include: 'Are Socialist Industries Inoculated against Innovation: A Case Study of Technological Change in Steel-making,' *Comparative Economic Studies* (Summer, 1989); 'The Consequences of Crisis for the Russian Far East Economy and for the Russo-Japanese Economic Relationship,' (with Alexander Temkin), in *Russia and Japan: An Unresolved Dilemma between Distant Neighbors*, ed. by Tsuyoshi Hasegawa *et al.* (Berkeley: University of California Press, IAS International Research Series, No. 87, 1993), pp. 299–339; 'Recent Changes in the Environment for Investment in Russia and the Asian Newly Independent States,' in *Recent Changes in the Environment for Investment in Russia*, Report for Russell 20–20, The Foundation for Russian-American Economic Cooperation (September 1992), pp. 1–17; 'Russian Industry and Air Pollution: What Do the Official Data Show?' (with Andrea Hagan), *Comparative Economic Studies*, Vol. 34, No. 2 (Summer, 1992), pp. 19–37.

Meredith Woo-Cumings

Meredith Woo-Cumings is Associate Professor of Political Science at Northwestern University. She is author, under the name Jung-en Woo, of *Race to the Swift: State and Finance in Korean Industrialization* (New York: Columbia University Press, 1991). She has also coedited two books—*Past as Prelude: History in the Making of New World Order* and *Financial Liberalization in Interventionist States*. Her current project, which critically examines the 'developmental state' argument, will culminate in an edited book entitled *The Developmental State in Comparative Perspective*.

Kozo Yamamura

Kozo Yamamura is the Job and Gertrud Tamaki Professor of Japanese Studies and Professor of East Asian Studies, Henry M. Jackson School of

International Studies, University of Washington. He is author of numerous works on Japanese economic history and on many issues in postwar economic growth and policy. Most recently, he has been a contributing editor to *The Political Economy of Japan, Volume 1: The Domestic Transformation* (Stanford: Stanford University Press, 1987); *Japanese Investment in the United States: Should We Be Concerned?* (Seattle: Society for Japanese Studies, 1989); *Japan's Economic Structure: Should It Change?* (Seattle: Society for Japanese Studies, 1990); and *Land Issues in Japan: A Policy Failure?* (Seattle: Society for Japanese Studies, 1992).

Introduction

This volume has developed from a World Bank project on the evolution, character, and structure of the Japanese civil service and its roles in shaping the interrelationship between the government and the private sector. The project was initiated and managed by the Economic Development Institute of the World Bank, and its central goal was not to produce a collection of essays dealing with selected analytic issues primarily of academic interest to social scientists specializing in Japan or comparative political economy. Rather, the aim was to present descriptions, discussions, and perspectives that would be useful to those managing the economic growth of developing nations.

The premise of this project is that there have been links between Japan's phenomenally successful economic growth and the character of its civil service. Furthermore, the project began with the assumption that an understanding of those links can be of practical use to those who are today managing the economic growth of currently industrializing countries. This is true, the project contends, even though the specific situations and problems these current policymakers confront are significantly different in important specifics from those Japan faced in various earlier time periods.

Although we believe that in Japan, as in most countries, the links between governments and markets are profoundly important for economic development, this book attempts to avoid many of the overly simplistic analyses that often dominate contemporary discussions of government–business relations in Japan. Too frequently, these revolve around the question of government versus markets: has the competitiveness of Japanese industry been improved because of, despite, or irrespective of government involvement? The research papers in this work, we believe, take no collective and unambiguous position on such a question, primarily because the answer depends so heavily on identifying specific industries, time periods, government involvements, and the like. As a consequence, the book represents no embrace of neoclassical interpretations of Japanese governmental agencies. Nor is it an industrial policy tract attempting to validate alleged and unwaveringly positive contributions made by the Japanese civil service to the nation's economic success.

For us, the more interesting questions concern how and in which specific ways the structures, incentives, and policies of the Japanese civil service have interacted with market forces. When and in what ways have features of the Japanese civil service been conducive to, and equally importantly, been inconducive to, positive economic development in Japan? With these in mind, we have sought to address questions concerning the sorts of lessons that policymakers in other countries might draw from the Japanese experience in confronting their own specific developmental difficulties.

We believe that there are at least four broad areas in which these essays offer particularly positive contributions. First, there is a wide array of new factual information linking the Japanese civil service and economic development. Second, there is a constant message that one of the major reasons for the success of the Japanese civil service has been the extent to which competitive forces have been built into the entire framework of the civil service. Third, the broad formal scope of authority given to most Japanese governmental agencies is combined with limited formal power to 'force' its will on unwitting client groups, or on the business and political sectors as a whole. As a consequence, much of the strength of individual agencies and of the civil service in combination relies on the power to convince, cajole, bargain, and otherwise act as 'political' rather than 'purely administrative' agencies. Finally, the book makes it clear that many of the most successful contributions made by the civil service to economic growth have been those that have been congruent with, rather than designed to overcome, market forces. While the book offers many more specific facts and lessons, these broad suggestions run constantly through the bulk of the chapters and provide a useful way of summarizing much of the book's potential value.

New Information

One of the more important contributions made by this study is the simple accumulation of new information about the structures, functioning, and policymaking activities of the Japanese civil service. While there is some Western-language material on the civil service generally, and more detailed information on specific agencies or policy arenas, this project brings together a range of new information and data, most of it unavailable in Western languages. A significant portion of the work involves original research and is consequently unavailable even in Japanese.

The essays in the first part of the volume provide the broad context and framework for the entire project. The opening essay by T. J. Pempel and Michio Muramatsu examines the Japanese bureaucracy within a comparative context. It examines the general pitfalls to which bureaucracies are prone and demonstrates why Japan's seems to have done better than most. The essay provides a succinct discussion of the political context within which Japan's civil service has operated for the past 125 years, covering a range of extensive and integrated details on the organization of the civil service; the methods by which it promotes its competence, coordination, and creativity; and the budgetary and other mechanisms with which the size of the civil service has been controlled. It also offers a broad argument as to how these components have provided positive links between the Japanese civil service and macroeconomic policies.

John Haley follows this with an examination of the legal framework for the Japanese civil service. His focus is on the postwar legal structure of public administration, and he provides a variety of new information on how the legal structure insulates the implementation of laws from political intervention and how the relative autonomy of the ministries from political control helps to generate a corps of professional civil servants. The legal system maintains accountability to the public and manages to provide for the redress of grievances both through individual agencies and through the judicial system.

Rounding out the first section, Kozo Yamamura offers a broad historical overview of the reasons for the success of Japan's 'catch-up' economic growth from 1880 to 1973. Focusing on the role of institutions and ideology, Yamamura shows how these two combined to encourage innovative activities and capital formation. Throughout, he argues, the civil service played a crucial and active role in promoting the 'catch-up' ideology and in increasing Japan's abilities to adopt new technologies, to save, and to take risks. This chapter also provides descriptions of numerous specific policies and practices mobilized for Japanese growth since the country began its industrialization.

Part Two concentrates on the evolution, over the prewar and postwar periods, of relations between the civil service and the private sector. Rather than seeking to demonstrate the supremacy of one sector over the other, the essays in this section show unambiguously how the two have been successfully fused within the Japanese experience. With an examination of competing types of bureaucratic rationality and their role in political stabilization, Bernard Silberman provides considerable information on the institutionalization of a rational state bureaucracy in early Meiji Japan (1868–1912). For him, bureaucratic rationality represents an organizational and institutional equilibrium reached as a means of resolving the persisting problems between politics and markets.

Silberman's focus on early Meiji is followed by an examination by Michio Muramatsu and T. J. Pempel of the evolution of the Japanese bureaucracy and its relations to civil society from the early twentieth century through World War II. A period on which there is little data, even among students of the Japanese civil service, this time was critical particularly in so far as political patronage was purged from the civil service and the career aspirations of individual civil servants were harmonized with broader national goals.

Yutaka Kosai also examines the relationship between government and business, primarily in the period since the first oil shock of 1973. In addition to providing a knowledgeable survey of the changes in relations between government and business over time, he demonstrates why macroeconomic policies were so relatively effective in the 1970s but were less so in the following decade. His analysis shows that, as economic coordinator and rule-setter, the civil service has simply become less welcome and less effective in the eyes of the private sector due to the fact that the national economy has become vastly more deregulated and competitive than it was in earlier periods. The economic successes of individual Japanese firms in the 1990s are simply no longer automatically guaranteed to correspond with what the government perceives to be desirable macroeconomic policies and what it defines as the national interest.

The post-retirement policies of *amakudari* are examined by its leading student, Takenori Inoki. Under *amakudari*, upon retirement officials 'descend from heaven' to take high-level positions in public corporations and in the private sector, usually around age 55. Inoki provides a great deal of information on the various practices that have prevailed historically and their consequences for government-business relations. Most importantly, he demonstrates how *amakudari* functions as an important incentive for individuals to attain high-level positions within the civil service.

In the final chapter in this section, Mitsutoshi Ito explores the persistent efforts by the Japanese government to maintain a small, efficient civil service. Again, this is an area that has not been subjected to extensive research in the West. Yet, as Ito demonstrates, these efforts have provided a vital mechanism for controlling the size and cost of Japan's civil service. Collectively labeled 'administrative reform,' these efforts have taken a variety of forms over time, including limits on personnel and agency budgets, the simplification of regulations, and the reduction of agency authority. Most recently, and parallel to efforts in other advanced democracies, Japan has worked toward the privatization of once publicly owned and operated corporations, including the national telephone system and the national railways. Reform efforts have also been targeted at the public pension program. All of these are extensively detailed by Ito.

Following this broad overview, Part Three includes a series of cases that elucidate the character, motivation, constraints, effectiveness, and changes in the policies, functions, and behavior of the bureaucracy and bureaucrats.

Yukio Noguchi provides a detailed description of Japan's 'second budget,' the Fiscal Investment and Loan Program (FILP). This program represented 3.5–4.0 per cent of GNP during the 1950s and early 1960s, increasing to over 5 per cent of GNP in the mid- to late 1960s and rising to 7-plus per cent in the 1970s and early 1980s. It clearly has formed an integral part of the national budget and the total economy since 1973. In his analysis, Noguchi shows how monies generated as a consequence of Japan's high personal saving rates were channeled into the FILP, and in turn were used to aid economic growth, to redress regional and sectoral disparities, and to meet changing infrastructural needs. These, he shows, were of vital importance for the development of heavy industry in the early 1960s.

Masaru Mabuchi follows with an analysis of the positive interconnections between Japan's Ministry of International Trade and Industry and the Ministry of Finance in the allocation of bank funds to specific industries. Providing a valuable description of the banking system, the Bank of Japan, and these two ministries, he shows how competition between Japan's two major 'economic agencies' and their private-sector networks have in fact forced them to generate a complementary and positive interplay between one another and consequently between Japan's industrial and financial sectors.

The Ministry of Labor is examined by Ikuo Kume in a way that is different from the usual focus on labor-union control and the resolution of labor–management disputes. Kume provides detailed descriptions of government efforts in the early postwar period to address widespread unemployment, of policy changes that occurred in subsequent decades in response to changes in the economy, and of the segregation of labor market and social welfare policies. He shows how ministry policies have reduced unemployment and prevented the development of a semipermanent underclass in Japan, while at the same time reducing reliance on public-sector jobs as the employment vehicle of last resort. This 'market-oriented' labor market policy grew, paradoxically, out of active political intervention but in the long run was highly conducive to the development and maintenance of a highly skilled national labor pool.

A good deal of new information on the links among local and central governmental agencies and among small and medium-sized industries and Japan's larger conglomerates is provided by the next three essays. Kengo Akizuki gives an extensive description of the financial relationship between the two levels of government through a focus on the Ministry of Home Affairs. This agency has managed to exert a stabilizing effect on local governments through its oversight functions and also at times to serve as the 'national voice' of local governments. In spite of local governments' dependence on the national budget, they are still able to initiate policies, pursue their own goals, and be politically autonomous.

Toshiya Kitayama examines the linkages between local governments and Japan's smaller and medium-sized enterprises (SMEs). Local governments, he argues, have sought to encourage the development and growth of such firms as a means of aiding their own regional economies. Using new and detailed information from both Osaka and Kumamoto Prefectures, he analyzes the policies of local governments, particularly their use of low-interest loans as opposed to outright grants, as a means to guide and generate effective new industries in specific regions. The entrepreneurship of these firms, local governmental policies, and linkages to larger Japanese firms have all been positively fused as a means to national economic development, he argues.

A dissenting view is provided by Yoshiro Miwa's chapter. Although he accepts the notion that local governments have indeed created the kinds of policies described by Kitayama, he contends that the economic effectiveness of these policies has not been particularly impressive. In his eyes, the success of the SMEs, while of great import to the overall national growth of the country, has not been discernibly connected to local governmental policy initiatives. Furthermore, he points out that the profit rates of SMEs, their relations with larger firms, and the increase in their numbers indicate that smaller firms have been neither exploited nor victimized by what some call the 'dual structure' of Japan's economy.

The combined impact of these chapters is to provide a great deal of new and detailed information on the structure, character, and functioning of the Japanese civil service, with particular reference to the ways these have been connected to Japan's economic performance over time. They are followed by four essays in Part Four that put the Japanese experience into comparative perspective. Here too is something of a substantially new perspective, since Japan is so frequently analyzed in isolation.

Meredith Woo-Cumings looks at the Korean civil service and shows how, rather than being a simple mirror-image of the Japanese civil service, it has its own rich history and tradition. Yet, 35 years of Japanese colonization (1910–45) has worked in conjunction with conscious Korean efforts to emulate the Japanese model. The result is that of all the other civil services in the world, Korea's probably bears the closest similarity to that of Japan.

Judith Thornton examines the Japanese experience in comparison to the Russian links between civil service and economic development. She shows how the two countries followed divergent paths since the early twentieth century, yet suggests that the former Soviet Union and the other command economies of Eastern Europe may now be looking to Japan for lessons on how to structure themselves for future, market-driven economic growth. However, she warns these countries against focusing on those formal properties of Japan's civil service that seem superficially closest to those with which they are most familiar, e.g., close government–private sector ties, public and quasi-public production facilities, industrial groups and oligopolies, and tight regulation of foreign trade and investment. Such an orientation, she argues, could easily serve as a barrier to the kinds of pro-market changes these countries now need.

Peter Hall provides a comparison of the Japanese experience in light of that of Western Europe, his own area of expertise. In highlighting some of the major contributions of the earlier papers, he also draws in the experiences of many European countries to show how so many aspects of the Japanese experience differentiate its history from that of many currently industrializing countries. Most particularly, Japan did not have to confront major problems of public order, serious ethnic and religious tensions, a hostile military, or massive inequalities in distribution. But with regard to the civil service itself, he demonstrates that many of the most valuable lessons to be drawn from the Japanese experience parallel those of the best experiences of its European counterpart.

The final essay in the volume is by Hyung-Ki Kim, who views the Japanese experience from the perspective of one who managed development policy in his own country and who, as a World Bank official, has advised and assisted other countries on their development policies and projects. Kim begins with a review of the academic literature that seeks to explain the roles played by the Japanese government in promoting economic development. Then he reexamines the historical record and proceeds to offer his own view that is in accordance with the Alexander Gerschenkron's generalization that governments' roles in the economies of their countries are dictated by the historical circumstances that countries find themselves in. Kim traces the major features of the historical circumstances that have shaped the evolving role of government in Japan around an underlying strong and historically persistent political imperative of catching up with and surpassing the West.

Japan's response to its historical situation helped to shape a civil service that was designed to facilitate the implementation of the country's strategic vision on the development of the economy. Kim outlines the features of this strategic vision and shows how the civil service has been able to deal with changing circumstances through timely changes in policies and institutions. In Kim's view, the good performance of the civil service has been based on the purposeful creation and maintenance of an elite with its own *esprit de corps* and with considerable autonomy from day-to-day political considerations.

Competition in the Japanese Civil Service

The Japanese civil service from its very start in the last third of the nineteenth century has been structured to recruit the nation's most highly talented personnel (as measured by educational achievements). These individuals have been recruited through meritocratic rather than political or personalistic criteria. Once in government agencies, those recruited have typically served in single agencies for the bulk of their professional careers, demonstrating high degrees of loyalty to these agencies and to their profession. They have been relatively well paid and have been given wide scope in carrying out their duties. This will strike many as congruent with Weberian notions of bureaucratic rationality, and indeed, for the most part, Japan, like France and Germany, developed civil services that were patterned after the Weberian ideal.

Yet, as Silberman points out in his contribution to the volume, there is no evidence of a direct relationship between such a form of bureaucratic rationality and economic development. Indeed, in the United States and Britain, economic achievements were made under alternative conceptions of 'bureaucratic rationality,' that hinged centrally on the individual 'professionalism' of those in the civil service, a personalistic set of achievements largely divorced from the structure of the bureaucratic institutions themselves.

One of the larger lessons that emerges from this study is the fact that unlike Weber's ideal bureaucracy, Japan's civil service has been marked by high levels of internal competition that have fostered improved performances. This competition has been built into the civil service, both in terms of personnel and in terms of agency-to-agency relations. In many respects, Japan's civil service is the embodiment of the most elementary principles of market competition.

As noted above, Japan's civil service from its very origins in the late nineteenth century, has attracted the country's 'best and brightest,' at least as measured by the nation's highly competitive educational system. Civil servants are recruited through a national testing system administered by the National Personnel Authority. Extensive internal training is available to civil servants. Through the system, most civil servants work long and hard, competing vigorously with one another for the rewards of promotion and ever higher and more responsible positions. This provides a dimension of competition and initiative throughout the personnel system. Meanwhile, retirement comes relatively early and with apparent grace, leaving top positions free from gerontocracy, and open to be filled by individuals in their late 40s and early to mid-50s. And, as the Inoki chapter makes clear, many retiring civil servants relocate to new positions, thereby bringing their skills into the service of the private sector while they are still at ages that allow them to make major, active contributions.

Furthermore, the quality of the specific positions to which retirement occurs varies greatly, introducing still another degree of personal competition into the process: those whose careers have proven to be the most valued by the civil service's leadership wind up with the best post-bureaucratic posts. The post-retirement 'carrot' serves more effectively as a personal motivation for many civil servants than any harsher 'stick' of top-down control and formal rules.

As a consequence of this mixture of traits, the personnel system in Japan's civil service works exceptionally well to attract, retain, train, and subsequently put to productive use, a highly skilled group of individuals. The civil service also utilizes them in ways that bring out some of their most valuable inherent traits. And throughout their careers, individuals are constantly engaged in a bounded, but quite real, competitive situation that encourages them to demonstrate high degrees of loyalty, diligence, and initiative.

Competition among agencies, and among levels of government, as with individuals, is also extensive, building another layer of inventiveness and competition throughout the civil service that is often lacking in public-sector agencies in other countries. In addition to the competition among individuals noted above there is intensive competition among agencies, and among levels of government—all of which has been generally conducive to overall governmental efficiency and ultimately to economic growth.

Thus as Mabuchi points out, the Ministry of Finance (MOF) and the Ministry of International Trade and Industry (MITI) have long been competitive with one another for overall power and influence. But MOF has its primary strengths in the development and allocation of capital and it is in the banking, securities, and insurance industries that its closest ties exist. Meanwhile, MITI's strengths have been in technological analysis and market conditions for manufactured products and raw materials. It is there that the agency has its closest ties, and in those areas that it has been most adept. Yet this competition and balance of strengths works together positively since the two agencies have historically been forced to cooperate with one another in the allocation of funds to specific firms and industrial groups, with the knowledge and expertise of each agency providing an essential ingredient to industrial funding, as well as a potential check over the competing knowledge and expertise of the other agency.

Rather different is the competition that exists between the national and the local levels of government. Akizuki, for example, notes how the Ministry of Home Affairs (MHA) serves primarily as a financial overseer of local governmental budgets, ensuring the kind of local governmental responsibility that has not been found in many other countries. Furthermore, the agency has been the simultaneous supporter of the specific industrial aims of many local governmental agencies and a strong advocate of local autonomy *vis-à-vis* the national government. Hence, despite Japan's image as a country with a strong central, and a weak local, system of government, local government initiatives in fact are quite frequent. These in turn allow for a good deal of testing and competition among local governmental projects, with the best and most efficient serving as subsequent models for national governmental policy formulation.

Building from similar notions of local competition and competition between national and local government agencies, Kitayama's study points out how different local governments in various regions have dealt quite differently in their efforts to encourage the development of various small and medium-sized firms in targeted industrial sectors. In many instances, these have encouraged the development of drastically different forms of industrial organization which have in turn proven successful challenges to the dominant mass manufacturing, Fordist principles that prevailed in many other countries. These new manufacturing techniques, in turn, have led to significant reorganization of manufacturing production facilities in both the large and small firms in Japan, with significant overall increases in national productivity.

Furthermore, Japan's is a competition that involves real winners and real losers; agencies shrink and agencies die; others are created anew; budgets change radically over time; individual bureaucrats find their careers and rewards are linked to their performance. This point is brought out perhaps most forcefully in Ito's discussion of administrative reform. Throughout its modern history the Japanese civil service has been kept quite small in comparative terms through a series of reform measures that have required cutbacks in personnel, reductions in bureaus, simplification of procedures, and, most recently in the late 1980s and early 1990s, the privatization of various governmentally run services such as telecommunications and the national railways.

Throughout these administrative reform efforts, high levels of intra- and interagency competition have been built in. Many of the reforms were predicated on allowing individual agencies to make their own determinations of how to achieve cuts, so long as nationwide or agency-targeted goals were achieved. (See, for example, the Law concerning the Number of Personnel in Administrative Agencies of May 1969.) Agencies were thus forced continually to assess, and prune themselves. They had to shuck their less critical functions, and reassign their own personnel, in ways designed to deal with potentially more important socioeconomic problems. Moreover, agencies which could capture new tasks as 'their own' were provided with additional resources to tackle such new problems. Hence, agencies benefited differentially from their respective abilities to reform themselves on a continual basis.

In all of these ways, competition creates a systemic bias within the Japanese civil service that leaves it in sharp contrast to the normal association with what Michel Crozier has called 'the vulgar and frequent sense of the word "bureaucracy"' which, as he notes, 'evokes the slowness, the ponderousness, the routine, the complication of procedures, and the maladapted responses of "bureaucratic" organizations to the needs which they should satisfy, and the frustrations which their members, clients, or subjects consequently endure.'[1] Instead, what one gets is the creation of what Pempel and Muramatsu call a 'proactive' civil service. In order to win in the many competitions among agencies and individuals, the entire civil service is forced to remain sensitive to changing conditions in the economic markets, in the political arena, and in the areas over which they have jurisdiction.

Scope and Authority

Still a second broad conclusion from this volume concerns the limited but specific legal mandates under which Japan's various governmental agencies operate, as Haley notes in his contribution on Japan's legal framework. Agencies are given rather specific spheres of influence by law, and these include rather broad definitions of the kinds of actions they may take within those spheres. The powers of regulation of many agencies are quite elaborate and extensive; thus, the Ministry of Transport has nearly 2,000 specific licensing and approval powers. Local governments need national permission to alter local bus routes, fares, or the location of bus stops. Such controls are hardly conducive to rapid adjustments to changing conditions or to economic efficiency.

At the same time, within the Japanese system, as many administrative units with responsibilities in broadly defined jurisdictional fields as possible are combined within a single comprehensive agency. This achieves consistency by fostering compromise in the event of any substantial conflicts in the policies recommended or pursued by its separate sections. In many instances, the potential for conflict will be identified and resolved within the ministry.

Broad mandates have an important impact on the private sector in many respects, but one of the most important is that the industries which the government has regulated the most stringently—finance, transportation, distribution and trucking, among others—are at the heart of the entire economy. Hence actions within these more regulated areas tend to shape actions within the less regulated segments of the economy as well.

Despite such formal authority, Japan's governmental agencies are far from autonomous; they cannot typically exert rigid formal control over their respective spheres of influence. At a minimum, there is constitutional provision that government agencies be responsible to the elected governments. This ensures a broad degree of public responsiveness.

In addition, there is limited capacity for direct political interference with most Japanese governmental agencies, most of the time. In particular, as several papers make clear, there is little opportunity for direct pork barrel projects to find their way into most governmental policies.

[1] Michel Crozier, *The Bureaucratic Phenomenon* (Chicago: University of Chicago Press, 1964), p. 3.

Moreover, individual and judicial redress exists for those who believe they have been treated unfairly by government agencies.

As a consequence of this mixture of powers and limitations, Japan's governmental agencies must rely heavily on persuasion and the generation of consent, both with the constituencies they oversee and with the politicians who oversee them. It is rare that an agency will attempt to effect important policies through simple fiat.

Yet in the bargaining process, government agencies are not without useful tools, both 'hard' and 'soft.' Among the more important mechanisms of persuasion is 'administrative guidance,' with which agencies may utilize the broad scope of the laws under which they were established, or under which they are currently operating, to make 'suggestions' for appropriate behavior by groups under their jurisdiction. These are by no means always followed, but not all of those being overseen are quick to challenge such suggestions on a regular basis.

There is also a good deal of information-sharing among businesses, industrial groups, quasi-public corporations, government agencies, and the like, and here the government agencies are usually the holders of the most powerful informational cards in the political game. In addition to allowing agencies to operate from a basis of strength in facts, such information flow also allows for a degree of ease in working out compromises, at least in so far as everyone is working from a comparable information base. Furthermore, while good information by no means ensures 'good' economic policies, it does help to generate more 'coordinated' economic policies.

Finally, it is clear that a good deal of the coordination in Japanese economic policies and whatever coherence has been shown among government agencies grew out of the long-term rule by the Liberal Democratic Party (LDP). From its formation in 1955 until its split and replacement by a coalition government in 1993, the LDP held virtually 2:1 majorities over the next largest party in the Diet and virtually all cabinet positions. As a probusiness party with a strong commitment to economic growth, the LDP had every incentive to encourage the civil service to pursue similar policies and the civil service had every reason to follow such guidelines. Furthermore, because government agencies typically had technical expertise over the specific areas, and political authorities rarely had the staff or the structural incentives to challenge these agencies on the details of the policies they pursued, the agencies were typically accorded a good deal of political space in their actions. Most importantly for the overall direction of Japanese economic policies, neither side had many significant incentives to compete with, or to undermine, the long-term interests of Japanese economic development.

The LDP, during its long tenure, and particularly toward the end of that tenure, was constantly revealed to have been wide open to all forms of bribery and corruption, and indeed the party split in part as a result of its own inability to deal with such corruption. Yet, one of the more surprisingly positive features of the links between the LDP and the civil service is that while the LDP was open to corruption, there is little evidence that such patterns spilled over to the civil service. Indeed, the national bureaucracy has constantly been relatively corruption-free, marking it as quite different from the civil services in many other parts of the world.

Market Conformity

The policy contributions of the Japanese civil service to economic growth have occurred in a variety of areas. Most fundamentally, the book argues, the civil service has done a generally good job of setting macroeconomic conditions favorable to the high value-added segments of Japanese business. The book outlines numerous of these policies, including policies related to the national currency, the national budget, inflation, research and development, capital and technology allocation to industrial sectors, and the like.

Japan's civil service has been particularly sensitive to the ways in which the development of a broad and positive infrastructure can contribute more to national economic growth than specific interventions in the microeconomy. At least two different layers of infrastructure have been important. First, there is the standard economic infrastructural elements that are used by many different industries—harbors, roads, transportation links, communications facilities, and others.

A second contribution can be found in the government's contributions to what might be thought of as the nation's human infrastructure. This comes out most particularly in the analysis of Japan's labor market policies. The Ministry of Labor pursued a labor market policy designed to keep most individuals in the active work force through retraining and the encouragement of intrafirm reorganizations, rather than creating massive public works programs and using the government as the employer of last resort. Japan followed a market-oriented approach to occupational training, public works, and unemployment.

Whether consciously thought through or not at the time, such policies allowed Japan to keep unemployment low without burdening the national treasury with an unending expansion of costly tasks designed at least partially to absorb the nation's unemployed. Rather, the policies continuously restructured the labor market to train workers for new jobs and to move them into the private sector as frequently as possible.

The Japanese government has never been reluctant to attempt to 'soften' the immediate impact of market forces. Usually, however, there have been strict time and cash limits on its support, designed primarily to give firms the time needed to restructure to meet such new market forces effectively. In addition, Japan's entire economy was marked by a rather unusual mixture of market conformity and market insulation, particularly during Japan's early postwar (and much of its prewar) industrialization. On the one hand, government policies were often designed to insulate critical Japanese industries from the potentially damaging consequences of international competition. This was done at least until they were perceived to be capable of competing effectively in the international marketplace. At the same time, most of the domestic Japanese market remained highly competitive, as among Japan's largest conglomerates. In this way, domestic market share of an individual firm was heavily linked to its ability to provide a more efficient and more desirable product to the consumer. And ultimately, once it could do this for the Japanese market, it was better positioned to try its most effective strategies and products in the export market.

Among the specific ways the civil service played an important role in this regard was in its mixed treatment of firms and industries. As Kosai points out, Japan's civil service has generally intervened to favor specific industries as a whole—allowing for some elements of industrial policy—but at the same time has treated (large) firms within a single industry relatively equally—again allowing market principles and efficiencies to prevail.

Much of the Japanese government's intervention has also been market compatible. Note, for example, that both national and local governmental assistance to targeted industries has most frequently involved low-cost loans with long-term payback arrangements; rarely has it involved direct grants. Furthermore, government assistance has most often been conditional on individual firms restructuring, diversifying, or dissolving in ways designed to create greater overall conformity to long-term market conditions. Although this has been changing somewhat in recent years, Japan's governmental agencies have had only limited capacity to act in favor of long-term protection for declining industries, except as in many industrialized countries, in the areas of agriculture and distribution.

Another major way in which the Japanese government managed to act in market-conforming ways involved its own continued efforts to reduce its size and its costs. This necessitated a conscious opting out of any moves toward the creation of a large social welfare state, such as had begun to take root in much of Western Europe. With its long-term conservative-dominated political framework, and with tight constraints over the size and scope of the civil service as well as over the national budget, Japan maintained the industrial world's smallest and least costly government.

On the one hand, this low-cost government freed up capital for use in the private sector. It also allowed the Japanese government to escape from the high cost of deficit finance that has consumed scarce capital resources in many other countries and from which many of these countries are now struggling to escape. And finally, it also prevented Japan from becoming locked into an ever-expanding set of entitlement programs such as those that have begun to cause such financial havoc in Scandinavia and much of the rest of Europe, and even in the generally low-cost governmental countries of the United States and Canada.

Japan's has hardly been an economy structured along pure neoclassical market principles. But then again, few countries are. What is most striking about the Japanese case in this analysis is that Japan, which has won a public reputation as having a highly protectionist and antimarket-oriented civil service has in many of the above ways built in certain features of market competition that have been highly beneficial to the national economy and to long-term national economic growth.

One final brief conclusion that emerges from the combined papers is that there is nothing particularly significant about any allegedly unique aspects of Japanese culture. Neither the civil service itself, nor Japan's specific economic performance, is seen by any of the authors as the out-growth of some particularistic and endemic Japanese national character that prevents others from attempting specific replication of Japan's experience in other contexts. Much of what Japan underwent historically was the result of conscious emulation of other systems; still more was the result of changes superimposed on Japan during the Allied Occupation (1945–52). It is important to remember such matters so that the Japanese case does not emerge as *sui generis* and without comparability or applicability elsewhere. This point is explored in great detail throughout the book and in particular in the final section where the particular lessons from the Japanese experience are highlighted for various contemporary policymakers.

Finally, we wish to express our gratitude to the following organizations and individuals who made this volume possible: The Society for Japanese Studies, Seattle, as an organizational cosponsor of this project was helpful in the efficient administration of the various workshops and publication of this volume. In Japan, staff at Kyoto University were of great assistance in organizing a preliminary workshop in Mishima. For their roles as discussants at the final workshop, we are grateful to Susan B. Hanley of the University of Washington; Hideyuki Takahashi, formerly of Japan's Ministry of Construction; and several representatives from the World Bank, Oladipupo Adamolekun, Ed Campos, Masaaki Kaizuka, and Gary Reid. The editors are especially grateful to Martha L. Walsh of the Society for Japanese Studies for providing indispensable and truly professional assistance in administering the project and editing manuscripts. Hyung-Ki Kim expresses his special thanks to Christopher Willoughby who, during his tenure as Director of the Economic Development Institute of the World Bank, initiated the Program for the Study of Japan's Development Management Experience, and to Latifah Alsegaf who provided highly efficient administrative support. He also gratefully acknowledges the kind advice of Masahiko Aoki, Ronald Dore, and Hugh Patrick in shaping the Program.

The Editors

PART ONE

FRAMEWORK AND CONTEXT

1

The Japanese Bureaucracy and Economic Development:
Structuring a Proactive Civil Service

T. J. PEMPEL

MICHIO MURAMATSU

For centuries, cross-national investigation has been a vital lens through which people have gained insights on their own societies. From Aristotle to Tocqueville, individuals have studied other societies with an eye toward improving their own. In the contemporary world, policymakers and scholars alike examine the experiences of various countries searching for learnable lessons.[1] This search is particularly vigorous among statemakers involved in actively structuring, or restructuring, their own societies, such as is happening today in many of the developing countries and in Eastern Europe. But it is widespread among more well-established regimes as well, as politicians and policymakers search continually for better ways to achieve their desired ends.

With its tremendous economic performance both before World War II and in the period from the 1950s until the late 1980s, Japan has been seen by many as an enviable source of such comparative inspiration. In particular, with its history of late industrialization, and with cultural roots unlike those of the major powers of Europe and North America, Japan resonates more closely with the experiences of current state-builders and rebuilders who are outside the Anglo-European tradition.

The country might appear less worthy of emulation given its economic downturn in the early 1990s; for many, the poor performance of the Japanese stock market, the collapse of land prices, and the decline in the asset values of many Japanese banks during the early 1990s raised ques-

T. J. Pempel wishes to acknowledge the research assistance of Jack Keating and Todd Landman in various aspects of preparing this paper. He also wishes to thank Don Kettl, Ellis Krauss, Richard Samuels, and those who provided useful feedback in a seminar on this topic on December 10, 1992 at the Center for Comparative Politics, University of Colorado, Boulder. Michio Muramatsu would like to thank F. Takahashi and T. Kitamura for their help.

[1] A particularly informative study of the problem of lesson-drawing across nations can be found in the collected articles in *Journal of Public Policy*, Vol. 11, No. 1 (Jan.–Mar. 1991). See in particular Richard Rose, 'What is Lesson-Drawing?', pp. 3–30.

tions as to how inevitable the Japanese miracle really was.[2] Such events also opened up numerous questions about the inherent character of the entire Japanese political economy. This is not the place to enter into a full-scale discussion of such issues. Suffice it to say, the structural character-istics of Japan's economy remain fundamentally sound. Moreover, regardless of how the future of Japan's political economy plays out, the country's overall economic performance has unquestionably been among the most impressive in the world for the past 100 years and certainly warrants the designation made by *The Economist* in 1981: economically, the magazine declared, Japan is clearly 'The Best at the Game.'[3]

Japan's economic success poses many questions for both pundits and scholars; the most intriguing, and also the most divisive, revolve around the causes behind the country's economic achievements. The central question has been 'How did Japan accomplish its miracle?' with the subtext being 'Could it be replicated here as well?' For some, the answer lies in Japan's allegedly unique culture, with the automatic implication that it is therefore beyond replication.[4] For others, the success owes less to Japan itself and more to the timidity and/or stupidity of its trading partners and economic rivals.[5] Others concentrate instead on the import-ance of business behavior and market forces.[6] Some seek to pick and choose from among the more appealing elements of the Japanese experience.

This is not the place to engage such arguments. We do, however, find our own views compatible with many of them.[7] Our point here is that one

[2] One of the more compelling recent works is Christopher Wood, *The Bubble Economy: Japan's Extraordinary Speculative Boom of the '80s and the Dramatic Bust of the '90s* (New York: Atlantic Monthly Press, 1992).

[3] *The Economist*, July 18, 1981.

[4] Michio Morishima, *Why has Japan 'Succeeded'? Western Technology and the Japanese Ethos* (Cambridge: Cambridge University Press, 1982); Junichi Kyogoku, *The Political Dynamics of Japan* (Tokyo: University of Tokyo Press, 1987), especially Chap. 6. See also Ezra Vogel, *Japan as Number 1* (Cambridge, Mass.: Harvard University Press, 1979). A critique of such ap-proaches can be found in Peter N. Dale, *The Myth of Japanese Uniqueness* (London: Croom Helm, 1986).

[5] Among others, see Clyde Prestowitz, *Trading Places: How We Allowed Japan to Take the Lead* (New York: Basic, 1988); Pat Choate, *Agents of Influence* (New York: Knopf, 1990); Karel van Wolferen, *The Enigma of Japanese Power* (New York: Knopf, 1989); James Bovard, *The Fair Trade Fraud: How Congress Pillages the Consumer and Decimates American Competitiveness* (New York: St. Martin's Press, 1991); and, most recently, in a category that might be labeled 'pseudo-fiction,' Michael Crichton, *Rising Sun* (New York: Knopf, 1992).

[6] Among the foremost works in this vein, but one that is more sensitive than most purely economic treatments, is Hugh T. Patrick and Henry Rosovsky, eds., *Asia's New Giant: How the Japanese Economy Works* (Washington: Brookings Institution, 1976). See also Ryūtaro Komiya et al., eds., *Nihon no sangyō seisaku* (Tokyo: University of Tokyo Press, 1984); Philip H. Trezise, 'Industrial Policy is Not the Major Reason for Japan's Success,' *Brookings Review* (Spring 1983), pp. 123–56. For a more extensive review of this material, see the chapter in this volume by Kozo Yamamura.

[7] In particular we share the view of Richard Samuels that relations between the civil service and business have most frequently involved a process he labels 'reciprocal consent.' Richard Samuels, *The Business of the Japanese State: Energy Markets in Comparative and Histori-

particular aspect of Japan warrants particular attention in supporting Japan's economic growth, namely, its civil service. Widely touted as having played a critical role in Japan's modernization and subsequent economic success, the Japanese civil service undoubtedly holds out a variety of lessons on the links between a nation's bureaucracy and its economic performance. We find the existing evidence overwhelming that the Japanese government, Japanese governmental policies, and the Japanese civil service played a variety of critical roles in the long term, and in the more recent economic development of Japan.

Our argument, at the same time, is not a simple causal claim that the Japanese civil service planned, structured, and oversaw Japan's economic performance, much as a general contractor plans a building. Various Japanese government agencies undoubtedly made positive and direct contributions to Japan's economic performance. And indeed, the Japanese civil service has been highly 'proactive' in most areas related to the national economy. But our overall claims relate as much to the indirect links between the civil service and economic success, links that involve the personnel, size, budget, and competitiveness of the civil service. Moreover, our claims are tied to the ways in which the Japanese civil service is woven into the broader fabric of the Japanese political economy and its interconnected role with other organizations vital to Japan's economic performance.

By way of a quick overview: Japan's civil service has long attracted the country's 'best and brightest.' Extensive internal training is available to civil servants. Throughout the system, most civil servants work long and hard, competing vigorously with one another for the rewards of promotion and subsequent reemployment. This builds in a dimension of competition and initiative throughout the personnel system. The national bureaucracy is comparatively small and has deliberately been kept that way; it has been quite responsive to democratic political controls; petty corruption is minimal; retirement comes relatively early and with apparent grace, leaving top positions free from gerontocracy and open to be filled by individuals in their late 40s and early to mid-50s. Meanwhile, many retiring civil servants relocate to new positions, thereby bringing their skills into the service of the private sector.[8] In short, the personnel system seems to work exceptionally well in terms of attracting, retaining, and subsequently putting to productive use a highly skilled group of

cal Perspective (Ithaca: Cornell University Press, 1987), pp. 8–9. We also find ourselves largely in agreement with Daniel Okimoto, *Between MITI and the Market: Japanese Industrial Policy for High Technology* (Stanford: Stanford University Press, 1989).

[8] This phenomenon known as *amakudari*, or 'descent from heaven,' has been widely studied in Japan. See, e.g., Michio Muramatsu, *Sengo Nihon no kanryōsei* (The postwar Japanese bureaucratic system) (Tokyo: Tōyō Keizai, 1981), pp. 78–82; Kent Calder, 'Amakudari,' *Leviathan*, No. 6 (1991) as well as Chapter 7 in this volume.

individuals and utilizing them in ways that bring out some of their most valuable inherent traits.

Competition among agencies, as with individuals, is also extensive; this builds in an inventiveness and competition throughout the civil service that is often lacking in public sector agencies in other countries. The Japanese civil service stands in sharp contrast to the normal association with what Michel Crozier has called 'the vulgar and frequent sense of the word "bureaucracy"' which, as he notes, 'evokes the slowness, the ponderousness, the routine, the complication of procedures, and the maladapted responses of "bureaucratic" organizations to the needs which they should satisfy, and the frustrations which their members, clients, or subjects consequently endure.'[9]

In contrast, the exceptionally high degree of competition that is layered throughout the Japanese civil service—competition among individuals, among agencies, and among levels of government—has been generally conducive to overall governmental efficiency and ultimately to economic growth.

Furthermore, Japan's is a competition that involves real winners and real losers: agencies shrink and agencies die; others are created anew; budgets change radically over time; individual bureaucrats find their careers and rewards are linked to their performance.[10] In this sense, competition in Japan's civil service is quite different from that associated with, say, the branches of the US military. When those agencies 'compete' with one another, the end result has typically been that each branch gets a large proportion of what it demands, even when what it is demanding overlaps or conflicts with the demands of the other branches. For a long time in the 'game' of US military competition, there were rarely any losers. The end result was a never-ending spiral of expanding budgets, personnel, weapons systems, promotions, and paperwork.

In the Japanese case, the extremes of competition are mitigated to some extent by broad coordination mechanisms designed to foster intra-agency cooperation. There is competition between national and local administrative agencies as well, resulting in additional creative competition. Yet, national and local administrative agencies also work with reasonably high levels of coordination rather than conflict. And standing as the ultimate coordinator of competing interests has been the political power of the long-ruling Liberal Democratic Party (LDP).

[9] Michel Crozier, The Bureaucratic Phenomenon (Chicago: University of Chicago Press, 1964), p. 3.

[10] This viewpoint is at odds, for example, with the budgetary analysis of John C. Campbell, Contemporary Japanese Budget Politics (Berkeley: University of California Press, 1977). But cf. Mathew D. McCubbins and Gregory W. Noble, 'Perceptions and Realities of Japanese Budgeting,' in Peter Cowhey and Mathew D. McCubbins, eds., Structure and Policy in Japan and the United States: An Institutionalist Approach (Cambridge: Cambridge University Press, forthcoming).

Much of this creative competition, as we will argue in detail below, results from the strict outer limits set on the size, budgets, and programmatic expansiveness of individual bureaucrats and the various agencies. As a result, individuals, agencies, and levels of government compete against one another for different slices of a pie that is relatively fixed in size. Japanese agency competition is rarely resolved through a simple expansion of the budgetary or personnel pie.

Rather, Japan's civil service has been kept systematically small, through a series of deliberate policies. And a small civil service, other things being equal, costs taxpayers far less than a large civil service. Low-cost government, of which Japan's is undoubtedly the industrial world's most conspicuous, by extension, provides a positive stimulation for long-term economic growth for the nation as a whole.

Japan's civil service thus emerges as an apparent exception to the purported laws of bureaucratic imperialism.[11] Instead, the Japanese national bureaucracy has been kept much smaller than its counterparts in other advanced democracies.[12] These outer limits prevent Japan's agencies from expanding inordinately, requiring that periodic reexaminations of goals and internal organization be made, and moreover that these be done under fixed or decreasing limits on personnel and budgets.

Despite all of these positive attributes, to assert any simple causal link between Japan's civil service and national economic performance is at best dubious and at worst absurd. The Japanese civil service was but one in a series of important political and social forces contributing to high economic growth. Japan's economic success in many ways is overdetermined; it has been the result of a fortuitous mixture of many elements, not the least of which was luck.[13]

Whatever contributions the civil service has made to Japanese economic success have occurred in a broader political and economic context. Japan's economy has not succeeded simply because one or more government agencies were charged with that task and then given an array of administrative tools to insure that the goal was reached. Rather, economic growth has been fostered by an interlocking and compatible set of institutions and organizational principles, as well as a deeply entrenched ideology,

---

[11] The first such measures required major austerity measures of the Japanese government and were known collectively as the Dodge Line, after Detroit banker Joseph M. Dodge, their architect. On the general problem and how it affected the civil service, see T. J. Pempel, 'The Tar Baby Target: 'Reform' of the Japanese Bureaucracy,' in Robert E. Ward and Yoshikazu Sakamoto, eds., *Democratizing Japan* (Honolulu: University of Hawaii Press, 1987); on subsequent reforms see T. J. Pempel, *Policy and Politics in Japan: Creative Conservatism* (Philadelphia: Temple University Press, 1982), Chap. 7, as well as the Ito chapter in this volume.

[12] See the chapter in this volume by Mitsutoshi Ito on administrative reform for details.

[13] Among the more useful examinations of Japan's economic success, see Yasusuke Murakami and Hugh T. Patrick, eds., *The Political Economy of Japan*, 3 volumes (Stanford: Stanford University Press, 1987–92); Patrick and Rosovsky, eds., *Asia's New Giant*.

throughout Japanese society.[14] Consequently, we offer no simple suggestions implying a one-to-one relationship between the Japanese civil
service and economic success, the kind implicit in popular notions that 'if
we want economic success, we should simply create a Ministry of International Trade and Industry here in Country X.' The Japanese experience
is far more complicated and contextually rooted than any such simplistic
punditry, or bureaucratic blueprinting, might suggest. At the same time,
it is certainly true, as James March and Johan Olsen have observed,[15] that
we can learn from other models that evolved in different contexts. Indeed,
as Eleanor Westney has demonstrated convincingly, many aspects of
Japan's government organization itself were efforts at modified replication of models in other historical contexts.[16] Moreover, functional
equivalents are often possible when mirror-image replication is not. Thus,
although the Japanese civil service does not represent a replicable cook-
book model of 'how to do it' organization that can be emulated elsewhere
regardless of historical context or social organization, we do believe it
offers some positive lessons for use elsewhere.

Furthermore, as we will endeavor to demonstrate, there are many
negative dimensions endemic to Japan's bureaucracy that must also be
recognized, lest the fascination with its positive potential blind us to
concomitant flaws. Before turning to the Japanese case, however, it is
important to examine the situation of bureaucracies and civil services in
general. In many countries the contributions of the civil service to economic growth have been far less clear-cut, if not overtly negative. If, as we
wish to argue, bureaucracies can, and in the Japanese case do, play a major
role in advancing national economic development, why have there been
such widespread criticisms of civil servants in so many other areas of the
world? Why are there so few success stories showing positive links between economic attainments and national or local bureaucracies? The next
section explores that problem.

Bureaucracy and Economic Development

At one level, the essential tasks of any civil service are simple: create the
climate, the infrastructure, and the policies that will redound to long-term

[14] For example, the pattern of so-called 'lifetime employment,' practiced by many large
Japanese firms, contributes to job stability, long-term planning by firms, and a reduction
in the pressures on government for expensive unemployment programs. On the broader
question of an ideology of growth, see Richard J. Samuels, *Rich Nation, Strong Army: National
Security and the Technological Transformation of Japan* (Ithaca: Cornell University Press,
1994).

[15] James G. March and Johan P. Olsen, *Rediscovering Institutions: The Organizational Basis of
Politics* (New York: Free Press, 1989).

[16] D. Eleanor Westney, *Imitation and Innovation: The Transfer of Western Organizational
Patterns to Meiji Japan* (Cambridge, Mass.: Harvard University Press, 1987).

improvement of the economic situation of the country and its citizens.[17] But, how to achieve these admirable goals is rarely self-evident. Perhaps the principal lesson of any civil service regarding economic growth should be taken from the Hippocratic oath administered to physicians: first, do no harm. Poorly organized, inept, and/or bloated and inefficient civil services have contributed greatly to the long-term economic stagnation of numerous countries. In their efforts at economic transformation, many countries have found their civil services to have been part of the problem rather than part of the solution.

A variety of detailed examples could be listed for different countries and regions, but the extensive list of problems typically breaks down into two rather different categories: first, problems of structure, organization, and personnel—problems that relate to the presumably 'inefficient' organization of the civil service itself; and second, problems concerning the relationship between the civil service and the broader political and economic system within which it functions. Solutions proposed for the first set of problems generally involve structural and organizational changes: change the pay scales, alter compression ratios, promote on the basis of formal testing, reorganize organizations along more 'relevant' lines, provide for more data bases, rely on a single (or a collegiate) executive, limit (or expand) the scope of control, make clear distinctions between line and staff, etc. Although there is rarely agreement on the specific solutions, there is usually agreement on where to search for them—within the civil service itself.[18]

The second set of problems are usually more difficult, involving as they do a restructuring of relations between the civil service and its environment. Most typically, this involves problems of boundary maintenance, particularly with politics. Typically, the call is to keep 'politics' out of 'administration.' In this view 'politics' is the enemy of organization and of the civil service. Bureaucracy means efficiency; politics, meanwhile, is seen as the opposite. Bureaucrats seek the best (technical) solution to problems. Politicians, on the other hand, because of their narrower, more particularistic considerations, force bureaucrats away from such correct and logical paths.[19]

Within the organization of the bureaucracy itself, at least four major

[17] Joseph J. Spengler, 'Bureaucracy and Economic Development,' in Joseph LaPalombara, ed., *Bureaucracy and Political Development* (Princeton: Princeton University Press, 1963), pp. 224–5.
[18] On this general problem, see, e.g., Ibrahim F. I. Shihata, 'Administrative Reform in Developing Countries: Some General Observations,' and Gary J. Reid, 'Public Sector Human Resource Management in Latin America and the Caribbean,' background papers, World Bank Conference on Civil Service Reform in Latin America and the Caribbean, Washington, May 20–1, 1993.
[19] An important contrast in perspective is Joel D. Aberbach, Robert Putnam, and Bert A. Rockman, *Bureaucrats and Politicians in Western Democracies* (Cambridge, Mass.: Harvard University Press, 1981).

difficulties predominate as technical or structural problems: competence, coordination, creativity, and checks on the expansion of bureaucratic cost and size. Problems of competence center on attracting and retaining a cadre of highly skilled and well-motivated individuals for careers in the civil service. In many countries, acquiring and retaining the nation's most well-qualified individuals for the civil service is particularly difficult because of the greater attractiveness of alternative private sector careers because of differences in financial or psychological rewards. Competence also involves ensuring that corruption and personal gain do not become the driving ambitions behind a civil servant's career; instead, service to broad national goals must be institutionalized as the predominant goal of government officials.

A second perennial problem endemic to all organizations, both private and governmental, is that of coordination. Too often multiple governmental agencies pursue competing and often mutually antagonistic objectives. Many civil services, particularly those in ex-colonial regimes, manifest elaborate categorization, exceptional compartmentalization, complicated and elaborate pay and grade scales, overlapping spheres of influence, gaps between central and local administrators, and what one Pakistani official characterized as a tendency for officials to 'delight in disagreeing with each other' and 'flourish[ing] their knowledge of rules only to differ and demolish.'[20] Frequently the upshot is stagnation and/or continued expansion. Yet, too often no mechanisms function effectively to coordinate the activities of such stagnant or multiplying agencies. Actions begin to duplicate and/or contradict one another, in turn necessitating the creation of additional coordinating mechanisms to resolve the new duplications or contradictions.

How can organizations limit the effects of 'turf wars' among agencies and establish coordination and clear lines of authority? Is leadership too concentrated to allow officials more directly in contact with day-to-day problems to take autonomous initiatives? Or conversely, is it too diffuse to offer any central guidance to confused local officials? Both problems of course can be found.[21]

Still a third structural problem, and one closely related to coordination, is that of creativity. How can government agencies be encouraged to transcend the temptations toward routine that are built into all large organizations? How, instead, can they become the generators of new ideas and innovative solutions to complicated and ever-changing problems? At least two dimensions are involved—personal and organiz-

[20] As quoted in Ralph Braibanti, 'Public Bureaucracy and Judiciary in Pakistan,' in LaPalombara, ed., *Bureaucracy and Political Development*, p. 397.

[21] See, for example, Roy Ramashray, *Bureaucracy and Development: The Case of Indian Agriculture* (New Delhi: Manas Publications, 1975), for a study which, while highlighting the problems of taking initiative in the field, also stresses the overall rigidity of the entire administrative system.

ational. First, how can individual initiative and imagination be encouraged when so much governmental work demands breaking down complex tasks into 'depersonalized' administrative behavior and actions that are repetitive, routine, and 'by the book'?[22] And more broadly, at the organizational level, how can the entire governmental apparatus function as an instrument oriented toward creative approaches to a changing array of social problems, including economic development, when again routine and repetition are inherently more valued?

A compelling explanation for the alleged lack of creativity in government agencies is offered by business leaders and neoclassical economists: civil servants and public agencies lack competition. Within the 'real world' of business and economics, they argue, the market disciplines all players with the harsh lash of competition. Failure to adapt to changing circumstances—indeed failure to anticipate change with creative and imaginative solutions—leads to unprofitability, the loss of one's job or one's markets, and, in extreme cases, to an individual's firing or a firm's bankruptcy and collapse. In contrast, within the public sector, all too frequently, the most unimaginative and inflexible individuals seem to gain preeminence while government agencies face no possibility of shrinkage, dismemberment, or collapse. James Q. Wilson aptly sums up this criticism: 'The Ford Motor Company should not have made the Edsel, but if the government had owned Ford it would still be making Edsels.'[23]

Thus a third major technical problem for national bureaucracies involves instilling creativity. How can a civil service overcome parochial goals and fuse individuals and agencies into the creative service of coherent national objectives? How does it ensure that it can control agencies on the one hand, while at the same time not stifle creativity and initiative on the other?

Finally, one of the most important problems endemic to any civil service is the tremendous internal pressures to expand its size.[24] Many countries (particularly those countries emerging from colonial controls) find that the only substantially well-trained, educated, and nationally minded organizations they possess are their national bureaucracies. As a consequence, it becomes very tempting for political leaders to entrust all manner of problem-solving to the one group that seems remotely capable of solving them, namely the civil service. Yet, as the problems handed over to the civil service begin to mount, so does its size and the number

[22] On this problem, see, e.g., Michel Crozier, *The Bureaucratic Phenomenon* (Chicago: University of Chicago Press, 1964).

[23] James Q. Wilson, *Bureaucracy: What Government Agencies Do and Why They Do It* (New York: Basic Books, 1989), p. 227.

[24] This problem of bureaucratic imperialism is by no means limited to agencies in the Third World. See William A. Niskanen, Jr., *Bureaucracy and Representative Government* (Chicago: Aldine/Atherton, 1971), for a rational-choice-based argument for why all agencies seek to expand.

28   *T. J. Pempel and Michio Muramatsu*

and scope of the problems it deals with. Not infrequently, the cycle is completed by a downward spiral in the effectiveness with which all tasks are handled.

Within many countries, especially those with small private sectors, the civil service is also one of the few areas that can provide even marginally satisfactory employment to an ever-increasing population. These countries face what Braibanti has called a 'simple adverse Malthusian ratio: the supply of poorly trained, unsuitable manpower seeking employment far exceed[s] the work which government [is] able to organize for itself.'[25] Government service becomes the employment vehicle of last resort, and for reasons of politics and domestic stability, political leaders find it all but impossible to curtail the continued expansion in the number and size of government agencies.

Perhaps even worse, the excessive confiscation and eventual depletion of economic and human resources from the rest of society leaves these areas devoid of the resources required for private initiative. A gargantuan, costly national bureaucracy can rapidly diminish the resources available for economic improvement through the private sector. This is the principal reason why most advocates of 'free markets' are skeptical of governmental efforts to provide economic 'help.'

In sum, the fourth major structural way in which bureaucracies impede growth comes from the temptation toward an unending expansion of bureaucratic agencies and bureaucratic personnel. How can a civil service be kept down to a 'reasonable' size so that not all of a nation's talent and financial resources will be absorbed into an ever-expanding and decreasingly effective public sector?

In contrast, there are at least three importantly different levels at which government and a public bureaucracy can make significant positive contributions to economic development. First, they can foster and attempt to inculcate widespread citizen belief in the possibilities of material growth and the desirability of delayed gratification in the interests of long-term, personal, family, regional, and national economic success. As a great deal of study of the process of development has shown, one of the most fundamental prerequisites for economic growth is a widespread belief in its very possibility. Peasants who for generations have known only subsistence levels of economic existence are predisposed to resist the kind of compromise, deferral of gratification, and socially (rather than individualistically) oriented behavior that is part of a flourishing economy.[26] Yet, through the power of example, as well as through education, socialization, rural assistance programs, expanded communication, and

[25] Braibanti, 'Public Bureaucracy and Judiciary in Pakistan,' p. 384.

[26] See, e.g., Edward Banfield, *The Moral Basis of a Backward Economy* (New York: Free Press, 1958); Daniel Lerner, *The Passing of Traditional Society: Modernizing the Middle East* (New York: Free Press, 1958).

the like, a growth-oriented government can play a major psychological role in transforming the attitudes of its citizens.

As a second contribution, governments are perhaps the only organizations that can create the vital infrastructural underpinnings essential to a dynamic economy. Government action is almost always needed to create roads, harbors, rail lines, airports, communication networks, educational systems, health care, sanitation, irrigation projects, and a host of other essentials to economic success.[27] In addition, as part of its infrastructural contribution, a government must also ensure such basics as law, order, and security; a suitable monetary and banking system; minimal standards of public health and education; and possibly, to the extent that they cannot be generated domestically in the short run, an influx of foreign talent and capital.[28] And even more directly, a civil service can provide a great deal of assistance in the development and maintenance of a viable economy, particularly in setting favorable macroeconomic conditions and in helping to ease the impact of market failures.

If national governments, through their civil servants, make progress on just these two simple goals, the long-term benefits to economic growth can be enormous. But there is still a third way in which governments potentially play a positive economic role. This involves their most controversial role, namely, specific growth-oriented policies that have their most immediate impact less at the level of the entire national infrastructure and the macroeconomy and more at the level of specific industries and/or firms. At least three such means are typically used, often in complex mixtures: (1) direct programs aimed at stimulating specific firms or industries through subsidies, 'industrial policy,' or 'picking industrial winners'; (2) indirect incentives such as tax deductions or tax credits that change market incentives; and (3) incidental results and side effects, such as civilian spin-offs from military research.[29]

All of these potentially positive roles involve actions that go beyond the sphere of the civil service itself. Unlike the technical problems dealt with above that can be isolated as internal and structural, many of the most critical problems related to economic growth are linked to the delicate relations between the civil service and the broader world in which it functions. This is particularly true of relations between the civil service and the world of politics. Despite the delicacies and ambiguities involved, such relations are critical to a nation's overall economic development. Civil servants typically resist what they perceive to be unwarranted political interference in the technical performance of their duties. Politicians, on

---

[27] An important contribution to the economic significance of such infrastructure can be found in Robert Reich, *Work of Nations* (New York: Knopf, 1991).

[28] Much of this basic logic is drawn from Spengler, 'Bureaucracy and Economic Development,' pp. 205–6.

[29] We are grateful to Donald F. Kettl for this distinction.

the other hand, see it as their right to ensure 'political responsiveness' by civil servants. At least two different forms of political intervention can impede civil servants.

The first of these, what might be called the 'eyes over the shoulder' problem, usually means that a civil servant must somehow 'solve' a politician's problem, typically by acting 'inefficiently' in some macro sense; it involves adding numerous microlevel costs to any activity. Instead of one national airport, build three to accommodate the political demands of the three main politicians whose eyes are over the bureaucrat's shoulder.

Still another pervasive political interference is more broadly systemic in nature. This involves structuring the civil service in ways designed to serve a particular political leadership, rather than the presumably clear-cut national interest, at least part of which should include economic development. When a political leadership can mobilize the bulk of the civil service to its own political ends, and when these ends are narrowly nongrowth or antigrowth, there are major problems.[30] Under such conditions, even the most developmentally oriented, creative, and imaginative bureaucrat or agency is stymied and prevented from acting in any way that challenges the broad antigrowth agenda of the political system within which it exists. The most perfectly structured civil service can do little for economic development if the broader political economy is unfavorable to such ends. Indeed 'perfect' administrative structures can impede economic development just as surely as they can advance it: 'Efficient administrative machines can be used to prevent as well as to promote development, and much of the effort that it takes to produce the appearance, if not the reality, of improvement in public administration can become . . . a means of concealing inability or unwillingness to undertake needed action on other fronts.'[31]

Yet, in a democratic political system, elected officials have the responsibility for determining the broad direction of public policy. Civil servants are not expected to choose the goals they pursue; rather, they are charged with determining the methods for reaching externally set political goals. In short, the system should function in the classic manner described by

---

[30] It is important to realize that politicians frequently oppose growth—or at least the kinds of economic growth that might impede their hold on power. Military dictators rarely favor growth in civilian industries that might challenge the use of scarce resources for military equipment. Powerful landlords rarely favor land reform measures that would free their peasant labor force to work cheaply in urban industries. Many manufacturers favor protection from overseas competition, even if it might benefit macroeconomic growth for the country at large, etc.

[31] Malcolm B. Parsons, 'Performance Budgeting in the Philippines,' *Public Administration Review*, Vol. 17, No. 3 (Summer 1957), pp. 173–9, as cited in Fred W. Riggs, 'Bureaucrats and Political Development: A Paradoxical View,' in LaPalombara, ed., *Bureaucracy and Political Development*, p. 126.

Max Weber.[32] This is hopelessly idealistic. Rarely is the division between politics and administration so cleanly established. The British civil service was once held up as the ideal of the depoliticized bureaucracy. Despite a vigorous two-party system with frequent changes in cabinets, the civil servant was expected to demonstrate loyalty to the national interest by serving either one of his two probable masters with neither personal nor administrative conflict. Thus, in a major study of what happened to a conservatively oriented civil service when a left-leaning Labour government came into power following long years of Conservative rule, Kingsley showed Labour nationalized industry and carried out a host of other dramatically different projects and the civil servants —despite being from presumably conservative backgrounds and educations at Oxford and Cambridge—dutifully followed their new masters.

Yet the realities proved different when Margaret Thatcher took office in 1979. Bypassing the presumably neutral civil servant, Thatcher brought a cadre of policy advisors into top positions whose advice was congruent with the policies she sought to have implemented.[33] Similarly, in Germany under the Social Democratic–Liberal coalition in 1969, large transformations of the civil service took place especially in the Chancellery's civil service.[34] Then again, following 14 years of such rule, a new party government swept out virtually all senior Chancellery officials who had been associated with the prior government.[35]

Such patterns of political direction and reorganization of the civil service are far more common than the simple presumption that 'any civil servant can equally well serve any master.' Invariably, political leaders seek to gain leverage over purportedly slow-moving, if not directly antagonistic administrative organizations.

Certainly this has been the situation in the United States and most other presidential systems where, in the words of Hugh Heclo, politicians have long felt the need to 'layer in' levels of politically sensitive experts between the executive head of a department and the civil service.[36] By doing so, Aberbach and Rockman argue, the US civil service is largely ignored in providing policy advice to the executive; but simultaneously, the process 'helps to politicize the administration itself by making it more

---

[32] Max Weber, 'Bureaucracy,' in H. H. Gerth and C. Wright Mills, eds., *From Max Weber: Essays in Sociology* (New York: Oxford University Press, 1958), pp. 196–244.

[33] Joel D. Aberbach and Bert A. Rockman, 'Political and Bureaucratic Roles in Public Service Reorganization,' in Colin Campbell, SJ, and B. Guy Peters, eds., *Organizing Governance: Governing Organizations* (Pittsburgh: University of Pittsburgh Press, 1988), p. 83.

[34] Ibid., p. 83.   [35] Ibid., p. 86.

[36] Hugh Heclo, *A Government of Strangers: Executive Politics in Washington* (Washington: Brookings Institution, 1977), especially Chap. 2.

fully responsive to real or anticipated political directions and needs at the top.'[37]

A major reason why most political leaders change so many layers of civil service is the fear that their policy goals will be impeded by the civil service. Richard Neustadt, in examining the US presidency, concluded that 'the power of the president is the power to persuade.'[38] And certainly many US presidents have found it almost impossible to push their favorite policy items through recalcitrant government agencies. The need for loyalists in government agencies—individuals who actually share the goals of the executive, rather than simply accept them reluctantly as the price they must pay for their job—is particularly acute when the goals of public policy shift with high levels of frequency. This is most typically the case when one political party, or dominant electoral coalition, replaces another. Suddenly, anti-inflationary policies give way to budgetary expansionism; tight constraints over eligibility for health care or social benefits are replaced by far looser standards; the bridge, armory, science laboratory, or highway that was to be constructed in district A is moved to district B or cancelled outright. Can the civil servant who has labored for years in pursuit of one set of policies suddenly reverse direction and pursue with equal vigor a completely contrasting set of objectives? Human nature suggests this is highly unlikely, and many government leaders act on that perception and endeavor to insinuate their loyalists into key administrative positions.

It is difficult to find an ideal balance between political responsiveness on the one hand and technical expertise on the other. Presumably, when a regime is democratically elected and progrowth, most of us would prefer to see the civil service turned into political and progrowth agents. In different regimes with different goals, our preferences might well be different.

This then returns us to the much broader point ultimately at issue, namely, the goals of the regime and the structures of the civil service that support them. To the extent that political leadership embraces economic development for the nation, presumably the civil service will be mustered in all its force to achieve these goals. And to the extent that the civil service is well structured internally, those goals are more likely to be achieved than when it is poorly structured. Yet all too frequently, the political leadership itself is weak, venal, self-serving, and rapacious, using administrative structures to impede rather than enhance national economic development. It is this weakness at the political level that may well serve as the most serious impediment to national economic growth.[39]

---

[37] Aberbach and Rockman, 'Political and Bureaucratic Roles,' p. 82.

[38] Richard E. Neustadt, *Presidential Power* (New York: John Wiley, 1960).

[39] In a poignant observation of the Liberian bureaucracy, hardly one that is widely admired as an example of efficiency and developmental orientation, David Brown suggested

Economic development must be recognized as a concomitant of political will and national development, rather than simply as a 'job' that can be turned over to one or several agencies of government. One of the greatest frustrations in the linkage between bureaucracy and economic development for many late developers and recently independent states is that at the time of independence, a relatively well-established bureaucracy was in place, but there was no parallel development of a legitimate political/ electoral mechanism. The result has often been chaos with a politically neutral civil service expected to 'solve economic problems,' yet with no agreement over who would provide the broad political direction and specific economic policy objectives to that service.[40]

There is no doubt but that a well-organized and motivated civil service can play a major role in advancing economic development; conversely, a poorly organized and unmotivated civil service can be a major impediment to a nation's economic well-being. As Lyndon Johnson said in a speech before the US Civil Service Commission's 1962 awards ceremony: it is an 'inescapable fact that in the modern world, no nation—new or old—can have unity and prosperity without a trained civil service.'[41] At the same time, such a trained civil service is only a necessary, but never a sufficient, condition for economic success. Economic development is a function of far more than bureaucratic adeptness or incompetence; rather it is a task that requires not only a very able and committed civil service, but also a political environment that embraces, and political resources that are dedicated to, the goals of economic development.

It is in this mixture that Japan offers the most positive lessons. Throughout the country's modern history, both the nation's politicians and its business leaders have been strongly committed to economic growth. In this sense, any contribution by the Japanese civil service has been made in a broader climate conducive to economic improvement. It is our belief

that the problems of many such bureaucracies may be as much political as structural. The bureaucracy, he notes, faces innumerable internal and organizational problems: 'the over-definition of its external boundary; the weakness of its internal boundaries; the relative insignificance of specialized expert knowledge to bureaucratic roles; and the idiosyncratic nature of the bureaucratic career.' At the same time, he notes that 'the Liberian administration was arguably effective in relation to certain goals, even if these were not ones which would have applied in the [Weberian] ideal-typical case.' This is so because 'these goals were essentially political and must be understood in relation to political constraints, rather than—as is often suggested in studies of Third World management—as 'cultural' phenomena. Attempts to improve public sector managerial performance in the Third World need to give as much attention to operational issues as to conventional targets.' David Brown, 'Bureaucracy as an Issue in Third World Management: An African Case Study,' *Public Administration and Development*, Vol. 9 (1989), p. 369.

[40] This point has perhaps best been made by Samuel P. Huntington, *Political Order in Changing Societies* (New Haven: Yale University Press, 1968).

[41] *The Federal Employee*, Vol. 47 (March 3, 1962), p. 10, as cited in Fritz Morstein Marx, 'The Higher Civil Service as an Action Group in Western Political Development,' in LaPalombara, ed., *Bureaucracy and Political Development*, p. 65.

that the Japanese civil service is structured in ways that have facilitated the nation's successful economic performance. Moreover, we will attempt to show that the Japanese bureaucracy has performed a variety of activities and carried out specific policies that have made major positive contributions to Japan's economic success. Many of these, we feel, can be emulated elsewhere, once sufficient adjustment is made for differences in broad political and economic conditions. It would therefore be wise to look first at the political context within which Japanese economic success has occurred. Our emphasis is on the importance of viewing the civil service as part of a set of institutional arrangements, including political and economic arrangements, that are committed to economic development.

The Japanese Political Context

Japan's political and economic leaders have rather consistently embraced economic development as a national goal since the Meiji Restoration in 1868 and with redoubled vigor in the years immediately following World War II. Politicians, whether elected or not, have almost unswervingly identified their long-term viability as dependent on achieving high levels of national economic growth.[42] In this sense, Japan's economic growth and improvement has rarely been opposed by the nation's rulers. Furthermore, the national civil service has generally been utilized as a major instrument to achieve those goals. The overriding psychological and ideological climate within which the Japanese civil service has functioned has been biased toward rapid economic growth. That the civil service has been shaped by that ideological climate is unmistakable.

During the Meiji period (1868–1912), as Bernard Silberman points out in his contribution to this volume, the civil service was explicitly designed as an extension of Japan's ruling elite. One of its major charges was to carry out the technical aspects of the country's industrialization and modernization. Political responsiveness to 'transcendental' national goals was partially ensured by efforts to insulate the civil service from 'partisan' electoral politics. Indeed, Japan's bureaucrats were officially designated

---

[42] This is by no means intended to imply that politicians have not been venal, self-serving, or oriented toward pork barrel projects. None of Japan's early *genrō*—the small group of unofficial, behind-the-scenes advisors to the emperor during the late nineteenth and early twentieth centuries—died poor; politicans such as Hara Kei were highly skilled in bringing pork barrel politics to Japan; Japan's postwar politicians have long adhered to the political maxim that 'all politics is local politics,' and have sought to represent themselves as a 'pipeline to Tokyo' through which benefits to their districts would flow. Corruption scandals have been a mainstay of Japanese electoral politics. Still, the basic orientation of such politicians has typically been that it is much easier to provide such narrow benefits to themselves or their districts if the size of the total national economic pie is expanding than if the pie must be recut.

'servants of the emperor,' rather than 'civil servants.' The Japanese bureaucracy was created with explicit guidelines designed to minimize the kinds of patronage that permeated the civil services of the United States and parts of Western Europe.[43] Macropolicy was insulated from political micromanagement.

Even after political parties began to gain influence over the formation of cabinets in the 1910s and 1920s, explicit patronage and the spoils system remained minimal. Top positions in various ministries were at times reallocated following changes in government. But for the most part, this meant replacement of one career civil servant by another. Even so, a considerable number of civil servants were formally affiliated with political parties during the 1920s, the highpoint of prewar party government. The years of the Taisho period (1912–26), for example, showed an increased partisanship in the lower echelons of local governments, where even postmasters were replaced when a new party gained power. Political micromanagement penetrated the civil service to such an extent that many 'progressive' bureaucrats, frustrated with the process of politicization, were receptive to the 'non-partisan' authoritarian climate of the 1930s. Such politicization continued until the end of World War II. (Furthermore, even though prewar politicians were generally weak policymakers, they did begin to accumulate the kinds of experiences and expertise that could be called upon in postwar politics.[44])

In the postwar period, there was widespread democratization of all aspects of politics. Most notably, cabinets had to be formed by parliamentary vote. Thus, the struggles between 'political responsiveness' and 'technical expertise' continued but with much greater weight given to elected officials. Despite the fact that 'politicians' and 'bureaucrats' are often treated in studies of Japanese politics as living in two separate worlds, where they nurture a basic disdain for the values and norms of one another, in fact the divisions between them have been far less problematic than in many other industrialized democracies. This is because the same political coalition dominated Japanese politics from the formation of the Liberal Democratic Party (LDP) in 1955 until at least 1993. The ultimate loyalty of the civil service to LDP policy objectives was never a major issue.[45] (And in a similar fashion, LDP politicians rarely wavered in their trust of the civil service.)

[43] An excellent study of the links between parties and civil service patronage cross-nationally is that of Martin Shefter, 'Party and Patronage: Germany, England and Italy,' *Politics and Society*, Vol. 7, No. 4 (1977), pp. 403–51.

[44] A·famous example of this involves the Policy Affairs Research Council of the Liberal Democratic Party, which for all intents and purposes was a carry over of the prewar Seiyūkai party appartus.

[45] Some would argue that the conservative coalition indeed traces back without serious interruption to the Meiji Restoration at least in spirit and personal connections if not in organizational structure. Regardless, in comparison with other industrialized democracies,

Meanwhile, the Japanese left has been fragmented and Japan is the only industrialized democracy never to have had an independent left-of-center government in its entire history. Consequently, it has never had a government committed to the establishment of a welfare state and to massive economic redistribution. Rather, Japan's ruling conservatives have pursued what they have called a 'Japanese style welfare *society*.'[46] Therefore, the national ideological climate has been highly conducive to progrowth policies as developed and/or implemented by the Japanese civil service.[47]

As a consequence, political leaders in both prewar and postwar Japan have never found it desirable, or necessary, to 'layer in' numerous political loyalists in the civil service. Quite the contrary, in the early postwar years, the civil service and former bureaucrats were 'layered in' to conservative party politics. Under the oversight of the Allied Occupation, the Japanese civil service was central in both shaping and carrying out the comprehensive policies originally designed to help the Japanese economy recover from the massive war damages and to begin the long process of regaining world economic strength. Moreover, in the late 1940s, Prime Minister Yoshida, confronting the Occupation's political purge of numerous prewar party officials, tapped into the upper reaches of the Ministries of Finance and Foreign Affairs and other agencies to recruit new party leaders for the Liberal Party he headed. It was under this alliance between new politicians and former bureaucrats that the early policy agendas of the currently ruling conservatives were laid out.

Collaboration rather than confrontation between the worlds of 'politics' and 'bureaucracy' has been a dominant political motif in postwar Japanese policy formation, particularly in economic matters. The earliest lines of cleavage over economic policy did not pit these two worlds against each other; rather, the main division was between coalitions composed of individuals from both worlds in a struggle over the appropriate direction for economic policy. On one side were Yoshida and his supporters where the central focus was on the development of export industries that could secure comparative advantage. Vital to this strategy was the adoption and implementation of industrial policies centered around the Japanese financial system, with a heavy reliance on the Japan Development Bank. Opposed to that program were bureaucrats in the Ministry of International Trade and Industry, the Ministry of Agriculture, Forestry, and

Japan until the early 1990s almost never saw major changes in the character and aims of governments when cabinets changed. This made Japan, along with a very small number of other democracies, quite unusual. T. J. Pempel, ed., *Uncommon Democracies: The Politics of One-Party Dominant Regimes* (Ithaca: Cornell University Press, 1990).

[46] Japan, Economic Planning Agency, *New Economic and Social Seven-Year Plan* (Tokyo: EPA, 1979).

[47] This point is elaborated in Pempel, *Policy and Politics in Japan: Creative Conservatism*, Chap. 2.

Fisheries, the Economic Stabilization Headquarters, and other economic agencies, with their political allies, seeking to make the public corporation the principal vehicle for economic reconstruction. The former group sought to focus on smaller businesses such as textiles, where Japan enjoyed a comparative world advantage; the latter group was more concerned with regular intervention in the economy and had heavy industry as a main target of official nurturance.

During the 1950s, these two coalitions competed vigorously with one another. Many prewar politicians, able to return to political life once the Occupation's purge was lifted, were highly critical of Yoshida's orientation. Under the leadership of conservative prime ministers Hatoyama, Ishibashi, and Kishi, this group pressed for more Keynesian demand stimulus that favored full employment and national market expansion. This direction continued until Ikeda became prime minister in 1960, when the Yoshida approach was rekindled. Competition between the two schools eventually resulted in policies that satisfied both groups in the form of export-led heavy industry, but with strong support for many smaller and medium-sized industries, a policy Kume calls 'developmental policy without losers.'[48]

This example illustrates how the combination of bureaucrats and politicians with their different orientations and attributes helped to create public policies. Vital to understanding the process is the realization that the two sides have traditionally reinforced, rather than competed with, one another. The basic division has been for politicians both to set broad macroeconomic goals, and to seek their own specific micropolitical goals within that broader context, leaving the bulk of middle-level policy formation and implementation to the various economic agencies of the national bureaucracy. Certainly one group has not been 'progrowth' and the other resistant.

Low levels of political intervention are partially ensured by the very fact that politicians are essentially not 'layered in' to the national bureaucracy. It is simply administratively difficult for 'politicians' to intervene on the regular basis that would be possible if their surrogates permeated the top layers of the bureaucracy.

For example, only the top two or three individuals in a government agency are political appointees—the minister and usually one, but in a few agencies two, political vice ministers. Meanwhile, even though roughly one-fourth of the Liberal Democratic Party has been composed of former bureaucrats, few Japanese bureaucrats enter the political world

[48] Ikuo Kume, 'Party Policies and Industrial Policy: A Case of Japan,' paper presented to an international conference, the English Science Research Council Research Initiative on Government–Industry Relations, May 20–2, 1992. The analysis of the competition of the two schools is developed in Yasuko Kono, 'Yoshida gaiko to kokunai seiji' (Yoshida diplomacy and domestic politics), in Michio Muramatsu, ed., *Sengo kokka no keisei to keizai hatten* (Postwar state formation and economic development) (Tokyo: Iwanami Shoten, 1992).

while in office. Unlike in France, Japanese civil servants do not serve as formal advisors to the cabinet, to ministerial cabinets, nor to elected local officials. Nor is there a *Grands Corps* concept allowing Japanese civil servants to move freely between administrative and political posts, or to run for office while retaining bureaucratic status.[49] Unlike those of Germany, Japan's bureaucrats cannot sit simultaneously in parliament while holding civil service posts, and in contrast to the United States, they do not serve on Japanese equivalents to 'presidential teams' made up of politicians, administrators, and admixtures of both. The lines separating politics and administration are in principle clear and unambiguous in Japan, and the only appointed political officials are the minister and parliamentary vice minister(s). This ensures that the civil service is not easily forced to surrender technical expertise in the interests of the more narrow political interests of individual politicians or the party as a whole. Formally, these appointed politicians have every right and power to supervise and intervene with the civil service. But in practice, most serve in their posts for periods of only one year to 18 months. Indeed, one comparative study of cabinet duration shows Japan's to have been consistently among the most short-lived in the major industrialized countries. The average duration of cabinets in Japan was 1.9 years, compared to 3.4 years for France, 4.6 years for Britain, and 3.0 years for the United States.[50]

Technical competence and political power of political appointees is by no means negligible; however, the administrative vice minister and the various bureau chiefs have typically spent more than 25 or 30 years getting to know the insides and outs of the agency. On most semitechnical matters, therefore, administrative efficiency prevails over political expediency. At the same time, Japan's politicians typically make a good deal of effort to gain broad knowledge over the spheres they allegedly control. Furthermore, with the LDP in control of the government from 1955 to 1993, more than 100 LDP politicians have had cabinet/ministerial experience, which gave the LDP a cumulatively high level of policy expertise. Attuned as they have been to electoral and political demands, these politicians have also been sensitive to the probable political ramifications of major agency actions. Consequently, it was rare for bureaucratic activity to proceed when key LDP officials were opposed.

Nevertheless, on most technical and nonpolitical matters, bureaucratic efficiency prevails over political expediency. Political intervention occurs usually with the setting of major goals and occasionally on specific, politically salient elements of an agency's activities. It does not emerge on each and every petty item in an agency's budget. It is the bureaucrats who draft

[49] Ezra Suleiman, *Politics, Power, and Bureaucracy in France* (Princeton: Princeton University Press, 1974).
[50] Jean Blondel, *Government Ministers in the Contemporary World* (London: Sage, 1985), appendix 2.

most legislation; it is they who set up and staff most policy advisory commissions; they have great leverage in drafting administrative ordinances that frequently interpret, embellish, or circumvent existing laws.[51]

Thus, political influence and oversight in Japan remains quite real, but largely on broad principles rather than day-to-day decision making. Since its formation in 1955 until its splintering in 1993, the Liberal Democratic Party was the single dominant electoral force in the country. Typically outpolling its nearest opponent party by margins of 2:1, the LDP formed all cabinets and had (often substantial) majorities in both houses of parliament throughout that time period, with the exception of the Upper House starting in 1989. Senior Japanese administrators would have been foolhardy to act contradictory to the interests of the LDP. But at least since the mid-1950s the LDP was a party whose leadership was committed to policies designed to ensure high growth and sound economics. The party tied its fortunes to expanding the national economic pie (and thus increasing its total intake of pie) rather than trying to take ever larger slices for itself and its supporters from a pie of a fixed size.

In this objective, the LDP did not confront a civil service hostile to its programs. Elected politicians did not have to bludgeon a reluctant administration to adhere to the party's policy goals. Obviously, as in any politically volatile situation, there have been differences of opinion over public policy directions, and the Japanese civil service is by no means an unthinking agglomeration of automatons, readily carrying out any and all directions from the top. However, the LDP was so strongly in control of the electoral offices of the national government that few career-minded civil servants would ever have anticipated attempting to block LDP-initiated efforts on policies with great significance. Indeed, by the time they reached important levels, most Japanese civil servants were socialized into pro-LDP approaches to policy for 20 years or more. Long-term LDP hegemony and the party's strong support for, and dependence on, a dynamic business sector all combined to create a climate of opinion that fostered the civil service's orientation toward economic growth and increased international competitiveness.

---

[51] Indeed, Japanese bureaucrats themselves consider that it is they rather than the elected politicians who are solving the nation's general policy problems. This is true even though most would disdain seeing themselves as 'political.' One study showed that 80 per cent of Japan's top bureaucrats felt that it was they who were most responsible for the formation of public policy, a figure drastically above the 21 per cent of British administrators and the 16 per cent of German administrators who felt similarly. Akira Kubota and Nobuo Tomita, 'Nihon seifu kōkan no ishiki kōzō' (The structure of consciousness of Japan's higher civil servants), *Chūō kōron*, No. 1079 (Feb. 1977), pp. 192–3. Another survey on higher civil servants, however, suggests that they are almost the same in perceiving their policy roles as Western civil servants. Joel Aberbach *et al.*, 'Comparing Japanese and American Administrative Elites,' *British Journal of Political Science*, Vol. 20 (Oct. 1990), pp. 461–88.

As the party's time in office continued to mount, so did its mechanisms for influence over the bureaucracy. Most notable were the Policy Affairs Research Council and the Executive Committee of the LDP. Moreover, the LDP developed many individual party officials with technical expertise on specific policy matters who attempted to keep watch over bureaucratic actions in the areas they knew best.[52] High-level promotions within the civil service must be approved by the cabinet, which in turn was dominated by LDP members. Finally, Diet hearings allow political investigations into the actions of government agencies. In short, what appeared to be a high level of bureaucratic autonomy from politics reflected instead an LDP so powerful *vis-à-vis* the broad outlines of the civil service, its policies, and its personnel as to make day-to-day intervention unnecessary.[53]

The Structures of the Japanese Civil Service: Competence, Coordination, and Creativity

The Japanese civil service has historically functioned in a system where its resources have been scarce but its prestige high. Civil servants as individuals, and ministries and agencies as organizations, have consequently been forced to work exceptionally hard to acquire whichever of those scarce resources they could. Action, rather than passivity, has been the mindset essential to success, both within the personnel system and throughout the organizational structure of the civil service. The successful civil servant, and the successful bureaucratic agency, is not the one waiting patiently for rewards and resources to be bestowed; rather, success demands a stance that is 'proactive.' And within the Japanese context discussed above, this proactivity works best when it is conducive to the broader political and economic goals of economic success.

Since both individuals and agencies are engaged in such proactive behavior, and since the available resources, such as promotions, new programs, or budgetary allocations, are scarce, the system is one that builds in a high level of creative competition. Individuals desirous of promotions more rapid than their peers must prove themselves constantly through hard work, better ideas, and greater follow-through. Agencies that seek to expand their budgets or their spheres of influence must beat out potential competitors through similar behavior. In this way, elements of competitively generated initiative and creativity are instilled into the system.

[52] Takashi Inoguchi and Tomoaki Iwai, *'Zokugiin' no kenkyū* (A study of 'tribal parliamentarians') (Tokyo: Nihon Keizai Shinbun, 1987).

[53] Muramatsu, *Sengo Nihon no kanryōsei*, p. 7. See also the treatment of this relationship in J. Mark Ramseyer and Frances McCall Rosenbluth, *Japan's Political Marketplace* (Cambridge, Mass.: Harvard University Press, 1993).

And finally, to round out the picture, the system is one in which resources, particularly in the form of personnel slots and budgetary allocations, are periodically reduced even further. This, in turn, has generally heightened the internal competition, and has generally fostered even further positive results in terms of civil service efficiency.

To examine how these elements interact, it is valuable to begin by examining the structural features of the Japanese civil service. Several deserve special attention in any discussion of the linkages between bureaucracy and economic growth. These enhance civil efficiency in the pursuit of national economic goals. From our perspective, the civil service has been structured and has evolved in ways that provide a positive balance among competence, coordination, and creativity. In this way, Japan's civil service has built in attributes that make it something of an exception to many of the negative structural characteristics of 'bureaucracies' noted above.

The national civil service in Japan has traditionally attracted some of the country's most able talent. By virtually any standard, the individuals who staff Japan's various agencies are highly competent. And, as will be noted subsequently, they are also highly competitive with one another, a process that instills a strong dose of creativity and individual responsibility. At the same time, this individual competition is subject to various forms of checks and coordination so that it does not completely undermine agency objectives.

Organization and Personnel: Ensuring Competence

The National Civil Service Law (October 21, 1947) and the National Government Organization Law (1948, revised in 1986) provide the main legal outlines of Japan's national bureaucratic service. There are twelve ministries, ten agencies, and seven independent regulatory commissions at the ministerial level. Twenty cabinet ministers are in charge of these ministries, agencies, and commissions.

The fundamental structures of Japan's national civil service have been in place since the early 1950s, as have the bulk of the structures introduced under the Occupation. Yet, the broad trend toward decentralization of administration introduced by the Allied Occupation was reversed, particularly in areas of education and police. In addition, the antimonopoly biases of early Occupation policies were revised. Since then a few additional changes have occurred: the Economic Planning Agency was created in 1955 to play a role in macroeconomic planning. In 1970, the Environment Agency was added to deal explicitly with problems of pollution. In 1974, land prices and land development became political issues and the National Land Agency was created. The Ministry of Agriculture and Forestry was reorganized as the Ministry of Agriculture, Forestry, and Fisheries in the late 1970s. But for the most part, structurally,

Table 1.1 Trends in Government Employment,
1980–90 (percentage of total employment)

	1980	1985	1988	1989	1990
Australia	16.0	17.5	16.5	15.6	15.6
Austria	17.6	19.4	20.9	21.1	20.8
Belgium	18.7	20.2	—	—	—
Canada	19.4	20.8	20.3	20.3	20.6
Denmark	28.3	29.7	29.4	29.8	29.9
Finland	17.2	19.2	20.6	20.6	20.9
France	20.0	22.7	22.9	22.8	22.6
Germany	14.6	15.6	15.5	15.4	15.2
Greece	8.9	9.9	10.1	10.4	10.2
Iceland	15.7	16.5	16.9	16.8	17.3
Ireland	16.4	18.8	18.4	17.9	17.2
Italy	15.7	16.8	17.3	17.4	17.2
Japan	8.8	8.7	8.3	8.1	7.9
Netherlands	14.8	16.0	15.4	15.1	14.9
New Zealand	17.2	14.9	—	—	—
Norway	25.3	29.2	29.3	30.8	32.0
Portugal	10.7	13.2	14.1	14.1	14.3
Spain	10.5	13.4	14.1	14.3	14.5
Sweden	30.7	32.9	31.8	31.5	31.8
Switzerland	10.1	10.3	10.5	10.6	10.6
Turkey	10.5	9.1	9.1	9.1	9.3
United Kingdom	21.3	21.7	20.7	19.5	19.1
United States	16.4	15.3	15.1	15.1	15.5

Source: OECD Report, *Public Management Development*,
Annex II (Paris: OECD, 1991), p. 74.

the central government agencies have been largely untouched for more than three decades.

Article 8 of the National Government Organization Law allows for the establishment by ordinance of a variety of additional councils, research institutes, laboratories, and cultural, educational, and medical institutions.[54] In addition, Japan has a number of public corporations directly responsible to individual cabinet-level agencies. Finally, there is an extensive local governmental service and about 100 public corporations. Together these employ over 5 million full-time public employees. This number represents nearly a tenfold increase in the size of Japan's bureaucracy since the 1940s. However, despite the fact that Japan is often thought of as a bureaucratized country, it actually has fewer public sector employees per capita than most other major industrialized countries. As Table 1.1 makes clear, government employees represent approximately

---

[54] Bureaus and sections within offices and ministries used to be established by law, but since 1984, they can be established by government ordinance. This is in keeping with the recommendation of the Second Provisional Administrative Reform Commission. As a result

15–20 per cent of the total employment of the United States, France, Germany, and Britain; in Japan the figure is only 7.9 per cent.[55]

Furthermore, as will be discussed at length below, a series of administrative reforms, starting in the early 1950s and continuing through the Second Provisional Administrative Reform Commission efforts of the mid-1980s and into the early 1990s, have deliberately kept down the size of the Japanese civil service. These initiatives have come from outside the civil service itself, largely through political programs aimed at meeting business demands to shrink a potentially expanding bureaucracy and to keep it small. As a result, there has been almost no substantial growth in the number of Japan's national civil servants over the last three decades. At the same time, there has been a substantial devolution of activities to local governmental levels. The number of local civil servants increased from about 2.94 million in 1975 to 3.22 million in 1990 (see Figure 1.1).

The most senior civil servant in each agency is the administrative vice minister, in charge of oversight of all administrative matters within his ministry. Below him stretch a limited number of relatively clean lines of hierarchy. Each ministry is typically divided into six to twelve functionally arranged bureaus, and these in turn are either subdivided into departments or divided directly into sections. These sections, employing anywhere from 20 to 30 people, form the working units of each ministry.

Competition to enter the higher civil service is intense and examination for the civil service as a whole is separated from recruitment to individual agencies. For the most part the actual recruitment procedures and the examination system have not changed substantially since the prewar period.[56] Three classes of examinations serve as the basis for all significant bureaucratic recruitment and are administered by the National Personnel Authority for the civil service as a whole. The Class I examination recruits 'high flyers,' those expected eventually to assume the top posts in the various ministries. All the evidence suggests that the written portions of the exam are judged fairly and that there is little potential for corruption or bribery to advance one's case. Less clearly neutral are the oral portions of the examination where subjectivity is more evident. A good deal of evidence suggests that those who do well on the oral examination are those who most mirror existing biases and norms within the civil service. Those who pass the Class I exam will then be subsequently recruited by

of this change, individual ministries and agencies are allowed to make organizational reforms on their own initiative without parliamentary approval. However, the law also provides a maximum number of bureaus (128) that can be established to prevent their infinite expansion.

[55] See also Tomiko Kato, 'Present Problems Concerning Managerial Personnel in the Public Sector,' *Local Government Review*, Vol. 5 (1977), pp. 17–35.

[56] On the examination system as it occurred under the Allied Occupation, see Maynard N. Shirven and Joseph L. Soeicher, 'Examination of Japan's Upper Bureaucracy,' *Personnel Administration*, Vol. 14, No. 4 (July 1951), pp. 48–9.

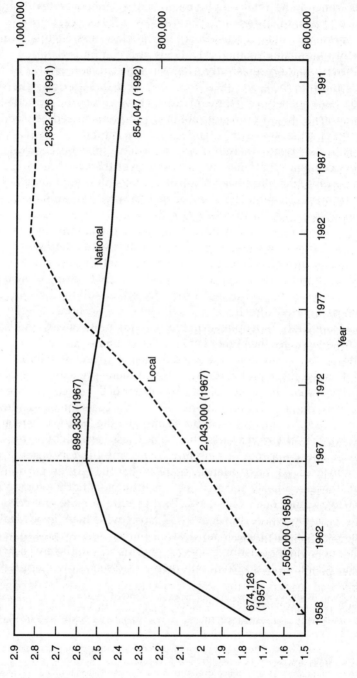

Fig. 1.1. Number of Central and Local Governmental Employees

individual ministries and they can expect appointment at a relatively low level followed by rapid advancement to higher positions, usually to one of the top three levels, at worst, before retirement. Those who fail the exam must seek employment elsewhere.

The Class II examination is used to select middle-level civil servants. The Class III exam covers all other positions. At times more than 55,000 individuals have competed for just over 1,300 positions in the Class I examinations. This meant a competition ratio of nearly 43 individuals for each post filled. This competition has lessened somewhat since the late 1970s, but even in 1992 there were nearly 15 test-takers for each successful applicant. (See Table 1.2.)

The Japanese civil service recruits broadly educated generalists from a small number of the nation's best universities. There is a heavy preference for law graduates, and those from the University of Tokyo tend to be disproportionately numerous in the top bureaucratic posts. (Table 1.3 provides competition rates for graduates.) Although there has been some reduction in the dominance of the civil service by University of Tokyo graduates, roughly 35–40 per cent of the successful applicants continue to be Tokyo graduates. Usually only 15 or so of Japan's 460–odd universities see 10 or more of their graduates succeed in the exams. Thus, there has been some democratic broadening of the recruitment process since the prewar period but past biases remain influential.[57]

Furthermore, recruitment is designed to ensure that those who enter through the exam system, rather than political appointees, the economically powerful, or any other 'non-administrative' group, gain access to the most senior positions. As noted above, ever since its establishment, the civil service has been almost completely immune to horizontal entry into its top or middle ranks. Rather, most recruitment occurs after the completion of university education in one's early 20s—'victory after a trial by educational fire'—and after that, promotion involves a long and fairly predictable series of steps up the career ladder leading eventually to 'retirement' from an agency before one's mid-50s.

Entrance and promotion are based on examinations. It is useful to note that top-level officials themselves perceive the process of bureaucratic recruitment to be open and nonascriptive. In reply to a question concerning whether people from a certain segment of society are inherently suitable to become leaders of the state, the negative replies of Japanese bureaucrats far outdistanced those of their counterparts in Britain, Germany, and Italy. Negative or more or less negative response in Japan

[57] Results of the 1991 civil service examination revealed that University of Tokyo graduates comprised just over 50 per cent of the successful Grade 1 level civil service exam-takers. Waseda University was next with 11.8 per cent, and Kyoto University graduates made up 7 per cent of the successful examinees. *Far Eastern Economic Review* (March 12, 1992), p. 72.

Table 1.2 Competition Rates for Japanese Higher Civil Service

	Number of Applicants	Total Number Successful	Ratio	Law Graduates		Ratio
				Number of Applicants	Number Successful	
1960	16,364	981	16.7	4,403	262	16.8
1961	11,743	1,133	10.4	3,284	308	10.7
1962	14,059	1,218	11.5	3,947	316	12.5
1963	16,329	1,366	12.0	4,077	298	13.7
1964	15,904	1,434	11.1	3,807	298	12.8
1965	21,125	1,624	13.0	4,411	299	14.8
1966	24,799	1,507	16.5	4,843	290	16.7
1967	21,567	1,364	15.8	4,293	269	16.0
1968	20,483	1,313	15.6	4,332	266	16.3
1969	17,973	1,306	13.8	4,032	251	16.1
1970	17,637	1,353	13.0	3,998	252	15.9
1971	23,532	1,401	16.8	5,093	261	19.5
1972	27,429	1,349	20.3	5,238	242	21.6
1973	30,129	1,410	21.4	5,866	262	22.4
1974	30,688	1,375	22.3	6,227	249	25.0
1975	37,825	1,206	31.4	7,556	237	31.9
1976	44,518	1,136	39.2	8,238	235	35.1
1977	48,514	1,206	40.2	8,729	240	36.4
1978	55,972	1,311	42.7	10,630	245	43.4
1979	51,896	1,265	41.0	10,034	229	43.8
1980	45,131	1,254	36.0	9,694	229	42.3
1981	40,770	1,361	30.0	9,644	226	42.7
1982	36,856	1,383	26.6	8,834	237	37.3
1983	34,854	1,478	23.6	8,421	221	38.1
1984	34,089	1,562	21.8	8,321	220	37.8
1985	36,072	1,655	21.8	8,915	242	36.8
1986	32,675	1,718	19.0	8,043	251	32.0
1987	32,308	1,696	19.0	7,666	250	30.7
1988	28,833	1,814	15.9	6,728	266	25.3
1989	27,243	1,983	13.7	6,443	270	23.9
1990	31,422	2.047	15.4	7,341	271	27.1
1991	30,102	2,200	13.7	6,955	287	24.2
1992	30,789	2,075	14.8	7,008	286	24.5

Source: Japan, National Personnel Authority, annual reports.

totaled 100 per cent, in contrast to negative responses ranging from 50 per cent in Italy to 80 per cent in Britain.[58] In this regard, the Japanese civil service is 'open' and is perceived as such by its members; social class per

[58] Kubota and Tomita, 'Nihon seifu kōkan no ishiki,' p. 195.

Table 1.3   Total Number of Applicants for the Civil
Service Examination

	Law and Other Graduates	*Engineering Graduates*	*Agriculture Graduates*
1978	23,326	25,567	7,079
1979	22,331	22,532	7,033
1980	20,440	18,272	6,419
1981	19,526	14,991	6,253
1982	18,355	12,609	5,892
1983	17,072	11,719	6,063
1984	16,884	11,491	5,714
1985	18,555	11,838	5,679
1986	16,704	10,776	5,195
1987	16,105	11,088	5,055
1988	14,076	9,969	4,788
1989	13,210	9,600	4,433
1990	16,888	9,937	4,597

Source: Japan, National Personnel Authority, annual
reports.

se plays little real role in recruitment although, as in most countries, there
is a far greater chance of gaining a position in the civil service if one is born
into the middle class within a metropolitan area than if one has blue-collar
parents and is from a rural area.[59]

Civil servants themselves evince a high degree of self-sacrifice in speaking about their high prestige jobs. Asked to choose from ten possible reasons for choosing their careers, virtually none of Japan's top-level civil servants answered that they took the position for the powers it held or as a possible springboard to a subsequent career. The most cited reasons were 'suitability to one's own character' (21 per cent), 'breadth of vision' (18 per cent), 'to serve the state' (16 per cent), and 'to serve the public' (12 per cent). Only after these did 'security of position' enter the picture with 10 per cent.[60] In effect, the civil service members manifest a strong degree of 'professionalism' and dedication to their tasks.

The bulk of the recruits to top positions could be categorized as generalists rather than specialists.[61] At the university, most majored in

[59] The fathers of higher civil servants represent a significantly higher proportion of professionals and university graduates than for the general public (and also for fathers of parliamentarians). Muramatsu, *Sengo Nihon no kanryōsei*, pp. 48–50.

[60] Yasuo Watanabe, 'Kōkyō komuin no ishiki,' in Bakuji Ari *et al.*, eds., *Gendai gyōsei to kanryōsei* (Contemporary administration and the bureaucratic system) (Tokyo: Tōkyō Daigaku Shuppankai, 1974), p. 429.

[61] This is in sharp contrast, for example, to the United States where most civil servants are originally hired as specialists and then must struggle to overcome this 'handicap' of specialization as they rise to higher levels.

subjects such as law, business, or administration rather than the sciences, engineering, or economics. Recruits are chosen by individual ministries and, although they may be dispatched to another agency for special training for a limited time period, virtually all remain within the agency into which they were recruited for the bulk of their careers. In this regard too they are highly professional and usually specialists in one area of government (even though they usually span the functions within that agency quite broadly).

There is virtually no movement from one agency to another, except on a temporary basis. In effect, one enters a specific agency in one's early 20s or one does not enter at all, and once in that agency, one's entire governmental career is spent there. This provides for a good deal of cohesiveness within each government agency; at the same time, this of course has the drawback of fostering agency consciousness over a consciousness of the civil service as a whole. Moreover, it prevents agencies from tapping into other segments of society to bolster their ranks from among proven talents.

Interesting are the cases where a new ministerial agency, such as the Environment Agency, the Economic Planning Agency, or the Land Agency, is created. Staffing these new agencies requires related ministries to provide some of the organizational units and the administrative personnel. As a consequence, these older ministries feel free to exercise certain 'territorial' claims over the new agencies to the extent that they were forced to sacrifice their own organization's resources to enable the new one to be created.

As can readily be imagined from all of the above, the members of the national civil service are highly homogeneous. With almost no significant ethnic, religious, and linguistic differences in Japan, such categories are virtually meaningless in hiring and promotion. Adding to the overall homogeneity otherwise created, most recruits are male, although by the beginning of the 1990s, a small but increasing number of females were being recruited and promoted along with their male counterparts. With most senior officials sharing a relatively common educational background, and a common socialization within their agencies, homogenization is further reinforced.

A good deal of professional training is available to most civil servants throughout their careers. Most are given a variety of positions throughout the agency with which they work.[62] Transfers occur once every two years or so, and are designed, among other things, to assure that all senior officials will be broadly familiar with most of an agency's or ministry's complete functions by the time they reach the top. During his or her career, an individual has many opportunities to acquire additional skills.

[62] Akira Kubota, *Higher Civil Servants in Postwar Japan* (Princeton: Princeton University Press, 1969). Muramatsu, *Sengo Nihon no kanryōsei.*

Various courses in foreign languages, computers, economics, and the like are often given by an agency. There is lots of room for the development and flourishing of individual talents within each agency. In addition, the National Personnel Agency maintains a program for potential high flyers to be sent abroad for two years of advanced education, including language training.

The most successful individuals can expect to achieve the position of section chief after approximately 15 years of service, assistant bureau chief after 22–5 years, and bureau chief after 25–8 years. The position of administrative vice minister, available only to the top individual out of two or three entering cohorts, is usually achieved after 28–30 years. Typically, this position is held for two or three years after which the vice minister and any remaining members of the group that entered the agency with him will retire. Retirement comes relatively early, usually before age 55, hence ensuring promotional opportunities and also highly responsible decision-making possibilities to relatively young officials.

Throughout all of this, loyalty to one's agency is inculcated and takes priority. This goes a long way toward overcoming the kind of fundamental alienation from authority that Crozier finds so pervasive in the French organizational culture which, far more heavily than Japan, relies on unbending rules and rigid 'dehumanizing' formalities:

> When one believes that human activities depend on the feelings and sentiments of the people involved, and on the interpersonal and group relationships that influence them, one cannot expect that imposing economic rationality on them will bring constant and predictable results. The functioning of a bureaucracy can never henceforth be totally explained by the combination of impersonality, expertness, and hierarchy of the 'ideal type.'[63]

The Japanese system, by way of contrast, is geared toward encouraging what Chester Barnard called 'the process of inculcating points of view, fundamental attitudes, [and] loyalties, to the organization . . . that will result in subordinating individual interest . . . to the good of the cooperative whole.'[64]

Petty corruption is relatively rare among Japan's civil servants, despite its deep and embarrassing pervasiveness within the long-ruling LDP. In effect, the civil service works smoothly without the grease of financial emoluments to its members. At the same time, Japan's civil service is not without a vague acceptance of 'token' gifts which are at least normally expected, although their offering does not automatically ensure favorable consideration of one's claims, nor does the failure to make the offer ensure that one's claims will be ignored. Yet, ingratiating oneself to an official is

---

[63] Crozier, *The Bureaucratic Phenomenon*, p. 179.
[64] Chester Barnard, *The Functions of the Executive* (Cambridge, Mass.: Harvard University Press, 1942), p. 279.

widely believed to be important to business success. Jack Huddleston provides an interesting example of how subtle pressures predominate throughout the system:

The general manager of a major European subsidiary remarked that every New Year he visits his appropriate ministry, takes a name card into an office after waiting in line, bows to an unattended desk, and leaves the name card on a tray. When he asked what would happen if his name card was not on the tray next year, his senior Japanese staff members suggested it would not be a good idea to find out.[65]

Most probably, there is an element of ironic humor and perhaps unneeded anxiety in this vignette, but there is no question that many individuals subject to administrative oversight are reluctant to test the blurry limits of official authority.

Salaries for civil servants are usually slightly below those for comparable private sector positions. In 1990, a newly entering civil servant received ¥168,000 per month; the private sector equivalent was usually about 10 per cent higher. Pay scales are determined by the parliament under advice of the Civil Service Commission. The commission uses a complex formula linked to private sector salaries to make its recommendations.

While civil service salaries are somewhat lower than those in the private sector, post-governmental remuneration, in the form of both pensions and subsequent employment opportunities created by one's agency, can be high. As Ramseyer and Rosenbluth suggest, the civil servant is thus 'bonded' for the future, and hence has diminished incentives toward petty corruption or toward major deviation from agency goals.[66]

Competition and Creativity

To return to the central theme of why the Japanese bureaucracy is 'so efficient,' it is useful to highlight the intense competition among individuals within these agencies, despite the broad levels of loyalty to the agency itself. This competition begins with the exam, and indeed with the long educational competition that precedes it. By the time they have secured posts, most of Japan's recruits have internalized values and norms of hard work, intense dedication, and high competition.

Such internalized norms are furthered by the personnel system which is designed to enhance and reward individual efforts congruent with agency or national goals. A great deal of individual competition is built into the Japanese civil service. Generally, the kind of wage competition

[65] Jackson N. Huddleston, Jr., *Gaijin Kaisha: Running a Foreign Business in Japan* (New York: M. E. Sharpe, 1990), p. 96.
[66] Ramseyer and Rosenbluth, *Japan's Political Marketplace*.

that might prevail in the private sector is minimal. Promotions are regular and somewhat standardized; salaries are tied to seniority. Nonetheless, the internal merit system is designed to ensure that the best jobs go to those individuals who, in the eyes of their superiors, have proven themselves in earlier positions. These better jobs also afford individuals increased opportunities for higher levels of training, greater opportunities to increase their competence, and, in the long run, an even greater chance to shine in the eyes of superiors as time goes on. Furthermore, subsequent post-civil-service employment for the civil service's highest flyers is also a consequence of how well they have performed in their official positions.

The attributes that are central to success are most interesting. One survey on civil servants shows that the most desirable trait for high-flying civil servants is 'ability to persuade' (71 per cent), followed by 'ability to plan' (24 per cent) and 'ability to negotiate with politicians' (4 per cent).[67]

In contrast, those who receive lesser assignments early on in their careers, and those who fail to develop the needed leadership traits, run the risk of losing out on many of these opportunities and ultimately finding themselves less well rewarded financially and professionally. The closed nature of recruitment intensifies the competitive process: one knows precisely who one's competitors are; the absence of horizontal entry limits the competing group.[68] In effect, personnel competition in Japanese governmental agencies becomes a life-long proposition.[69]

Throughout this process, the 'carrot' of future successes hangs always just ahead. Even those who in one way or another fall behind their peers in the promotion competition know that further promotions are probable; they will not be fired; nor will they be passed over by younger high flyers; continued hard work will be rewarded, albeit perhaps not as quickly as for their competitors, nor as rapidly as they might prefer. And ultimately, their post-retirement careers will also be a function of their perceived abilities and dedication to their agencies.

The consequence is a high level of competition, initiative, aggressiveness, and dedication to the major tasks of the agency.[70] Positive performances, however nuanced, are allegedly seen, rewarded, and provide a further basis for improved opportunities to perform even better the next

---

[67] Muramatsu, *Sengo Nihon no kanryōsei*, pp. 75–6.

[68] It is worth noting that the total lifetime earnings for these most successful individuals may not differ tremendously from that of their less successful colleagues. But the pressure remains intense because careers in second jobs and later can usually account for major salary differences. One could be promoted to the presidency of the Bank of Japan, for example, while another might become a less well-paid member of the Board of Directors of a large private company.

[69] This idea draws on the work of Naohiro Yashiro, 'Nihon no kanryō shisutemu to gyōsei kaikaku' (The Japanese bureaucratic system and administrative reform), JCER Paper No. 18 (Dec. 1992).

[70] Ibid.

time around. In effect, individuals can find themselves swirling upward in a 'positive cycle of reinforcement,' or downward in its reverse.

This competition continues for postcareer rewards, as well. Those who serve loyally for 25 or 30 years can expect to be generously rewarded in such jobs, the best of which can be quite lucrative and prestigious.[71] Personal interest thus dictates that individual civil servants work hard and effectively throughout their careers in order to ensure their long-term pensions and postbureaucratic positions. A major consequence of this system is to link individual career fortunes to hard work, approval of superiors, competition with one another, and a long-standing dedication to one's agency. All of this is conducive to the overall efficiency of each agency and in turn to the civil service as a whole.

Personal frustration and withdrawal might be the anticipated consequence of such a severe system of competition. Yet, within most agencies, there is close coordination and management from above. The General Secretariat of each agency has extensive powers over personnel, internal budgets, organization, and drafting of related laws and ordinances.[72] As a consequence, these units are principal organs for internal agency cohesion and coordination. They provide chosen individuals with opportunities to develop contacts in the broader political and economic arenas (through attendance at LDP meetings, business symposia, study groups, interministerial talks, travel abroad, and the like). They also place them in situations demanding increased competence, and fraught with competitive challenges. The General Secretariat is something of a permanent handicapper in the ongoing horse race among its thoroughbred civil servants.

Still a second layer of competition, creativity, and coordination takes place in agency-to-agency relations. As noted above, an individual civil servant's principal loyalty is to his particular agency. Consequently, one of the more serious problems in Japan is that of sectionalism. In many bureaucratic systems, numerous agencies with competing missions engage in activities that duplicate or, worse still, completely contradict those of other agencies. Agency A does not know what Agency B is doing or, if it does know, it works in total disregard of the second agency's activities. Coordination at higher levels is weak or ineffective. McConnell, Lowi, and others have characterized the United States in such a fashion.[73] Laegreid

[71] The second careers of national civil servants are extensively examined in a good deal of literature. Known as *amakudari*, the process of matching retiring civil servants to appropriate jobs in the private or semi-private sector is one to which the personnel sections of all government agencies devote considerable time and effort. Of particular importance in this process is the development of longstanding relationships between a government agency and its clients.

[72] Daiichi Itō, *Gendai Nihon no kanryōsei bunseki* (An analysis of the contemporary Japanese bureaucracy) (Tokyo: Tōkyō Daigaku Shuppankai, 1982).

[73] Grant McConnell, *Private Power and American Democracy* (New York: Vintage, 1966); Theodore J. Lowi, *The End of Liberalism* (New York: Norton, 1969).

and Olsen's phrase 'Key Players—On Different Teams' suggests the same phenomenon for Norway.[74] Moulin and Lorwin have identified the problem as comparably endemic to the Belgian civil service.[75]

Such sectionalism is also pervasive in Japan. Both horizontally across agencies and vertically between central and local governments, Japan has at least as many problems of competition and coordination as any other large government bureaucracy. In Japan, as elsewhere, the quest for bureaucratic coordination becomes one of the most sought-after goals. Seidman suggests, in fact, that 'the quest for coordination is in many respects the twentieth-century equivalent of the medieval search for the philosopher's stone. If only we can find the right formula for coordination, we can reconcile the irreconcilable, harmonize competing and wholly divergent interests, overcome irrationalities in our government structures, and make hard policy choices to which no one will dissent.'[76]

In Japan, competition among agencies is at least as stringent as that among individual civil servants. Most agencies have their 'natural constituencies' of interest groups and socioeconomic sectors. To the extent that these societal interests compete, that competition is typically reflected in agency-to-agency competition as well. In effect, elements of Japan's societal diversity are manifested in agency competition.

Similar competition prevails in relations between the central government and local governments. Japan has had a long history of relatively strong central control over its local prefectures and cities. In this regard it manifests much more of a continental than an Anglo-American pattern of control. The prewar Ministry of Home Affairs appointed prefectural governors and also exercised overarching control over the functions of the various national ministries within various regions. The result was a rather clear hierarchy from the center down to the smallest locality. Fusion of national and local activities was thus ensured, with the local governments given high degrees of discretion in their activities so long as these did not conflict overtly with national laws or the extremely strong policy preferences of the national government.

In the period since the war, local governmental units have gained considerable autonomy from the center, despite many criticisms to the contrary. When it comes to finance, local units of government carry out far more administrative tasks than is true of their counterparts in other

[74] Per Largreid and Johan P. Olsen, 'Top Civil Servants in Norway: Key Players—on Different Teams,' in Ezra Suleiman, ed., *Bureaucrats and Policymaking* (New York: Holmes and Meier, 1984), pp. 206–41.

[75] See Leo Moulin, 'The Politicization of the Administration in Belgium,' in Mattei Dogan, ed., *The Mandarins of Western Europe: The Political Role of Top Civil Servants* (New York: John Wiley/Sage, 1975), pp. 163–86, and Val Lorwin, 'Segmented Pluralism, Ideological and Political Cohesion in the Small European Democracies,' *Comparative Politics*, Vol. 3, No. 2 (Jan. 1971), pp. 142–55.

[76] Harold Seidman, *Politics, Position, and Power: The Dynamics of Federal Organization* (New York: Oxford University Press, 1970), p. 164.

advanced industrialized democracies. This can be seen from an examination of the relationship between revenue and spending in Japan. The ratio of national to local revenue in Japan is roughly 7:3. The national government, principally through national taxes, takes in 70 per cent of all government revenue in the country while prefectures, cities, towns, and villages collect the remaining 30 per cent, largely through local taxes of one form or another. But by way of contrast, the ratio of national expenditures to local expenditures is about 3:7, indicating that the central government transfers considerable sums from its annual revenues to local government units for eventual expenditure. These transfers come primarily in the form of the 'local distribution tax' and various grants-in-aid and direct subsidies.

Because the transfers from center to periphery are so vast, the national government has a strong incentive to press its policy goals down onto the local areas and can exert an element of national coordination over local policy actions. At the same time, local entities are not without their own independent political agendas which they seek to press upward onto the national government. The result, quite frequently, is a sharp conflict between local autonomy and central control.

Given the agency-to-agency and center-to-periphery competition within Japan's civil service, there is obviously a great need for both horizontal and vertical coordination throughout the system, although these two layers are not always complementary.[77] Part of the coordination results from the proliferation of data shared widely throughout the government and indeed throughout society as a whole. Japan's is a bureaucracy based on the extensive collection and sharing of common data, from which decision-making consensus, at least on the parameters of the problem being confronted, can be created. This point is ably made by Jeff Broadbent in an extensive quantitative study of organizational density in Japan, Germany, and the United States. He shows that the various social and network formations among the business, labor, and bureaucratic sectors in Japan were far more concentrated and centralized than in the other two countries, and a major role in such concentration was played by information control.[78] A good example of how such coordination operates in economic policy is provided by Mabuchi's chapter in this volume, dealing with the information trade-offs between the Ministries of Finance and International Trade and Industry.

[77] For an interesting treatment of how these two levels interact, see Richard J. Samuels, *The Politics of Regional Policy in Japan: Localities Incorporated?* (Princeton: Princeton University Press, 1983).

[78] Jeff Broadbent, 'The Japanese, German and US Labor Policy-Making Process: Structural Differences in the Representation of Business, Labor and other Organizations,' unpublished manuscript, University of Minnesota, 1992; see also David Knoke *et al.*, 'Policy Networks and Organizational Influence Reputations in the U.S., German and Japanese Labor Policy Domains,' unpublished manuscript, University of Minnesota, 1992.

To bolster the coordination that emerges from shared information, a number of structures exist to bridge sectionally generated cleavages. Within each agency—but rarely across agencies—various advisory committees are widely used to bring together bureaucratic and non-bureaucratic actors to discuss various policy problems. Under Article 8, Section 1 of the National Administrative Organization Act of 1949, government agencies are empowered to create advisory commissions to provide policy input and advice. Such advisory commissions provide a useful way for civil servants to gather opinions for 'client' groups, and at times to impose their own agenda on such groups. In the mid-1980s, bureaucrats made up about 21 per cent of the membership of these bodies; former bureaucrats made up another one-fifth.[79] And as noted above, the bureaucratic agency that establishes the committees typically chooses its membership, provides the staff for its meetings, and writes the eventual report. Throughout the process, coordination and opinion-sharing allow movement toward a policy consensus at least between the agency and its client groups.[80]

In addition to such bodies that coordinate intraagency, and agency-to-private-sector opinions, there are other mechanisms to deal with the inevitable agency-to-agency controversies that crop up. At the horizontal level across agencies there are section chief conferences, bureau chief conferences, and, if seriousness warrants, even vice-ministerial conferences whose mission is to resolve any interministerial conflicts.

In terms of local–central coordination, as Muramatsu has demonstrated, the interactions between the two levels of government also involve a great deal of mutual penetration and a high degree of bargaining and coordination. Initiatives take place at both levels and are frequently welcomed at the other, again largely because of the large amount of information sharing and the high degree of commonality of interest.[81]

A good example of this latter point concerns garbage collection. Normally a local government function, this aspect of government service became problematic during the early 1970s when local governments found it difficult to finance the disposal of large amounts of industrial

[79] Yasunori Sone *et al.*, *Shingikai no kiso kenkyū: kinō, taiyō ni tsuite no bunseki* (Basic research on advisory committees: An analysis of their function and condition) (Tokyo: Keio University, 1985).

[80] On the advisory committee system, see T. J. Pempel, 'The Bureaucratization of Policymaking in Postwar Japan,' *American Journal of Political Science*, Vol. 18, No. 4 (Nov. 1974), pp. 647–64. Also, Yasunori Sone, *Shingikai kenkyū* (report of the Keio University Sone Seminar), 1989; Muramatsu, *Sengo Nihon no kanryōsei*, pp. 124–9. Frank Schwartz, 'Of Fairy Cloaks and Familiar Talks: The Politics of Consultation,' in Gary D. Allinson and Yasunori Sone, eds., *Political Dynamics in Contemporary Japan* (Ithaca: Cornell University Press, 1993).

[81] Michio Muramatsu, 'Central Local Political Relations in Japan: A Lateral Competition Model,' *Journal of Japanese Studies*, Vol. 12, No. 2 (Summer 1986); Michio Muramatsu and Akira Nakamura, 'Myth and Reality in Local Policy Implementation in Japan,' in Douglas Ashford, ed., *Discretionary Politics: Intergovernmental Social Transfers in Eight Countries* (Greenwich, Conn.: JAI Press, 1990).

waste. They successfully persuaded the national government to undertake a coordinated policy action to deal with this problem. The result was
a nationally coordinated policy, but one that had clearly arisen in response to local initiatives. Moreover, local 'testing' of various programs
provided a useful mechanism by which the central government could
choose among possible alternatives.

In a similar vein, regional development was coordinated in part
through local industrial policies. Individual agencies within the national
government provided guidelines for local economic development designed to blend local plans with those of the center. The national government also put together a law, for example, creating a number of 'New
Industrial Cities' in 1962. These received subsidies, favorable borrowing
terms and incentives to merge with other municipalities, all as a means of
fusing various local developmental requirements. In short, the broad history of local–national governmental relations in Japan also suggests high
levels of close and positive interaction, substantial local creativity to
which the national government is willing to defer, and yet a level of
overall coordination that keeps both levels of government moving in
complementary directions.

Ultimately, however, when either horizontal or vertical conflicts were
irreconcilable among agencies, it was the ruling LDP, either directly or
through the cabinet, that provided the final coordination. In this, the
expertise of various LDP members was helpful. Since serious problems of
coordination are almost inevitably rife with political implications, a political decision aimed at a final solution is the logical outcome. But as many
instances have shown, when the LDP intervened, it typically did so in
favor of one ministry and against another; it did not usually provide
'winnings' to the two or more competing agencies.[82]

In most instances, whether at the central or the local level, all bureaucratic agencies seek to avoid the interjection of political choices into what
are seen as administrative matters. Again, this is by no means a uniquely
Japanese response. Bureaucrats the world over, despite their differences,
unite as a body when politicians threaten to interfere with their presumed
technical decision making prerogatives. In the United States this has been
labeled 'cooperative feudalism'—the sense that politicians are the en-
emies of bureaucrats, despite their separate agencies and missions. Agencies 'are at one where it comes to combating attempts by outsiders to
encroach upon their fiefdoms. Outsiders include lay administrators and

[82] A good example of this is provided in the area of telecommunications and the battles
between the Ministry of International Trade and Industry and the Ministry of Posts and
Telecommunications. See Chalmers Johnson, 'MITI, MPT, and the Telecom Wars: How
Japan Makes Policy for High Technology,' in Chalmers Johnson, Laura D'Andrea Tyson, and
John Zysman, eds., *Politics and Productivity: How Japan's Development Strategy Works* (New
York: Harper Business, 1990), pp. 177–240.

competing professions, but the most feared are elected executives charged with representing the broader public interests.'[83]

Japanese bureaucrats are by no means unique in seeking to protect their collective turf against intruding politicians. In turn, elected officials have done their best to ensure greater responsiveness to perceived political needs by civil servants. As far back as 1962 the Liberal Democratic Party, in an effort to ensure political responsiveness among the civil service, created its Executive Council in an attempt to provide political oversight before proposed matters reached the cabinet.[84] There is a great deal of evidence emerging to suggest that the LDP became increasingly capable of providing greater direct oversight and input into bureaucratic decisions by the mid-1970s.[85] Furthermore, locally elected national politicians are frequently enlisted by local administrative units to press their specific cases at the national level. This provides another instance of coordination between politics and administration, but one that is vertical, rather than horizontal, in nature. Such political coordination had become particularly important to the LDP as Japan's budgetary constraints and political pressures came into greater conflict.[86] But again, this increasingly political influence must be seen in the broader context of a generally high level of congruence between 'political' and 'bureaucratic' goals.

Just as competition among individuals has its positive face, so too does competition among agencies or among levels of government. One of the central problems that vex most bureaucracies is that of adjusting to changing times and hence to new missions. When agencies have clear and fixed missions, it is very tempting as Michel Crozier has long noted for France, for them to adhere strictly to existing rules and patterns of behavior, resisting new approaches to changing social problems.[87]

Because the missions of each agency are spelled out in rather vague and general terms, and because the tasks of local governments are likewise vaguely configured, when a new social problem arises, it is not automatically clear which agency will be given responsibility for attempting to deal with it. Nor is it clear that the national government, rather than some local

[83] Seidman, *Politics, Position, and Power*, p. 136.

[84] Kazuo Kojima, *Hōritsu no dekirumade* (Drafting a law) (Tokyo: Daiichi Hōki, 1976).

[85] See, for example, Seizaburō Satō and Tetsuya Matsuzaki, *Jimintō seiken* (The LDP administration) (Tokyo: Chūō Kōronsha, 1986); Hideo Ōtake, ed., *Nihon seiji no sōten* (Political issues in Japan) (Tokyo: Sanichi Shobō, 1984).

[86] T. J. Pempel, 'The Unbundling of 'Japan, Inc.': The Changing Dynamics of Japanese Policy Formation,' *Journal of Japanese Studies*, Vol. 13, No. 2 (Summer 1987), pp. 271–306; Michio Muramatsu and Ellis Krauss, 'The Conservative Party Line and the Development of Patterned Pluralism,' in Kozo Yamamura and Yasukichi Yasuba, eds., *The Political Economy of Japan, Volume 1: The Domestic Transformation* (Stanford: Stanford University Press, 1987); Ellis Krauss and Michio Muramatsu, 'Bureaucrats and Politicians in Policymaking: The Case of Japan,' *American Political Science Review*, Vol. 78, No. 1 (March 1984), pp. 126–46; Calder, *Crisis and Compensation*; Ramseyer and Rosenbluth, *Japan's Political Marketplace*, inter alia.

[87] Crozier, *The Bureaucratic Phenomenon*.

governmental unit, will be the first to respond. Indeed, local initiatives often outpace those from the center. Consequently, on many new problems there is often a marketplace approach to their solution: various agencies and levels of government, in effect, 'bid' on the problem in an attempt to sweep it into their sphere of influence. Thus, for example, when biotechnology became a buzz word in the early 1980s, the Ministries of Agriculture, Forestry, and Fisheries, Education, International Trade and Industry, and Health and Welfare all established research projects and/or administrative subdivisions to begin examining problems and possibilities in biotechnology. The ultimate target was to establish a claim over the administrative responsibility and the budgets that would eventually be expanded to deal with biotech.

'Internationalization' has created much the same response as multiple agencies have attempted to adjust internally to a nationally identified goal that will clearly bring with it resources and prestige. In such a manner, the inherent proclivity toward sectionalism carries with it a competitive process under which agencies compete with one another to tackle emerging problems and to stay abreast of changing social circumstances. In so doing, they also provide for a good deal of internal regeneration that works to overcome at least the worst cases of institutional sclerosis.

From the local level, one can easily point to the initiation of the national pension program as having begun with local governmental programs to provide 'pensions for the respected elderly' as early as 1951 and the national program not being created until 1959. Children's allowances began with a program in Musashino City in April 1967; by the end of 1969 some 171 local governments had adopted similar programs. Only in 1972 did the national government adopt the program nationwide. In like fashion, it was local governments that began providing free medical care for the elderly—starting with the small town of Sawauchi in Iwate Prefecture in 1960—and the national government adopted such a plan only in 1973.[88]

In a similar way, and with more direct and immediate relevance to economic policy, Japan's policies of industrial zones began partly with national initiative, but were responded to vigorously by various local entities, each competing for the monies to attract desired industries.[89] Much the same was true of subsequent policies concerning the creation of so-called 'technopolises.' Initially proposed by the Ministry of International Trade and Industry, the program attracted 40 prefectural bids for the new centers, with the ministry eventually choosing 20 sites in 19 prefectures.

Thus, the broad picture that emerges is of a civil service structured in ways that build in a variety of lines of competition—among individuals

[88] Calder, *Crisis and Compensation*, Chap. 8.
[89] See, e.g., Samuels, *Politics of Regional Policy*, especially Chap. 4.

and among agencies—that are conducive to unleashing self-interested creativity. At the same time the system provides coordination mechanisms that mitigate some of the detrimental possibilities of completely unrestrained competitiveness and the consequent frustrations felt by competition's losers.

One additional structural feature of the Japanese civil service is also important, namely, the strict outer limits that have been set on bureaucratic expansion. This feature is particularly important in that it continues to limit the resources available to the civil service, thereby intensifying the system's overall competitiveness.

Checks on Expansion

Many government bureaucracies find it comparatively easy to recruit qualified individuals, set up mechanisms for coordination, and to mesh politics and the civil service. The simplest means, however, often result in a never-ending spiral of growth—in both agencies and governmental cost. The end result is massive and costly government that becomes inherently inefficient and, more importantly, drains away limited national resources from potentially growth-producing endeavors. It has proven difficult in most countries to check the expansion of the civil service and to reorganize and downsize on a regular basis. The Japanese experience presents a striking contrast. There the merits of limiting bureaucratic expansion have been widely accepted and, most significantly, such limits have been effectively institutionalized. In the Japanese case, two sets of limits have been crucial: those carried out annually through the budget process, and those carried out periodically to reduce the size of the bureaucracy as a whole.

Japanese Budget Controls

One of the most important powers of the Japanese Ministry of Finance (MOF) is the power over the budget.[90] On an annual basis the ministry's various budgetary officials fan out through the Kasumigaseki area of Tokyo, which houses most national government offices, to oversee the budget-making process of Japan's individual government agencies. For our purpose, one power is central: the power to set a finite limit on the expansion, from one year to the next, of any agency's budget. One of the first tools used in such limits involves an absolute ceiling on the increase in the amount requested from one year to the next. During the high growth period of the early 1960s, this limit was relatively generous, as

---

[90] Campbell, *Contemporary Japanese Budget Politics*.

high as 50 per cent. Still, it was a limit of some sort. But from the mid-1960s until the mid-1970s this was reduced to 25–30 per cent growth in total requests. From then on, the ceiling on requests was progressively lowered and for several years involved absolute shrinking of administrative budgets, and only 1–2 per cent increases for other activities. Since 1983, actual budget expenditures have been virtually zero over the previous year. (See Table 1.4.)

Moreover, until 1966 MOF was able to maintain balanced (or overbalanced) budgets. Never completely successful from its own standpoint in ensuring fiscal responsibility, MOF still has stood as a major power forcing individual agencies to set their own internal priorities concerning the programs and activities they seek to carry out. The ministry has then been able to coordinate the whole process and to keep the entire national budget under relatively strong control.[91] During the mid-1980s, the limits MOF sought to set were further enhanced by sweeping administrative reform efforts. As a consequence, agencies for several years were required to submit, variously, low-growth, zero-growth, and negative-growth budget proposals.[92] The consequence was that strong outer limits were established over the presumably natural tendency of bureaucratic agencies, in their competition with one another, to 'solve' their problems at the expense of 'efficiency' through unchecked programmatic add-ons. Instead, the budgetary process has provided a sharp, mandatory, and effective incentive for agencies to cut programs rather than simply adding them.

Administrative Reform

A second mechanism that has set outside limits on the size of the civil service has been administrative reform. A central problem that has existed in almost all governments has been the proliferation of agencies and bureaucrats. Few countries have demonstrated any significant ability to shrink their civil services. Somehow, the tasks demanded of them expand geometrically with the result that agencies and numbers of government personnel expand similarly quickly. As noted above, Japan has been a significant exception to this general pattern. It has maintained a very small government at the national level with relatively fixed numbers of agencies and personnel since the early 1960s. How has this been carried out? The chapter by Mitsutoshi Ito deals with this problem in greater detail. At this point suffice it to say that the process has involved the interesting complementarity of outside political initiative to ensure regular restruc-

---

[91] For a less sanguine viewpoint, see Jiro Yamaguchi, Ōkura kenryō shihai no shuen (The end of Ministry of Finance dominance) (Tokyo: Iwanami Shoten, 1987).
[92] See, for example, Muneyuki Shindō, Gyōsei kaikaku to gendai seiji (Administrative reform and contemporary politics) (Tokyo: Iwanami Shoten, 1986).

turing of the national bureaucracy designed to keep it small, plus a willingness to allow individual ministries and agencies a great deal of latitude in their actual restructuring processes. The only requirement has been congruence with overall goals concerning size and expenditure. This process strikes us as meshing the best of two worlds: outside oversight on broad limits, but inside reorganization on specific details. This allows an agency to meet oversight goals in ways that an agency itself can recognize as highly efficient.

The first major cuts in the Japanese bureaucracy came toward the end of the Allied Occupation as a part of the so-called Dodge Line, an economic belt-tightening that was designed to balance the Japanese governmental budget, reduce inflation, and put the nation's financial system on a sound footing. Although the program was initially developed by the Americans, it was implemented with vigor by the Yoshida government. Some 300,000 government employees were laid off, most in the highly unionized public corporations such as the National Railways, Nippon Telephone and Telegraph, and the Postal Service.

A less draconian set of measures was undertaken in 1964, involving a freeze on most major governmental expansion and a semipermanent reduction in the filling of vacancies. Among other things, this set of measures led to the passage of a Law on the Total Number of Public Personnel, which set an outer limit on the total size of the civil service.

In 1967 these measures were expanded to require that all agencies and ministries eliminate one of their bureaus. Which bureau to cut was a decision again left to the individual agency. In addition, a 5 per cent reduction in the fixed number of personnel was ordered to take place over a three-year period (1969–71). Most of these cuts were achieved through retirement, death, relocation, and other forms of natural attrition. Again the agencies were allowed to reorganize internally to deal with this shrinkage. Furthermore, various government commissions and public corporations were subject to elimination or downsizing.[93]

Curbing the natural tendency toward bureaucratic sprawl has allowed the conservative government to maintain one of the lowest-cost governments among the industrialized democracies as a per cent of GNP (see Table 1.5). The merits of small government came increasingly to be recognized by elected officials, if for no other reason than that it meant a relatively low tax burden on Japan's recovering businesses was possible.[94] Small government has also contributed to the overall competitiveness and efficiency of the agencies and personnel still in place.

The most important move toward shrinking the civil service came in the middle of the 1980s when Japan was facing major problems with national

[93] These processes are detailed at length in Pempel, *Policy and Politics in Japan*, Chap. 7.

[94] The key agency within the Ministry of Finance that was responsible for this small government orientation was the Tax Collection Agency.

Table 1.4 Increases in Budget Ceilings, Budget Requests, and Initial Budgets (as a percentage of previous year's budget)

Fiscal Year	Ceiling on Request (%)	Ministries Requests (%)		Initial Budget (%)	
		general account	general expenditures	general account	general expenditures
1961[a]	50	48		24.4	
1962	50	40		24.3	
1963	50	38		17.4	
1964	50	35		14.2	
1965[b]	30	26.0	24.9	12.4	12.8
1966	30	25.8	23.6	17.9	20.4
1967	30	27.6	23.2	14.8	12.0
1968	25	24.2	22.4	17.5	14.9
1969	25	22.5	20.9	15.8	13.3
1970	25	22.1	21.5	18.0	16.9
1971	25	23.3	—	18.4	17.4
1972	25	21.5	—	21.8	25.2
1973	30	28.1	24.4	24.6	22.5
1974	25	22.4	21.8	19.7	19.0
1975	25	23.5	15.5	24.5	23.2
1976	15	16.8	10.8	14.1	18.8
1977[c] administrative expenditures	10				
others	15				
	14.5 (in total)	18.7	16.0	17.4	14.5
1978 administrative expenditures (excluding the research)	0				
others	13.5				
	13.2 (in total)	15.9	14.6	14.5	13.4

Category					
1979 administrative expenditures (excluding research) others	0 13.5 13.8 (in total)	14.5	13.4	12.6	13.9
1980[d] administrative expenditures others	0 10 9.8 (in total)	13.7	10.5	10.3	5.1
1981[e] administrative expenditures others	0 7.5 7.9 (in total)	12.5	8.6	9.9	4.3
1982 (excluding expenditures for defense, ODA, pension, measures for energy and science and technological promotion)	0	5.7	1.8	6.2	1.8
1983 (excluding aforementioned exceptions and investment expenditures)	1.9 (in total) -5	0.9	1.5	1.4	0.0
1984 current expenditures	1.46 (in total)	3.8	1.0	0.5	-0.1
investment expenditures	-10 -5 1.01 (in total)				

Table 1.4 Continued

Fiscal Year		Ceiling on Request (%)	Ministries Requests (%)		Initial Budget (%)	
			general account	general expenditures	general account	general expenditures
1985	current expenditures	−10	8.2	0.9	3.7	0.0
	investment expenditures	−5				
		0.86 (in total)				
1986	current expenditures	−10	7.4	1.5	3.0	0.0
	investment expenditures	−5				
		1.5 (in total)				
1987	current expenditures	−10	6.7	0.5	0.0	0.0
	investment expenditures	−5				
		1.0 (in total)				
1988	current expenditures	−10	12.5	1.8	4.8	1.2
	investment expenditures	0				
		1.8 (in total)				
1989	current expenditures	−10	13.0	2.8	6.6	3.3
	investment expenditures	−5				
		2.8 (in total)				
1990[f]	current expenditures	−10	11.4	3.0	9.6	3.8
	investment expenditures	−5				
		3.0 (in total)				

Note: General account means the total amount of government expenditures except those under the special accounts which the government separately established for specific purposes. General expenditure means expenditures that exclude bond expenditures and local allocation tax from the general account.

[a] For 1961–4: John C. Campbell, *Contemporary Japanese Budget Politics* (Berkeley: University of California Press, 1977); Campbell first compares the ceiling rate with the increasing rates of actual requests by the ministries and of the actual budget (general account) made at the beginning of each fiscal year.

[b] After 1964, see the accounts published each year in *Nihon keizai shinbun* and also see Y. Nakajima, 'Tokurei Kōzai izon kara no dakkyaku Heisei 2 nendo yosan ni tsuite' (On the emerging 1990 annual budget with attention to its special features), *Fainansu,* March 1990, pp. 4–12.

[c] From 1977, the local allocation tax, bond expenditures, and natural increments of pensions were exempt from the ceiling constraint. From 1977 to 1980, the ministries' requests did not include the bond expenditure.

[d] During the making of the budget in the 1980 fiscal year, MOF used the term 'general expenditure' for the first time. (The general public expenditure in each previous year was calculated and publicized by MOF thereafter.)

[e] From 1981, only the local allocation tax was excluded from the ministries' requests.

[f] For the first time since the 1975 fiscal year supplementary budget, the 1990 fiscal year budget did not depend on the special issuance of deficit bonds.

Source: Junko Kato, 'Bureaucratic Rationality in Question: Tax Politics in Japan' (Ph.D. diss., Yale University, 1993), Table 2–1.

Table 1.5 Trends in Government Current Disbursements, 1976–89 (percentage of GDP)

	1976	1980	1985	1986	1987	1988	1989
Australia	29.8	30.7	34.1	35.2	35.0	34.2	—
Austria	42.4	46.4	48.5	48.2	47.9	47.0	—
Belgium	40.1	42.7*	45.9	45.1	45.4	44.4	—
Canada	35.8	36.2	38.7	39.5	40.0	40.1	39.6
Denmark	46.9	52.2	56.5	58.3	58.8	58.6	57.4
Finland	41.0	35.8	40.5	41.8	39.7	40.0	39.9
France	41.8	44.5	47.6	46.9	47.4	46.8	46.5
Germany	44.0	44.7	45.6	44.9	44.4	43.8	44.6
Greece	29.5	30.5	34.6	35.6	36.5	34.0	31.8
Iceland	33.0	33.3	32.5	32.1	32.1	35.4	36.6
Ireland	37.9	38.8	43.6	43.5	43.7	—	—
Italy	—	33.0	38.0	39.0	39.2	39.6	41.1
Japan	23.6	27.6	31.2	31.5	33.4	34.3	
Luxembourg	50.2	53.3	55.9	52.9	—	—	—
Netherlands	49.5	52.8	54.3	53.0	53.6	52.4	50.1
Norway	49.8	53.2	55.1	54.7	55.2	55.1	—
Portugal	—	31.4	35.9	37.6	—	—	—
Spain	—	29.7	34.5	35.0	—	—	—
Sweden	—	56.3	59.5	60.4	62.2	61.9	—
Switzerland	33.9	32.8	34.4	35.0	34.5	35.0	34.1
United Kingdom	39.7	39.9	42.2	41.2	40.6	40.2	39.7
United States	29.5	30.8	31.3	31.4	—	31.6	—

Source: OECD Report, *Public Management Development, Annex II* (Paris: OECD, 1991), p. 74.

budget deficits and massive expenditures to cover national debt payments. Under the so-called Second Administrative Reform Commission, business and political leaders embarked on a program that led to massive privatization of the railways, the telecommunications industry, the tobacco and salt monopoly, parts of Japan Airlines, and other public corporations.[95] In addition, as noted above, national budgets were kept at fixed and low (and occasionally zero and negative) rates of growth which again impeded bureaucratic expansion both of programs and of personnel.

In the early 1980s, the national bureaucratic agencies were once more mobilized to participate in the reorganization, and the result was the rapid capping of what had been a systematic and regular expansion in government expenditures. In addition, the size of the bureaucracy was frozen at relatively small levels. And meanwhile a number of rather inefficient government corporations were privatized, enhancing governmental efficiency and revenue intake.

[95] On the national railways, see Atsushi Kusano, *Kokutetsu kaikaku* (Privatization of the national railways) (Tokyo: Sōgō Rōdō Kenkyūjō, 1989).

As noted, this matter is taken up in much greater detail in Ito's chapter. At this point it is worthwhile simply to highlight the fact that the Japanese experience demonstrates that there is nothing inevitable about bureaucratic expansionism. A strong government committed to the maintenance of a small bureaucracy can certainly accomplish such a task if sufficient political will is mobilized. Moreover, by allowing government agencies to play a major role in the reallocation of their own personnel, following mandatory reductions in size, it is also possible to enhance internal efficiency. Surely if there is bloat in any agency, those most likely to know its location are the senior civil servants. Providing them with incentives to reduce that bloat has been a highly positive measure in enhancing overall bureaucratic efficiency.

Direct Policy Influences

Most of the discussion to this point concerning the links between Japan's civil service and the nation's successful economy has been focused on indirect ways in which the structure of the Japanese civil service has contributed to overall national efficiency. Other papers in this book are devoted to examining some of the more direct links between bureaucratic action and economic performance. Still, this overview would not be complete without some discussion of the ability of Japanese civil servants to play a direct role in influencing national economic policy. The first point to establish is that Japanese bureaucrats are willing to take such actions. This is of course not automatically true of civil servants in various parts of the world. Peter Hall, for example, in a comparison of bureaucratic attitudes in France and Britain found that 'French civil servants felt responsibility for the direction of industry, generally capable of undertaking it and entitled to do so, when their British counterparts were far more hesitant.'[96] In this sense, the Japanese officials are far more like their French, than their British, counterparts.

The tools for bureaucratic influence over policy formation are considerable in Japan. In many countries the mechanisms for influence are indirect and implicit, e.g., tax code provisions designed to provide economic incentives. Japanese civil servants have access to such instruments as well. But many of the tools available to Japanese bureaucrats are direct, such as, for example, widespread influence over most aspects of the macroeconomy, including budgets, interest rates, and to some extent exchange rates. In addition, they have the authority to create various forms of cartels, to regulate (or deregulate) specific industries, to provide direct research and development subsidies, to control access to various tech-

---

[96] Peter Hall, *Governing the Economy: The Politics of State Intervention in Britain and France* (New York: Oxford University Press, 1986), p. 279.

nologies, and so forth. Bureaucratic influence is also noteworthy in the oversight of advisory committees, in the drafting of legislation, and in the discretionary implementation of such legislation. Partly as noted above, such extensive powers were the result of a willingness by LDP politicians to allow such 'technical' details of policy formation to be left to the national bureaucracy. Under the dominant party system that prevailed in Japan, the LDP was happy to delegate various powers to the bureaucracy and to attempt subsequently to influence bureaucratic implementation of such powers. In that way, many issues could be kept out of the parliament where opposition party influence is more institutionalized.[97] (That parliamentarians have small parliamentary staffs provides another strong incentive.[98])

Japanese governmental agencies have been masters of cooptation which has long been a major source of power to any agency, public or private. On one level, of course, they 'serve' various constituent groups, and to the extent that they do so, these groups are willing to accede to bureaucratic authority. But at the same time, government agencies also utilize these very same groups to advance their own policy and organizational ends.[99] So long as policy outcomes are moving in directions compatibly acceptable to both sides, an element of ambiguity about the specifics of bureaucratic authority is desirable.

Local neighborhood associations have been important in this regard. Most powerful during the prewar period, today they still distribute various monthly journals providing significant information concerning new welfare programs, free health checks, changes in the dates of garbage collection, and so forth. Informally, this is their only official function. Yet when local governments are interested in contacting local citizens, the neighborhood association is an invaluable organization for citizen mobilization.

Still another mechanism through which government agencies can get early information on problems as well as head off potential opposition has been the advisory commission. The debate over the role of advisory commissions in Japan has been rather extensive, with many contending that they indeed represent organizational opportunities for groups otherwise outside the arenas of power to exert substantial influence over policy formation. This has been particularly true of many business groups which have used the advisory committees as a way to influence government standards for industrial products and overall government policies toward specific industries.[100]

---

[97] Muramatsu, *Sengo Nihon no kanryōsei*, p. 201.

[98] Ramseyer and Rosenbluth, *Japan's Political Marketplace*.

[99] Michio Muramatsu *et al.*, *Sengo Nihon no atsuryoku dantai* (Pressure groups in postwar Japan) (Tokyo: Toyo Keizai Shinposha, 1986), Chap. 5.

[100] e.g., Hidetake Satō, 'Shingikai seido kaikaku no kokuminteki kadai: Kokka dokusen shihonshugi to rippō, gyōsei kikan' (The national task of reforming the advisory committee

We do not completely disagree with this point of view. Yet, we would rather note that several biases of the advisory commission system favor bureaucratic influence. First, it is the agency that determines the areas to be investigated; committees are not free to expand their scope of discussion beyond the bureaucratic mandate. Second, in most instances it is the organizing agency that determines the membership of each committee. Third, civil servants staff the committees, do most of the research required, and (drawing heavily on input from the interest organizations they monitor) provide virtually all the data used in deliberations.[101] Fourth, it is the civil servants who draft the final reports.[102] Thus, we would conclude that at a minimum, the advisory committee system provides an important source of bureaucratic influence over policy formation.

As still another important influence for central agencies, we would cite the drafting of legislation. As in most parliamentary systems, it is the bureaucratically crafted, government-sponsored bills that provide the main agenda for the legislature. And in Japan, most bills are drafted first by government agencies. It would be a mistake to miss the important links between the LDP and the bureaucratic agencies in this process: agencies did not draft bills opposed by the government; rather they served as an extended staff of the LDP. But the drafting process is again a powerful one, and agencies could exert a great deal of influence over substance through this seemingly 'neutral' process.

Finally, there is great discretion in the implementation of Japanese law. Most laws in Japan are drafted in vague and ambiguous language, leaving high levels of discretion in their enforcement. Again, governmental agencies have various ways in which to exert real policymaking power through such implementation. Ministerial ordinances and implementation directives explaining 'how' laws are to be interpreted are one such measure. 'Administrative guidance' is another.

'Administrative guidance' typically involves a series of recommendations from a government agency to specific firms and, more often, to an entire industry over a sustained period of time. It is advice that the agency believes to be in the best general interests of the industry. Since it is not legally binding, such guidance, to be successful, requires cooperation by both sides. And since any such guidance is likely to engender some

system: State monopoly capitalism, law, and administrative organs), *Keizai*, Vol. 174 (1978), pp. 123–50. See also Samuels on 'reciprocal consent' in *The Business of the Japanese State*.

[101] An interesting case of bureaucratic dependence on data from industry is provided in Richard J. Samuels, 'The Industrial Destructuring of the Japanese Aluminum Industry,' *Pacific Affairs*, Vol. 56, No. 3 (Fall 1983), pp. 495–509.

[102] Pempel, 'Bureaucratization of Policymaking,' pp. 659 ff. Disagreeing viewpoints can be found in Ehud Harari, 'Japanese Politics of Advice in Comparative Perspective: A Framework for Analysis and a Case Sudy,' *Public Policy*, Vol. 22 (1974), pp. 536–77, and in Schwartz, 'Of Fairy Cloaks and Familiar Talks.'

resentment, particularly by firms or industries that might see themselves as disadvantaged by the specific advice, government officials will typically talk extensively with industry leaders to iron out such differences. Such guidance provides government agencies with far more flexibility than they would have simply through their licensing prerogatives. Such statutory provisions, important as they may be, leave little room for the kinds of detailed instructions that the bureaucracy has felt necessary in guiding various industries.

Administrative guidance was used most extensively in the 1950s and early 1960s, largely to fortify Japan's smokestack industries. Throughout this process, the bureaucracy worked closely with individual industrial sectors and specific firms. To make its advice effective, the government gave the targeted industries access to the nation's limited foreign exchange reserves. The petrochemical and automobile industries, meanwhile, were given fiscal, financial, and tax breaks in order to further their development. The textile industry is another classic case in which administrative guidance was put to work. When the market turned sour, the government routinely helped the industry adjust its supplies by issuing advice calling for production cuts or lower capital investment. Finally, during the 1970s, the Ministry of International Trade and Industry issued guidance calling for Japan to shift its industrial structure toward 'knowledge-intensive, resource-conserving' industries. The Ministry of Finance has actively used administrative guidance in overseeing the banking and securities industries as well.

John Haley makes an interesting observation about the Japanese bureaucracy that relates to the problem of administrative guidance. As he puts it, 'Japanese bureaucrats enjoy widespread public acceptance of their authority to govern, an authority that . . . is symbolic and does not necessarily denote the powers of actual rule.'[103] Yet, over time, symbols take on reality and the symbolic power of the Japanese civil servant is often translated into 'suggestions' to various segments of the private sector about 'appropriate' behavior. As Haley notes, such actions do not pack the full force of law, but within Japan they carry considerable weight and are used and respected by those over whom guidance is exerted with close to the force of actual law. Although not all agree on its overall effectiveness, as has frequently been noted, administrative guidance has been a major tool in Japanese industrial policy.[104]

The subsequent chapters will play a major role in fleshing out the ways in which direct bureaucratic influence is exerted over public policy, particularly over policies that have an impact on economic growth. Clearly,

[103] John Owen Haley, *Authority Without Power: Law and the Japanese Paradox* (New York: Oxford University Press, 1991), p. 154.
[104] On the broad issues of administrative guidance and industrial policy, see Chalmers Johnson, ed., *The Industrial Policy Debate* (San Francisco: ICS Press, 1984).

however, the Japanese bureaucracy has by no means been reluctant to take on such roles in general. Whether or not the Japanese bureaucracy exerts considerably more influence over policy formation than bureaucracies in other advanced democracies is a matter of some dispute. It is doubly difficult to isolate bureaucratic power because it has rarely been exercised 'against' the LDP and/or the ruling politicians. Nor is it often exerted against Japan's powerful economic interests. But what is certainly clear from the above is that in contrast to many other countries, the Japanese civil service enjoys both an environment and a set of policy tools that in combination allow it to play a considerable role in Japan's economic growth.

The Negative Face of the Japanese Civil Service

The Japanese civil service is not without its flaws. Lest the above portrait seem too laudatory, it is important to examine briefly some of the major problems endemic in the Japanese bureaucracy. Most of these emerge as the negative aspects of the traits examined above.

There is no question that Japanese civil servants operate with high levels of competition, for example. And as we noted, this frequently can lead to exceptional motivation and quality performance far beyond that coming from the more noncompetitive, security-minded civil service posts throughout the world. At the same time two things should be noted. First, as Table 1.1 makes clear, the levels of competition for Class I civil service positions has been declining. It is not at all clear that competition rates in themselves equal high quality. But for a variety of reasons, many able graduates from quality universities no longer aspire to be civil servants, preferring work in the private sector. Furthermore, there have been recent reports that a number of young high flyers drop out of bureaucratic careers in their mid-30s in order to enter different occupational paths.[105]

There is also increased evidence that many civil servants, rather than opting for behavior patterns filled with creative, if often high risk action, are instead becoming oriented toward a strategy of 'risk minimization.' Getting into trouble out of the desire to make an outstanding contribution is not always worth it, in the eyes of many civil servants. Better to perform one's job safely and peacefully than to risk failing miserably and visibly. This tendency has become increasingly true when civil servants act in areas with high political visibility, such as in agencies dealing with local

[105] An interesting example of this concerns a former MITI official, Jun Okawa, who left MITI in his late 30s because of frustration with Japanese efforts to prevent foreign sales of metal baseball bats. Furthermore, as he pointed out, he was frustrated by 'a poor salary. I could not sustain my lifestyle.' Since gaining a business degree at the University of Chicago, he has been working with Western companies attempting to enter the Japanese market by teaching them how to get around MITI regulations. *Wall Street Journal*, May 11, 1993.

government, construction, education, agriculture, and even securities regulation, all of which are areas of great political concern to elected members of the government.

Just as individual competition has injected creativity into individual agencies, so agency-to-agency and central-to-local policy competition played a positive and creative role in many policy areas. Trying to get the mandate for a new program, or attempting to be selected as a positive pilot program, gives agencies and local governments the incentive to push beyond safe, predictable, and lethargic approaches to governance. At the same time, competition and sectionalism can lead to inefficiencies and frustrating overlaps as well.[106]

Moreover, the budgetary rigidities of the Ministry of Finance and the overall focus on low-cost government has prevented many active ministries from taking new initiatives in various policy areas, including cultural activities and social welfare. There is a tendency for the Japanese government to maintain existing programs and existing budgetary shares, even if this reduces adjustment to new problem areas.

Competition between ministries over 'turf' is standard, such as that between the Ministry of International Trade and Industry and the Ministry of Posts and Telecommunications in the Telecom War. Consider, too, the relations between the banking and securities industries. In Japan, both come under the jurisdiction of the Ministry of Finance, but through two separate bureaus. These two bureaus fought viciously over the 'intrusion' of banks into the securities business and the securities industry into banking. The end result was a slowdown in Japanese financial liberalization that has contributed heavily to the lack of international competitiveness of both industries.[107]

Because Japanese government agencies and bureaus are often closely tied to the social groups they oversee, they frequently become their protectors despite any consequent economic irrationality.[108] To appreciate this point, one need only consider the Ministry of Agriculture, Forestry, and Fisheries and its longstanding advocacy of rice price support for farmers and a resistance to agricultural liberalization; the long-standing support from the Ministry of International Trade and Industry for the continuation of restrictions on large-scale stores; the protective nurturing of the pharmaceutical industry by the Ministry of Health and Welfare; or

[106] Thus, for example, MITI and MPT both have almost duplicate programs at the local level to introduce high-definition television (HDTV) because each agency is competing for control over the industry. Our thanks to Ellis Krauss for pointing out this example.

[107] See Frances Rosenbluth, *Financial Politics in Contemporary Japan* (Ithaca: Cornell University Press, 1989) and James Horne, *Japan's Financial Markets* (Sydney: George Allen and Unwin, 1985).

[108] This point is implicit in Eisuke Sakakibara and Yukio Noguchi, 'Ōkurashō Nichigin ōkiku no bunseki' (An analysis of the Ministry of Finance-Bank of Japan dynasty), *Chūō kōron* (Aug. 1977). See also Hideo Ōtake, *Gendai Nihon no keizai kenryoku seiji kenryoku* (Economic power and political power in contemporary Japan) (Tokyo: Sanichi Shobō, 1979).

the restrictions on liberalization of the securities industry by the Securities Bureau of the Ministry of Finance.

The Banking Bureau has been a close protector of the nation's banking industry, following a so-called 'convoy approach.' Just as war ships move in a convoy at a speed determined by the slowest ship, so Japan's commercial banks were effectively regulated in ways designed to protect the most fragile banks. The Ministry continually refused requests from the most competitive institutions to upgrade their services or to raise their interest rates to savers.

To see how close and often negative these relationships can become, the securities industry also provides a good example. Among other things, when financial liberalization was proposed by the Securities and Exchange Council to the Securities Bureau, a noteworthy figure in the securities industry, formerly a Ministry of Finance official, was given a draft of the report which he read at home, adding some 40 modifications. In a similar fashion, the Ministry of Finance secretly allowed major securities houses to compensate major shareholders for stockmarket losses, in effect allowing their best customers to buy stocks with virtually no downside risk. When this matter became public it caused a major scandal in relations between Nomura Securities and the Ministry of Finance. Thus it is clear that oftentimes, agency competition and close coordination with the private sector can have effects that are seriously detrimental to the economy, and that they do not automatically produce added digits on the GNP.

We have also noted that local initiatives and agency competition have often worked in a positive way to create competition among agencies eager to tackle new social problems and regions anxious to try new policy approaches. Still, it would be a mistake to assume that all issues have been equally attractive in encouraging such initiatives. Many problems are highly sensitive politically, fostering the natural instincts among most bureaucrats to keep one's head down and to avoid risk-taking. This was certainly the case for most of the late 1960s concerning the mounting environmental problems faced by the country. Despite an overt 'problem,' agencies were reluctant to compete with one another to take it on. Rapidly escalating land prices in the 1980s and 1990s were similarly avoided by most agencies. In some instances, the fact that no post-bureaucratic jobs appear likely to result from tackling an issue (or that potential post-bureaucratic jobs will be threatened if an issue is taken up) serves as a big disincentive to taking on new problems, no matter how severe they may be for society as a whole.

Finally, although the national government has been kept relatively small in size, the number of local governmental personnel has expanded rather substantially. (See Figure 1.1.) Many of the tasks that might once have been handled at the center have simply been pushed down to the level of local government. It is impossible to tell just from the statistics anything about the effects on Japan's economy or its bureaucratic efficiency. Yet, it is clear that small national government has come at the price of an expanding local governmental service.

Finally, one additional negative aspect must be noted: Japan's civil service has not been structured with an explicit eye toward benefiting or protecting the individual citizen. Japan's economic policies have been oriented toward Japan's producers, rather than toward its consumers. It is difficult for individual citizens to gain a serious hearing in the civil service, particularly at the national level. Again, Japan is hardly unique in this regard, but the point deserves articulation.

The overall message we wish to convey is that Japan's civil service has by no means been an unadulterated success. Indeed, many of the structures and processes that have been so positively conducive to efficiency and economic growth have their negative faces that must also be recognized. This is particularly true for anyone seeking to draw lessons from the Japanese experience. It would be wise to recognize that any efforts at emulation of the Japanese civil service in the hopes of eliminating real or imagined problems in one's own government, might well engender new problems even greater than those targeted for reform. Overall, we think the Japanese civil service has been largely a plus for Japan and for Japanese economic development. Any realistic assessment of its role, however, must stop short of utopian portraits of unblemished perfection. There are real costs to many aspects of the Japanese civil service but these are more than counterbalanced by its positive features.

Conclusion

Japan's economic success, we have tried to argue, has been greatly assisted by the character of the nation's civil service. The remaining chapters will deal in considerable detail with the hows and whys of bureaucratic influence. The central point here is that whatever powers the Japanese civil service has been able to exert have operated within a broader political and social context that has itself been highly conducive to rapid economic growth. In effect, the Japanese civil service would have been able to do little 'by itself' in this area, although in some very important ways, various agencies have been highly conducive to overall economic success. At a minimum, any progrowth orientation within the civil service has been bolstered by the comparable orientation of the country's dominant conservative coalition.

Still, the Japanese civil service offers a variety of lessons about ways in which economic growth can be catalyzed, enhanced, and advanced. What is clear from our work, and what we hope will be clear from the subsequent chapters, is that the Japanese civil service has been instrumental in creating and maintaining a climate conducive to growth. The bureaucracy has also played a major role in the creation of a progrowth economic infrastructure throughout the country. And finally, as we have tried to suggest, various agencies have had the formal and informal power to take even more direct measures in advancing a progrowth economic strategy. Again, all of these points will be bolstered by the case studies to follow.

For those looking to Japan for lessons, we think two different points stand out. First, Japan offers numerous positive lessons regarding how the technical details of bureaucratic organization can be made conducive to economic growth. In particular, the quality of recruitment and the high degrees of built-in competition among individuals, agencies, and levels of government are all conducive to hard work, creativity, and generally positive outcomes, administratively and economically. In addition, the systematic limitations that check bureaucratic expansion are worthy of consideration by any political leadership anxious to see resources freed up from the public sector and made available to the private sector.

Yet, such techniques will themselves be virtually meaningless unless any potentially imitative civil service operates in a political and economic climate that allows the civil service to utilize its powers in ways that are actually growth-enhancing. Japan does not represent a bureaucratic template that can be applied to any other society desirous of emulating the Japanese experience. Rather, Japan's civil service is indicative of precisely the complex ways in which the organization and behavior of any multifaceted institution are significantly shaped by the historical context in which it has evolved.

What is, perhaps, capable of being carried over into other contexts, is Japan's pattern of 'bounded competition' within its bureaucracy. Structured to encourage rivalry among individual bureaucrats, as well as among agencies, and levels of government, the Japanese civil service provides tremendous incentives for creativity, imagination, hard work, and dedication. At the same time, this competition exists in a world of real winners and losers, set partially by the Ministry of Finance, partially by politics, and partially by the private business sector. Because limits are set on bureaucratic expansion, two goals are served.

The first goal is that the bureaucracy is kept smaller, but still hard working and creative. The individual who fails to accept the norms of diligence and initiative will not necessarily be fired, but he will hold posts of diminishing importance and prestige and will not be likely to have as challenging and rewarding a second career. For an agency, to fail to be hard working and creative is to be doomed to shrink and decline in size, mission, and capability.

The second goal that is served is one particularly critical for long-term economic growth: government is kept relatively small and relatively low in cost. If nothing else, this ensures that national resources are not consumed in vast quantity by the public sector, but are in fact, freed up for use in the potentially expandable segments of the private economy. In this regard, too, Japan offers a positive example.

2

Japan's Postwar Civil Service:
The Legal Framework

JOHN O. HALEY

However contentious many of the issues may seem regarding the postwar role of Japan's civil service, few question the basic proposition that Japan's economic bureaucracies played a significant if not defining part in Japan's stunning economic recovery and growth. The paradox may remain of an interventionist civil service ostensibly directing industrial and financial policies alongside a vigorously competitive market economy as well as a political system seemingly dominated by bureaucratic interests that was equally often acutely responsive to the demands of national and local constituencies, political leaders, and business enterprises. Yet the ubiquitous presence of a policy-directing civil service is a fundamental premise in nearly all analyses of Japan's postwar economic performance.

Other chapters in this volume deal with particular policies and related characteristics of Japan's political and administrative processes at both the national and local levels and the tensions they produce. They collectively identify salient contributions of postwar Japanese public administration at the municipal, prefectural, and national levels to Japan's economic growth. These include (1) the domination of competitive market forces over state-directed policies as a result of participation by the private sector in both the formulation and implementation of economic policies; (2) the capacity to develop and carry out at least relatively coherent policies with minimum cost; and (3) a constructive balance between administrative autonomy and political accountability. In the words of Paul S. Kim: 'Japan's contemporary public bureaucracy is one of the smallest and least expensive systems in the world. Yet it is an efficient, well-coordinated, and responsive public sector.'[1]

As in most other parliamentary systems, Japan's modern administrative law framework has appeared since its inception in the late nineteenth century to provide for strong centralized control. Most administrative agencies have also enjoyed extensive formal authority as well as a high degree of freedom from political interference. These features have

[1] Paul S. Kim, *Japan's Civil Service System: Its Structure, Personnel, and Policies* (Westport, Conn.: Greenwood Press, 1988), p. 1.

contributed greatly to the coherence of national economic policies in Japan. Yet, Japanese public bureaucracies in the postwar period increasingly have had to rely heavily on various means of persuasion and consensus in all stages of formulating and implementing policy. Legal command and formal coercive power to ensure compliance and conformity with policy objectives are rarely available or used. Moreover, despite apparently extensive autonomy'from direct legislative or judicial intervention, Japan's civil service remains distinctly accountable for high standards of behavior. Each of these features is reinforced if not determined by the postwar legal structure of public administration in Japan. My aim here is to analyze in broad brush how this occurred and, in so doing, to suggest the elements of this legal structure that could be effectively transferred as a model for other systems.

Context and Caveats

The Japanese civil service operates within an institutional structure created and controlled by constitutional, statutory, and regulatory law.[2] The organization of the civil service, its authority and coercive powers, the scope of its discretion and accountability, as well as the less formal levers it wields in the formulation and implementation of public policy are all grounded in law. Rule by law has long been a fundamental premise of Japanese governance. As Elise K. Tipton observes in her assessment of this aspect of Japanese police behavior in the interwar period, 'Japanese legalism' mandates 'that there should be legal boundaries to the scope of official discretion' and requires 'a legal basis for [official] action.'[3] Thus the legal framework along with the mechanisms for law-making and change are critical to any understanding of the performance and role of Japan's civil service and the factors that foster or inhibit its performance. Indeed, I argue here that the legal structure within which Japan's civil service operates has been instrumental in defining its role in the economy and channeling its behavior. Like the banks of a fast-flowing stream, the legal institutions of postwar Japan have determined the direction and often the intensity of bureaucratic activity.

[2] The literature describing the structural features of public administration in Japan is voluminous in English as well as Japanese. Among the best recent publications are: Kim, *Japan's Civil Service System*; B. C. Koh, *Japan's Administrative Elite* (Berkeley: University of California Press, 1989); and, somewhat earlier, Kiyoaki Tsuji, ed., *Public Administration in Japan* (Tokyo: University of Tokyo Press, 1984). John C. Campbell also provides an excellent summary of the most salient characteristics in 'Democracy and Bureaucracy,' in Takeshi Ishida and Ellis S. Krauss, eds., *Democracy in Japan* (Pittsburgh: University of Pittsburgh Press, 1989).

[3] Elise K. Tipton, *Japanese Police State: Tokkō in Interwar Japan* (Honolulu: University of Hawaii Press, 1990), p. 69.

At the outset, however, several propositions or caveats underlying my analysis are best clarified to avoid unnecessary repetition and possible misunderstanding. The first is that no institutional system or set of laws can assure correct policies or honest and fair administration. When we favor a particular policy, we are apt to describe the institutional arrangements that produce it as a virtue of the system. We are equally quick to condemn the same configuration when we think the policy bad. Seldom, however, does institutional structure deserve the full measure of either praise or blame. Law and institutions may dictate how policies are made and implemented but cannot determine the wisdom and honesty of those who ultimately make them. The most we can ask of law is that it establish institutions and processes that operate in foreseeable ways and that provide incentives for fair, honest, and efficient governance—in other words, that our constitutions, statutes, and regulations do in fact enable good government by creating systems with predicable patterns and appropriate incentives. The choice among systems, however, involves more guesswork than judgment as we attempt to decide which arrangements are most likely to produce better policies overall. Some institutions, for example, will be more responsive to immediate majoritarian demands. Others will ensure greater deliberation and consensus. None, however, will prevent mistakes or preclude success. We should also bear in mind that labels often mislead. Consistency and continuity are after all merely positive expressions for inertia and stagnation.

Second, Japan's laws and the institutions these laws have created must be understood as a hybrid of Western institutions—themselves a largely unplanned mix of various European and American models—introduced only within the past century. Thus unlike Japan's industrial peers, contemporary Japan's most basic legal and political institutions were either borrowed or imposed. Although widely accepted as legitimate, they did not evolve from within. Most of these alien institutions were of course purposefully introduced and adapted to achieve specific results. Many were also analogous to preexisting institutions and practices. Yet the consequences of their interplay within the Japanese cultural environment—an environment they also influenced and partially changed—could not have been fully predicted or forecast. Hence neither the institutions nor the patterns of governance that emerged in the course of time as a result of the constitutional and other legal reforms of the late nineteenth century or as modified and restructured by an occupying military conqueror in the mid-twentieth century were produced by either internal historical evolution or a coherent agenda of structural change. Rather they reflect a complex and often elusive mixture of selective borrowing and cultural adaptation. The result is a hybrid that should not be mistaken for its origins nor be evaluated in their terms.

For the period after World War II, this problem of evaluation is compounded by the complexity of the Allied Occupation and its contribution
to Japan's institutional mix. Unlike the reforms of the Meiji period (1868–
1912), for the most part the institutional changes introduced in the immediate postwar period were imposed by an alien occupying army in
order to effect drastic reform of what were perceived to be fundamental
flaws in Japan's political and legal processes. Needless to say, the occupation army's assessment of both the problem and the cure was imperfect.
Thus to attempt to evaluate the legacy of these reforms solely in terms
of what they were designed to achieve without careful and critical
reexamination of the assumptions on which they were based risks futility.
The Occupation reforms are more meaningfully evaluated instead by
looking backward from what they in fact accomplished and contributed to
the postwar Japanese experience.

For the Japanese civil service the contribution of the Occupation reforms is difficult to exaggerate. As detailed below, the basic structure of
governance in postwar Japan, including the role of the civil service, was
the creation of a constitution and series of statutes enacted under the
active supervision and often forceful direction of the Occupation authorities. Although, as Silberman details in his chapter in this volume, the
legal structure for a modern (Westernized) civil service was in place by
the turn of the century, nearly all of contemporary Japan's most fundamental regulatory statutes, from foreign exchange and foreign trade controls to securities regulation, were enacted with the participation and
instruction of the Occupation authorities and their advisors. Notwithstanding frequent assertions to the contrary,[4] prior to the 1930s Japan had
not experienced the degree of administrative intervention in the economy
that had become commonplace in most other industrial states at least by
the end of World War I if not before.[5] The contribution of the Meiji legal
reforms was to create an infrastructure for a market economy with only
limited, and that largely promotional, direct governmental intervention
and almost no regulation. Until the Occupation, the principal civilian
bureaucracies were those for home affairs and justice whose tasks were
defined more in terms of maintaining governmental control and public
order rather than economic performance. Even the Ministry of Finance

[4] See, e.g., Seymour Martin Lipset, 'Pacific Divide: American Exceptionalism—Japanese
Uniqueness' (unpublished paper presented to a conference of the Research Committee on
Comparative Sociology of the International Sociological Association at Kurashiki, Japan,
July 5, 1992), pp. 8–10. In light of U.S. legislative grants of land, mining, and timber rights in
the 1870s as well as the introduction of antitrust and other regulatory controls in the 1880s
and 1890s, Lipset is surely incorrect that 'the United States developed with much less
government involvement in the economy than almost all other now industrialized countries'
(pp. 9–10), particularly Japan.
[5] For fuller explication of Japan's relative freedom from regulatory intervention in the
economy prior to the 1930s, see John Owen Haley, *Authority Without Power: Law and the
Japanese Paradox* (New York: Oxford University Press, 1991), pp. 142–3.

(MOF) and its formal and informal controls over financial institutions were not fully developed until the 1930s. Not until the Occupation was the full array of administrative controls that would prevail over the postwar economy introduced.

The Allied Occupation did not, however, change Japan's basic continental law orientations. Despite the abolition of the administrative court system, administrative law in Japan as in continental Europe remained dominated by French concepts of separation of powers and the organizational role of administration within the overall juridical structure and German definitions of justiciable administrative actions. Absent was the emerging American emphasis on administrative procedure and judicial relief. Under the Occupation no American-styled administrative procedure law was introduced and little attention was paid to the problems of the role of judicial review and the capacity of the regular courts to grant adequate remedial relief in cases involving administrative mistake or improper conduct beyond constitutional and statutory provision for damage actions.[6]

The Japanese contribution to the Occupation reforms, it should be emphasized, was significant. Many of the most critical reforms in Japan's administrative system, including the creation of an independent, nonpolitical administrative personnel agency, in fact reflected prewar Japanese reform efforts and were achieved as a result of Japanese initiative. At least one notable reform—state liability for damages resulting from official error and misconduct—was initially rejected by the Occupation authorities. Equally important, however, the organizational features introduced under the Occupation proved to be remarkably enduring. A largely imposed constitution seems to have become almost amendment-proof, and, with few exceptions, a regulatory structure designed in part in response to emergency postwar conditions still stands. Whether because of resistance from the interests these reforms favored or the peculiar fragmentation of political power they fostered or some combination of these and other factors, only rarely has any significant modification in their basic design been possible.

A third caveat simply underscores observations previously made by Muramatsu and Pempel: the patterns of governance in contemporary Japan, particularly the role of the civil service, are in many respects determined by its parliamentary system. Hence Japan shares with most other industrial states, except the United States, certain attributes common to all parliamentary regimes. Some features of Japan's political and administrative processes that may therefore appear to be unusual or 'unique' from

[6] For further detail on administrative law reforms under the Allied Occupation, see John O. Haley, 'Toward a Reappraisal of Occupation Administrative Reforms: Administrative Accountability,' in Koichirō Fujikura, ed., *Eibei ronshū* (Essays on Anglo-American law) (Tokyo: University of Tokyo Press, 1987), pp. 543–67.

an American point of view in reality merely reflect the oddities of the American governmental system. Such misinterpretation has become especially acute in postwar American assessments of the role and influence of the Japanese bureaucracy. Little evidence, for example, supports the common view that the Japanese bureaucracy is any more influential in formulating public policy than the bureaucracies in at least half a dozen European states, including France, Germany, and the United Kingdom. In fact, from a European perspective the dominant characteristics of Japan's civil service may well be a relative coercive weakness, lack of direct legislative presence, and breadth of the state's legal liability for official mistake.

Summary of Argument

These propositions stated, the principal argument of this chapter can be summarized. The legal framework governing the organization and performance of the national civil service in postwar Japan, in my view, has enabled Japan on the one hand to develop a considerably more coherent set of economic policies at less cost than regimes in which either the role of the state is minimized or legislative interests prevail. On the other, this structure has also permitted Japan to avoid the overriding rigidities characteristic of more coercive administrative regimes exemplified by centralized and segmented—that is, selectively regulated—economies. This is not to say that all administrative agencies (a term used here in a generic sense to include all administrative units) achieve this balance uniformly. Some are considerably more responsive if not beholden to outside constituencies; others enjoy greater autonomy. By and large, however, the basic pattern holds and the differences that do exist are useful in aiding analyses of the consequences of disequilibrium in either direction.

As a model, therefore, the legal framework for national public administration in Japan includes the following features:

1. A parliamentary system of governance with cabinet accountability to a democratically elected legislature and an independent judiciary.
2. Constitutionally guaranteed freedom of political expression and freedom of the press in addition to redress (state liability to compensate) for official misconduct and gross error.
3. An autonomous, nonpolitical agency responsible for establishing the standards for entry into the public service, comprehensive qualifying examinations, compensation, and disciplinary action.
4. Comprehensive legislation establishing the basic organization for all executive units of government in addition to separate statutes that

delineate the functions and jurisdictional authority for each executive unit.

5. The reduction of governmental units into as few comprehensive departments or ministries and as little overlapping jurisdiction as feasible.

6. Placement of responsibility for the preparation of the national budget and broad allocations of resources in an administrative unit that demonstrates the highest professional standards and relative insulation from arbitrary political demands.

7. A nonpolitical agency accountable to the cabinet with the necessary legal competence and expertise responsible for professional review and final drafting of all legislation.

8. Broad public and political acceptance of the principles that, first, governmental policies are most effective when based on consent and implemented by persuasion and nonadversarial approaches rather than coercion and, second, that correspondingly the coercive powers of administrative agencies should be more limited in scope than their authority to intervene.

The argument presented here is developed in two parts. The first begins with a descriptive account of the basic legal structure for the organization and authority but remarkably limited coercive powers of the Japanese civil service. It continues with an examination of the laws affecting civil service recruitment, professionalization, and what is perhaps best called community allegiance. The first section concludes with an explanation of the significance of this structure to Japan's capacity to achieve coherence as well as to a dependence on consensus in public policy. The focus shifts in the second part to the issue of accountability, both political and legal. It includes an analysis of political controls, the contribution of one-party rule, as well as the role of judicial review through both direct review of formal administrative actions and the more pervasive use of damage claims against the state as a mechanism for regulating civil service performance. The paper concludes with an attempt to integrate the analyses in both parts in developing the model legal framework outlined above.

Structure and Authority

With the notable exception of Japan's few 'independent' specialized agencies formally constituted under the aegis of the Prime Minister's Office, all public administration in Japan is conducted today by internal departments or separate but attached agencies of eleven ministries (see Table 2.1), each of which is headed by a politically appointed cabinet minister. This basic structure is the product of the 1947 National Administrative

Table 2.1 Government of Japan, Executive Branch, Cabinet (Ministers of State)

Agency/Ministry/Office (*headed by Minister of State)	Personnel Positions (March 1992)
Board of Audit	1,206
National Personnel Authority	701
Cabinet	174
Cabinet Legislation Bureau	68
Prime Minister's Office	555
Fair Trade Commission	460
Imperial Household Agency	1,057
Environmental Disputes Coordination Agency	40
National Public Safety Commission*	
National Policy Agency	7,968
Management and Coordination Agency*	3,739
Hokkaido Development Agency*	8,413
Economic Planning Agency*	496
Science and Technology Agency*	2,084
Environment Agency*	883
Okinawa Development Agency*	1,103
National Land Agency*	454
Defense Agency*	[274,652]
Defense Facilities Administration Agency	92
Ministry of Justice*	45,919
Public Prosecutors	[2,049]
Public Security Examination Commission	4
Public Security Investigation Agency	1,785
Ministry of Foreign Affairs*	4,239
Ministry of Finance*	14,384
Mint Bureau	14
	(1,481)
Printing Bureau	16
	(6,162)
National Tax Administration Agency	54,447
Ministry of Education*	129,983
Agency for Cultural Affairs	724
Ministry of Health and Welfare*	58,498
Social Insurance Agency	16,961

Organization Law (Law No. 120, 1947, as amended), and the various 'establishment laws' for each of Japan's administrative units. As enacted in 1947 the original statute provided for a considerably less coherent system. Following American models, it created an administrative structure that included many free-standing regulatory agencies. One of the first changes made when Japan regained full sovereignty in May 1952, however, was to amend the National Administrative Organization Law and related statutes to subsume most of the separate units within a compre-

Table 2.1 *Continued*

Agency/Ministry/Office (*headed by Minister of State)	Personnel Positions (March 1992)
Ministry of Agriculture, Forestry, and Fisheries*	22,804
Food Agency	12,903
Forestry Agency	1,341
	(19,348)
Fisheries Agency	2,047
Ministry of International Trade and Industry*	5,436
Agency for Industrial Science and Technology	3,543
Agency of Natural Resources and Energy	582
Patent Agency	2,266
Small and Medium-sized Enterprise Agency	190
Ministry of Transport*	18,351
Central Labor Relations Commission for Seafarers	51
Marine Safety Agency	11,730
High Marine Accidents Inquiry Agency	246
Meteorological Agency	6,277
Ministry of Posts and Telecommunications*	2,747
	(296,438)
Ministry of Labor*	24,723
Central Labor Relations Commission	120
Ministry of Construction*	24,820
Ministry of Home Affairs	324
Fire-Defense Agency	128
Total	497,122
	(323,429)

Note: Figures in brackets [ ] are for military personnel and government prosecutors, neither of which are considered to be civil service employees. Figures in parentheses ( ) are for civil service employees subject to special statutes, such as forest and postal service employees.

Source: *1992 Public Employees White Paper*, pp. 298–9; *Nihon no tōkei 1992/1993* (Statistics of Japan (1992/1993) (Tokyo: Sōmuchō Tōkei Kyoku, 1993), pp. 294–7, for figures in brackets.

hensive cabinet-level ministry. For example, Japan's initial Securities and Exchange Commission, created in 1948 under the Securities Transactions Law (Law No. 115, 1948), was subsumed along with a variety of other independent boards within the Ministry of Finance in 1952 (Law No. 270, 1952) as an internal bureau. The pattern was repeated in other ministries.[7] The only major entirely separate regulatory agencies to remain were the National Personnel Authority and the Fair Trade Commission.

[7] See Hideo Wada, 'Gyōsei iinkai' (Administrative commissions), *Jurisuto*, No. 361 (1967), pp. 70–3.

The American model, it should be noted, does not fit comfortably within a parliamentary system. A primary concern in creating independent agencies in the United States was to reduce presidential control over the direction of regulatory policy. In turn, however, accountability to Congress was increased. The constitutional position of these agencies in the United States is still a debated issue. In contrast, the direct accountability of the cabinet to the Diet under Japan's postwar constitution eliminates this peculiarly American tension between the legislative and executive branches of government. That said, however, a second justification for independent boards, commissions, and other regulatory agencies is to reduce all forms of direct political control. Thus the creation of independent regulatory agencies is premised on a determination that coherence in overall policy should be sacrificed in the interest of more effective regulatory policies formulated and implemented by those with specialized expertise with only limited, indirect political accountability. As explained below, the Japanese model resolves this problem of assuring adequate outside control without statutory rules governing administrative procedures or broad direct judicial review.

The Japanese Fair Trade Commission (FTC) is an instructive example of the inherent problems of adapting the American model to the Japanese context. The FTC remains the only significant policymaking agency today without cabinet representation (see Table 2.1). The problems of conflict between the competition policies set out in Japan's Antimonopoly and Fair Trade Law (Law No. 54, 1947), to be implemented by the commission and the industrial policies underlying much of Japan's postwar economic legislation are well known. The result has been a continuing tension and inconsistency in antitrust enforcement. The relative weakness of the commission is at least in part explained by its anomalous position as a separate agency without ministerial status. These tensions have also led to at least an attempt to achieve some indirect control over the commission through the commissioner appointment process, dominated by the Ministry of Finance. Countervailing such controls the commission has tended to rely for support on outside constituencies, evident in both its protective role for Japanese licensees of foreign technology since 1968 and use of foreign, primarily American, political influence, most recently evident in the Bush administration's Structural Impediments Initiative.

In comparison, the Japanese model differs primarily in its underlying preference for consistency and coherence. As argued below, the differences in accountability—political or legal—are less significant than superficially they may appear. The decision to combine as many administrative units with responsibilities in broadly defined jurisdictional fields as possible within a single comprehensive ministry achieves consistency by forcing compromise in the event of any substantial conflicts in the policies recommended or pursued by its separate sections. In many instances the potential for conflict will be identified and resolved within the ministry, if necessary, by upward appeals to higher levels of authority. As a result, Japan is able to achieve a greater degree of consistency than the United States in both formulating and implementing most national policies.

This is not to say that Japan is able to avoid all conflict and inconsistency. At the ministerial level the Japanese system replicates the problems intrinsic to the fragmented American structure. Overlapping jurisdiction coupled with bureaucratic rivalry, made more intense by personnel socialization within each ministry and lack of mobility among agencies, hinder cooperation and coherence.

Viewed as a whole the establishment laws in effect divide nearly all sectors of the nation's economic and social life into spheres of responsibility allotted to individual ministries. The seemingly—at least in American eyes—precatory language of the initial articles of these statutes is more properly understood as binding legislative mandate that defines the competence of the ministries in terms of their respective spheres of authority as well as the nature of their roles and administrative tasks. For example, the Ministry of International Trade and Industry (MITI), under its 1952 Establishment Law (Law No. 275, 1952) is granted broad responsibility for the 'promotion' and 'adjustment' of Japanese commerce and industry (art. 3[1]), the authority to adjust, inspect, and promote the consumption, distribution, and production of mining and industrial products (art. 3[2]). In article 3(3) MITI is given the authority to foster the rationalization and 'appropriateness' of commercial, mining, and industrial activities. Its responsibilities in these areas of Japanese economic life include planning (art. 3[4]) and the adjustment of output and supply (art. 3[12]), especially in energy-related resources (art. 3[5&6]). The same article gives MITI the authority to provide 'guidance' for the promotion of small and medium-sized enterprises (art. 3[9]) and its jurisdiction over foreign exchange controls (as related to commerce and industry) (art. 3[1]), industrial standards (art. 3[11]), intellectual property rights (art. 3[8]), publicly owned enterprises (art. 3[13]), the alcohol monopoly (art. 3[13]), and oversight over technical schools for mining (art. 3[10]). The term 'regulation' is not used at all.

Similarly, the Ministry of Agriculture, Forestry, and Fisheries (MAFF) Establishment Law (Law No. 153, 1949) delegates to MAFF expansive authority to foster production by Japanese agriculture, forestry, and fisheries (art. 3[1&2]); to promote the welfare of Japanese farming, forestry, and fishery households (art. 3[1&5]); and to ensure the stability of foodstuffs for the nation (art. 3[1]). Its authority includes planning, adjustment, rationalization, inspection, testing, and research related to agriculture, forestry, and fisheries as well as 'oils' and specialized equipment for these industries. Again, no mention is made of 'regulation' or regulatory controls.

In contrast, the Ministry of Health and Welfare (MHW) is explicitly empowered in article 4 of its establishment law (Law No. 151, 1947) to regulate all drugs and pharmaceuticals in addition to its responsibilities for managing social welfare, social security, and public health programs. Also carefully delineated is the exclusion from MHW jurisdiction of labor pension and annuity programs, the administration of which is delegated to the Ministry of Labor (see article 4 of the Labor Ministry Establishment Law, Law No. 162, 1949). The MOF Establishment Law (Law No. 144, 1949) lists 129 separate areas subject to MOF authority (art. 4), many with explicit delegation of authority for managerial control. Included is MOF's exclusive responsibility for preparing the national budget for Diet approval, management of revenues and all national assets, and prior approval authority for the most basic contractual arrangements by other ministries and governmental units.

Legislative policy is formulated in Japan like other parliamentary systems within the ministries with subject-matter jurisdiction (see Figure 2.1). Nearly all statutory law in Japan and other parliamentary governments is first introduced as cabinet bills with most supplementary regulation prepared simultaneously. Roughly 90 per cent of all enacted legislation in Japan is based on bills introduced by the cabinet, a lower percentage than many European states, the United Kingdom included.[8] This is not to say, however, that the policies are *made* by administrative officials. Some are and some are not, depending upon their content and the extent to which issues of national importance are involved. As in all industrial states today the influence of the civil service on policy is substantial.

What distinguishes the legislative process in Japan is the extent of parliamentary and public participation. As explained below, agreement by those most concerned with a particular policy is essential in Japanese policymaking. The need for consensus involves the Diet, especially the standing Diet committees, to an extent that gives real meaning to Diet assent. This aspect of the Japanese legislative process is viewed by some as its distinguishing feature.[9] For this reason too the Japanese policymaking structure also includes an unusually large number of advisory committees, ad hoc policy groups, and similar vehicles for developing consen-

---

[8] See Ezra N. Suleiman, 'Toward Disciplining of Parties and Legislators: The French Parliamentarian in the Fifth Republic,' in Ezra N. Suleiman, ed., *Parliaments and Parliamentarians in Democratic Politics* (New York: Holmes and Meier, 1986), pp. 87–8. Virtually all legislation enacted in the United Kingdom begins as government-sponsored bills, and between 1945 and 1978, a remarkable 96.6 per cent of all government bills were approved. More striking is the extent to which government bills are enacted without even minor amendment in the course of legislative action. Between 1946 and 1966 a mere 7 per cent of all government bills were altered in any form. Even during the period of the minority Labour Government (1974–8), 59 per cent of the government-sponsored legislation was enacted without change of a single clause. Richard Rose, 'British MPs: More Bark than Bite?' in Suleiman, ed., *Parliaments and Parliamentarians in Democratic Politics*, pp. 11–12, 28–9.

[9] Fukase Tadakazu, 'Nihon no rippō katei no tokushoku' (Distinctive features of the Japanese legislative process), *Jurisuto*, No. 805 (1984), pp. 16–24.

sus. Indeed, as noted in many of the case studies that constitute this volume, characteristic of Japan's administrative structure is the number of statutory advisory commissions, committees, and boards. Each has its own history and function. Some, like many of those attached to the Ministry of Finance as noted above, reflect post-Occupation transformation from independent regulatory agencies to ministry sections or advisory committees. Some perform prefunctionary tasks and have seemingly little significance. Most, however, provide a formal channel for private sector participation in the consensus-building process that nearly all administrative organs in Japan require in formulating and implementing policy.

The formulation of legislative policy should not be confused, however, with the more technical aspects of legislative drafting. Whereas the two are intertwined in the United States with many constituencies in and out of government contributing language to bills in process, in Japan a single agency—the Cabinet Legislation Bureau—has responsibility for the final version of all cabinet bills. The process has been described in detail by Mamoru Seki, former Director of the bureau's Second Division.[10] As explained by Seki, the bureau works closely with members of the ruling party's policy board, ministry officials, and concerned Diet members from the earliest stages of the process of drafting. One result is a consistency of terminology and form enhancing both the certainty and clarity of law in Japan.

Finally, mention should be made of an additional but often neglected factor that underlies the structure of Japan's postwar civil service: the lack of a politically significant military establishment. The constitutional order of postwar Japan effectively subjects a potentially potent military to civilian control. Thus unlike prewar Japan the military does not challenge the civilian bureaucracies for status or influence.

Autonomy

The influence of Japan's civil service on public policy is also a function of its ability to act with limited direct political influence. But for the relative autonomy of Japan's civil service, Japanese public officials would exert considerably less effective influence on public policy as either negotiators or arbiters. This relative autonomy is in part a feature of most parliamentary systems, within which direct political direction must generally be channeled through party leaders and the politically appointed ministers in charge in contrast to the United States where legislative policy is made in congressional committees. As noted below, the lack of party rivalry has

---

[10] Mamoru Seki, 'The Drafting Process for Cabinet Bills,' *Law in Japan: An Annual*, Vol. 19 (1986), pp. 168–87, translated by Daniel H. Foote from 'Naikaku teishutsu hōritsuan no ritsuan katei,' *Jurisuto*, No. 805 (1985), pp. 25–39.

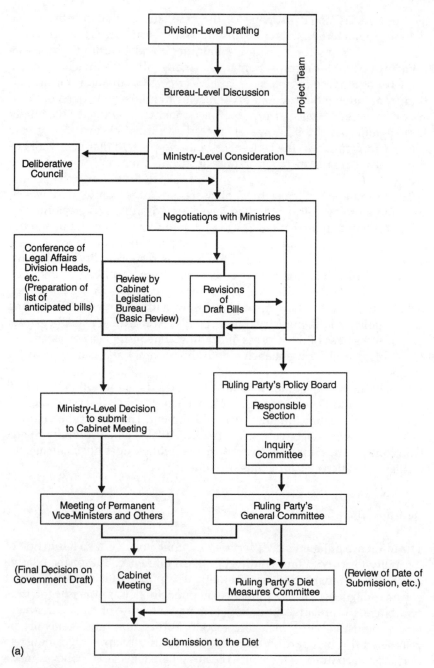

Source: *Law in Japan: An Annual,* Vol. 19 (1986), p. 173.

Fig. 2.1. The Legislative Process in Japan
        (*a*) Drafting Process for Cabinet Bills

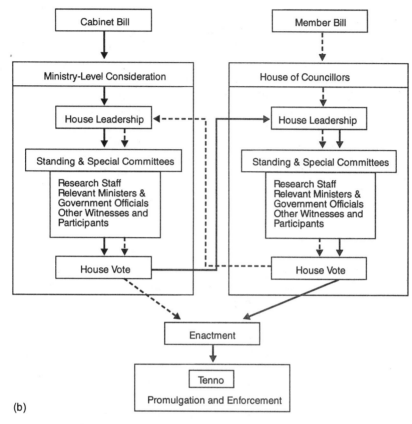

Source: Adapted from *Jurisuto*, No. 805 (1984), p. 19.

Fig. 2.1. *Continued*
(*b*) Diet Deliberation and Action

tended to obscure the extent of political influence and corresponding accountability of the civil service in the case of Japan.

Nevertheless, other institutional features in the Japanese administrative structure reinforce the insulation of the civil service from direct legislative interference. Among the most important is the limited number of administrative positions available for political appointment. In addition to the minister there are at most only two other political appointments for each ministry: the office of political or 'parliamentary' vice minister. This position is ranked alongside the office of administrative vice minister, the senior career administrative position in each ministry. Except for MOF, MAFF, and MITI, each of which has two parliamentary vice ministers, no ministry has more than one. As a result, career civil service personnel occupy all but the highest administrative positions with corresponding freedom from direct supervision by political appointees.

Another source of general administrative autonomy is the delegation of decisions relating to compensation and tenure to a separate, nonpolitical administrative agency, the National Personnel Authority (NPA). The NPA is generally considered one of the few remaining autonomous agencies established under the Occupation. Notwithstanding its creation as a principal component of the Occupation's rather limited civil service reform effort,[11] the establishment of a central administrative department in charge of civil service personnel recruitment, compensation, and discipline originated in prewar reform efforts at least as early as under the first Konoe cabinet (1937–39).[12] As described in articles 3 and 4 of the National Public Employees Law (Law No. 120, 1947, as amended), which serves as its establishment law, its functions include the administration of the general public service examinations; recommendations to the Diet of compensation schedules for all categories of national public employees, including elected officials; adjudicatory review by appeal of disciplinary measures against civil service employees, as well as administration of public employee training and benefit programs.

The importance of the NPA to the effective performance of Japan's civil service is substantial. The professionalization of the Japanese civil service owes much to the NPA and the basic statute governing national public service employees it administers. Within the Japanese context it has assured that civil service positions have been filled on the basis of generally applied standards of competence in lieu of personal or partisan considerations. Its authority over recommendations for public service compensation gives the agency a degree of leverage that is difficult to exaggerate. Above all else, however, the NPA has ensured that compensation decisions for national public service are made in terms of prevailing general private sector standards and not political or public pressures. As a result, Japanese public employees are well paid by international standards[13] but not excessively so in relation to Japan's private sector or, for that matter, local public employees. Indeed, the comparison of national and local government employee compensation is an instructive illustration of the role of the NPA.

As noted by Yukio Noguchi, on average the compensation of local government employees by 1987 was 6 per cent higher overall in comparison to national public employee compensation rates. Moreover, in 33

---

[11] See Justin Williams, Sr., *Japan's Political Revolution under MacArthur: A Participant's Account* (Athens: University of Georgia Press, 1979), p. 65; T. J. Pempel, 'The Tar Baby Target: "Reform" of Japanese Bureaucracy,' in Robert S. Ward and Sakamoto Yoshikawa, eds., *Democratizing Japan: The Allied Occupation* (Honolulu: University of Hawaii Press, 1987), pp. 157–87.

[12] See Koh, *Administrative Elite*, p. 33.

[13] For example, in 1992 the average section chief was 46 years old and earned a base salary of ¥534,057 or $4,272.46 U.S. (at ¥125 per $1 US) per month. Jinji'in (National Personnel Authority), *Kōmuin hakusho* (Public employees white paper) (Tokyo: Ōkurashō Insatsu Kyoku, 1992), p. 216.

municipalities the local rates were 20 per cent higher.[14] What Noguchi does not mention is that for the vast majority of local public employees living costs are considerably lower than for at least national (and local) government workers in the Tokyo metropolitan region.[15] The contrast in levels of compensation between local and national government employees is an indication of the role of the NPA as a central agency in restraining civil service demands for higher compensation while simultaneously avoiding countervailing taxpayer pressures to maintain civil service compensation at unreasonably low levels in relation to private sector rates.

Ministry of Finance control over the national budget has had similar effect in restraining growth in the number of national public employees. As noted at the outset, Japan has one of the smallest civil service establishments in the world. While most of Japan's industrial peers have witnessed substantial increases in the number of national government employees during the postwar period, Japan has managed to maintain a relatively constant number of national public employees during the past four decades and actually to reduce the size of its national bureaucracy since the mid-1980s.[16] This phenomenon has not, however, been true for Japan as a whole. The number of local government employees has increased.[17] Again, the restraining influence of a central agency responsible for recommending resource allocations can be viewed as a principal factor.

No single prerogative of any ministry is as critical to its overall influence and the effective coordination of Japanese policymaking as MOF's

[14] Yukio Noguchi, 'Public Finance,' in Kozo Yamamura, *Policy and Trade Issues of the Japanese Economy: American and Japanese Perspectives* (Seattle: University of Washington Press, 1982), p. 204.

[15] In 1990 the average monthly expenditure per household in Japan for food, housing, utilities, clothing, medical care, transportation, education, and recreation was ¥311,174. However, in the Tokyo-Yokohama metropolitan area the average expenditure was ¥354,641. In contrast the average for the Kyoto-Osaka-Kobe metropolitan area was ¥308,001 with northern Kyushu at ¥298,079. On a regional basis, the Tokyo region (Kanto) was again the highest with an average expenditure of ¥346,605 as compared to a regional low of ¥234,957 for Okinawa, followed by ¥268,970 for Shikoku, ¥277,281 for Kyushu, and ¥279,792 for Tohoku. Statistics Bureau, Management and Coordination Agency, *Japan Statistical Yearbook 1991* (Tokyo: The Mainichi Newspapers, 1991), p. 534.

[16] In 1965 Japan had a total of 834,391 general account national public employee positions. By 1989 the number had decreased to 824,769. The number of all budgeted national employee positions in 1970 was 1,992,793. By 1991 the number had decreased even more dramatically to 1,180,700. *Japan Statistical Yearbook 1991*, pp. 703, 705. See also *Asahi nenkan 1992* (Asahi year book 1992) (Tokyo: Asahi Shinbunsha, 1992), p. 470. As of March 31, 1992, Japan had a total of 4,528,637 public employees, of whom 1,169,292 were national and 3,359,345 were local. *1992 Public Employees White Paper*, p. 297. Of the budgeted national public employee positions, approximately 26 per cent are for postal workers, 24 per cent uniformed personnel in the Self Defense Forces, and 12 per cent in national educational institutions.

[17] In contrast to the decrease in the number of both general account and total budgeted national public employee positions, the number of local government employees increased from 2,213,000 in 1965 to 3,225,000 in 1989. *Japan Statistical Yearbook 1991*, p. 703. See also Noguchi, 'Public Finance,' pp. 219–20.

responsibility for preparation of the national budget. In the words of Campbell, 'the balance of [national] revenues and expenditures is kept under tight MOF control,' and the preservation 'of the ministry's autonomy, elite status and jurisdictional boundaries' is considered its highest priority.[18]

Persuasion and Consent

Reliance on consensus in the formulation and implementation of public policy in Japan is no myth. The structure of the Japanese legislative system, as explained above, necessitates efforts to achieve agreement within the Diet for measures worked out within the ministries. Similarly, in implementing policy the weakness of enforcement powers in Japan requires the assent of those subjected to governmental controls.

As unrivaled for influence and as extensive as the statutory delegations of authority to Japan's civilian ministries may appear, they do not include equally extensive coercive powers. MOF alone exercises full managerial control over most subjects within its jurisdiction. Even MOF, however, must rely upon special statutory provisions for coercive controls over the banking, securities, and insurance industries subject to its supervision. In turn, few of Japan's regulatory statutes provide for the full range of coercive powers common to most industrial states. Typically, a ministry will be granted the authority to intervene and supervise but not to issue binding legal orders subject to sanctions for failure to comply. As a result, the most important levers of power exercised by a ministry are encompassed within its licensing and approval authority.

To add to the examples of these levers detailed in other contributions to this volume, particularly that of Mabuchi, MITI's authority to intervene 'to adjust' energy supply pursuant to national energy policies does not include coercive powers to regulate energy prices or to allocate output. Through the use of import licensing and approval powers under the 1949 Foreign Exchange and Foreign Trade Control Law (Law No. 228, 1949), the ministry was able to negotiate energy policies and, at least relatively, effectively mediate between Japan's various producers and principal industrial users.[19] However, MITI's ability to direct energy policies was limited by both Diet and MAFF intervention to protect agricultural

[18] John C. Campbell, *Contemporary Japanese Budget Politics* (Berkeley: University of California Press, 1977), p. 373.
[19] See, e.g., Richard Samuels, *The Business of the Japanese State: Energy Markets in Comparative and Historical Perspective* (Ithaca: Cornell University Press, 1987); Laura F. Hein, *Fueling Growth: The Energy Revolution and Economic Policy in Postwar Japan* (Cambridge, Mass.: Harvard University Press, 1990); Martha Ann Caldwell, 'Petroleum Politics in Japan: State and Industry in a Changing Policy Context' (Ph.D. diss., University of Wisconsin-Madison, 1981).

users,[20] industry and labor demands,[21] as well as, ultimately, antitrust constraints.[22] From the perspective of Japanese energy policy, in the words of Samuels, 'the activist Japanese state has failed at nearly every juncture—in peace and war—as early as 1902 and as recently as 1984—to entice the private sector to consolidate on its terms and under its control.'[23] In contrast to MITI's postwar energy policies, MOF has been able to control Japan's financial policies with less deference to outside pressures as a result of its ability to restrict entry effectively through licensing requirements and its more general controls over monetary and fiscal policies. However, MOF too is constrained by ministry rivalry and industry needs. The internationalization of capital markets, for example, forced MOF to make significant changes in regulatory policies affecting the banking industry. The limits of MOF control extend even to monetary policy in that the postal savings system, under the Ministry of Posts and Telecommunications not MOF, accounts for a third of all Japanese personal savings.

The result is an unusual degree of administrative weakness in the process of negotiating compliance with public policy, a weakness masked by the pervasive nature of administrative intrusion and ubiquity of official participation in almost all sectors of national economic and social life. The weakness of administrative power in Japan is critical to an understanding of the process of making and implementing public policy. All governments rely upon negotiated consent, particularly in enforcing policy. Such consent, however, is often obtained from the otherwise recalcitrant recipients by the threat of coercion. Thus formal grants of coercive powers provide the principal means of implementing regulatory policies more in their threatened use than actual exercise. Knowledge that officials can and will use coercive measures to enforce desired policies induces compliance. The relative lack of such coercive threats forces Japanese officials to resort to an array of more indirect but seldom as effective means of persuasion. As a result, policies that require extensive direct compulsion tend to be avoided. Voluntary compliance can best be assured, however, by negotiating for consent in the process of formulating policies rather than only in their enforcement. Hence the apparent paradox of extensive authority with limited coercive power produces a predominant pattern of negotiated consent and compromise between officials and the private sector in both the formulation and implementation of public policy in Japan. As a result, administrative procedure in

[20] See Caldwell, 'Petroleum Politics,' pp. 78–9.

[21] Laura Hein cites the example of a 1963 statute restricting the use of oil in heavy boilers that was so weakened as a result of electric-power industry opposition that it became almost totally 'ineffectual.' Hein, *Fueling Growth*, p. 384, note 3.

[22] See, e.g., *Idemitsu Kōsan K.K., et al.* v. *Japan*, 38 Keishū 1287 (Sup. Ct., 2nd P.B., Feb. 24, 1984).

[23] Samuels, *The Business of the Japanese State*, p. 225.

Japan also tends to be informal, unregulated, and opaque with little private sector demand for legislated formalities or greater transparency.[24]

In implementing promotional economic policies, the pattern of official intervention tends to take the form of governmental intermediation among competing private interests. With voluntary compliance ordinarily a given, officials play a monitoring role in the allocation of resources and mediating conflicts. As Yasusuke Murakami observed, Japanese administrative agencies have discovered that they are more effective as arbiters rather than enforcers of legal rules.[25]

Consensus does not mean unanimity. Rather, in the context of Japanese policymaking, it involves agreement among those whose cooperation will be essential in the process of legislating and implementing policy. It thus truly empowers the participants. Unlike majoritarian decision making, consensus in effect gives veto power to each party in the circle of those whose assent is required. As a result, many of the political tensions in Japan relate to demands for participation in that circle and the countervailing concern that any expansion will result in the inability to act. To be effective, therefore, Japanese civil servants must have finely honed skills as negotiators, mediators, and persuaders. Above all else, they must protect their status as the representatives of the national interest and the common good on which rest their authority and capacity to persuade.

Legal Accountability

The rule of law is a fundamental principle of Japan's postwar public law system. However, those who seek to find in postwar Japan legal controls over administrative actions equivalent to those in the United States or European legal systems will be disappointed and are more than likely to conclude that public administration in postwar Japan is notably free from legal constraints. As recently construed by the Japanese Supreme Court in a landmark case arising out of the opposition to the Tokyo International Airport at Narita,[26] the 'due process' guarantee of article 31

---

[24] Private sector preference for informal administrative processes where an agency is forced to rely on consensus helps to explain the contrast between decades of fruitless effort to enact an American-styled administrative procedure act but successful imposition of formal procedural controls over FTC decision-making processes under the 1977 amendments to Japan's Antimonopoly and Fair Trade Law. For further detail see note 26 below.

[25] Yasusuke Murakami, 'Toward a Socioinstitutional Explanation of Japan's Economic Performance,' in Yamamura, ed., *Policy and Trade Issues of the Japanese Economy*, p. 17.

[26] In a Grand Bench decision in 1992, the Japanese Supreme Court rejected the argument that the due process provision of article 31 applies only to criminal proceedings, although the majority opinion narrowed its application to administrative proceedings that share the characteristics of criminal cases. *Sanrizuka Shibayama Rengō Kūkō Hantai Dōmei* v. *Japan* (Sup. Ct., B.B., July 1, 1992), *Jurisuto*, No. 1006, pp. 155, 157).

of Japan's postwar constitution does not apply to administrative proceedings in general. Only after prolonged efforts has Japan been able to enact even a weak statute governing administrative decision-making and enforcement.[27] Nor, despite postwar constitutional reforms abolishing the administrative court system and explicitly empowering the regular courts with the prerogative of judicial review, direct judicial review of administrative actions remains bound by restrictive prewar doctrines developed in European administrative jurisprudence but abandoned there in favor of more liberal approaches. Largely ignored, however, are features of the Japanese system that assure more extensive review of administrative conduct than in any other industrial state, except perhaps South Korea and Taiwan, which have both recently adopted the Japanese approach.

The primary means for direct review of administrative behavior in Japan are direct appeals from formal administrative actions under the

[27] For the seminal study in English on Japan's lack of any general statutory requirements or uniform practice regarding administrative procedures, see Nathaniel L. Nathanson and Yasuhiro Fujita, 'The Right to a Fair Hearing in Japanese Administrative Law,' *Washington Law Review*, Vol. 45 (1971), pp. 273–334. On the most recent recommendations for a national administrative procedure law, see Hiroshi Shiono, 'On the Occasion of the Publication of the Administrative Procedure Law Study Commission Report,' *Law in Japan*, Vol. 19 (1986), pp. 90–124.

Although the arguments in favor of generally applicable standards and greater uniformity are compelling, the contrast with U.S. law practice is considerably less significant than may first appear. U.S. formal procedural controls, particularly those that require 'judicialized' hearing procedures, are generally essential to enable effective judicial review—a core concern of U.S. administrative law. Judicial review in the United States is generally akin to appellate review of a trial court proceeding in which the appellate court has only limited authority to reconsider the factual issues decided by the court of the first instance. Without engaging in a *de novo* examination of the factual or evidentiary basis for the administrative agency's action, the courts would not be able to determine whether the administrative decision satisfied even the most basic requirements of rationality and good judgment, much less substantive statutory requirements unless the agency has acted pursuant to formal proceedings in which a record for review was developed. Greater administrative discretion is allowed within the bounds of constitutional requirements of due process, however, whenever *de novo* judicial review is followed. In contrast, in Japan the first appeal in civil, criminal, as well as administrative cases ordinarily gives the parties an opportunity to retry the facts *de novo*. Thus one of the principal aims in requiring formal hearings in the United States does not apply in Japan. Nor, it might be added, do the proposals for a Japanese Administrative Procedure Act envision as complete a 'judicialization' of administrative proceedings as currently mandated by U.S. federal and state law.

Measured by the standard criteria of accuracy, efficiency, and fairness, the Japanese emphasis on informal procedures is difficult to fault. First, there is no evidence that in general the lack of formal procedural requirements produces significantly less responsible or accurate administrative decisions. Procedural controls do not always produce the best results. The flexibility of informality in fact has significant gains in terms of both accuracy and efficiency. Fairness is therefore the central issue. Yet public demand for greater procedural controls has not been as strong in Japan as in the United States or, apparently, Europe. This suggests that 'procedural fairness' is less important or, perhaps, is defined differently in Japan, or that, as argued above, the necessity for some degree of negotiated consensus produces results that in most instances the Japanese public considers to be just and appropriate.

1962 Administrative Case Litigation Law (Law No. 139, 1962). However, restrictive prewar doctrines derived from German administrative law continue to dominate the interpretation of the courts' authority to adjudicate direct appeals. As a result, the judiciary generally limits appeals to cases involving only formally binding administrative actions. Informal measures, especially any non-binding administrative measures, such as internal policy directives and various forms of 'administrative guidance,' are ordinarily not justiciable. Moreover, the 1962 statute limits the remedial authority of the courts essentially to revocation of administrative decisions and dispositions or declarations affirming their illegality or invalidity. Japan like continental Europe does not include Anglo-American notions of equity power in its definition of judicial authority. Nor do Japanese, or continental European courts, exercise contempt powers. The restrictive scope of direct judicial review of administrative actions is thereby compounded by equally limited forms of relief and means of coercion. Neither Japanese nor continental European courts therefore play a partnership role with administrative agencies as in the United States and the United Kingdom in interpreting and enforcing administrative regulations. Finally, delay in obtaining judicial relief when available has also been a significant barrier to direct relief. In 1991, for example, over 10 per cent of the administrative appeals in district courts (first instance adjudication) had been pending for over five years, and over half had been pending for over a year.[28]

Direct appeals of administrative measures are supplemented, however, by the extensive availability of private damage actions under the National Compensation Law (Law No. 120, 1947). No industrial state provides more extensive relief in the form of monetary compensation for as wide a range of administrative misfeasance. The statute makes the state liable for all manner of 'negligent' conduct by public authorities, local as well as national, as well as all 'defects' in the 'management of public facilities' (art. 2). Judicial interpretations of the law have also been quite expansive. As a result, the courts routinely review a variety of judicial as well as administrative actions that would be immune from judicial scrutiny in the United States and in Europe. Remedial restrictions remain, however. The National Compensation Law only provides for after-the-fact compensatory damages. It does not empower the courts to take preventive measures or to order agencies to act. Nevertheless, the law does ensure the legal accountability of Japan's civil service. Within the context of Japanese administrative culture, this threat of judicial condemnation for misfeasance can be viewed as significant.

[28] Saikō Saibansho, Jimu Sōkyoku (Supreme Court, General Secretariat), *Shihō tōkei nenpō* (Annual report of judicial statistics), Vol. 1 (Tokyo: Ōkurashō Insatsu Kyōku, 1992), pp. 192–3.

Political and Social Controls

Formal legal accountability is not the principal mechanism for ensuring responsible public administration in Japan. Informal mechanisms of social control constitute a dominant characteristic of Japanese society. As John Braithwaite argues,[29] social disapproval is the principal means of societal regulation. Political embarrassment is an equally effective form of social 'shaming' as most Japanese officials will admit. It is especially effective for a hierarchical bureaucracy in which senior officials are considered to be responsible for the acts of those under their supervision. Consequently whenever official misconduct is exposed in the courts, the media, or the Diet, the impact is felt throughout the agency concerned as senior officials, ministers included, suffer the social consequences of the resulting public disapproval. Litigation therefore is more important as a catalyst for the social penalty rather than the process through which the formal, legal remedy is applied.

Whether the Japanese experience can be effectively used as a model for other states depends largely upon the extent to which the institutional and legal framework of the Japanese civil service is determinative in helping to produce a bureaucratic 'culture' in which public and political 'shaming' serve as effective means of ensuring accountability and control. Unfortunately, Braithwaite's argument has yet to be fully tested empirically and his basic propositions, at least as applied to bureaucratic behavior, run counter to the shared values, habits, and expectations of American—and perhaps more broadly Western—lawyers and social scientists, for whom there seem to be few if any substitutes for formal prohibitions backed by coercive sanctions. It should be added that the effectiveness of more formal approaches also remains largely untested and is equally accepted as a matter of political ideology and faith. Comparison between Japanese bureaucratic conduct and the behavior of what appears to be the American bureaucracy most similarly constituted—the United States Forest Service—does, however, strongly suggest that certain organizational features do result in similar responses.[30] Like elite Japanese civil service personnel, the Forest Service responds quickly to public criticism and legislative concerns, yet it remains one of the most self-contained of American bureaucracies. Every director in its history has come from within the service. Mobility into other agencies is extraordinarily rare. It shares an ethos as an elite corps that serves—and is responsible for

[29] John Braithwaite, *Crime, Shame, and Reintegration* (Cambridge: Cambridge University Press, 1989).

[30] See John O. Haley, 'Mission to Manage: The U.S. Forest Service as a "Japanese" Bureaucracy,' in Koichiro Hayashi, ed., *The US-Japanese Economic Relationship: Can It be Improved?* (New York: New York University Press, 1989), pp. 196–225.

defining—the public interest. And it has a strong sense of its managerial mission and autonomy. The internalization of standards of professional conduct is achieved by techniques of mentoring and socialization within the service that have uncanny resemblance to Japanese patterns.[31]

Single-party rule in Japan for nearly a half century has tended to obscure the efficacy of both formal and informal political controls over public administration. The Liberal Democratic Party's monopoly of postwar governance has produced an extraordinary continuity in policies and long-term programs. These do not require further political intervention to implement. Much of Japan's public administration has thus become a matter of routine, and the degree of political control that actually exists is not felt except in the rare instance of significant change. As Young H. Park points out, cabinet ministers can exert significant influence on the ministries they direct, especially by virtue of their control over ministry personnel decisions, but they 'seldom deviate from paths charted prior to [their] appointment. To do so would be to go against not only the agency but also the party and its divisions (and *zoku*) involved in agency policy-making.'[32]

The political accountability of Japanese public administration depends above all on a constitutional structure in which legislators are themselves ultimately accountable to the electorate, the freedom of the press is guaranteed, and an independent judiciary does exercise the authority of judicial review of legislative and administrative actions. Without such fundamental legal protection, it is doubtful that less formal and direct means of control would be able to operate.

Conclusion

The legal framework of public administration in Japan has two predominant effects. The first is to insulate the implementation of law from political direct intervention. The relative autonomy of Japan's ministries from routine political control ensures that a corps of professional civil servants is in charge of daily implementation of established policies. A relative lack of coercive powers coupled with the largely promotional aims of Japan's economic policies also enables those subject to administrative direction to have a voice by forcing officials to rely more on persuasion than power. A considerably greater degree of political direction is evident in the formation of policies. Coercive weakness also means that policymaking in Japan

[31] See Herbert Kaufmann, *The Forest Ranger: A Study in Administrative Behavior* (Baltimore: Johns Hopkins Press, 1954).
[32] Young H. Park, *Bureaucrats and Ministers in Contemporary Japanese Government* (Berkeley: University of California, Institute of East Asian Studies, Center for Japanese Studies, 1986), p. 186.

requires a substantial degree of consensus in order to enable effective enforcement. As a result Japanese officials both enjoy and rely upon a managerial authority cast in terms of their role as representatives of the common national interest. Without such authority their ability to persuade and their autonomy would be significantly reduced.

A second effect is to create conditions under which civil service accountability to the public is assured. Again, the autonomy and authority of the civil service are crucial elements. The availability of a vehicle for individual redress in court for official mistake and misconduct functions in the Japanese context to check arbitrary action and any abuse of discretion. The mechanisms of judicial redress provide an effective means for public scrutiny that, coupled with the potential of public disapproval and ultimate political accountability, promotes responsible public administration by threatening the principal prerogatives Japanese bureaucracies seek to protect: their authority and autonomy. The end result is an interdependence of discretion and accountability that underlies the balance of coherent and responsive policymaking in Japan.

3

The Role of Government in Japan's 'Catch-up' Industrialization: *A Neoinstitutionalist Perspective*

KOZO YAMAMURA

Did the Japanese government, its central bureaucracy in particular, make a substantive positive contribution to the transformation of a late nineteenth-century agrarian economy into an economic superpower of today? If so, are there lessons the governments of developing nations around the globe can learn from the Japanese experience? Joining a large majority of students of the Japanese economy, I answer the first question in the affirmative.[1] And although many answer the second question negatively, my answer to it too is affirmative.

The goal of this essay is to explain my answer to the second question and to suggest what lessons can be learned; the essay proceeds as follows. The first section offers analytic perspectives I believe important in understanding the reasons for Japan's economic performance, thus important in seeking lessons from the Japanese experience for developing nations. Drawing on these analytic perspectives, the second section describes and examines selected aspects of the Japanese economic experience. The third section discusses the political and economic 'costs' imposed by the government in its efforts to promote economic performance; argues that the contribution made by the government exceeded the costs; and suggests that the Japanese experience, like those of other nations, offers useful lessons to the policymakers and civil services of developing nations.[2]

---

[1] The majority consists of most scholars of the Japanese economy who contributed works cited in the footnotes below. The minority of scholars who answer this question negatively are those neoclassical economists who argue either that the Japanese economy achieved its performance despite policies adopted by the government or that the policies were ineffective. Since the goal of this chapter is not to engage in analytic-methodological discussion, no effort is made to rebut either the minority view in general or specific analytic criticisms that can be readily anticipated on numerous analyses and observations I offer in this chapter.

[2] By 'government,' I refer to the executive, legislative, and judicial branches and the bureaucracy. However, in a dozen cases in this chapter, I use such expressions as the government and the bureaucracy in particular or the government (ministries) to emphasize the bureaucracy—within the above broad definition of the government. Also, civil service is used interchangeably with bureaucracy.

The period of the Japanese economic experience discussed in this essay is from the Meiji Restoration of 1868, when Japan's efforts to industrialize began, to the early 1970s, when the productive efficiency of most Japanese industries had either reached or surpassed that of their Western counterparts. Examining Japan's economic experience in this period (and not focusing only, for example, on the postwar period) is necessary because, as is made evident below, the reasons for Japan's (or any other nation's) economic performance were (and are) shaped by its past, i.e., it is 'path dependent.'

Analytic Perspectives and the Roles of Government

The analytic perspectives I believe essential in understanding the reasons for Japan's economic success, and especially the government's roles in helping the economy to achieve that success, can be summarized as follows.

1. Institutions, broadly defined as 'humanly devised constraints on human actions that determine the structure of incentives,'[3] are of crucial importance in determining the performance of the economy because they collectively shape the motivations of individuals and groups to save, innovate, take risks, and cooperate. Put differently, institutions—laws, policies, social norms, and many other things satisfying the above broad definition—determine transaction costs,[4] which are the costs of obtaining the information necessary to measure the valuable attributes of what is being traded and the costs of specifying and enforcing property rights (in the broad sense of the phrase, including those in human capital). In an economy in which such costs are high, citizens are less motivated to save and invest or to innovate and take risks by making a commitment of resources. In an economy where such costs are low, the opposite will be the case.

Although one can illustrate in many ways the importance of institutions in determining transaction costs—and thus the importance of the above-noted motivations of individuals and groups in determining the performance of an economy—let me present the following to clarify this important analytic perspective. Individual A 'owns' a parcel of land, but how fully he can realize all possible gains from the parcel depends on his costs in obtaining information regarding all possible valuable attributes of the parcel that can be used for generating varying amounts of income over

---

[3] Douglass C. North, *Institutions, Institutional Change, and Economic Performance* (Cambridge: Cambridge University Press, 1990), p. 3.
[4] For an analytically comprehensive definition of transaction costs, see Thrainn Eggertsson, *Economic Behavior and Institutions* (Cambridge: Cambridge University Press, 1992), pp. 14–16.

time when used for possible alternative purposes (such as agriculture, residential development, or mineral exploitation). Each alternative use requires particular, extensive information regarding pertinent technology, the specific attributes of land required for that use, the magnitude and flow of expected income, whether the expected income stream can be controlled and at what cost, market conditions, etc. His success in maximizing income also depends on the enforcement costs incurred within the existing structure of property rights (consisting of laws, the reliability of their enforcement, social conventions and norms constraining the use of land, etc.).

This is to say that the existing structure of property rights can impose on A extremely high transaction costs in his attempt to fully specify and enforce the rights to all valuable attributes of the parcel, thus to capture the fullest possible gains from the parcel. To the extent he is unwilling or unable to incur those costs, some of the potential gains from the parcel are left in the public domain, i.e., are unappropriated by A, inviting someone other than A to invest resources to capture such unappropriated gains. This costliness, thus the motivation of A to assume the costs of obtaining information, depends on institutions or the 'property rights structure.' That is, the structure of property rights affecting the costs that A must incur in capturing gains from the parcel determines his motivation to make the most efficient use of the parcel.[5]

2. Institutions that determine economic performance in substantive ways as just noted are 'path dependent.' That is, a political economy comes to possess specific institutions because of past developments (due to unique historical circumstances), and existing institutions can and do constrain or shape how institutions evolve or are changed within the political economy. One must discuss the performance of an economy with a long-term perspective because institutions, being path dependent, change only slowly.[6] (Note that even revolutions rarely change all institutions, and the path-dependent nature of institutions explains why an economy can and often does follow a path of either growth or stagnation over a long period.)

3. While competition is essential for economic growth, cooperation, too, is crucial in enabling a political economy to achieve higher economic performance because it reduces transaction costs (i.e., reduces or

[5] Note that saving, risk-taking, and innovative efforts over time too are affected by the structure of property rights which change the incentives to engage in these activities. For a lucid discussion of transaction costs and their relation to property rights, see Yoram Barzel, *Economic Analysis of Property Rights* (Cambridge: Cambridge University Press, 1989).

[6] Among the by-now large body of literature on the subject, the most important in the context of this chapter is Paul David, 'Clio and the Economics of QWERTY,' *American Economic Review*, Vol. 75 (1985), pp. 332–7. (QWERTY refers to the arrangement of letters in the top row of the typewriter keyboard which was set in the late nineteenth century and has not changed since then despite attempts to replace it with a more efficient arrangement.) Also see North, *Institutions, Institutional Change, and Economic Performance*, pp. 92–104.

eliminates the inefficient use of resources as typified in the example provided in 1 above). For instance, cooperation enables firms to pool physical and human resources for R&D activities or to avoid wasteful duplicative investment; enables employers and employees to minimize losses due to labor disputes or, more importantly, due to efficiency-reducing rules needed because of lack of cooperation; and enables government and firms to devise jointly and put into effect policies that best balance public needs and firms' profit incentives in order to best use resources over time.

It should be stressed here that cooperation is a long-term concept because it is a means to increase efficiency by reducing transaction costs, and reduction in costs is achieved when the 'game' is played repetitively *over time*. Cooperation is often made much easier (i.e., the costs of cooperating are minimized) when there is a third party (e.g., government) capable of enforcing the rules of the game at the lowest possible costs[7] and even more importantly when the citizens in an economy have shared ideology, values, or norms.

4. Although they are a part of institutions as defined above in the broadest terms, it is essential to realize the importance of shared ideology, values, and social norms in determining how well most institutions work and how much cooperation can be achieved in an economy. This is because, for example, citizens who abide by laws because of shared social norms reduce monitoring and enforcement costs in myriad situations; cooperation can be achieved much more easily among citizens who have shared values than in cases in which citizens' values differ; and if many citizens in an economy have an instrumentalism orientation (a willingness to forgo current consumption and other forms of gratification for the sake of long-run improvements in living standards and/or socio-economic status), the economy is likely to have large savings that can be invested in capital goods or in education.[8]

[7] The insights useful for cooperation are found in the game theory literature, most of which is highly technical. In the context of this chapter, the most useful work is Robert Axelrod, *The Evolution of Cooperation* (New York: Basic Books, 1984).

[8] The analytic bases of the preceding perspectives are both the accumulated insights of many economists and political scientists who examined the effects institutions have on the structure of incentives and the neoinstitutional economic analysis emerging as an increasingly coherent analytic perspective today and adding fundamental new insights to challenge the orthodox neoclassical economic analysis itself in substantive ways. Accumulated insights refer to those contributed during the past 30 years by the large number of scholars who have examined the political and economic behavior of individuals and groups by adopting many overlapping paradigms and theories (e.g., property rights, information, transaction, monitoring and/or enforcement, public 'choice,' 'collective actions,' 'game,' 'new' industrial organization, etc.). In political science, these insights are adopted or adapted to give rise to 'positive political economy' which emphasizes both economic behavior in the political process and political behavior in the marketplace. And, an increasing number of economists, drawing upon these insights, are succeeding in evolving what has come to be called neoinstitutional economic analysis, i.e., a generalized price theory that focuses its attention on transaction costs and is applied to economic and political institutions and to changes in these institutions over time. Because they share the same set of accumulated

5. In an economy where industries do not yet possess the most advanced technology in the world (Japan before the early 1970s and all developing nations today), firms can continue to increase productivity over time by successively adopting more advanced foreign technology. This is to say that such an economy can pursue what may be called a strategy of achieving dynamic technological efficiency, i.e., successively adopting, as rapidly as possible, new (Western) technology in order to increase the capabilities of manufacturing industries so that they can produce and export increasing quantities of steadily more technologically advanced (higher value-added) products.[9]

If the preceding perspectives are valid, they together suggest that the government, especially its central bureaucracy, can play an important role in determining the performance of an economy. This is because the government can be the most effective definer of institutions and enforcer of property rights, and thus can determine how efficiently resources in the society are used. And it can play active roles in shaping and inculcating ideology, values, and social norms to reduce the costs of cooperation.

For governments of developing economies, the roles suggested by the above are many and must include enacting and enforcing laws and otherwise doing everything possible to reduce the costs of maintaining property rights. But one of the most important roles is enabling firms to pursue dynamic technological efficiency (hereafter, DTE) as effectively as

insights, if somewhat differently, 'positive political economy' and neoinstitutional analysis overlap extensively.

For those interested in learning about (1) what I referred to as accumulated insights, (2) how they helped give rise to neoinstitutional analysis, and (3) the essential analytic approaches and perspectives of neoinstitutional analysis, by far the best book to consult is Eggertsson, *Economic Behavior and Institutions*. North, *Institutions, Institutional Change, and Economic Performance*, is an excellent work that also provides rich discussions of (1) and (3) by a leading scholar of neoinstitutional analysis. For a good description of 'positive political economy,' see Peter C. Odershook, 'The Emerging Discipline of Political Economy,' in James E. Alt and Kenneth A. Shepsle, eds., *Perspectives on Positive Political Economy* (Cambridge: Cambridge University Press, 1992), pp. 9–30.

[9] Dynamic technological efficiency differs from dynamic economic efficiency in that the latter refers to increasing the efficiency of all resources over time to make the economy as a whole more efficient. In addition to the long-run increase in productivity by adopting new technology (making fixed investment necessary) as discussed in the text, firms can also increase productivity by 'tracing' the declining part of the short-run cost curve. Achieving an increase in productivity in this manner can be an important way to maintain the pace of productivity increase over time when the next level of technology can be adopted only after a delay for whatever reasons in an economy. For a full analytic discussion of the preceding, see Yasusuke Murakami and Kozo Yamamura, 'A Technical Note on Japanese Firm Behavior,' in Kozo Yamamura, ed., *Policy and Trade Issues of the Japanese Economy: American and Japanese Perspectives* (Seattle: University of Washington Press, 1982), pp. 113–21. This article also contains an analysis showing that firms' efforts to maximize market share also enable them to maximize profits when they are 'tracing' the declining part of the long-run average cost curve. This analytic observation is important in explaining how 'coordination' of investment made by the government in Japan by permitting price-fixing cartels did not limit competition for market share by product quality, services, terms of financing, and/or delivery, etc. (as discussed in the second section of this paper).

possible by adopting policies[10] that directly or indirectly make available the largest possible amounts of capital at the lowest possible cost to the firms. This is because the capital market, if left 'unguided' by policy, will not allocate capital in the maximum amounts possible at low enough costs to enable firms to most effectively pursue the strategy of DTE and thus to maximize the long-run performance of the economy. Such policies include, along with progrowth macroeconomic policy, tax and other policies that increase saving and make savings available at the lowest possible cost to firms attempting to adopt new technology successively over time.

What needs to be realized is that the cost of information in the capital market is high in regard to the long-run returns capital could earn by realizing gains from exploiting declining long-run costs, i.e., pursuing DTE. Because of this, the market, if left unguided by policy, will allocate more capital to less socially desirable (i.e., less growth-promoting or even growth-impeding over time) short-run, rent-seeking activities (for which information costs are lower). The examples of such activities include use of resources to gain monopoly rights, acquisition of properties for speculative profits, and rent-seeking takeovers of firms. 'Rent-seeking' activities refer to attempts by individuals and groups to increase their own income/wealth while at the same time reducing the net wealth of their society.[11]

The above is to say that when information costs in the capital market are high, government intervention to change the structure of property rights (e.g., tax policy or capital market regulation), which will alter the distribution of income for the sake of enabling firms to increase their productive efficiency over time, can make a positive contribution in effectively increasing national income.[12]

How well government 'guides' and makes policy to preferentially allocate capital to firms pursuing DTE depends on the ability of those directly involved—political leaders, bureaucrats, and firms—to reduce information costs. This is because more information—increased understanding by citizens of the long-run gains that result from allocating capital to maximize the gains of declining long-run costs—will reduce the political costs of the policy. That is, an informed public, aware of the long-term gains that result from the guidance and policy, is more willing to accept

---

[10] Policies too are a part of institutions and change the structure of property rights.

[11] A useful survey on rent-seeking is Robert D. Tollison, 'Rent-seeking: A Survey,' *Kyklos*, Vol. 35, No. 4 (1982), pp. 575–602. See also Anne O. Kreuger, 'The Political Economy of the Rent-seeking Society,' *American Economic Review*, Vol. 64, No. 3 (June 1974), pp. 291–303.

[12] Note that even in neoclassical analysis, which supports protection for infant industries, imperfection in the capital market is implicitly recognized. If the capital market is 'perfect' (zero information costs), firms in an infant industry can borrow funds and pay them back after they become internationally competitive. That is, no protection is needed even for infant industries if the capital market is 'perfect.'

the short-run sacrifices that result in many forms due to the guidance and policy.

Another very important contribution government can make is to prevent monopolists from emerging, or to regulate them (as in public utilities), and to 'guide' oligopolists, who pursue the strategy of achieving DTE and typically dominate those industries important in increasing an economy's international competitiveness, to coordinate their respective investments (with others in the same industry). Such guidance is necessary because, in attempting to achieve DTE (i.e., faced with declining long-run costs), they will overinvest (create excess capacities) and engage in competition for market share, which will result in resource-wasting bankruptcies[13] or even in the emergence of a monopolist. Given this fact, a government wishing to increase the productive efficiency and capacity of innovating firms in oligopolistic industries over time needs to guide firms to slow the pace of investment at times by coordinating their respective investments.

This means that, when excess capacity becomes large enough to threaten the collective viability of firms in an industry, the output of each firm needs to be reduced (operating at below optimum output). Should this occur, in order to assure that oligopolists earn sufficient profit to make future investments, price-fixing cartels may need to be allowed. So long as oligopolist firms pursue the strategy of DTE, periodic output reduction or cartelized prices need not result in welfare loss to the economy *over time* because as investment resumes (as demand 'catches up' with supply capacity), costs, thus long-run prices, will decline, benefiting consumers and increasing the international competitiveness of the firms. If investment in the next round is coordinated on the basis of each firm's current market share, even when prices are cartelized, competition for market share—in quality, service, product variety, terms of financing, and in other ways—will result.[14]

In discussing the 'guidance' of oligopolists, it is important to note that guidance can err and permit rent-seeking activities by oligopolists (e.g., cartelized prices may be higher and cartels may last longer than necessary to achieve the policy goal). How quickly or slowly such errors are corrected to minimize rent-seeking by oligopolists depends on characteristics of government (ministry)-business relations, the ability of government to obtain and use relevant information, products cartelized, and other factors.[15] For the guidance to be effective, trade policy needs to be adopted to limit foreign imports at below cartelized price: advanced low-cost

---

[13] In neoclassical economic analysis, bankruptcies do not 'waste' resources because, in the world of zero transaction costs, resources will be used elsewhere immediately.

[14] In strict analytic terms, these forms of competition too constitute 'price competition.'

[15] Each of these factors is not elaborated here because they will be further discussed with examples in the following section. The ability of government to obtain and use information, of course, is crucially determined by the quality of bureaucracy.

exporters will be permitted to export as long as they do not cause the cartelized price to decline. Less advanced high-cost producers may export at cartelized price.[16]

To be successful, the coordination of investment and the trade policy just described require that bureaucracy and industry have a shared ideology and that the bureaucracy has sufficient information regarding technology (cost functions), market conditions (both at home and abroad), profits being earned by oligopolists, and other relevant aspects of the industry in which investment is being coordinated. That is, to implement successfully both coordination and trade policy, close cooperation between bureaucracy and the firms involved is necessary. Such cooperation can be obtained only if the goal of these policies is understood and shared by the bureaucracy and the firms.

In concluding this section, it is important to stress that there is no guarantee that the roles played by government will always be positive (growth-promoting) in net terms. While many actions of a government may contribute positively to reducing transaction costs and increasing the supply of capital to, and guiding, innovating oligopolistic firms, they may be growth-impeding because government (ministries) may engage in rent-seeking activities. Such activities may be motivated by its desire to (1) increase its command over resources to retain power (or to safeguard or increase ministerial turf); (2) serve the interest of its own or its supporters' ideology or values; and/or (3) behave as a 'discriminating monopolist,' i.e., act to distribute gains to various groups according to the political and financial support each provides in enabling the government ministries to retain their power (turf). Also important is that a government can increase transaction costs 'unintentionally,' i.e., some of its actions may be intended to reduce transaction costs but result in increasing costs later on in unexpected ways.[17]

The degree to which a government's actions are positive or negative in reducing transaction costs in net terms and the extent of rent-seeking activities in an economy (including those by the government) substantively determine the nation's structural production frontier, the maximum output a nation can produce (with a given resource

---

[16] For the trade policy described to be successful, there are many other economic analytic and political economic issues that need to be discussed because the policy raises many issues similar to those raised in discussing the strategic trade policy. However, these issues are not pursued since the intent of offering the preceding discussion is to better understand the coordination and trade policies adopted by Japan discussed in the second section. For useful essays discussing the theory and political-economic issues of the strategic trade policy, see Paul R. Krugman, ed., *Strategic Trade Policy and New International Economics* (Cambridge, Mass.: MIT Press, 1986).

[17] On these observations, two useful analytic articles by Douglass C. North are 'A Framework for Analyzing the State in Economic History,' *Explorations in Economic History*, Vol. 16, No. 3 (July 1979), pp. 249–59, and 'Government and the Cost of Exchange in History,' *Journal of Economic History*, Vol. 44, No. 2 (June 1984), pp. 255–64.

endowment and technology). The more positive a government's actions (i.e., a positive net contribution in reducing transaction costs) and the less rent-seeking behavior is possible, the closer the economy's structural production frontier is to the technological production frontier (the upper limit of output a nation can produce given its level of technology and resource endowment). This is to say that a nation with institutions that induce a nonproductive or low productive use of resources will grow at a rate far below that of the technological production frontier, while a nation having institutions that encourage the productive use of resources can grow at a rate substantially nearer the technological production frontier.[18]

The Japanese Experience

This section argues that what mattered substantively in enabling Japan to achieve its economic performance were the shared ideology of catching up with the West as rapidly as possible; the political decision to catch up by adopting progrowth institutions (including activist policies instead of *laissez-faire*); and the use of cooperation (between the government/bureaucracy and business, among firms, and between management and labor) to better enable progrowth institutions (including policies) to achieve their goals.[19] As evident from the discussion in the preceding section, these reasons for Japan's economic success were interdependent and mutually reinforcing.

Before discussing these reasons for Japan's economic experience, let us note that numerous institutions (in the narrower sense of the term) were created by both the prewar and postwar governments to reduce transactions costs. As is well documented, many of the most important were created during the early Meiji years, often modeled after Western counterparts, and they continued to be revised in subsequent decades to meet the changing needs of the economy. These included laws recognizing private property ownership (including in rice paddies); commercial codes; laws establishing banks and other financial institutions, insurance companies, and accounting procedures; and patent laws. Except for substantial changes under the Allied Occupation (a constitution granting equal rights to women, labor laws guaranteeing rights to collective bargaining, and others), postwar changes to all of these laws can be characterized as

[18] The concepts and discussions of the two frontiers are adapted from Douglass C. North, *Structural Change in Economic History* (New York: Norton, 1981). Also see Eggertsson, *Economic Behavior and Institutions*, pp. 317–26.

[19] Although it will be made evident in the following, this is not to say that entrepreneurship, firms' wide-ranging efforts to increase productivity, and competition among firms were not essential in enabling Japan to achieve its economic performance.

revisions rather than fundamental changes in the legal bases of the economy.[20]

Ideology

Few would disagree that, for the political leaders and bureaucrats of Meiji Japan (1868–1912), one overriding ideology determined the character and effectiveness of institutions: Japan had to increase its economic capabilities as rapidly as possible to maintain its sovereignty in 'the age of imperialism' and then become a 'first-rate' nation, an industrial power capable of participating in the political and economic arenas of the early decades of the twentieth century.

The national desire to achieve rapid industrialization was sustained throughout the Meiji years because the Japanese were constantly and forcefully reminded of their 'second-rate' status by a series of international developments. Most significant were: in 1895 Japan was forced to relinquish the Liaotung Peninsula, a spoil of the Sino-Japanese War, because of the Triple Intervention (Russia, Germany, and France); a 'humiliating treaty' mediated by US President Theodore Roosevelt and signed to end the Russo-Japanese War of 1904–5 gave Japan no war indemnity and caused a major riot by 30,000 people in the heart of Tokyo; and 'unequal' treaties signed with Western powers early in the Meiji period could not be renegotiated until 1911 to eliminate extraterritoriality and regain tariff autonomy.

Japan's desire to become a first-rate nation remained unchanged into the interwar decades as it continued to suffer what it believed were the results of being a second-rate nation. Let me cite only a few of these results. At the Versailles Conference in 1919, what Japan gained fell considerably short of what it had hoped for and participants in the conference showed little interest in discussing a clause sought by Japan guaranteeing racial equality. In the several treaties signed in the 1920s to determine the relative standing of the naval forces of the world powers, Japan had little choice but to accept what it regarded as a force too small for a 'first-rate' nation. And Japan's efforts, throughout the 1930s, to realize its ambitions in China and Southeast Asia met strong, and in some cases successful, resistance from the Western powers. That is, throughout the interwar

---

[20] For further description, see Marius B. Jansen and Gilbert Rozman, eds., *Japan in Transition: From Tokugawa to Meiji* (Princeton: Princeton University Press, 1986); Takafusa Nakamura, *The Postwar Japanese Economy: Its Development and Structure* (Tokyo: University of Tokyo Press, 1981), and *Economic Growth in Prewar Japan* (New Haven: Yale University Press, 1983); Kozo Yamamura, *Economic Policy in Postwar Japan: Growth Versus Economic Democracy* (Berkeley: University of California Press, 1967); and the useful citations in Marius B. Jansen, ed., *The Cambridge History of Japan, Volume 5: The Nineteenth Century* (Cambridge: Cambridge University Press, 1989), and in Peter Duus, ed., *The Cambridge History of Japan, Volume 6: The Twentieth Century* (Cambridge: Cambridge University Press, 1988).

years, Japan was repeatedly reminded that it had to continue to upgrade its industrial capability as rapidly as possible by accumulating capital and absorbing Western technology.

The desire to catch up with the West was no less strong in the postwar period. Defeated and demoralized, postwar Japan's national goal well into the late 1960s was to wage a 'total war' for rapid economic recovery and growth, i.e., 'there was no politics in the sense of the competitive advocacy of the fundamental goal of society' because rapid growth be-came a 'war to be won, the first total war in Japanese history for which all of the nation's resources were mobilized voluntarily.'[21] This meant there was a national consensus for adopting policies and creating institutions to help achieve rapid growth throughout the 1950s and 1960s despite the burdens imposed in various forms on many by the progrowth policies adopted by the conservative Liberal Democratic Party (LDP) and by the institutions created or evolving to facilitate rapid growth. The consensus that kept the LDP in power weakened visibly by the late 1960s, but the nation's strong desire to become an even more efficient 'factory to the world' showed little sign of wavering well into the 1970s and, many argue, even to this day.

Without this 'catch-up' ideology, the two most crucial interdependent institutional realities of Japan—the dominance of a progrowth coalition and the orientation toward instrumentalism of the citizens in both prewar and postwar politics—cannot be explained. The ideology provided a principal explanation for the dominance of the coalition consisting of political and business leaders and civil servants committed to achieving growth over time, thus to creating and maintaining institutions to achieve the goal. And, because of the ideology, citizens' orientation toward 'instrumentalism,' which substantively affects their willingness to save and invest in education, can be observed in the postwar decades as well as the Meiji period. To be sure, this orientation was a combined result of their belief in the ideology, the 'politicization' (or 'use') of the ideology by the progrowth coalition (with the Ministry of Education and other agencies of the government taking well-documented, visible roles),[22] and 'path

---

[21] Eisuke Sakakibara and Yukio Noguchi, 'Ōkurasho-Nichigan ōcho no bunseki' (An analysis of the dynasty of the Ministry of Finance-Bank of Japan), *Chūō kōron* (Aug. 1977), p. 110.

[22] There is a substantial amount of literature on how the 'catch-up' ideology was 'politi-cized' by political leaders, the bureaucracy (especially the Ministry of Education), business leaders, and mass media to reduce the political costs of the dominance of the progrowth coalition and its policies and to nurture an 'instrumentalism' orientation both in the prewar and postwar periods. The most useful literature includes: Carol Gluck, *Japan's Modern Myths: Ideology in the Late Meiji Period* (Princeton: Princeton University Press, 1985); Teruhisa Horio, *Educational Thought and Ideology in Modern Japan* (Tokyo: University of Tokyo Press, 1988); Michio Morishima, *Why Has Japan Succeeded? Western Technology and Japanese Ethos* (Cambridge: Cambridge University Press, 1982); Robert J. Smith, *Japanese Society* (Cambridge: Cambridge University Press, 1983); Kenneth B. Pyle, 'The Future of Japanese Nationality: An

dependence.' That is, many Japanese were willing to make sacrifices because they were convinced of the need or desirability of catching up with the West; Japan's political and economic leaders 'politicized' it— propagated and inculcated the ideology—in order to create and maintain progrowth institutions; and Japan had a heritage of Confucianism and other socio-cultural traditions of instrumentalism.[23]

Strategy and Policies

The national goal of prewar Japan to become a rich and first-rate nation called for a national strategy. The strategy adopted was one of active government involvement in the market in order to achieve import substitution as rapidly as possible, i.e., to make the maximum effort in pursuit of dynamic technological efficiency. Achieving import substitution and pursuing DTE were the same because each meant that Japan had to make a long-term, sustained effort to increase both the output and productive efficiency of its manufacturing industries. This was the strategy of *bōeki rikkoku*—building a nation capable of producing products increasingly competitive in international markets—articulated repeatedly by political leaders and in numerous official pronouncements of the prewar period.[24]

Wishing to achieve rapid recovery and growth, the government of postwar Japan was no less vigorous in its activist orientation. There was

Essay in Comparative History,' *Journal of Japanese Studies*, Vol. 8, No. 2 (Summer 1982); Ronald P. Dore, *Education in Tokugawa Japan* (Berkeley: University of California Press, 1965); Herbert Passin, *Society and Education in Japan* (New York: Columbia University, Teachers College Press, 1965); William K. Cummings, *Education and Equality in Japan* (Princeton: Princeton University Press, 1980); and Thomas P. Rohlen, *Japan's High Schools* (Berkeley: University of California Press, 1983).

[23] On Japan's cultural and Confucian heritage and its influence on contemporary society and ideology, see for example: Horio, *Educational Thought and Ideology in Modern Japan*; Gluck, *Japan's Modern Myths*; Frank Upham, *Law and Social Change in Postwar Japan* (Cambridge, Mass.: Harvard University Press, 1987); *Daedalus*, Vol. 119, No. 3 (Summer 1990), a special issue on 'Showa: The Japan of Hirohito'; Thomas P. Rohlen, 'Order in Japanese Society: Attachment, Authority, and Routine,' and Lois Peak, 'Learning to be Part of the Group: The Japanese Child's Transition to Preschool Life,' *Journal of Japanese Studies*, Vol. 15, No. 1 (Winter 1989); and John O. Haley, 'Consensual Governance: A Study of Law, Culture, and the Political Economy of Postwar Japan,' and Robert J. Smith, 'The Cultural Context of the Japanese Political Economy,' in Shumpei Kumon and Henry Rosovsky, eds., *The Political Economy of Japan, Volume 3: Cultural and Social Dynamics* (Stanford: Stanford University Press, 1992). For an excellent analytic discussion of 'instrumentalism,' see Yasusuke Murakami, 'The Age of New Middle Mass Politics: The Case of Japan,' *Journal of Japanese Studies*, Vol. 8, No. 1 (Winter 1982).

[24] For example, Odaka, in reviewing Japanese economic growth, wrote: 'What was accomplished made it evident that during the 110 years from the start of the Meiji period to 1980, Japan single-mindedly pursued the path of *bōeki rikkoku* except during the war years.' Konosuke Odaka, 'Seichō no kiseki (2)' (The path of growth [2]), in Yasukichi Yasuba and Takenori Inoki, eds., *Kōdo seichō* [Rapid growth], Vol. 8 of *Nihon keizaishi* (Economic history of Japan) (Tokyo: Iwanami Shoten, 1989), p. 154.

no need to become a 'strong nation' militarily and national efforts could now be focused on becoming a 'rich nation' by means of increasing the international competitiveness of manufacturing industries. The vigor and effectiveness as well as the character of the strategy changed by the early 1970s because of the ending of the catch-up process (much less Western technology to borrow) and for other reasons (weakening of the consensus for rapid growth, criticism of industrial policies by trading partners, and others). But, as the institutions created for the strategy evolved to meet the needs of changing political and economic conditions both at home and abroad, they continue to this day to increase Japan's share in the international markets of increasingly more technologically advanced products.

In pursuit of the strategy, numerous policies were adopted (and all policies invariably affected cooperation as discussed below) in both the prewar and postwar periods. The policies adopted in the prewar period can be divided into those promoting the transfer of Western technology, those providing capital at the lowest possible cost in the largest possible amounts to manufacturing firms, and those assisting increases in exports while restricting imports. Since all these policies are well documented, the following will only illustrate their principal characteristics.

Throughout the Meiji period, the government employed a large number of Western engineers, technicians, and foremen to work in government-built pilot plants and other projects adopting Western technology. It also imported many types of machinery used in military ordnance, textile, iron and steel, and several other industries, and played many other visible roles in importing and disseminating Western technology, including holding numerous 'technology fairs' throughout the Meiji period.

After World War I, the roles of government in promoting the adoption of Western technology changed because large innovating firms in the chemical, machinery, and other industries were signing an increasing number of contracts with Western firms to obtain their technology and managerial guidance.[25] As a result, the principal policies adopted to increase the pace of adoption of Western technology became those providing low-cost capital and enabling firms to minimize the risks of investment as described below. However, a wide-ranging policy inaugurated to promote science and education during this period is worthy of our special attention. Under this policy, the government created a dozen research institutions—some under the control of government and others affiliated with universities—to promote scientific research in chemistry, metallurgy, aviation technology, and other areas, and sharply increased

[25] This is fully discussed in Kozo Yamamura, 'Japan's Deus ex Machina: Western Technology in the 1920s,' *Journal of Japanese Studies*, Vol. 12, No. 1 (Winter 1986), pp. 65–94.

the numbers of (i.e., funding for) middle and high schools, especially high schools of 'practical learning and skills.'[26]

Policies adopted to provide capital to industries took many forms. In both the Meiji period and the interwar years, subsidies were provided directly and indirectly in the forms of outright grants; public expenditures to improve infrastructure primarily for the benefit of industrial firms; sale of government-established pilot plants using Western technology at a fraction of the cost the government had incurred to build them; imposing only a very modest tax on corporate and individual incomes (while obtaining revenues from taxes on salt, tobacco, *sake*, and the like, on imported consumer goods, and on services); adopting monetary and fiscal policies to minimize the cost of capital (although at the cost of steady inflation); and, as will be discussed further, limiting increases in wage rates by severely constraining the rise of labor union activities.

To minimize the risks of capital investment which were high because of the 'lumpy' investment required in adopting new technology, policies adopted in the Meiji and interwar years included the government purchase of the output of an industry during its initial years (typified in the cases of iron and steel, many types of machinery, automobiles, ships, woolen cloth, Western paper, etc.); acquiescence to and even promotion of cartels when excess capacities resulted due to recessions, too rapid a pace of competitive investment, or unanticipated sudden decline in exports; a series of laws on behalf of the chemical, iron-steel, and other industries, exempting them from corporate taxes and import duties (on raw materials and imported machinery for as long as 10 years); and of course the policies to reduce the cost of capital described above and policies promoting exports and restricting imports (described below) also helped to further reduce the risks of investment.

The government during the Meiji and interwar decades was also active in implementing many policies that directly or indirectly increased exports and limited imports of products that competed against Japanese 'infant' industries. Among these policies, the most notable included subsidies to the Japanese shipbuilding industry and shipping lines, tariff and tax measures to promote trade with Japan's colonies, tariffs and other policies to restrict importation of many consumer and producer goods, and finally an exchange rate policy to boost exports and minimize the trade deficit.[27]

[26] Juro Hashimoto, 'Kyodai sangyō no kōryū' (The rise of the giant industries), in Takafusa Nakamura and Kōnosuke Odaka, eds., *Nijū kōzō* (The dual structure), Volume 6 of *Nihon keizaishi* (Economic history of Japan) (Tokyo: Iwanami Shoten, 1989), p. 98.

[27] For the observations contained in this and the preceding paragraphs, a few examples of useful sources are Nakamura, *Economic Growth in Prewar Japan*, pp. 51–76; Johannes Hirschmeier and Tsunehiko Yui, *The Development of Japanese Business, 1600–1973* (Cambridge, Mass.: Harvard University Press, 1975), pp. 70–227; and Kozo Yamamura, 'The Japanese Economy, 1911–30: Concentration, Conflicts, and Crises,' in Bernard Silberman

Because of the abundance of literature on the industrial policy of post-war Japan, let me highlight only its major pillars.[28] Until the late 1960s the government adopted numerous policies and marshaled all of its resources to help, in direct and indirect ways, Japanese firms to acquire and make the most effective use of Western technology. The most important among these policies included the gathering and dissemination by several ministries of all manner of information regarding Western technology; research on and experiments with Western technology conducted by government-owned or -sponsored agencies, the fruits of which were disseminated to firms at no cost; and providing direct subsidies to firms attempting to find ways to adopt or improve imported technologies.

However, because firms were principal agents in seeking new technology and adopting it, a much more important role played by the postwar government in an effort to achieve DTE was that of making available to firms the largest possible amount of capital at the lowest possible cost. This role was performed effectively during the rapid growth period (1950–73) by such policies as (1) the 'low interest rate disequilibrium policy,' under which both loan and deposit rates were controlled (low, controlled deposit rates made it possible for banks to make low-rate loans to firms, and the excess demand for loans due to below-equilibrium loan rates enabled the Bank of Japan and private banks to engage in credit rationing to direct funds to innovating firms making rapid capital investment); (2) a consistently pursued policy to provide loans preferentially

and H. D. Harootunian, eds., *Japan in Crisis* (Princeton: Princeton University Press, 1974), pp. 84–112. Those who wish to study the prewar economic history of Japan are referred to Kozo Yamamura, 'Recent Research in Japanese Economic History, 1600–1945,' in Paul Uselding, ed., *Research in Economic History* (Greenwich, Conn.: JAI Press, 1977), Supplement I, pp. 221–45.

[28] Of the numerous works on Japan's postwar 'industrial policy' and the roles of the bureaucracy in formulating and administering the policy, some useful examples are: Nakamura, *The Postwar Japanese Economy* and *Economic Growth in Prewar Japan*; Edward Lincoln, *Japan's Industrial Policies* (Washington: Japan Economic Institute, 1984); Ira C. Magaziner and Thomas H. Hout, *Japanese Industrial Policy* (Berkeley: University of California Press, 1980); Hugh T. Patrick and Henry Rosovsky, eds., *Asia's New Giant* (Washington: The Brookings Institution, 1976); Marie Anchordoguy, *Computers Inc.: Japan's Challenge to IBM* (Cambridge, Mass.: Council on East Asian Studies, Harvard University, 1989); Daniel I. Okimoto, *Between MITI and the Market: Japanese Industrial Policy for High Technology* (Stanford: Stanford University Press, 1989); Chalmers Johnson, *MITI and the Japanese Miracle: The Growth of Industrial Policy, 1925–75* (Stanford: Stanford University Press, 1982); T. J. Pempel, ed., *Policymaking in Contemporary Japan* (Ithaca: Cornell University Press, 1977); Daniel I. Okimoto and Gary R. Saxonhouse, 'Technology and the Future of the Economy,' George C. Eads and Kozo Yamamura, 'The Future of Industrial Policy,' and Masu Uekusa, 'Industrial Organization: The 1970s to the Present,' in Kozo Yamamura and Yasukichi Yasuba, eds., *The Political Economy of Japan, Volume 1: The Domestic Transformation* (Stanford: Stanford University Press, 1987); Chalmers Johnson, Laura D'Andrea Tyson, and John Zysman, eds., *Politics and Productivity: The Real Story of Why Japan Works* (Cambridge, Mass.: Ballinger, 1989); and Hugh T. Patrick, ed., *Japan's High Technology Industries: Lessons and Limitations of Industrial Policy* (Seattle: University of Washington Press, 1986).

to innovating firms at below market rates;[29] (3) tax policies allowing generous deductions for R&D expenditures, rapid depreciation of capital investment and many kinds of reserves, and exempting capital gains and interest income from taxation (the latter became taxable in the early 1960s but continued to be taxed at a lower fixed rate separately from personal income); and (4) monetary and fiscal policies that carefully attempted to balance the twin goals of providing capital to manufacturing firms at the lowest possible cost and minimizing inflation and trade deficits.[30]

Since 1973, reliance on these policies by firms has declined slowly but steadily because of the decelerated growth rate and the increased ability of large innovating firms to finance their capital needs. As a result, the low interest rate disequilibrium policy has been gradually abandoned in practice, low-interest loans made by government-owned or -controlled banks have declined, and many provisions in the tax policy favoring capital accumulation and saving have changed gradually.

In addition to reductions in the risk of capital investment achieved by the above-described policies that helped to reduce the cost of capital itself to all innovating firms, the government took a few other significant actions to further minimize the long-term risks of adopting new technology and increasing productive capacity. They included the adoption of numerous industry-specific laws and a procartel policy.

Of the scores of industry-specific laws enacted in the rapid growth period, those enacted for the machine tool industry, an industry that played a pivotal role in helping to increase the productivity of all other industries, are most useful in illustrating the policy goals of these laws: to substantially reduce the risks of rapid expansion of productive capacity and to promote adoption of Western technology. The first of the laws for the industry (a five-year, temporary law) was enacted in 1956 to provide low-cost loans to firms in the industry. Under the law, those firms (producing 19 broad categories of machine tools by benefiting from the loans) were required to inform the Ministry of International Trade and Industry (MITI) of the specific character of their technological progress and to produce products observing various standards set by the ministry for each category of machinery and machine tools. The law also permitted the firms to engage in 'coordinated activities' in regard to prices, quantity, and types of machinery and machine tools produced.

This law, widely recognized to have played a crucial role in reducing the risks of rapid adoption of new technology and achieving standardiz-

---

[29] See, for example, Thomas F. Cargill and Shoichi Royama, *The Transition of Finance in Japan and the United States: A Comparative Perspective* (Stanford: Hoover Institution, 1988), pp. 20–57, and Henry C. Wallich and Mable I. Wallich, 'Banking and Finance,' in Patrick and Rosovsky, eds., *Asia's New Giant*, pp. 249–315.

[30] See, for example, Joseph A. Pechman and Keimei Kaizuka, 'Taxation,' in Patrick and Rosovsky, eds., *Asia's New Giant*, pp. 317–82; and Yamamura, *Economic Policy in Postwar Japan*, pp. 35–53 and 129–51.

ation of machinery and machine tools, was renewed twice 'to cope with
the liberalization of international trade and capital markets.'[31] Then, in
1971 a law differing little in substance from its precursors was enacted
under the name of the Temporary Law for the Promotion of Specified
Electronics Industries and Specified Machine Tool Industries, only to be
replaced in 1978 by the Temporary Law for the Promotion of Specified
Machinery and Information Industries. Even in the 1970s, a score of similarly significant industry-specific laws remained in effect along with
many other laws that helped various industries achieve more narrowly
specified goals such as limiting entry, output, or restricting or controlling
prices and/or investment.[32]

In the interest also of reducing the risks of adopting new technology
and expanding productive capacity, the Antimonopoly Act of 1947 was
amended in 1949 and 1953 to permit two types of authorized cartels—
'recession' and 'rationalization' cartels—enabling many firms in a large
number of industries to invest in large-scale and more efficient productive
capacities. These were the cartels that enabled firms to fix prices and/or
output in times of excess capacity resulting from recession, too rapid a
pace of investment, or increased international competition. Although
their numbers steadily decreased by the late 1970s, the total number of
these cartels in manufacturing industries that were exempted from the
Antimonopoly Act and other cartels authorized by industry-specific laws
in late 1971 stood at 36.[33]

When the preceding and other policies to promote capital investment
and reduce the risks of investment were being pursued to increase the
international competitive ability of manufacturing industries, many other
policies were adopted to increase exports and limit imports more directly
in the rapid growth period. As fully discussed in the very large amount of
literature on these policies, most important among those promoting exports were policies providing many types of tax incentives, permitting
export cartels, assisting exporting firms in obtaining market information,
and overcoming legal and other difficulties encountered abroad. And,
from the long list of policies limiting imports, the most notable were
stringent quota and tariff policies of the 1950s and early 1960s, policies
limiting imports of capital until late in the 1960s, inspection and product
standard policies that imposed high costs for foreign exporters to Japan
until the late 1970s, and many others.[34] By the late 1970s most of these

[31] Yutaka Kosai, 'Kōdo seichōki no keizai seisaku' (Economic policy of the rapid growth
period), in Yasuba and Inoki, eds., *Kōdo seichō*, p. 239.

[32] For industry-specific laws, useful sources in English are Lincoln, *Japan's Industrial
Policies*, and Magaziner and Hout, *Japan's Industrial Policy*.

[33] Kozo Yamamura, 'Structure is Behavior: An Appraisal of Japanese Economic Policy,
1960 to 1972,' in Isaiah Frank, ed., *The Japanese Economy in International Perspective* (Baltimore:
Johns Hopkins University Press, 1975), pp. 67–100.

[34] Eads and Yamamura, 'The Future of Industrial Policy.'

policies had been curtailed, and by the early 1980s Japan could claim, for example, that it had one of the lowest mean effective tariff rates among the industrial economies and was imposing no quota on the import of industrial products.

In concluding the discussion of strategies and policies adopted by the government to help Japanese firms pursue DTE, I must add the following brief observations on the dual structure and the roles that government played in creating and maintaining it. An examination of the size distribution of firms, measured in terms of assets, employment, capital-labor ratios, and various measures of productivity reveals that Japanese manufacturing industries maintained a dual structure—an extremely small number of very large firms and a very large number of small firms—that is not seen, at least in this exaggerated bifurcated form, in other industrial nations.[35] This dual structure was most pronounced during the interwar years and the rapid growth decades of the 1950s and 1960s.[36] In order to better understand how this structure was fostered and maintained by many policies as an effective means to pursue the strategy of DTE, let us first acquaint ourselves with the following facts.

When the pertinent data are closely examined, as Blumenthal has done, it is found that the ratio of wages to rental cost of capital (costs of interest and depreciation)—the wage–rental ratio—was much higher for large firms relative to that for small and medium-sized firms, principally because the cost of capital was lower for large firms relative to that for small and medium-sized firms. That is, although wage rates were higher for large firms than for smaller firms, the disparity in the cost of capital between large firms and small and medium-sized firms resulted in this difference in the ratio. The difference was more pronounced during the interwar years and the rapid growth period than in the early decades of the twentieth century. This is to say that large firms had significantly higher capital–labor ratios than did small and medium-sized firms after the late 1880s (when data become available) and that the differential in the capital–labor ratio was largest during the rapid growth period.[37]

The main reasons for the difference in the ratio are obvious. In the prewar period, it was due to the ready access to capital (i.e., to the *zaibatsu* and other large banks) enjoyed more by the large firms than by the small and medium-sized firms and to the government subsidies provided to the

[35] For data and analyses of the dual structure, see Yasukichi Yasuba, 'The Evolution of Dualistic Wage Structure,' pp. 249–98, and Ryoshin Minami, 'The Introduction of Electric Power and Its Impact on the Manufacturing Industries: With Special Reference to Smaller Scale Plants,' pp. 314–20, both in Hugh Patrick, ed., *Japanese Industrialization and Its Social Consequences* (Berkeley: University of California Press, 1976), and Tuvia Blumenthal, 'Factor Proportions and Choice of Technology: The Japanese Experience,' in *Economic Development and Cultural Change*, Vol. 9 (1980).

[36] Blumenthal, 'Factor Proportions and Choice of Technology,' p. 558.

[37] For a good analytical discussion of the observations contained in this paragraph, see ibid.

largest firms in many ways as discussed earlier (such as the sale of government-built pilot plants at bargain prices and direct subsidies). And in the
postwar period, the large disparity in the ratio resulted from loans made
preferentially to the largest firms (by *keiretsu* banks and government-
controlled banks), government subsidies granted in many forms, and tax
exemptions and reductions that benefited large, innovating—rapidly investing—firms much more than smaller firms. These reasons tell us that
the dual structure emerged and continued to exist because it was an
important institution in pursuing the strategy of achieving DTE in a labor-
abundant economy like prewar Japan and in an economy in which, although labor ceased to be abundant, the costs of capital remained high
relative to those of labor, as was the case in Japan during the rapid growth
period.

In creating and maintaining the dual structure by adopting the policies
described above and many others (such as those relating to the labor
market), Japan was going against the advice that many (neoclassical)
economists would give, that is:

as long as there is a marked discrepancy between factor endowment and factor
utilization, given a particular state of the arts, innovations should be 'biased' in a
labor-using direction, as a learning effort in the use of the country's relative
abundant resource (i.e., labor) and in conserving the relatively scarce resource (i.e.,
capital).[38]

Japan ignored such advice because both its political and economic
leaders and the officers of economic ministries, wishing to make Japan 'a
factory to the world' as rapidly as possible, had little doubt that giving
preferential access to capital to a small number of the largest firms would
help realize their goal as effectively as possible. These leaders and officers
could not have stated what they believed as well as Blumenthal has:

The choice of technology is a long-range decision because changes in technology
take a long time to be implemented. The reason lies in the need to disseminate
information, train labor, overcome vested interests, change the attitude of management, and create the necessary physical capital in which new technology
is embodied. An early introduction of capital-intensive techniques, though inefficient in the short run, prepares the economy for the time when changing
factor proportions set in. Moreover, capital-intensive technology imported from
more advanced countries may well have a quicker pace of technological improvement since such improvements, made in the exporting country, can also
be introduced. The long-term dynamic advantage more than offsets the static
disadvantage.[39]

---

[38] John C. H. Fei and Gustav Ranis, 'Less Developed Country Innovation Analysis and the
Technology Gap,' in Gustav Ranis, ed., *The Gap between the Rich and the Poor Countries* (New
York: Macmillan Publishing Co., 1972), p. 315, as quoted in Blumenthal, 'Factor Proportions
and Choice of Technology,' p. 555.
[39] Blumenthal, 'Factor Proportions and Choice of Technology,' p. 556.

Cooperation

Cooperation between the government (ministries) and firms, among firms, and between management and labor played a crucial role in helping Japan achieve its economic performance. Although the cooperation between government and business has been discussed indirectly already in the preceding subsection, let me begin this subsection with the following on cooperation between government and business.

Government and Business   It is well known that the Meiji government worked closely with bankers, and the shared ideology and the economic gains that business leaders realized through cooperation were powerful glues to cement the close relationship that evolved. The cooperation became more effective in the interwar decades because various economic ministries gained more skills and knowledge, and developed administrative structure necessary in cooperating with manufacturing firms in formulating and administering tax, monetary, fiscal, exchange rate, and other policies to best pursue the strategy of achieving DTE.

Defeat in the Pacific War transformed Japan in numerous significant ways, including the 'democratization' that proceeded under the new constitution. But, the substance of the postwar government–business relationship changed remarkably little from that of the prewar decades. The changes that did occur were in the ways cooperation was achieved, i.e., the new relationship built on the skills and knowledge acquired in the interwar decades was more organized, systematic, and multifaceted than its prewar counterpart to meet the more complex political and economic needs of both the 'democratized' Japan and the economy attempting to recover and grow from devastating defeat (as can be readily seen in the preceding descriptions of policies adopted in the postwar period).

The avenues for cooperation included, besides the policies adopted, 'economic plans' and 'administrative guidance.' The former—from the first plan for the 1955–60 period (the Five-Year Plan for Economic Self-Support) to the latest, the eleventh plan, for the 1988–92 period (Economic Management within a Global Context)—consisted only of broadly stated economic goals and descriptions of how the plan was to be achieved.[40] As economic plans in a capitalist economy, they were 'indicative' and not those that 'command.' This, however, is not to say that such plans were merely statements of national economic goals and thus had no import. These plans helped to justify the policies adopted and helped banks and firms know what types of and how much assistance would be forthcoming from the government if and when the banks chose to make loans to the industries 'targeted' in the plans for rapid growth and if and when the

---

[40] On these plans, see Yutaka Kosai, 'The Politics of Economic Management,' in Yamamura and Yasuba, eds., *The Political Economy of Japan, Vol. 1*, pp. 555–92.

firms adopted the new technology or engaged in the new ventures called for by the plans as necessary means to achieve the planned goals. In short, these plans 'worked' because they articulated national economic goals and facilitated cooperative efforts between the economic ministries and firms that were required in pursuing the strategy of DTE.

The 'administrative guidance'—ministerial directives and suggestions provided without explicit legal power of coercion—that many specialists argue played an important role in aiding the rapid growth of postwar Japan is characterized as follows by a Japanese economist:

Administrative guidance usually takes the form of 'notification' which contains 'recommendations.' This guidance, issued by the Ministries of Finance, International Trade and Industry,... and other governmental agencies, conveys 'advisory remarks,' 'requests,' 'notices,' and 'opinions' from these agencies to private industries and businessmen. Such administrative guidance is usually effective in accomplishing the goals of the governmental agencies.... The number of 'notifications' issued by the ministries is immense. For anyone wishing to analyze the effects of these notifications, it may take several years just to examine the notifications.[41]

Since much has been written already on the guidance and how it 'worked,' here let me only reemphasize the importance of the shared ideology and the well-informed bureaucracy in making administrative guidance achieve its goal with the fewest possible rent-seeking activities on the part of both those guiding and those being guided.

Japanese-type Interfirm Relations This refers to the interfirm relations (as typified by those maintained among firms in the prewar *zaibatsu* and postwar *keiretsu*) among Japanese firms that are demonstrably more intensive and longer-term than those of their counterparts in the West. As demonstrated by numerous recent works both in 'new' industrial organization, which explores the roles of transaction costs in affecting the organization and behavior of firms, and in an increasing number of analytic studies on Japanese firms and industrial organization, Japanese-type interfirm relations are better able than Western-type interfirm relations to reduce transaction costs. They are thus more successful in using resources and knowledge more cooperatively to maintain a higher level of performance.[42]

[41] Ueno Hiroya, 'Wagakuni sangyō seisaku no hassō to hyōka' (The reasons for, and an evaluation of, the industrial policy of Japan), *Kikan gendai keizai*, Vol. 20 (Winter 1975), p. 17.

[42] These aspects of interfirm relationships are discussed and analyzed extensively in Michael Gerlach's *Alliance Capitalism: The Social Organization of Japanese Business* (Berkeley: University of California Press, 1993); in his 'Keiretsu Organization in the Japanese Economy: Analysis and Trade Implications,' in Johnson, Tyson, and Zysman, eds., *Politics and Productivity*; and in his 'Twilight of the *Keiretsu*? A Critical Assessment,' *Journal of Japanese Studies*, Vol. 18, No. 1 (Winter 1992). Also see Masu Uekusa, 'Industrial Organization: The 1970s to the Present,' in Yamamura and Yasuba, eds., *The Political Economy of Japan, Vol. 1*;

Close, intensive, and long-term interfirm relations reduce transaction costs because they are, in the final analysis, lasting cooperation based on mutual 'trust' and on 'hostages' that enable firms to capture 'quasi-rent.' This is to say that firms, in the interest of growth and profitability over time, exchange 'hostages' (human and physical resources 'dedicated' exclusively to the specific interfirm relation) and realize 'quasi-rent' (returns from the specific hostages that are above what the specific hostages could earn in alternative uses in a competitive spot market) that can be shared by firms maintaining Japanese-type interfirm relations. As the technological complexity of production in Japan increased and risks of increasingly large investment—necessary in adopting successively more advanced 'lumpy' technology—rose, the value of long-term cooperative relations grew more important.[43]

Few would dispute that the bureaucrats of economic ministries were crucial in giving rise to and maintaining Japanese-type interfirm relations, as they were in the case of the dual structure. Had it not been for the efforts of bureaucrats in drafting and implementing laws relating to the workings of the capital market and, more importantly, in exercising their discretionary power of 'guidance' to allocate credit to the largest firms in both the prewar and rapid growth periods (via the *zaibatsu* and the *keiretsu* 'main banks'), Japanese-type interfirm relations (as well as the dual structure) could not have emerged and continued to exist to the extent and in the ways they did.

The above is to say that because of preferential access to capital given to large firms by the Ministry of Finance and the Bank of Japan (by pro-*zaibatsu* bank policies of the prewar period, the 'window guidance' of the

---

Paul Sheard, 'The Economics of Interlocking Shareholding in Japan,' *Ricerche Economiche*, Vol. 45 (1991); Paul Sheard, 'The Main Bank System and Corporate Monitoring and Control in Japan,' *Journal of Economic Behavior and Organization*, Vol. 11 (1989); Iwao Nakatani, 'The Economic Role of Financial Corporate Grouping,' and Masahiko Aoki, 'Aspects of the Japanese Firm,' in Masahiko Aoki, ed., *The Economic Analysis of the Japanese Firm* (Amsterdam: North-Holland, 1984); Masahiko Aoki, 'Toward an Economic Model of the Japanese Firm,' *Journal of Economic Literature*, Vol. 28 (March 1990); Aoki, *The Co-operative Game Theory of the Firm* (Oxford: Oxford University Press, 1984); Aoki, *Information, Incentives and Bargaining in the Japanese Economy* (New York: Cambridge University Press, 1988); Banri Asanuma, 'Manufacturer-Supplier Relationships in Japan and the Concept of Relation-Specific Skill,' *Journal of the Japanese and International Economies*, Vol. 3 (1989); Richard Caves and Masu Uekusa, *Industrial Organization in Japan* (Washington: The Brookings Institution, 1976); Ronald Dore, *Flexible Rigidities* (Stanford: Stanford University Press, 1986); Mark Fruin, *The Japanese Enterprise System: Competitive Strategies and Cooperative Structures* (Oxford: Oxford University Press, 1992); and Japan Fair Trade Commission, 'Long Term Relationships among Japanese Companies: A Report by the Study Group on Trade Frictions and Market Structure' (1987).

[43] See Oliver E. Williamson, 'Credible Commitments: Using Hostages to Support Exchange,' *American Economic Review*, Vol. 73 (Sept. 1983); Paul L. Joskow, 'Contract Duration and Relationship-Specific Investments: Empirical Evidence from Coal Markets,' *American Economic Review*, Vol. 77, No. 1 (March 1987); and Paul Milgrom and John Roberts, 'Economic Theories of the Firm: Past, Present, and Future,' *Canadian Journal of Economics*, Vol. 21, No. 3 (Aug. 1988).

rapid growth period,[44] and many other policies and 'guidance'), Japan's capital market continued to be 'segmented' in favor of the large firms that grew rapidly by adopting new technology. Many of these firms were the core firms among the *zaibatsu* and *keiretsu* groups of firms which became parent firms of Japanese-type close parent–subsidiary interfirm relations providing access to capital (loans, equity participation, or trade credit) to their respective subsidiaries.[45]

'Familism' and 'Dual Control' of Firms Many volumes on Japan's labor–management relations have extensively documented that, by international standards, the labor–management relations of Japanese firms are characterized by 'familism,' an ideology stressing the family-like characteristics of a firm (especially 'permanent employment'), which is maintained to this day (despite increasing difficulties in doing so). This is not to say that 'familism' has prevailed unchallenged since the Meiji period; the leftist union movement had to be suppressed in the prewar period and frequent and serious confrontations between management and unions occurred during the 15 or so years following the end of World War II. However, when Japan's labor–management relations are examined, especially comparatively *vis-à-vis* the experiences of other industrialized nations, one is justified, I believe, in observing that this ideology played an important role in 'muting' or even effectively eliminating labor–management confrontation.[46]

Although I am unable to enter into the discussion it merits, we should note that the 'firm as family' ideology is more easily sustained because the power of stockholders is weak in Japan (relative to that in Western firms) and because the firms are 'dually controlled' by management (promoted from within a firm) and the permanent employees of the firm. As analysis by Aoki and others has persuasively shown, the weakness of stockholders can only be explained by the extensive dependence of firms on bank loans

---

[44] 'Window guidance' refers to ceilings placed by the Bank of Japan on new lending by private banks. The rationale for this 'guidance' was to control the major channels of funds when a tight monetary policy was being pursued. See Koichi Hamada and Akiyoshi Horiuchi, 'The Political Economy of the Financial Market,' in Yamamura and Yasuba, eds., *The Political Economy of Japan, Vol. 1*, pp. 244–5.

[45] Nakamura, *Economic Growth in Prewar Japan*, pp. 51–76; Hirschmeier and Yui, *The Development of Japanese Business*, pp. 70–227; Yamamura, 'The Japanese Economy, 1911–30,' pp. 84–112; Lincoln, *Japan's Industrial Policies*; and Magaziner and Hout, *Japanese Industrial Policy*.

[46] See Andrew Gordon, *The Evolution of Labor Relations in Japan: Heavy Industry, 1853–1955* (Cambridge, Mass.: Harvard University Press, 1985); Byron K. Marshall, *Capitalism and Nationalism in Prewar Japan: The Ideology of the Business Elite, 1868–1941* (Stanford: Stanford University Press, 1967); Sheldon Garon, *The State and Labor in Modern Japan* (Berkeley: University of California Press, 1988); Andrew Gordon, *Labor and Imperial Democracy in Prewar Japan* (Berkeley: University of California Press, 1991); and Haruo Shimada, 'Japan's Industrial Culture and Labor-Management Relations,' in Kumon and Rosovsky, eds., *The Political Economy of Japan, Vol. 3*.

instead of equity capital, due significantly to various policies already described.[47]

Also not to be forgotten is that in both the prewar and postwar periods, the bureaucracy, especially the Ministry of Education, played a major role in 'politicizing' the ideology of 'familism.' As many specialists have noted, this politicization took such forms as laws and guidance promoting the emperor as the head of the Japanese 'family' (in the prewar period), efforts to determine the content of textbooks, and aid in many direct and indirect ways to opinion leaders and organizations (including the mass media) expressing views defending or promoting the ideology. It is well known that throughout the prewar period and in the 1945–60 period, the bureaucracy seized every opportunity to promote 'familism' and enterprise unions as the basis of labor–management relations.[48]

To conclude this review of the important roles played by the ideology of catch-up, the activist strategy and policies, and cooperation, let me offer the following observation and what I believe were the reasons for it. Many of the policies adopted were anticompetitive (e.g., preferential allocation of capital, 'coordination' of investment that included cartels, direct and indirect promotion of the dual structure, *zaibatsu* and *keiretsu*) and so was the cooperation between the government and firms and among firms (e.g., 'economic planning' and 'administrative guidance' were often made for the benefit of the large innovating firms).

However, most knowledgeable observers of the Japanese economy believe that firms and groups of firms (*zaibatsu* or *keiretsu*) competed, often 'excessively,' to increase productive efficiency, i.e., to promote economic growth. Thus, among such observers making many similar observations, Lockwood characterized the intense competition waged by prewar firms in the same industry but belonging to different *zaibatsu* as 'dog-eat-dog' competition.[49] Nakamura noted that even in the industries that were increasingly concentrated during the interwar years, firms in many markets 'saw rather stronger competition.'[50] And Murakami, who made an extensive study of the anticompetitive policy of the postwar period, concluded that 'although cartels did exist during the intermittent short recessions' (i.e., excess capacity developed), 'competition in terms of price and quality was intense during prosperity—probably more intense than that in the same industries in most other industrial nations.'[51]

---

[47] Aoki, 'Aspects of the Japanese Firm,' 'Toward an Economic Model of the Japanese Firm,' *The Co-operative Game Theory of the Firm*, and *Information, Incentives and Bargaining in the Japanese Economy*.

[48] See, for example, Gordon, *The Evolution of Labor Relations in Japan*, pp. 346–8, and Clark, *The Japanese Company*, pp. 40–1.

[49] Lockwood, *The Economic Development of Japan*, p. 232.

[50] Nakamura, *Economic Growth in Prewar Japan*, p. 202.

[51] Yasusuke Murakami, 'The Japanese Model of Political Economy,' in Kozo Yamamura and Yasukichi Yasuba, eds., *The Political Economy of Japan, Vol. 1*, p. 54.

There are, I believe, two reasons for this seeming paradox: competitiveness exhibited despite presumably anticompetitive policies, and cooperation among firms and groups of firms. One is the fact that Japanese firms were pursuing dynamic technological efficiency and the other is the low information cost between the bureaucracy administering the policies and the firms.

Since one of the reasons has already been discussed earlier in explaining the usefulness of the 'guidance' to 'coordinate' investment, I need to add only the following. Oligopolistic firms pursuing DTE can increase profits by increasing market share (i.e., larger output leads to reduction in cost, thus increased competitiveness). This means that such firms have strong motivations to engage in price competition to increase market share except when there is a large industry-wide excess capacity (due to too rapid an increase in capacity, recession, or a slow increase or even a decline in exports). This is because price competition in such a case can lead to 'excessive competition' or even to bankruptcies.

The above is to say that oligopolistic firms pursuing DTE compete for market share, even when the 'coordination' of investment (i.e., price-fixing or output-limiting cartels) is in effect, by product quality and variety, service, terms of financing, and delivery, etc. as many studies have shown. Also, as was frequently seen in both prewar and postwar cartels, the most efficient firms in a cartel often 'cheated' as evidenced in the fact that the ministries and/or trade associations found it necessary to monitor and enforce the terms of cartels.

The other reason is the low information cost of anticompetitive policies, i.e., the policies entailed only a minimum possible or a limited reduction in competitiveness because the government (ministries) over the years acquired the skills and expertise necessary to obtain and use a wide range of pertinent information required in administering the policies as effectively as possible and because the industries have learned through experience that providing information to the government and refraining from rent-seeking activities better enables them to pursue DTE with the aid of policies. The above is not to say that competition was not limited at times and in various industries by the anticompetitive policies and rent-seeking activities of firms but to observe that despite this fact the Japanese economy maintained vigorous competition most of the time and in all industries.[52] No economy can achieve sustained growth without competition and the Japanese economy is no exception.

[52] Why and to what extent the Japanese economy was competitive is a crucial question deserving much more discussion than I am able to present in this chapter. Readers interested in pursuing this question are referred to Murakami and Yamamura, 'A Technical Note on Japanese Firm Behavior'; Lockwood, *The Economic Development of Japan*; Nakamura, *Economic Growth in Prewar Japan*; Murakami, 'The Japanese Model of Political Economy'; and Uekusa, 'Industrial Organization: The 1970s to the Present.'

Costs, Net Contributions, and Lessons

Japan's economic success was far from cost-free. Costs resulted because members of the political economic coalition—political and business leaders and the central bureaucracy, which promoted the national strategy of pursuing dynamic technological efficiency—'overexploited' the reasons for Japan's economic performance and engaged in rent-seeking activities to maintain or increase their power. The intent of this section is to present examples of those costs and to argue that the contributions made by the government (and the central ministries in particular) in promoting Japan's economic performance exceeded, substantially and demonstrably, the costs it imposed directly and indirectly on the economy and citizens.

Few would doubt that the ideology of catch-up was overexploited in the prewar and postwar periods. In the prewar years, the ideology was politicized and used by the government, for example, to suppress, at times ruthlessly, leftist ideology and the trade union movement, and to mute or stifle prevalent complaints against real wages that rose more slowly than did labor productivity. In the postwar period, despite a new constitution, the ideology continued to be overexploited to weaken leftist-led unions (in the 1950s and early 1960s), to justify what many in Japan regard as excessive intervention in education, to delay efforts to redress the increasingly serious pollution of air and water, and to neglect investments in housing and public amenities. Those familiar with Japanese history can add many more examples with little difficulty.

Both the policies to provide the maximum amount of capital at the lowest possible cost to firms adopting new technology (thus also to help create and maintain the dual structure) and the 'guidance' given to oligopolistic firms to help them continue to increase productive capacity and efficiency imposed costs on the economy and citizens in numerous direct and indirect ways. And, for both the pre- and postwar periods, the examples of these costs (which can also be seen as costs of government-business cooperation) included fiscal and tax policies favoring savers and investors to the detriment of low-income earners and consumers; the cartelized prices consumers were required to pay for many manufactured products; the high costs of borrowing for the purposes of consumption and acquiring houses; conspicuous differentials in working conditions and wage levels between large and small firms; and a slow increase in public expenditures for the 'safety net' (social security, pensions, unemployment compensation, and the like). Again, these examples could be easily multiplied by anyone familiar with the path and pattern of Japanese economic growth since the Meiji years; sacrifice was demanded of citizens in many forms in order to enable firms to more effectively pursue the strategy of achieving DTE.

Cooperation among firms and between management and labor also imposed costs in numerous obvious and subtle ways. Both *zaibatsu* of the prewar years and *keiretsu* of the postwar years exerted market power in a variety of forms. To cite only a few examples among many, the oligopolistic power possessed in a market by a firm within each *zaibatsu* or *keiretsu* group could be and was often used to increase the market power of the firms in the same group in other markets (e.g., a steel maker required an importer of coal to use a shipping line of the same *keiretsu*); entry into a market was made more difficult because group relations were maintained (e.g., non-group firms, domestic or foreign, found that trading preference was given to firms in a group in various ways); and large manufacturers exerted undue pressure (to reduce prices, meet more stringent delivery schedules, accept less favorable terms of payment, etc.) on smaller subsidiaries who were dependent on the former as buyer of their product and/or as supplier of capital and/or technology.[53]

The costs of Japanese-type management and labor relations are as well known as its contributions. Thus, here, let me make only the following two broad observations. In discussing these costs one must be aware that the vaunted benefits of the relations (employment security, opportunity for skill acquisition, fringe benefits, etc.) were enjoyed only by employees of the larger firms (increasing since the 1920s to approximately 20–25 per cent of total employees by the 1970s). The remaining employees of small and medium-sized firms received significantly fewer similar benefits. This was especially the case in the prewar period when 'familism' was invoked as a substitute for unionism. A second observation is that both in the familism of the prewar period and in the company-based (rather than industry- or skill-based) enterprise unions of the postwar period, cooperation between management and labor contributed to economic growth as noted in the preceding section. But the contribution was made possible at a cost to employees: their acceptance of work rules and conditions, overtime, and intrusions into their private lives in many forms by the employer that would not likely be accepted in less 'cooperative' relations.

However, the performance of the economy achieved at all of these costs was impressive indeed, as the following quickly demonstrates. Real GNP grew at the annual average rate of 3.15 per cent during the 1889–1938 period and the rate was substantially higher—nearly 9 per cent—in the 1950–72 postwar period. Per capita real income, as a result, rose at an annual average rate of 2.14 and 7.61 per cent in the same prewar and postwar periods and this was why Japanese per capita income in 1965 dollars rose from $136 in 1886 to $10,084 in 1981, easily

---

[53] Subsidiaries include distribution outlets at both wholesale and retail levels.

the best performance among the 14 industrialized nations Minami compared.[54]

This performance of GNP and per capita income was due to another performance: the rapid increase in Japanese exports that included an ever-larger proportion of high value-added manufactured products. That is, the average annual growth rate of exports in the prewar period (1889–1938) was 8 per cent and in the postwar period (1956–80), 12.9 per cent.[55] Even more impressive was the radical change that occurred in the product mix of exports: the product categories that accounted for the largest proportion of exports in 1877 were primary (agricultural) products, 47.1 per cent, and textiles, 38.6 per cent but by 1970 heavy and chemical manufactured products accounted for as much as 85.6 per cent of total exports with textiles and other products of light industries and primary products contributing only 6.8 and 1.1 per cent, respectively.[56]

The export performance was in turn due to the high performance achieved in the national effort to save and invest. Among the major industrial nations, Japan's investment rate (real fixed capital investment as a proportion of real GNP) was consistently very high during the 1880–1960 period, i.e., despite the fact its income was still substantially lower than that of such advanced nations as Germany, the United States, and the United Kingdom, Japan's investment rate was either only slightly below or even a little higher than that of these nations. And for the 1961–79 period, only the investment rate of West Germany (26.6 per cent) came near the rate Japan achieved (30.9 per cent), with others managing only substantially lower rates (e.g., 17.7 for the United Kingdom and 17.4 for the United States).[57]

The real significance of all these indicators is better seen when we examine how the standard of living and quality of life of Japanese citizens improved because of these performances made possible by the roles government played. Reflecting the rapid increases in GNP and per capita income, real personal consumption expenditure rose at the annual average rate of 2.53 per cent for the 1889–1938 period, and 6.99 per cent for 1956–80. (The rate was nearly 8 per cent during the rapid growth period of 1950–73.) These rates range from high to very high in comparison to those achieved by other industrial nations during comparable periods.

Because of such rates of increase in the level of personal consumption, the patterns of consumption changed, reducing the Engel coefficient substantially over time. From 1921 when reliable data became available, the coefficient ranged from 35 to 37 per cent in the 1920s and most of the 1930s

[54] Ryōshin Minami, *The Economic Development of Japan: A Quantitative Study* (London: The Macmillan Press Ltd., 1986), p. 13. In making the comparison, Minami selects different years for each country compared for the beginning of modern economic growth (e.g., 1834 for the United States and 1765 for the United Kingdom).

[55] Ibid., p. 219.   [56] Ibid., p. 227.

[57] For a comparison of investment rates between 1881 and 1979, see ibid., p. 184.

and declined to 27.8 by 1980. In contrast, the expenditure category identified as 'miscellaneous'—total expenditures minus those incurred for food, housing, heat and light, and clothing; i.e., funds available for education, entertainment, medical care, and the like—rose from 29–30 per cent in the interwar years to 49.2 per cent by 1980.[58] It should be noted, however, that the improvement indicated in the Engel coefficient fails to show the steady improvement in the quality and mixes of food consumed. For example, annual per capita consumption of animal protein (meat and fish) rose from 2.0 kg. of meat and 13.9 kg. of fish in the 1930s to 23.8 kg. of meat and 34.2 kg. of fish in the mid-1980s.[59]

Better diet, improving medical care, and other changes over time jointly raised many indicators of the quality of life. Life expectancy for males rose from 42.8 years during the 1891–98 period to 73.4 by 1980 and for females from 44.2 to 78.8 during the same period. The infant death rate, for which reliable national data become available in 1920, declined from 166.2 per thousand live births in 1920 to a mere 7.5 in 1980. As is well known, these accomplishments are not exceeded by any large industrialized Western nation.[60]

Further, the Japanese also became better educated principally because of rising income. The percentage (within age cohort) of students enrolled in compulsory education rose from 28.1 per cent in 1873 to virtually 100 per cent in the postwar years (99.6 in 1940 and 99.8 in 1980), despite the fact that the number of years of compulsory education rose from four years in the early Meiji period to nine in the postwar period. No less significantly, those completing at least two years of higher education beyond the high school level steadily rose from a few per cent of the cohort group in the Meiji years to 38.5 per cent by 1980 (the latter figure is exceeded only by the United States). Indeed, the quality of life in Japan in 1980 bore little resemblance to that in 1867 when the nation under the new government resolved to pursue the strategy of dynamic technological efficiency.[61]

Such data and many others that could be readily added led Minami to describe Japan's economic performance as follows:

When, after closing her shores to the world for more than two hundred years (1641–1854), Japan recommenced intercourse with other countries the majority of

---

[58] See, for the data contained in this and the preceding paragraph, ibid., pp. 37–8, and Kosai and Ogino, *The Contemporary Japanese Economy*, p. 9.

[59] *Asahi shinbun*, Jan. 1, 1985.

[60] Life expectancy data are from *Hundred Year Statistics of the Japanese Economy* (Tokyo: Statistics Department, Bank of Japan, 1966), p. 17, and *Nihon keizai tōkei nenkan* (Annual statistics of the Japanese economy) (Tokyo: Statistics Bureau, Management and Coordination Agency, 1989). The infant death rate is from Irene B. Taueber, *The Population of Japan* (Princeton: Princeton University Press, 1966) and Ichiro Yano, ed., *Sūji de miru Nihon no 100-nen* (One hundred years of Japan seen in numbers) (Tokyo: Kokuseisha, 1981), p. 273.

[61] Minami, *The Economic Development of Japan*, p. 19, and Yano, ed., *Sūji de miru Nihon no 100-nen*, p. 361.

the world's people did not even know of her existence. Economically Japan was a long way behind the advanced nations of the west. According to one estimate, in 1870 Japan's GNP per capita was only a quarter of that of the UK. After several wars and phenomenal economic growth, particularly after the Second World War, Japan has gradually made itself known to the peoples of the world. Her GNP per capita is now on a par with the advanced industrial nations of the west, and today a description of the state of the world's economy without reference to Japan would be impossible.[62]

And, *The Economist* observed recently:

Few would deny that what Japan achieved was indeed an economic miracle: to lift an economy from ruins to parity with the world's richest countries in the span of a single generation, to go on in the next to attain world leadership in many industries, to do this under the rule of democracy (however flawed) and to spread the economic benefits widely across the population is a stunning achievement.[63]

On the basis of what has been summarized in this and the preceding section, I argue, as many have done, that the Japanese government made substantive contributions in enabling the economy to achieve the performance we have seen and in helping very significantly to improve the standard of living and quality of life of its citizens. I also maintain the costs the government imposed on its citizens in efforts to aid firms in their pursuit of the strategy of achieving DTE did not exceed the contributions made by the government in increasing the living standard and quality of life of citizens. An important support to this claim is found, I submit, in the fact that many of these costs were borne, in both similar and different ways, by citizens of such developed nations as the United Kingdom and the United States where government played a significantly lesser role in the process of industrializing the respective economies.[64]

If the government did indeed make a positive net contribution in enabling Japan to achieve its high economic performance, what can the government, and the bureaucracy in particular, of developing nations of today learn from the Japanese experience?

One possible answer is that there is little developing nations can learn from the Japanese experience or that of any other developed nations because: (1) each developing nation's institutions, as defined broadly at the outset of this chapter, are path dependent and complexly interwoven, thus no 'piecemeal' adaptation of Japanese or another developed nation's experience is possible; (2) population and natural endowments, the degree and types of ethnic and religious diversity, and numerous other political, economic, and social conditions and characteristics of each

---

[62] Minami, *The Economic Development of Japan*, p. 3.

[63] Clive Crook, 'A Survey of the Japanese Economy,' *The Economist*, March 6, 1993, p. 10.

[64] Some may be prepared to make the stronger assertion that these Western economies in which governments were less activist than in Japan imposed more economic costs on their citizens.

developing nation differ from those of Japan and other developed nations; and (3) the international political and economic (especially technological) conditions the developing nations have faced in recent decades and will continue to face in coming years also differ from those faced by Japan as it attempted and succeeded in catching up with the West and those faced by Western nations as they successfully industrialized as 'leaders.'

However, another possible answer is that, despite the force of the above answer in explaining the tremendous difficulties encountered by developing nations in their efforts to achieve economic development, the governments of these nations can, and thus should be encouraged to attempt to, adapt (not adopt or emulate) some or any of the policies and practices of the Japanese government that made a substantive net contribution in Japan's efforts to catch up with the West.

As do many who search for useful lessons for developing nations, I subscribe to the latter answer because I am persuaded that the governments of developing nations can adopt policies and otherwise take actions that are similar in varying degrees to those adopted or pursued in Japan, and can do so benefiting from the knowledge gained by closely examining the Japanese experience. This is to suggest that developing nations can fruitfully continue to attempt to learn how economic growth was achieved and at what costs by all developed nations and especially by Japan which succeeded in its 'catch-up' industrialization. What must not be forgotten, however, is that an effort to learn from the experiences of Japan can be rewarded not with a detailed map to follow but only with a diary describing how a determined traveler managed, with hardship and sacrifice, to complete his journey successfully.

PART TWO

THE PROCESS OF EVOLUTION

4

The Structure of Bureaucratic Rationality and Economic Development in Japan

BERNARD S. SILBERMAN

The relationship between state administration and economic development has been a subject of fitful and sometimes anxious concern ever since Max Weber first called attention to the relationship between organizational rationality and the development of modern capitalism and society. Despite a great deal of writing there has not been much success in showing precisely what constitutes this relationship. Weber, in a fit of functionalism, argued that organizational roles characterized by specific rules defining hierarchy, hierarchical authority, specialization, differentiation, career, expertise, and the possession of office were required, if by nothing else, by the sheer size and complexity of modern society and its capacity for engendering resources.[1] Furthermore, Weber argued, this rationalized structure of administration was the most efficient form of administration.[2]

Thus, since Weber, the assumption has been that successful economic development was linked to the existence of a rational bureaucratic structure and role. The problem here is that neither Weber nor his successors have provided us with a specific description or analysis of how the rise of capitalism or economic development was linked to the institutions of rational role structure nor the ways in which the role structure is related to efficiency. This is especially significant for the study of state bureaucracies where the claim has been consistently made that national economic development requires a highly rational state bureaucracy. But here too we have little in the way of substantive support for this view.

The prototypical view on how the 'efficiency' of bureaucratic rationality produces successful developmental outcomes stresses the expertness of the bureaucratic role and the capacity of the rational structure to acquire and organize information in appropriate categories. This capacity, it is

[1] Max Weber, *Economy and Society*, edited by Guenther Roth and Claus Witich (Berkeley: University of California Press, 1978), Vol. 1, pp. 217–21.
[2] Ibid., p. 223.

thought, makes possible the selection of policies that have long-range goals rather than the short-range ones that may be efficiently achieved by the market. This kind of rationality stresses direct intervention—the capacity to pick winners as against losers. Here the argument is that as economic systems develop they require guidance by expert, neutral state agents. This is an argument that says bureaucratic expertise is the basis for the utilitarian superiority of state constraints on markets in allocating resources and outputs. What it comes down to is the belief in the obtuseness of the private sector in terms of the long run in societies seeking economic development or growth.[3]

This view is reflected in the emergence in the early 1950s and 1960s of the idea of 'development administration.'[4] Basically the literature that emerged from this movement was a response to cold war pressures. The Western, especially American, attempt to find a more or less comprehensive approach to economic development that could compete with communist or socialist concepts of planned development led a large number of scholars and public administrative experts to the Weberian notion of rationality. Weber's views had the advantage of being a theory that linked legitimacy, rationality of decision making, and organizational rationality in a manner that appeared to make possible economic growth and development within the framework of capitalism. From this perspective development administration took the next step and argued that societies with underdeveloped economies tended to fail in economic growth because of the absence of such rational bureaucracies and the legitimacy that rested on the idea of expertise.[5]

The 1950's was a wonderful period. The 'American Dream' was the 'World Dream'—and the best and quickest way to bring that dream into reality was through the mechanism of public administration.[6]

From this approach emerged the view that a rationalized bureaucracy is far more capable of providing adequate structures of allocation and coordination because of its legal-rational organizational characteristics.[7] That is, successful development occurs as a consequence of the rational bureaucracy's greater organizational capacity to provide infrastructure and facilitate coordination by removing obstacles to allocation. The bureauc-

---

[3] Brian Hindley, 'Empty Economics in the Case for Industrial Policy,' *World Economy*, Vol. 7, No. 3 (Sept. 1984), pp. 286–7.

[4] Ferrel Heady, *Public Administration: A Comparative Perspective* (New York: Marcel Dekker, Inc., 1979), pp. 12–30.

[5] See Bert Hoselitz, 'Levels of Economic Performance and Bureaucratic Structures,' and Joseph J. Spengler, 'Bureaucracy and Economic Development,' in Joseph LaPalombara, ed., *Bureaucracy and Political Development* (Princeton: Princeton University Press, 1967), 2nd ed., pp. 168–99.

[6] William J. Siffin, 'Two Decades of Public Administration in Developing Countries,' *Public Administration Review*, Vol. 36, No. 1 (1976), p. 61.

[7] Weber, *Economy and Society*, Vol. 1, pp. 224–5.

racy's efficiency stems from its capacity to reduce the transaction costs due to market inefficiencies. What this comes down to is the assurance that there will be a minimum of arbitrary state intervention by political leaders and civil servants pursuing their own interests.[8]

As it turned out, bureaucracies did not exist in a vacuum. On the state bureaucracy's ability to pick winners, Hindley has put it neatly:

> Although the claim supporting an industrial policy is likely to be that its activity is designed to pick winners, its actual objective may be different. Probably the most popular hypothesis in this class is that industrial-policy choices are dictated by purely political considerations; although rationalised in terms of finding neglected winners, the policy is in fact a means of propping up losers whose failure would raise political problems for the government. It is quite likely that clients selected on such a basis will fail to outperform the market.[9]

As another scholar has put it in the case of Japan 'Their [MITI's] criteria for industry selection may have been simply cosmetic.'[10]

The attribution of success to the view that bureaucracies are more efficient because markets don't always perform well is based on the observation of so-called less developed countries where patronage bureaucracies are seen as major obstacles to economic development because they pursue private interests.[11] But lest we now think that bureaucratic rationality is a necessary although not a sufficient cause, it turns out that, upon examination, industrial development was not inevitably tied to rational administration. The United States and Great Britain are cases in point. Both had come to the rationalization of administrative roles considerably *after* industrial development had entered mature stages. In the case of the United States the rationalization process was not completed until the early 1920s. In Great Britain the rationalization process did not begin to reach maturity until the end of the 1870s and the beginning of the 1880s.[12] The case of Brazil is, perhaps, equally instructive here. Ben Ross Schneider convincingly argues that industrial development in Brazil occurred rapidly in the 1970s and 1980s precisely *because* of the presence of personalism and patronage at the higher levels of the state bureaucracy.[13] Thus, it seems that, historically, rational state administrations appear to be a

---

[8] S. N. Eisenstadt, 'Bureaucracy and Political Development,' in LaPalombara, ed., *Bureaucracy and Political Development*, pp. 109–10.

[9] Hindley, 'Empty Economics,' pp. 288–9. On the expertness of expertise, see David Faust, *The Limits of Scientific Reasoning* (Minneapolis: University of Minnesota Press, 1984).

[10] Masahiro Okuno-Fujiwara, 'Industrial Policy in Japan: A Political Economy View,' in Paul Krugman, ed., *Trade With Japan: Has the Door Opened Wider?* (Chicago: University of Chicago Press, 1991), p. 280.

[11] See Fred W. Riggs, *Administration in Developing Countries: The Theory of Prismatic Society* (Boston: Houghton Mifflin, 1964).

[12] Bernard S. Silberman, *Cages of Reason: The Rise of the Rational State in France, Japan, the United States, and Great Britain* (Chicago: University of Chicago Press, 1993), pp. 156 ff.

[13] Ben Ross Schneider, *Politics within the State: Elite Bureaucrats and Industrial Policy in Authoritarian Brazil* (Pittsburgh: University of Pittsburgh Press, 1991).

necessary condition for successful economic development under only *some* but not all conditions.

The historical record provides little help in the other direction. Writers have pointed to Japan and Germany and, sometimes, to France as apparent exemplars of how the rationalization of state administration was correlated to rapid economic development. In these countries a rationalized bureaucratic role had indeed emerged *prior* to significant levels of industrial development and therefore prior to demands from various groups in the society. It has become a stock argument that this chronology reflects the self-conscious aim of political leaders to achieve economic development through rationalization of the state bureaucratic role. But it is hard to know why any of the political leaders of these states chose to pursue rationalization of a specific kind when there were no models to guide them in their choices. In the first half of the nineteenth century neither France under Napoleonic rationalization nor Prussia under a mandarin-like rationalization was particularly successful in the encouragement of industrial development.

Nor was there any theory available to even suggest a correlation between bureaucratic rationalization and economic development. There existed a theory of state *intervention*—mercantilism or neomercantilism—but this theory was neither very coherent nor historically very successful and it was in no way coherently related to administrative rationalization. Moreover, the early attempts of state administration in both these countries to *intervene* in economic policy were hardly unmitigated successes.[14] At the same time there is considerable criticism of the state's abilities in this regard in modern and contemporary Japan.[15] The will to pick winners may have been and may still remain in place but there is considerable question about the state's capacity to construct a usable standard of evaluation.

The historical record seems to undercut the basic assumptions that link state rationality as represented by a rationalized bureaucracy as either a necessary or sufficient cause to economic development. The variation in timing of the relationship between state bureaucratic rationalization and economic development in such places as the United States and Great Britain at one end of the scale and France, Germany, and Japan at the other end clearly suggests that coordination and allocation problems in the economy were not driving forces in the rationalization process or in the success of economic development. That is, there is historically no *direct* relationship between state bureaucratic rationalization and economic development.

[14] Frank B. Tipton, Jr., 'Government Policy and Economic Development in Germany and Japan: A Skeptical Reevaluation,' *Journal of Economic History*, Vol. 41, No. 1 (March 1981).
[15] Hiroyuki Odagiri, *Growth through Competition, Competition through Growth: Strategic Management and the Economy in Japan* (Oxford: Clarendon Press, 1992), pp. 278–309; Richard J. Samuels, *The Business of the Japanese State: Energy Markets in Comparative and Historical Perspective* (Ithaca: Cornell University Press, 1987), pp. 8–22, 285–90.

This ambiguity only points up the fact that there continues to be a major lacuna in our understanding of the emergence of the rational bureaucratic role and its relation to economic development. Strangely enough, despite the theoretical and practical significance of understanding this relationship, there have been few attempts to engage in systematic comparative analyses of how economic development and the rationality of state bureaucracy are related.[16] The problem is made more difficult by the observation that there are two types of rational administrative role in modern industrial societies: professionally oriented as in the United States and Great Britain, and organizationally oriented as in Japan, France, and Germany.

At the heart of the difficulty is the failure, I believe, to perceive that the affiliation between state bureaucratic rationality and economic development centers on the structural relationships between policy and organization. What I mean by this is that when *policy* is viewed in structural terms, we are talking about the systematic character of: decision-making processes leading to intervention, decision-making roles, and the constraints on these processes and roles. When there are well-defined rules governing the process and structure of decision-making then we also have a structure of accountability governing political leaders and administrators with regard to policy.

When we talk about *bureaucracy* in structural terms we mean the administrative *role* and its constraints. When these constraints on the role are ruleful and systematic so as to produce predictable outcomes both in terms of career and in terms of restraining individual opportunism so that resources are allocated on a 'public' basis, then the role may be said to be rational and accountable.

What ties policy and bureaucracy together is the system of constraints that defines the bureaucratic role. That is, the rules governing the selection, appointment, advancement, and range of discretion of bureaucrats responsible for making the most significant decisions are the rules that also restrain individual opportunism, produce predictability about decision making, and create the structure of accountability. As Weber indicated when he stressed role characteristics over administrative structure, role structure is central to our understanding of organizational rationality and, therefore, to the formation of policy.

At the heart of the role structure is the idea of impersonality—*sine ira et studio*, without hatred or passion, as Weber put it[17]—that is, behavior governed by systematic rules of office or profession that allow or force

---

[16] B. Guy Peters, 'Public Policy and Public Bureaucracy,' in Douglas E. Ashford, ed., *History and Context in Comparative Public Policy* (Pittsburgh: University of Pittsburgh Press, 1992), pp. 283–5; Robert Wade, *Governing the Market: Economic Theory and the Role of Government in East Asian Industrialization* (Princeton: Princeton University Press, 1990), p. 345.

[17] Weber, *Economy and Society*, Vol. 1, p. 225.

individuals to be alienated or separated from their private interests. This alienation is the sign of 'publicness.' In this manner the rules governing and defining role behavior serve as the means of bridging the gap between state and society; they are the instrumental means and symbolic structures for insuring the dominance of public interests. In short, legitimacy stems from the construction of depersonalized roles—ones in which patronage or clientilistic selection is replaced by 'objective' rules.

Bureaucratic rationality is the means by which individual opportunism in the *political* realm is overcome. It is this rationality that legitimates and defines the extent of state intervention in the 'public interest.' This clearly implies that bureaucratic rationality is related primarily to problems of 'political efficiency' and not economic efficiency. The question is, however, where do the structures of depersonalization come from? If they do not arise out of systemic demand as the historical record shows, then from where?

If bureaucratic intervention in economic policy formation is politically driven, who or what is doing the driving? If political leaders are decision makers, then we can assume that they are, in good part, driven by the desire to maintain their status. If intervention in the economy is politically driven then successful or unsuccessful intervention, when it occurs, is a product of political choices aimed at reducing uncertainty about political leaders' incumbency rather than purely economistic choices.

We can conclude from this reasoning that (1) the main historical significance of the emergence of bureaucratic rationality is its integrative capacity, but (2) successful economic development does require a minimal set of rules governing the relationships between individuals and state and society in a systematic and predictable manner. Then we might argue that economic development, once set in motion by historically contingent forces or events, is sustained over the long term by the systematic and ruleful structure of the relations between state and society mediated by the bureaucratic role. Rationalized bureaucracy is not the only such systematic and ruleful structure that makes integration possible but it is the one that, in two variants, became dominant in the nineteenth and early twentieth centuries. Bureaucracy in this sense came to function as, and represent modes of, state-society integration. It is this rise to dominance in one of its two forms in the case of Japan that this chapter addresses.

The Modes of Bureaucratic Rationality

Much of the metaphysical pathos that surrounds Weber's and myriads of his successors' views of bureaucratic rationality stems from the belief that the rationalization of the bureaucratic role would produce only one kind of state-society integration. Weber grimly saw no basic difference between a liberal or socialist society in which bureaucratic rationality, as he defined it, was essentially the same. This mode of integration was an administrative structure that provided the bureaucracy with the autonomy to dominate society and its policies regardless of its other political characteristics.

The singular grimness of the 'iron cage,' however, has never been quite fulfilled. Historically, advanced industrial societies have not produced the same definitions of the rational role. Even a cursory glance indicates that there have been different organizational outcomes in state development in the nineteenth and twentieth centuries. Despite a number of similarities in the definition of the rationalized administrative role, all bureaucratic roles and organizational structures did not end up alike.[18]

Indeed, when we examine the literature on organizations, especially state administration, it suggests that there are two basic ways in which the bureaucratic role can be organized. Despite the particular historical forms that state bureaucratization has taken, there appear to be at least two types of role systems governing the form and structure of the rationalized administrative organization: organizational and professional orientations.

Organizational Orientation

In this mode organizational rules dominate the structure of information, determining what information is appropriate and what is the appropriate use of the information. This is reflected in the presence of rules governing the criteria for higher offices. These stress entry into the organizational career prior to appointment to office. The stress placed on early commitment by the individual is reflected in the establishment of severe

---

[18] Students of comparative and developmental public administration have long noted this anomaly (Heady, *Public Administration;* Brian Chapman, *The Profession of Government: Public Service in Europe* [London: Allen and Unwin, 1959]; John A. Armstrong, *The European Administrative Elite* [Princeton: Princeton University Press, 1973]; Ernest Barker, *The Development of Public Services in Western Europe: 1660–1930* [London: Oxford University Press, 1944]; Guy B. Peters, *The Politics of Bureaucracy: A Comparative Perspective* [New York: Longman, 1978]; Michel Crozier, *La Societé bloquée* [The grid-locked society] [Paris: Éditions du Seuil, 1970]; Fritz Morstein-Marx, *The Administrative State* [Chicago: University of Chicago Press, 1957]) but have provided no convincing arguments as to why a supposedly universal process results in different structural outcomes. The difficulties surrounding categorization can be resolved to a large extent if we view the Weberian characteristics not as a series of scalar indices of structure but rather as a description or definition of role characteristics. The question then is no longer whether an administrative structure is more or less rational but whether an essential constellation of role characteristics is present. This allows us to ask whether there are different ways of arriving at this constellation of 'rational' role characteristics (Arthur L. Stinchcombe, 'Bureaucratic and Craft Administration of Production,' *Administrative Science Quarterly*, Vol. 4 [1959], pp. 168–87; Marshall W. Meyer, 'Two Authority Structures of Bureaucratic Organizations,' *Administrative Science Quarterly*, Vol. 13 [1968], pp. 211–28; John Child, 'Predicting and Understanding Organization Structure,' *Administrative Science Quarterly*, Vol. 18 [1973]). This focuses our attention on the following aspects: the quantified and qualified definitions of eligibility, recruitment, appointment, promotion, career, and discretion primarily of upper civil servants.

restrictions on eligibility and recruitment. These take the form of limiting eligibility to those who have: (1) passed through highly specific courses of university training, usually legal training; and/or (2) attended schools designed to train, formally or informally, upper civil servants; and/or (3) served in some form of apprenticeship program before being appointed to office. Whatever the particular form of the requirement, the general result is that individuals are asked to forgo other opportunities and give themselves over to the idea of a bureaucratic career early in their educational careers.[19]

Such early commitment requires incentives because of opportunity costs. These incentives take the form of career predictability. There are two aspects to this predictability. One takes the shape of limiting entry into higher office only to those who have made the prescribed early commitment. This makes appointment by other means such as lateral entry or promotion from the lower civil service very rare. Early commitment thus assures the individual of eligibility for high office. The second aspect takes the form of highly predictable patterns of promotion based on seniority. This provides a minimal assurance of career advancement for the individual.

In combination these two incentives help shape the organizational structure. Departmental specialization is one outcome. Movement across ministries is likely to be viewed with disfavor by both superiors and subordinates since it produces a discordant note of career unpredictability. Furthermore, knowledge acquired in one ministry or department is not always easily transferable. Nor is transfer with promotion looked on favorably by the recipient or new colleagues. Equals or subordinates are uneasy about how to integrate the newcomer and about the consequences for promotion. Superiors have to rearrange promotion patterns and face the morale consequences.

This emphasis on hierarchy as predictability is also evident in personal terms. Monopoly of higher offices by those who committed themselves to a bureaucratic career while still pursuing their education creates stratification within the organization based on education. This provides predictable boundaries that cannot be easily crossed. As a result, there are a narrow range of entry-level offices and these require pretty much the same skills and experiences. Seniority emerges as the means for ensuring the persistence of the incentives to give up alternative careers; it does so by providing a highly visible means of predicting early career advancement. Seniority provides predictability without negative overtones. Distinctions in rank, authority, and status in the early career are seen as the products of impersonal conditions. Early career commitment thus produces a set of incentives which in turn produces a homogeneous corps of

---

[19] Armstrong, *The European Administrative Elite*, p. 201.

upper-level administrators and a role structure with specific predictable characteristics. The specification of the career role is consciously dominated by the organization through its emphasis on hierarchy and specialization. Restricted entry into the highest offices, high organizational boundaries formed by early role commitment, departmental specialization, and career all contribute to the definition of the rational bureaucratic role as one in which organizational commitment is crucial and the reward for this commitment is high levels of predictability about status and career. Where such restrictions exist we can conclude that the organization can resist outside intervention. Its lack of permeability makes it difficult for outsiders to manipulate. The autonomy of this condition makes the higher civil servant an admired figure. Major examples of this type are Japan, France, Germany, Spain, Italy, and the former Soviet Union.

Professional Orientation

This mode stresses the individual as the basic unit for the possession and allocation of appropriate information. This results in a role characterized by the rule that professional or preprofessional training is the primary criterion for holding higher administrative office.[20] The *assumption* of the professional role and its accompanying status is considered sufficient and, indeed, superior to its organizationally oriented counterpart. The professionally oriented bureaucratic role stresses the possession by the individual of an expertise that is accompanied by a public service orientation with a distinctive ethic that justifies the privilege of self-regulation and a status that underscores autonomy and prestige.[21]

Where professional orientation is stressed, the bureaucratic organization takes advantage of the existing high social and economic incentives for individuals to take on professional training and roles. By recruiting professionals or those with preprofessional training the organization need not offer high incentives for early commitment to the bureaucratic career. The promised rewards of a professional career already provide such incentives. Instead, incentives are directed toward recognizing the status of the professional role through salary, flexibility of access (lateral entry and/or promotion through the ranks—the latter indicating that professional status has been achieved), flexibility of assignment, and greater

---

[20] By preprofessional training, I mean the existence of a formal or informal rule that the individual acquire a specific kind of higher education in order to undertake professional training. Thus, for example, an education at a leading university in England seemed to be a requirement for passing on to the higher status professions of barrister as opposed to solicitor, physician as opposed to surgeon, and high-level administrator as opposed to lower-level ones.

[21] Magali Sarfatti Larson, *The Rise of Professionalism: A Sociological Analysis* (Berkeley: University of California Press, 1977), pp. x–xii, 187–207; Eliot Friedson, *Professional Powers: A Study of the Institutionalization of Formal Knowledge* (Chicago: University of Chicago Press, 1986), pp. 20–38.

discretion and autonomy.[22] In this arrangement career structures are less systematic and predictable. Seniority plays a role but a much lesser one in determining promotion. So-called 'fast tracks' exist that take advantage of and offer incentives for higher levels of professional capacity. As one might expect, organizational specialization and hierarchy tend to suffer in this context.

It cannot be emphasized too strongly that in this kind of organizational environment the professional or the preprofessional training has defined the *individual* and not the organization as the means by which information is transmitted and as the source for the decision about the conditions under which it can be used. The internalization of complex integrated skills and the norms for their use by the individual considerably reduces the necessity for the organization to define these aspects through career experience and formal rules. Moreover, the individual's internalization of the criteria for the appropriate use of his or her skills produces high predictability of role behavior. Since predictability is high, organizational definition of hierarchy and differentiation as means of delimiting opportunism need not be heavily emphasized.[23] Precisely because the professionally oriented bureaucratic role is governed by norms derived mostly from extraorganizational sources, the organization is more permeable than it is in the organizationally oriented mode. The emphasis on professional training makes public and private bureaucratic roles relatively interchangeable. This capacity for interchangeability makes possible greater inter- and intraorganizational vertical and horizontal mobility. In this organizational mode it is the *profession* not the bureaucrat that is highly valued. In this sense the bureaucratic role as an integrative one stems from its being one of a number of roles open to the professional. The United States, Great Britain, Canada, and Switzerland are examples of this mode.

In sum, we can distinguish between two patterns of institutionalization of the rationalized bureaucratic role that emerged at the end of the nineteenth and beginning of the twentieth centuries and, as a consequence, two modes of state-society integration.

In one mode emphasis is placed on the role of organizations in determining tasks. Rules, especially those that quantify and qualify bureaucratic role, operate to define tasks and the conditions of application of whatever skills the individual possesses. In the absence of internalized norms of discretion and practice, organizational rules perform these tasks.

---

[22] Thomas Hammond and Gary J. Miller, 'A Social Choice Perspective on Expertise and Authority in Bureaucracy,' *American Journal of Political Science*, Vol. 29 (1985), pp. 1–28.

[23] Charles Perrow, *Complex Organizations: A Critical Essay* (New York: Random House, 1986), pp. 22–3; Eliot Freidson and Buford Rhea, 'Knowledge and Judgement in Professional Evaluations,' *Administrative Science Quarterly*, Vol. 10 (1965), pp. 107–24.

In this mode integration of state and society is achieved or at least sought through the establishment of the 'publicness' of organizational structure and role. The emphasis on rules defining the bureaucratic role and decision making are seen as the means of removing private interests from public policy or as a means of transforming an array of private interests into a public one. Rational organization comes to represent the public interest—administration substitutes for politics. State-society integration is achieved, in a sense, mechanically through an identity of formal organizational structure and representations. The state bureaucracy comes to be viewed as a value, a symbol, the true representative of the public interest and not simply as an instrument. Leaders in private organizations view this organizational structure both as a source of legitimacy and as a means of reducing uncertainty about their status and thus reproduce the organizational mode of rationalization in the private sector. It is this instrumental isomorphism or mirror-imaging of public and private organizations that provides the basis of state-society integration. It is reflected in the homogeneity of the socialization, education, and training of 'public' and 'private' elites.

In the other professional the role is characterized by the individual acquisition and control of a complex task. Where this mode is dominant the training is entrusted to the individual who is assumed to be better suited to determine the conditions of its use than any organizational structure. State-society integration is achieved or sought through a system or systems of voluntary structure. The social institutions of education culminating in the voluntaristic structure of professions provides one basis for the integration of state organization to society: the means of determining eligibility for public service and other occupations. Political leadership via parties is often the other basic structure underlying integration—parties serving as the means for recruitment and selection of professionals for the highest levels of decision making. If the organizational mode is 'mechanical' then this mode might be described, à la Durkheim, as 'organic.' The professional role, of which the bureaucratic role is a by-product, integrates the state with society through the two voluntaristic social structures of professional education and party.

The existence of these two patterns—organizational and professional—indicates that there are two types of rational administration. To the extent that successful economic development occurred and has continued to occur under both types (as it did, for example, in the United States after 1920 and in Japan and Germany in the post-World-War-II period), this suggests that economic developmental success was not necessarily a consequence of the particular structure of bureaucratic rationality that had emerged in either Japan or the United States by the end of the nineteenth and early twentieth centuries. Rather, it indicates that economic development was affected by the degree to which the bureaucratic role served to integrate state and society in a number of states or the same state at varying times and under varying conditions.

In short, I argue that state-civil society integration in the modern industrial state was a consequence of the rationalization of the administrative role either directly as in the organizationally oriented mode or indirectly as in the professionally oriented mode. Furthermore, it is the varying level of integration that helps explain the different capacities or contributions of civil bureaucracy to economic development. The existence of two forms of bureaucratic role rather than one suggests that rationalization was not driven by the supposedly universal systemic economic demands of industrialization or modernization but by continuing problems of political leadership role definition and integration.

Uncertainty, Modes of Bureaucratic Rationality, and the Case of Meiji Japan (1868–1912)

To explain how the institutionalization of rational state bureaucracy came to serve as the integrative link between state and civil society, the operational problem is to explain why rational bureaucratic organization developed in these two modes across different polities at different stages in their social and economic development.

When we examine the extensive literature on complex organizations in the fields of economics, sociology, political science, and history, there appears to be no adequate explanation of why different modes of bureaucratic rationalization occur.[24] Despite the considerable differences between explanations, there seem to be several common themes. First, all the explanations stress some aspect of uncertainty: uncertainty about availability or proper allocation of resources, about legitimate authority, transaction costs, organizational stability or managerial power or status. Second, there seems to be common agreement that limited or bounded rationality—that is, limitations on the availability of information and the limited capacity to search for the best solution—of decision makers is a major factor in bureaucratic rationalization. Bureaucratic organizations are seen as the response to the continuing problem of imperfections of individual decisions in situations where neither perfect information nor a perfect market exists. Third, all of the explanations implicitly or explicitly assume that rationalization is a process of institutionalizing opportunistic advantages by those who lead private or public organizations. Finally, in line with the preceding themes, all the explanations appear to agree that internalization is the processual means by which bureaucratic rationaliza-

---

[24] An extended survey of this literature is available in Silberman, *Cages of Reason*, Chap. 1.

tion occurs. It is either a process of internalizing possible sources of profit or efficiency or of internalizing transaction costs, or it is the internalization of information and resources generally. The internalization process is seen as the primary mechanism of response. Internalization accounts for the emergence of hierarchy, specialization and differentiation, career structures, and utilization of formal rules—organizations thus exhibit the structured role characteristics implied by Weber's description.

In this context rational bureaucratization may be seen as the result of the persistence of uncertainty or risk in the environment which reveals the unsuitability of the old rules for making decisions and thus provokes attempts to provide new rules and greater predictability. The process by which this occurs is the institutionalization of opportunistic advantages which in the case of the state are claimed as monopolies. Rational bureaucratization emerges, I argue, as the result of strategic choices made within a context of persistent decision-making problems. The solution to these problems is constrained by the existence of other structures governing choices and possible outcomes—in short, the environment. From this perspective I argue that the two different forms of bureaucratic rationalization represent different strategies of choice by agents for dealing with the same specific recurring problem(s) within different environments.

The common recurring problem(s) in a large number of nineteenth-century states that appears to have produced the rationalized administrative role was not allocational efficiency since there was no market to test efficiency in price terms.[25] Precisely because the state is a monopoly and the state administration has no competition (except intramurally) and its agents are capable, therefore, of disguising political choices as objective economic ones, efficiency of its operations cannot be a recurring problem

[25] Although attempts have been made to apply cost–benefit analysis, the difficulty is that no reasons are given as to why redistribution decisions made by government officials should be considered as efficient even when goals are specified. See: Richard Zeckhauser and Elma Schaefer, 'Public Policy and Normative Economic Theory,' in Raymond A. Bauer and Kenneth J. Gergen, eds., *The Study of Policy Formation* (New York: Free Press, 1968), pp. 27–102; Aaron Wildavsky, 'The Political Economy of Efficiency: Cost Benefit Analysis, Systems Analysis, and Program Budgeting,' in Austin Ranney, ed., *Political Science and Public Policy* (Chicago: Markham Publishing Co., 1968); C. D. Foster, 'Social Welfare Functions in Cost–Benefit Analysis,' in John R. Lawrence, ed., *Operational Research and the Social Sciences* (London: Tavistock, 1966); R. Layard, *Cost–Benefit Analysis* (Harmsworth: Penguin Books, 1972); Thomas E. Borcherding, 'The Sources of Growth of Public Expenditures in the United States, 1902–70,' in T. E. Borcherding, ed., *Budgets and Bureaucrats* (Durham: Duke University Press, 1977), pp. 45–70; Alan Abouchar, *Project Decision Making in the Public Sector* (Lexington, Mass.: Lexington Books, 1985); George Downs and Patrick D. Larkey, *The Search for Government Efficiency: From Hubris to Helplessness* (New York: Random House, 1986); Dennis J. Palumbo, 'Organization Theory and Political Science,' in Fred I. Greenstein and Nelson Polsby, eds., *Handbook of Political Science* (Reading, Mass.: Addison-Wesley, 1977), pp. 319–69; Brian J. Loasby, *Choice, Complexity and Ignorance* (New York: Cambridge University Press, 1976); and P. M. Jackson, *The Political Economy of Bureaucracy* (Totowa, NY: Barnes and Noble, 1983), pp. 176–210.

148   *Bernard S. Silberman*

(except, of course, to members of the political opposition) to which the response is rationalization. Nor was operational efficiency a notable cause. In the cases of Japan, France, and Great Britain there was no public outcry or demand for efficiency nor was there anything but the most ambiguous notion of what efficiency meant. Only in the United States was there a public outcry about administrative corruption but this was primarily confined to the problems created by patronage and the difficulties encountered in rationalizing patronage.[26]

If the central recurring problems of state organizational life were neither allocative efficiency nor operational efficiency, what then remains? One clue is provided by the historical conditions under which the two modes of bureaucratic rationality were institutionalized. The organizationally oriented examples all share a common road to bureaucratic rationalization—the occurrence of a revolutionary condition. Organizationally oriented bureaucracies emerged in France after 1789 and Japan after 1868, following revolutionary situations in which there were total successions of leadership.[27]

[26] This is reflected well in several aspects of the role structure often associated with rational bureaucracy. Role hierarchy and hierarchical responsibility are not always high or even positively correlated with other aspects of role structure. See: Stanley H. Udy, Jr., '"Bureaucracy" and "Rationality" in Weber's Organization Theory,' *American Sociological Review*, Vol. 24 (1959), pp. 591–5; and D. S. Pugh *et al.*, 'Dimensions of Organizational Structure,' *Administrative Science Quarterly*, Vol. 13 (1968), pp. 65–105.

Furthermore, there is a considerable literature eager to show us that rational-legal characteristics as described by Weber produce inefficiency and conflict. See: Alvin W. Gouldner, *Patterns of Industrial Bureaucracy* (Glencoe, Ill.: Free Press, 1954); Mancur Olson, Jr., *The Logic of Collective Action* (Cambridge, Mass.: Harvard University Press, 1968), p. 62; Robert Michels, *Political Parties* (New York: Free Press, 1966), p. 71; Oliver Williamson, *Markets and Hierarchies: Analysis and Antitrust Implications* (New York: Free Press, 1975), p. 125; Joseph R. Monsen, Jr., and Anthony Downs, 'A Theory of Large Managerial Firms,' *Journal of Political Economy*, Vol. 73, No. 3 (1965), pp. 221–36; Harry Braverman, *Labor and Monopoly Capital* (New York: Monthly Review Press, 1974); Dan Clawson, *Bureaucracy and the Labor Process: The Transformation of U.S. Industry* (New York: Monthly Review Press, 1980).

Such criticism is also widespread in the literature evaluating the performance of public bureaucracies. Finally, arguments about operational or x-efficiency as the main recurring problem do not explain why distinctly different patterns of rational organizational roles should emerge (Harvey Leibenstein, 'Aspects of the X-Efficiency Theory of the Firm,' *The Bell Journal of Economics*, Vol. 6, No. 2 [1975], pp. 580–606; Harvey Leibenstein, *Inside the Firm: The Inefficiencies of Hierarchy* [Cambridge, Mass.: Harvard University Press, 1987]). If operational efficiency were the recurring problem it seems reasonable to expect that the limited variables related to operational efficiency would result in very similar structural outcomes for organizational roles. See: Harvey Leibenstein, 'Allocative Efficiency vs. X-Efficiency,' *American Economic Review*, Vol. 56, No. 3 (1966), pp. 392–415; Harvey Leibenstein, 'Allocative Efficiency, X-Efficiency and the Measurement of Welfare Losses,' *Economica*, Vol. 30 (1969), pp. 304–9; and Harvey Leibenstein, *General X-Efficiency Theory and Economic Development* (New York: Oxford University Press, 1978).

[27] For descriptions of state development following these crises of leadership succession see, on France, Ezra N. Suleiman, *Politics, Power, and Bureaucracy in France: The French Administrative Elite* (Princeton: Princeton University Press, 1974); Jacques Leon Godechot, *Les Institutions de la France sous la Revolution et l'Empire* (The Institutions of France under the Revolution and Empire) (Paris: Presses universitaires de France, 1968); Clive H. Church, *Revolution and Red Tape: The French Ministerial Bureaucracy, 1770–1850* (Oxford: Oxford University Press, 1981); Guy Thuilier, *Bureaucratie et bureaucrates en France au XIXᵉ siècle* (Geneva:

The connection between crises of leadership succession such as that which occurred in Japan after 1868 and a process that led to the organizationally oriented outcome is related to the fact that leadership succession implies the substitution of one means of, and criteria for, selecting leaders by other means and criteria. When such substitutions are made there must be new institutional arrangements for the selection process and for acquiring the criteria for selection. This replacement process has, historically, been one of increased differentiation as achievement characteristics were substituted for ascribed ones and officeholding was no longer a property right. Total successions of leadership offer clear opportunities for the reconstruction of administrative systems and for the relationship between state and society.[28] These observations suggest that the continuing problem facing many nineteenth- and early twentieth-century states was the dilemma of the succession of political leaders and the level of uncertainty regarding their incumbency or possession of power. This leads us to conclude that: rational bureaucratization may be construed as a consequence of strategic choices by those holding political power in environments of greater or lesser uncertainty.[29]

Librairie Droz). On Japan, see Bernard S. Silberman, 'Bureaucratic Development and the Structure of Decision-Making in the Meiji Period: The Case of the Genrō,' *Journal of Asian Studies*, Vol. 27 (1968), pp. 81–94; Bernard S. Silberman, 'Bureaucratization of the Meiji State: The Problem of Succession in the Meiji Restoration, 1868–1900,' *Journal of Asian Studies*, Vol. 35 (1976), pp. 421–30; Bernard S. Silberman, 'The Bureaucratic State in Japan: The Problem of Authority and Legitimacy,' in Tetsuo Najita and J. Victor Koschmann, eds., *Dimensions of Conflict in Modern Japan* (Princeton: Princeton University Press, 1982), pp. 226–57; Robert M. Spaulding, Jr., *Imperial Japan's Higher Civil Service Examinations* (Princeton: Princeton University Press, 1967); Einosuke Yamanaka, *Nihon kindai kokka no keisei to kanryōsei* (Bureaucracy and the structure of the modern Japanese state) (Tokyo: Kobundo, 1974); E. Herbert Norman, *Japan's Emergence as a Modern State* (Westport, Conn: Greenwood Press, 1975; originally published in 1940); W. G. Beasley, *The Meiji Restoration* (Stanford: Stanford University Press, 1972). On Germany, see John R. Gillis, *The Prussian Bureaucracy in Crisis, 1840–60: Origins of an Administrative Ethos* (Stanford: Stanford University Press, 1971); Rolf Engelsing, 'Zur politischen Bildung der deutschen Unterschichten, 1789–1863' (The political formation of the German non-elites, 1789–1863), *Historische Zeitschrift*, Vol. 206, No. 2 (April 1968), pp. 337–69; Tibor Sule, *Preussische Burokratic Tradition: zur Entwicklung von Verwaltung u. Beamtenschaft in Deutschland 1871–1918* (The Prussian bureaucratic tradition: The development of administration and civil service in Germany 1871–1918) (Göttingen: Vandenhoeck u. Ruprecht, 1988); Albert Lotz, *Geschichte des deutschen Beamtentums* (History of the German civil service) (Berlin: R. V. Decker's Verlag, 1909); Reinhart Kosseleck, *Preussen zwischen Reform und Revolution: Allgemeines Landrecht, Verwaltung und soziale Bewegung von 1791 bis 1848* (Prussia between reform and revolution: The legal code, administration, and social movements from 1791 to 1848) (Stuttgart: Klett, 1967).

[28] Professionally oriented bureaucracies, such as those in the United States and Great Britain, emerged under conditions in which there were relatively well-defined and well-regulated rules governing the succession of political leadership. These rules were processual in character, producing high levels of predictability about the consequences for winners and losers but did not provide certainty about outcomes of any specific election. Thus uncertainty for political leaders existed but at a much lower level than for those emerging from a revolutionary condition. Silberman, *Cages of Reason*, pp. 66–84.

[29] Greater or high uncertainty is a situation in which there is relatively little information about the possible forms of rules covering decision making but sufficient information is available to assign probabilities to the outcomes of some but not all choices. Total succession

Utilizing these two aspects of uncertainty it is possible to deduce two quite different strategies: the strategy of political leaders in low uncertainty situations produces a professionally oriented rational bureaucratic role while high uncertainty situations produce organizationally oriented rationality.

Bureaucratic rationalization was the consequence of political acts by those seeking to secure their incumbency to positions of power and status. Political leaders did not set out to create a rationalized structure because they perceived it as an instrument of social efficiency. Rather they engaged in a series of strategic actions to defend their incumbency. Each of these choices produced new problems which required resolution. These acts in turn created other problems. At each strategic choice the possibilities of further problems and choices were narrowed. Out of this Markov-like chain there finally emerged an equilibrium of structural relations based on role definition. It was this equilibrium that became the institutional forms of rationalized bureaucracy. Political leaders did not intend the final outcome. Their actions over time produced an outcome, however, that resulted in the reduction of uncertainty about their and their successors' incumbency. Rationalized bureaucracy thus was not a function of economic market failures but of political 'market' failures—the failures of custom to provide predictability about political leadership and its actions under new conditions of uncertainty. Bureaucratic rationalization therefore cannot be seen, historically, as the instrument of emergent rationality with either the goal or the direct capacity of rationalizing market allocations.

This is readily seen in the strategy that emerged from conditions of high uncertainty such as those facing the would-be leaders of the Meiji Restoration in 1868. Under conditions of high uncertainty the lower samurai who now sought to claim power because of their role in bringing down the old rules faced a dilemma. They had destroyed the old rules governing political leadership and in doing so stripped themselves of the means for sustaining themselves in positions of leadership. They were left with few choices about securing their status, power, and material resources. They could not resort to a franchise system since they had no assurance voters would choose them—voters being notoriously fickle. This was all the more true in Japan where there was no experience with voting and as a consequence leaders had no idea on what grounds individuals might make choices if left to themselves.

---

of leadership or major leadership succession crises is one of those conditions where high uncertainty reigns. Lesser or low uncertainty is that in which there is considerable information available in the form of operating rules about the probabilities of the outcomes of choices. Elective systems of determining leadership succession are one condition of low uncertainty because the procedural rules are well articulated but the specific outcomes are not. See Silberman, *Cages of Reason*, pp. 42–3.

Given this state of affairs, putative political leaders such as the lower samurai who came to dominate political power in Meiji Japan had to engage in a strategy of 'strategic replacement.' On the one hand, this strategy allows the putative leaders to strategically replace those at the secondary and tertiary levels of decision making with those who are loyal to them while, on the other hand, it allows them to produce a well-defined administrative career role that results, in the long term, in a homogeneous cadre of decision makers devoted to the organization above all personal obligations. Achieving the first requires not only replacement of individuals; it also means the internalization (or centralization might be an alternative word) of a wide range of localized or decentralized offices which often characterized secondary and tertiary levels of decision making in prerationalized states. The problem here is that the samurai leaders had no place to go for replacements other than their friends and loyal supporters.

Loyalty, however, as a criterion for selecting incumbents to decision-making roles is at best indifferent and at worst a powerful source of disruption and disorder. Loyalty provides no guidelines in itself for decision making other than self or patron interest. Nor was it possible, as the samurai leaders found, to make any but the most gross distinctions between levels of loyalty, thus creating conflict among those claiming to be loyal. Loyalty could not be the source for organizational continuity once the event that served as the measure of loyalty was long gone. Moreover, loyalty could not provide for uniformity of decision making or implementation. Finally, continued reliance on loyalty provided challengers to the samurai leadership with ammunition to charge that private rather than public interest was being served. Thus, the imminent strategy had to give way to the long-term strategy if there was to be any organizational continuity and, therefore, continuity of the leadership as well.

The resolution to many of these problems was the resort to rules to specify the boundaries of decision making, the procedures, and the appropriate information to be used in arriving at decisions. The problem for the Meiji leaders was to show that these rules were not arbitrary nor served private interest. How could decision making be made to appear to be public in character without resort to the franchise? Rationalization of administrative roles—the structure of decision making—provided the Meiji leaders with the only organizational solution.

By reliance on rules the Meiji leaders created a uniformity that made administrative roles a function of *organizational* rather than individual characteristics. The publicness of the rules was assured in Meiji Japan, as it was in other cases, by positing in nature the existence of a body of rules governing the physical as well as the social world which were capable of being discovered and understood. That is, there is the claim that systems of knowledge exist that allow their possessors to appropriately order priorities and their implementation. Reliance on expertise removes issues from politics. Science or scientism is substituted for personal esoteric knowledge and interest; administration is substituted for politics. From this point of view administration not only substitutes for politics, it also becomes the representative of the public interest.[30] Political *cum* administrative leaders under the condition of critical leadership succession thus become committed to the restructuring of the decision-making role not only because they wish to retain their power, status, and material goods but also because they have come to believe in the superior capacity of these new organizations to determine the public interest. The public interest in their eyes, as in the case of Meiji Japan, is too important to be left to the public.

In order to maintain the integrity and continuity of the organization, the Meiji leaders were increasingly induced to seek systematic public means for gaining access to the administrative role while maintaining sufficient closure or boundaries to external interference. This can and could be resolved most easily by making access to the administrative role dependent on the acquisition of a body of knowledge that can be objectively tested. Merit thus becomes in Meiji Japan as in other similar cases the test of eligibility and assures the public rather than private character of organizational access. The use of knowledge as the test of merit assures the utilitarian equality of the bureaucratic role. Expertise is public and by its nature should provide the best solution for the greatest number of people. By providing only limited access to the acquisition of appropriate educational standards, the Meiji leaders were assured of a supply of uniformly trained individuals. Education and expertise became the means by which the public interest was depoliticized.

The strategy of emphasizing merit measured by acquired education results as it did in Meiji Japan in the emergence of specific structural qualities. To get individuals to commit themselves to this kind of opportunity-cost education, organizational incentives have to be offered. The easiest strategy in such cases is to assure the individual of both short-term and long-term job advantages. The former takes the shape of promises of commensurate reward for the sacrifices of early commitment to education—the higher the education, the higher the earlier appointment level. The long-term advantage is most easily taken care of by creating a highly predictable career structure in which movement through a series of offices is based on objective grounds such as seniority. The emphasis in such a strategy must be on predictability of career and the result of this is increased specialization since horizontal mobility from department to

[30] For a rich explanation of the political character of science or its political uses see Yaron Ezrahi, *The Descent of Icarus: Science and the Transformation of Contemporary Democracy* (Cambridge, Mass.: Harvard University Press, 1990).

department or ministry to ministry creates a bewildering set of career possibilities.

In short, the strategy that began with an attempt to replace loyalty ended in the case of Meiji Japan as elsewhere with a structure that looked like the Weberian conception of organizational rationality. The ad hoc tactics or strategies the Meiji leaders pursued in order to insure their incumbency resulted in the creation of what appears to be a highly autonomous organizational structure in which role is well defined and enumerated.

Rationalization of the Meiji State, 1868–1900

How this strategy worked out in real life is readily observable in the Japanese case. There emerged within the span of a generation after 1868 an administrative structure that has continued to be the basis for civil service up until the present.[31] The characteristics of this structure are very much like those of the French upper civil service. Like the French system, the Japanese structure was and is characterized by a highly insulated internal labor market. After entrance, allocation of offices is almost

---

[31] The basic features of this upper civil service role might be described as follows:

(1) Higher education in law or the so-called policy sciences—political science, economics, public finance—as the basis for eligibility to the senior general administrative service. This is distinct from eligibility for the technical administrative roles in such areas as agriculture, communications, science, and public works where higher education in the civil sciences is the basis for eligibility.

(2) Passage of tests, both written and oral, designed specifically for entry into the upper civil service. Passage of these exams is essential for recruitment into the upper civil service. There is no linkage between the upper and lower civil service which allows mobility from the lower service to the higher one. These examinations originally centered on law but later came to include the policy sciences for those entering the senior administrative service. Furthermore, sufficient knowledge to pass these exams has required, in effect, the possession of a university degree from one of a limited number of universities. Possession of a degree from the University of Tokyo has had the greatest predictability aspect. Far more than a simple majority of administrative senior civil servants have been consistently recruited from this premier Japanese university. Smaller percentages are recruited from other state universities and several private universities.

(3) Entrance into a distinct upper civil service career beginning at the lowest level of the upper civil service and moving through a series of hierarchically linked offices at a highly predictable rate.

(4) Advancement largely on the basis of seniority until the middle levels (section chief or equivalent) and after this, as offices become fewer, selection by vice-ministerial level officials on the basis of performance and seniority.

(5) A career centered primarily within a single ministry with specialization arising systematically as a function of the degree to which individuals ceased to advance and remained in one office or section.

(6) A service-wide uniform career period (20 years service or 60 years of age), completion of which has provided the person with a vested interest in a retirement income or pension.

(7) A career structure in which officeholders have been protected from arbitrary dismissal. The grounds for dismissal have been well defined in laws and regulations, and the administration of disciplinary measures has been in the hands of senior civil servants.

completely independent of external forces until a person reaches the highest levels of office as vice minister. As a result, skills have been highly
organization-specific. Moreover, the constraints of the career structure,
which have kept most people within the same ministry throughout their
careers, very often render their skills to be not only organization-specific,
but specific to various sub-units of the organization.

Entry into the civil service was, by 1900, governed by a set of clearly
defined rules. An informal but major precondition of entry was training in
law. To a considerable degree this continues to be the case despite the
inclusion of policy sciences. Legal or policy science training in itself has by
no means been sufficient to secure entrance since passage of oral and
written exams are essential. The ability to pass these exams, however, has
not been widely distributed among graduates of a great many universities. Indeed, from the very beginning, graduates of Tokyo Imperial
University (now less regally known as the University of Tokyo) have
dominated the lists of successful examinees.[32] Kyoto and several other
state universities have made inroads over time but they remain minority
contributors to the lists of successful examinees.

Since the number of schools providing successful candidates has consistently been small and the desire for high-status careers so high, the
demand for positions in the entering classes of the University of Tokyo
and Kyoto University have been proportionally high since the 1880s.
Successful entry to these universities was, and still is, dependent on
passage of an examination. Very early it became evident that significant
numbers of successful entrants came from a relatively small number of
higher schools—the 'numbered' state higher schools which were the first
to be established between 1877 and 1908.[33] Thus, if one had ambitions to
become a senior civil servant, commitment to the career had to come at the
point of entrance to the higher schools in the individual's mid-teens.
Entrance to these schools became prized as well. Astute parents soon
sought out middle schools that had reputations for preparing students
successfully for entrance into the 'numbered' higher schools. In effect,
commitment to career was often not the choice of the person but rather of
his parents. However it occurred, the commitment to an upper civil service career had to be made long before a person came to sit for the civil
service examinations.

Having successfully passed the upper civil service exams, the individual set out on a career course that was well defined. One moved
through a series of hierarchically organized offices at very regular inter-

[32] Robert M. Spaulding, Jr., *Imperial Japan's Higher Civil Service* (Princeton: Princeton University Press, 1967), pp. 131–2, 267–70; Michio Muramatsu, *Sengo Nihon no kanryōsei* (The
postwar Japanese bureaucratic system) (Tokyo: Tōyō Keizai Shinpōsha, 1981), pp. 56–82;
Akira Kubota, *Higher Civil Servants in Postwar Japan: Their Social Origins, Educational Backgrounds and Career Patterns* (Princeton: Princeton University Press, 1969), pp. 67–76.
[33] Kubota, *Higher Civil Servants*, pp. 60–3.

vals. This movement has been governed by adherence to the formal and informal rules of seniority. The career structure has assured everyone of a minimal level of promotion, usually to section chief or its equivalent.[34] Specialization and differentiation have largely been a matter of internal training through career service and not a product of pre-entry training. The insulation of the career from external constraints was established in 1899 by the creation of autonomous disciplinary committees within the civil service.[35] These committees or their successors have by and large continued to be autonomous, made up mostly of senior civil servants who have rarely dismissed anyone from the service except on grounds of illness and disability.

The creation of uniform retirement and pension rules, beginning in 1884 and revised in 1890, formed the basic continuing structure of career completion. This very early assured the senior official of a predictable career cycle.[36] For those who were forced to retire early by rising to the highest posts such as vice minister, or failing to achieve those posts when colleagues of equal seniority reached them, the completion of the career cycle has consistently been extended into the postcareer period through second careers.[37] There have been very clearly understood rewards for early commitment and successful entry into the upper civil service since the completion of its institutionalization in 1899 through the *Chokunin* (senior level of the upper civil service) Appointment, Civil Service Status, and Civil Service Disciplinary Ordinances of that year.[38]

The Strategy of High Uncertainty

If we now turn to the dynamics of the strategies that produced the above outcomes, we can begin in February 1868 when the Imperial Court, led by the young Emperor Meiji, stripped the head of the Tokugawa House, Keiki, of his court rank, and thus brought an end to the old regime—the so-called *bakuhan* system, a form of highly integrated feudalism closely approaching federalism. In administrative office in the domains and the *primer inter pares* domain, the Tokugawa was based on inherited family rank. Within this category, appointments were based on unsystematic and

---

[34] Ibid., pp. 127–28.

[35] *Hōrei zensho* (Collected laws; hereafter, *HZ*), Imperial Ordinances 68 and 69, 1899.

[36] *HZ*, Dajōkan Ord. 1, 1884; Law 43, 1890; Law 48, 1923.

[37] Chalmers Johnson, *MITI and the Japanese Miracle: The Growth of Industrial Policy, 1925–75* (Stanford: Stanford University Press, 1982), pp. 63–73; Chalmers Johnson, *Japan's Public Policy Companies* (Washington: American Enterprise Institute, 1978), pp. 101–18; Bernard S. Silberman, 'The Bureaucratic Role in Japan, 1900–45: The Bureaucrat as Politician,' in Bernard S. Silberman and H. D. Harootunian, eds., *Japan in Crisis: Essays in Taisho Democracy* (Princeton: Princeton University Press, 1974), pp. 183–216.

[38] Bernard S. Silberman, 'Bureaucratic Development and the Structure of Decision-Making in Japan: 1868–1925,' *Journal of Asian Studies*, Vol. 29 (1970), p. 349.

unpredictable patterns of patronage and merit.[39] In place of the old regime, the emperor and the court administration were 'restored' to govern a unified administration directly. This restoration brought to the fore a group of men the majority of whom could not have held such high office under the previous regime. The group included domain lords and upper samurai but was dominated by lower samurai.[40] By 1875 these lower samurai had proved to be indispensable through their knowledge of who could be considered loyal and their knowledge of the West. The former had resulted in the creation of factions in the new central government built around domain identity. The latter had resulted in the almost complete displacement of the traditional *kuge* (court aristocracy) and *daimyō* (feudal lords) leadership.

The new putative leaders faced the dilemma of providing an acceptable reason for the high level of exclusiveness that the domain-identified factions (*hanbatsu*) represented in the new government. This exclusiveness evoked opposition among a spectrum of loyal claimants. To overcome this opposition the putative leaders engaged in two strategies. The first was the internalization and increasing specification of local government. Beginning in 1871 with Imperial Ordinance 353 (July 14) the domains were dissolved and replaced by a system of urban and rural prefectures (*fu-ken*). Between 1871 and 1878 the process of delineating and completely integrating local governmental administrative roles into the central government was accomplished. The capstone to the structure—the Local Administration Ordinance of 1878—came only after the Satsuma Rebellion of 1877 had been put down.[41] This completed the 'strategic replacement' of local officials all the way up to the central ministries. The new governors were almost entirely drawn from the ranks of samurai (86.2 per cent).[42] Furthermore, about 40 per cent were drawn from the four cliques whose leaders dominated the central government.[43]

The emergence of the 'People's Rights' movement and the rise of party and proto-party politics in the 1870s and 1880s clearly revealed to the new

[39] For a fuller description of this system, see Silberman, *Cages of Reason*, Chap. 6.

[40] Approximately two-thirds of them had participated actively in the attacks on the old regime in the name of their loyalty to the emperor. Altogether almost 75 per cent of this group had either been politically active against the regime and/or also had acquired some Western knowledge. Almost two-thirds (62 per cent) of this group, predominantly lower samurai (52 per cent), could not have held such posts under the preceding regime. In short, the appointment of lower samurai and some upper samurai to imperial court positions revealed a revolutionary change: experience and achievement in the loyal service of the emperor was of more importance than rank accorded by birth. Bernard S. Silberman, *Ministers of Modernization: Elite Mobility in the Meiji Restoration, 1868–73* (Tucson: University of Arizona Press, 1964), pp. 52–72.

[41] HZ, Imperial Ordinances 17 (July 22, 1878) and 32 (July 25, 1878).

[42] Silberman, 'Bureaucratic Development and the Structure of Decision-Making,' pp. 347–62.

[43] See appendix for data on civil service appointments in this period and the post-1900 period.

leaders that they continued to face the problem of explaining why they should govern without the participation of others just as loyal and equal. The problem was exacerbated as the governmental leadership became narrower with the passage of time. By the early 1880s a number of the original leaders had died or been expelled from the leadership: Takamori Saigō, Taisuke Itagaki, Toshimichi Ōkubo, and Shigenobu Okuma being the most prominent. The most visible of the remaining leaders proved to be those who came to be known later as the *genrō* or elder statesmen. The narrowness of the leadership gave challengers the opening to accuse them of pursuing private ends. Thus, while the emergence of the *genrō* as the basic leadership institution resolved the immediate problems of uncertainty for political leaders it did little to resolve the long-term problems of uncertainty resting on the questions of legitimacy and accountability.

Indeed, the *genrō* could not be formalized or given constitutional existence since to do so would raise the question of inequality of access to decision making among those who had supported the Restoration. In effect, the emergence of the *genrō* underscored the problems of leadership selection, power and legitimacy. Were the *genrō* an indication that there was no distinction between bureaucratic and government leadership? If no distinction existed what was the relationship of bureaucratic officials to the emperor? Finally, given the powers the *genrō* had arrogated to themselves who and what was the emperor? In short, the existence of the *genrō* raised the question of what the relationship was between political/bureaucratic leadership and society and how they could be integrated.

Faced with the attack on their legitimacy on just such grounds by the People's Rights Movement and the political parties that followed, the leadership engaged in a two-pronged strategy. The *genrō* set out consciously to answer this challenge by constructing a role of administrative/political leadership that was depoliticized while, at the same time, extraordinarily sensitive to the possible charge of *lèse-majesté*. They sought to construct a predictable and defined structure of accountability between administrative role and imperial power.

In 1881, coincident with the crystallization of the *genrō*, the movement toward integration began with the announcement that a constitution and a national assembly would be granted by 1890. The leaders viewed this as the formal means that would define the relationship of emperor to state and society, the administration to the bureaucracy, and the individual to the state. This kind of definition would establish that the integration of state and society would rest on the public character of the emperor—'the axis of the nation' as Hirobumi Itō, one of the senior imperial advisors, would write in 1888.[44] State and civil society would be integrated by the transcendent character of the emperor.

[44] Joseph Pittau, *Political Thought in Early Meiji Japan: 1868–1889* (Cambridge, Mass.: Harvard University Press, 1967), pp. 177–8.

Essential to this project was the search for the appropriate rhetoric of state definition. For this purpose Hirobumi Itō was sent off to Europe by his *genrō* colleagues to study European governments and constitutions and most especially Germany where he discovered the delights of statist legal positivism—precisely the kind of state definition that put power in the hands of the state bureaucracy. Meanwhile, his compatriots back home began a campaign of creating a public emperor charismatically defined by a carefully constructed persona. The emperor was first put on public display and then, after 1881, placed in increasingly splendorous and awe-inspiring contexts.[45] As the leadership did so, they began the process of constructing the emperor as a sovereign who was both ideologically and legally the ultimate source of authority, the embodiment of the national interest, and thus the only source of accountability for the civil and military services.

While Itō was learning the language of imperial sovereignty, his colleagues at home began the production of an imperial sovereign whose will had no natural restraints—who ruled directly and to whom all were accountable. This was reflected in a line of imperial rescripts directed at establishing an emperor before whom all were socially but not politically equal. The Imperial Rescript to Soldiers and Sailors (1882) established the emperor as the direct sovereign over a people who were held to a set of precepts regardless of social origin.[46] The imperial rescript promulgating the constitution as a gift further clarified the emperor's position as the state and the source of accountability. The Rescript on Education of 1890 established the emperor as the source of moral authority and reinforced the understanding already inherent in the earlier rescripts and in the constitution itself that the emperor was the only *natural* institution and that all other institutions existed as a function of his will, mediated by his civil and military servants.[47]

By 1890, the Meiji leaders had successfully defined the emperor as the symbol of publicness, the embodiment of public interest. By his elevation, both legal and moral, the emperor was depersonalized and transformed into *the* institution of legitimacy. In this process the Meiji leaders also turned their attention to the problem of establishing the publicness of the emperor's servants and thus establishing a continuous link from imperial authority, accountability, and executive power to the bureaucratic role and its relation to society.

[45] Carol Gluck, *Japan's Modern Myths: Ideology in the Late Meiji Period* (Princeton: Princeton University Press, 1985), p. 75; David A. Titus, *Palace and Politics in Prewar Japan* (New York: Columbia University Press, 1974), pp. 48–9.

[46] Centre for East Asian Cultural Studies, ed., *Meiji Japan Through Contemporary Sources* (Tokyo: Centre for East Asian Cultural Studies, 1972), p. 237.

[47] Gluck, *Japan's Modern Myths*, p. 121.

At the same time the Meiji leaders were faced by the challenges of the nascent party opposition, the uncertainties over the recruitment of further leadership, lack of uniformity in the implementation of decisions, and the fears of the second- and third-level leaders over the absence of any systematic and predictable career structure. It became clear, by the early 1880s, that recruiting a state bureaucracy on the basis of loyalty to the new regime was insufficient to produce an orderly exercise of authority and power. Faced with these problems the Meiji leaders had little choice about how publicness—the commitment to a public interest—would be achieved.

Already committed to the concept of imperial authority and accountability the Meiji leaders could resolve the problem of publicness only by avoiding a bureaucratic role that depended for its legitimacy on the personal will of an emperor or its accountability to a popularly elected body of officials. To do either was to invite charges of patronage and self-interest. Rather, they had to create a set of rules that carefully delineated objective criteria for holding public office. These criteria had to be based on a standard of merit, one that would be sufficiently exclusive without being manifestly socially based. The only such exclusionary device was education. For the Meiji leaders educational stratification became a basic policy for education and provided the means for creating a highly exclusionary system of higher education. At the same time the role structure required careful definition if it is was to provide a predictable and transparent structure for movement into and up through the administrative structure.

The first steps in this direction were taken in 1884 with the creation of the regulations for the recruitment and appointment of judicial officials and the creation of a pension plan for civil officials. Both of these were harbingers of the emergence of the career structure.[48] These were followed in 1887 by regulations creating an examination system for administrative civil servants—regulations clearly favoring graduates of Tokyo Imperial University.[49] The favoritism shown to Tokyo graduates evoked charges that led to the revisions of 1893–94.[50] This reorganization established the distinction between the lower and upper civil service as career entry points, thus providing differentiated levels of incentives for stratified

---

[48] See Spaulding, *Imperial Japan's Higher Civil Service*, pp. 53–6. Also *HZ*, Dajōkan tasshi 102 (Dec. 26, 1884); *HZ*, Imperial Ord. 1 (Jan. 4,1884). Later revisions: *HZ*, Law 43 (June 20, 1890); *HZ*, Law 48 (April 13, 1923).

[49] *HZ*, Imperial Ord. 37, 38 (July 23, 1887); *HZ*, Cabinet Ord. 20 (July 23, 1887); *HZ*, Imperial Ord. 57, 58 (Nov. 5, 1887); *HZ*, Cabinet Ord. 25 (Dec. 21, 1887); *HZ*, Imperial Ord. 63, 64 (Dec. 24, 1887); *HZ*, Cabinet Ord. 28 (Dec. 1887).

[50] The revisions are encompassed in the following regulations: *HZ*, Imperial Ord. 126, 183, 187, 197 (Oct. 31, 1893); Imperial Ord. 54 (May 24, 1894); Cabinet Ord. 2 (May 7, 1894); Foreign Ministry Ord. 7 (June 22, 1894).

levels of education. While the regulations did not formally require any specific level of education for entry into the upper civil service, the nature of the examination system made it self-evident that a university education in law was required.

With the 1894 examination regulations, the path to a bureaucratic career became relatively well defined, well known, and, within a very few years, highly predictable. Bureaucratic recruitment at the senior level now came to require not only a university education in law, but also, as a prerequisite to university entrance, a higher school education as well. Entrance to Tokyo and, later, other imperial universities was dependent on passing an examination that required a higher school education. The exclusiveness of these criteria was intensified by the Meiji leaders. They sought to create an eligibility pool for administrative office that was homogeneous in character and that excluded as much as possible those trained in private universities where faculty selection was outside direct government regulation. The degree to which they were successful is reflected in the dominance of Tokyo Imperial University faculty and/or graduates among administrative examiners and those who passed the upper civil service examinations.[51] The creation of the higher school system in 1886 and its reformulation in 1894 as the primary preparation for entrance to Tokyo Imperial University provided further means for reinforcing the straitness of the gate to the civil service career.[52] By 1900 the commitment to a civil service career or any career the state now defined as requiring a university education had to be made before the age of 17 when one sought to pass the examinations for entry into one of the numbered higher schools.[53] The examination system and the corresponding stratified system of education as it was organized between 1884 and 1894 created well-defined preservice and entry-level career paths for the lower and upper civil service.

Two new pressures that emerged in the mid-1890s led to the completion of the career path structure. One was the concern of upper civil servants about the predictability of their careers and the other was the continued challenge of political parties to the Meiji leadership. The first step in resolving the problem of career predictability was taken by linking the various levels of upper civil service rank through the mechanism of seniority.[54] The final elements of the career structure were put in place as

---

[51] See tables 4.7–9.

[52] Kokuritsu Kyōiku Kenkyūjō, *Nihon kindai kyōiku hyakunenshi* (One hundred years of modern Japanese education) (Tokyo: Kyōiku Kenkyū Shinkōkai, 1974), Vol. 4, pp. 454–64.

[53] See tables 4.7–11.

[54] Beginning in 1892, a series of ordinances created a system of promotions within the *sonin* rank (middle rank of highest civil service) in which each advance in grade required at least two years of service in the previous grade. By 1895 patronage appointment at *sonin* rank had formally come to an end. This produced higher costs for transfers since they upset expectations. The longer one stayed in the same ministry the greater the cost of transfer to the ministry since accumulated skills and knowledge would now be lost. The transferee would

a response to political party attempts to come to power through parliamentary majorities. The conflict between the *genrō* and the parties rose in intensity throughout the 1890s. Differences between the two leading *genrō*, Aritomo Yamagata and Itō, over how to deal with the obstructionism of the parties led Itō to invite Shigenobu Okuma and Taisuke Itagaki, whose parties had just united to form the Kaishintō, to take over the cabinet and thus create the first party cabinet (June 30, 1898).

The cabinet lasted long enough (until November 8, 1898) to stoke the fires of anxiety in Yamagata. As prime minister following the first party cabinet, Yamagata, seeking to protect and maintain *genrō* control over political leadership and leadership succession, instituted a series of regulations which completed the career structure. The Civil Service Appointment Ordinance (March 28, 1899) linked the highest civil service levels to service in the ranks below them.[55] To further protect the upper civil service from possible unlinking of senior appointments from lower levels, Yamagata created, for all intents and purposes, a tenure system through the promulgation of the Civil Service Discipline Ordinance and the Civil Service Status Ordinance.[56] These two ordinances made it almost impossible to engage in any kind of replacement or purge of senior officials except at the vice-ministerial level.

To secure these regulations beyond possible reform by party politicians, Yamagata resorted to the stratagem of having the emperor issue an imperial message outlining categories of legislation requiring Privy Council approval. Included were regulations and legislation relating to the appointment, examination, dismissal, and ranking of civil servants.[57] With these acts Yamagata completed the structure of a career that now began in

also lose since he would be behind his new colleagues in information and skills peculiar to his new home. In other words these new systematic promotion structures based on seniority resulted in role specialization. *HZ*, Imperial Ord. 96 (Nov. 14, 1892); Imperial Ords. 123, 124 (Sept. 21, 1895); Imperial Ords. 196, 197 (June 22, 1897).

[55] *HZ*, Imperial Ord. 61. The ordinance provided that officials at the highest civil service levels (*chokunin*) could be recruited only from: (1) former and incumbent lower officials of the third (highest) grade *sōnin*; (2) former *chokunin* officials with at least one year's service in *chokunin* rank excluding years served as a technician or teacher and excluding those appointed under special regulations; (3) former *chokunin* officials who had passed the higher civil service examinations or had two years' service as a *sōnin* rank official; (4) former or incumbent *chokunin* procurators; (5) former or incumbent *chokunin* judges who could be appointed only in the Ministry of Justice; (6) former or incumbent *chokunin* professors who could be appointed *chokunin* only in the Ministry of Education; (7) flag officers who could be appointed as *chokunin* only in the Army or Navy Ministries.
These regulations were changed slightly in 1913 to include those who passed the newly instituted diplomatic examinations and those ex-*chokunin* who received approval of the Upper Civil Service Commission for reinstatement. See *HZ*, Imperial Ord. 261 (July 31, 1913).

[56] The Discipline Ordinance is *HZ*, Imperial Ord. 62, and the Status Ordinance is *HZ*, Imperial Ord. 63, both of March 28, 1899.

[57] Eigo Fukai, *Sūmitsu-in jūyō giji oboegaki* (Major protocols and proceedings of the Privy Council) (Tokyo: Iwanami Shoten, 1953), pp. 472–5.

one's middle teens and was highly predictable. The 'internal labor market' character of this career is reflected in the career structures of prefectural governors after 1899. The degree to which the careers of senior civil servants became predictable after approximately 1900 is easily observed in the data on prefectural governors.[58]

In the end then, the rationalization of the bureaucratic role was not a consequence of direct concern about economic efficiency, administrative efficiency, or economic development. Rather it had emerged as the consequence of the high uncertainty faced by the early Meiji leaders. As they resolved each imminent source of uncertainty about their status and power, new problems were raised. The resolution to these problems raised new ones. Each nest of new problems constrained the nature of the next set. Finally, by 1899 with Yamagata's fear-inspired rules, the bureaucratic role had become extraordinarily hedged in by a systematic body of rules. The coherency of these rules and their integration with a systematically stratified structure of education produced an institutional equilibrium which, it is fair to say, has yet to be destabilized despite the numerous changes in regimes since 1900.

Conclusion

The central conclusion to be drawn here with regard to the question of the relationship between bureaucratic rationality and economic development is that bureaucratic rationality is an organizational and institutional equilibrium arrived at as a consequence of persisting problems of state-society integration. These problems are best represented by those dealing with political leadership, political leadership succession, and accountability. In the case of Japan, those who came to power after 1868 were constrained by the very nature of revolutionary uncertainty to engage in a series of strategic acts that led them to create an emperor who came to be defined as the embodiment of the public—the emperor as the state. With the emperor as the sole source of accountability, the Meiji leaders were able to avoid any notion of popular sovereignty as the source or means of defining the public interest. Instead, to confirm the emperor as the embodiment of the public the Meiji leaders created a civil service whose rules and career structure made it seem self-evident that its incumbents were restrained from pursuing any private interest. Precisely because the bureaucratic role was rooted in an educational structure which seemed to insure the absence of arbitrary private interest, the role was seen as representing the collective good. State and society were integrated in a seamless organizational web of collective as opposed to private good.

[58] See tables 4.4, 4.5, and 4.12–18.

The degree to which this integration existed may be seen in the character of private large-scale organizations as they evolved in Japan after 1900. Between 1900 and 1930 large-scale organizations increasingly took on the character of the state bureaucracy. Clear distinctions between white-collar workers and white-collar management were created primarily on the basis of differing levels of education. White-collar management was increasingly recruited through examinations similar to those of the state bureaucracy—even down to competing for the same kinds of university graduates despite the fact there seemed to be little use for law in private management. The same patterns of career structure emerged: internalized labor markets emphasizing departmental specialization. It is evident that private organizations sought these structural forms because they had acquired institutional status and legitimacy from their state origins while at the same time these forms helped to resolve problems of labor supply and shop floor control.

This set of organizational characteristics became the legitimate symbol of collective and public interest. For this reason it was relatively easy, as in the case of Germany prior to World War I, to isolate labor. Lacking, by its very nature (the pursuit of group as opposed to collective interest), the capacity to construct an organization that had the characteristics of publicness, labor was and still is relatively easily placed on the defensive margins of Japanese society. This isolation had, of course, powerful economic consequences. It produced, in a rather short time, a relatively docile (in the sense of teachable as well as, perhaps, the sense of passive) labor force. It was also a labor force that, when not made docile by isolation, was easily coopted into the bureaucratic organization through its inability to defend itself against the legitimacy of the organizational structure.

Successful economic development in post-1900 Japan occurring simultaneously with the institutionalization of the rational state bureaucracy was not, therefore, a total coincidence. Rather, one might argue that the emergence of the bureaucracy as the integrating mechanism between state and society through its highly organizationally structured rule systems also reduced the capacity of outlier interests (those directly or indirectly opposed to industrial development) to intervene in decision making while at the same time it provided a public channel for integrating 'appropriate' or excluding 'inappropriate' interests. Similarly, one could argue that the simultaneity of postwar economic development and the integration of the bureaucracy to the new party system—the system of 1955— came at a propitious time for economic development.[59] This was a period charged with labor conflict which became outflanked by the single-party

[59] Junnosuke Masumi, 'The 1955 System: Origin and Transformation,' in Tetsuya Kataoka, ed., *Creating Single-Party Democracy: Japan's Postwar Political System* (Stanford: Hoover Institution Press, 1992), pp. 47–51.

dominance of the LDP through its capacity to form strong bonds with the state bureaucracy.[60] Recent disarray in the LDP suggests that party politics in Japan is undergoing serious decay as the corollary instrument of integrating state and society which must leave the bureaucracy in an increasingly strong position as the primary integrating role.

On the level of structure the integrative status of the bureaucratic role as it exists in both public and private (or it might be said that there is no private bureaucratic role in places such as Japan, France, or Germany since they are isomorphic) organizations sets boundary lines that exclude a variety of obstacles not the least of which has been those who seek to put an end to organizational profits from the absence of consumer accountability. Thus, individual organizations or even groups might resist state direction successfully but only within limited boundaries. Those boundaries are rarely crossed because the organizational structures are based on a bureaucratic role that is homogeneous across organizational lines and is, therefore, consensual about the manner in which decisions ought to be made and how they are to be held accountable.

There are, of course, prices to be paid for this kind of integration. Marginalization of some groups is the most evident of these prices. Perhaps more important socially and economically is the isolation of group *interests*. Isolating or marginalizing these, I believe, has reduced the cost and increased the speed of economic development.[61] In short, the price of economic development for societies whose political leaders faced or now face high uncertainty is the creation of powerful bureaucracies which swallow up the political space, which is held by interest groups in those societies where low uncertainty dominated or dominates. The result is that individuals in such societies are paid in the coin of the 'long run.' That is, in the absence of interest groups capable of pressing individual choices, individuals must settle for the promise of better things to come. This, indeed was the promise held out by the Meiji leaders—a promise which many believe has only been partially fulfilled at least in terms commensurate with the effort and sacrifice.[62]

[60] Junnosuke Masumi, 'The 1955 System: Origin and Transformation,' in Tetsuya Kataoka, ed., *Creating Single-Party Democracy: Japan's Postwar Political System*, pp. 47–8.

[61] Olson, Jr., *The Logic of Collective Action*, pp. 232–37.

[62] It is no coincidence that Japan and the United States not only have the most marginalized examples of organized labor, but also have the lowest levels of taxation and social welfare of all of the advanced industrial societies. This clearly suggests that a major transformation may be occurring in the United States. A sign of this transformation is that the United States has undergone, over the past generation, a decline in the way professions serve as the integrative structure linking parties and bureaucratic role. This has led to an increasing marginalization of organized labor and greater emphasis on internal labor markets, powerful declines in the autonomy of professional life, and vastly diminished dominance of professions in organizational structure. On these grounds it is perhaps possible to argue that convergence between Japanese and American organizational life may be in the offing. This may produce a new spurt of economic growth in the United States but it will also produce a new crisis in the structure of state-society integration.

Table 4.1 Number of Offices Held Prior to Appointment of pre-1900 Appointees

No. of Offices	N	%
0	31	38.7
1	10	12.5
2	7	8.7
3	11	13.8
4	9	11.2
5	5	6.3
6	4	5.0
7	1	1.2
8 and over	2	2.4
Totals	80	100.0

Note: The data in this table are derived from an analysis of the backgrounds of a simple random sample of 80 (25 per cent) prefectural governors appointed to office between 1868 and 1900. The methods used to select the sample and the sources of information are detailed in Bernard S. Silberman, 'Bureaucratic Development and the Structure of Decision-Making in Japan: 1868–1925,' *Journal of Asian Studies*, Vol. 29 (1970), pp. 347–62.

Table 4.2 Number of Offices Held Prior to Appointment to High Civil Service Offices of 1875–1900 Appointees

No. of Offices	N	%
0–1	8	10.5
1	20	26.3
2	12	15.8
3	12	15.8
4	8	10.5
5	5	6.5
6	7	9.2
7–10	4	5.3
NA		
Totals	76	99.9

Note: The data here are based on the analysis of those who entered the civil service prior to 1873 and achieved offices in the highest levels of the civil service. This group amounted to 50 per cent (76) of the total population of those who had held such offices prior to 1900. The original group was selected on the basis of a simple random sample and would thus seem to be a relatively fair representation of the total population of the highest civil servants in this period.

Table 4.2 *Continued*

Source: See Bernard S. Silberman, 'Bureaucratic Devel-
opment and the Structure of Decision-Making in the
Meiji Period: The Case of the Genrō,' *Journal of Asian
Studies*, Vol. 27 (1967), pp. 81–94.

Table 4.3 Number of Ministries of Service for Those
Holding the Highest Civil Service Positions, 1875–1900

No. of Ministries	N	%
1	1	1.3
2	2	2.6
3	7	9.2
4	10	13.1
5	13	17.1
6	13	17.1
7	12	15.8
8	5	6.6
9	3	4.0
10	1	1.3
11	2	2.6
NA	7	9.2
Totals	76	99.9

Source: See Table 4.2.

Table 4.4 Level of First Appointment to Office of pre-1900 Gubernatorial
Appointees

Level of Office by Civil Service Rank	N	%
Lower Civil Service *hannin* rank	11	14.0
Upper Civil Service *sōnin* rank, grades 8–6	16	20.0
Upper Civil Service *sōnin* rank, grades 5–3	17	21.0
Upper Civil Service *chokunin* rank, grades 2–1	20	25.0
Military service	7	9.0
NA	9	11.0
Totals	80	100.0

Source: See Table 4.2.

Table 4.5 Length of Service as Governor of pre-1900 Appointees

Years of service	N	%	Years of service	N	%
1 or less	13	16.2	11	0	0.0
2	15	18.7	12	2	2.5
3	6	7.5	13	0	0.0
4	5	6.2	14	2	2.5
5	13	16.2	15	2	2.5
6	3	3.8	16	0	0.0
7	2	2.5	17	1	1.2
8	3	3.8	18	1	1.2
9	2	2.5	19	2	2.5
10	1	1.2	20+	7	8.7
Totals				80	100.0

Source: See Table 4.2.

Table 4.6 Type of Education of Upper Civil Servants, 1868–99

	Education					
	Traditional		Western		NA	
	N	%	N	%	N	%
Sample I (central administration)	23	30.3	46	60.5	7	9.2
Sample II (perfectural government)	58	72.5	18	22.5	4	5.0
Combined Totals	81	52.0	64	41.0	11	7.0

Source: See Table 4.2.

Table 4.7 Recruitment of Administrative Examiners, 1894–1941

Status at Time of Appointment	1894–1905	1906–1917	1918–1928	1929–1941
Professors				
Tokyo Imperial University	46.0	66.0	44.6	41.2
Kyoto Imperial University	3.7	19.1	22.8	24.9
Other Public Colleges	2.1	4.1	2.2	14.8
Other Universities	0.0	0.0	0.0	8.0
Serving Officials	48.2	10.8	30.4	11.1
Total	100.0	100.0	100.0	100.0
N	189	194	224	687

Source: Modified from Robert M. Spaulding, Jr., *Imperial Japan's Higher Civil Service Examinations* (Princeton: Princeton University Press, 1967), p. 249.

Table 4.8 University Training of Higher Examiners (in percentage of total number of appointments to committees)

Education	Judicial		Administrative			
	1893–1907	1908–1922	1894–1905	1906–1917	1918–1928	1929–1941
Tokyo Imperial University	44.8	78.0	72.5	95.9	85.7	67.5
Justice Ministry Law School	41.4	6.4	19.0	3.1	0.0	0.0
Kyoto Imperial University	0.0	5.2	0.0	0.0	8.9	24.2
Other State Colleges	0.0	0.0	0.0	0.5	0.0	3.2
Private Universities	0.0	7.5	0.0	0.0	5.4	5.1
Foreign Universities	0.0	0.0	4.8	0.0	0.0	0.0
No Higher Education	13.8	2.9	3.7	0.5	0.0	0.0
Total	100	100	100	100	100	100
N	174	173	189	194	224	687

Source: Modified from Robert M. Spaulding, Jr., *Imperial Japan's Higher Civil Service Examinations* (Princeton: Princeton University Press, 1967), p. 251.

Table 4.9 Administrative Examination Results, 1894–1901 (by Tokyo Imperial University graduates versus others)

Year	University	Taking Prelim Examination	Taking Main Examination	Passed Main Examination
1895	Tokyo	0	42	25 (59.5)
	Other	84	39	12 (30.7)
1896	Tokyo	0	66	42 (63.6)
	Other	144	43	8 (18.6)
1897	Tokyo	0	51	26 (51.0)
	Other	259	95	28 (29.5)
1898	Tokyo	0	51	26 (51.0)
	Other	373	163	18 (11.0)
1899	Tokyo	0	71	22 (31.0)
	Other	344	103	9 (8.7)
1900	Tokyo	0	94	39 (41.5)
	Other	377	94	19 (20.2)
1901	Tokyo	0	70	16 (22.8)
	Other	396	101	26 (25.7)
Totals	1894–1901			
	Tokyo	0	450	193 (42.9)
	Other	2,022	657	126 (19.2)

Source: Modified from Robert M. Spaulding, Jr., *Imperial Japan's Higher Civil Service Examinations* (Princeton: Princeton University Press, 1967), p. 131.

Table 4.10 University Education of Gubernatorial Appointees, 1900–45

University	N	%
Tokyo Imperial	115	85.2
Kyoto Imperial	10	7.4
Hitotsubashi (state university)	2	1.5
Hosei (private university)	1	0.7
Foreign	2	1.5
No degree	5	3.7
Totals	135	100.0

Table 4.11 Comparison of Ordinary to Higher Middle Schools by Number and Enrollment, 1886–1902

Year	Ordinary		Higher	
	No.	Students	No.	Students
1886	56	10,300	2	1,585
1889	53	11,530	7	3,837

Table 4.11 *Continued*

Year	Ordinary		Higher	
	No.	Students	No.	Students
1892	62	16,189	7	4,443
1895	96	30,871	7	4,289
1898	169	61,632	6	4,664
1901	242	88,391	8	4,361
1902	258	95,027	8	4,781

Source: Kokuritsu Kyōiku Kenkyūjo, *Nihon kindai Kyōiku hyakunenshi* (One hundred years of modern Japanese education) (Tokyo: Kokuritsu Kyōiku Kenkyūjo, 1974), Vol. 4, pp. 13–15.

Table 4.12 Enrollment at Various Levels of the Educational System, 1886–1902

Year	Primary	Ordinary Middle	Higher	Imperial-Universities
1886	56	10,300	2	1,585
1889	53	11,530	7	3,837
1892	62	16,189	7	4,443
1895	96	30,871	7	4,289
1898	169	61,632	6	4,664
1901	242	88,391	8	4,361
1902	258	95,027	8	4,781

Source: Kokuritsu Kyōiku Kenkyūjo, *Nihon kindai kyōiku hyakunenshi* (One hundred years of modern Japanese education) (Tokyo: Kokuritsu Kyōiku Kenkyūjo, 1974), Vol. 4, pp. 15–16.

Table 4.13 Level of First Office Held by Gubernatorial Appointee, 1900–45

Level of Office	N	%
Lower Civil Service *hannin* rank	0	0.0
Upper Civil Service *sōnin* rank, grades 8–6	111	82.0
Upper Civil Service *sōnin* rank, grades 5–3	13	10.0
Upper Civil Service *chokunin* rank, grades 2–1	0	0.0
Military service	0	0.0
NA	11	8.0
Totals	135	100.0

Table 4.14 Number of Offices Held Prior to Appointment as Governor, 1900–45

No. of Offices	N	%
1	0	0.0
2	0	0.0
3	2	1.5
4	1	0.75
5	7	5.0
6	21	15.5
7	31	23.0
8	21	15.5
9	14	10.0
10	12	9.0
11	9	6.5
12	5	4.0
NA	12	9.0
Total	135	99.75

Table 4.15 Years of Service by Number of Offices Held Prior to Appointment as Governor, 1900–45

No. of Offices	Years of Service prior to Appointment						Total	
	0–5	6–10	11–15	16–20	21–25	26 + NA	n	%
1	0	0	0	0	0	0	0	0
2	0	0	0	0	0	0	0	0
3	0	1	1	0	0	0	2	1.5
4	0	0	0	1	0	0	1	0.75
5	0	0	5	2	0	0	7	5.0
6	0	0	10	10	1	0	21	15.5
7	0	0	14	13	4	0	31	23.0
8	0	0	9	10	2	0	21	15.5
9	0	0	2	10	1	1	14	10.3
10	0	0	2	9	1	0	12	9.0
11	0	0	0	6	3	0	9	6.7
12	0	0	0	3	1	1	5	3.75
NA							12	9.0
Total *n*	0	1	43	64	13	2		
%	0	0.75	31.8	47.4	9.6	1.5	9.0	100

Table 4.16 Length of Service of Governors, 1868–99;
1900–45

Length of Service in Years	Period of Appointment			
	1868–1899		1900–1945	
	n	%	n	%
1–5	20	25.0	0	0
6–10	16	20.0	3	2.0
11–15	4	5.0	0	0.0
16–20	4	5.0	28	20.5
21–25	11	14.0	47	35.0
26–30	10	12.5	17	13.0
31–35	5	6.0	12	9.0
35+	3	3.75	2	1.5
NA	7	8.75	26	19.0
Total	80	100.0	135	100.0
Median	10.5		23.0	
Mean	18.0		25.4	

Table 4.17 Retirement Age of Gubernatorial Appointees, 1900–45

Age in 5-year Interval	N		%	
20–24	0	(0)	0.0	(0.0)
25–29	0	(2)	0.0	(2.5)
30–34	3	(5)	2.0	(6.0)
35–39	0	(5)	0.0	(6.0)
40–44	16	(6)	12.0	(7.5)
45–49	48	(2)	35.5	(2.5)
50–54	42	(10)	31.0	(12.5)
55–59	15	(24)	11.0	(30.0)
60–64	5	(9)	3.5	(11.5)
65–69	0	(3)	0.0	(4.0)
70+	0	(1)	0.0	(1.5)
NA	6	(13)	4.5	(16.0)
Total	135	(80)	99.5	(100.0)
Mean	46.6	(55)		
Median	49.0	(56.8)		

Note: 1868–89 figures are in parentheses.

Table 4.18 Post-service Occupations of Governors, 1900–45

Occupation	N	%
Business Industry	30	22.0
Politics–Local and National	38	28.0
Law Practice	6	5.0
Government Advisor	8	6.0
Volunteer Activities	11	8.0
No Occupation	11	8.0
NA	31	23.0
Total	135	100.0

Source: Bernard S. Silberman, 'Ringi-sei: Traditional Values or Organizational Imperatives in the Japanese Upper Civil Service: 1868–1900,' *Journal of Asian Studies*, Vol. 32 (1973), pp. 251–64.

5

The Evolution of the Civil Service before World War II

MICHIO MURAMATSU

T. J. PEMPEL

The bureaucracy was one of the few Japanese institutions that did not undergo massive alterations during the Allied Occupation following World War II. As a consequence, there is far greater continuity between the postwar civil service and its prewar antecedents than is seen among other institutions. Furthermore, the prewar civil service played a major role in the overall economic planning and development of Japan as a modern nation. However, little scholarly work has been done to establish the continuities (and differences) between the prewar and postwar civil services or their specific roles in national economic advancement.

Silberman's essay in this volume indicates that the development of Japan's civil service system took place at an early stage in Japan's efforts to modernize, that it succeeded in recruiting competent young men through the introduction of an open selection examination system, and that the civil service system was relatively independent from politics. This essay deals with the response of the civil service system to the first wave of democracy, which swept Japan during the Taisho period of the 1920s, and the activities of the system during World War II. It then seeks to make certain tentative links between the prewar bureaucratic experiences and Japan's postwar civil service. This chapter is supplementary to the Silberman chapter on two points. First, it is concerned primarily with the political aspects of the civil service. Second, it attempts to bridge some of the chronological gap between the earliest years of the Meiji period and the end of World War II.

The Prewar Civil Service and the Broader Political System

In the early years of the Meiji period (1868–1912), when Japan established its first civil service system, government personnel were recruited largely from among individuals belonging to the powerful regional clans which had toppled the Tokugawa regime (1600–1868). By 1920, however, the key personnel of the bureaucracy were no longer from the old feudal clans and their factions, but rather were those who had passed the Upper-Level Civil Service Examination, mostly University of Tokyo graduates. This changing composition of the civil service reflected changes in the political system and the growing influence of party politics during the prewar period.

In order to insulate the bureaucracy from political party influences, Japan's Meiji constitution (1889) explicitly declared that public officials were 'servants of the emperor' and all matters pertaining to such officials were to be determined by imperial decree rather than by the parliament. Public officials were accorded a higher social position, as pointed out by Silberman, and were divided into three ranks depending upon the degree to which the emperor was formally involved in their appointment: (1) those appointed through imperial investiture; (2) those appointed through imperial decree; and (3) those appointed on the basis of recommendations by the prime minister. In addition to their high social position, which was backed by the authority of the emperor, a number of other measures were taken to make civil service jobs attractive. These included large salaries, good pensions, and job security. Furthermore, when a disciplinary measure was taken against any imperial investiture or imperial decree official, not only did the reasons for doing so have to be stated clearly, but a resolution by a disciplinary committee, consisting of a member of the appointed Privy Council and five other persons, was required. Protected by such regulations, public officials had wide latitude when engaging in policymaking activities.

The regulations that limited the involvement of politics in hiring and assigning personnel also played a crucial role. Protected by these regulations, public officials were able to take action 'aloof from' politicians and the public.

After the Sino-Japanese War of 1894–5, however, the bureaucracy began to feel the influence of party politics. The years after the war saw the growing power of political parties, particularly in the parliament. Japan's first party cabinet, formed in 1898 under Shigenobu Ōkuma, revised the Civil Service Appointment Ordinance to make it possible for party politicians to be appointed as imperial decree officials. This act was further revised in 1899 by a non-party prime minister, Aritomo Yamagata, to prevent candidates for imperial decree positions from being selected freely by the parties. They now had to be selected, as a rule, from among those who had passed the Upper-Level Civil Service Examination, after which they then would have accumulated a certain degree of job experience. This revision by Yamagata was extremely important. The civil service system, which had been created by Hirobumi Itō, was thus strengthened by Aritomo Yamagata. In this sense both men played critical roles not only in the Meiji Restoration generally, but in the subsequent civil service creation and reform more specifically.

The era of Taisho democracy (1912–32), however, brought subsequent challenges to the strict merit system and the job security of bureaucrats. During the Gonbei Yamamoto cabinet (1913), the Civil Service Appointment Ordinance was revised once again, so that within each ministry (except for the Army and Navy Ministries) parliamentarians could be appointed to the post of vice minister and many other key positions. In addition, the requirements were eased for imperial decree officials, officials appointed by the recommendation of the prime minister, and officials appointed by the ministries using the delegated authority of the emperor, thereby making such positions accessible to a wider range of candidates.

During this period, the knowledge deemed desirable for public officials underwent constant review and change. The subjects covered by the selection examinations were changed frequently, in response to advances in academic research and the needs of a changing world. The revisions of the Upper-Level Examination Act made under the Giichi Tanaka cabinet of the late 1920s serve as an example. Prior to the Tanaka cabinet, the main portion of the Upper-Level Civil Service Examinations consisted of both a written and an oral exam, with the latter administered only to those who passed the former. In 1873, for example, the mandatory subjects on the written exam were constitutional law, criminal law, civil law, administrative law, economic law, and international public law, while the elective subjects were public finance, commercial law, criminal procedure law, and civil procedure law. (The examinee was required to take one of the elective subjects, in addition to all six mandatory subjects.)

As a result of the revisions under the Tanaka cabinet, however, those taking the test for administrative positions now had to take, as mandatory subjects, constitutional law, administrative law, civil law, and economic law, while they were required to choose three out of the following 20 elective subjects: philosophy, ethics, logic, psychology, political science, sociology, history of economics, Japanese history, political history, classical Japanese and Chinese, commercial law, criminal law, international public law, civil procedure law, criminal procedure law, public finance, agricultural policy, commercial policy, industrial policy, and social policy. Examinees therefore had a wider range of subjects to choose from. While such revisions resulted in some changes in the curriculum within the faculties of law in Japanese universities, the revisions never seriously undermined the advantage held by graduates of law faculties in the application for civil service positions.

The conflict over revisions of the civil service regulations reflected a deeper conflict in the political elite between elected party politicians, on the one hand, and the Meiji founding fathers and their administrative disciples, on the other. The two camps, the elected and the non-elected, battled ceaselessly for control of the cabinet and public policy. For example, the non-elected camp led by Yamagata, fought back when a Seiyūkai party leader, then Home Minister in the Saionji cabinet, proposed to abolish the county (gun) level of administration (the counterpart of the Kreis in Prussia). County administration was targeted by the political parties because it permitted strict control of all towns and villages. The county level was also deemed unnecessary at this point because towns and villages were in the process of being consolidated. In 1908, a proposal to abolish the county level was defeated, but in 1921 the same proposal finally passed the parliament under the Hara cabinet.

Another famous battle between these two camps was over the issue of lower taxes on land. In this case, the elected camp was defeated. As the non-elected leaders began to feel the new tide of democracy, they were more eager to defend the bureaucracy from opponents by changing the regulations concerning the recruitment of party politicians to the highest positions and by adapting the desirable knowledge possessed by the bureaucrats to the changing environment.

In 1941, under wartime conditions, the subjects on the selection examinations were further widened under the Fumimaro Konoe cabinet. Particularly noteworthy is the fact that, reflecting the trends of the time, greater emphasis was placed on Japanese history. As the military situation turned increasingly against Japan, however, and as more and more young men were drafted into the military or sent to work in factories, it became increasingly more difficult to hold such selection examinations, and the civil service system, which had prided itself on the strictness of its selection process, lost its substance. Around 1940, the Selection Committee for Civilian Officials started to conduct its selection process by first asking applicants to submit resumes, and on the basis of those resumes asking those it thought suitable to write theses at home. These theses then became the basis for selection by the committee.[1] This marked the lowest point of the civil service system up to World War II.

In sum, after the enactment of the Civil Service Appointment Ordinance, despite efforts by Yamagata and others to place the bureaucracy beyond the influence of party politics, the Japanese civil service gradually became more democratized, a trend that was not reversed through two world wars. The level of involvement in the bureaucracy by the nobility and the former oligarchs was drastically reduced. The influence of the feudal clans and factions declined. In their place, as Masa'aki Takane has argued, the key positions within the bureaucracy came to be held by those who had passed the merit-based selection examinations.[2]

---

[1] Komuin Seido Kenkyūkai, ed., *Kanri/Komuin seido no hensen* (History of the Japanese civil service) (Tokyo: Daiichi Hoki, 1980).

[2] Masaaki Takane, *Nihon no seiji eriito* (Japanese political elites) (Tokyo: Chuokoronsha, 1977), pp. 37, 68–70.

As the higher civil service developed, conflicts and competition in policymaking among former regional clan leaders and their related bureaucratic factions decreased, and the ministries developed their own autonomous institutional identities and interests. This phenomenon has been seen in many governments, and is caused by the fact that each ministry possesses its own 'clients' and perspective on public policies. From this basis, a modern form of interministry competition emerged in prewar Japan.

Interministerial conflicts also arose because there was no unified set of civil service laws and because the hiring, classification, duties, and other aspects of the civil service were regulated by separate laws. The Civilian Official Examination Committee was responsible for the selection examinations. The Civilian Official Disciplinary Committee was charged with the discipline of public officials. The Selection Committee for Civilian Officials was charged with the selection and hiring of personnel other than those who came through the selection examinations. Many academics and others felt this was a problem, but no specific reform efforts were made until a proposal in 1939 called for the establishment of a Personnel Bureau (or Department) within the cabinet. This organ would have been responsible for the unified administration of personnel matters. This proposal sought to improve efficiency and unify administrative work, but the resistance from ministries was strong, and the Central Personnel Bureau was never realized. This suggests the procedural mechanisms prior to World War II for solving conflicts over division of authority and the difficulty in Japan of establishing an agency to coordinate the bureaucracy as a whole.

When Japan's economic development is discussed, the development of Japan's politics, laws, and social order are often neglected. The bureaucratic agency charged with political and social order was the Home Ministry,[3] and its bureaucrats attained a position of great importance in prewar Japan. Since the end of World War II, aspirants to the national bureaucracy have typically named the Ministry of Finance as their highest preference for postings, but in the prewar period such elites more often chose the Home Ministry. The Home Ministry assigned governors to all 47 prefectures and thus exercised effective control over local affairs. It also maintained law and order through its control of the police. This ministry was involved in all public construction in urban and rural areas, such as roads, bridges, and railroads. Its influence was enormous, and this was a major reason why the Home Ministry was largely dismantled by the Occupation, which divided it into several ministries, including the Ministry of Construction, the National Policy Agency, the (Tokyo) Metropolitan

---

[3] Kasumi Kai, ed., *Naimusho-shi* (History of the Ministry of Home Affairs), Vols. 1–4 (Tokyo: Chiho Zaimu Kyokai, 1971). This is a detailed history of the Ministry of Home Affairs, totaling 3,500 pages.

Police Department, the Ministry of Labor, and later the Ministry of Home Affairs (not to be confused with the prewar ministry).

Economic ministries such as the Ministry of Finance and the Ministry of Commerce and Industry were naturally major participants in the policymaking process before the war, but in terms of the budget-making process, the influence of the Army and Navy Ministries was also considerable. Government spending for the army and navy was a key determinant of the total budget size. Depending upon the issue, the Imperial Household Ministry also had a say in the determination of policy. After the war, the Imperial Household Ministry was scaled down to the Imperial Household Agency, losing its political influence in the process. These changes left the Ministry of Finance as the single administrative agency with significant budgetary influence.

In addition, the advisory Privy Council was abolished, and the upper parliamentary chamber was changed from an appointed to an elected body. Political power in Japan after the war was thus divided between the power of the parliament and the power of the bureaucracy. This made it easier to make policy innovations after the war; it also increased the efficiency of the policy process.

Stratification by Origin

The democratization of the civil service had its limits, including stratification by social origin. The decline in the importance of feudal families and other pre-Meiji forces of influence is extremely marked. In place of these old 'social classes' came graduates of the University of Tokyo. The government's public characterization of the civil service was that the Upper-Level Civil Service Examination provided a fair test for the selection of these elites. Capable young men from around the nation could take this examination, regardless of their origins, and by passing it they could both serve their country and open the way for their own social advancement. Young men from various regions believed this proposition, went to Tokyo, and eventually wound up at the University of Tokyo, where the training of bureaucrats was carried out. In this way, an almost religious belief took root in society that upper-level bureaucrats were an especially superior group that had survived a rigorous selection process.

This characterization, however, was no more than a half-truth. According to Takane's research, one characteristic of the prewar political elite was the coexistence of heredity-based and merit-based systems.[4] This came about because the leaders of the Meiji period, after considering the social costs of trying to eradicate the pre-Reformation elite, continued to

---

[4] Ibid., pp. 90–7.

provide them with certain roles. This compromise with the old elites made possible the gradual, relatively peaceful modernization of Japan. That members of the old nobility and feudal families were given certain roles is evident from the appointment of prime ministers such as Kinmochi Saionji and Fumimaro Konoe, both of whom were members of the nobility. According to Takane's data, many of those who had achieved high social standing as of 1920 had deep roots in the old regional clans of the Tokugawa period. Furthermore, many who had attained success not only had origins in these old clans, but were also graduates of the University of Tokyo. Merit was not the sole criterion for placement. The door to social advancement remained closed to those who did not already have a foot in the door. Takane also points out that the problem during the Meiji period was not the overapplication of a merit-based system, but rather the fact that the merit-based system was not thoroughly adhered to, and that Japanese public administration was not fully freed from various biases even by the 1920s and 1930s.

Wartime Developments

During the wartime period, Japan's civil service showed several new developments. First, the bureaucracy and industry developed a closer relationship. In order to wage total war, businesses were organized into compulsory cartels, and regulatory means for use by the bureaucracy were developed for each industry. Some of these regulatory means, including administrative guidance, survived into the postwar years, forming the basis for postwar public administration. The most persuasive example can be seen in the area of monetary and financial policy. Yukio Noguchi and Eisuke Sakakibara have pointed out that the foreign exchange laws established in 1942 survived in essentially the same form after the war. The principle that guided both wartime and postwar monetary policy was 'regulation as a rule, non-regulation as an exception.'[5] Also in 1942, the Reorganization Act for the Banking Industry was formulated. Under the guidance of the Ministry of Finance, the number of banks, which had been more than 500, was reduced to 61. The ministry then placed these banks under its guidance and supervision.

Many of the basic forms of postwar control and the postwar priority production system implemented under the economic bureaucracies find their roots in controls instituted during the war. The ideas for the Law for the Procurement of Emergency Funds and the Emergency Measures Law concerning Exports and Imports were formed in 1937, even before Japan plunged into all-out war. Under the former, Japan's industries were

[5] Yukio Noguchi and Eisuke Sakakibara, 'Ōkurasho-Nichigin ōcho no bunseki' (An analysis of the Ministry of Finance-Bank of Japan dynasty), *Chūō kōron*, Aug. 1977.

divided into three categories, and plans were made whereby industries of Group One, which included steelmakers and shipbuilders, were given priority for the allocation of funds and industrial growth. The government would cooperate on a case-by-case basis with industries of Group Two, which included textiles and papermaking companies, regarding the procurement of funds by such industries. Finally, the plant and facilities investments of Group Three industries would be held back.

The second of these two laws was the basis for similar controls on exported and imported products. In order to carry out these policies, the government used its regulatory powers and forced the industries into control associations, which were single-industry cartels. These associations were then entrusted with the responsibility for implementing controls. In other words, an attempt was made to realize the objective of state control while incorporating as much as possible the participation of privately owned businesses.

The behavior of high-level bureaucrats was particularly noteworthy during this period. As Japan expanded its sphere of influence in Manchuria, and as various indicators increasingly pointed toward the outbreak of war, Japan's so-called 'progressive bureaucrats' emerged. These bureaucrats communicated closely with one another and came to play leading roles in the policymaking processes within their respective ministries. Many gathered in new, interministerial policy planning organs within the cabinet.

Despite being called 'progressive bureaucrats,' these individuals were often politically reactionary in that they tended to look down upon the mandate of the parliament; many in effect pursued 'state socialism' as their goal. This group developed a definition of the national interest that was different from that developed by elected officials, and they attempted to participate in the policymaking process based upon their specific definition of this national interest. Those in this group were characterized by idealism and quickness of action. As a shortcut to the realization of their policies, these bureaucrats ultimately joined forces with the military. They aspired to form a core of power, but one different from the earlier bureaucrats who were to be 'aloof from' politics. Typical and leading examples of such bureaucrats were Nobusuke Kishi of the Ministry of Commerce and Industry, and Shirō Tohata and Hiroo Wada of the Ministry of Agriculture and Forestry.

The Ministry of Commerce and Industry was established in 1925 when the Ministry of Agriculture and Commerce, established in 1881, was divided into two ministries.[6] As Japan faced new international conditions, many of its industries, which had grown during the 1920s, primarily through the advancement of light industries, began to encoun-

---

[6] Chalmers Johnson, *MITI and the Japanese Miracle* (Stanford: Stanford University Press, 1982).

ter difficulties. Kishi, Yoshino, and other bureaucrats of the Ministry of Commerce and Industry believed that securing natural resources and introducing new technologies were necessary for Japan's national success in the new age. The Ministry of Commerce and Industry prepared a policy for the 'Rationalization of Industries.' Kishi together with the other ministry bureaucrats and middle-ranking soldiers attempted to press actively for Japan's advance into Manchuria as a means of securing national resources. In the minds of such bureaucrats, elected politicians were unreliable. Yet these progressive bureaucrats were well aware of the influence of politics and therefore felt that it was necessary for them to participate actively in the political process.[7]

Bureaucrats in the Ministry of Agriculture and Forestry shared the same spirit as Kishi and the other progressive bureaucrats within the Ministry of Commerce and Industry. They placed great importance on the conflict between landowners and tenant farmers, mainly as an obstacle to increasing food production. Consequently, they prepared an aggressive land reform plan. The top officials of the Ministry of Agriculture and Forestry had reached a consensus that agricultural land reform was necessary to create more landed farmers so as to increase food production. The experience such bureaucrats gained by such progressive policies—aimed at both increasing food production and destroying the old, feudalistic system—formed the foundation for the land reforms subsequently carried out under the Occupation after World War II.

The Postwar Period

The Occupation's dismemberment of the Home Ministry, along with policy emphasis on economic development by the Japanese government, enhanced the status of the economic ministries, particularly the Ministry of Finance. In addition, some leading politicians and bureaucrats felt that the Japanese government had implementation problems due to the lack of a high-level central agency responsible for intergovernmental relationships. Recognizing the need for a counterbalance to the Ministry of Finance, and knowing the importance of stable and efficient policy implementation at the local level, the Japanese government decided to create an analog to the prewar Home Ministry by expanding the status of the Local Finance Commission which had been created in 1946. In 1949, the commission became an agency at the cabinet ministerial level, and in 1960 it was finally given ministerial status as the Ministry of Home Affairs. The ministry is responsible for the coordination of local interests and horizontal ministerial interests concerning local governments.

[7] On these so-called progressives, see Takashi Itoh, *Taishōki kakushin-ha no seiritsu Taishō jidai* (Formation of the Taisho period progressives) (Tokyo: Hanawa Shobo, 1978).

During the last years of the Occupation and especially after the Occupation forces left Japan, the conservative government sought to reverse and restructure the political system toward greater centralization. Those changes have remained nearly intact. For instance, a public corporation for telephone and telegraph service was organized as an arm of the Ministry of Posts and Telecommunication. This system remained in place until the public corporation was privatized in 1985.

Most important were changes in the direction of centralization in the areas of police and education. Labor laws were changed, and the Antimonopoly Law was revised in order to lift many of its restrictions. In short, an effort was made to decrease the effects of increasing participation by means of greater centralization. The Japanese government made efforts in this way to modify the system that had been imposed on it, even if the aim of the effort was not achieved to the extent expected.

The basic postwar system has remained intact, but adaptation has continued. In 1955 the Economic Planning Agency was created to play a role in macroeconomic policymaking. In 1970 the Environment Agency was organized to respond to citizens' movements demanding improvements in the environment. In 1974, when land prices and land development became political issues, the National Land Agency was established. In 1966 the name of the Ministry of Agriculture and Forestry was changed to the Ministry of Agriculture, Forestry, and Fisheries to express its new priorities. These evolutionary and adaptive organizational reforms largely stopped in the 1970s, and the Second Provisional Administrative Reform Committee represented an attempt to break the stalemate in administrative innovation.[8]

Concluding Remarks

Before World War II, Japan had an authoritarian political system, modeled after Prussia's. As long as the elder statesmen, who had created the Meiji constitution and had the ability to work in close cooperation with the emperor, were active, this system was an important driving force behind Japan's efforts to modernize. Once these elder statesmen had retired from the front line of politics, formal authority remained concentrated in the emperor, but in reality various advisors each took policymaking initiative in their respective jurisdictions. This, in turn, introduced the dangers of political fragmentation.

This constitution could not function properly unless certain conditions were met. Of course, it can be said that all political systems require favorable conditions to operate correctly. Japan's prewar imperial system

[8] For more information on this committee, see the chapter in this volume by Mitsutoshi Ito.

was one of the more difficult systems to operate, however, because it made the emperor into a living god, and thus did not permit the existence of a 'leader,' like a postwar prime minister, who could function as a politically integrating force.

We argue that Japan's prewar bureaucracy had the characteristic of being 'extensively involved in society and having a pervasive influence upon society, but not being thoroughly involved in society.' From the beginning of the Meiji period, Japan's bureaucracy took on a wide range of activities, which were aimed at the promotion of rapid modernization, utilizing what few resources it had. As Haley's essay indicates, Japan had few means to exercise its coercive powers as a state, because it had to disperse its resources among a wide variety of activities. Thus, while Japan's bureaucracy had extensive jurisdictional range, i.e., jurisdiction covering many areas or activities, its coercive powers with respect to any given field of policy were weak.[9] Nevertheless, Japan's bureaucracy was highly capable and performed relatively well. Undeniably, Japan's bureaucracy played a major role in the Westernization of Japan in this short period.

The bureaucracy faced a problem, however, in that while it was able to raise an issue, it could not effectively resolve that issue according to its wishes once another influential party interfered. This was a source of frustration for the bureaucracy, and was also one of the underlying causes of the emergence of the progressive bureaucrats. Another characteristic of Japan's prewar bureaucracy was, as Kiyoaki Tsuji has observed, the fragmentation it displayed in the policymaking process.[10] Many would say that the cause of such fragmentation lay in the fact that jurisdiction over the civil service system itself was fragmented.

In comparison, the postwar bureaucracy has been better integrated into its political environment. Political stability and integration was first secured by the Occupation authorities. Long-term, stable rule by the Liberal Democratic Party (LDP) followed. More instrumental than anything else in the integration of politics was the fact that the prime minister's position and influence were guaranteed by having been built into the constitution. For a period after the war, politicians, whose foundation of power lay in the Diet, were rated very poorly by the general public (and many in the civil service) for the same reasons as before the war. Postwar politics has, however, positioned the Diet to be the dominant organ of government. Anything said by this group which constitutes the 'highest organ of state power' automatically has influence. Moreover, the LDP accumulated a

---

[9] Michio Muramatsu, 'Patterned Pluralism under Challenge: The Policies of the 1980s,' in Gary Allinson and Yasunori Sone, eds., *Political Dynamics in Contemporary Japan* (Ithaca: Cornell University Press, 1993).

[10] Kiyoaki Tsuji, *Shinpan Nihon kanryōsei no kenkyū* (A study of the Japanese bureaucracy) (Tokyo: University of Tokyo Press, 1952).

vast amount of information on policy during its long-term rule, and gradually it became a powerful ruling party and secured superiority *vis-à-vis* the bureaucracy.

As mentioned above, the civil service system successfully enabled the hiring of competent persons, who were then formed into a highly capable, competent group. In this respect, it is the same as the prewar civil service system. It is also the same as the prewar system, however, in that the postwar bureaucracy is fragmented. The basic cause for this fragmentation is the practice of hiring new personnel, in which the passing of the selection examinations by an applicant, and the actual score achieved on the test, is completely separate from the actual appointment of the applicant into the civil service. Consequently, the loyalty of the bureaucrat remains, not to public service as a whole, but to a particular ministry or agency. The devotion that accompanies this loyalty is the only thing that can bridge the gap between the political parties and the bureaucracy, and the gap that naturally forms between the various ministries and agencies. The bureaucracy's work hours, which normally last late into the evening, are also a physical means of filling in such gaps. The discrete personnel administration policies and practices of each individual ministry and agency thus acquire great importance.

To put it simply, such personnel administration policies and practices treat all civil servants as elites. Therein lies the importance of the secretariat of each ministry and agency. It is commonly said that agencies are driven by 'the three section chiefs in the bureau of the secretariat of each ministry.'[11] Among these, however, the importance of the section chief of personnel (or the section chief of the secretariat) is especially great. A key feature of the personnel administration policies and practices of the central ministries and agencies is to prevent any bureaucrat from dropping out from 'the smooth promotion system' for 30 years after his appointment to the civil service. The objective is to ensure that, among bureaucrats of the same age group, the most highly successful individuals maintain a high degree of motivation, while the less successful are not left with a feeling of frustration. In fact, Japan's central ministries and agencies have succeeded in carrying out this sort of personnel administration. For those successful bureaucrats at the top of their class, in the case of the Ministry of Finance, for example, the road is not closed to the position of president of the Bank of Japan, or the head of the Tokyo Securities Exchange. In the case of the Ministry of Transport, successful bureaucrats might become president of Japan Air Lines or any of the six Japan Railways. Innumerable bureaucrats of the Ministry of International Trade and Industry have gone on to become presidents and vice presidents of major private companies. For bureaucrats of the Ministry of

---

[11] See, for example, Masaru Nishio, *Gyōseigaku* (Public Administration) (Tokyo: Yuhikaku, 1993), p. 150.

Home Affairs, governorships of Tokyo Prefecture and other big prefectures are attractive second jobs.

Even 'less successful' bureaucrats achieve social as well as financial positions much better than other individuals of their age group who went directly from college to a private corporation and who have successfully climbed the corporate ladder. In other words, elegant and stable second jobs await even those who are 'less successful' in the intra-bureaucratic race. The ministries and agencies thus secure the loyalty of their respective bureaucrats.

This practice of *amakudari* (literally, 'descent from heaven'),[12] however, is the target of public criticism, as can be seen by the treatment it gets in the press. The central ministries and agencies have countered with the argument that such a practice involves merely the redistribution of human resources beneficial to society. Such criticism is all the more reason why, in order to ensure that such *amakudari* is not seen as high-handed, efforts must be made to hire the most capable persons and to train them in ways that will increase their capabilities. While the Japanese government initially trained its bureaucrats through on-the-job training, the importance of off-the-job training has recently become apparent and is systematically being carried out.

Two things should be mentioned about the practice of *amakudari*. First, the frequency of *amakudari* to private companies has decreased, and is still declining. Second, it is not automatic that able bureaucrats will find a second job, even a good one. The cabinet has the power to authorize appointments to government-owned companies. In the case of *amakudari* to private companies, negotiation and a selection process are involved. Furthermore, regulations by the National Personnel Agency forbid bureaucrats from taking second jobs closely related to their jobs in the ministries.

The difference between success and failure is thus small. Naohiro Yashiro has focused on the fact that one feature of the competition among bureaucrats for promotion and career advancement is that even such small differences are perceived as significant.[13] Such competition within Japan's upper-level bureaucrat group is vicious, for two reasons. First, the atmosphere makes even small differences seem significant. The second is that there is a virtuous cycle and a vicious cycle at work: conditions for speedy promotions and advancement are good for those who were first assigned to a good position, while conditions are continuously bad for those who started out in a bad position. At stake in the competition are assignments to the good positions, which can make all the difference in a bureaucrat's career.

---

[12] This practice is described in detail in this volume by Takenori Inoki.

[13] Naohiro Yashiro, 'Nihon no kanryō-shisutemu to gyōsei kaikaku' (The Japanese bureaucratic system and administrative reform), JCER Paper No. 18 (Dec. 1992).

In addition to the above, there were also important differences between wartime and postwar economic administration. First of all, the conditions under which postwar industrial policies were formulated and implemented were different from those of prewar policies. Industrial policies function in an entirely different way in a democracy and a market economy. It is never certain that private industries will follow such policies, because the government does not have the strong authority it had in wartime. Second, when promotional industrial policies are adopted, their effect may not be very great, because the society and the economy are not operating under overall control, as they were before and during the war. The effect of such policies on Japan's overall postwar economic growth are not at all clear. The industry that showed the greatest growth and profits after the war was the light electric appliance industry, which did not receive much positive government support, an example that provides an immediate counterweight to notions that the bulk of Japan's economic growth was attributable to civil service policies.

Two conclusions follow from the study of Japan's wartime economic controls and their postwar impact. First, the jurisdiction of the bureaucracy was enlarged. As Samuels says, however, jurisdiction does not equal control.[14] In a period when the influence of democracy comes from below, the enlarging of jurisdiction has the potential of weakening powers of control. Second, an atmosphere was created that made it easier for the bureaucracy to involve itself in the economy. The belief spread that economic development was not just an effect of market forces, and that the bureaucracy could participate in and contribute to the economy. In all of these ways, the wartime experience was extremely important with respect to the development of the proactive bureaucracy that continued into the postwar period.

[14] Richard J. Samuels, *The Business of the Japanese State* (Ithaca: Cornell University Press, 1987).

6

Government–Business Relations and Competitiveness:
The Japanese Case

YUTAKA KOSAI

Japan's promotion of industrial competitiveness is often regarded as having rewarded cooperation between the public and private sectors. As is usual with a 'success story,' however, myth and reality are so mingled that it is difficult to determine whether the competitiveness of Japanese industries has been improved because of, irrespective of, or in spite of, governmental involvement, and, if so, to what extent. A quick glance at the theories presented and facts documented by previous researchers makes one hesitant to draw a simplistic conclusion.

First, all Japanese industries cannot be regarded as competitive; it is impossible to make every industry competitive, as is taught by comparative advantage theory. This point can be illustrated within the framework of the flexible exchange rate regime in the following way. Suppose that Japan succeeds in promoting the competitiveness of industry A by government measures. The resultant increase in the export of A from Japan will bring about the appreciation of the yen, which in turn will harm the competitiveness of industry B. In fact, Japanese agriculture, the distribution sector, and some service industries are inefficient and heavily protected. Those manufacturing industries that are competitive have become more and more concentrated. As shown in Table 6.1, in 1970 one quarter of Japan's exports were in light industry goods, foodstuffs, and other products; by 1990 the share dropped to one-tenth. Machinery accounted for most major items of export from Japan in 1990, while the importance of other commodities has decreased since 1970 (see Table 6.2). It may well be that industry A is strategically more important than industry B due to the existence of externalities and so on. But the concentration of exports in a few industries suggests that the law of comparative advantage really works.

This chapter was first written for the Senior Policy Seminar on International Competitiveness: Public Sector/Private Sector Interface, held at Seoul, Republic of Korea, on April 18–21, 1990, and revised on June 20, 1993.

Table 6.1 Structure of Japan's Exports (percentages)

	1970	1980	1990
Foodstuffs	3.4	1.2	0.6
Raw Materials and Fuels	1.0	1.0	0.8
Light Industry	22.4	12.2	9.7
Heavy and Chemical Industry	72.4	84.4	87.3
Others	0.8	1.2	1.6

Source: Research Bureau, Economic Planning Agency, ed., *Keizai yōran* (Economic statistics handbook) (Tokyo: Printing Bureau, Ministry of Finance, 1981, 1992).

Table 6.2 Main Items of Export from Japan (US$ millions)

	1970	1980	1990
Motor Vehicles	1,337	23,273	50,959
Office Machinery	—	2,280	20,618
Thermionics, etc.	—	2,307	13,347
Iron and Steel Products	2,844	15,454	12,509
Scientific and Optical Equipment	498	4,526	11,554
Tape Recorders	451	3,305	7,846
Power-Generating Machinery	—	2,548	7,731
Vessels	1,410	4,682	5,566
Metal Products	714	3,947	4,632
Plastic	427	1,867	4,386
Radio Receivers	695	3,008	2,474
Synthetic Fabrics	626	2,254	1,824
Foodstuff	648	1,588	1,646
Clothing and Clothing Accessories	462	500	564
Total Exports	19,318	129,807	286,948

Source: Japan Tariff Association, *The Summary Report, Trade of Japan* (monthly), various issues.

It is also noteworthy that the Japanese government has not concentrated on promoting the competitiveness of industries. If measured by the number of laws passed and the amount of money expended, more effort has been spent on the protection of politically privileged, declining, or comparatively disadvantaged industries. Furthermore, not all industrial policy has succeeded. Some industries have performed rather well without significant or with relatively little government intervention.

However, the major concern in this essay will be the bright side of Japanese government–industry relations, leaving the cases of failure aside, as we are seeking positive lessons from successful cases. The task to find the optimal mode (if any) of public–private interaction remains important, interesting, and still open with respect to Japan.

The organization of this chapter is as follows. After a short survey of existing views of government–business relations and their effects on the competitiveness of Japanese industries, I discuss the improved competitiveness after the oil crisis in the 1970s and the sharp appreciation of the yen in the latter half of the 1980s. Some reflective remarks conclude the chapter.

How to Explain the Effects of Public–Private Relations in Japan

Conventional View

Although no exact count of opinions has been made, the majority or conventional view of public–private sector relations and their effects on the competitiveness of Japanese industries seems to be that of Japan Inc., modified and widely interpreted. The powerful Ministry of International Trade and Industry (MITI) is the headquarters of Japan Inc., with respective industries as its subordinate departments.[1] Japan has been regarded as the originator of industrial policy, a shrewd practitioner of industrial targeting, and a prototype of the capitalist developmental state[2] where bureaucrats play a major role in promoting the nation's industrialization. It has a 'formidable set' of weapons of sectoral intervention.[3] The many scholars who have taken this perspective have emphasized different aspects of the system.

This view has recently been popularized by the so-called revisionists and Japan-bashers in the wake of rising tensions and friction over US-Japan trade issues. Japanese industrial policy has gained academic sophistication through the works of strategic trade theorists. They in particular emphasize the importance of set-up costs, learning effects, and technological externalities. Some feel that Japanese industrial policy was justified by this new brand of international economics.[4]

[1] US Department of Commerce, *Japan: The Government–Business Relationship* (Washington: Government Printing Office, 1972).
[2] Chalmers Johnson, *MITI and the Japanese Miracle: The Growth of Industrial Policy 1925–75* (Stanford: Stanford University Press, 1982).
[3] Peter J. Katzenstein, ed., *Between Power and Plenty* (Madison: University of Wisconsin Press, 1978), Introduction.
[4] See Paul Krugman, 'The U.S. Response to Foreign Industrial Targeting,' Brookings Papers on Economic Activities (1984), and Laura D'Andrea Tyson, *Who's Bashing Whom? Trade Conflict in High-Technology Industries* (Washington: Institute of International Economics, 1992).

Counterexamples

This majority view has been challenged by counterexamples. Milton Friedman, for example, pointed out that the industrialization of Japan in the late nineteenth century was achieved under (because of, according to Friedman) exceptionally low rates of tariff protection (Japan was forced to concede the right to decide tariff rates autonomously in treaties to open the country immediately before the Meiji Restoration of 1868).[5] Before the 1930s, the primary Japanese industry for half a century had been textiles, and its importance seemed to be in exact accordance with the nation's factor endowment: natural resources were poor, capital was scarce, but labor was abundant and cheap. This view implies that Japan did not make great leaps forward. From time to time the nationalistic leaders of Japan in the prewar period did confess their aspirations to make great leaps forward but their dream did not come true until the 1930s.

For the postwar period, many counterexamples against the ruling role of government have been given. Let me mention a few of those most often cited.

In 1955 MITI announced a plan to make a national car that would meet certain technical and cost standards. MITI intended to integrate the competing automakers into one by offering government support to the national car maker in order to make it competitive by realizing economies of scale. Technical goals embodied in the plan provided stimulus to designers and engineers in the automobile industry. However, the idea of one integrated national car manufacturer failed because none of the automakers in Japan would give up its independence. MITI was far from omnipotent.[6]

A group of former Japanese naval engineering officers established a company after the war called Totsuko that would later develop into the Sony Corporation. Totsuko, a small company not well known in the early 1950s, applied for MITI's permission to import foreign technology. Skeptical of the importance of the technology Totsuko wanted to import and of the technical capability of Totsuko to digest the imported technology, MITI remained hesitant to give permission and delayed its decision for two years.[7] MITI's foresight was far from perfect in this case.

---

[5] Milton Friedman and Rose Friedman, *Free to Choose: A Personal Statement* (New York: Harcourt Brace Jovanovich, 1980), Chap. 2.

[6] *Kokuminsha*, here translated as national car, is sometimes translated as people's car. See Hiromichi Mutoh, 'The Automotive Industry,' in Ryutaro Komiya, Masahiro Okuno, and Kotaro Suzumura, *Industrial Policy of Japan* (Tokyo: Academic Press Japan, 1988). The corresponding word in German may be *Volkswagen*. A more detailed discussion is found in Toshimasa Tsuruta, *Sengo Nihon no sangyō seisaku* (Postwar industrial policy of Japan) (Tokyo: Nihon Keizai Shinbunsha, 1982).

[7] Phillip Trezise and Yukio Suzuki, 'Politics, Government and Economic Growth in Japan,' in Hugh Patrick and Henry Rosovsky, eds., *Asia's New Giant: How the Japanese Economy Works* (Washington: Brookings Institution, 1976), p. 798.

In the early 1960s MITI prepared a bill aimed at promoting the competitiveness of certain industries by realizing economies of scale through mergers and agreements. The effort failed because some business leaders were antagonistic and the Ministry of Finance, the other powerful agency in the government, was believed to be unsympathetic to the idea. The 'establishment' was not monolithic in Japan.[8]

In addition to these examples, Ryutaro Komiya has listed a group of industries whose exports perform very well without much help from MITI, including cameras, bicycles, watches, tape recorders, magnetic tape, and so on.[9]

So far the debate has been based on case studies or anecdotes. In terms of the number of laws passed and money spent, high-growth sectors have received much less help from government compared with other industries. Public utilities, agriculture, small and medium-sized firms, and declining or comparatively disadvantaged industries have received more support and guidance from the government. The inefficiency of government regulation and intervention has long been criticized and prompted deregulation through administrative reform, a movement in which business leaders were deeply involved.[10]

Based on quantitative data, some pioneering works have tested the validity of government intervention in promoting the competitiveness of industries in Japan. For example, Gary Saxonhouse showed that the profit rate has not been raised by participating in government-sponsored joint research and development programs.[11] Whether these types of studies will result in complete refutation of the conventionally held view of Japan Inc. remains to be seen.

Japan has not been alone in trying to help high technology industries. Daniel Okimoto impressively showed that government support for this sector in Japan was smaller than in other advanced nations.[12] One may interpret such findings as showing the inadequacy of the simplistic ver-

[8] Toshimasa Tsuruta, 'Rapid Growth Era,' in Komiya *et al.*, eds., *Industrial Policy of Japan*, pp. 63–70.

[9] Komiya *et al.*, eds., *Industrial Policy of Japan*, pp. 6–9.

[10] A comprehensive survey of Japanese legislation on industry was made by Hiroya Ueno, *Nihon no keizai seido* (Economic institutions in Japan) (Tokyo: Nihon Keizai Shinbunsha, 1978). For a quantitative survey of taxes, subsidies, and fiscal loans, see Seimitsu Ogura and Naoyuki Yoshino, 'Tokubetsu shōkyaku, Zaisei Tōyūshi to Nihon no sangyō kōzō' (Rapid obsolescence, Fiscal Investment and Loan Program, and Japanese industrial structure), *Keizai kenkyu*, April 1985. Most studies on Japanese industrial policy have been based on anecdotal evidence, which has been criticized by Richard Beacon and David E. Weinstein, 'MITI and the Japanese Myth: Growth, Economies of Scale, and Targeting in Japan (1950–90),' unpublished manuscript, 1993.

[11] Gary R. Saxonhouse, 'Japanese Cooperative R&D Ventures: A Market Evaluation,' University of Michigan, Research Seminar in International Economics, Paper No. 156 (1985).

[12] Daniel I. Okimoto, *Between MITI and the Market: Japanese Industrial Policy for High Technology* (Stanford: Stanford University Press, 1989).

sion of government-led promotion of competitiveness in Japan, or as showing the extraordinary effectiveness of government intervention in Japan. We need new models to explain how government intervention really works in Japan, and Okimoto's book tried to supply one.

Alternative Explanations

If Japan's success in promoting competitiveness should not be explained mainly by government intervention, it must be explained in other ways. If other hypotheses could explain well the increasing competitiveness in Japan, we would not need to rely on the role of government for that purpose. In other words, the value of the government role in promoting competitiveness is at least partially dependent on the value of alternative hypotheses.

One obvious alternative to the government-led promotion of the competitiveness hypothesis should be that of market-led competition. As mentioned earlier, Friedman was a pioneering advocate of this view, and Yoshiro Miwa's devastating criticism of the majority opinion left room for no conclusion other than that the market works.[13] Kosai and Harada have tried to reconsider Japanese economic development in light of the functioning of the market mechanism.[14] Although a pure market-oriented explanation remains a minority view, more emphasis on the role of the market mechanism relative to the conventional view has characterized a number of recent authoritative works.

More and more attention has focused on the role of firms in Japan, with their specificities of labor–management relations, relationship banking, parts supplier–assembler relations (*keiretsu*), and the long-term perspective of management.[15] The achievement of these works has been notable, and has intentionally or unintentionally lessened the dominance of government–business relations in explaining improvements in competitiveness in Japan.

---

[13] See Yoshiro Miwa, 'Coordination Within Industry: Output, Price, and Investment,' in Komiya *et al.*, eds., *Industrial Policy of Japan*, and his *Nihon no kigyō to sangyō soshiki* (Firms and industrial organization in Japan) (Tokyo: University of Tokyo Press, 1990).

[14] Yutaka Kosai and Yutaka Harada, 'Economic Development in Japan: A Reconsideration,' in Robert Scalapino, Seizaburo Sato, and Jusuf Wanandi, eds., *Asian Economic Development: Present and Future* (Berkeley: University of California, Institute of East Asian Studies, 1985).

[15] Among others, see Masahiko Aoki, *Information, Incentives and Bargaining in the Japanese Economy* (Cambridge: Cambridge University Press, 1988); Ken-ichi Imai and Hiroyuki Itami, 'Interpenetration of Organization and Market: Japan's Firms and Market in Comparison with the U.S.,' *International Journal of Industrial Organization*, Vol. 2, No. 4 (Dec. 1984), pp. 285–310; William Ouchi, *Theory Z: How American Business Can Meet the Japanese Challenge* (Reading, Mass.: Addison-Wesley, 1981); and James Abegglen and George Stalk, Jr., *Kaisha: The Japanese Corporation* (New York: Basic Books, 1985).

Efforts for Reconciliation

Currently, the existence of these opposing views has resulted in a stalemate. The simplistic and stereotyped version of the Japan Inc. hypothesis
is unsatisfactory. The nihilistic version of the anti-Japan Inc. hypothesis
has also failed to persuade many observers who still feel that there are
some elements of truth in the hypothesis so widely spread (echoing the
Japanese proverb that says 'no smoke without fire'). The emphasis on the
role of Japanese firms with their specific characteristics (which are often
referred to as the J-firm) has been a significant achievement in recent years
but there remains the task of clarifying government–business relations
peculiar to J-firms.

In the search for ways out of the stalemate, reconciliatory, synthetic,
and/or complementary theories have already been proposed. Four efforts
in that direction are surveyed here. Although no simplistic view can fully
explain the effects of relations between the public and private sectors,
theoretical views are important in suggesting the direction of empirical
observations.

Development Stage Theory   Development stage theory has a long tradition,
originating in the German historical school in the nineteenth century. It
long dominated the thinking of Japanese economists and policymakers
and still has some influence; it remains relevant in the current debate.

Infant industries need state protection to be nurtured, according to the
historical school. Similarly, in an economy in its developmental stage,
government plays a much greater role than in a mature economy, in
which a liberal market order prevails. The rule applies to Western countries: Britain protected its trade by the Navigation Act under Cromwell to
challenge the advanced position of Holland; Germany as well as the
United States were high tariff countries in the nineteenth century when
they were catching up with Britain. Japan and the newly industrializing
economies in Asia are tracing the mercantilist footsteps of Western
economies.

The Policy Innovation Forum, a group of eminent Japanese economists
led by Yujiro Hayami, published a statement regarding Japanese government–business relations as an institution for modernization in late developing nations but urged that Japan should be a liberal market economy as
it has already graduated from its developmental stage. These economists
expressed the expectation that the Asian newly industrializing economies
would follow the same step soon.[16]

Relations between the public and private sectors may change over time,
and it is important to study more carefully the changing character of

[16] Seisaku Kōso Foramu (Policy Innovation Forum), 'Sekai shisutemu no saikochiku ni
mukete' (Toward the reconstruction of the world system), 1990.

government–business relations. The stage-of-development approach is valuable in stimulating such studies. However, to define the infant stage or graduation remains difficult; there is no simple test. As a result, the extent to which the importance of government intervention corresponds to (and can be justified by) the stage of development remains ambiguous.

Furthermore, public–private interactions still exist with specific national characteristics after an economy matures. The stage of development may be an important factor that determines government–business relations, but it may not be the sole factor.

Compartmentalized Competition   Yasusuke Murakami proposed a sophisticated view of reconciliation and synthesis.[17] He admits that both industrial policy and interfirm competition helped Japan's swift industrialization. Government selects target industries, and then announces measures to promote the targeted industries such as special tax treatment, finance from government financial institutions, and subsidies and legislation for protective measures in a limited number of cases. The government thus prepares the playground. Once the playground is readied, firms can compete with each other as fiercely as circumstances allow. Entrepreneurship and ingenuity are fully exploited. Government administrative intervention used to be indicative rather than mandatory (weak guidance hypothesis) and was equally and impartially applied among the firms within each industry ('theorem of fairness within an industry'). In other words, industries are treated differently while firms in each industry are treated equally. Thus Murakami proposed his compartmentalized competition hypothesis.

In this framework, control of new entries in a specific industry is important from the viewpoint of sectoral industrial policy. I found that Murakami tends to exaggerate the limitations imposed on new entries; they have been frequent in postwar industrialization since the *zaibatsu* combines were dissolved by the Allied Occupation. Examples of new entrants include some of the great Japanese industrial corporations: Kawasaki Steel, Sumitomo Metal, and Kobe Steel (iron and steel); Honda (from motorcycles to passenger cars); Sony (electronics); etc. The degree of compartmentalization can be argued.

While several aspects remain to be criticized with respect to Murakami's view, there is no doubt that he offered an interesting hypothesis combining sectoral industrial policy with interfirm competition in each industry. The intervention–competition mix should be regarded as an important element in public–private sectoral relations in postwar Japan.

---

[17] Yasusuke Murakami, 'The Japanese Model of Political Economy,' in Kozo Yamamura and Yasukichi Yasuba, eds., *The Political Economy of Japan, Volume 1: The Domestic Transformation* (Stanford: Stanford University Press, 1987).

Bureaupluralism   Masahiko Aoki, who has contributed much in theorizing about the characteristics and structure of Japanese firms (J-firm), also offered an insightful hypothesis with respect to the roles played by bureaucrats and the working of bureaucracy in Japan. He calls his view 'bureaupluralism.'[18] He recognizes two facets of bureaucratic entities: one is the way they delimit national interest and the other is their role as an agent representing the interests of its jurisdictional constituents *vis-à-vis* other interests. The first characteristic is emphasized in developmental state theory, while the second is in accordance with market supremacy-pluralist theory. By admitting both elements and asserting that both theories remain only partial, Aoki tries to offer a hybrid view of the Japanese polity. The role of bureaucrats is dualistic in this framework. They must work as agents of jurisdictional interests, but in order to represent the interests of principals effectively, they have to prove that their assertions serve national interests legitimately. Thus each bureaucratic entity represents the interests of its own jurisdiction but all administrative entities still share values, speak the same language, and obey the same rules of the game. That is, coordination among bureaucratic entities is achieved through quasipluralistic interministerial bargaining within the bureaucratic process. Bureaucrats play the role of mediator between national and private interests, as the managers in Aoki's theory of the J-firm mediate the interests of stockholders and employees. Similarity or isomorphism between bureaucrats and managers provides consistency and coherence in Aoki's general view of the Japanese political economy.

Mediators, moderators, or arbitrators play a very important role in the process of adjustment. It is not difficult to detect a tendency to conservative inertia in their behavior and it seems difficult to explain their role as innovators. The essence of the process of development lies in industrial innovation. While Aoki's contribution is undeniably important, the question of where entrepreneurship came from in postwar innovation in Japan remains to be fully resolved.

Market Failures and the Theory of Industrial Policy   A group of economists, headed by Komiya, made a joint study of the industry policy of Japan;[19] theoretical parts of the work were written by four young (now middle-aged) economists (sometimes called the Gang of Four: Motoshige Itoh, Kazuharu Kiyono, Masahiro Okuno, and Kotaro Suzumura). They tried to theorize industrial policy, or to find cases (if any) where industrial policy might be useful, instead of evaluating the performance of actual industrial policy. These four seemed more sympathetic to industrial policy than either the older generation of economists or the contributors of most of the

---

[18] See Aoki, *Information, Incentives and Bargaining*.
[19] The work was later published as Komiya *et al.*, eds., *Industrial Policy of Japan*.

empirical chapters of the book, who remained more dubious about the effectiveness of industrial policy in Japan.

These four relied on market failure as justification for government intervention in industry. They emphasized several types of externalities as being more relevant than others, such as learning-by-doing, the set-up cost of an industry, spill-over effects of research and development, and the necessity to rise up the ladder of industrial development. At this point their familiarity with newly developing trade and growth theory (à la Krugman) became clear. Their theory might serve as a common ground for debating industrial policy in Japan as well as elsewhere.

In that and other senses their contribution remains undeniably important. However, they have merely shown the possible usefulness of industrial policy under some circumstances, as they set out to do. They have not provided us with the conditions on which the success or failure of actual industrial policy depends.

Recent Japanese Experiences in Public–Private Interactions and Their Effect on Competitiveness

The majority of the works described above are concerned with experiences of the 1950s and 1960s, when Japan grew rapidly and its competitiveness was dramatically improved. This section will discuss more recent experiences, that is, the 1970s and 1980s. In this period, the competitiveness of an industry in Japan depended more on the behavior of firms than on government-business relations, although concern here is with evolving public–private sectoral interactions and their possible effects on promoting productivity.

Let us begin with a general picture of the period. Japan suffered severely from the repeated rises in oil prices in the 1970s. A sharp appreciation of the yen in the latter half of the 1980s threatened the competitiveness of many industries in Japan. But still Japan survived. Japanese industries invested much abroad while maintaining their industrial base at home. In several important industries, Japan's competitive edge was further sharpened and Japanese industries came to be characterized by rapid productivity gains, quality improvement, and efficient development and design of new products.

It is important not to praise excessively the Japanese miracle. As already mentioned, not all Japanese industries are competitive and the divergence between competitive and uncompetitive industries is more and more apparent. Some industries were severely hurt by the oil crisis and the sharp rise in the value of the yen. Industries such as aluminum refining, nonferrous metals, coal, etc. have all but disappeared from Japan. Japan's competitiveness is now maintained by fewer and fewer industries.

Japan's economic power is also exaggerated by the expansion of its financial wealth. It is true that the saving rate is still high in Japan, but the extraordinary increase in the financial wealth of Japan in the late 1980s was brought about by a set of extraordinary conditions at that time. Due to the appreciation of the yen, the unusually low cost of capital during the latter half of the 1980s, and the skyrocketing increases in land and stock prices, Japan was able to buy a large amount of foreign assets very cheaply. The situation is now clearly changing, as a result of crashes in land and stock prices and the accompanying deterioration of the financial position of banking institutions in Japan.

Recently, a more sober evaluation of the competitiveness of major Japanese industries has become prevalent. The Japanese level of productivity is not high when expressed in per capita GNP in dollar terms, if purchasing power parity instead of the market exchange rate is used in the comparison and if long working hours are taken into consideration. The Japanese personal computer industry, previously protected by the fact that developing Japanese-language software was difficult for foreign producers, is now faced with severe competition from foreign competitors who have succeeded in technological improvements in hardware as well as in developing superb software in Japanese. Language barriers have disappeared, and the dominance of domestic producers in the domestic market has been shaken. In the semiconductor industry, the United States replaced Japan as the largest producer in the world market, and Japan's weakness in the development and production of high-quality chips became apparent. A skeptical view of the competitiveness of the Japanese automobile industry is also emerging as the United States and other auto producers have learned Japanese management technology while the Japanese are forced to abandon some of their strategic business practices such as frequent and rapid development of new models. The effects of the appreciation of the yen in early 1993 will severely test the competitiveness of Japanese industry. It may well be that Japan is losing its strong industries while protecting its low productivity sectors such as agriculture and service industries.

With these cautions in mind, this section focuses on possible favorable relations between government and business in promoting competitiveness; negative lessons of government intervention are in excess supply the world over.

How the Oil Crisis Was Overcome

Brezinski once characterized Japan as 'a fragile blossom,' particularly emphasizing its weak energy and resource bases.[20] The oil crises in 1973

[20] Zbigniew Brezinski, *The Fragile Blossom: Crisis and Change in Japan* (New York: Harper and Row, 1972).

and 1979 hit directly at the root of Japan's weakness. The Japanese economy faltered, naturally, but somehow survived. How? What was done by the government and how did the private sector react?

Government did several things. First, it adopted a very stringent monetary and fiscal policy in 1974 and 1980 to stop inflation. In both cases, these policies played a key role in controlling inflation. As the risk of economic and social disintegration—which, if developed, might have reduced the competitiveness of the economy—was mounting under the pressure of rampant inflation, it was imperative for government to put inflation under strict control. Sound monetary and fiscal policies were in this sense a prerequisite for maintaining competitiveness, while not directly promoting the competitiveness of any specific industry.

Government also took steps to control the prices of a number of specific commodities in 1974. Standard prices were announced for some petroleum and other products, on the basis of existing laws, while the producers of some 60 important commodities were asked to give the government advance notice of any intended price changes, on the basis of administrative guidance.[21] But these measures were limited in scope and duration. They were regarded as a temporal emergency measure and were not repeated in 1980 on such a large scale. Oil prices set by OPEC were passed through fully to domestic prices in Japan, without much government intervention. No other measure would have been sensible, as Japan was almost completely dependent on imported oil. This makes an interesting contrast to the experiences of oil price controls in the United States, which surely mitigated the inflationary effects of the first rise in oil prices but failed to conserve energy. The amount of oil consumption required to attain 1 per cent growth in GNP dropped rapidly in Japan after the first oil crisis while that in the United States declined significantly only after the control of oil prices was removed (finally in 1982).

A third government action was to ask trade union leaders not to demand high wage increases. In the spring wage negotiations in 1974, wages increased by 32.9 per cent, thus sharply raising the unit labor cost and relative share of labor. This in turn caused an increase in unemployment. To restrain wage increases within a reasonable range was seen as important in order for the economy to avoid stagflation (unemployment cum inflation combined). Wage increases in the spring of 1975 decreased to 13.1 per cent. To some observers, this showed the working of income policy in a Japanese style.[22]

The existence and effectiveness of Japanese income policy at that time has since been a controversial issue. Statutory or compulsory measures were never taken; only moral persuasion was used. Econometric studies

---

[21] See Yutaka Kosai, *The Era of High-Speed Growth* (Tokyo: University of Tokyo Press, 1986), pp. 189–91.

[22] Murakami, 'The Japanese Model of Political Economy,' pp. 72–5.

show that the wage increase in 1975 could be explained in terms of rates of unemployment and inflation, without introducing specific proxy or dummy variables that represented income policy.

It was true that government tried to persuade trade union leaders to restrain their demand for increases in wages, and to accept a moderate increase in wages, in exchange for a government promise to keep the rate of inflation under control. However, given the existence of enterprise-based trade unionism in Japan, where wages were to be settled at the enterprise level (not the national level), national union leaders may have had little influence on wage determination. They accepted the moderate wage increase imposed on them by market forces such as a rising unemployment rate, squeezed profits, declining rate of inflation, etc., and took advantage of the government promise to keep inflation under control as a good excuse to save face.

Still, an important fact was that good management–labor relations had not been destroyed during the oil crises in spite of the rise in unemployment and restraint of wages at the time. Management tried to avoid layoffs and labor made concessions in demanding wages. Mutual trust enabled both parties to act not from the viewpoint of short-run conflict of interests but of long-term mutually beneficial cooperation. Government worked for strengthening mutual trust by putting inflation under control within a short time.

A fourth area for government involvement were efforts to substitute oil with nuclear and other new energies. In 1974 MITI launched the Sunshine Project aimed at promoting R&D in new energies. Wind, solar, ocean, biomass, and geothermal energies were studied, and more effort was spent on the development of nuclear energy including government support for building nuclear electric power plants.

Nuclear energy occupies an important place in Japan's total supply of electricity. However, construction of nuclear plants meets strong resistance from nearby residents. Construction has often been delayed by citizen resistance, a fact that refutes a stereotyped version of the Japan Inc. hypothesis. According to a plan authorized by MITI in 1979, the capacity of nuclear plants for electric generation was to be expanded to 51–3 million kilowatts by the end of 1990 from 12.7 million at the end of 1978. The actual capacity attained by 1990 was 31,645,000 kilowatts, three-fifths of the target, although the utilization rate was raised thanks to technical improvements (see Table 6.3).

Meanwhile, development of new energy failed as estimated costs remained prohibitively high. Government policy toward new energy sources seems preoccupied with technology and lacks the economic incentives to promote demand.[23]

[23] Ken-ichi Imai, 'Industrial Policy and Technological Innovation,' in Komiya *et al.*, eds., *Industrial Policy of Japan*.

Table 6.3 Nuclear Electrical Generation

	Capacity (thousand kilowatts)		Supply (billion kilowatt hours)	
	Planned	*Actual*	*Planned*	*Actual*
1978	1,270	1,270	59	59
1985	29,000	24,686	146	160
1990	52,000	31,645	280	202
1995	76,000	—	432	—

Source: Keizai yōran 1981, pp. 355–6; *Keizai yōran 1992*, pp. 84–5. Planned figures are from the Interim Report of the Electricity Council, December 1979.

Fifth, the government helped industries seriously affected by the oil price increase to adjust. A Specific Depressed Industries' Adjustment Law was passed, and firms in designated industries were allowed to scrap excessive productive facilities, to formulate rationalization plans, etc., as a joint action. Unemployment relief and special measures to promote regional development of depressed areas were also provided.[24] How efficient these measures were remains to be discussed. But government did (or could) not introduce protectionism in order to help troubled industries, a fact to its credit.[25]

None of the government measures so far mentioned was directly concerned with conserving energy. Energy saving, however, was the most important means by which Japan could overcome the oil crises and, again, the government did several things. It called upon the people through the mass media to save energy, ordered the closing of gasoline stations on Sundays, curtailed radio and television broadcasts after midnight, and began the Moonlight Project to promote R&D in energy conservation. However, these government efforts were marginal at best in explaining the unexpected progress in conserving energy after the oil crises. The

[24] See Sueo Sekiguchi, 'An Overview of Adjustment Assistance Policies in Japan' and 'Industrial Adjustment and Cartel Actions in Japan,' both in Hong W. Tan and Haruo Shimada, eds., 'Troubled Industries in the United States and Japan,' A Rand Study, St. Martin's Press, 1994; Sueo Sekiguchi and Toshihiro Horiuchi, 'Trade and Adjustment Assistance,' in Komiya *et al.*, eds., *Industrial Policy of Japan*; Atsushi Seike, 'The Employment Adjustment in Japanese Manufacturing Industries in the 1970s,' *Keio Business Review*, Vol. 22, No. 3 (1985); and Eiko Shinotsuka, 'Employment Adjustment in Japanese Manufacturing,' *Japanese Economic Studies* (Spring 1987).
[25] Japan protects agriculture and other industries. The closedness of Japanese domestic markets, which are formally open, is often criticized. Still, government did not try to defend the declining manufacturing industries. See Abegglen and Stalk, *Kaisha*, p. 33, for an evaluation of this point.

Table 6.4 Primary Energy Consumption per Million Dollars of GNP

				Tons of oil equivalent/US$ million			
	1975	*1980*	*1985*	*1986*	*1987*	*1988*	*1989*
Japan	213	188	161	159	153	156	153
United States	520	481	418	406	409	408	399
Germany	278	269	250	246	243	238	224
						1975 = 100	
Japan	100	88	76	75	72	73	72
United States	100	93	80	78	79	78	77
Germany	100	97	90	88	87	86	81

Note: Primary energy covers oil, coal, natural gas, hydroelectric, and atomic energy. US$ millions are expressed at the constant price of 1987.

Source: International Energy Agency, *IEA Statistics* (annual), various issues; World Bank, *World Tables* (annual), various issues.

business sector began to save energy, apparently at its own initiative under market forces.

Government contributed to conserving energy significantly not by any positive action but mostly by non-action, by not imposing price controls for long. This non-action led to a high price for oil, to which the business sector responded by reducing the amount of oil consumed. The energy consumption required for GNP growth dropped more quickly and sharply in Japan than in the United States or Germany, as shown in Table 6.4. The reduction was made possible by utilizing recently developed microelectronic devices for energy saving. It was also promoted by mobilizing employees' initiative and cooperation, quality control activities, an employees' proposal system, small-group debates, and so on. On the industry level, a shift in the industrial structure from energy-using sectors to an energy-saving sectors contributed much to the reduction of oil consumption. Thus, the limited role of government in overcoming the oil crises shows again the limited relevance of the stereotyped Japan Inc. hypothesis.

Yen Appreciation and Restructuring

In the latter half of the 1980s, the yen appreciated sharply against the dollar and other currencies. The exchange rate of approximately 260 yen per dollar in early 1985 rose to approximately 120 yen per dollar toward the end of 1988. It was feared that the higher yen would seriously damage the competitiveness of the exporting industries, bringing about domestic depression and a shift of productive facilities (and employment opportunities) from home to abroad. The fear was exaggerated in that it ignored the effect of yen appreciation on favorable terms of trade, which were further improved by the simultaneous fall of oil prices.

At the same time, firms sought to rationalize and restructure Japanese industries in order to cope with the appreciation of the yen. Again, managerial resources—including cooperative relations between labor and management, between assemblers and parts suppliers, as well as between banks and industrial firms—were fully mobilized. Firms played a dominant role in the process of industrial adjustment after the appreciation of the yen, as had been the case in the process of the adjustment after the oil crises. Government helped firms directly or indirectly in their efforts to rationalize and restructure.

The first thing government did was to expand domestic demand through monetary and fiscal stimuli. The Bank of Japan reduced its official discount rate to a historical low of 2.5 per cent. Although the government was pursuing fiscal consolidation and reconstruction in the mid-1980s as its most important policy task, expansionary supplementary budgets were passed in the fall of 1986 and spring of 1987. The measures pursued after the rise of oil prices and after yen appreciation were not the same, but both were intended to secure economic stability against external shocks.

Government also helped industrial adjustment by allowing designated cartel and unemployment relief. Measures initially intended to help depressed industries adjust to the oil shocks were extended and applied to those affected by the appreciation of the yen; the lists of major depressed industries differed little after these two events, and the aluminum refinery, coal, and electric furnace industries were faced with virtual extinction.

These government measures helped Japanese firms to rationalize and restructure. Domestic demand substituted for foreign markets and was expanded by fiscal and monetary policies. The low cost of capital made it easy for firms to obtain funds for rationalization and restructuring. Firms were also able to sell their assets at high prices and write off the losses they incurred as a result of changes in the value of the yen. Toward the end of the 1980s when the appreciation of the yen began to stabilize, Japanese industries reemerged as competitive as ever. The quality of their products had improved considerably and new products had been developed. The reputation of the lean management of Japanese firms was heightened during the latter half of the 1980s.[26] While investment abroad rose sharply, domestic investment also increased vigorously, thus bringing a fear of hollowing in domestic industries. Figure 6.1 suggests that investments at home and abroad were complementary in Japan, while substitutable in the United States, in the 1980s.

[26] Michael L. Dertouzos, Richard K. Lester, and Robert M. Solow, eds., *Made in America: Regaining the Productive Edge* (Cambridge, Mass.: MIT Press, 1989).

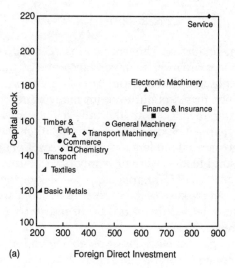

(a)   Foreign Direct Investment

Note: International Economy Unit, Planning Bureau, Economic Planning Agency. I thank the Agency for permission to use its calculation. The calculation is based on the following sources: Ministry of Finance, *Taigai chokusetsu toshi todokede jisseki* (Report on foreign direct investment), various years; Department of National Income, Economic Research Institute, Economic Planning Agency, *Shihankibetsu minkan kigyō shihon sutokku sokuhō* (Quarterly report on private business capital stock), various issues.

Fig. 6.1A. Capital Stock and Foreign Direct Investment by Industry in 1991 (fiscal year 1985 = 100)

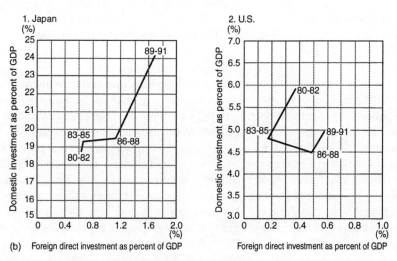

(b)   Foreign direct investment as percent of GDP   Foreign direct investment as percent of GDP

Note: The Japanese data are on a fiscal-year basis, while the US data are on a calendar-year basis.

Source: See Figure 6.1A for Japan. The calculation for the United States is based on the following sources: US Department of Commerce, Survey of Current Business, various issues; Organization of Economic Cooperation and Development, Flows and Stocks of Fixed Capital, 1991.

Fig. 6.1B. Domestic Investment and Foreign Direct Investment by Japanese and US Manufacturing Industries (as percentage of gross domestic product)

From the viewpoint of 1993, one might argue that the bubble economy of the late 1980s did more harm than good in the long run. Japanese firms, in pursuit of high value-added product development, lost the lean management, which they had nurtured for many years, particularly after the oil crises. Higher prices of labor and land measured in dollars, although partly mitigated by cheaper rates of interest, pushed up the cost of production and deprived Japanese industries of some of their competitive edge. The low cost of capital appeared to give rise to wasteful investment, which brought about a high break-even point and lowered the financial position of firms. As a result of lowered rates of interest combined with heightened asset prices in Japan, a large-scale capital outflow took place, reversing the trend of the appreciation of the yen. The value of the yen fell to approximately 150 yen per dollar toward the end of the 1980s. An illusion of excessive competitiveness among Japanese industries has been formed due to the bubble-induced depreciation of the value of the yen. Simultaneous increase in investment at home and abroad paved the way for excess capacity, as can be seen in the automobile industry. The competitiveness of Japanese industries will be tested again in the face of the revaluation of the yen that began in early 1993. Whether Japanese industries have really overcome the appreciation of the yen remains to be seen.

Deregulation and Privatization

Government–business relations in Japan were to a considerable extent affected by the move toward deregulation during the 1980s. Due to the prolonged recession after the oil crises, tax revenues decreased drastically and the government was forced to launch fiscal and administrative reforms to limit the size of government. Deregulation was one aspect of the reform and was pushed through upon the recommendations of the Administrative Reform Commission. Another source of pressure for deregulation were US demands on Japan to open its domestic markets. The Structural Impediments Initiative provided a comprehensive framework in which the United States could negotiate with the Japanese government on the liberalization of domestic institutions.

Measures for deregulation were taken in such industries as finance, telecommunications, air transport, trucking, and retail (see Table 6.5). Deregulation went hand in hand with privatization in the case of telecommunications, as the Nippon Telegraph and Telephone (NTT) Public Corporation was demonopolized and denationalized to allow entry of new common carriers. The national railway was also divided and privatized to enhance regional competition and to improve service. The Antimonopoly Law was strengthened by increasing the penalty imposed on illegal cartels.

Table 6.5   Selected Measures for Deregulation

Finance
    Gradual liberalization of interest rate controls
    Deregulation of foreign exchange
    Banks' and security firms' entry into each other's business allowed in part

Air Transport
    Monopoly of international routes by Japan Airlines abolished
    Competition in domestic routes promoted by two or three carriers per route
    Privatization of Japan Airlines

Telecommunications
    Telecommunications industry law passed
    Privatization of Nippon Telegraph and Telephone

Trucking Industry
    Licensing system changed to permit system
    Abolition of supply–demand adjustment regulation
    Integration of categories of activities
    Fare permit system replaced by notification system

Distribution
    Amendment of Large-scale Retail Stores Law
    Reduced period for coordination processing

Source: Mitsuru Taniuchi *et al.*, *Nihon keizai gokanen yosoku* (Japan's economic outlook for fiscal years 1993–7) (Tokyo: Japan Center for Eonomic Research, 1992).

The effects of these deregulation measures have already been felt in lower charges, freer entry, increased services, and activization of business activities in related fields.[27] For example, charges for long-distance phone calls were lowered drastically (by half between Tokyo and Osaka). The number and floor area of large-scale retail shops sharply increased immediately after the amendment of the Large-scale Retail Stores Law. There should be no doubt that deregulation is working to promote competition and efficiency in Japanese industries.

One important feature of the process of deregulation in Japan is how extremely gradual it has been. The liberalization of interest rates began with the introduction of certificates of deposit in 1979, and it took 15 years for full liberalization to be reached. The rule assigning domestic air routes to specific air transport companies was abolished and competition was allowed, while regulation of airfares including the principle of equal airfares for equal distances was strictly maintained. The number of regulations has actually increased during the period of deregulation as many detailed regulations were added for precautionary purposes when the broadly defined power of government intervention was

[27] Mitsuru Taniuchi *et al.*, *Nihon keizai gokanen yosoku* (Japan's economic outlook for fiscal years 1993–7) (Tokyo: Japan Center for Economic Research, 1993).

removed. This gradualism may help diminish the transitory harms of deregulation but definitely slows the permeation of the effects of liberalization.

The move toward liberalization was countered at least in part by the increased role of government intervention in solving trade disputes with the United States, European Community, and other countries. MITI set upper limits on the number of automobiles to be exported to the United States or EC by individual auto producers in order for the voluntary export restraints to be workable. MITI also worked hard to persuade automakers to build plants abroad or to increase the use of auto parts from abroad. Administrative guidance has reemerged as a weapon of bureaucratic control. It should be noted that this type of government intervention may weaken the competitiveness of Japanese industries. In the case of automobiles, the voluntary export restraint guaranteed higher profits for automakers in both countries, gave incentives for Japanese car makers to produce luxury cars to increase sales amounts with the same number of cars exported, and tempted them to expand their productive capacities beyond demand in order to get around trade barriers. Government involvement in such a manner would be counterproductive in promoting the competitiveness of industries.

More Positive Interaction: R&D

So far we have been concerned with the broad question of how Japan overcame the oil crises and yen appreciation. In general, the dynamism of business behavior with good management–labor relations was emphasized, while the importance of government's role in maintaining macroeconomic stability was recognized. On the other hand, microlevel interaction between government and firms which aimed at promoting competitiveness appeared to be less important at this time compared to the earlier period. Policy measures such as subsidies, special tax treatment, and government loans were not as widely or intensively in use after 1970 as in the 1950s and 1960s.

Still, there has been interaction between government and business for promoting industrial competitiveness. The most important seems to be in the research and development projects in which the government collaborated with business firms as a financial supporter, organizer and coordinator, or research participant. An often-cited example in this category is the Very Large Scale Integration (VLSI) Technology Research Association which was established in 1976.[28] A technology research as-

---

[28] References include Ryuhei Wakasugi, *Gijutsu kakushin to kenkyū kaihatsu no keizai bunseki* (Economic analysis of innovation, research, and development) (Tokyo: Tōyō Keizai Shinpōsha, 1986); Imai, 'Industrial Policy and Technological Innovation'; Akira Goto and Ryuhei Wakasugi, 'Technology Policy,' in Komiya *et al.*, eds., *Industrial Policy of Japan;*

sociation is a framework for a number of firms to join in a specific research project, set up under the Mining and Manufacturing Technology Research Association Law of 1961. Among the technology research associations established during 1961–90, the VLSI Technology Research Association was one of the most important, in the size of its expenditures, number of researchers mobilized, and also in its contribution to technological breakthroughs.

The purpose of the VLSI Technology Research Association was to develop the technology needed to manufacture VLSI, i.e., to try to place memory of one megabyte on a single chip, a technique IBM was said to be in the process of developing at the time. The association was given four years to accomplish the task. MITI took the initiative and urged five rival electronics companies (Fujitsu, Hitachi, Mitsubishi, NEC, and Toshiba) to form the association. The ministry sent researchers from its Electro-Technical Laboratory to the association's Joint Research Institute. Research money amounted to ¥72 billion, of which ¥29 billion came from the government as a subsidy. The R&D expenditure by the association amounted to about one half of the total R&D expenditures in the semiconductor industry in 1976–80. Development of common and basic technologies such as microprocessor and crystal technologies was assigned to the Joint Research Institute where a hundred researchers from five companies, MITI, and NTT worked together. Research on applied technologies that were closer to product development (such as design technology) were carried out by two separate groups of firms (Fujitsu, Hitachi, and Mitsubishi on one hand and NEC and Toshiba on the other). The association finished its task within the allotted four years. Several technical breakthroughs were made and more than 1,000 patents were obtained by the association.

The association's aims were specific. Its duration was limited. Its organization combined cooperation between firms and government for the development of the common and basic technology with competition among rival companies in the development of product-related technologies. The association brought together researchers from companies and government to work together toward the same research goals, and gave opportunities to access and transfer the information among the participants. Thus the association was an interesting case where government and firms worked together to promote research and development, and where concerted effort produced positive results in strengthening the competitiveness of Japanese industries.

Okimoto, *Between MITI and the Market*; Marie Anchordoguy, 'A Challenge to Free Trade? Japanese Industrial Targeting in the Computer and Semiconductor Industries,' in Kozo Yamamura, ed., *Japan's Economic Structure: Should It Change?* (Seattle: Society for Japanese Studies, 1990); and Fumio Kodama, *Haiteku gijutsu no paradaimu* (Paradigm of high technology) (Tokyo: Chūōkōronsha, 1991).

It is not correct, however, to regard the promotional measures for high technology industries as specific to Japan. Daniel Okimoto showed that every measure practiced in Japan to promote the competitiveness of the high technology industry was more widely or more intensively practiced in other major countries.[29] It should also be mentioned that not all of the technology research associations were successful. According to Wakasugi, the VLSI Association was the most successful among such associations ever established.[30] It is said that the firms used to send their inferior research staff to the associations while keeping the best researchers at their own research laboratories. Failure of the mission of the associations would be a natural consequence if companies did not fully cooperate with each other.

The project for Developing the Basic Technologies for the Next Generation Computers could be regarded as a successor to the VLSI project as a national theme for a technological break-through. Some of the useful results obtained in the project have already been made available. The usefulness of the core concept of the fifth-generation computer remains to be seen.

Conditions for effective public and private interaction remain subtle and difficult to generalize. Some say that the personal leadership of the director mattered most in the success of the VLSI project.

An ironic case of government intervention and business reaction could be added here. The standards of limiting the carbon monoxide concentration in emissions were set at the same levels specified in the US Muskie Act (the Clean Air Act Amendment of 1970) in Japan in 1975. The targets were expected to be difficult to achieve and were strongly opposed by automobile producers. However, the standards were met by 1978, enabling Japanese automakers to meet the strictest regulatory standards at that time in the world. Emission control and energy conservation became a source of strength for Japanese automobile producers. The intervention that was initially regarded as anti-industry promoted the competitiveness of the industry.[31] It is worth mentioning that the targets were achieved first not by the largest maker but by relatively new firms. This shows that competitive industrial organization is conducive to increased competitiveness in the industry.

Concluding Remarks

Following this short glance at theories and recent experiences on government–business relations in Japan, what can be said? Although it seems

[29] Okimoto, *Between MITI and the Market.*
[30] Wakasugi, *Gijutsu kakushin to kenkyū kaihatsu no keizai bunseki*, p. 178.
[31] Mutoh, 'The Automotive Industry,' pp. 311–12.

premature to draw any definitive conclusion, some afterthoughts should be recorded to suggest further explorations in the future.

We have seen that any simplistic version of the Japan Inc. hypothesis is unsatisfactory. This is true for the high growth period of the 1960s but even more so for the 1970s and 1980s. The formidable set of weapons for sectoral policy that once characterized Japan is shown to be in wide use among other nations including advanced countries, and most of the weapons are no longer intensively used in Japan. Also, Japan is no longer monopolizing the success story of rapid industrialization. The newly industrializing economies of Asia are providing a variety of experiences in promoting competitiveness in the late twentieth century with varying degrees of government involvement.

The situation gives us the opportunity to make an imaginary experiment in more purified, ideal conditions. Suppose Japan succeeded in promoting competitiveness even after its formal involvement in industries decreased. What was left in government–business relations after many of the measures for direct intervention were no longer in use might be the essential element in the Japanese experience throughout the periods of rapid and moderate growth.

If government can influence the competitive performance of industries, this must be so through the actions and reactions of government and business firms. This proved more true in light of economic changes in the post-rapid-growth period. The tendency for recent studies to emphasize the behavior of firms more than the dominant role of government seems well justified by recent government–business relations. The direction of research examined in the second section of this paper is useful in view of the facts presented in the third section.

In order to contribute to the analysis of government–business relations in view of recent developments in theories and situations, let me conclude with four observations. First, the importance of macroeconomic policy for the stabilization of industrial competitiveness cannot be overemphasized. Government actions may give rise to fluctuations in exchange rates under the flexible exchange rate regime, thus affecting the competitiveness of industries. When the policy taken is unsustainable, short-run deviations in exchange rates might produce an illusory improvement or deterioration in competitiveness. The situation might be worsened if investment were based on the illusion. Of course one can reject this fear by assuming rational expectations on the part of business firms. Still, fluctuations take place under almost-rational behavior of modern economic agents.

During the high growth period, under a fixed exchange rate system and with small reserves of foreign currencies, Japan had little scope for manipulating macroeconomic policy measures. Now with freedom for macroeconomic policy actions, Japan's risk of mismanagement is greater.

It is simplistic to say that macroeconomic policy after the oil crises succeeded while policy after the appreciation of the yen failed. There is no denying, however, that the bubble economy at least partly induced by macroeconomic policies in the latter half of the 1970s produced the illusion of strengthened competitiveness of Japanese industries. Asset inflation was not a purely financial phenomenon but affected the real sector in several ways. For its failure to control asset inflation in the late 1980s, Japan will pay the price after the bubble bursts when appreciation of the yen reemerges. How to expand domestic demand without risking the stability of asset markets remains to be seen.

My second observation is concerned with the increasing role of government as a deregulator or a setter of new rules for competition. The finance industry, telecommunications, trucking, and the distribution industry belong to a sort of network infrastructure for other industries. The industrial competitiveness of the Japanese economy as a whole depends on the level of efficiency in the working of the infrastructure. Many of the above-mentioned industries are classified as public utility industries and were strongly regulated by government. Innovation of technology, particularly that related to information, opened the way for the introduction of more competition in these fields. How fast and smoothly government deregulates or sets new rules for competition affects the competitiveness not only of the industries directly concerned but also of the economy as a whole.

Government in Japan efficiently played the role of collaborator with industries, or so it is believed. An emerging issue is the possible conflict between the roles of collaborator and rule-setter. Some distancing of government and business may be required for the latter. The extreme gradualism may have the advantage of avoiding transitory confusion but the disadvantage of delaying adjustment to changed situations. Government–business relations are being put to the test.

Third, credit should be given to the fact that industrial adjustment after the oil crises and yen appreciation took the forms of restructuring, diversification, or dissolution of businesses, instead of introducing protectionism. The trade surplus in Japan's current account made it impossible to turn to protectionism. Still, protectionism in agriculture and other regulated industries remains strong. Trade friction has sometimes resulted in the increased intervention of the government in rationing the volumes of exports or imports in order for voluntary export restraints or import expansion to be effective. The temptation to meddle in industrial coordination without hope for innovation in industry seems counterproductive, but it is clearly increasing.

Finally, it seems to be repeatedly shown that, in order to perform well the role of promoter of competitiveness, government must rely on competition among firms through successful technology development.

Shared goals and mutual trust are important assets inherited from the rapid growth experience, but the problem now arising in Japan is whether these assets can be maintained without damaging other important roles in macroeconomic management and rule-setting.

7

Japanese Bureaucrats at Retirement: *The Mobility of Human Resources from Central Government to Public Corporations*

TAKENORI INOKI

The basic functioning of modern industrial society can be viewed from three analytical angles: how the various roles in society are structured, how human resources are allocated among these roles, and how the resources are compensated or rewarded for the roles they fulfill.[1] If human resources are allocated and compensated according to rational principles, to a certain extent the best and brightest in society will flow into those roles that assure the highest economic and/or non-economic compensation. This speculation generally held true in pre-World-War-II Japan where the talented elite went into the public service, which on the average offered them higher salaries than business or politics. Attracting the most capable members of the labor force, who were endowed with intelligence and public virtue, the prewar Japanese bureaucracy was relatively free from corruption, and the morale and morality of government officials were high.

We can observe similar trends in postwar Japan, in spite of the fact that compensation for government officials, at least in economic terms, is no longer high. The question thus arises of why the best and brightest still go into public service. There may be a number of reasons, such as high social prestige or the strong political power they enjoy because of their office. This explanation, however, does not fully consider an economic aspect (incentive mechanism) of this problem that is particularly important for analyzing the effective functioning of the so-called 'clean' bureaucracy and the efficient allocation of human resources in a national economy. We must consider whether it is appropriate to compare simply the level of *current* salaries received by government officials with that of other sectors when we consider *total* compensation. *Lifetime* income, including salaries earned after retiring from the core government ministries, may make a more appropriate comparison. This leads us to analysis of the practice of *amakudari* in the Japanese bureaucracy.

[1] Kazuo Koike, *Shokuba no rōdō kumiai to sanka* (Participation and unions on the shop floor) (Tokyo: Tōyō Keizai Shinpōsha, 1977), p. 16.

It is often pointed out that a bureaucracy–industry link in Japan is formed by the practice of *amakudari* (literally, 'descending from heaven'), the movement of retired officials of the central government to jobs in business. *Amakudari*, however, is not confined to this direct government–business link. Another important and indirect type is the movement of central government officials to public corporations established by the national government by special laws as instruments for activities by the state. A third type also exists in the mobility of officials from the central government to local government.

These elaborate formal and informal networks of human resources have been said to facilitate systematic exchanges of information between central government officials and representatives of non-government sectors or industries.[2] Such networks seem to operate as a basic means for disseminating information between central government and non-government sectors through direct mobility of human resources, which is promoted by the early retirement of public servants in the national government. As officials retire from central ministries, they carry both information and power to public corporations or to business, and in the process form human channels between the sectors.

This chapter focuses on the *amakudari* of the second variety, i.e., the movement of top officials to public corporations, and analyzes the economic *raison d'être* of these public corporations as a device for human resource management within the Japanese bureaucracy. My basic hypothesis is that *amakudari* not only maintains and reinforces the connection between government and non-government sectors, but that it also vitalizes human resources by incorporating a strong competitive mechanism into bureaucracy.

This chapter is organized as follows. The first section provides a brief description of *amakudari*, a short history of regulations imposed upon this practice, especially in the late 1970s, and a list of the pros and cons of *amakudari*. The second section surveys general trends and structures of *amakudari* networks observed after the 1960s. The public corporations around which the second type of *amakudari* has developed are given special legal status and assist government or other *activities* by performing special functions, sometimes for limited periods. No research done to date has clarified whether this practice emerged as 'make-work' for retired officials or whether it really enhances the economic efficiency of human resource allocation in the bureaucracy and among various economic sectors in Japan. The latter proposition implies that *amakudari* fully utilizes the rich talents of officials throughout their working lives without

---

[2] See Chalmers Johnson, *Japan's Public Policy Companies* (Washington: American Enterprise Institute, 1978). Johnson's work is a standard reference that emphasizes the close human network relationships between central government officials and business on the one hand, and Diet members on the other.

hampering the work incentives of young officials in the central government.

In considering these structures we have to distinguish several categories of mobility: Are these middle-level managing officials or top officials? Does the pattern differ by ministry? Is the depth and extent of this government/non-government connection affected by each ministry's regulatory power over industry?[3] We also have to bear in mind that this mobility need not take the form of a one-step movement from government to semi-governmental corporations, but very frequently it is a multistep path (sometimes figuratively called 'migratory birds' movement), from large to small corporations or rotation among various corporations, like migratory birds resting in several places. This paper focuses mainly on the *amakudari* of top officials (not middle-management officials under age 50) into public corporations and identifies established career paths of officials in various ministries, making it possible to compare the nature of mobility in these ministries. Three ministries were chosen for this purpose: the Ministry of Finance, the Ministry of International Trade and Industry, and the Ministry of Labor.

The third section discusses and tests two basic hypotheses concerning *amakudari* movement from central government to public corporations. The final section provides some concluding remarks and policy implications.

Amakudari: Description, Comparison, and Criticism

One type of *amakudari* is the transfer of retired government officials to private firms, or to trade associations of these private firms. However, the direct transfer of bureaucrats to these private (for-profit) organizations is prohibited in principle by article 103 of the National Public Service Law, which regulates the behavior of national public servants. The law provides that public servants in the central government may not enter the private sector for two years after retirement from office and are not permitted to take jobs 'closely connected' to their jobs during the last five years of public service. This prohibition clause, when applied, also specifies the categories and qualifications of public servants, the reasons for their separation, and the posts they will obtain in the private sector. As demonstrated by Table 7.1, which shows the approved number of these officials reemployed in private companies in three periods, this provision has loopholes. It is also true that complete regulation is difficult to achieve because it may sometimes violate the freedom of occupational choice, which is guaranteed by the constitution.

---

[3] This implies that a recent move toward 'deregulation' may reduce the asset value of these officials in business and change the present trend and structures of this practice. We need, however, a long observation period in the future in order to test this hypothesis.

Table 7.1 Approved Number of Reemployed Officials in Private Companies (3-year average)

Ministries	1969–71 average	1979–81 average	1989–91 average
Finance	40.7	47.7	58.7
International Trade and Industry	25.7	22.0	25.7
Transportation	20.7	25.7	17.7
Posts and Telecommunications	9.7	16.0	19.3
Construction	17.3	26.7	25.3
Labor	2.3	1.3	1.3
Agriculture, Forestry, and Fisheries	18.3	22.3	23.3
Health and Welfare	4.0	6.3	3.3
Education	0	5.3	11.0

Source: National Personnel Authority, *Kōmuin hakusho* (White paper on government employees), various issues.

The second type of *amakudari*, transfer to public corporations, is not prohibited by law. This type, the subject of this essay, is of great interest because these public corporations do not have autonomous power concerning the appointment of directors who are systematically deployed under the complete supervision of the secretariat of each ministry. In this respect, it is indeed questionable whether or not these public corporations are outside the central government. They may be considered inside the central government because salaries of employees in most public corporations are paid from taxes. These corporations are non-profit organizations established by the national government, and their fields of operation cover economic policy as well as social policy areas. Examples of the former, for instance, include the Japan External Trade Organization (overseen by the International Trade Administration of the Ministry of International Trade and Industry), the Japan Highway Public Corporation (overseen by the Road Bureau of the Ministry of Construction), and the Housing and Urban Development Corporation (overseen jointly by the Ministry of Construction and the Ministry of Transport). Examples of the latter are the Pension Welfare Service Public Corporation (overseen by the Pension Bureau, Ministry of Health and Welfare), the Labor Welfare Corporation (overseen by the Labor Standards Bureau, Ministry of Labor), and the like. *Amakudari* to these public corporations is outside legal controls.[4]

According to the official explanation, these public corporations are established 'primarily when particular activities are better managed in the

---

[4] A somewhat puzzling example is that government officials can move freely into NHK (a non-profit broadcasting organization), but they are not permitted to obtain jobs in private broadcasting corporations.

form of a profit-enterprise, when efficiency in performance is more likely to be achieved than under direct operation by the national government agencies, or when more flexibility in financial or personnel management is required than is normally possible under the laws and regulations pertaining to government agencies.'[5] But the organizational structure, the mode of control by the national government, and other features of these corporations vary according to the nature of operations.

As of April 1, 1992, there were 92 such corporations with 784 managing directors and approximately 600,000 employees. Approximately 60 per cent of their managing directors had been appointed from among retired bureaucrats, and on average more than half of the middle managers in these public corporations were transferred from related ministries.

We can complete our classification of *amakudari* with the third variety, the dispatch of national government officials to local government. This type of movement was formerly associated with retired officers of the Ministry of Home Affairs, but in recent years it has gradually been extended to other ministries. Vice governors of prefectures appointed from the Ministry of Finance (MOF), the Ministry of International Trade and Industry (MITI), or the Ministry of Labor (MOL) are typical examples.

Countering these three types of *amakudari* there are flows of human resources *toward* the national government, which raise problems of a different nature. This flow of human resources toward the center is sometimes called *amaagari* (literally, 'ascending to heaven'). The temporary transfer or loan of bank employees and construction companies to the Economic Planning Agency, the dispatch of local government officials to MOL, and transfer of officers from the Bank of Japan and public corporations are examples. The merits and demerits of this exchange have been pointed out from the perspective of government and business or public corporations. Although I do not take up these questions in this paper, it is worth noting how such an 'osmotic' network has formed in postwar Japan. Tsujinaka explains this phenomenon in the following manner: 'Denied the path to a strong state based on hierarchical centralization and control under a statist ideology, the state bureaucracy turned toward the osmotic network system whereby more sophisticated and indirect means of control could be developed and systematized.'[6] *Amakudari*, he believes, is one of these means of control along with administrative guidance, advisory councils, and the like.

[5] Institute of Administrative Management Under the Supervision of Management and Coordination Agency, Prime Minister's Office, Government of Japan, *Organization of the Government of Japan* (1992), p. 108.

[6] See Yutaka Tsujinaka, 'Rengo: The Final Participant in Japan's Osmotic Corporatism: A Network Interpretation of Its Strength,' paper presented at the 42nd Annual Meeting of the Association for Asian Studies, April 7, 1990, Chicago.

Table 7.2 *Pantouflage* and *Amakudari*: France and Japan

	France (1972)	Japan (1974)
Samples	Presidents of largest 100 firms	Top managers of largest 100 firms
Number of Observations	96	1,050
Rate of *Pantouflage/Amakudari* (per cent)	33.3	3.5

Sources: Dominique Monjardet, 'Carrière des dirigeants et contrôle de l'enterprise' (Executive careers and business management), *Sociologie du travail*, April–June 1972; Takao Nomura, 'Amakudari keieisha wa ze ka hi ka' (Is *amakudari* right or wrong?), *Nihon no keiei bunka*, Vol. 3 (Tokyo: Chuo Keizaisha, 1974); and Masaru Yoshimori, *Furansu kigyo no hasso to kodo* (Way of thinking and behavior of French firms) (Tokyo: Daiyamondo-sha, 1984).

International and Historical Comparison

Amakudari is not unique to postwar Japan. A similar practice in France, known as *pantouflage* (coming from the word 'pantoufle,' meaning 'slipper') is estimated to be about ten times more frequent than in Japan. Approximately one-third of the presidents in large French corporations are reported to 'descend from government/bureaucracy.' At least two studies, though now slightly outdated, have been published on the French case.[7] Table 7.2 is a summary and comparison of the French and Japanese practices. According to these studies, a noteworthy difference between France and Japan is the timing of the transfers: *amakudari* takes place at retirement, typically when the manager is in his 50s after almost 30 years of service; about 40 per cent of *pantouflage* is observed among bureaucrats with less than 10 years of service.[8]

Amakudari in Japan is more or less a postwar phenomenon. It is reported that a certain portion of prewar national government officials also obtained jobs in business or public corporations such as the Manchurian Railway Company, Korean Bank, or Formosan Bank. The number of such cases was not small in prewar Japan, but *amakudari* was not yet systematically established as a personnel management method.[9] As Tables 7.3, 7.4, and 7.5 show for the three ministries of this study, a substantial number of public corporations were established in the 1950s and 1960s. Although *amakudari* is not unique to postwar Japan, its social significance has greatly

---

[7] See Yve Jannin, 'Profil des administrateurs de contrôle des grandes sociétés françaises' (Profile of managing directors of large French firms), *Humanisme et enterprise*, No. 2 (1975).

[8] Ibid.

[9] A general structure of retirement behavior of career officials in both pre- and postwar Japan is thoroughly explained in Michio Muramatsu, *Sengo Nihon no kanryōsei* (Bureaucracy in postwar Japan) (Tokyo: Tōyō Keizai Shinpōsha, 1981), pp. 79–80.

Table 7.3 Public Corporations of the Ministry of Finance 1992

	Date of Establishment	Number of Managing Directors	Number of Employees
Central Bank for Commercial and Industrial Cooperatives	Nov. 30, 1936	11 (2)	5,643
People's Finance Corporation	June 1, 1949	8	4,702
Housing Loan Corporation	May 6, 1950	9	1,146
Export-Import Bank of Japan	Dec. 28, 1950	8	523
Japan Development Bank	April 20, 1951	10 (6)	1,086
Agriculture, Forestry, and Fisheries Finance Corporation	April 1, 1953	8	927
Small Business Finance Corporation	Aug. 20, 1953	8 (1)	1,721
Fund for Promotion and Development of Amami Islands	Sept. 10, 1955	3 (2)	27
Hokkaido-Tohoku Development Corporation	June 8, 1956	7 (1)	288
Finance Corporation of Local Public Enterprise	June 1, 1957	5	76
Small Business Credit Insurance Corporation	July 1, 1958	6 (1)	403
Environmental Sanitation Business Finance Corporation	Sept. 2, 1967	4 (1)	56
Okinawa Development Finance Corporation	May 15, 1972	5 (1)	223
Japan Tobacco Inc.	April 1, 1985	28 (1)	24,150
Total: 14 Public Corporations		120 (16)	40,971

Note: Numbers in parentheses are part-time directors not included in the official count.

Source: *Tokushu hōjin sōran* (Directory of public corporations) (Tokyo: Management and Coordination Agency, 1992).

increased in the past four decades because of its systematic and widespread practice in all ministries. Not until the 1960s was the word *amakudari* coined and used widely in everyday language.[10]

[10] A common understanding on the origins of this practice has not yet been reached. Chalmers Johnson and Kent Calder have pointed out the important momentum brought about by the National Total Mobilization Order after 1941. (See Chalmers Johnson, *Japan's Public Policy Companies* [Washington: American Enterprise Institute, 1978], p. 114, and Kent E. Calder, 'Elites in an Equalizing role: Ex-Bureaucrats as Coordinators and Intermediaries in the Japanese Government–Business Relationship,' *Comparative Politics*, Vol. 21, No. 4 [1989].) In a Japanese dictionary published in 1934 (Heibonsha's *Dai-jiten*), the word *amakudari* is listed as meaning only that 'a superior commands his men to do something, or an argot, meaning a strong recommendation from an authority.' However, the movement of government officials into the business sector was observed even in the Meiji period (1868–1912). Roan Uchida (1868–1929), a popular novelist and social critic, used the term *amakudaru* (whose noun form is *amakudari*) in this contemporary sense in his social criticism, titled *Shakai hyakumensō* (Society in kaleidoscope) published in 1902.

Table 7.4 Public Corporations of the Ministry of International Trade and Industry, 1992

	Date of Establishment	Number of Managing Directors	Number of Employees
Central Bank of Commercial and Industrial Cooperatives	Nov. 30, 1936	11 (2)	5,643
Electric Power Development Co., Ltd.	Sept. 16, 1952	21	2,739
Small Business Finance Corporation	Aug. 20, 1953	8 (1)	1,721
Japan Bicycle Racing Association	Oct. 1, 1957	8 (1)	273
Small Business Credit Insurance Corporation	July 1, 1958	6 (1)	403
Japan External Trade Organization	July 25, 1958	9	876
Institute of Developing Economies	July 1, 1960	5 (2)	259
Water Resource Development Corporation	May 1, 1962	11 (1)	1,905
Japan Motorcycle Racing Association	Oct. 1, 1962	5	77
Metal Mining Agency of Japan	May 20, 1963	6 (1)	215
Coal Mine Damage Corporation	July 1, 1963	7 (1)	330
Environmental Pollution Control Service Corporation	Oct. 1, 1965	5	180
Japan National Oil Corporation	Oct. 2, 1967	11	343
Pollution-Related Health Damage Compensation Association	June 10, 1974	3 (2)	71
Japan Regional Development Corporation	Aug. 1, 1974	13	722
Japan International Cooperation Agency	Aug. 1, 1974	12 (2)	1,064
Japan Small Business Corporation	Oct. 1, 1980	8 (1)	475
New Energy and Industrial Technology Development Organization	Oct. 1, 1980	11	742
Total: 18 Public Corporations		160 (15)	18,038

Note: Numbers in parentheses are part-time directors not included in the official count.

Source: *Tokushu hōjin sōran*, 1992.

Criticism of Amakudari

The mobility of retired officials to business or public corporations was called into question during the drafting of the National Public Service Law in 1947. The draft prepared by the General Headquarters (GHQ) of the Supreme Commander for the Allied Powers originally prohibited the transfer of retired officials to private business in the first two years after retirement. During revision of the draft, GHQ gave way to the Japanese government which insisted that *amakudari* to a 'representative'

Table 7.5 Public Corporations of the Ministry of Labor, 1992

	Date of Establishment	Number of Managing Directors	Number of Employees
Labor Welfare Corporation	July 1, 1957	6 (1)	13,084
Japan Institute of Labor	Sept. 15, 1958	5 (1)	133
Small Enterprise Retirement Allowance Mutual Aid Corporation	July 1, 1959	6	229
Employment Promotion Corporation	July 1, 1961	9 (1)	4,710
Retirement Allowance Mutual Aid Association for Construction, the Sake Brewing Industry, and Forestry	Oct. 1, 1981	6 (3)	68
Japanese National Railway Settlement Corporation	April 1, 1987	8	2,515
Total: 6 Public Corporations		40 (6)	20,739

Note: Numbers in parentheses are part-time directors not included in the official count.
Source: *Tokushu hōjin sōran*, 1992.

post in a private firm be prohibited only when the post was 'closely connected' to the post occupied in national government in the last five years of service.[11]

The law, however, contained overly ambiguous provisions concerning the distinction between permissible and impermissible cases of *amakudari*, and as a result it accelerated and systematized the practice so extensively as to cause severe attacks on *amakudari* from opposition parties in the Diet which claimed that *amakudari* had many negative effects.

First, they claimed, it tended to infringe on the autonomy of public corporations by keeping their operations within the influence of the central government. This negative effect may sometimes turn out to be positive, especially when the network of human resources between government officials and non-government sectors operates as an efficient means to disseminate information through the direct mobility of human resources. But when the problem of 'regulation' comes in, it is always difficult to avoid the collusion between officials and rent-seeking corporations or businesses that has caused many political scandals in postwar Japan. As is often pointed out, the real value of retired officials to a business firm exists in their network of connections in the bureaucracy, 'which make it possible for them to influence the way regulations are

[11] See Takashi Harada, 'Amakudari no motiv' (Motif of *amakudari*), *Soshiorogi* (Kyoto University), Vol. 34, No. 3 (Jan. 1990).

enforced. The bureaucrats, in turn, look forward to jobs in the industries they regulate.'[12]

A second negative effect identified by the opposition parties was that once a position (director or middle manager) has been held through *amakudari*, it tends to be occupied subsequently by retired officials from the same ministry (the so-called 'hereditary' property of *amakudari* positions). Such routinized political appointments from government to public corporations naturally lower the work incentive of capable staff members which would otherwise be enhanced by the system of internal promotion. Third, salaries received by retired officials working in public corporations are said to be too high, especially when these officials' productivity after retirement from central government is considered.

The practice of *amakudari* has been and still is severely criticized by the general public and mass media. Besides the negative effects mentioned above, critics point out the 'excessively' high salaries and retirement payments received by reemployed retired officials. Many expose-type books on *amakudari* have been published, either in the form of journalistic *reportage* or as 'true story' style novels.[13] The most steady and fierce attacks, however, come from the federation of labor unions of those public corporations obliged to receive new managers from among retired central government officials. This federation since 1972 has published annual white papers on *amakudari* and disclosed statistical data and documents concerning labor disputes related to *amakudari* practices. These white papers frequently criticize the undemocratic personnel management policies in the bureaucracy, the unreasonable practice of making Diet members out of bureaucrats, the halfhearted effort to train young managers in public corporations, and, above all, possible collaboration between politicians and the bureaucracy and between the bureaucracy and business.

These arguments have brought about a number of political attacks from opposition parties in the Diet, which in turn have resulted in several decisions by the cabinet. Examples of these decisions are: (1) a reduction in the number of directors in public corporations by 20 per cent (August 25, 1981); (2) a reduction in the percentage of *amakudari* directors to less than half the total number of directors (December 18, 1979); (3) prohibition of multistep transfers of retired officials among public corporations

[12] This quotation is taken from an article in *This is Yomiuri*, (Nov. 1992), pp. 52–61. (An English translation appeared in *Japan Echo*, [Spring 1993].)
[13] Well-known and readily available examples are as follows: Kiyoshi Asai, *Yakunin no seitai* (Life mode of government officials) (Tokyo: Gakuyō Shobō, 1971); Taisuke Yuki, *Shōsetsu Ōkurashō* (The Ministry of Finance: A novel) (Tokyo: Bungei Shunjū-sha, 1971); Nihon no Kanryo Kenkyūkai, ed., *Oyakunin sōjūhō* (How to control bureaucrats) (Tokyo: Nihon Keizai Shinbunsha, 1971); Shin Sataka, *Nihon kanryō hakusho* (White paper on civil servants in Japan) (Tokyo: Kōdansha, 1986). One example written from the point of view of a retired high official is Saburō Ōkita, *Nihon kanryō jijō* (Situations of Japanese bureaucrats) (Tokyo: TBS Britanica, 1984).

with a one-time exception only when definitely necessary (December 18, 1979); (4) age limits on directors (65), with a limit of 70 for presidents and vice presidents of public corporations (December 23, 1977); and (5) limits on the length of service of these directors to six years for general directors and eight years for presidents and vice presidents (December 23, 1977).

These cabinet decisions seem to have had almost no binding force and have brought few results consistent with these decisions. In particular, decisions (2) and (3) have not been strictly observed, although the practices they are supposed to regulate began to decline slowly in the late 1980s. The *amakudari* rate (the number of *amakudari* directors divided by the total) dropped from 65.9 per cent in January 1985 to 56.5 per cent in February 1991. The so-called 'migratory bird' type of transfer reaping multiple retirement payments decreased slightly from 30 cases to 26.

Rational Aspects of Amakudari

Other arguments, however, have attempted to rationalize this practice from the point of view of human resource management. It is maintained, for instance, that the efficient and flexible operation of public corporations requires an infusion of valuable human resources, with broad and deep knowledge of regulations and administration, from the national government. These resources are particularly valuable when public corporations are subject to governmental control and regulation, which in turn require repeated negotiations with relevant ministries.

The merits of this practice to the receiving organization are similar to the demerits already mentioned. In *private* companies that employ retired government officials, for example, a new manager who has 'descended' from the central government and is well acquainted with bureaucratic 'esoterics' usually does have close ties with officials in the ministry. These ties constitute a real asset both as information channel and as human resource.

Another important aspect of *amakudari* is that it contributes to the vitality of the bureaucratic organization by creating an incentive mechanism in the personnel management of bureaucrats. The level of salaries earned by officials *before* retirement from a ministry is definitely low compared to the private sector, and salary differentials among and within various ministries are virtually non-existent because nearly all salaries are regulated and standardized by the salary revision scheme of the National Personnel Authority.[14] *Amakudari*, therefore, can be considered as a form

[14] In this context a comparison of *average* salaries earned by government officials and in the private business sector in general does not make much sense. It must be a comparison between salaries earned by officials (which vary little anyway) and the upper half or the first quartile of salary distribution in the business sector. The best and brightest, if they do not go

of deferred compensation whose values are determined on the basis of two factors: the officials' actual performance in ministries, and the rank or prestige of various ministries.[15] This hypothesis is further explored in the remainder of this paper. If found tenable, it will confirm the existence of an incentive mechanism in the *amakudari* practice for both young and middle-aged bureaucrats, which is thought to make competition within public office more effective. And it can be maintained that the total present value of compensation earned by 'descending' officials between their retirement from government and retirement from the final job in their careers should be considered a cost of vitalizing the bureaucratic system by incorporating a competitive mechanism, even if it may not be a payment for their 'productive' service after retirement.

According to this hypothesis, the greatest merit of *amakudari* to society, in spite of its demerits, lies in its effects in building an incentive mechanism into the government employment system, regardless of what *amakudari* officials do after obtaining their second jobs post-retirement.[16]

General Trends and Structure of *Amakudari*

This section provides an overall picture of *amakudari* and its change over time.[17] Out of the total of approximately 780 managing directors in public corporations as of February 1991, about 410 came from the central ministries and 122 were considered to be 'migrant' high officials who obtained these jobs as the second or third in their careers. The number of these 'migratory' ex-officials did not decline over the 1980s, in spite of the various cabinet decisions enumerated above, but rather increased in absolute number.

One aspect of my hypothesis is that the higher one's final post in a ministry at the time of retirement, the higher one's post in a public corporation[18] and the longer one's stay in this corporation. One simple indicator that can be used to test a necessary condition of this hypothesis is the length of service in the second (*amakudari*) job. It is unambiguously

into public service, go into business after graduating from top-notch universities and generally earn higher salaries than the average salaries in business.

[15] The initial deployment (who goes to which ministry) is determined by the results of the National Public Service Examination, which consequently forms a ranking of ministries through this screening process.

[16] This point is mentioned in Tuvia Blumenthal, 'The Practice of Amakudari with the Japanese Employment System,' *Asian Survey*, Vol. 25, No. 3 (March 1985). Blumenthal, however, does not explicitly mention the concept of 'deferred payment.'

[17] See Muramatsu, *Sengo Nihon no kanryōsei*, pp. 78–82.

[18] This 'law' is also pointed out by Aoki, who writes: 'Obviously, the longer a bureaucrat survives in the ranking hierarchy of the ministry, the better are his/her prospects for post-bureaucrat *amakudari* positions. Thus *amakudari* positions are provided as the final prize in the competition among bureaucrats in the ranking hierarchy.' See Masahiko Aoki, *Information, Incentives, and Bargaining in the Japanese Economy* (Cambridge: Cambridge University Press, 1987), p. 266.

observable that there is a significant difference in the length of service between the president/vice president group and the ordinary director group: the average length of service in the former group was 44 months as of February 1991 while the latter was 30 months (see Table 7.6). The number of former presidents and vice presidents whose length of service exceeded 73 months (i.e., more than six years) was 16 while the number of directors staying longer than 73 months was reported to be only 3. The average age of ordinary directors was 56.4, while that of presidents and vice presidents was 61.0 and 35 per cent were over age 60 (see Table 7.6).

As mentioned in the previous section, reduction in the number of managing directors was one of the pressing issues of administrative reform in the 1980s. This task, however, was not sufficiently achieved in the 1980s. Although the number of public corporations decreased from 111 to 92 between 1979 and 1989, full-time managing directors decreased only slightly from 787 to 775 during the same period.

The ministries providing the largest numbers of *amakudari* officials to public corporations (as of 1991) are MITI (60), the Ministry of Agriculture, Forestry, and Fisheries (43), and MOF (28) (see Table 7.7). The Ministry of Labor and the Ministry of Foreign Affairs show smaller numbers, 18 and 14, respectively. MOL and the Ministry of Transport hold assured, vested posts in certain public corporations where as many as 90 per cent of directors' positions are occupied by high officials descending from these ministries. In this respect, MOL and the Ministry of Transport are exceptional. It is also interesting to note that *amakudari* is not frequently found in the Ministry of Foreign Affairs, where most career officials retire at approximately age 62 or 63, after having served as ambassadors stationed in more than three countries.

In this chapter I have selected MOF, MITI, and MOL as three typical ministries to study in greater detail to determine the inflow of retired officials to public corporations, particularly the timing, and their length of stay and remuneration as directors. Each ministry has a certain number of public corporations within its oversight, though some are overseen jointly by more than one ministry. Tables 7.3 to 7.7 present basic data on all public corporations under the supervision of the three ministries studied here. The number of directors indicated in these tables does not reflect the total number of posts occupied within each ministry since some corporations are managed jointly by more than one ministry.

MOF, MITI, and MOL

The testable hypothesis presented here is divided into two propositions that can be explained using Figures 7.1 and 7.2.[19]

---

[19] Some officials retire from the government at an early stage in their careers (from around their early 40s) and change their places of employment several times. These individuals are

Table 7.6 Average Length of Service and Average Age of Directors in Public Corporations (as of February 1, 1991)

Type of Public Corporation	Number of Public Corporations	Presidents & Vice Presidents			Ordinary Managing Directors		
		Number of Persons	Average Length of Service (Mos.)	Average Age	Number of Persons	Average Length of Service (Mos.)	Average Age
Large-scale Public Investment	13	25 (25)	32	60.2	80 (92)	28	56.1
Medium-scale Public Investment	17	28 (28)	36	61.5	79 (92)	30	57.3
Public Credit Institution	9	15 (15)	39	61.7	43 (45)	24	56.3
Cooperative Finance and External Banking	3	6 (6)	35	63.0	19 (24)	24	56.5
Metropolitan Transit	1	2 (2)	59	63.5	6 (11)	24	56.9
Cigarette, Railroad, Etc.	12	20 (33)	69	58.1	35 (195)	42	55.1
Others	37	40 (45)	45	62.9	113 (164)	31	57.5
Total	92	136 (154)	44	61.0	375 (623)	30	56.4

Note: All figures are those identified by the Federation of Unions of Public Corporations. Figures in parentheses are total number officially reported.

Source: Amakudari hakusho (White paper on *amakudari*) (Tokyo: Seirōren, 1992).

Table 7.7 *Amakudari* and Internally Promoted Officers in Public Corporations (October 1, 1991)

Ministries Sending Officials to Public Corporations	Amakudari		Internally Promoted	
	No.	%	No.	%
Construction	23	82.1	5	17.9
Agriculture, Forestry, and Fisheries	43	82.7	6	11.5
Science and Technology	12	50.0	10	41.7
Finance	28	63.6	16	36.4
Education	19	76.0	2	8.0
International Trade and Industry	60	78.9	13	17.1
Labor	18	90.0	2	10.0
Health and Welfare	15	83.3	1	5.6
Foreign Affairs	14	82.4	2	11.8
Transport	25	96.2	0	0

Note: Because the origins of some officers are unknown or they are from the private business sector, the percentages for some agencies or ministries do not necessarily add up to 100.

Source: *Amakudari hakusho*, 1992.

1. There exists an order or sequence of retirement that is essentially determined by internal competition within each ministry. The sequence has, at least among career officials, one regularity: the timing of the transfer from the central government to an outside corporation comes late as long as one continues to win in this internal competition (Figure 7.1).

2. The higher the final post in a ministry, the longer the stay in a public corporation. This relation was quantitatively verified, though not completely, in the previous section: the job tenure of president is on average longer than that of an ordinary director. This holds true for remuneration as well: when one's final post in a ministry is high, remuneration in a public corporation is also high (Figure 7.2). This constitutes one of the conditions necessary to sustain the theory that *amakudari* is a form of deferred payment to reward competition in the bureaucratic hierarchy.

Promotion and the Process of 'Attrition'

Before investigating specific cases of *amakudari* to public corporations, it may be useful to present, as an example, a so-called promotion model for career bureaucrats within MOF. As one climbs higher up the ladder of promotion, fewer of one's peers will be left in the ministry and competi-

not included in this comparison, which focuses only on a more or less 'elite' group of officials who successfully remained in office even after their 50s.

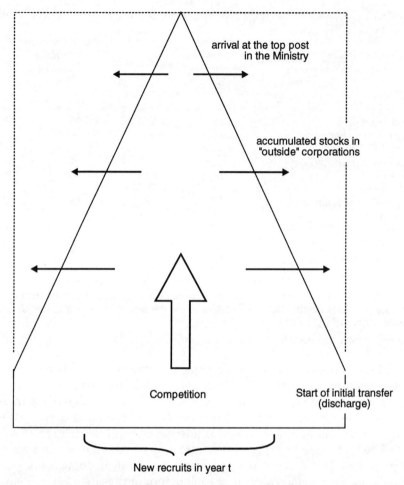

arrival at the top post
in the Ministry

accumulated stocks in
"outside" corporations

Competition

Start of initial transfer
(discharge)

New recruits in year t

Fig. 7.1. Competition and Exclusion Process 'Inside' and 'Outside' Central Ministries

tion grows keener. The shaded area in Figure 7.3 roughly corresponds to the accumulated stock of retired bureaucrats who leave MOF each year.

Let us now consider four cases of *amakudari* from ministries to different public corporations. Case 1 (Table 7.8) is from MOF to the People's Finance Corporation, established in 1949 to finance small amounts of money to the general public for cost of living expenses or education and administered by the Banking Bureau in MOF. There are eight managing directors in the People's Finance Corporation and four of these positions, including the president and vice president, are filled through *amakudari*. The remaining four directors are promoted internally. In this case we can clearly confirm our hypotheses concerning the age of retirement and

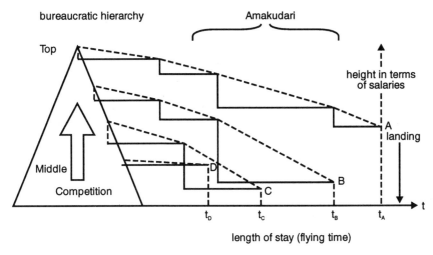

Fig. 7.2. Economic Structure of *Amakudari:* Length and Height of Compensation

Table 7.8 *Amakudari* from the Ministry of Finance to the People's Finance Corporation (October 31, 1990)

Post in the People's Finance Corporation	Age at Retirement from MOF	Present Age	Estimated Monthly Salary (¥)	Post at Retirement
President	58	60	1,275,000	Vice Minister
Vice President	58	59	1,047,000	MOF to Secretary of Tax Administration Agency
Director	50	54	875,000	Councilor of Secretariat and Chief of MITI's Basic Industries Bureau
Director	52	55	875,000	Head of Tokyo Taxation Bureau

Source: Amakudari hakusho, 1992, and *Shokuinroku* (Directory of government employees) (Tokyo: Ministry of Finance Printing Office, various issues).

salaries offered by this corporation. (Note that one of the directors comes from MITI.)

Case 2 (Table 7.9) may serve as an example of several *amakudari* posts occupied by officials from two ministries, i.e., MITI and MOF, in the Japan Regional Development Corporation, which was established for development of local cities and industries in 1974. It is noteworthy that the last director listed in Table 7.9 moved to this corporation in his early 40s as a middle manager and was promoted internally to the post of managing

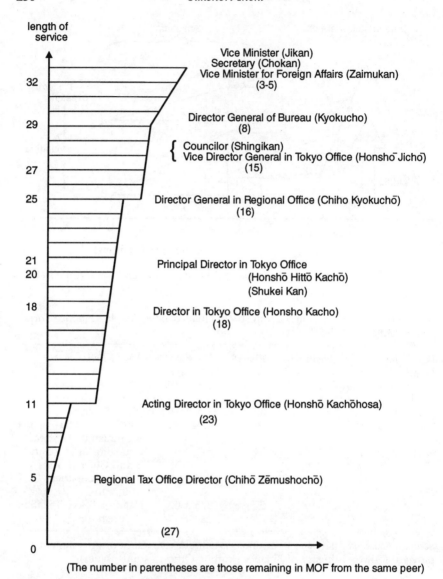

Fig. 7.3. Promotion Model: The Ministry of Finance

director. The data on all other directors support my basic hypotheses that
the more highly promoted ministry officers tend to be assigned to higher
posts in public corporations in the *later* stages of their careers.

Case 3 (Table 7.10) is an informative example that verifies the differential treatment existing among different corporations administered by the

Table 7.9 *Amakudari* from MITI and MOF to the Japan Regional Development Corporation (October 31, 1990)

Present Post in the Japan Regional Development Corporation	Age at Retirement	Retired from	Present Age	Estimated Monthly Salary (¥)	Career and Post at Retirement
President	57	MOF	63	1,275,000	MOF → Vice Minister of National Land Agency[b]
Director	50	MOF	51	875,000	MOF → Superintendent of National Tax College
Director	51	MITI	52	875,000	Councilor of MITI Secretariat
Director	55	EPA[a]	57	875,000	MITI → EPA Councilor
Director	early 50s	MITI	62	875,000	MITI → middle manager of Japan Regional Development Corporation

Notes:
[a] EPA = Economic Planning Agency
[b] The arrows → indicate a change of office.

Source: See Table 7.8.

Table 7.10 *Amakudari* from MITI to Coal Mine Damage Corporation (October 31, 1990)

Present Post in the Coal Mine Damage Corporation	Age at Retirement	Present Age	Estimated Monthly Salary (¥)	Post at Retirement
Chairman	52	59	1,104,000	Head of Coal Division of Agency of Natural Resources and Energy, MITI
Vice Chairman	49	54	983,000	Councilor of Secretariat, National Land Agency
Director	50	54	850,000	Director of Inspection Institute, MITI
Director	44	61	850,000	Deputy Chief of Coal Planning Section, Coal and Mining Bureau, MITI
Councilor	?	59	665,000	Budgeting Inspector, Budget Bureau, MOF

Source: See Table 7.8.

Table 7.11 *Amakudari* from the Ministry of Labor to the Employment Promotion Corporation (October 31, 1990)

Present Position in the Employment Promotion Corporation	Age at Retirement from MOL	Present Age	Estimated Monthly Salary (¥)	Post at Retirement
Chairman of the Board of Directors	58	63	1,104,000	Vice Minister
Vice Chairman	54	57	983,000	Secretary General of Labor Relations, Commission for Public Corporations
Director	?	58	850,000	Division Head of Labor Market Center in Employment Security Bureau
Director	52	54	850,000	Secretary General of Central Labor Relations Commission
Director	54	59	850,000	Labor Standards Bureau, Director of Hyogo Office
Director	?	56	850,000	Secretary General, Central Labor Relations Commission
Director	52	52	850,000	Secretary General, Central Labor Relations Commission
Director	51	53	850,000	Division Head, Tax Administration Agency, MOF

Source: See Table 7.8.

same ministry. The chairman in Case 3 left MITI for the Coal Mine Damage Corporation at the age of 52 and earns a lower salary than the chairman or president of other large corporations. Furthermore, the vice chairman and directors of the Coal Mine Damage Corporation all left MITI at earlier periods in their careers. However, the overall results listed in Case 3 still confirm the basic hypothesis.

The Ministry of Labor has only six public corporations under its supervision, but the percentage of *amakudari* officials in these six ranks as one of the highest among all the ministries. Case 4 (Table 7.11) describes the situation in the Employment Promotion Corporation which has nine full-time managing director posts, seven of which are occupied by *amakudari* officials from MOL. The former vice minister of MOL obtained the position of chairman in this corporation at the age of 58, though his salary is not as high as the salary of chairmen of some other public corporations.

What we have observed in these four cases supports the hypothesis presented in the previous section. *Amakudari* to public corporations, therefore, can be considered as a form of deferred compensation whose values are determined on the basis of two factors: the actual performance as officials in ministries, and the rank or political importance of their ministries. In this essay, however, it has been possible only to show that necessary conditions for our hypothesis are being satisfied. Thus we cannot reject the hypothesis that *amakudari* is a device to vitalize bureaucratic organization by inducing early retirement, and the data do not contradict the proposition that the levels of salaries earned by *amakudari* officials in public corporations can be a form of deferred compensation according to the performance of each official and the relevant prestige of his ministry.

Policy Implications

No economic system can operate properly without appropriate steering by the central government, though the degree of steering, i.e., intervention, is a major policy issue in the effort to balance economic freedom and equality. It goes without saying, however, that the central government definitely needs rich human resources who possess high intellect and public virtues to provide proper judgment on external as well as domestic policy issues.

In order to obtain such rich human resources, the Japanese government has recruited able young graduates from prestigious universities. Finding talented candidates, however, is never sufficient to maintaining the effective functioning of the bureaucracy. It is important to have a system that can train and stimulate these competent young bureaucrats by giving proper incentives to turn their abilities into performance. Otherwise, any new recruit's potential would wither without being proven and the whole bureaucracy would suffer from inefficiency and corruption. In this sense, *amakudari* vitalizes human resources in the bureaucracy by its built-in mechanism of a deferred payment element and early retirement, both of which seem to provide strong incentives to actualize the potentially rich resources in the Japanese bureaucracy. At the very end of their careers, officials' efforts and subsequent rewards will have secured their financial standing, and their social status and lifetime economic conditions will coincide. Despite the negative aspects outlined earlier, *amakudari* contains an implicit mechanism that can attract the most capable members of the labor force who are endowed with intelligence and public virtue, by providing them with proper compensation for their performance in ministries.

Needless to say, there are at least two kinds of costs in the practice of *amakudari*. One is favoritism on the part of the official toward the private company to which he is about to 'descend' (which results in government–business collusion). This cost will definitely distort the system of fair competition and it is hard to avoid this cost unless the official is fully conscious of fairness and public virtue. A second cost lies in the agencies that receive former officials. Because of the political appointments from outside, the morale of employees in these agencies is greatly reduced. Some public corporations are said to have been established mainly to create employment opportunities for retiring officials.

In this respect, the *amakudari* system does incur certain costs to the entire society. Considering, however, the various benefits this system assures to society such as the high morale and morality of the officials, we can surmise that the benefits may exceed the costs, and the problem is thus how to calculate these costs and quantitatively compare them with the total benefits *amakudari* assures. In sum, unless we can contrive any other compensation mechanism alternative to *amakudari* (such as a higher and more differentiated salary structure), we must admit that the *amakudari* system plays certain positive roles in human resource allocation between government and non-government sectors and in the proper functioning of the entire bureaucracy.

8

Administrative Reform

MITSUTOSHI ITO

Since the end of World War II, the Japanese government has carried out significant administrative reform three times: in 1949, the 1960s, and the 1980s. These reforms were attempts to limit the size of government, increase the efficiency of administration, and promote economic development. Small, efficiently managed government has been a vital factor in Japan's economic growth.

For government agencies, administrative reform means adapting to changes in the environment in order to justify their continued existence. It is difficult for a government agency to justify maintaining its policies—even maintaining the agency itself—if demand for them has declined, and changing an agency's policies enables it to respond to changes in the environment. However, adapting to change is not easy for government agencies, particularly when reform reduces the scale of the organization. Administrative agencies in any country have a tendency to maintain or expand their size and thus face a dilemma when confronted with administrative reform.

The incentive to resolve this dilemma comes from outside the administrative agency, usually from political executives (in the case of Japan, the prime minister). The responses of government agencies to outside pressures for reform are varied: some respond positively to such demands; others resist administrative reform, forcing the intervention of political executives; still others may succeed in avoiding change.

Japan's experience with administrative reform demonstrates the diversity of agencies' responses to reform. In this essay, I briefly explain the characteristics and history of the administrative reforms carried out in Japan since World War II, and then focus on the drastic administrative reform of the 1980s, giving examples of some of the agencies reformed. It is significant that the thoroughgoing reform of the 1980s was actually carried out, albeit not perfectly successfully, despite the presence of both political and administrative vested interests in government.

The Politics of Administrative Reform

Administrative reform in Japan has included measures to curb the number of personnel and size of budget for individual government agencies, to simplify regulations in order to improve administrative efficiency, and to reduce the authority of ministries with respect to permits and licenses. Government agencies, however, perceive issues such as their orientation and organization as well as the behavior of their bureaucrats as areas of their own concern and, by nature, they tend to avoid reform or at least try to maintain the status quo.[1] However, continued efforts to maintain or expand a government organization are not always easy, because only limited resources, particularly financial resources, are available for the government as a whole. The Ministry of Finance (MOF), which is responsible for government finance, tries to check the growth of each ministry during the budget-drafting process.

The primary means of overcoming this bureaucratic inertia is intervention by political executives, who forcibly demand that bureaucrats reform their organizations and policies. The politicians' motive is the acquisition and expansion of political power. By incorporating administrative reform into political platforms, they make it an important political issue, and through its realization they increase their control over government and their ability to stay in power. While the bureaucracy has a narrow range of clients, the constituencies of leading political executives, such as the prime minister, are a broad range of the general public.[2] Voters see administrative reform as a means of lightening their own burdens and are eager to support reform efforts. The prime minister thus has both legal authority and popular support in attempting to reform the bureaucratic system. Government agencies are given the right to autonomy only within the scope of (implicit) commission, and only if they act in anticipation of and accordance with the prime minister's interests in a particular policy area.[3]

Another effective resource available to the prime minister in guiding administrative reform is the so-called 'state-maintenance ministries' or 'coordinating agencies.' In Japan, these are MOF and the Administrative Management Agency (precursor of today's General Affairs Agency). Unlike 'line ministries' (e.g., the Ministry of International Trade and Industry

---

[1] Masahiko Aoki, *Information, Incentives and Bargaining in the Japanese Economy* (Cambridge: Cambridge University Press, 1988), pp. 268–9; B. Guy Peters, *Comparing Public Bureaucracies: Problems of Theory and Method* (Tuscaloosa: University of Alabama Press, 1988), pp. 146–7; Joel D. Aberbach, Robert D. Putnam, and Bert A. Rockman, *Bureaucrats and Politicians in Western Democracies* (Cambridge, Mass.: Harvard University Press, 1981), pp. 241–2.

[2] Peters, *Comparing Public Bureaucracies*, pp. 146–7, 175–6; Aberbach *et al.*, *Bureaucrats and Politicians*, pp. 224, 241–2.

[3] Samuel Kernell, 'The Primacy of Politics in Economic Policy,' in Kernell, ed., *Parallel Politics: Economic Policymaking in Japan and the United States* (Washington: The Brookings Institution, 1991), pp. 370–2.

and the Ministry of Transportation) and social service ministries, they are more sensitive to the intentions of political executives.[4] MOF, which is relatively free of clientelism, provides stable financial management. The Administrative Management Agency endeavors to engender an efficient, well-coordinated administration. These coordinating agencies constitute part of a policy network and the information they gather is a political resource that weakens the line ministries' monopoly on information. Provisional committees installed by the prime minister for administrative reform have also been part of this policy network.[5]

In responding to pressures from political executives, line ministries in return rely on ruling-party Diet members and interest groups as clients to help defend their agencies. The union of these three groups resembles the iron triangles seen in the United States or what we can consider small, semi-independent 'sub-governments.' Ruling-party Diet members can sometimes limit the leadership of the prime minister, who is dependent on support from ruling-party Diet members and factions. On the other hand, the prime minister can to some extent control ruling-party Diet members because of his authority to support specific candidates in elections and to distribute posts.

The establishment by law of the Provisional Committee for Administrative Reform was a device to circumvent the pluralism of the ruling party and the central government as well as to centralize power. In the political process of administrative reform in the 1980s, the coalition of the prime minister, MOF, and business (plus salaried city-dwellers who represent the majority of the people) were rivals with the sub-governments or iron triangles.[6] Which policy of which ministry is subjected to administrative reform, and to what extent, is a function of the political process and involves various factors such as the visibility of issues and the importance of a particular clientele as a constituency of the ruling party.

Ministries have developed three methods for coping with the dilemma of whether to maintain the status quo or modify their policies. One response is to carry out the policy reform, including cutbacks in financial and other resources, and adapt the organization to changes in the environment. This pattern of 'anticipated reaction' avoids outright intervention by top political executives in the policy and personnel affairs of the ministry. In this pattern, it is relatively easy to preserve the ministry's autonomy. The 1980s reform of the pension system, discussed below, was a good example of this pattern. In the second pattern for coping with this dilemma, ministries fail to adequately respond to external change and

---

[4] Peters, *Comparing Public Bureaucracies*, pp. 151–2, 175–6; Aberbach *et al.*, *Bureaucrats and Politicians*, pp. 210–11.

[5] Peters, *Comparing Public Bureaucracies*, pp. 128, 167.

[6] As for the political coalition model, see Cathie Jo Martin, 'Business Influence and State Power: The Case of U.S. Corporate Tax Policy,' *Politics and Society*, Vol. 17, No. 2 (1989).

reform is carried out by political power. This pattern is illustrated in the privatization process of the Japanese National Railways in the 1980s. And in a third pattern, ministries manage to maintain their organizations without major reform. In the administrative reform in the 1960s, for example, a budget bureau directly affiliated with the prime minister was proposed to facilitate comprehensive coordination of policies. MOF strongly opposed this bureau, which would have removed budget formulation from MOF control, and this item was eventually excluded from the proposal.[7] The attitudes of ministries toward administrative reform depend on the political resources available to them and their recognition of the political process concerning the issue facing them.

The political and administrative systems of Japan have gradually become pluralistic. Individual ministries have been given certain discretionary powers and autonomy, and, together with Diet members and interest groups, they constitute the sub-government. However, if they fail to respond to environmental changes by modifying their policies or organization, the prime minister will at times modify the policy or organization in the name of administrative reform. This occurred to a certain extent in the administrative reform of the 1980s. This interplay of bureaucratic and political forces has been evident throughout Japan's postwar administrative reform efforts.

Earlier Administrative Reforms in the Postwar Period

The Japanese bureaucracy has been highly efficient since the Meiji Restoration of 1868,[8] a condition attributable both to historical factors and to the achievements of early administrative reform. The Japanese government has been successful in containing the size of its bureaucracy. Let us briefly examine how administrative agencies have changed since World War II and what kind of administrative reform the government has carried out. Generally speaking, changes in Japan's postwar administrative system have occurred in four phases:[9] institutionalization (from 1945 to the mid-1950s); expansion (from the mid-1950s to the mid-1960s); restraint (from the mid-1960s until the early 1970s); and large-scale reform (1980s).

During the early years of institutionalization (when Japan was occupied by Allied forces, 1945–52), a new constitution was promulgated, the old authoritarian prewar systems such as the Ministry of Internal Affairs and

[7] Kaoru Ōta, *Yakunin o kiru* (A dissection and criticism of bureaucrats) (Tokyo: Tōyō Keizai Shinpōsha, 1980), pp. 42–8.

[8] T. J. Pempel, *Policy and Politics in Japan: Creative Conservatism* (Philadelphia: Temple University Press, 1982), pp. 255–95.

[9] Gyōsei Kanri Kenkyūkai, *Gendai gyōsei zenshū 3, gyōsei kanri* (The complete works of contemporary administration, Vol. 3: Administrative management) (Tokyo: Gyōsei, 1984), pp. 38–66.

the military were abolished, a parliamentary system was established that made the Diet the highest organ of state power, bureaucrats became servants not to the emperor but to the people, and it was determined that the rules and regulations governing administrative agencies would be made by laws enacted by the Diet. In other words, various systems of administration were democratized. In the latter half of this period, the administrative agencies that would become the Prime Minister's Office, the Ministry of Justice, the Economic Planning Agency, the Ministry of Home Affairs, and the Self-Defense Force were established or their organizational status was raised. Thus, basic administrative agencies in postwar Japan were institutionalized in this period.

During the first years of the Allied Occupation of Japan, Japan rapidly increased the money supply (i.e., printed currency) to grant subsidies to such key industries as coal, iron and steel, and electric power. The result was rampant inflation in the 1945–49 period. Against this background, the 'Dodge Line' was adopted in 1949. Named for Joseph M. Dodge, the US banker dispatched to Japan by the Truman administration, the major objective of the Dodge Line was to adopt a single, stable exchange rate by controlling inflation, thereby establishing basic conditions for the expansion of Japan's foreign trade and industrial production. To realize this objective, Japan stopped providing key industries with direct financial assistance. Through these measures and also by maintaining a balanced budget, inflation was held in check.[10]

The Dodge Line meant the conversion of postwar economic rehabilitation from a controlled economy to a free-market economy.[11] From that time on, industrial funds were no longer provided directly by the government, but by banks in the private sector. As part of the 1949 administrative reform that was part of the Dodge Line, many employees in the public sector were dismissed to reduce expenditures. Immediately after the war, the Japanese government had recruited veterans and civilians who had been demobilized or returned to Japan from abroad, and had increased the number of administrative personnel to carry out economic control. However, under a restrictive fiscal policy adopted in 1949 by the Yoshida administration, the number of administrative personnel was reduced from 1,600,000 to 1,400,000. Labor unions resisted in vain the dismissal of 160,000 civil servants. In addition, the number of bureaus within each ministry was reduced by 30 per cent on average. The number of personnel was reduced again in 1951 and 1954, also under Prime Minister Yoshida.[12]

[10] See Kozo Yamamura, *Economic Policy in Postwar Japan* (Berkeley: University of California Press, 1967), pp. 29–31, for further discussion and details of the Dodge Line.
[11] Kimihiro Masamura, *Sengoshi*, Vol. 1 (Postwar history) (Tokyo: Chikuma Shobō, 1985), pp. 230–44.
[12] Gyōsei Kanri Kenkyūkai, *Gendai gyōsei zenshū 3*, p. 46.

Temporary economic and social crises, including an increase in the number of unemployed, occurred as a result of the government's deflationary policy. Enterprises surviving these crises in the early postwar period became the major driving force for rapid economic growth in later years.

A balanced budget policy was the basic financial principle of the conservative administration until Keynesian deficit finance was introduced in the mid-1960s. The Dodge Line played an important role in controlling growth in the size of the government. By keeping the financial scale of the government at a low level, funds were made available to the private sector, thus becoming an important stimulus for rapid economic growth. The small shares of defense and social security expenditures made it possible to limit the financial scale of the government.[13]

After the mid-1950s when tax revenues rose steadily because of the rapid economic growth that followed the Korean War, the size of the government was expanded, due to the new administrative agencies established to help Japan catch up with Western nations in terms of social capital and the level of welfare. For example, the organ that later became the Economic Planning Agency gained agency status (1955); the Atomic Energy Commission, the Agency of Science and Technology, and the Pension Bureau of the Ministry of Health and Welfare were established in 1956, 1956, and 1959, respectively; the Prime Minister's Office was separated from the cabinet and the posts of Director General of Administrative Affairs and Deputy Director General of Administrative Affairs were established (1960); the Agency of Local Autonomy became the Ministry of Home Affairs (1960); and many public corporations were established in order to expand the social capital.

The 1960s brought Japan continued rapid economic growth, and in 1964 Japan acquired Article 8 status in the International Monetary Fund. With this development, the Japanese market was opened further to outside firms, requiring Japanese enterprises to increase their international competitiveness. During the same period, business leaders had begun to feel that delayed rationalization in the public sector, compared to advances in the private sector, were major obstacles to further economic growth. For example, the burdensome customs procedures for imported products was a roadblock for industries, and they asked the government to simplify administrative procedures and increase administrative efficiency. Business leaders also requested a general reduction in the number of government personnel, while demanding enactment of a law that would permit the flexible reallocation of human resources so that the personnel of government agencies in charge of economic development—the

---

[13] The shares of defense and social security expenditures in total account expenditures were 9.4 and 13.3 per cent, respectively, in 1960. Yukio Noguchi, *Zaisei kiki no kōzō* (The structure of fiscal crisis) (Tokyo: Tōyō Keizai Shinposha, 1980), pp. 162–3.

Ministry of International Trade and Industry, for instance—could be increased.

With this strong impetus for rationalization in the public sector, the Administrative Council on several occasions made proposals for increased flexibility in administration, simplification of administrative management, increased efficiency, and reduction of expenditures, to live up to ever-increasing administrative needs. Unfortunately, however, few of these proposals for administrative reform were put into practice. In 1960, under the Ikeda administration, the Fifth Administrative Council had proposed the establishment of the authoritative First Provisional Administrative Reform Council (FPARC), which was modeled after the Hoover Commission of the United States, in order to carry out drastic administrative reform. FPARC, established in 1961, attempted to address many of the concerns of business in its proposal,[14] submitted to the government in 1964. The proposal stressed the need to reinforce the general coordination function of the central government through establishment of the Cabinet's Office, to restrain expansion of the size of government, and to promote efficiency of administrative management.

In the late 1960s, some of the proposals made by FPARC were put into practice. To limit the size of government, two important devices were introduced. The first was the enactment of a law to abolish one bureau in each ministry, under the order of Prime Minister Satō in 1968. As a result, 18 of the total 120 bureaus were abolished. After that, the so-called 'scrap and build' system was established under which no new bureau could be established to respond to any socio-economic change, unless a comparable bureau of diminished need or relevance was abolished. Under this system, the number of bureaus in the central government remained more or less the same, except for the increases caused by establishment of the Environment Agency (1971) and the National Land Agency (1974). Some have criticized this system as irrational, in that there was no prioritization among ministries and agencies in abolishing one bureau in each ministry or agency. However, because of the equity of making each ministry choose one bureau to abolish, this system effectively mitigated resistance from bureaucrats.

Another device to limit the size of the government was the Law Concerning the Number of Personnel in Administrative Agencies (May 1969). Before its enactment, the number of personnel in each administrative agency had been determined by the law governing it. Under the new law, however, the total number of national service personnel employed in all

---

[14] Atsushi Sato, 'Sō-teiin ho no seiritsu to gyōsei kaikaku' (The enactment of the law concerning the number of personnel in administrative agencies and administrative reform), *Juristo*, No. 429 (Aug. 1, 1969); Bakuji Ari *et al.*, 'Discussion: Gyōsei kokka no isō' (The situation of the administrative state), pp. 6–30, and Hirobumi Uzawa *et al.*, 'Discussion: Gyōsei kaikaku' (Administrative reform), pp. 86–112, *Jurisuto, Zōkan sōgō tokushū*, No. 29 (1983).

ministries and agencies was fixed, and the number of personnel employed in each ministry or agency was determined by government ordinance. This allowed the government to reallocate personnel quickly and flexibly in response to changes in administrative need. Coupled with this law, a personnel reduction plan was implemented to prevent the expansion of the number of government personnel. The first step of this plan was begun in 1967, followed by several subsequent steps in later years. Through this plan, surplus personnel generated as a result of rationalization and increasing efficiency were pooled and reallocated to agencies where additional human resources were needed to respond to increasing administrative needs. As a result, the number of personnel working in all administrative agencies was reduced from 899,333 in 1967 to 887,022 in 1983. The number of personnel in almost all government agencies was reduced, although there were increases in national universities (about 28,000) and national hospitals (about 7,800). Since the Law Concerning the Number of Personnel in Administrative Agencies was designed to reduce the number of personnel by the same percentage in all ministries, it too did not disadvantage any specific ministry and met little resistance from ministries.

These measures to abolish one bureau in every ministry and to reduce personnel, both made in response to the FPARC proposal, were significant in that they made it possible to live up to new administrative demand while checking the growth of administrative agencies.

The Second Provisional Administrative Reform Committee and Political Leadership

Having survived the two oil crises of the 1970s relatively successfully and become an 'economic superpower,' the Japanese had begun to recognize the need to make contributions to the international community. Specifically, Japan felt the need to increase expenditures for overseas economic assistance and to carry out administrative deregulation to open up the Japanese market to foreign exporters. These measures were considered necessary to prepare favorable conditions enabling Japanese firms to become increasingly competitive internationally and to conduct business in a more liberal manner in both domestic and overseas markets.

In addition to the rising expenditures for overseas assistance, in the 1970s Japan had also rapidly increased public expenditures for social welfare (e.g., social security and old-age pensions). However, maintaining the increasing level of these expenditures placed heavy burdens on both society and business enterprises. As a consequence, an attempt was made to slow the growth of government expenditure through large-scale administrative reform.

Advocates of administrative reform in the 1980s were not satisfied with previous reforms of the administrative system, which had focused narrowly on increased efficiency of administrative management and reduction of the number of civil servants. The aim in the 1980s was large-scale reform of the existing administration through measures ranging from elimination of political vested interests to changes in the awareness of the people. Supporters believed that it was necessary to change not only the administration but also politics at large, if Japan were to adequately cope with the changes, both domestic and overseas, it faced or was expected to face in the future. For this reason, this 'administrative reform' became a mix of short-term objectives such as restriction of government budget, medium-term objectives including drastic reform of the social security system, privatization of public corporations (including the Japanese National Railways), and promotion of deregulation; and long-term objectives such as establishment of a system that would permit Japan to make positive contributions to international society. In order to achieve these objectives, the promoters of administrative reform tried to change the dominant ideology in society from one placing importance on welfare by the government to 'neoliberalism' which stresses the importance of self-help and a market economy. They also tried to transform Japan into a state prepared to bear the cost of maintaining international peace and order, or into a state whose presence could be recognized internationally.[15]

The principal advocate of administrative reform in the 1980s was the Second Provisional Administrative Reform Committee (SPARC), which was established following a sequence of events during the 1970s that made administrative reform the top priority for the Japanese government. In the economic recession triggered by the first oil crisis of 1973, tax revenue dropped sharply in the following years. Thus, by 1975, the dependence of the central government's general account on public debts rose to 26 per cent. The dependence continued to climb, and by fiscal year 1979, it had risen to 40 per cent. The first strategy the government employed to reduce the budgetary deficit was the introduction of a broad-based consumption tax, but the ruling Liberal Democratic Party (LDP), which had proposed the tax, suffered a serious setback in the 1979 general election, making it politically impossible to introduce any new tax of this type in the immediate future.

Under these circumstances, the government was forced to shift its strategy for reducing the budget deficit to curtailing expenditures. Many people, business leaders in particular, demanded a reduction in government expenditures by carrying out administrative reform before increas-

---

[15] For more information on this reform effort, see Shumpei Kumon, 'Japan Faces Its Future: The Political Economics of Administrative Reform,' *Journal of Japanese Studies*, Vol. 10, No. 1 (Winter 1984), pp. 143–65.

ing taxes. Many business leaders wished to avoid an increase in the corporate tax. Salaried workers, who represent most of the work force in Japan, were dissatisfied with the tax system that imposed on them what they believed was an unfairly heavy burden and also with the priorities in national expenditures that favored less developed sectors, such as agriculture and small and medium-sized enterprises, and undeveloped regions at the cost of neglecting public amenities for salaried city-dwellers. In this way, 'fiscal reconstruction without tax increase' became an important factor in initiating administrative reform.

In 1981, the members from the private sector of the Administrative Management Committee, which had been established to deliberate on administrative reform based on the proposal submitted by FPARC in 1965, made the following proposal:

This committee has submitted many ideas and opinions regarding administrative reform since its foundation. Most important, however, is their implementation. Implementation of administrative reform tends to face strong opposition not only from governmental agencies but also from various interest groups. To successfully carry out administrative reform, overriding this opposition, the prime minister and cabinet members must exhibit strong leadership.

It is very important to establish a top-level organ to stress administrative reform. Members should include not only the prime minister and cabinet members but also representatives of political parties and the private sector. Around this organ, a system for materializing administrative reform should be built.[16]

The chairman of the Administrative Management Committee at that time was Yasuhiro Nakasone, who concurrently served as director general of the Administrative Management Agency. At a cabinet meeting in July 1980, Nakasone officially proposed establishment of SPARC, and on March 16, 1981, SPARC was established. At that time, Nakasone, who had just failed in his attempt to become prime minister, was not satisfied with his position as director general of the Administrative Management Agency, which at that time was generally regarded as a minor agency. Nakasone thought that success in administrative reform would serve as an ideal political stepping stone in his aspirations to rise to the post of prime minister.

SPARC was made up of nine members, under whom 21 expert members, about 50 councillors, and about 70 executive office staff members performed various duties. The members included three representatives from business, two representatives from labor unions, one journalist, one scholar, one representative of local government, and one representative of the central bureaucracy. It was very significant that the government appointed Toshio Dokō, former chief executive officer of

[16] Masaru Kanbara, *Tenkanki no seiji katei: Rinchō no kiseki to sono kinō* (The political process of a turning point: SPARC and its functions) (Tokyo: Sōgō Rōdō Kenkyōsho, 1986), p. 4.

Toshiba and chairman of the Japan Federation of Economic Organizations, as chairman of SPARC. Dokō had demonstrated his ability to
rationalize business, and many people were attracted by his austere lifestyle and exemplary character. Under Dokō's leadership, SPARC gained
strong support not only from business but also from the general public,
making the SPARC proposal all the more valuable and meaningful. For
this reason, government agencies would not be allowed to resist outright
the proposals and recommendations made by SPARC.[17]

The expert members and councillors were also selected from different
sectors, and there was little difference between their roles and duties in
three or four subcommittees. There, they conducted research, deliberated
on administrative reform, and submitted their findings to SPARC. There
was some criticism that certain ex-bureaucrat expert members and councillors were hindrances to research and deliberation. However, as one
former senior bureaucrat in the Administrative Management Agency observed, these people were helpful as intermediaries in the exchange of
information between SPARC and government agencies, and they helped
formulate proposals most likely to be implemented by government
agencies.[18]

It is important to note that Nakasone, then director general of the
Administrative Management Agency, appointed many friends and
academic advisers as expert members and councillors. In a cabinet meeting, Nakasone made the following statement: 'The Administrative Management Agency will investigate any reports of attempts by government
agencies to obstruct administrative reform, report them to the prime
minister and the chief of the ministry or agency concerned, and ask them
to take appropriate disciplinary measures. I request your understanding
and cooperation.'[19] To some extent this restrained ex-bureaucrat expert
members and councillors from expressing opinions in favor of and for the
benefit of the administrative agencies to which they once belonged.

Because of the individuals who comprised SPARC, it was an authoritative organ that made very effective policy proposals. In Japan, the ordinary
policymaking process is bottom-up: policies are drafted by bureaucrats,
then deliberated and approved in divisions of the LDP Policy Affairs
Research Council and in the Diet. This process made it difficult to formulate an administrative reform policy that would drastically change the

[17] Useful for discussion of SPARC are: Kumon, 'Japan Faces Its Future'; Michio
Muramatsu, 'In Search of National Identity: The Politics and Policies of the Nakasone
Administration,' *Journal of Japanese Studies*, Vol. 13, No. 2 (Summer 1987), pp. 307–42;
Toshiyuki Masujima, 'Gyōsei kaikaku no tetsuzuki' (Procedures of administrative reform),
Nenpō seijigaku 1985: Gendai Nihon no seiji tetsuzuki (1986), pp. 147–69; Haruo Sasaki, 'Rinji
gyōsei chō sakai no katsudō no keika to seika' (Progress and results of SPARC actions), *Nenpō
gyōsei kenkyū*, No. 19 (1985), pp. 1–28; and Kanbara, *Tenkanki no seiji katei*.
[18] Masujima, 'Gyōsei kaikaku no tetsuzuki,' p. 154.
[19] Muramatsu, 'In Search of National Identity,' p. 321.

status quo because of the various interests involved. By contrast, SPARC followed a top-down system. Political executives ordered relevant government agencies to implement policies proposed by SPARC. In this process, called 'council politics,' little consideration was given to vested interests, and policies for drastic reform could be made relatively easily.

Other factors also contributed to the success of SPARC. One was that SPARC refrained from making idealistic, ambitious, yet unrealistic proposals and instead made practical proposals that seemed potentially realizable. Unrealistic proposals for administrative reform, such as establishing a cabinet budget bureau and concentrating power in the cabinet agency, were unlikely to be realized given the strong opposition from the Ministry of Finance and other ministries and agencies. A second factor was that SPARC included representatives of interest groups as expert members and councillors and provided for coordination among these groups. This facilitated implementation of proposals made by SPARC. A third factor was that SPARC made proposals consecutively on five different occasions, instead of making all its proposals in one package at the end of its term. Thus, SPARC could adjust its position by carefully observing the responses from the government, mass media, and the public. This also made it possible for the government to put proposals into practice on a piecemeal basis, as much as practicable. This gradual implementation helped sustain the interest and support of the mass media and the general public.[20] It should be added that the policies and ideas for administrative reform proposed by SPARC were followed by the First, Second, and Third Provisional Councils for the Promotion of Administrative Reform, which were established in 1983, 1987, and 1990, respectively, to follow up the progress of the proposals of SPARC and to study further reform.

Following the establishment of SPARC, Prime Minister Suzuki made administrative reform his cabinet's top priority and expressed his determination to promote administrative reform by saying: 'I shall carry out administrative reform even at the risk of my political life.'[21] Nevertheless, the most important political executive promoting administrative reform was Nakasone, who became prime minister in late November 1982 and continued the emphasis on administrative reform. The most important reason why SPARC, which was just one of many councils, had far-reaching influence on governmental agencies and also on the ruling LDP was that the prime minister clearly expressed his determination to carry out administrative reform and became a strong supporter of SPARC.[22]

[20] Kumon, 'Japan Faces Its Future,' pp. 146–7, and Masujima, 'Gyōsei kaikaku no tetsuzuki,' pp. 157–8.
[21] Kanbara, *Tenkanki no seiji katei*, p. 18.
[22] Masujima, 'Gyōsei kaikaku no tetsuzuki,' p. 151.

Political executives of the government and the LDP established their own body to promote administrative reform when SPARC was created. Organs of this type began to be established in the 1970s to deal with important political issues and became the nucleus of political power in Japan. This body was headed by the prime minister and had 14 executives who represented the cabinet and the LDP. Its strong influence clearly indicates the political executives' strong commitment to administrative reform in the 1980s. Every time SPARC made a proposal, this body and the cabinet gave it full consideration and worked to implement it as quickly as possible. LDP executives continued surveillance over politicians, and cabinet members kept an eye on bureaucrats to forestall their resistance.

SPARC Proposals and Their Consequences

Almost all the policies and ideas for administrative reform proposed by SPARC were contained in the first three of its five proposals. Let us look briefly at these three proposals.

The first proposal (July 1981) concentrated on measures for fiscal reconstruction. Some of its major recommendations were reduction of subsidies in general, reduction of personnel and expenditures, and reduction in the number of public corporations and rationalization of their management. The second proposal (February 1982) concentrated on measures to consolidate and rationalize permits and authorizations by the government. Major elements included simplification of procedures for renewal of drivers' licenses and simplification of inspection procedures for imports and exports and reduction in the number of items to be inspected. The third proposal (July 1982) reflected the basic philosophy of administrative reform and thoroughly reexamined both domestic and external policies. Specifically, the third proposal included (1) reinforcement of the cabinet's authority to comprehensively adjust and coordinate the activities of individual ministries and agencies, (2) establishment of a Comprehensive Administrative Agency for coordination among all government agencies in terms of both personnel and organization, and (3) drastic reform of public corporations and their privatization in particular.[23]

Underlying these reform proposals was the philosophy of 'neoliberalism,' the idea that burdens borne by the people must be minimized and the vigor of the private sector must be utilized most effectively by reducing the size of government and increasing the efficiency of administration. The promoters of administrative reform feared that Japan might, someday in the future, contract the so-called 'advanced country

[23] Kumon, 'Japan Faces Its Future,' pp. 161–2.

disease,' which includes excessive government intervention in or protection of the private sector and a resultant weakening of the private sector. There were exceptions to this philosophy, however. We must remember that budgets for defense and overseas economic cooperation were increased substantially in order to make a 'positive contribution to international society.'

To consider the extent to which the government put into practice the proposals made by SPARC, let us begin with the short-term objectives: fiscal reconstruction and reduction of the national debt. Beginning in 1982, the Ministry of Finance adopted the SPARC-supported principle of 'zero ceiling,' under which the growth of a budget request over the previous year's budget had to be zero. As a result, the growth rate of expenditures in the General Account budget was reduced to 1.8 per cent in fiscal year 1982, to 0 per cent in fiscal year 1983, and even to −0.1 per cent in fiscal year 1984. Along with this development, the budget deficit declined remarkably, lowering dependence on public debt from 32.6 per cent in fiscal year 1980 to 15.6 per cent in fiscal year 1982.[24]

Despite FPARC's recommendation for realignment and rationalization, the number of items subject to permit and authorization by administrative agencies increased from about 7,000 at the time of FPARC to 10,045 in 1981. The figure further increased to 10,169 in 1988, despite the SPARC proposal. Thus, the government reinforced its control over activities in the private sector by means of permits and authorization. There was resistance from ministries and agencies when an attempt was made to rationalize permits and authorization in the 1980s. For example, the Automobile Inspection Association and certain LDP members exerted pressure to strengthen control by adding to the law a provision that automobile owners who failed to have their vehicles inspected regularly would be required to pay a penalty of ¥100,000, in exchange for extending the period between inspections. The major reason why rationalization of permits and authorization is hard to promote, in contrast to the considerable success in budget and personnel cuts, can be found in the narrow range of actors who are subject to permits and authorization, which lowers the visibility of the issue.

SPARC deliberated the idea of consolidating the Economic Planning Agency, the National Land Agency, the Hokkaido Development Agency, and the Okinawa Development Agency into one organ to be called the Comprehensive Planning Agency as a measure to eliminate sectionalism in administrative agencies and to strengthen the comprehensive coordination function of the cabinet. However, this idea was not included in the SPARC proposal, because of the resistance of ex-bureaucrats in these government agencies. Nevertheless, the idea of consolidating part of the

---

[24] Yukio Noguchi, 'Budget Policymaking in Japan,' in Kernell, ed., *Parallel Politics*, p. 121.

Prime Minister's Office and the Administrative Management Agency into one organ called the Comprehensive Administration Agency was included in the proposal, and this specific proposal was implemented, resulting in the birth of the Management and Coordination Agency in 1984. The establishment of this new agency was the product of compromise between the promoters and opponents of administrative reform. Some of the most significant results of the administrative reform in the 1980s, including drastic reform of public corporations and social security program, will be discussed in the remaining sections of this chapter.

Reform of the Japanese National Railways

Reform of the Japanese National Railways (JNR) was one of the most significant results of the 1980s administrative reform. The need for reform had been stressed for many years, yet its realization was believed to be next to impossible. Before privatization, JNR was managed as a public corporation under the Japanese National Railways Law. Under this law, the income and expenses of JNR, including fares and investment in plant and equipment, were treated as a special account and required Diet approval, and salaries paid to JNR employees were not determined by bargaining between labor and management, but by an external administrative committee. In other words, JNR could not make decisions independent of political considerations and ultimate Diet review, even with respect to basic internal matters.[25] JNR's first deficit was in 1964, and the deficit was not rectified in the years that followed; by the 1980 fiscal year, it exceeded ¥1 trillion. In fiscal year 1981, JNR's cumulative debts grew over ¥16 trillion, which represented almost 30 per cent of the General Account budget. Thus, reform of JNR had become an urgent issue.

Why did the JNR deficit grow so large? SPARC cited four causes for the deterioration of JNR management in its third proposal. First, JNR could not adequately cope with changes in the transportation structure, namely, rapid increases in the use of private automobiles and commercial trucks. Although JNR should have concentrated its efforts and specialized in areas where its advantages could be fully utilized (intercity and metropolitan passenger transportation, in particular), it failed to quickly respond to this change. Second, JNR executives lacked an entrepreneurial spirit. Since the government and the Diet intervened extensively in JNR management, its executives were not fully responsible for railway management, and even when the JNR began to operate at a loss, they expected that the government would extend support. Third, relations between JNR

[25] For discussion of the JNR reform, see Atsushi Kusano, *Kokutetsu kaikaku: Seisaku kettei geimu no shuyaku tachi* (JNR reform: Actors in a policy decision game) (Tokyo: Chūō Kōron-sha, 1989).

labor and management included both conflict and behind-the-scenes dealings. Neglect of roles and duties, which lowered the morale of employees, hampered rationalization of JNR management and lowered productivity. Fourth, JNR's personnel expenses were abnormally high in comparison to its income, and the aging of JNR employees resulted in larger payments for retirement allowances and pensions. Executives had attempted to reform management several times, but in vain; both management and labor had grown accustomed to counting on the government and were reluctant to change that attitude. This condition continued into the 1980s until SPARC was established.

In 1980, JNR had worked out the JNR Management Improvement Plan. The contents of this plan were very progressive by the conventional standards of JNR, and included a drastic reduction in employees and a switch from train to bus transport in rural areas where the operation of JNR trains was inefficient. SPARC, however, believed that the problems facing JNR could not be resolved as long as JNR was managed as a public corporation. Thus, SPARC's third proposal to the government included the suggestion that JNR be divided into several smaller units and privatized. In other words, SPARC demanded that JNR stop depending on the government and make a fresh start as an efficiently managed private enterprise.

The Ministry of Transport (MOT), which had jurisdiction over JNR, at first supported the JNR Management Improvement Plan, under which JNR was to remain a public corporation, but gradually accepted SPARC's proposal to divide and privatize JNR. At first, MOT felt that its interest was in maintaining the public corporation status of JNR, but there was little sense of solidarity between the ministry and JNR. Ministry officials gradually realized that privatization of JNR would not result in a substantive loss of influence for the ministry. In fact, JNR developed most of its policies on its own, except for important decisions requiring approval of the Diet or the cabinet: the task of the Ministry of Transport was simply to confirm them. MOT could not surpass JNR in its information-collecting and policymaking abilities. There was also a historical factor. Before the war, both the Ministry of Transport and JNR constituted the Ministry of Railways. When the Ministry of Railways was divided into the Ministry of Transport and JNR after the war, the most expert employees opted to work for JNR and thus the ministry could not dominate JNR by employee talent, either.[26] This seems to be the primary reason why the Ministry of Transport accepted the proposal of privatizing JNR with little resistance. MOT began to think the proposed division and privatization of JNR would give it an initiative in the policymaking process concerning railways.[27]

---

[26] Ibid., p. 228. See also Mamoru Sakamoto and Tsuyoshi Maeya, *Kanryō tachi no atsuki hibi* (Hot days for bureaucrats) (Tokyo: Aipekku, 1990), p. 173.

[27] Sakamoto and Maeya, *Kanryō tachi no atsuki hibi*, p. 196.

In 1982, the National Railways Reconstruction Committee, which was established in accordance with the SPARC proposal, directed JNR to supply the materials and data needed to work out a JNR reform plan, but JNR was reluctant to extend cooperation. Then, Prime Minister Nakasone dissipated opposition by reassigning members of the upper echelon of JNR who had opposed the idea of dividing and privatizing JNR and had the National Railways Reconstruction Committee draft a reform plan. As a result, eight bills designed for the privatization of JNR passed the Diet in 1986. In April 1987 JNR was divided and privatized, giving birth to six new passenger railway companies in the private sector. There were several likely motivations for the group within JNR who wished to maintain the public corporation status of JNR: they could not face up to reality, underestimated the force behind administrative reform, adhered to their own vested interests, or feared that reform would generate a great number of dismissals. As a consequence, they failed in the organizational reform necessary for coping with the change in administrative demand.

Privatization of the Nippon Telegraph and Telephone Public Corporation

The Nippon Telegraph and Telephone Public Corporation (NTT) was privatized earlier than JNR, in April 1985. Before the 1980s, management of NTT was not regarded as a major issue because, unlike JNR, NTT recorded annual budget surpluses. In fiscal year 1979, for example, NTT recorded a surplus of ¥452.9 billion, while JNR's deficit was ¥82.8 billion. 'Preemptive' bureaucrats—bureaucrats attempting to 'preempt the costs of change through policies that pursue the structural transformation of their economies'[28] who thus felt the need to reform NTT management— did not emerge as early as they had in the case of JNR, either within NTT or in the Ministry of Posts and Telecommunications (MPT), which had jurisdiction over NTT.[29]

The idea of privatizing NTT was presented for the first time in SPARC's first proposal (1981), which made the following observations and suggestions: (1) The number of NTT employees had not been reduced in spite of the modernization of its facilities and equipment. This caused growth in

[28] Peter J. Katzenstein, *Small States in World Markets: Industrial Policy in Europe* (Ithaca: Cornell University Press, 1986), p. 23. See also Hideo Ōtake, 'Jiyūshugi kaikaku no naka no kōporachizumu' (Corporatism in liberal reform), *Leviathan* special issue (Summer 1992), p. 138.

[29] Useful for discussion of the privatization of NTT are: Michio Muramatsu, 'Min'eika, kisei kanwa to saikisei no kōzō: Denki tsū shin seisaku no henka' (The structure of privatization, deregulation, and reregulation: Changes in telecommunications policy), *Leviathan*, No. 2 (1988), pp. 118–35; Sakamoto and Maeya, *Kanryō tachi no atsuki hibi*, pp. 305–31; and Tahara, *Shin Nihon no kanryō*, pp. 35–60, and also his *Heisei Nihon no kanryō* (Bureaucrats of Heisei-era Japan) (Tokyo: Bungei Shunjū, 1990), pp. 89–111.

personnel expenses, which in turn created pressure for higher telephone charges. (2) Due to the public corporation status of NTT, the government and the Diet tended to frequently intervene in the management of NTT. For this reason, both labor and management were deprived of incentives for efficient management and had few opportunities to exhibit their entrepreneurship. (3) Remarkable progress is made every day in the telecommunications industry and any entity in the telecommunications business must respond flexibly to these changes. The management style of NTT thus required reform in the form of privatization.

In the summer of 1982, MPT expressed its opposition to the proposed privatization of NTT, fearing that its authority would be drastically reduced. MPT, however, was unsure whether this posture would bring real benefit to the ministry. Actually, it is said that since the previous year younger career bureaucrats in the Telecommunications Policy Bureau of MPT had been ordered to explore the ideal shape of the telecommunications industry in the future.[30] Among these younger bureaucrats, there was mounting support for the privatization of NTT, primarily on the following three grounds. First, the methods of telecommunication were being diversified remarkably due to rapid technological innovation, and it was expected that pressure to liberalize the telecommunications industry, or pressure to promote the participation of private-sector companies in the telecommunications industry, would inevitably grow. So long as NTT remained a public corporation, it would be unable to respond adequately to the new environment, for it was under the control of the government and the Diet. Therefore, NTT had to be privatized.

Second, if NTT were privatized, its scope of business could be expanded and diversified, which would certainly increase the power of MPT. Also, the Ministry of International Trade and Industry (MITI) was trying to expand its jurisdiction over the telecommunications industry. If MPT were too slow in responding to the new situation, new segments of the telecommunications industry might be put under the control of MITI. Furthermore, MPT could take this opportunity to grow into a ministry that could determine policies at its own discretion in wide-ranging areas.

Third, a relationship similar to that between the Ministry of Transport and JNR existed between MPT and NTT. Before World War II, MPT and NTT constituted two major parts of the Ministry of Communications. After the war, this ministry was divided into two organizations, which stood on equal footing. MPT did not in fact exert much influence on NTT's management policy. If MPT were to demonstrate its initiative in the privatization of NTT and the subsequent process of expanding its scope of business, it could raise the status of the ministry. In this way, a consensus

[30] Soichiro Tahara, *Shin Nihon no kanryō: Nippon dai kaizō* (Bureaucrats of new Japan: A big restructuring in Japan) (Tokyo: Bungei Shunjū, 1990), pp. 58–9, and Sakamoto and Maeya, *Kanryō tachi no atsuki hibi*, pp. 318–19.

was gradually formed within MPT to support the proposed privatization of NTT.

The response of MPT bureaucrats to the NTT privatization proposal made by SPARC had not been predetermined and should not be considered 'preemptive.' However, once the proposal for privatization was made, MPT tried to cope with thè new situation quickly and never insisted on maintaining the status quo. Bureaucrats in MPT demonstrated flexibility in responding to the new environment and were even positive in trying to transform a kind of crisis for the administrative organ into an opportunity for change.

How did NTT executives respond to SPARC's privatization proposal? At that time, the president of NTT was Hisashi Shindo, who had once served as president of a large private enterprise. The government had appointed Shindo with the expectation that he would exhibit his entrepreneurship in promoting efficient management of NTT. It is not clear whether Shindo had the idea of privatizing NTT from the very beginning, but immediately after becoming president, he secretly launched a project team (made up of more than a dozen younger elite supervisors) to conduct research on the management style of NTT.[31] Furthermore, it is said that this elite group actually developed the scenario for NTT privatization, and that SPARC proposed privatization of NTT with the cooperation of this team.[32] This reformist group and NTT shared one reason for privatization of NTT: if NTT were to remain a public corporation under the strict control of the government and the Diet, it would not be able to respond adequately to new needs of the telecommunications industry. Another reason this NTT group supported privatization was that the Diet had to approve the pay level for employees of NTT, which operated in the black, just as it did for JNR, which operated in the red. NTT was dissatisfied that, because both were public corporations, its pay level was the same as that of JNR and NTT intended to raise the salary levels of its employees by means of privatization. For this reason, the labor union of NTT began to support privatization, although it had initially been opposed.

On the management level, however, only a minority were in favor of reform. Technical managers in particular objected to privatization. The group who insisted on maintenance of the status quo had many vested interests in the process of procuring materials from a group of private enterprises which were often called the 'NTT family.' To make a breakthrough in this situation, President Shindo and his reformist group took advantage of the US request to open up the market to foreign suppliers to cut off the relationships between the opposition group and the NTT family.

[31] Tahara, *Heisei Nihon no kanryō*, p. 93. [32] Tahara, *Shin Nihon no kanryō*, pp. 52–3.

In the end, with assistance from political executives, LDP members and NTT officials opposing the privatization were persuaded and the privatization of NTT was carried out. The action taken by NTT's reformist group in pursuit of privatization had more or less the same characteristics as the flexible action of the reformist group within MPT.

Reform of the Public Pension Program

The reform of the public pension programs was an important achievement of administrative reform, comparable to the privatization of JNR. In 1961, all Japanese were entered in one of seven types of public pension programs offered for different types of employees (company employees in the private sector, public service personnel, etc.). In the process of administrative reform in the 1980s, reform of this public pension program surfaced as a political agenda, and SPARC offered the following recommendations in its third proposal: (1) differences in the levels of benefits among different public pension programs should be eliminated; (2) fragmented public pension programs should gradually be consolidated into one overall program; (3) pension finance should be stabilized in the long term through reduction in the growth of the overall pension expenditure, while restraining the benefit level, raising the age at which pensions begin to be paid, and increasing the amount of premiums.

Three factors contributed to making reform of the public pension program a political agenda.[33] First, it was recognized that the expansion of social insurance payments was one of the major causes of the financial crisis of the central government which began in the mid-1970s. Second, Japan's population was aging more rapidly than those of the United Kingdom, Germany, and France. Unless the public pension program were reformed, increasing social security payments would put an increasingly heavier burden on government finance. Third, it was predicted that unless the public pension program were reformed, the ratio of the people's burden (the sum of taxes and social security payments) to national income would rise to such an extent that the economic vitality of Japan would decline, as had already been witnessed in some European countries. While the ratio of the people's burden (tax plus social insurance) was somewhere between 50 and 60 per cent of national income in the United Kingdom, France, and West Germany in 1981, that of Japan was only 33.7 per cent. Yet many people predicted that Japan's figure would soon rise to the level of European countries. In this sense, most of the measures taken in the administrative reform, including the reform of the public pension

[33] For discussion of the reform of the public pension program, see Junko Kato, 'Seisaku kettei kenkyū no riron to jisshō' (Theories and empirical research from a policy decision process), *Leviathan*, No. 8 (1991), pp. 165–84.

program, were 'preemptive' in that they were intended to prevent troubles expected to occur in the future.[34] In this regard, Japan took advantage of being a latecomer.

In the administrative reform in the 1980s, the crisis of the government's pension finance became a political agenda. It had been possible to predict the coming of this crisis as early as the mid-1960s, because of the rapidly aging population of Japan. The major reason for the success in the reform of the public pension scheme in the 1980s was the fact that the Ministry of Health and Welfare (MHW) had recognized the need to drastically change Japan's public pension program 20 years earlier.[35] In 1976, the director of the Pension Bureau, concerned about the future of pension financing, pointed out that the benefit level was too high and suggested the need to reform the public pension program, including controlling the benefit level.[36]

Why was the reform not implemented until the administrative reform of the 1980s, despite the fact that a crisis in pension financing had been predicted much earlier? First, since the predicted crisis was not immediate but somewhere in the future, efforts to evade such a crisis were postponed for political reasons. In fact, the pension program reform proposal in 1980, which included raising the age at which pension payments began, was frustrated by opposition from both the ruling and opposition parties and from labor unions. It was only natural that labor objected to raising the age level, and political parties feared losing support from the general public. Given this development, MHW took the crisis of pension financing all the more seriously and held regular research meetings among younger bureaucrats in anticipation of reform. The establishment of SPARC and its proposals helped create an environment in which pension program reform seemed politically feasible.

The reform itself was a difficult task. The interests of individuals enrolled in different types of pension programs conflicted, and there was also a conflict of interest among ministries having control over the different types of pension programs. For this reason, it was extremely difficult to consolidate the different types of pension programs into one. Therefore, MHW developed a sophisticated, two-stage plan for the new public pension program. The idea was to establish a basic pension program that would be shared by all existing programs and then to add supplementary portions unique to the individual pension types. Thus, the foundation was laid for consolidating different types of pension programs into one in the future and checking the benefit level in general terms. MHW persuaded all concerned into thinking that this was the only proposal that would, if

[34] Ōtake, 'Jiyūshugi kaikaku no naka no kōporachizumu,' p. 138.
[35] Minoru Nakano, *Seisaku kettei katei* (Policy decision process) (Tokyo: Tokyo Daigaku Shuppankai, 1992), p. 29.
[36] Kato, 'Seisaku kettei katei kenkyū no riron to jisshō,' p. 170.

implemented, ensure the establishment of a public pension program that would remain stable in the long term. Finally, a consensus was formed through concession and compromise, and the law to reform the public pension program was enacted in 1985.

Thus, MHW succeeded in policy reform and maintenance of its organization without forcing intervention by political executives, by developing its own vision of reform and making necessary preparations.

Conclusion

Since the end of World War II, the Japanese government has maintained a relatively small, efficiently managed administrative system through three major administrative reforms. Because of this, the government has been able to contribute to Japan's high postwar economic performance. More resources were invested in the private sector than in the public sector, encouraging economic expansion. Accordingly, it is incorrect to perceive Japanese economic growth as growth based on massive government financial support to large enterprises in the postwar period. It was only during a short postwar period that the Japanese government extended heavy financial assistance to large enterprises. In fact, most government spending was directed to sectors suffering slow economic growth, or was used to mitigate the dissatisfaction of people in less developed regions in terms of economic growth. Such government spending was necessary for the conservative Liberal Democratic Party to obtain popular support and to maintain its political power. The demand for administrative reform grew only when it was widely recognized that too much government spending in undeveloped sectors or regions poses an economic burden on enterprises and taxpayers in general, or that inefficiency in government hinders the economic activities of enterprises.

Subjected to administrative reform were social services (including social security), agriculture, and the JNR, which had required massive government expenditures. Also, lifting regulations that hampered free economic activities of enterprises became one of the objectives of administrative reform. Generally, most policies of social service ministries are adopted to meet the social demand of the times, and they are policies necessary for the government to obtain support from the general public. Inevitably, however, policy priorities change in accordance with changes in the environment both in and outside Japan. For the government and ministries to survive, they have to modify their policies in accordance with these changes. Due to their incentive structure, however, it is difficult for administrative agencies to change their policies or organizations voluntarily, because by nature they are inclined to sustain the organization and maintain the status quo.

The force to make ministries carry out administrative reform comes from outside, particularly from top political executives. The drastic administrative reform around 1950 was carried out with the influence of the Allied Occupation forces. Then-Prime Minister Yoshida accepted the American policy and strongly committed himself to the policy to maintain a small government. Until the mid-1960s, the balanced budget policy, which was the basis of a small government, continued to be one of the basic principles of the conservative party. Pursuant to this principle, massive investment funds became available to the private sector, bringing about remarkable economic growth. In the 1960s, Prime Minister Satō introduced the policy to abolish one bureau in each ministry and the so-called Law Concerning the Number of Personnel in Administrative Agencies, checking the expansion of the size of the government. In the 1980s, Prime Minister Nakasone embarked on a large-scale administrative reform, restricting the growth of government size and realizing substantial deregulation.

The degree of success of administrative reform initiated by a prime minister depends on a combination of the intensity of social demand for reform, institutional authority of the prime minister, organizational structure of the ruling party, expertise and information the prime minister can obtain from the policy network, and the leadership of the prime minister himself. At times, society becomes discontent with the large size of government or its low productivity or the prime minister himself may take the lead in administrative reform. The prime minister has unparalleled authority, including the power to manage personnel affairs, and is capable of controlling ruling-party Diet members to some extent, supporting them in elections and exercising his authority to allocate posts. With respect to political resources such as expertise and information, the prime minister rivals line ministries, taking advantage of the coordination ministries (e.g., MOF and the Administrative Management Agency), councils, and individual staff members. To successfully carry out a large-scale administrative reform, the prime minister's strong leadership combining these factors in a most effective manner is required.

Ministries have their own political resources and allies, to ensure continuance of the organization and maintain the status quo. Whether actual change is made with respect to issues subjected to administrative reform depends on the political process, which is affected by various factors. Ministries' attitudes toward administrative reform depend on their recognition of the political forces at work in the ongoing administrative reform. In the process of administrative reform in the 1960s, MOF succeeded in frustrating the attempt to shift the budget-making authority from MOF to the cabinet. MOF's expertise in budget-drafting seems to have served as a political resource to frustrate the attempt. The reform attempt to curtail ministries' authority concerning licenses and permits was not successful.

One reason for the latter failures may have been that these issues were invisible to the general public, since many of these authorities concerning licenses and permits were minor. On the other hand, the drastic reform of privatizing JNR and other public corporations was successful. The high-ranking executives of JNR persistently opposed the proposed division and privatization of JNR and were reassigned. Generally, attempts to control expansion of national finances and government personnel were also successful. Throughout the process of reform in the 1980s, MHW drafted the reforms of the public pension program and medical care system at an early stage and successfully coped with changes in the environment, without inviting government intervention.

The administrative reform of the 1980s showed that any motivated, competent prime minister can carry out administrative reform in a system like Japan's, characterized by pluralism of society, politics, and administration. Yet it is not certain whether Japan will adequately respond to its aging society and the rapid changes in the international community it now faces. The Third Provisional Council for the Promotion of Administrative Reform submitted its final proposal to the government in October 1993. This proposal emphasizes two objectives: (1) central-local and local-level reforms in the direction of greater local autonomy, and (2) deregulation aimed at curtailing permits and authorizations by administrative agencies. Emphasis is also given to restraint of the expansion of government, reform of the public financing system and public corporations, and reinforcement of the cabinet's coordinating function. The result is yet to be seen. Under these circumstances, there is growing opinion that a system permitting the prime minister to exert stronger leadership should be established.

In closing, I want to emphasize that administrative reform is difficult because of democracy, not in spite of democracy. Administrative reform, whether in budget-cutting or abolishing licenses, may easily lead to the loss of support from some voters during an election. This is true in any democratic society. The iron triangles formed around vested interests are a chronic disease of democracy and are most deeply rooted in the United States. Japan was successful to a considerable degree in promoting administrative reform and overcoming distorted democracy. Many Japanese scholars believe administrative reform was a challenge to cure distorted democracy, not to limit democracy.

PART THREE

CASES

9

The Role of the Fiscal Investment and Loan Program in Postwar Japanese Economic Growth

YUKIO NOGUCHI

Japan's Fiscal Investment and Loan Program (FILP; Zaisei Tōyūshi Keikaku) is a unique financing system operated by the government and is frequently referred to as 'the second budget.' It has been used by the government as a policy instrument in a manner similar to the regular budget to achieve policy objectives, but the FILP is different from the regular budget (the General Account budget) in terms of source of funds, type of projects financed, and nature of legislative control. In this latter sense, it can be said that the FILP has given the Japanese government a unique and powerful policy tool not possessed by the governments of other countries.

Two sets of questions arise in considering the role and implementation of the FILP. First, in what sense was it different from the regular budget? What advantage was given to the Japanese government because of the use of the FILP? Second, how was resource allocation affected by the FILP? In particular, how important was the FILP in the postwar economic growth of Japan?

To address these questions, I first offer a brief explanation of the FILP and how it functions,[1] and then review its structure and history. In assessing the role of the FILP, I compare actual resource allocations with hypothetical resource allocations that might have been realized in the absence of the FILP. The final section focuses on lessons from the Japanese experience and considers whether a similar system could be introduced in other countries, especially developing nations or former socialist countries. In order to answer this question, it is necessary to analyze conditions under-

---

[1] For general descriptions of the budget-making process in Japan, see Yukio Noguchi, 'The Development and Present State of Public Finance,' in T. Shibata, ed., *Public Finance in Japan* (Tokyo: University of Tokyo Press, 1986); Yukio Noguchi, 'Public Finance,' in Kozo Yamamura and Yasukichi Yasuba, eds., *The Political Economy of Japan, Volume 1: The Domestic Transformation* (Stanford: Stanford University Press, 1987); and Yukio Noguchi, 'Budget Policymaking in Japan,' in Samuel Kernell, ed., *Parallel Politics: Economic Policy Making in Japan and the United States* (Washington: Brookings Institution, 1991).

lying the FILP and to identify whether these conditions are unique to Japan.

The basic view presented in this chapter is that the FILP performed important and appropriate roles at various stages of Japan's economic development. It provided funds to basic industries and to the construction of industry-related infrastructure during the early stages of rapid economic growth (mainly during the 1950s). However, after this early stage of economic growth, many industries were able to 'graduate' from the FILP, i.e., they began to be able to sustain the growth of their firms with no further aid from the FILP. After the late 1960s, the FILP shifted its emphasis toward rectifying the distortions brought about by economic growth by providing funds to sectors with low productivity and for improving the social infrastructure related to citizens' standard of living and quality of life. It should also be emphasized here that the FILP was able to exist and function only under the very special macroeconomic conditions of postwar Japan, and hence it would not be easy to introduce a similar system in other countries, particularly where the private saving rate is low.

Outline of the FILP

The FILP is a government-operated financing system composed primarily of the long-term loan of funds accumulated in the Trust Fund Bureau of the Ministry of Finance. The sources of this Trust Fund are deposits in the postal savings system and the reserves and surpluses of such special accounts as welfare insurance and national pensions.[2] Organizations that receive FILP financing include various other special accounts, government-affiliated financial institutions, local governments, public corporations, and other public institutions. These agencies can be classified into two categories: financial institutions, such as the Japan Development Bank and the Japan Export-Import Bank; and public corporations that undertake public works, such as the Japan Highway Corporation. Table 9.1 shows the breakdown of FILP spending for 1991 and shows the source of

---

[2] At the end of fiscal year 1992, the outstanding amount of postal savings was about ¥156 trillion, or about 31 per cent of the total amount of household deposits to financial institutions. It should be noted that the Japanese postal savings system, under the jurisdiction of the Ministry of Posts and Telecommunications, is recognized as the largest financial institution in the world. Japanese citizens, who have long maintained a very high saving rate, are attracted to the postal savings system by its nationwide network and competitive financial products. For more information on the postal savings system as well as pensions and other special funds, see for example: Kent E. Calder, 'Linking Welfare and the Developmental State: Postal Savings in Japan,' and Stephen J. Anderson, 'The Political Economy of Japanese Saving: How Postal Savings and Public Pensions Support High Rates of Household Saving in Japan,' both in *Journal of Japanese Studies*, Vol. 16, No. 1 (Winter 1990); and Kazuo Sato, 'Saving and Investment,' in Yamamura and Yasuba, eds., *The Political Economy of Japan*, Vol. 1.

funds—including Trust Fund loans of more than five years as well as other sources—for each recipient of FILP support.

The actual structure of the FILP is somewhat more complicated, however. Although about 80 per cent of total FILP funding in recent years has come from Trust Fund lending, other government financing operations are also included. As shown in Table 9.2, lending from the Special Account for Postal Life Insurance and the investment operations of the Industrial Investment Special Account is also included in the FILP. The final source of FILP funds is government-guaranteed bonds issued by public corporations. The payment of the principal of and interest on these bonds is guaranteed by the national government.

The size of the FILP as a percentage of GNP is shown in Table 9.3. It must be noted that the FILP does not disclose the entire financing operation of the Trust Fund because neither short-term loans (mainly those for special accounts) nor the purchase of national bonds is included in the FILP.[3]

The FILP is formulated in tandem with the compilation of the national budget. While the budget is drafted by the Budget Bureau of the Ministry of Finance, the FILP is prepared by the same ministry's Finance Bureau. For both the regular budget and the FILP, requests filed by ministries and organizations are reviewed by MOF examiners, and the final program for the next fiscal year which begins in April is usually determined in December.

Since the 1973 fiscal year, the program has been submitted to the Diet for approval as an integral part of the national budget.[4] When necessary, such as during an inflationary period when a stimulus package is called for, the original plan may be revised. Before 1973, the FILP was under some degree of Diet control in the sense that the budgets of related special accounts such as the Trust Fund Special Account and the Industrial Investment Special Account as well as those of the government-affiliated agencies had to be approved by the Diet.[5] The control was only indirect, however. For example, in the case of the Trust Fund Special Account, only

[3] In fiscal year 1991, ¥600 billion of the Trust Fund was allocated by the Ministry of Finance for the purchase of national bonds. This amounted to about 4.5 per cent of the total issue of national bonds. During the early 1980s, more than one-fourth of national bonds were purchased by the Trust Fund.

[4] Lending programs with maturities longer than five years from the Trust Fund and the Postal Insurance Fund are to be listed in the General Chapter of Special Accounts. In order to retain flexibility, changes in programs are allowed without further approval of the Diet for up to 50 per cent of the original plan. For details, see Zaisei Chosakai, *Kuni no yosan* (The national budget) (Tokyo: Dōyū Shobō, 1973).

[5] In this respect, there is a difference between government-affiliated agencies such as the JDB, JEIB, and other government banks on the one hand and public corporations such as the JHC and other institutions included in the FILP on the other. While the budgets of the former have to be approved by the Diet, those of the latter are out of Diet control.

The initiation of Diet oversight in 1973 was primarily a formal acknowledgment of changes that had already been taking place, i.e., the increasing influence of politicians. In this sense, the 1973 reform was a consequence and not a cause of the change.

Table 9.1 Allocations of the Fiscal Investment and Loan Program (FY 1991, ¥billion)

	Industrial Investment Special Account	Fund of Trust Fund Bureau	Postal Life Insurance Fund	Government-Guaranteed Bonds and Loans	Total
Special Accounts[a]	—	4,662.9	65.7	—	4,728.6
Government-Affiliated Agencies					
HLC	—	6,267.4	135.6	—	6,403.0
PFC	—	1,914.0	321.0	—	2,235.0
SBF	4.5	1,385.1	557.4	20.0	1,967.0
AFF	—	388.5	56.5	—	1,967.0
IFM	—	—	—	1,135.0	1,135.0
JDB	—	1,196.1	64.4	—	1,260.5
JEIB	—	1,111.2	59.8	—	1,171.0
Others[b]	4.5	443.4	88.7	—	536.6
Public Corporations					
HUDC	—	519.3	151.0	220.0	890.3
PWS	—	4,183.0	—	—	4,183.0
EPCSC	—	68.3	—	—	68.3
JRDC	1.8	67.4	11.0	—	80.2
JHPC	—	837.9	1,075.0	144.8	2,057.7
MEPC	—	99.7	256.0	—	355.7
HEPC	—	87.1	227.0	—	314.1

JRCPC	—	54.9	20.0	55.0	129.9
OECF	—	689.9	37.1	—	727.0
Others[c]	48.4	1,011.9	2,031.9	168.5	3,437.0
Local Government (Local government bonds and loans)	—	3,285.0	1,080.0	—	4,365.0
Special Companies					
SCB	6.5	77.2	—	—	83.7
TBBCC	—	—	—	42.6	42.6
EJR	—	3.7	11.3	46.9	61.9
KIAC	—	—	—	63.6	63.6
EPDC	—	74.0	19.0	—	93.0
Others[d]	—	19.9	25.0	3.6	48.5
Total	65.7	28,534.9	6,305.0	1,900.0	36,805.6

[a] Includes Urban Development Loan SA, National Hospital SA, National School SA, National Property Special Consolidation Fund SA, Specific Land Improvement SA, Postal Services SA, and National Forest Services SA.
[b] Includes the Small Business Credit Insurance Corporation, Environmental Sanitation Business Finance Corporation, Hokkaido-Tohoku Development Finance Corporation, and the Okinawa Development Finance Corporation.
[c] Includes Employment Promotion Projects Corporation, Teito Rapid Transit Authority, Japan Private School Promotion Foundation, and the Water Resources Development Public Corporation.
[d] Includes Central Japan Railway Co., Ltd.; West Japan Railway Co., Ltd.; Japan Freight Railway Co., Ltd.; and the Organization for the Promotion of Urban Development.

Abbreviations:
  HLC: Housing Loan Corporation
  PFC: People's Finance Corporation
  SBF: Small Business Finance Corporation
  AFF: Agriculture, Forestry, and Fisheries Finance Corporation

Table 9.1 *Continued*

JFM: Japan Finance Corporation for Municipal Enterprises
JDB: Japan Development Bank
JEIB: Japan Export-Import Bank
HUDC: Housing and Urban Development Corporation
PWS: Pension Welfare Service Public Corporation
EPCSC: Environmental Pollution Control Service Corporation
JRDC: Japan Regional Development Corporation
JHPC: Japan Highway Public Corporation
MEPC: Metropolitan Expressway Public Corporation
HEPC: Hanshin Expressway Public Corporation
JRCPC: Japan Railway Construction Public Corporation
SCB: Shōkō Chūkin Bank
TBBCC: Tokyo Bay Bridge Construction Co., Ltd.
EJR: East Japan Railway Co., Ltd.
KIAC: Kansai International Airport Co., Ltd.
EPDC: Electric Power Development Co., Ltd.

Source: Ministry of Finance, *Zaisei kin'yū tōkei geppō* (Fiscal and monetary statistics), No. 471 (Tokyo: Government Printing Bureau, July 1991).

Table 9.2 Sources of Funds in the FILP (¥ billion)

	FY 1955	1965	1975	1980	1985	1991
Industrial Investment Special Account	34	43	66	17	31	66
Trust Fund Bureau	153	1,187	9,800	19,939	23,642	29,135
Postal Savings	82	465	5,050	9,487	8,739	8,800
Welfare Insurance and National Pension	31	370	2,132	4,660	5,325	6,430
Interest Receipts and Loan Repayments	39	353	2,618	5,792	9,578	13,904
Postal Life Insurance Fund	48	110	1,014	1,689	2,577	6,305
Government-Guaranteed Bonds and Loans	52	437	463	1,567	3,181	1,900
Total	298	1,776	11,343	23,211	29,432	37,406

Note: Part of the Trust Fund is used for the purchase of national bonds. This is the reason for the discrepancy between figures in Tables 9.1 and 9.2.

Source: Ministry of Finance, *Zaisei kin'yū tōkei geppō* (Fiscal and monetary statistics), No. 471 (Tokyo: Government Printing Bureau, July 1991).

Table 9.3 The Size of the FILP and Its Share in GNP

Fiscal Year	FILP (¥ billion)	Share in GNP
1955	297.8	3.4
1960	625.1	3.9
1965	1,776.4	5.3
1970	3,799.0	5.1
1975	10,561.0	6.9
1980	18,103.6	7.4
1985	20,495.0	6.3
1990	35,815.8	8.2

Source: Ministry of Finance, *Zaisei kin'yū tōkei geppō* (Fiscal and monetary statistics), No. 471 (Tokyo: Government Printing Bureau, July 1991).

such items as interest revenue, interest payments, and other expenses were included in the budget. The lending program itself was not included in the budget and hence was out of the Diet's control. Similar limitations were true for the budgets of government-affiliated agencies. For this reason, it can be said that the FILP was relatively free from political influence and provided the government with considerable freedom of action in policymaking. In the case of lending from government-affiliated banks such as the JDB, considerable autonomy is granted to individual institutions with regard to the selection of projects.[6] Thus the decision-making process for the FILP is more decentralized than that of the regular budget.

Financing before FILP Existence

During the period immediately after World War II, the government played an important role in the reconstruction of industries that had been totally destroyed during the war. Through the Priority Production Policy, a special financial institution called the Reconstruction Finance Bank (RFB), an independent organization entirely owned by the government, was established in 1947 to give priority to the reconstruction of strategic industries. The share of RFB lending in total lending of financial institutions was about one-fourth, and as high as three-fourths for investment funds. The RFB allocated about 70 per cent of its funds to the 'six basic industries': coal, iron and steel, fertilizer, electric power, shipping, and textiles. In these industries, more than 80 per cent of investment funds was supplied by the RFB.

The source of these funds was government subsidies and the revenue from bonds purchased by the Bank of Japan, which created (i.e., printed) currency to purchase the bonds. Combined with the deficit of the national budget, this inevitably caused hyperinflation. The rate of increase in consumer prices became as high as 80 per cent per annum in the 1949 fiscal year. Reconstruction of basic industries was thus achieved by a substantial drop in the purchasing power of money, i.e., by forced savings caused by hyperinflation.

This policy was terminated in 1949 in accordance with the new policy direction, called the 'Dodge Line,' recommended by the American banker Joseph Dodge who was sent to Japan by the Truman administration to seek ways to improve the economic condition of Japan. Based on Dodge's recommendation, the Supreme Command of the Allied Forces compelled the Japanese government to terminate subsidies to industries and to balance the budget. Lending from the Reconstruction Finance Bank was also curtailed.

The predecessor of the Trust Fund, the Deposit Fund, had existed since before the war, but use of the fund in the immediate postwar years was restricted to the purchase of national and municipal bonds. Because of the termination of the Reconstruction Finance Bank and industries' increased need for funds, the government introduced several institutional reforms

[6] It is explicitly specified in the notification from the director general of the Banking Bureau of the Ministry of Finance to the governor of the JDB that all decisions concerning the selection of individual projects and the amounts of loans are left to the independent decision of the JDB.

in order to utilize the Deposit Fund more effectively. In 1950, the purchase of bank debentures issued by long-term credit banks was initiated. Government-affiliated banks were also established, including the Japan Export Bank (later renamed the Japan Export-Import Bank, JEIB) in 1950 and the Japan Development Bank (JDB) in 1951. The latter was established as a successor to the Reconstruction Finance Bank. Other institutions were also established during this period, as shown in Table 9.4.

In 1951, the Trust Fund Law was enacted, and the Deposit Fund was reorganized into the Trust Fund. This law established the basic principle that postal savings and other government funds should be accumulated in the Trust Fund, enabling it to oversee and coordinate the use of all the savings and funds. In 1953, the system of granting government guarantees to bonds issued by the Japan National Railway and Japan Telephone and Telegraph was introduced and the Industrial Investment Special Account was established. With this groundwork laid, the first FILP was formulated in FY 1953, and it has been formulated each year since then. Major activities of government financial institutions are shown in Table 9.5.

The FILP during the Rapid Growth Era (1950s and Early 1960s)

The FILP played a strategic role in rapid economic growth, especially in the 1950s, by providing huge amounts of funds to heavy and export industries through government-affiliated banks. In Table 9.6, this operation is classified as 'Basic Industries.' During the early 1950s, almost one-fourth of total FILP funds were allocated for this purpose. The importance of FILP funds in corporate finance is shown in Table 9.7. During the early 1950s, the FILP supplied 21.0 per cent of total funds, and for the four basic industries (electric power, shipping, coal, and iron and steel), the share was as high as 37.2 per cent. The share of the FILP declined in later years, but remained above 20 per cent for these four basic industries until the mid-1960s.

The JDB was the most important financial institution in performing this function. As shown in Table 9.8, the major targets of JDB lending were the electric power, shipping, and coal mining industries, which accounted for about three-fourths of total JDB lending in the 1950s. The JEIB was also critical in supporting the growth of export industries. As shown in Table 9.9, about one-half of its lending was directed to the shipbuilding industry, which grew rapidly after the mid-1950s and secured as much as a 50 per cent share in the world market in the mid-1960s.

Although not included in the FILP, a significant amount of bank debentures issued by long-term credit banks such as the Industrial Bank of Japan, which supplied funds to basic industries, was purchased by the Trust Fund. The share of bank debentures in the total assets of the Trust

Table 9.4 Government Financial Institutions

Institution	Year of Establishment	Supervising Ministries	Number of Employees	Outstanding Loans (end of 1989, ¥ billion)
Government Banks				
Japan Export-Import Bank	1950	MOF[a]	489	5,404.8
Japan Development Bank	1951	MOF	1,090	9,060.6
Public Finance Corporations				
People's Finance Corp.	1949	MOF	4,781	6,390.4
Housing Loan Corp.	1950	MOF	1,156	36,160.8
Agriculture, Forestry, and Fisheries Finance Corp.	1953	MOF, MAFF	951	5,282.1
Small Business Finance Corp.	1953	MOF, MITI	1,768	6,444.6
Hokkaido-Tohoku Development Corp.	1956	HDA, MOF, NLA	300	880.4
Japan Finance Corp. for Municipal Enterprises	1957	MOF, MHA	89	12,182.8

Small Business Credit Insurance Corp.	1958	MOF, MITI	396	385.2
Medical Care Facilities Financing Corp.	1960	MOF, MHW	183	—
Environmental Sanitation Business Financing Corp.	1967	MOF, MHW	61	629.0
Okinawa Development Finance Corp.	1972	MOF, ODA	236	896.2
Others				
Overseas Economic Cooperation	1961	EPA	1,956	—
Post Offices	1876	MPT	23,122[b]	—

[a] Abbreviations: MOF, Ministry of Finance; MAFF, Ministry of Agriculture, Forestry, and Fisheries; MITI, Ministry of International Trade and Industry; HDA, Hokkaido Development Agency; NLA, National Land Agency; MHA, Ministry of Home Affairs; MHW, Ministry of Health and Welfare; ODA, Okinawa Development Agency; EPA, Economic Planning Agency; MPT, Ministry of Posts and Telecommunications.
[b] The number of post offices.

Source: Ministry of Finance, *Zaisei kin'yū tōkei geppō* (Fiscal and monetary statistics), No. 471 (Tokyo: Government Printing Bureau, July 1991).

Table 9.5 Major Activities of Government Financial Institutions

Institution	Major Activities
Japan Export-Import Bank	Lending to residents and non-residents, and debt guarantees involving exports and imports
Japan Development Bank	Lending and payment guarantees for promotion of industrial development and socioeconomic advancement
People's Finance Corp.	Lending to small business and educational loans
Housing Loan Corp.	Loans for the construction, improvement, and purchase of houses
Agriculture, Forestry, and Fisheries Finance Corp.	Lending for maintenance and promotion of agriculture, forestry, and fishery production
Small Business Finance Corp.	Lending to small businesses for equipment and long-term operations
Hokkaido-Tohoku Development Corp.	Lending, investment, and loan guarantees for development programs in the Hokkaido and Tohoku regions
Japan Financial Corp. for Municipal Enterprises	Lending to municipal enterprises and subscriptions to municipal bonds
Small Business Credit Insurance Corp.	Insurance for loan guarantees for small business and lending to the Credit Guarantee Association
Environmental Sanitation Business Financing Corp.	Lending to environmental sanitation business entities and their associations
Okinawa Development Finance	Lending for promotion of industrial development in Okinawa

Source: Ministry of Finance, *Zaisei kin'yū tōkei geppō* (Fiscal and monetary statistics), No. 471 (Tokyo: Government Printing Bureau, July 1991).

Fund was 15.0 per cent in 1955 and 8.1 per cent in 1960 (the share has fallen to about 1 per cent since 1965).

FILP lending was important not only in quantitative terms as mentioned above, but also in qualitative terms measured by, for example, the maturity of loans and the lending rate in comparison with those offered by private financial institutions. The average term to maturity for investment loans was 2.6 years in the case of city banks, 5.7 for long-term banks, and as long as 11.5 for the JDB in 1965.[7] The lending rate of the Trust Fund

[7] This estimate by the JDB is quoted by Akiyoshi Horiuchi and Masayuki Ōtaki in 'Seifukainyū to ginkō kashidashi no jūyōsei' (The importance of government intervention and bank lending), in Koichi Hamada, M. Kuroda, and Akiyoshi Horiuchi, eds., *Nihon keizai no makuro bunseki* (Macroeconomic analysis of the Japanese economy) (Tokyo: University of Tokyo Press, 1987).

Table 9.6 Trends in the Allocation of FILP Funding (per cent)

	1953–1955	1956–1960	1961–1965	1966–1970	1971–1975	1976–1981
Basic Industries	23.6	16.6	9.9	6.3	3.7	2.9
Trade and Economic Cooperation	2.8	4.3	7.9	10.4	8.8	6.4
Regional Development	5.7	9.0	7.5	4.6	3.7	2.6
Industrial Infrastructure	26.4	21.6	26.1	24.3	23.2	18.1
Low Productivity Sectors	18.6	20.9	19.0	20.1	19.6	22.6
Small-Medium Enterprises	—	13.7	12.9	15.6	15.2	17.7
Improvement of Life	22.9	27.6	29.6	34.3	41.0	47.4
Total (¥ billion)	921	2,336	6,195	13,771	34,073	9,547

Source: Seiritsu Ogura and Naoyuki Yoshino, 'Zeisei to zaisei tōyūshi' (Tax and the FILP), in Ryūtarō Komiya, Masahiro Okuno, and Kōtarō Suzumura, eds., *Nihon no sangyō seisaku* (Industrial policy in Japan) (Tokyo: University of Tokyo Press, 1984).

Table 9.7 Shares of Various Sources Supplying New Funds to Industry (per cent)

	FY1952–55		FY1956–60		FY1961–65		FY1966–70	FY1971–75
	A	B	A	B	A	B	A	A
Capital Market	11.9	6.5	21.6	24.9	17.8	25.1	11.2	12.2
Stocks	10.0	4.8	15.3	16.3	13.0	15.0	5.9	4.6
Bonds	1.9	1.7	6.3	8.6	4.8	10.0	5.3	7.5
Financial Institutions								
Private	59.8	56.3	60.7	53.8	66.4	52.8	73.7	74.2
Banks	38.8	46.7	34.2	36.0	30.9	29.2	48.5	50.4
Others	21.0	9.6	26.5	17.8	35.5	23.6	25.2	23.7
FILP	28.3	37.2	17.7	21.3	15.8	22.1	15.1	13.7
Japan Development								
Bank	13.3	24.1	4.6	10.4	4.2	12.1	3.9	3.6
Others	15.0	13.1	13.1	10.9	11.6	10.0	11.2	10.0

Note: A is industry total; B is four basic industries (electric power, shipping, coal, and iron and steel).

Source: Amane Ishikawa and Toyoo Gyōten, *Zaisei tōyūshi* (The FILP) (Tokyo: Kin'yū Zaisei Kenkyū kai, 1977).

was more than 4 per cent less than the long-term prime rate during the 1950s and about 3 per cent less in the early 1960s. Although this difference decreased, it was consistently about 2 percentage points throughout the 1960s when the long-term prime rate was around 8 to 9 per cent. Government financial institutions were thus able to offer lending rates considerably lower than the market rates.[8]

In evaluating the effects of the FILP in lowering the cost of capital for firms, Ogura and Yoshino found the greatest impact in the shipping industry, in which the savings on interest payments due to FILP-related loans was on average over 20 per cent of the amount of investment being made by the industry during 1962–75. The next largest effect was in the manufacture of transport machinery (mainly shipbuilding) and in the electric power and coal-mining industries, for which the ratio was around 5 to 10 per cent. For such industries as iron and steel and wholesaling, the ratio was below 5 per cent. Most of these effects were attributable to JDB lending.[9]

It is important to note that the General Account provided virtually no subsidies to the operation of the Trust Fund. Both the Postal Savings

[8] The Housing Loan Corporation and the Agricultural, Forestry, and Fisheries Corporation receive significant amounts of subsidies from the national government to make the lending rate lower than the borrowing rate from the Trust Fund. The number of institutions that receive such subsidies has increased since the 1970s. In the case of the JDB, a huge amount of capital was supplied by the national government at the time of its establishment, which enabled the JDB to provide low-interest loans.

[9] Seireitsu Ogura and Naoyuki Yoshino, 'Zeisei to zaisei tōyūshi' (Tax and the FILP), in Ryūtarō Komiya, Masahiro Okuno, and Kōtarō Suzumura, eds., *Nihon no sangyō seisaku* (Industrial policy in Japan) (Tokyo: University of Tokyo Press, 1984).

Table 9.8 Trends in the Composition of Japan Development Bank Loans (per cent of total loans)

	1951–55	1956–60	1961–65	1966–70	1971–75	1976–80	1981–82
Energy	45.3	58.7	25.8	15.0	7.7	24.4	41.9
Electric power	38.8	39.0	16.6	7.4	—	17.7	14.5
Coal mining	6.5	9.7	8.5	3.4	—	—	—
Transportation							
Shipping	25.3	27.3	30.3	35.5	17.7	7.7	11.7
International competitiveness	—	12.1	14.6	8.4	—	—	—
Improvement of Balance of Payments	—	—	4.4	2.5	—	—	—
Regional development	—	2.6	21.5	27.5	30.9	30.5	25.8
Pollution control	—	—	—	0.6	19.1	21.3	8.5
Technology	—	—	—	8.3	10.6	11.1	9.2
Total (¥ billion)	274	302	672	1,363	2,827	4,535	2,239

Source: Seiritsu Ogura and Naoyuki Yoshino, 'Zeisei to zaisei tōyūshi' (Tax and the FILP) in Ryūtarō Komiya, Masahiro Okuno, and Kōtarō Suzumura, eds., *Nihon no sangyō seisaku* (Industrial policy in Japan) (Tokyo: University of Tokyo Press, 1984).

Table 9.9 Trends in the Composition of Japan Export-Import Bank Loans, in billion yen (per cent of total loans)

	1950–55	1956–60	1961–65	1966–70	1971–75	1976–80
Export total	133 (94)	282 (85)	663 (77)	1,382 (76)	1,719 (44)	2,251 (44)
Shipbuilding	88 (66)	184 (56)	419 (48)	822 (45)	727 (19)	534 (11)
Plants	44 (33)	97 (30)	244 (28)	560 (31)	992 (25)	1,715 (34)
Imports	0 (0)	2 (1)	6 (1)	60 (3)	685 (18)	1,104 (13)
Investment	1 (1)	26 (8)	44 (5)	143 (8)	639 (16)	650 (13)
Economic Cooperation	0 (0)	19 (6)	151 (17)	223 (12)	865 (22)	1,092 (21)
Total	134 (100)	330 (100)	866 (100)	1,809 (100)	3,909 (100)	5,098 (100)

Source: Seiritsu Ogura and Naoyuki Yoshino, 'Zeisei to zaisei tōyūshi' (Tax and the FILP), in Ryūtarō Komiya, Masahiro Okuno, and Kōtarō Suzumura, eds., *Nihon no sngyō seisaku* (Industrial policy in Japan) (Tokyo: University of Tokyo Press, 1984).

Special Account and the Trust Fund Special Account were operated on a self-sustaining basis—that is, operating expenses were paid out of interest revenues. Thus, if the combination of these two special accounts can be regarded as a bank, it accomplished the surprising feat of collecting deposits at commercial rates and lending funds at preferential rates on a self-sustaining basis. Several explanations, such as the tax-exempt status of postal savings, have been offered for this remarkable ability, but they do not completely explain the reasons behind it. The fundamental reason can be found in the fact that the financial market was strictly controlled. Because the number of banks was severely limited, and because interest rates were set at levels under which marginal financial institutions could survive, most banks must have experienced excess profits. Since the Trust Fund needed no such excess profit, it could provide loans at below-market rates.

A second role for the FILP has been to finance public capital formation. Distinction is made between projects financed by the FILP and by general revenues such as taxes and government bonds according to the profitability of the projects. For example, toll-free highways, local roads, and streets are constructed by the national and local governments using general revenues. (Revenue from the petroleum tax is the main source of funds for road construction, but revenue from other taxes and government bonds is also used.) The FILP covers toll highways through three public corporations established for this purpose: the Japan Highway Corporation, in charge of nationwide highways such as the Tōmei and Meishin; the Metropolitan Highway Corporation, in charge of inner-city highways in the Tokyo Metropolitan Area; and the Hanshin Highway Corporation, in charge of inner-city highways in the Hanshin (Osaka and Kobe) Metropolitan Area. Construction of these highways has been financed by loans from the FILP, which are redeemed by future toll revenues. Subsidies are also provided by the government to lower the cost of capital.

Similar distinctions are made for other types of social infrastructures such as ports, airports, and irrigation facilities. Those projects that are relatively profitable are carried out by public corporations and are financed by the FILP. In the case of public housing, low-rent housing for relatively lower-income people is supplied by local governments using general revenues, and relatively high-rent housing by the Japan Housing Corporation using the FILP. The FILP also finances railways and subways and plays an important role in financing public investments by local governments. This function is carried out both by purchasing local government bonds and by providing loans from the Japan Finance Corporation for Municipal Enterprises.

One of the important features of public investment in postwar Japan is that public corporations have made a relatively large share compared to that of the general government defined in the National Account Statistics (i.e., the part of the government that is financed by the general account budget and non-profit-yielding special accounts). As shown in Table 9.10, the share of the general government in total public capital formation, which was 68.2 per cent in 1954, declined to 52.9 per cent in 1956 and stayed below 60 per cent during the rapid growth period. On the other hand, the share of public corporations rose from 27.0 per cent in 1952 to over 30 per cent during the late 1950s and to 40.6 per cent in 1961. This represents the fact that the role of the FILP in public investment was significant, since most investments by public corporations were financed by the FILP.

This feature also implies that priority was given to profit-yielding and industry-related projects such as highways, ports, and airports rather than to non-profit-yielding projects unrelated to industry such as streets, sewers, and parks. As shown in Table 9.11, the relative share of infrastructures for the improvement of citizens' lives and the environment (sewers, housing, schools, and parks) was less than half that of transportation and communications-related facilities until the early 1970s. In Table 9.12, the share of public corporations in capital formation is shown to be high compared to that of the general government until the 1970s. This reflects the same bias.

Table 9.10 Composition of Government Capital Formation

Fiscal Year	Housing	General Government	Public Corporations	Inventory	Gov't. Gross Capital Formation
1951	4.2	62.7	27.5	5.7	346
1952	3.8	63.8	27.0	5.4	460
1953	4.9	67.2	29.5	−1.6	590
1954	5.1	68.2	28.8	−2.1	584
1955	4.4	48.7	29.7	17.2	714
1956	6.2	52.9	35.9	5.0	686
1957	5.3	57.2	38.8	−1.2	813
1958	5.7	55.9	35.7	2.7	944
1959	4.9	56.7	35.4	3.0	1,110
1960	4.3	58.2	34.7	2.8	1,315
1961	3.6	56.6	40.6	−0.8	1,717
1962	4.5	56.6	39.6	−0.6	2,185
1963	4.4	55.9	41.3	−1.6	2,448
1964	4.7	56.2	36.9	2.1	2,793
1965	4.9	54.9	37.3	2.8	3,333

Note: Gross Capital Formation is in billion yen; others are in per cent.

Source: Toru Hashimoto, *Nihon no zaisei kōzō* (Structure of public finance in Japan) (Tokyo: Tōyō Shinposha, 1968).

Table 9.11 Composition of Public Capital Formation (percentage share)

	1960	1965	1970	1975	1980
Life and the Environment					
Environment	7.0	7.2	7.9	12.6	12.3
Housing	4.1	4.7	5.4	5.4	4.0
Welfare Facilities	1.6	1.9	2.4	2.5	1.9
Schools	7.2	6.2	5.4	8.4	10.6
Subtotal	19.9	20.0	21.1	28.9	28.8
Transportation and Communication					
Roads	16.3	20.8	22.0	18.7	21.2
Railways	10.7	11.5	8.0	7.6	6.5
Ports	2.6	2.5	2.8	2.3	2.1
Airports	0.2	0.2	0.5	0.6	0.8
Telecommunications	11.0	10.6	10.0	8.8	6.4
Subtotal	40.7	45.6	43.4	38.0	37.0
National Land Conservation	8.7	6.2	6.5	5.8	6.9
Agriculture	5.4	5.5	6.1	6.7	8.4
Others	25.2	22.7	22.8	20.5	18.9
Total	100	100	100	100	100

Source: Toshika Kenkyū Koshitsu, *Shakai shihon no seibi katei to shōrai tenbō ni kansuru kenkyū* (A study of the process of social infrastructure construction and its future outlook), NIRA Report NRC-82-10, 1984.

Table 9.12 Composition of Gross Capital Formation (percentage share)

	1965	1970	1975	1980	1985	1990
Gross Capital Formation	100.0	100.0	100.0	100.0	100.0	100.0
Housing	20.5	19.6	24.2	20.8	17.5	18.9
Private	19.1	18.2	22.5	19.6	16.5	18.2
Public	1.4	1.4	1.7	1.1	0.9	0.7
Business Fixed Investment	64.0	67.4	59.4	59.9	65.3	65.5
Private	51.2	58.7	49.2	50.0	59.4	61.4
Public Corporation	12.8	8.7	10.2	9.9	5.9	4.1
General Government	15.5	13.0	16.4	19.4	17.2	15.6

Source: Economic Planning Agency, *Yearbook of National Account Statistics* (Tokyo: Economic Planning Agency, 1992).

The Changing Role of the FILP: The Latter Stage of Rapid Growth (after the Late 1960s)

After growth began to be achieved on a self-sustaining basis, large companies in the leading industries no longer needed government support. Rather, government intervention came to be perceived as an obstacle to further growth. The FILP changed the focus of its lending from basic industries to low-productivity sectors such as small firms, declining industries, agriculture, and less developed regions. As shown in Table 9.6, the share of FILP funds allocated to basic industries declined from 23.6 per cent during the early 1950s to 9.9 per cent in the early 1960s and to 6.3 per cent by the late 1960s. This followed the general shift in economic policies, as indicated by the major objectives of the Five-Year Economic Plans of the government. Whereas the emphasis of earlier plans was the promotion of economic growth, the Economy and Society Development Plan formulated in 1967 raised 'the adjustment of distortions caused by economic growth' as its most important objective. This change in FILP lending can also be confirmed in Table 9.7, where the share of FILP funds in the total supply of industrial funds is seen to have declined to about 15 per cent during the 1960s.

Corresponding changes can also be observed in JDB lending (Table 9.8). The share of the electric power industry, which was almost 40 per cent during the 1950s, declined sharply during the 1960s due to increased internal funds and funds raised by bonds. The iron and steel industry had 'graduated' from JDB loans earlier: whereas about 15 per cent of industry funds came from JDB loans under the First Rationalization Plan (1951–53), almost all funds after the Second Rationalization Plan (1956–60) were obtained from the capital market and from private financial institutions. JDB loans shifted to such areas as regional development and environmental control, reaching 30.9 and 19.1 per cent, respectively, of total JDB lending in the early 1970s.

The most important area in which private financial institutions, especially city banks, could not provide enough funding was for small and medium-sized enterprises (SMEs). In the FILP, funds for this sector are supplied by three major financial institutions: the People's Finance Corporation, the Small Business Finance Corporation, and the Commerce and Industry Associations' Financial Institution. Most lending by the Okinawa Development Corporation and the Environmental Sanitation Business Financing Corporation is also directed to SMEs. The share of FILP-related institutions in total loans outstanding to SMEs has been about 10 per cent since the mid-1960s.

A second important area was housing loans, provided by the Housing Loan Corporation. In 1965, the share of lending from this corporation was as high as about 67.8 per cent of total housing loans outstanding. A third area was agriculture and fisheries, where loans were carried out by the Agriculture, Forestry, and Fisheries Finance Corporation. The lending rate was kept significantly lower than the market rate. Regional development was also covered by various institutions: the above-mentioned regional development financing by the JDB, the Hokkaido and Tohoku

Development Bank, and the Okinawa Development Bank. The Regional Development Corporation provided financing for firms that relocated to former coal-mining regions.

Corresponding changes occurred in financing public capital formation, as reflected in the increases in the shares of the expenditure categories 'Improvement of Life' in Table 9.6 and 'Life and Environment' in Table 9.11. The latter, which was about 20 per cent until the early 1970s, increased to about 30 per cent in the late 1970s. The most remarkable change was observed for environmental and sanitation-related infrastructures (mainly sewers), whose share increased from about 7 or 8 per cent in the 1960s to greater than 12 per cent in the late 1970s.

There were several reasons for the above-mentioned shift in fund allocation. Demand for government finance from leading industries was decreasing, and industry-related infrastructures had been considerably improved thanks to investment during the earlier periods. Two additional reasons can also be pointed out. One was the need to rectify the income discrepancies or productivity differentials between the advanced and backward sectors. Because rapid economic growth was an imbalanced growth in which heavy and export-oriented industries grew more rapidly than other sectors and in which population and industrial activities became concentrated in urban areas, such sectors as SMEs, agriculture, and rural areas lagged behind. In order to prevent social tension from becoming serious, it was necessary to extend aid to these sectors.

A second reason was that as the relative power of politicians became stronger, it became more and more difficult to insulate fund allocation decisions from political pressure. Since most politicians find their political bases in such sectors as SMEs and agriculture, it was natural that fund allocation shifted to these sectors. Some of the best examples were the establishment of fragmented, sector- or region-specific institutions such as the Medical Care Facilities Financing Corporation established in 1960; the Environmental Sanitation Business Financial Corporation established in 1967 to target 'environmental sanitation businesses' (such as restaurants, coffee shops, barbers, beauty salons, hotels, boarding houses, public bathhouses, and laundries); and the Okinawa Development Finance Corporation established in 1972, when US occupation of the Okinawa islands ended, to stimulate development in these southernmost islands of Japan.

It is difficult to identify the source of the initiative for change in the relative share of public works. Probably the most important factor was the change in general economic conditions. As people became more affluent, the demand increased for improved infrastructures for services such as sewer systems. A general concern for the environment also arose in the 1970s.

Assessments of the Role of the FILP

In order to evaluate the effect of the FILP on resource allocation patterns and economic growth, it is necessary to imagine fund allocation mechanisms in hypothetical economies in which the FILP did not exist, and to compare the flow of funds that would have been realized in such economies with the actual flow. Here, I consider the following four types of hypothetical economies, assuming that household consumption is unaffected by government policies.

Case A: In this economy, neither the postal savings nor social security funds exist. Because of the above assumption, the amount of household savings would be the same as that in the actual economy, and all savings would be absorbed by private financial institutions such as banks.

Case B: This economy assumes the same conditions as case A, except that part of private savings is absorbed by the government in the form of national bonds and used for revenue in the national budget. I assume that the amount of revenue obtained by bonds is the same as that absorbed by the FILP.

Case C: This is an economy in which the postal savings and social security funds exist. I assume, however, that the Trust Fund allocates all its funds for purchasing national bonds so that the amount of budget expenditures is the same as in case B.

Case D: In this economy, the amount of budget expenditures is assumed to be the same as in cases B and C. In this case, however, I assume that expenditures are financed entirely by tax revenue. Due to the assumption concerning household consumption, the amount of household saving would be smaller than that in the actual economy.[10]

Decision-making organizations and the criteria for resource allocation would be different in these different cases. In case A, decisions are made by private organizations and hence the profitability of projects would be the most important criterion. On the other hand, decisions are made by the government in cases B, C, and D, and social welfare considerations

[10] Cases B and C differ in the way private savings are channeled into the government. Macroeconomic saving-investment balances are the same in these cases, and different in case D because household saving is smaller.

As for the decision criteria, the profitability condition is unnecessary in case D because the expenditure is financed by tax revenue. In cases B and C, it is necessary to redeem the national bond. But because the redemption is financed by future tax revenues, rather than fees or toll revenues, the profitability of the individual project is not required either. Thus there would be no difference in decision-making organization and criteria in these cases.

Some authors argue that the postal saving system is the same as national bonds because both are means to channel private saving to the public sector. This argument is correct in the sense that cases B and C are the same. However, as discussed in the text, the actual FILP is different from these cases in terms of both the decision-making organizations and criteria. Namely, because in the actual economy private savings have been channeled into the public sector by postal savings, decisions were made by government-affiliated institutions rather than the government itself, and profitability conditions were taken into account.

rather than profitability would become the important factor. At the same time, however, there is a danger in these cases that inefficient projects will be chosen because of political pressure. As discussed below, the system with the FILP can be characterized as one between these polar cases in terms of both decision-making bodies and criteria.

Let us first compare the actual system of the FILP with the case in which resource allocation is entirely determined by private institutions (case A). If this system had existed during the period before rapid economic growth (i.e., before the 1950s), the short-term profitability criterion would have been emphasized since the future prospects of heavy industries in Japan were uncertain at that stage. It is therefore quite possible that most private savings would have been allocated to such sectors as retail and wholesale business for which the gestation period is relatively short. It is also possible that capital flight to overseas markets might have occurred (in spite of government efforts to prohibit it) so that domestic capital formation would have been impaired. In these cases, economic growth led by heavy industry would not have materialized in Japan.

In the actual economy, the government was able to allocate resources to the heavy industries and export-oriented industries and to the construction of industry-related infrastructures such as highways and ports using the FILP system, thus contributing to the high economic performance of postwar Japan during the 1950s and early 1960s. It is thus possible to argue, as Ueno and Ito *et al.* have done,[11] that the FILP played strategic roles in fostering rapid economic growth similar to the role played by government finance in overcoming difficulties caused by incomplete information. Since lenders do not necessarily possess sufficient information about borrowers, loans from government financial institutions served as signals of government policy priorities and hence as implicit guarantees, thus increasing loans from private banks. The FILP not only allocated funds to strategic industries in their 'infant' stage but also played a 'pump-priming' role[12] by indicating the priority sector of the economy. The latter effect is said to have been particularly important for the JDB.[13]

Other scholars, however, question whether such an effect actually existed. Horiuchi and Ōtaki,[14] for example, concluded from their statisti-

[11] See Yūya Ueno, 'Wagakuni sangyō seisaku no hassō to hyōka' (The idea and evaluation of industrial policies in Japan), *Kikan gendai keizai*, No. 20 (1975), pp. 6–49; and Motoshige Ito, Kazunao Kiyono, Masahiro Okuno, and Kōtarō Suzumura, 'Shijō no shippai to hoseiteki sangyō seisaku' (Market failure and corrective industrial policy), in Komiya *et al.*, eds., *Nihon no sangyō seisaku*.

[12] On the 'pump-priming' effects of government loans, see: Ito *et al.*, 'Shijō no shippai to hoseiteki sangyōseisaku.' Some authors refer to this as the 'cowbell effect.' See Mikiya Hyūgano, 'Kyōchō yūshi to shinsa nōryoku—Nihon Kaihatsu Ginkō no keisu' (Corporative lending and the assessing ability of banks), *Keizaigaku ronshu*, Vol. 50, No. 1 (April 1984), pp. 70–80.

[13] Hyūgano, 'Kyōchō yūshi to shinsha nōryoku.'

[14] Horiuchi and Ōtaki, 'Seifukainyū to ginkō kashidashi no jūyōsei.'

cal analysis that such a function can be observed only for a limited number of industries such as iron and steel, agriculture, and transportation. In these industries, the effect of JDB loans was significant in obtaining loans from private banks and hence had an 'inducing effect.' However, for such industries as coal and machinery, the direction of causality was the opposite, i.e., variations in private lending caused the variation in JDB lending. In the case of the coal industry, this can be interpreted as JDB loans being used to help a declining industry.

As mentioned earlier, emphasis in the allocation of FILP funds has shifted since the late 1960s to housing, small and medium-sized enterprises, and to the construction of living-standard related social infrastructures in order to rectify distortions caused by rapid economic growth. If the FILP had not existed during this period, it is possible that such distortions would have been left uncorrected and hence social tensions would have been more serious.

On the other hand, it is possible to argue that some of the projects financed by the FILP during this period were not efficient from a pure economic point of view. For instance, loans from the Environmental Sanitation Business Corporation, the Agriculture, Forestry, and Fisheries Finance Corporation, and the Okinawa Development Finance Corporation may be regarded as political and hence a waste of resources. Such fund allocation would not have been realized in a purely private process. In this sense, the existence of the FILP may be regarded as having retarded the growth potential of the Japanese economy.

So far, comparison has been made with the case in which allocation of private savings is determined by private organizations (case A). It is also necessary to compare the FILP with the pure governmental processes, i.e., systems in which resource allocation is determined entirely in the framework of the national budget (cases B, C, and D).

In the pure governmental processes, the direct profitability of projects would not be considered in their selection. On the other hand, in the FILP, only those projects that can earn revenues may be selected because it is necessary to repay the loans. Moreover, the rate of return must be above a certain level in order to pay interest. For example, in the case of highways, only toll highways can be financed by the FILP and the selection of routes is affected by rate-of-return considerations.

It is frequently argued that the postwar Japanese economic structure placed too much emphasis on economic growth by neglecting the improvement of citizens' quality of life. It may be argued that in the pure governmental processes (especially case D), more resources would have had to have been allocated for public housing, living-standard related infrastructures, and welfare programs. In this sense, the existence of the FILP was one of the basic causes of the bias in the Japanese economic structure.

It must be noted, however, that the profitability condition does not necessarily imply the neglect of quality of life. Projects such as commuter trains, other public transportation, urban development, and renewal projects yield considerable cash revenues and improve the quality of life of urban citizens. Thus, depending upon the policy, different resource allocations were possible even with the FILP, and, as mentioned above, the priority of the FILP has shifted to these areas since the late 1960s.

It is also necessary to note that being able to be unconcerned with profitability in making resource allocations does not always imply the improvement of welfare. On the contrary, there is a danger in the pure governmental processes that policy decisions will be distorted by irrational political pressures. Thus, it is quite possible that in the pure governmental processes, considerable waste of resources would have been brought about in the form of excessively generous welfare programs, excessive protection of sectors of low productivity including agriculture, and irrational regional allocation of public facilities.

The FILP system differs from the pure governmental processes in several additional aspects. One is the flexibility in policy changes. In the case of the regular budget, strict restrictions are imposed on the use of the budget. Changes are not allowed unless a supplementary budget is approved by the Diet. On the other hand, more flexibility is permitted for the FILP. This was particularly true until the early 1970s while the FILP was in effect free from Diet control. Thus we may say that the Japanese government was able to adapt to the changing economic environment more flexibly than the governments in the hypothetical pure governmental economies.

Another important difference is the degree of decentralization in decision making. In the case of the pure governmental processes, detailed decisions must be made regarding the budget, hence decisions are highly centralized at the government level. In contrast, in the FILP, only broad decisions concerning the allocation of funds are made at the ministry level and the selection of individual projects is left to individual institutions. This is particularly true for financing. For instance, the JDB had considerable discretionary power in selecting its projects. This means that it is possible to use the 'on the spot information' emphasized by Hayek more accurately in decisions.[15]

Compared with case D in which expenditures are financed entirely by the general government using tax revenues, it was possible to maintain a low tax burden in postwar Japan because some of the functions that could have been performed by the General Account were executed by the FILP. The construction of social infrastructure is one example. In other words, the existence of the FILP has contributed to the continuation of a balanced

[15] F. A. Hayek, 'The Use of Knowledge in Society,' *American Economic Review*, Vol. 35 (1945), pp. 519–30.

budget for the General Account and to keeping the size of the general government small in postwar Japan.

It is often pointed out that the basic macroeconomic feature of the postwar Japanese economy was the high investment rate in the private sector. This was made possible because the tax burden was kept low and because the General Account budget did not swallow savings. In this sense, the FILP has contributed to forming the basic macroeconomic structure of the Japanese economy.

Concluding Remarks: Lessons from the Japanese Experience

In conclusion, let me consider the possibility of introducing government financing systems similar to the FILP in other countries, such as developing countries or the former socialist countries. It is first necessary to identify the conditions under which the FILP could exist and function in postwar Japan.

First, we must note that the FILP could function only under certain macroeconomic conditions that existed in postwar Japan. The most important of these was the high saving rate in the private sector. Without ample savings in the private sector, a financing system like the FILP cannot function since it is a system of channeling savings, rather than creating them. Thus, in an economy in which the private-sector saving rate is low, a system for raising the saving rate (possibly by using tax incentives) or creating forced saving will be required. The second important macroeconomic condition was the absence of a huge deficit in the government budget. Even if there are ample savings in the private sector, they cannot be used for a system like the FILP if they are absorbed by the government to finance a budget deficit.

It is also important to recall that the FILP not only provided financing in the quantitative sense but also in the qualitative sense, particularly in that the interest rate was lower than the market rate. I argued that this was made possible because the private financial sector was strictly regulated and that excess profits existed in private financial institutions. It was because of this that the FILP was able to provide preferential financing without receiving much subsidy from the General Account budget. If these conditions cannot be met, a system like the FILP cannot perform its policy-oriented function adequately. In fact, even in Japan, the strategic role of the FILP has diminished during recent years because these conditions are disappearing. In particular, the shrinking discrepancy between the Trust Fund lending rate and the long-term prime rate, brought about by growing competition in the financial market, makes it more and more difficult for the FILP to provide preferential financing. Whether or not 'elite bureaucrats' can guide the economy better than the market can is a controversial matter. While political scientists tend to give a positive answer, economists in general are skeptical.

The view presented in this chapter lies somewhere in between. I have argued that without government-led financing, resources would have been allocated during the early 1950s to projects yielding quick returns and, as a result, the heavy-industry-led economic growth would not have materialized.

On the other hand, we should recall that the FILP's significant role in the industrial development of Japan was limited to the early stage of rapid growth when industry was still in an 'infant' stage. When many industries became able to achieve sustained growth on their own—or 'graduated' from the FILP—the role of the FILP shifted to the adjustment of social tensions by providing financing to low-productivity sectors. This suggests that the role of a government financing system should not only be specifically tailored for the needs of a particular economy, but should also be different for different stages of economic development.

10

Financing Japanese Industry:
The Interplay between the Financial and Industrial Bureaucracies

MASARU MABUCHI

The nature of a country's financial system holds the key to the effectiveness of its industrial policy. In countries with mature capital markets, such as the United States and the United Kingdom, where equity capital is the predominant source of industrial funds, the state's capacity to implement industrial policy is limited. In contrast, in countries such as Japan and France where capital markets are less developed and where the state administers interest rates, banks play a prominent role as suppliers of funds and the state is thus in a much better position to expand its control of the industrial economy.[1]

The focus of this chapter is how two parts of Japan's bureaucracy, the Ministry of International Trade and Industry (MITI) and the Ministry of Finance (MOF), interact in allocating bank funds to industry. The relationship that has developed between these two rival ministries has improved the quality of industrial policies and decreased the probability of policy

---

[1] John Zysman has applied this line of argument to Japan, in *Governments, Markets, and Growth* (Ithaca: Cornell University Press, 1983), pp. 234–51. He argues that the state is all-powerful in allocating private funds to private companies through private banks because, he believes, of the allocation mechanism of the Japanese financial system. Because the Ministry of Finance (MOF) and the Bank of Japan (BOJ) establish artificially low interest rates, there is excess demand for money. A balance must be achieved by some form of credit rationing. Banks select the most desirable clients, but since part of their funds come from the BOJ, the banks in turn must be subject to BOJ credit rationing. Thus, in Japan, 'a rational banker *must* wish to follow the lead of the central bank. The government's industrial priorities of growth and exports will be met. The banks entangled with selected sectors will not be constrained by their ability to fund their loans, though banks in other sectors of the economy will be' (ibid., p. 248).

Zysman's comparative perspective offers a rough sketch of Japanese industrial finance. His argument, however, is advanced on many premises that do not hold in reality. The most critical is his assumption that the Ministry of International Trade and Industry and MOF act as if they constitute a single entity sharing their jurisdiction, i.e., they jointly and harmoniously administer both the industrial and financial sectors. However, in reality the two ministries each have their own jurisdictions in the financial and industrial sectors and they tend to have differing perspectives on the economy. This will be made clear in this chapter.

errors. Designed by MITI, industrial policies are not put into practice until they meet MOF approval.

In order to better understand this interministerial relationship as well as the role of the central bank in promoting industrial growth, I first examine the basic characteristics of the banking system in Japan. Loan practices and government regulation of the bond market have been instrumental in the government's ability to implement industrial policies through the banking sector. In the second section, I discuss the organization and roles of MOF, the Bank of Japan (BOJ), MITI, and other public bodies related to industrial finance. MOF was able to pursue a low-interest policy without constraints imposed by the BOJ, which is charged with the stabilization of currency, because of the dependence of the BOJ on MOF. In the third section, I examine the structure of the financial policy network linking financial authorities and the banking sector, and the structure of the industrial policy network connecting MITI and the industrial sector. I go on to show that the two networks were relatively independent and demonstrate how industrial policies formulated in MITI were often closely reevaluated and implemented by MOF. In the last section, I speculate on the role of the Liberal Democratic Party (LDP). The absence of the LDP in financial policymaking and financial administration, I argue, enabled both MOF and MITI to pursue growth-oriented financial policies instead of redistribution-oriented policies.

Because of the jurisdictions and controls—as well as the limits on their operations—of these two ministries, we see that MOF must rely on MITI for the formulation of policies but MITI in turn is dependent on MOF for the implementation of policies. The counterbalancing nature of their relationship holds an important key to the effectiveness of Japan's industrial policy.

Basic Conditions of the Banking System

Financial institutions, in any country, tend to be more strictly and widely regulated by the government than firms in the manufacturing and service industries. Indeed, it is difficult to envision a financial market independent of governmental regulation, and Japan is no exception. Banks in Japan are regulated, in part, by the Securities and Exchange Law of 1947, which prohibits banks from engaging in securities transactions other than those involving national bonds, thereby dividing the roles of banks and securities firms. The banking industry is comprised of 13 city banks, 63 regional banks,[2] 3 long-term credit banks, 7 trust banks, 71 mutual

---

[2] Both city banks and regional banks are categorized as 'ordinary banks' in the Banking Law. There are no legal provisions distinguishing them. See Shiro Makimura and Tsutomu Tamaru, *Chihō ginkō* (Local banks) (Tokyo: Kyoikusha, 1991), pp. 17–20.

banks,[3] 462 credit associations, 483 credit cooperatives, and a large number of agricultural cooperatives.[4] While the long-term credit banks raise capital by issuing financial debentures and offer long-term credit for use in investment by private corporations, other institutions rely upon the deposits made by their customers as a source of funds to lend and offer short-term credit. Only the trust banks are permitted to deal in trust and custodial services.

Loan practices vary among these institutions. City banks and other large banks act as a conduit to feed large sums from the household sector to leading industries. This characteristic is referred to as 'indirect financing' by banks and makes a striking contrast with Anglo-American financial practices, where most funds for industry are collected through the bond market or stock market.

The prevalence of 'indirect financing' by banks came into being mainly because MOF limited the issuance of bonds. That is, although the Temporary Fund Adjustment Law of 1937, which provided for legal control over bond financing, was abolished in 1948, MOF continued to 'guide' bond financing until the mid-1980s. The control lever of such guidance was the Bond Issue Committee, comprised of representatives of the largest banks and major securities companies, which had an obvious incentive to follow MOF guidance. The committee imposed stringent requirements regarding the financial soundness and size of firms that could attempt to issue bonds, and the rates the committee set for the bonds it allowed to be issued were extremely low. Thus, issuing bonds to obtain funds was made substantially less attractive than raising funds through bank loans whose interest rates were set at low levels.[5] In short, artificially low interest rates and strict regulation of bond issues blocked the direct flow of funds via the bond market from households to industrial firms, who are the final borrowers.

This 'indirect finance' system, whereby firms obtained funds indirectly through banks rather than directly via the bond market, enabled banks to exert significant influence on the business decisions of borrowers. Since part of banks' funds are borrowed from the Bank of Japan, further control is exerted by the government. This meant that MOF, having the power to affect the decisions of the BOJ, exerted its power over the financing of firms. Banks have supplied a large quantity of funds to firms, monitored firm activities carefully, and were able to change the policies of firms

---

[3] The mutual banks have been converted into regional banks since 1989 because their business was virtually indistinguishable from that of the regional banks and because they wanted to get rid of the smaller-scale business connotations of 'mutual bank.'

[4] See *International Banking: A Legal Guide, International Financial Law Review Special Supplement* (Sept. 1991), pp. 116–20.

[5] Koichi Hamada and Akiyoshi Horiuchi, 'The Political Economy of the Financial Market,' in Kozo Yamamura and Yasukichi Yasuba, eds., *The Political Economy of Japan, Volume 1: The Domestic Transformation* (Stanford: Stanford University Press, 1987), p. 236.

through various means, including dispatching bank executives to firms whose policies were deemed inappropriate.[6] Through the monitoring process, banks were able to obtain information about borrowers that would not otherwise have been accessible to outsiders. Information about borrowers gave banks an advantage over the financial authorities (MOF and BOJ) in responding appropriately to specific aspects of industrial policy.

Government Control

The Ministry of Finance

The Ministry of Finance is made up of seven bureaus, three of which are responsible for private-sector finance: the Banking Bureau, the Securities Bureau, and the International Finance Bureau, which oversees the foreign operation of Japanese financial institutions and the operations of foreign financial institutions in Japan. Because each bureau has its own jurisdiction and objectives, conflicts sometimes arise among them as they seek to protect the interests of their respective client industries. Several factors, however, do facilitate interbureau cooperation. The most important is the rotation of personnel, generally every year. A person who is a Banking Bureau official one year may be in the Securities Bureau the next. 'MOF is willing to sacrifice some degree of technical specialization to the higher goal of intraministerial coordination.'[7]

Regulatory power over the banking sector is monopolized by the Banking Bureau. In countries with a unitary banking system, such as Japan, regulatory power is shared by several authorities, including the central bank. The influence over banks wielded by the Bank of Japan (described below) is exercised under MOF supervision, and regulatory power over banks is centralized in MOF.[8] Overall, the postwar Japanese financial

---

[6] This was particularly true for 'main banks' (the city banks), which acted as the principal supplier of funds within an enterprise group, i.e., 'financial *keiretsu*.' M. Therese Flaherty and Hiroyuki Itami, 'Finance,' in Daniel I. Okimoto, Takuo Sugano, and Franklin B. Weinstein, eds., *Competitive Edge: The Semiconductor Industry in the US and Japan* (Stanford: Stanford University Press, 1984).

[7] Frances McCall Rosenbluth, *Financial Politics in Contemporary Japan* (Ithaca: Cornell University Press, 1989), p. 19.

[8] On the other hand, countries adopting the federal system, such as the United States, Canada, and Australia, have a dual banking system in which responsibility for bank regulation is divided between federal and state governments. (Louis W. Pauly, *Opening Financial Markets: Banking Politics on the Pacific Rim* [Ithaca: Cornell University Press, 1989], p. 19.) In the United States, for example, a state-chartered bank belonging to the Federal Reserve Board (FRB) is directly regulated by the state chartering agency and the Federal Reserve System; a state bank not belonging to the FRB is regulated by the state agency and the Federal Deposit Insurance Corporation; and a national bank is regulated by the Comptroller of the Currency and the FRB. (Arnold H. Heggestad and William G. Shepherd, 'The "Bank-

market has been regulated by MOF to the extent that the public has referred to it as a 'convoy system,' assuring the profitability of financial institutions. Just as transport ships are grouped together when crossing the high seas in wartime to enable fast cruisers and destroyers to protect the slower transports and cargo vessels, the Japanese financial system was characterized as one in which large, efficient banks followed the slower pace that had been set for small and inefficient banks.

MOF has three principal responsibilities. First, the ministry was and still is responsible for enforcing the boundaries between segments of the financial markets. Laws, orders, and administrative guidance limit the business activities in which each type of financial institution is permitted to engage. Enforcement is also segmented by the organizational division between the Banking Bureau and the Securities Bureau.[9] These bureaus are further subdivided, with the Banking Bureau, for example, divided into three sections, each responsible for a different subsector of banking. MOF is also responsible for maintaining order within each area of finance as defined by these boundary lines. The Banking Bureau controls the expansion of banks (the opening of new branches) and the types of financial instruments the institutions can offer. The Securities Bureau likewise exercises strong control over the opening of new branches by securities firms, new entry into the bond market, characteristics of the bond market, and returns on securities.

Second, MOF along with the Bank of Japan regulates interest rates in various submarkets of the capital market. The Temporary Interest Adjustment Law of 1947 gave the Policy Committee of the Bank of Japan the authority to set upper limits on interest rates on bank deposits in many different submarkets. In addition, interest rates not covered by this 1947 law, such as long-term prime rates, are set by MOF as administrative guidance. All this results in a highly regulated system in which all interest rates are tied to the official discount rate. The role of MOF in this field is to coordinate all other interest rates with the discount rate set by the BOJ.

Third, MOF has control over foreign parties operating in Japan. During the high growth era, financial officials tightly controlled the flow of foreign and domestic capital to and from Japan, by using the Foreign Exchange Law, in order to maintain Japan's international balance of payments at a given level. It was necessary to insulate the Japanese capital market from influences of foreign capital in order for domestic regulations to function effectively. If the inflow and outflow of capital were not regulated, the domestic system of regulated interest rates could easily be

ing" Industry,' in Walter Adams, ed., *The Structure of American Industry*, 7th ed. (New York: Macmillan Publishing Company, 1986), pp. 301–2).

[9] James Horne, 'Politics and the Japanese Financial System,' in J. A. A. Stockwin *et al.*, eds., *Dynamic and Immobilist Politics in Japan* (London: Macmillan Press, 1988), p. 173.

circumvented, thereby undermining the system. As Pempel has pointed out, the Japanese government stood between Japan and foreign countries and acted as a 'doorman' until the mid-1960s. It was able to determine what entered and left Japan, and under what conditions.[10] As a doorman, the Ministry of Finance was extremely selective and stubborn.

Although MOF's strength in the banking sector seems powerful today, even greater powers were vested in it during World War II. Postwar regulations, however, changed some of the ministry's wartime controls. Among others, the Emergency Funds Adjustment Law, which was enacted in 1937 to require banks to obtain governmental approval for large investments in order to choke off funding for non-essential industries, was nullified under the Allied Occupation (1945–52). Similar controls over the allocation of short-term credit, established in 1940, were also relinquished as the Occupation's programs of financial demilitarization proceeded.[11] Because the central regulation of credit has not been reestablished since the 1950s, MOF had to resort to administrative guidance to direct the lending practices of private banks in the postwar period. In short, MOF has had no formal power to direct banks to lend funds to specific firms and industries in the postwar era. To allocate credit selectively, therefore, MOF had to rely upon the Bank of Japan, which controls the supply of money to the economy.

The Bank of Japan

Since its foundation in 1882, the Bank of Japan has never been independent of the Japanese government. From 1931, it was increasingly used as a tool of militarist administrations to finance national aggression and support the central coordination of credit allocation. In 1942, the Bank of Japan Law was revised to confirm the Bank's subservience to the government. MOF was to issue direct orders to the Bank's management and dismiss any non-cooperative officers.[12] This law, modeled on the German 1939 Reichsbank Act, decreed that 'the Bank of Japan shall be managed solely for the achievement of national aims.'[13] The framework of the law was not revised during the Occupation and continues in effect today.

There are two ways to define the independence of a central bank. One is a behavioral definition. A central bank can be considered independent if it can set policy instruments without approval from outside authorities and if, for some minimal period of time, the instrument settings clearly

---

[10] T. J. Pempel, 'Japanese Foreign Economic Policy,' in Peter Katzenstein, ed., *Between Power and Plenty* (Madison: University of Wisconsin Press, 1978), p. 24.

[11] Jerome Cohen, *Japan's Economy in the War and Reconstruction* (Minneapolis: University of Minnesota Press, 1949), p. 85.

[12] Bank of Japan Law, Chapter IV.   [13] Ibid., Chap. I, Article 2.

differ from those preferred by the fiscal authority.[14] The other definition is institutional. Indication of institutional independence can be gleaned from the origins of governors appointed in the bank, their terms of office, their methods of reaching decisions, and so on. Statements of goals in the charter of a central bank may also help reveal its degree of independence. Such goals can range from a statutory duty to foster the general welfare of the country to specific requirements set by law—for example, controlling inflation, promoting full employment or production, or stabilizing the exchange rate.[15]

The Bank of Japan, according to the institutional definition, is one of the least independent central banks in the developed countries. The terms of the members of central banks' governing bodies vary from a high of 14 years to a low of 3 years. Three central banks are widely regarded as having some significant degree of independence—those in the United States, Germany, and Switzerland—and the terms for the United States (14 years) and Germany (8) are at the upper end of the scale.[16] In Japan, the official length of term in office for members of the central bank's governing body is four years, which is almost at the bottom of the scale. Among central banks in developed countries, only at the Bank of Japan is it clearly stated that top officials may be removed at the discretion of the appointing authority (the cabinet). Also, only the Bank of Japan is under the command of the government, specifically as well as generally. It is also audited by the government instead of an auditing authority more or less independent of the government. As for its goals, the Bank of Japan is expected to pursue 'national aims' rather than to stabilize the value of the currency.[17]

The institutional dependence of the BOJ on the government along with a traditional perception among the public regarding the relationship between the government and the central bank seems to have decreased its behavioral independence. During the Occupation, the Japanese banking system, including the central banking system, became a target of reform efforts. In 1948, the Finance Division of the General Headquarters of the Supreme Commander for the Allied Powers and the US Far East Command called for the establishment of a Banking Board with cabinet rank, to be independent of partisan and bureaucratic influence and vested with broad powers. Under this proposal, which aimed to reorganize the BOJ,

[14] John T. Wooley, 'Monetary Policy Instrumentation and the Relationship of the Central Banks and Governments,' *Annals of the American Academy of Political and Social Science*, Vol. 434 (Nov. 1977), pp. 170–2.

[15] King Banaian, Leroy O. Laney, and Thomas D. Willett, 'Central Bank Independence: An International Comparison,' in Eugenia Froedge Toma and Mark Toma, eds., *Central Bankers, Bureaucratic Incentives, and Monetary Policy* (Dordrecht: Kluwer Academic Publishers, 1986), p. 202.

[16] Nihon Ginkō Chosakyoku, *Chūō ginkō seido no shomondai* (Problems of the central banking system) (Tokyo: Nihon Ginkō, 1960), pp. 84–5.

[17] Bank of Japan Law, Chap. I, Article 2.

MOF, and their relationship, the BOJ was to have no policymaking role and was to be charged only with implementing programs determined by the Banking Board. The BOJ was also to be freed from domination by MOF. The Banking Board would have been much like the Board of Governors of the Federal Reserve in the United States. The proposal was to make the Japanese central bank independent of the government by recognizing 'the Banking Board as the architect and the Bank as the builder of Japanese monetary policy.'[18]

The proposal, however, was not realized. From the standpoint of policymakers in Washington, it was very doubtful that establishment of the Banking Board would have helped to resolve the most urgent problem facing the Japanese economy, that is, inflation. The Bank of Japan opposed the proposal because it feared being downgraded to a policy tool of the Banking Board. MOF also opposed the proposal because the Banking Board would have deprived MOF of regulatory powers over the banking sector and financial policymaking.

Although MOF's reaction to the proposal is understandable, the BOJ's is less clear. If the Banking Board had been established, the Japanese central bank would have acquired independent status for the first time. Considering the existing dependence of the BOJ on MOF, the BOJ's negative reaction to the proposal is still more incomprehensible. Even if the Banking Board had been established and BOJ put under its control, the position of the BOJ in the state would not have been altered significantly because the BOJ had already been under the control of MOF. But we must remember that the BOJ enjoyed de facto independence from MOF during the Occupation. Because MOF along with other central ministries was under attack by the Supreme Command of the Allied Powers and faced possible dismantling, it could not afford to control the BOJ.

As a compromise, a Policy Committee was organized within the framework of the BOJ to deal with policymaking. Its decisions would be carried out through the existing Bank mechanism. The legal organization of the BOJ was changed so that the Policy Committee could assume the position of what had previously been the role of BOJ governor, but the BOJ remained under the effective control of the governor for several reasons. First of all, the governor, who was the ex-officio member of the committee, was successful in his bid to become speaker of the committee. It was alleged that Bank executives, including then-Governor Ichimada, persuaded other members of the Policy Committee to vote for the governor. The first election established a precedent and since then the governor has automatically become speaker. Second, a secretariat was set up in the BOJ and the members of the committee did not have their own research staff. Third, Ichimada consciously broke communications between the

[18] William M. Tsutsui, *Banking Policy in Japan: American Efforts at Reform during the Occupation* (London: Routledge, 1988), p. 79.

committee and the working divisions of the BOJ so that the committee did not receive information it needed to decide financial policies by itself. All other efforts were devoted to restricting the activities of the committee. In short, the operational structure of the BOJ was left unaltered even after the committee was founded.

As for its relationship with MOF, some substantial monetary powers such as determination of the discount rate, establishment of rates of interest for financial institutions, and regulation of market operations were transferred from MOF to the BOJ Policy Committee. But the committee was not granted legal independence from the government because MOF maintained control over it; MOF control over the governor simply changed into control over the committee. Significantly, key supervisory responsibilities such as the authority to examine banks, grant licenses, and regulate the establishment of new branches were not transferred to the committee, but remained under the control of MOF. In short, the 'war time "chain of command" stretching from the bureaucracy to private-sector finance via the Bank of Japan was not broken.'[19]

Central banks, generally speaking, prefer economic stability, unlike governments, which prefer economic growth. If central banks were independent enough to behave as they wished, they would pursue a tight monetary policy rather than an easy monetary policy, even if the government were committed to a progrowth, low-interest policy.[20] The dependent status of the BOJ probably enabled the government to formulate a growth-oriented financial policy. First, the government could set both long-term and short-term loan rates and the rates paid on deposits at levels below market rates, the 'equilibrium' rates that would have resulted had these rates not been administered.[21] Second, because MOF and the BOJ maintained low-interest policies, 'indirect financing' took root in Japanese financial practices, as described at the beginning of this paper. Third, 'the credit-based, price-administered financial system'[22] encouraged excess demand for loans at the controlled rates and enabled MOF and the BOJ to allocate credit selectively to large firms in industries adopting new technology, increasing productivity, and expanding exports. Although economists are not agreed whether 'window guidance'— a form of moral suasion exerted by BOJ over banks to determine the rate of increase in loan funds available from banks for corporations—was

[19] William M. Tsutsui, *Banking Policy in Japan: American Efforts at Reform during the Occupation*, p. 86.

[20] See Alberto Alesina, 'Politics and Business Cycles in Industrial Democracies,' *Economic Policy*, Vol. 8 (April 1989), pp. 55–98.

[21] On how much or even whether or not these 'administered' rates differ significantly from market rates, see Hamada and Horiuchi, 'The Political Economy of the Financial Market.'

[22] Zysman, *Governments, Markets, and Growth*, p. 233.

effective in controlling the total amount of bank lending,[23] there seems to be a consensus that city banks mostly followed BOJ guidance although other banks did not. It is sufficient, therefore, to note here that the BOJ as a 'strong obligee'[24] was able to influence the lending patterns of city banks through window guidance to the extent that the BOJ had committed to industry strategies.

Before we examine the degree of commitment by financial authorities to industrial policies, let us briefly consider the third element of the state responsible for industrial policies through financial markets.

The Ministry of International Trade and Industry

Until the mid-1960s, MITI had a variety of tools for industrial policies at its disposal. Most important was the power to allocate foreign exchange (dollars) selectively, based on the Foreign Exchange Law in effect until 1964. Since most Japanese firms required imported raw materials and foreign technology, the ministry exercised this power by guiding firms in their decisions on the rate of capacity increase and to affect the timing, composition, and allocation of the flow of new technology.[25] However, MITI has been deprived of this power by the liberalization of trade that has developed gradually since 1961 when the first Joint Meeting of Economic Ministers of Japan and the United States was held in order to discuss conditions on opening the Japanese market. Since 1967, MITI has also lost its power to permit firms to introduce foreign technology, start joint ventures with foreign companies, and so forth, due to the process of liberalization of investment.[26]

Faced with the prospect of reduced legal powers, MITI tried in 1962 to enact a law that would have not only preserved its existing powers over the industrial sector, but would also have given it new powers over the banking sector. This was the Temporary Measure for the Promotion of Designated Industries.

[23] As for the recent controversy over the effectiveness of window guidance, see Akira Furukawa, 'Jissho bunseki: Madoguchi shido no yukosei to ginkojunbi no juokansu' (Empirical analysis: Effectiveness of window guidance and demand function of bank reserves), *Tōyō keizai rinji—zokan shirizu*, No. 54 (1980); Akiyoshi Horiuchi, 'Madoguchi shido no yukosei' (Effectiveness of window guidance), *Keizai kenkyū*, No. 28, No. 3 (July 1977); Iwao Kuroda, 'Madoguchi shido o meguru bunseki no saikento' (Reexamination of analyses concerning window guidance), *Kikan gendai keizai*, No. 37 (Winter 1979).
[24] Nihon Ginkō Chosakyoku, *Nihon ginkō: Sono kino to soshiki* (Tokyo: Nihon Ginkō, 1967), p. 80.
[25] George C. Eads and Kozo Yamamura, 'The Future of Industrial Policy,' in Yamamura and Yasuba, eds., *The Political Economy of Japan*, Vol. 1, p. 432.
[26] No description of MITI and its organization and function is provided here as it is readily available in English. See, for example, Chalmers Johnson, *MITI and the Japanese Miracle* (Stanford: Stanford University Press, 1982).

The basic plan of the temporary law was designed in the Organization Committee of the Industrial Structure Research Council set up in 1961 as an advisory body for the Minister of International Trade and Industry (the council was reorganized into the Industrial Structure Council in 1964). The organization committee consisted of seven members but did not include representatives of private banks or firms. The organization of the committee illuminated that MITI had no intention to listen to the voices of the affected interests in framing the plan.

After receiving the report of the committee, MITI embarked upon drafting the law. In the drafting process, a clause regarding fund allocation was the most controversial. A draft provided that representatives of industries and banks, ministers, and scholars should select industries that were strategically important in the international competition and decide the measures that would promote them. In this framework, banks would be required to supply investment funds to the targeted industries. Because the banks didn't want to be constrained in their lending practices by outsiders, however, they insisted that they would take part in shaping the measures but would not bear responsibility for implementing them. The banks repeatedly worked upon the drafters to loosen the binding force of the measures. Their efforts brought about a significant result. In the original draft, the banks were supposed to fund the targeted industries based upon the provision 'following the measures.' The provision was altered to 'respecting the measures' in the second draft and then was toned down to 'considering the measures' in the third. The final draft said that the banks fund 'taking the purport of the law into consideration.' The binding force of the clause was weakened in comparison with what MITI initially expected. If the law had been enacted, however, MITI would still have been able to administer banks' business.

MOF was negative toward the law proposed by MITI. Not only were they speaking for their clients in opposing MITI's proposal, but also they didn't want MITI to break into their jurisdiction. The banking sector was MOF's sanctuary where no one else was permitted to enter. It was also an important supplier of post-retirement jobs to financial officials. Moreover, MITI asked for more power than MOF had seized over banks. Even MOF had no authority to direct the banks to fund the specified industries. It was reasonable that MOF found even minor faults in the law and made complaints against it.

The bill, which was submitted to the Diet in 1963 after negotiations among the parties whose interests would be affected, granted MITI less power than the original plan assumed. Nonetheless, MITI encountered opposition from almost every direction. The industrial sector, whose representatives had not been invited to the deliberation process in the committee, dared not give government the key with which it could decide their life or death. The banks and MOF persistently managed to emasculate the law. The opposition parties harshly criticized the proposed law because it would violate the Antitrust Law. They also denounced the law as a relapse toward the prewar era during which the government coordinated credit allocations for munitions industries. Although the governing party or the Liberal Democratic Party (LDP) didn't oppose it overtly, it was not prepared to go so far as to steamroll the opposition of banks, industry, and the opposition parties.

The temporary measure was rejected by the Diet. Thereafter MITI submitted the same law to the Diet twice, only to trace the same path.

Thus an attempt of MITI to be a 'line agency' for financial policies ended in a failure. There was no other way left for MITI to take a role of a 'staff agency' which was attached to the financial authorities.

MITI obtained a lesson from this miscarriage. That is, in order to lead industries successfully, it had to consult them in advance. As many observers have pointed out, MITI has since then developed extensive networks with industries through such methods as inviting their representatives to councils. And MITI had to rely upon the MOF's administrative guidance to banks so that MITI could make banks supply investment funds to the strategically important industries.

The Structure of Policy Networks

Generally speaking, of all the ministries, MOF relies most heavily upon administrative guidance, although it is a ubiquitous process for enforcing public policies in Japan. Certainly the Banking Law enacted in 1927 vested MOF with regulatory authority over banks, but it was only a broad framework of 37 articles that left much to interpretation.[27] Administrative actions were carried out through administrative guidance, mostly in written form but on occasion orally. Notifications and other administrative guidelines issued by the ministry covered everything from regulations for the banking industry as a whole to regulation of the day-to-day operations of individual banks. A collection of notifications issued annually is published as a book with more than 1,000 pages.

The effectiveness of administrative guidance as a means for the government to encourage the private sector to take actions the government deems necessary has been emphasized by many scholars. It has been widely argued that although administrative guidance is an injunction

---

[27] This simplicity itself is a major reason why the old Banking Law was able to survive in the totally different political and economic environments of the prewar, wartime, and postwar periods. The Banking Law functioned with the support of such related laws as the National Mobilization Law and the Special Law for Military Finance during the prewar and wartime periods and was able to survive alongside such laws as the Antimonopoly Law mainly because the Banking Law was simple and left much to interpretation. The law was revised in 1982.

without coercive legal effect to encourage the regulated to behave in certain ways, the regulated know that yielding a little can reap rewards now and later in another aspect of their relationships with the ministries.[28]

As Haley has pointed out, however, 'administrative guidance should be treated as a generally weak means of enforcing governmental policy, one which absent formal controls and sanctions leaves room for maneuver and manipulation by those being regulated.'[29] Samuels has suggested that the extensiveness of administrative guidance should not be considered an indicator of state strength,[30] and this principle must apply even to MOF, alleged to be the strongest ministry in Japan's bureaucracy. If MOF issued a notification to regulate banks' lending practices, they could ignore it. In the case of ceilings on compensating balances—compulsory deposits that banks require customers to keep when banks lend money to them,[31] for instance, banks repeatedly failed to meet the ministry's guidelines without being subject to any sanctions. The effectiveness of bureaucratic discretion thus must not be exaggerated.

Rather than rely on its limited array of sanctions, each agency of the bureaucracy has sought to maintain close working relations with the sector under its jurisdiction, building up the credibility necessary to secure voluntary compliance.[32] MOF and the banking sector exchange their views in what Katzenstein calls 'nodes of the policy network,' that is, institutions connecting state and society.[33] In addition to the Federation of Bankers' Associations, the umbrella organization for the banking industry, each type of bank forms an association, such as the City Bank Roundtable, the Federation of Regional Bankers' Associations, and the Federation of Mutual Bankers' Associations. Credit associations and credit cooperatives organize their own national federations as well. All these voluntary organizations are forums where banks forge common positions *vis-à-vis* MOF and where the ministry can consult with them regarding financial policies. Representatives of banks are also given op-

---

[28] See Johnson, *MITI and the Japanese Miracle*, and John O. Haley, *Authority without Power: Law and the Japanese Paradox* (New York: Oxford University Press, 1991).

[29] John O. Haley, 'Administrative Guidance vs. Formal Regulation: Resolving the Paradox of Industrial Policy,' in Gary Saxonhouse and Kozo Yamamura, eds., *Law and Politics of the Japanese Economy: American and Japanese Perspectives* (Seattle: University of Washington Press, 1986), p. 122.

[30] Richard Samuels, *The Business of the Japanese State: Energy Markets in Comparative and Historical Perspective* (Ithaca: Cornell University Press, 1987).

[31] Banks used these compensating balances to increase their effective interest rate spreads. If, for instance, a bank lends ¥100 million to a corporation at the prime rate of 5.25 per cent and requires that 40 per cent of that be kept in a bank deposit getting 4 per cent interest, the corporation is in effect borrowing only ¥60 million for a net interest payment of ¥3.65 million, or an effective interest rate of 6.08 per cent. Rosenbluth, *Financial Politics in Contemporary Japan*, p. 41.

[32] Ibid., pp. 22–3.

[33] Peter Katzenstein, *Policy and Politics in West Germany: The Growth of a Semisovereign State* (Philadelphia: Temple University Press, 1987), p. 35.

portunities to express their opinions in MOF advisory councils, such as the Committee on Financial System Research and the Financial Problems Research Group.[34]

MOF and the banking sector thus make up the financial policy network. Their activities are intertwined in such a densely woven fabric that they must collaborate in order to function.

The industrial policy network, between MITI and industry, is more extensive than that of MOF mainly because MITI has less legal authority over related industries than does MOF. What Johnson called 'public policy companies' are examples of nodes of policy networks, such as public corporations, public units, government enterprises, special companies, and auxiliary organs.[35] There were 33 deliberation councils in MITI in 1981, including those formed as advisory councils having no legal standing. The Industrial Structure Council, the biggest and most famous, consists of several divisions such as the Iron Division and the Chemical Industry Division.

The practice of employing retired government officials as executives in private companies, that is, 'descent from heaven' (*amakudari*), is extensive within MITI as well as MOF.[36] Career mobility from government to business is usually interpreted as the consequence of government efforts to penetrate business decisions.[37] At the same time, however, it is the consequence of business efforts to influence government decisions. As Calder pointed out, in key industries such as banking, construction, and communications, retired officials descend to relatively small-scale companies rather than the leading companies that are strategically more important for MITI.[38] 'Descent from heaven' gives companies with otherwise weak influence access to the economic policymaking process in the government.

After MITI lost its legal authority over the industrial sector in the process of liberalization and failed to enact the Temporary Measure for the Promotion of Designated Industries, it was left with some effective tools for leading industries toward the ministry's purpose. Subsidies, tax exemptions, and governmental loans are examples. The ministry used these both as carrots and sticks in influencing firms' decisions. Most of the

[34] As for differences between the two bodies, see James Horne, *Japan's Financial Markets: Conflict and Consensus in Policy Making* (Sydney: George Allen and Unwin, 1985), pp. 79–84 and 96–7.

[35] Chalmers Johnson, *Japan's Public Policy Companies* (Washington: American Enterprise Institute for Public Policy Research, 1978), p. 25.

[36] For more discussion of *amakudari*, see the paper by Inoki in this volume.

[37] See, for example, Gerald L. Curtis, 'Big Business and Political Influence,' in Ezra F. Vogel, ed., *Modern Japanese Organization and Decision-Making* (Berkeley: University of California Press, 1975), p. 45.

[38] Kent E. Calder, 'Elites in an Equalizing Role: Ex-Bureaucrats as Coordinators and Intermediaries in the Japanese Government-Business Relationship,' *Comparative Politics*, Vol. 21, No. 4 (July 1989).

tools for industrial policies that MITI can mobilize are, however, not under MITI's exclusive control. In order to ensure subsidies for a targeted industry, for instance, MITI has to present a budget request to the Budget Bureau of MOF and get its approval. The amount of subsidies MITI can allocate to industries depends to a great degree upon MOF's decision. In the same way, in order to give tax exemptions to a certain sector, MITI must get the approval of the Tax Bureau of MOF. The determination of industrial policies through the manipulation of budgets and taxes is not decided solely by MITI but is 'settled in conjunction with the MOF'[39] in a linking of the industrial and financial policy networks.

MITI's capacity to implement industrial policies through the control of financial markets is still more limited by the presence of MOF and the BOJ. The banking sector, the main supplier of capital to industry in Japan, is under their jurisdiction. MITI lacks the tools it needs to influence the flow of funds from the banking sector to the industrial sector. It also has no effective interface with banks; in order to affect banks' decisions, MITI has to rely upon MOF's influence over them.

The most important fact concerning the implementation of industrial policies through the control of financial markets is that on one hand MOF has neither regulatory powers over nor communication circuits with the industrial sector, while on the other hand MITI has neither regulatory powers over nor communication circuits with the banking sector. That is, the two policy networks were patterned along the lines of established bureaucratic jurisdictions, a characteristic Muramatsu and Krauss have described for the Japanese political system as a whole.[40]

MOF's lack of interface with the industrial sector can be seen, for example, in its Budget Bureau. A target for pressure from all interest groups, including trade associations, this bureau tends to avoid direct contact with them mainly because budget examiners are afraid of being 'captured' by them. When an official of the bureau needs additional information to examine a MITI request for industrial subsidy, therefore, he sends questions to MITI officials rather than to representatives of the related industry.[41] The Finance Bureau handling 'the second budget' (the Fiscal Investment and Loan Program)[42] also stands at arm's length from

---

[39] Yoshihisa Ojimi, 'A Government Ministry: The Case of the Ministry of International Trade and Industry,' in Vogel, ed., *Modern Japanese Organization and Decision-Making*, p. 103.

[40] Michio Muramatsu and Ellis S. Krauss, 'The Conservative Policy Line and the Development of Patterned Pluralism,' in Yamamura and Yasuba, eds., *The Political Economy of Japan*, Vol. 1, p. 542.

[41] Although interest groups occasionally provided useful information to the Budget Bureau because their perceptions of their own interests might differ from those of the requesting ministry, as John C. Campbell has noted, such a meeting was held only in an *ad hoc* way. John C. Campbell, *Contemporary Japanese Budget Politics* (Berkeley: University of California Press, 1977), p. 59.

[42] The Fiscal Investment and Loan Program is the subject of Noguchi's paper in this volume.

industry for the same reason. According to Okimoto, the Tax Bureau decides on tax exemptions for industries after determining the total exemptions to be given to industry as a whole during negotiations with MITI. Thereafter, the Tax Bureau delegates to MITI the allocation of exemptions among industries; MITI can grant freely special tax exemptions in whatever amounts it deems appropriate for industries of its choosing as long as it stays within the limits of the agreed-upon aggregate ceiling.[43] This method is necessary also because the Tax Bureau lacks detailed information on the industrial sector.

The same holds true for three financial bureaus, the Banking Bureau, the Securities Bureau, and the International Finance Bureau. In order to understand the circumstances surrounding financial institutions, these three bureaus have built formal and informal networks with them. But because the three financial bureaus lack such networks with non-financial companies, they have little opportunity to obtain the information they need to form industrial policies, such as information on new industrial technologies, trends of markets, and promising industries for the future. MOF, in starkest terms, is not equipped for developing industrial policies and must therefore 'buy' them from MITI so that it is able to direct loans.

MITI in turn has no interaction with the banking sector. While eager to develop close working relations with industry, MITI has made no such efforts with the banking sector. Since the failure of the Temporary Measure for the Promotion of Designated Industries, MITI has refrained from breaking into MOF's turf. One exception was the Industrial Finance Committee, set up within the framework of the Industrial Structure Council. The committee, making one-year plans for coordinating banking loans with the investment needs of industry, was supposed to be an institution in which industrialists, bankers, and bureaucrats developed plans for coordinating investment. It was the sole body organized in MITI that elaborated policies for the allocation of financial resources through private banks. The committee, however, hardly functioned as an effective linchpin linking the financial policy network and the industrial policy network. First of all, banks sent very few representatives because they were cautious not to commit themselves to regulatory funding plans, as shown in the case of MITI's Temporary Measure for the Promotion of Designated Industries.

As a result, financial coordination through the committee was minimal. In the one-year period of the 1961 plan, for instance, lenders missed allocation targets by an average of nearly 6 per cent in most industries and by 11 per cent (cement) and 21 per cent (paper) in others. In 1962, planned investment targets were missed by over 10 per cent in the petroleum,

---

[43] Daniel I. Okimoto, *Between MITI and the Market: Japanese Industrial Policy for High Technology* (Stanford: Stanford University Press, 1989), p. 88.

petrochemical, ammonium sulfate, electronics, and paper industries, and in 1963 the targets for these industries were again missed by 6 per cent.[44] These discrepancies between planned and actual allocations suggests that banks, to a considerable extent, made loans according to their own criteria.

A more important point is that banks did not suffer MITI retaliation in spite of their failure to follow MITI-sponsored plans. MITI lacks retributive powers over uncooperative banks, either in the short or long run. In short, MITI is not equipped to implement industrial policies through action in financial markets and must therefore 'sell' them to MOF if it wants to realize such policies.

Industrial policies developed in MITI can be transmitted to MOF through several routes. Most important have been the special measures for targeted industries drafted by MITI, such as the Temporary Measure for the Promotion of the Machinery Industry and the Temporary Measure for the Advancement of Designated Electric and Machinery Industries. Although 'the promulgation of a regulation or a law is not the same as proof of its effectiveness,'[45] as Friedman pointed out, enactment of such industry-specific measures tends to be regarded by MOF as a sign of strategically important industries and is possibly used for guiding private banks' loans via the window guidance of the Bank of Japan. For the Japan Development Bank (JDB) as well, which has close ties with MOF rather than with MITI to which MOF dispatches many more officials than MITI, those special measures seem to be useful to know which industries are considered promising. The JDB, as one of its officials noted, furnished funds selectively to the industries promoted by special measures.[46] JDB loans, seen as indicators of industries the government was prepared to support in many other ways, helped those industries to extract loans from private banks.

The linkage among the enactment of special laws, JDB loans, and private bank loans is, however, not always straightforward. Even in the early stages of rapid economic growth, JDB loans were not as critical as might be expected in drawing money from private banks. This was illustrated by the Temporary Measure for the Promotion of the Machinery Industry of 1956. Among the five largest companies in the machine tool industry, all but one borrowed a significant share of investment funds from private banks before the law was enacted.[47] This suggests that banks decided on

[44] David Friedman, *The Misunderstood Miracle: Industrial Development and Political Change in Japan* (Ithaca: Cornell University Press, 1988), p. 207.

[45] Ibid., p. 4.

[46] *Nihon kaihatsu ginkō junen-shi* (Ten years of the Japan Development Bank) (Tokyo: Nihon Kaihatsu Ginkō, 1963), pp. 137–8.

[47] Minaru Sawai, 'Kosaku kikai,' in Shin'ichi Yonekawa *et al.*, eds., *Sengo Nihon keiei-shi dai 2 kan* (Postwar history of Japanese management) (Tokyo: Tōyō Keizai Shinposha, 1990), pp. 151–2.

their own criteria and made loans to industries before they were targeted. The main bank in an enterprise group (*keiretsu*) might supply funds to affiliated companies whether or not they belonged to a strategically important industry designated by MITI. It is relevant to note here that one of MITI's objectives with the Temporary Measure for the Promotion of Designated Industries had been to break the established financial practices in enterprise groups that tended to feed money to industries that MITI considered insignificant.

Following the enactment of a special measure, MITI submits to MOF a budget request containing subsidies and tax exemptions for the targeted industry, giving MOF a precise and concrete prioritization of MITI requests. Documents such as council reports and MITI white papers have also been useful in giving MOF an idea of MITI's long-term 'visions,' particularly since the 1970s,[48] provided that busy MOF officials take time to read them carefully.

It is important to note that MOF would not have complied with the industrial policies developed by MITI without making its own critical evaluation of such policies. MOF has developed its own way of examining other ministries' policies, including industrial policies. In their work on the British treasury, Wildavsky and Heclo have portrayed the ideal type of financial official as 'an able amateur': 'a great deal of his behavior can be deduced by assuming that he must make a large number of complex decisions in a short period of time without being able to investigate any of them fully. He relies on the ability to argue, to find internal contradictions, to pick out flaws in arguments whose substance he has not fully mastered and of whose subtleties he can only be dimly aware.'[49] Strictly speaking, this refers to the behavior of budget examiners in the financial ministry, but it is also applicable to MOF officials in charge of financial policies who attempt to examine industrial policies. They analyze MITI's policies with 'lay skepticism,' that is, mistrust of technical professions, self-serving private interests, and sophisticated quantitative analyses.[50] Some MOF officials might compare MITI's comments with information they happened to obtain from banks dealing with industrial firms. Although banks' information is usually firm-oriented rather than sector-oriented, it gives financial officials a vivid, though fragmented, image of industries that they cannot otherwise obtain. Such fragmented information may not be sufficient for financial officials to develop policies by themselves, but it is useful in criticizing MITI policies.

[48] Toshiya Kitayama, 'Tsushosangyosho ni okeru gyōsei sutairu no henka' (Changes in the administrative style of MITI), in Sōmucho, ed., *Shakai keizai no henka to gyōsei sutairu no hen'yo ni kansuru chosakenkyū hōkokusho* (Tokyo: Sōmucho, 1990), pp. 11–40.

[49] Hugh Heclo and Aaron Wildavsky, *The Private Government of Public Money: Community and Policy Inside British Political Administration* (Berkeley: University of California Press, 1974), p. 60.

[50] Ibid., pp. 44–5.

After MOF is convinced that a MITI policy is promising or at least will not damage banks' business, MOF in turn begins to persuade the banks to follow MITI's policies. The banks then examine the government's policies on their own criteria and may follow them when they are convinced such policies are acceptable. Even if the banks ultimately follow MITI's policies, there is a time lag between MITI's policy decision and the banks' implementation of such policies.

Because the financial policy network and the industrial network are coupled only loosely, industrial policies are decided and implemented through financial markets in what Lindblom 30 years ago called a 'disjointed manner.'[51] MITI develops industrial policies after extensive and intensive consultation with related industries. These are transmitted via several routes to MOF, which in turn examines and evaluates them from perspectives different from MITI's. Policies that gain MOF's confidence are passed to the BOJ or government-affiliated banks such as the JDB. The latter screen them on their own criteria, although the range of their discretion is not so wide. Finally, signals are sent to banks. Because banks—at least city banks—are sensitive to both MOF's administrative guidance and BOJ's window guidance, they will refrain from ignoring these signals completely, but when they think a government policy will be unprofitable or, worse, risky, they will manage to sabotage the policies.

Industrial policies implemented by banks, therefore, have been already endorsed by many related actors. It would be fair to say that the industrial policies that survive this long process are of proven quality.

The Role of the LDP

Within the financial policy network, an important role is also played by the governing party, the Liberal Democratic Party (LDP). One of the most important roles of the LDP has been consistently supporting low-interest policies as a means to help Japan achieve sustained economic growth. Without support from the LDP, usually latent but sometimes open, MOF would not have been able to influence the BOJ's decisions on interest rates. The LDP's role, however, stops there. The LDP delegates decisions regarding financial policies to MOF, whether or not they are related to industrial policies.

Banks, at least the big banks, have made large contributions to the LDP since its formation in 1955, making the industry one of the 'big three' private-sector funders of annual contributions to the LDP, along with the

---

[51] David Braybrooke and Charles E. Lindblom, *A Strategy of Decision: Policy Evaluation as a Social Process* (New York: Free Press of Glencoe, 1963).

electric power and steel industries.[52] The banks' total publicly reported political contributions have consistently amounted to about 20 per cent of private industry's combined contributions. Each of the city banks reported contributions to the LDP on the order of ¥65–75 million annually.[53] It may be assumed from this fact that the making of financial policy is highly politicized. LDP politicians seem to intervene heavily in the policy process to pay their debt to banks. The making of financial policy is, however, apolitical on the whole.

The banking industry has generally avoided becoming too close to individual politicians, even those with a great deal of influence, and has made lump-sum contributions to the LDP rather than contributing to individual influential politicians. Put differently, banks pay an insurance fee, as it were, for the generally favorable environment provided by the LDP's conservative and stable rule.

The LDP has left policy formulation and implementation in financial matters to the bureaucracy much more than it has in other policy areas and has avoided being involved in disputes on financial policies. This attitude of the LDP is in sharp contrast to that in the budgeting process. There are at least two reasons why LDP politicians refrain from intervening in financial policymaking, other than the seemingly plausible explanation that financial policy is too technical for them to comprehend. First, LDP politicians could not take rash steps toward helping banks because they must also protect banks' rivals, the securities firms, which are another important supplier of funds to the LDP. Securities companies have given less than banks in publicly reported annual donations but probably more through the 'back door.' It is widely alleged that securities companies have given politicians 'insider information' on good stock purchases, then effected price increases through concentrated efforts and told politicians when to sell for a handsome capital gain before the stock dropped.[54] The securities industry is, in short, another important constituency of the LDP. The most efficient way to maintain a balanced appearance had been for the LDP to not intervene in policy disputes affecting financial markets. 'Indeed, the LDP shows a strong preference for delegating to the MOF delicate balancing operations between Japanese banks and their rivals, the security houses, for fear of alienating either group. Delegation to the bureaucracy avoids or disguises political responsibility for the consequences of policy measures that may inflict some damage on supporters.'[55]

---

[52] Gerald Curtis, *The Japanese Way of Politics* (New York: Columbia University Press, 1987), p. 173.

[53] Tomoaki Iwai, *Seiji shikin no kenkyū* (A study of political contributions) (Tokyo: Nihon Keizai Shinbunsha, 1990), p. 115.

[54] Rosenbluth, *Financial Politics in Contemporary Japan*, p. 38.   [55] Ibid., pp. 26–7.

A similar explanation for politicians' lack of intervention in financial policymaking is that the LDP must also be concerned with the interests of banks' second greatest rivals, the postal service. It is important to mention here that although regulatory power over banks is concentrated in MOF, the Japanese savings system is divided into bank savings and postal savings. The Postal Savings Law of 1947, which has formed the basis for the operations of the postal savings system, established an independent decision-making framework for postal savings. While regulations relating to bank deposits are managed by MOF, postal savings matters are managed by the Ministry of Posts and Telecommunications (MPT). The Postal Savings Law directs MPT to take into account the interest rates offered on deposits by other financial institutions. However, the rates set by MPT were often marginally or appreciably higher than those set by MOF on deposits made in banks.[56] The differences in the rates remain a source of conflict between MPT and MOF. This conflict is especially acute when MPT fails to respond immediately on MOF plans to lower interest rates on bank savings that ask MPT to lower rates on postal savings.[57]

As I explain below, the influence of post offices in putting together a winning electoral coalition is believed to be immense, and thus their interests cannot be ignored. There are over 20,000 post offices in Japan, and a majority are categorized as 'special post offices' which differ from normal post offices in that their management receives commissions on sales. Because the position of postmaster is held in respect, the role of the post office network in the electoral support system for politicians can be significant. On average, there are about 400 post offices in each electoral district, and the support of the local postmasters' association can be of considerable importance to a politician, if used effectively.[58] These two sectors of the savings system have sometimes come into overt conflict regarding interest-rate decisions and the broader field of regulatory policies.

A relative lack of LDP involvement in financial policymaking seems to have a significant impact on the nature of the financial network. First, it has kept the opposition parties away from financial policies. Because the LDP rarely articulates its positions on particular issues in this area, the opposition could not find an opportunity to challenge government policies that affect people's well-being, such as low bank deposit yields or unfavorable terms of consumer credit. When the LDP was called to take a stand on the postal savings interest rate issue, the opposition parties were covertly allied with the LDP in supporting MPT. If the LDP were to

[56] See Yoshinobu Akiba, *Yūbinkyoku no chōsen* (Challenge of postal offices) (Tokyo: Nikishuppan, 1992), Chap. 2.
[57] For more information on the use of postal savings funds by the Japanese government, see the chapter by Noguchi in this volume.
[58] Horne, *Japan's Financial Markets*, p. 123.

intervene constantly in financial policymaking, the opposition would also be involved in it, as in the budget-making process.[59] One of the consequences that would likely result from LDP intervention in financial policymaking would be higher bank deposit rates, which would raise the cost of capital for industries.

Conclusion: Lessons from the Japanese Experience

We must be very careful in trying to draw lessons from the Japanese experience. Just because institutional arrangements of a certain country produce certain results in its own social, cultural, and historical contexts, we cannot expect to obtain the same or even similar consequences by simply transplanting those arrangements into other countries that have different backgrounds. We can neither export our cultural qualities to other countries nor import their social structure.

However, by examining the institutional arrangements for industrial policy that were discussed in this chapter in terms of their qualities that have decreased the probability of policy errors, however, we may be able to obtain several positive lessons from the Japanese experience. If the implementation of industrial policies through financial markets contributed to rapid economic growth in Japan, it is because those policies were developed from multiple viewpoints. Policies endorsed by MITI could not reach the financial sector unless they were accepted by conservative MOF officials; the separate financial and industrial policy networks have been loosely coupled since MITI failed to acquire legal power over banks. Therefore, Lesson One might be: Set up separately a ministry in charge of financial policies and a ministry in charge of industrial policies.

Industrial policies have not been developed solely by MITI but are the product of collaborative efforts by the ministry and the related industries. This is because MITI is empowered to guide industries in a certain direction, but cannot compel them to go where they are reluctant to go. MITI has made continued efforts to supplement its insufficient powers by consulting the industrial sector, which has resulted in good industrial policies. Thus Lesson Two might be: Vest a ministry of industry with such insufficient powers as to induce it to collaborate with industry.

BOJ's dependent relations with the government explain to a large extent the reason for continued low-interest policies, which have been critical for

---

[59] As Yukio Noguchi has pointed out, the basic function of the national budget in the rapid growth era was to adjust distortions caused by the imbalance of rapid growth (Yukio Noguchi, 'The Government–Business Relationship in Japan: The Changing Role of Fiscal Resources,' in Yamamura, ed., *Policy and Trade Issues*, p. 129.). This redistributional feature of the budget was brought in largely by competition between the government and the opposition.

the rapid growth economy. Following this simple causality, Lesson Three could be: Subordinate a central bank to the government. However, if the government had legal and effective authority to decide the discount rate and other interest rates, the decision-making process might have become highly politicized. Although it is difficult to evaluate the effects of a 'political business cycle' on economic growth, which might be caused by the politicization of financial policymaking, they probably distorted firms' investment decisions. Therefore, it seems appropriate to restate Lesson Three as: Subordinate a central bank to the government, but keep it away from partisan politics.

Although MOF is not empowered to command banks to adopt certain lending practices, it is influential enough to force banks to examine seriously those industrial policies MOF is convinced are necessary. This kind of relationship seems to enable banks to see the industrial sector in wider perspective. Lesson Four will thus be: Vest a ministry of finance with powers that induce banks to respect the ministry's guidance.

Japanese industrial policies are often characterized as market-conforming policies. Just because they are policies, they intend to guide Japanese industries in a certain direction. The market is ever-changing, and a policy direction should be finely tuned so that it can conform to the market and avoid committing errors. The Japanese institutional arrangement surrounding industrial policies induced the ministries and industry to examine them continuously from different angles. That behavior seems to have made the policies conform to ever-changing markets and to have led to Japanese economic success.

11

Institutionalizing the Active Labor Market Policy in Japan:
A Comparative View

IKUO KUME

In the postwar high growth period, most advanced industrial democracies made full employment an important political goal, and this commitment drove them to introduce various employment policies. A similar repertoire of employment policies is found in most of these countries. Despite policy similarities, however, unemployment rates diverged widely by the 1980s. In 1960–7, Japan, Germany, France, the United Kingdom, and smaller European countries—such as Austria, Belgium, Denmark, Finland, the Netherlands, Norway, and Sweden—boasted of unemployment rates below 2.5 per cent. However, only some smaller European corporatist countries—Sweden, Norway, Austria, and Switzerland—and Japan were able to keep their records of low unemployment into the 1980s.

Many studies have been conducted to explain this divergence.[1] One explanation is based on the countries' differing economic growth rates. For example, Japan achieved relatively high GDP growth after the 1973 and 1979 oil crises, and this evidently contributed to its low unemployment. In contrast, after the oil crises the economic growth rates in the smaller European countries were not as good as in Japan. A second explanation focuses on increases in public sector employment. This explanation is helpful in understanding several countries' low unemployment. Sweden, Norway, Austria, and, to a lesser degree, Switzerland significantly increased government employment after the oil crises and were able to absorb some would-be unemployed workers in the public sector.

These explanations, however, cannot fully explain the differences. First, the growth rate of the Japanese economy in 1974–9, although higher than

I would like to thank Peter Katzenstein, T. J. Pempel, Bruce Reynolds, Martin Kenney, and all the participants in this project for useful comments on this paper.

[1] See David R. Cameron, 'Social Democracy, Corporatism, Labour Quiescence, and the Representation of Economic Interest in Advanced Capitalist Society,' in John H. Goldthorpe, ed., *Order and Conflict in Contemporary Capitalism* (New York: Oxford University Press, 1984), pp. 143–78.

other countries', was lower than those of the high unemployment countries of the 1960s (e.g., the United States). Second, government employment increased in Belgium as much as in Austria, but the former suffered from greater unemployment. In sum, although economic growth and government employment are important factors in explaining low unemployment respectively in Japan and in the smaller European countries, some additional factors must be introduced to explain them as exceptions. Some scholars recently have used such factors as work organization, union strategy, corporate culture, and wage negotiation patterns to explain low unemployment in these countries.[2] Some economists try to explain the lower level of Japanese unemployment by focusing on an allegedly 'unique' Japanese factor, i.e., the abundance of marginal jobseekers, mainly female, who readily stop searching for jobs during economic downturns, and of underemployed workers who, while not satisfied with their jobs, retain them nonetheless.[3]

Such explanations miss the political and governmental contribution to low unemployment in Japan. In this chapter, I will focus on government employment policy as an important additional contribution to Japan's low unemployment. Sweden and Japan are famous for their extensive and consistent employment policy development, while the United States allegedly fails to deploy any consistent policy. In postwar Japan, we can identify three stages of employment policy development. Between 1945 and 1960 the main employment policy involved a public job creation program. Then from the 1960s to the first oil crisis (1973), employment policy became more market-oriented and active. This was designed to help job seekers find decent jobs through a nationwide placement service and intensive job training. Obviously the tight labor market contributed to this policy change. This, however, was not just reactive, but was instead a proactive change. It aimed to promote mobility of unemployed workers to reduce serious regional differences in employment rates.

Then, after the first oil crisis, the Ministry of Labor (MOL) developed a new employment policy to prevent unemployment. This provided employers with various incentives to retrain their employees for new job openings within the company, and for employers to hire redundant workers in targeted industries. This was an innovative extension of the active labor market policy of the 1960s, because it has attempted to stimu-

[2] See, for example, Ronald Dore, *Flexible Rigidities: Industrial Policy and Structural Adjustment in the Japanese Economy 1970–80* (London: Athlone Press, 1986); Lowell Turner, *Democracy at Work: Changing World Markets and the Future of Labor Unions* (Ithaca: Cornell University Press, 1991); Kuramitsu Muramatsu, 'Koyōchōsei no kettei yoin' (Determining factors of employment adjustment), *Nihon Rōdō Kyōkai zasshi*, No. 262 (1981), pp. 14–25.

[3] This explanation has some weaknesses because it is difficult to distinguish underemployed workers and marginal job seekers from ordinary ones. In addition, no extensive comparative study is available to conclude that the underemployed are abundant in Japan. See Isao Ōhashi, Kazuhiro Arai, Hiroyuki Nakajima, and Masuyuki Nishijima, *Rōdō keizaigaku* (Labor economics) (Tokyo: Yuhikaku, 1989), pp. 272–83.

late the market to reduce unemployment rather than simply creating public relief jobs. I argue that these employment policies have to some degree contributed to Japan's low unemployment.

Studies on government employment policy, however, do not agree on the specific impact on lowering the unemployment rate. For instance, one labor economist analyzed the unemployment rate and the employment adjustment subsidies designed to help structurally depressed companies retrain their workers through intracompany training and job reassignments. She then concluded that the policy was not very effective in reducing unemployment.[4] Against this view, MOL has argued that because this policy is designed to *preempt* possible unemployment within companies, the policy outcome could not be measured by unemployment statistics. Consequently, the ministry contended, she underestimated the effectiveness of official policy.[5] Employment policy in Japan has become so market oriented that its functioning is embedded within the market. Without understanding this, we tend to underestimate the effectiveness of the active labor market policy in Japan. A substantial number of economists now seem to agree on the effectiveness of employment policy especially after the oil crisis.[6]

The picture of the 1960s seems somewhat different. High economic growth was the main cause for low levels of unemployment. However, the government policy to facilitate labor mobility seems to have reduced unemployment by reducing the costs of job searches and recruitment. In the early 1960s, partly in response to the strong union movement in the declining coal mining industry, the government introduced a new set of employment policies to facilitate the mobility of redundant workers from coal mining to new jobs in other sectors. This policy worked fairly well. In 1963, for instance, 59,800 unemployed miners sought new jobs. Among them, 67 per cent found new jobs in other industries that year, 34 per cent were employed through the public placement service, and 19 per cent were employed through the mining companies' placement efforts.[7] The

---

[4] Eiko Shinozuka, 'Koyōchōsei to koyōchōsei joseikin no yakuwari' (Employment adjustment and the role of the subsidies for that adjustment), *Nihon Rōdō Kyōkai zasshi*, No. 317 (Oct. 1985), pp. 2–18.

[5] Eiko Shinozuka, *Nihon no koyō chōsei: oiru shokku ikō no rōdōshijō* (Employment adjustment in Japan: Labor market conditions after the oil crisis) (Tokyo: Tōyō Keizai Shinpōsha, 1989), Chap. 6.

[6] Haruo Shimada, *Rōdō keizaigaku* (Labor economics) (Tokyo: Iwanami Shoten, 1986). The analysis of the employment adjustment coefficient shows that Japanese companies are more reluctant to lay off workers in order to reduce output than are their American counterparts. Kuramitsu Muramatsu tried to find the causes of this difference and concluded that union organization is one determinant. His analysis did not include any policy variables, but there is a possibility that Japanese employment can be an additional determinant of the difference, given the absence of such a policy in the United States. Muramatsu, 'Koyō chōsei no kettei yōin.'

[7] Ōhara Shakai Mondai Kenkyūsho, ed., *Nihon rōdō nenkan* (Annual of Japanese labor) (hereafter *Nihon rōdō nenkan*) (Tokyo: Rōdōjunpō-sha, 1966), p. 476.

government's active labor market policy seemed to help the market function smoothly in absorbing unemployed workers. This leads us to the second and politically more important aspect of Japan's employment issue.

Japan and Sweden succeeded in preventing the emergence (or reducing the size) of an 'underclass'[8] while the United States, in spite of its economic prosperity in the 1950s and 1960s, failed to reduce the problem of such a semi-permanent underclass. Margaret Weir attributes this US failure to unsuccessful institutionalization of government employment policy and to inconsistency in implementation, despite many innovative policy ideas within the policy community.[9]

On the other side of the coin, in Japan we can find the consistent development of an active but market-oriented employment policy. In Sweden too, we find consistent institutionalization of an active labor market policy supported by a centralized national union federation, Landsorganisationen (LO), and the Social Democratic government.[10] Such a market-oriented active employment policy in Japan and Sweden has contributed not only to reducing unemployment, but also to preventing the emergence of an unemployable underclass. The policies sought to help as many unemployed as possible to take available job openings across the nation rather than providing them with public relief jobs where they used to be employed. In other words, Japan and Sweden created national labor markets while the United States, by providing the urban poor with public employment, impeded the development of a truly national labor market.

This is not just a result of economic growth. Historical experiences, such as those in Latin America, show that economic growth alone does not necessarily contribute to the abolition of the underclass. The case of the United States also suggests a similar point. In the midst of US prosperity, we can still find the persistent existence of an underclass. The lack of institutionalization of a national employment policy in the United States has resulted in its poor employment performance. More important, the sporadic development of public job creation programs allegedly resulted in both pork-barrel politics and, more seriously, in the creation of a segregated urban poor dependent on such public jobs in most urban areas. These experiences show that just the existence of economic growth

[8] Postwar Japan's income distribution is among the most egalitarian. In addition, we can find almost no 'underclass' that can be distinguished by demographic or other characteristics. See Toshimitsu Shinkawa and T. J. Pempel, 'Occupational Welfare and the Japanese Experience,' in Michael Shalev, ed., *Occupational Welfare and the Welfare State in Comparative Perspective* (New York: Plenum, forthcoming).

[9] Margaret Weir, *Politics and Jobs: The Boundaries of Employment Policy in the United States* (Princeton: Princeton University Press, 1992). Cf. Gary Mucciaroni, *The Political Failure of Employment Policy, 1945–82* (Pittsburgh: University of Pittsburgh Press, 1992).

[10] Hugh Heclo and Henrik Madsen, *Policy and Politics in Sweden: Principled Pragmatism* (Philadelphia: Temple University Press, 1987), pp. 46–79.

or a tight labor market does not necessarily let the labor market function well nor improve the conditions of the underclass.

This leads us to a political explanation. The labor market is a political creation rather than a given, as neoclassical economists typically presume it to be. Political action or inaction influences the nature of the labor market. In postwar Japan, an active employment policy played an important part in preventing the emergence of an underclass and, to some degree, in reducing unemployment. This policy was due to at least two factors. First, in Japan the members of the employment policy community were deeply concerned about unemployment due to Japan's 'unbalanced' economic development. This pessimism forced the government to formulate an active employment policy and served as a precondition for policy. But in addition, a second factor was the Ministry of Labor as a civil service institution. Various policies related to employment, e.g., occupational training, unemployment insurance, and unemployment-related public works, were all developed within MOL. These otherwise unrelated policies were linked to one another through the institutional framework of the Ministry of Labor and formed the core of an active market-oriented employment policy.

Moreover, these policies combining as they did to eliminate or shrink Japan's underclass and to generate low unemployment rates contributed substantially to Japan's economic dynamism and to reducing public demands for high government spending on a variety of welfare services. In this chapter, I will try to analyze how and why such a market-oriented employment policy was formulated and successfully implemented in postwar Japan. First I will review the development of employment policy in Japan, focusing on its shift from a state-centered to a market-oriented policy. Then I will analyze why this policy development was possible in brief comparison with the US and Swedish experiences.

Employment Policy in Postwar Japan

In this section, I will describe how Japanese employment policy changed from state-centered to market-oriented, that is, from a public job creation program to an active labor market policy. Figure 11.1 shows that the number of persons eligible for the Unemployment Relief Public Works (URPW) decreased drastically in the 1960s. In 1971 new legislation ensured that no newly unemployed individuals became eligible for the URPW. Yet MOL remained active in employment policy. Figure 11.2 shows the budget increase for employment security and public job creation. Since 1960 expenses for employment security policy have increased steadily, while those for the URPW have not. Therefore, a tight labor

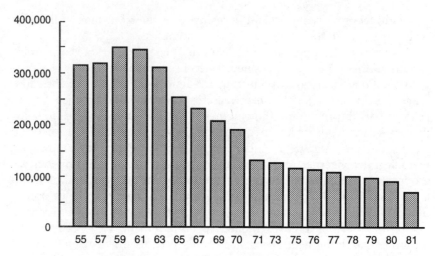

Source: Masami Takatsuji and Kiyoaki Tsuji, eds., Gendai gyōsei zenshū 10: Rōdō (Collection on modern administration, Vol. 10: Labor) (Tokyo: Gyōsei, 1984), p. 32.

Fig. 11.1. Number of Persons Eligible for URPW

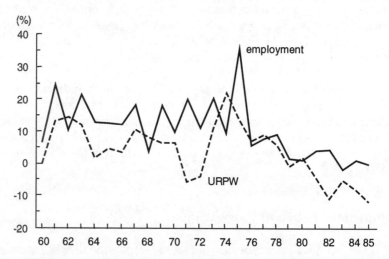

Source: Calculated from Bureau of Statistics, Office of the Prime Minister, ed., Japan Statistical Year book (Tokyo: Mainichi Shinbunsha, annual).

Fig. 11.2. Budget Growth of Employment Security and URPW

market did not result in a drastic decrease in the need for the state to intervene in the market.

Figure 11.3 shows organizational developments within the Ministry of Labor and indicates the changing strategy of MOL in the field of employment policy. The Bureau of Occupational Training was established from

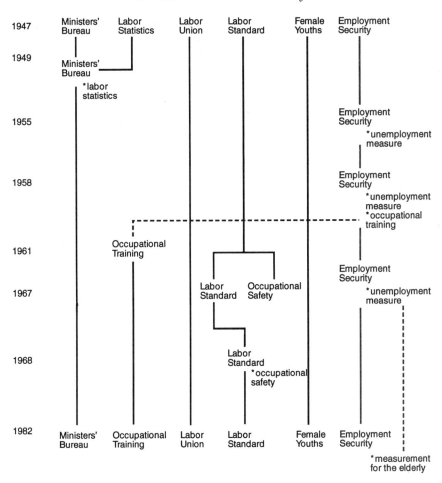

Source: Masami Takatsuji and Kiyoaki Tsuji, eds., *Gendai gyōsei zenshū 10: Rōdō* (Collection on modern administration, Vol. 10: Labor) (Tokyo: Gyōsei, 1984), p. 32.
Fig. 11.3. Ministry of Labor: Internal Bureaus and Sub-bureaus

the Employment Security Bureau in 1961, and these two bureaus are the main policy implementors of Japan's active labor market policy. On the other hand, the Sub-bureau on Unemployment Measures, which had been in charge of public job creation, was eventually converted into the Sub-bureau on Measures for the Elderly. Evidently, in the 1960s employment policy changed from state-centered to market-oriented. Let us review how this change occurred.

The Program for Public Jobs Creation

Japan's postwar constitution, formulated under the strong auspices of the Allied Occupation forces, has strong prolabor clauses. The rights to organ-

ize unions and to bargain collectively with employers are, for instance,
identified as fundamental rights of the people in the constitution. They
were legislated into the Labor Union Law of 1945. Furthermore, the
constitution has an employment rights clause. The new constitution requires a government commitment to full employment, although not its
immediate realization. Consequently, in the field of labor policy, major
institutional and policy developments were made after World War II.
In 1947 the socialist Katayama cabinet established the Ministry of Labor
from the labor policy and safety bureaus in the Ministry of Welfare and
legislated laws concerning public employment security, unemployment
insurance, and labor standards. To implement these laws, MOL, reorgan-
izing the prefectural labor policy offices, set up its own network of
local branches. The Public Employment Security offices were put in
charge of unemployment insurance and public occupational placement,
while 334 Labor Standards offices were assigned to regulate working
conditions.

However, constitutional provisions and the above policy developments
could not automatically achieve full employment. The devastated postwar economy was a long way from full employment. In 1946 the number
of fully employed was 1,590,000 and there were many underemployed or
potentially unemployed persons. Some 965,000 worked less than one
week per month; 995,000 worked in family enterprises without pay; and
2,448,000 worked 8–19 days a month.[11] Faced with this economic situation
and increasing unemployment as a result of the postwar demobilization,
the government first decided to implement public works projects as a way
to reconstruct the economy and to provide the unemployed with jobs.
However, the resulting public works projects did not absorb many of the
targeted unemployed. In 1948 the Public Employment Security offices
recruited only 20 per cent of the employed for the project. This is partly
because the locations of public works projects were often far from the
urban high unemployment areas. In 1946 almost 70 per cent of all public
works were implemented in rural areas.[12] Such projects were aimed principally at reconstructing the infrastructure of the economy rather than at
creating public relief jobs. This preference is clearly articulated in the
Cabinet Decision on the Urgent Public Employment Measure of February
15, 1946. It stated that this measure should not be allowed to degenerate
into simply poverty relief but should contribute to the reconstruction of
the Japanese economy.[13]

[11] Ministry of Labor, *Shitsugyō taisaku nenkan* (Annual of the Unemployment Public Relief
Work) (Tokyo: Ministry of Labor, 1951), p. 3.

[12] Yoshitaka Imaki, 'Shittaijigyo hōsei no enkaku' (History of the legal framework of the
Unemployment Relief Public Works) in Sōgō Rōdō Kenkyūsho ed., *Gendai rōdōhō kōza*, Vol. 13
(1984), pp. 253–4.

[13] Kazuo Ōkouchi, ed., *Shiryō sengo 20 nenshi 5: Rōdō* (Documents—twenty years after the
war, Vol. 5: Labor) (Tokyo: Nihon Hyōronsha, 1966), p. 3.

However, until 1949 when the disinflationary Dodge Line was implemented,[14] real unemployment was thought to have been covered up, to a great degree, in the heavily subsidized economy.[15] Then the members of the policy community predicted that the Dodge Line would change this situation dramatically and inevitably increase unemployment. Administrative reform and rationalization in the private sector in those days resulted in a substantial jump in unemployment. From 1948 to 1950 the number of the fully unemployed increased from 240,000 to 440,000.[16]

Predicting an increase in unemployment and recognizing its subsequent sociopolitical costs, the government, following the cabinet decision of March 4, 1949, quickly submitted a bill on Urgent Relief Measures for the Unemployed to the parliament, which passed it immediately. The basic idea was that although unemployment should be solved by developing the national economy, it would be necessary, given the economic difficulties of the times, to create public jobs for the unemployed. Consequently, the government started the Unemployment Relief Public Works Program as a project separate from existing public works projects. Noteworthy is the fact that the goal of this new project shifted from economic reconstruction to the temporary creation of jobs for the unemployed. The cabinet decision of 1949 described this new category of public works as involving relief measures for the unemployed, with priority being given to public jobs.[17] This program was quickly developed in subsequent years and created many public jobs for the unemployed (see Figure 11.4).

Problems and Possibilities

The number of the fully unemployed did not increase as was predicted. This was partly the result of the economic boom caused by the Korean War of 1950. Instead, underemployment came to be regarded as an important problem by members of the policy community. In 1953 MOL's Deliberation Committee on the URPW published a report on underemployment. The report defined underemployment as a situation in which workers were employed in unreasonably bad conditions of very low

[14] For more information on the Dodge Line, see the paper in this volume by Ito.

[15] In 1945 and 1946 it was very difficult to recruit workers in the coal mining and textile industries. This was because, with hyper-inflation and the prevalence of the underground economy, people just did not have enough motivation to work in the productive sectors. Yasutsuna Nakajima, *Shokugyō antei gyōseishi* (Administrative history of employment security) (Tokyo: Koyomondai Kenkyūkai, 1988), pp. 165–8. In 1946 the Ministry of Welfare conducted a survey of 400,000 unemployed workers and found that only 23,000 wanted to be employed. Also in 1946 only 68 per cent of job openings were filled. Keizai Antei Honbu, *Keizai jissou hōkokusho* (1947), cited in Ōkouchi, ed., *Shiryō sengo 20 nenshi*, p. 1.

[16] Sorifu Tokeikyoku, *Rōdōryoku chōsa*, cited in *Shiryō sengo 20 nenshi*, p. 530.

[17] *Nihon rōdō nenkan*, 1950, p. 793.

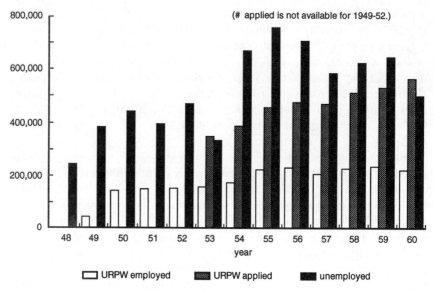

Source: *Nihon rōdō nenkan*, 1961, pp. 375–76.
Fig. 11.4. URPW and Unemployment

wages and/or for short and volatile terms. It proposed that MOL should develop a comprehensive employment policy to make all workers better off by targeting not only the fully unemployed but also the underemployed.

In this context the issue of underemployment requires that employment policy be integrated with overall economic policy. In the early 1950s there was, however, no consensus on how to solve the unemployment problem in this broader economic policy among the party politicians or within the policy community. Roughly speaking, three types of solution were considered, although advocates for all three agreed upon the necessity of the URPW program. The first involved the socialist idea of emphasizing the state's responsibility to ensure full employment. From this perspective, state ownership was often proposed to deal with unemployment. The nationalization of the coal mining industry was a typical example of this policy orientation. The second perspective involved a 'liberal' idea, emphasizing market mechanisms as a fundamental tool for dealing with unemployment. Liberals with such a view typically regarded public job creation for the unemployed as a necessary but temporary or exceptional measure. For them, unemployment was to be solved through economic development, which could be realized only through market competition. The third view could be labeled a 'democratic planning' perspective and proposed more 'planning' and state intervention. From such a view, an integrated industrial policy was necessary to develop the Japanese economy with minimum unemployment.

After the Katayama and Ashida Socialist-Democrat coalition governments (May 23, 1947–October 7, 1948) collapsed and as the left wing gained power within the Japan Socialist Party (JSP), the socialist idea lost any possibility of being realized.[18] Thereafter, it was between the liberal and the democratic planning perspectives that significant political discourse on employment policy was exchanged. The parliamentary discussion in the early 1950s demonstrated a typical difference between these two ideas on employment policy. Labor Minister Hori of Prime Minister Yoshida's liberal government stated that although everyone would want full employment, it should not be given first priority as a political goal. He argued that any increase in employment should come after economic development. At that time, the government supported management's rationalizing efforts within private companies. Unions, on the other hand, were militantly opposed to any such rationalization and the unemployment that resulted. For the liberals, it seemed to be necessary to have 'frictional' unemployment, which the future rationalized economy could absorb. For this purpose, the liberals saw the unions' power to resist rationalization as the most serious problem. In 1954 the Yoshida cabinet's Minister of Labor Kosaka bluntly proposed an overtly antilabor policy. He argued that the government should reduce protection for the unions and advocated deregulation of labor standards, although he did simultaneously propose new legislation to control layoffs. His idea was somewhat similar to the neoliberal idea of the 1980s, presuming that if the market functioned freely and the economy developed, the unemployment problem (although not unemployment per se) would eventually disappear.

The democratic planners criticized this liberal idea as a form of *laissez-faire* capitalism that was insensitive to the economic problems of both workers and small and medium-sized companies. For instance, Shuji Kawasaki of the Democratic Party, criticizing Hori's labor policy, advocated integration of a full employment goal into the government's economic development plan.[19] Politicians in this democratic planners' camp were critical of Yoshida's liberal government and were eager to fuse the goals of full employment and industrial policy.[20]

This democratic planning idea was introduced into the labor policy of the Hatoyama cabinet, especially under Labor Minister Kuraishi, after the merger of the Liberal and Democratic Parties in 1955. In the parliament, Kuraishi proposed that labor policy be integrated into broader economic

[18] These are the only cabinets the JSP has formed in the entire postwar period, as of July 1993.

[19] *Nihon rōdō nenkan*, 1952, pp. 638–9.

[20] Shinsuke Kishi and Tanzan Ishibashi are among the politicians who strongly advocated full employment and an industrial policy against Yoshida's 'laissez-faire' capitalism. Shinsuke Kishi, *Kishi Shinsuke kaikoroku* (Reminiscences of Shinsuke Kishi) (Tokyo: Kouseidō, 1983).

322 *Ikuo Kume*

policies.[21] Against the economic-growth-comes-first idea, he argued that economic development and an increase in employment should be pursued simultaneously in the government economic development plans. Then he flatly denied any necessity to reduce protection for workers by reforming the Labor Standards Law as a means to increase employment. This was the first time a labor minister proposed government intervention to make the labor market function so efficiently as to absorb as many of the unemployed as possible. This represented the start of a new policy idea toward a market-oriented employment policy.

In the following year, Labor Minister Kuraishi proposed a more comprehensive policy package to solve the unemployment problem. It consisted of three proposals. The first was to develop the economy by supporting the 'productivity movement' of the Japan Productivity Center. The second involved passage of the new Basic Law on Employment.[22] The objective of this legislation was to require the government to consider maximization of employment in formulating every economic policy. The third proposal involved a new Minimum Wage Law. The common goal of these three policies was to develop the economy in ways that included maximum employment and better working conditions. The logic ran as follows: to increase productivity by rationalization might result in a marginal increase in unemployment. In response the government should introduce policies to facilitate economic development which would provide those unemployed with better jobs in the more successful industries. In this policy package, MOL tried to transform its employment policy into a market-oriented policy. It emphasized expansion of the economy as a major mechanism to achieve maximum employment rather than emphasizing the government's direct creation of jobs for the unemployed.

This market-oriented employment policy was further consolidated by Labor Minister Ishida in the Ikeda cabinet. In July 1960, when he was reappointed as Minister of Labor, Ishida said, 'Labor policy hereafter will focus more on the role of labor in the broader economy, e.g., on wages and employment, rather than on policy toward labor unions.'[23] At the time, MOL recognized three main challenges: (1) an increase in young job seekers; (2) difficulty in finding jobs for middle-aged people, despite a persistent labor shortage of skilled workers; and (3) continued severe unemployment in some regions. Therefore MOL advocated an active labor market policy (originally called the developmental employment policy). This consisted of two specific policy goals, i.e., increasing labor mobility across the nation to solve regional unemployment problems

[21] *Nihon rōdō nenkan*, 1956, p. 640.
[22] This was finally legislated as the Employment Measures Law in 1966, as described in the main text.
[23] *Nihon rōdō nenkan*, 1961, p. 369.

and helping workers to acquire the skills necessary to gain jobs in the prospering manufacturing sectors.

This new employment policy finally resulted in the Employment Measures Law of 1966, which prescribed that the government should pursue the goal of full employment in formulating and implementing public policies. This was not the first legislation articulating such a commitment to full employment; this commitment had been made earlier in the Law to Establish the Deliberation Committee on Employment in 1957. However, the 1966 law is very important in that it was the basic law that required the government to coordinate its policies with the goal of maintaining full employment. It required the government to set up a Basic Plan to Facilitate Employment at the cabinet level, in which economic and industrial policies were coordinated with employment policies such as occupational placement service and measures regarding skill formation.

Among others, the Subsidies for the Change of Jobs Program, introduced by the Employment Measures Law, showed the characteristic nature of this active labor market policy. Two categories of persons were targeted by this program: those who could not find jobs easily, such as the handicapped and the middle-aged, and those who lost their jobs in industries targeted by the government for restructuring. After receiving unemployment insurance compensation, such persons were eligible to receive additional allowances for living, training, and job search trips. Moreover, the program provided their employers with subsidies to hire and train them. The basic idea behind this program was that the government would try to increase the 'value' of the unemployed in the labor market and to help them to find appropriate jobs. Therefore this was clearly an 'active' labor market policy, in contrast to the previous policy mix of public job creation and unemployment insurance. The latter presumed a clear demarcation between market and government, with the government providing emergency shelter, outside the labor market, for the unemployed looking for job openings by themselves or waiting for the next upturn in the economy. The former policy meant active government intervention in the functioning of the market. It required that employment policy be a part of economic policy. This therefore represented a major change in the nature of employment policy from state-centered to market-oriented.

However, these two policies differed on another important point. The latter explicitly facilitates labor mobility across the entire nation, while the former was largely indifferent to such moves. One of the reasons for the URPW legislation was to reduce serious unemployment in some regions by creating jobs in that area rather than moving the unemployed to areas where there were job openings. The market-oriented active employment policy that followed was also a policy designed to create a nationwide labor market.

New Policies

No grand design for a new employment policy actually guided this change; rather, it was a patchwork policy development. Yet three policy areas—occupational training, unemployment relief public works, and unemployment insurance—all show similar moves toward a market orientation. These evolved somewhat independently but the result was an integrated active labor market policy in the form of the Employment Measures Law of 1966 and later in the Employment Insurance Law of 1974.

Occupational Training   Before the Occupational Training Law of 1958, there was no comprehensive program for occupational training. Two types of policy related to training, one each under the jurisdictions of the Labor Standards Bureau and the Occupational Security Bureau. The Labor Standards Bureau had a program to promote a modern training system within companies. Its main objective was to abolish the premodern 'exploitative' apprentice system in the private sector and to protect newly employed youths. The Occupational Security Bureau had an occupational guidance program whose purpose was to teach skills to the unemployed. The former was mainly a regulatory policy, while the latter was part of the relief measures for the unemployed. The occupational guidance policy, for instance, was originally implemented in response to short-term needs. A typical goal was to provide the unemployed with skills necessary for public works, such as carpentry and construction skills. What was missing was the link of occupational training to broader economic policy.

However, this occupational guidance gradually became part of long-term economic policy. First, the program began teaching skills for machinists, who were necessary for Japanese economic development. Second, MOL set up the Comprehensive Occupational Guidance Center to implement a coordinated public occupational training program. Third, MOL started a training program for occupational instructors who could conduct intracompany training.

Following these incremental developments, the Occupational Training Law was legislated in 1958. It consolidated the training programs of the Labor Standards Bureau and the Occupational Security Bureau under the jurisdiction of the Occupational Training Sub-bureau (which eventually became a bureau in 1961). The objective of the legislation was to reorganize occupational training under a single explicit goal, namely, economic development through skill formation among workers and by supplying enough skilled workers to industry.[24]

---

[24] In large companies in Japan, there exists a 'lifetime' employment system, and thus training is usually done within the firm. Therefore, this public job training is mainly for small and medium-sized companies, which have difficulty establishing their own training programs because of their size and high labor turnover.

In this new system, the public occupational training institutions were hierarchically reorganized: the General Occupational Training Office at the prefectural level; the Comprehensive Occupational Training Office, for advanced training, at the national level; the Central Occupational Training Center for training instructors and for occupational research; and the Occupational Training Center for the Handicapped at both the prefectural and national levels. This reorganization aimed to set national standards for skills and to decrease the transaction costs between employers and job-seekers. The national examinations for various skills and a subsequent skill certificate system were established for this objective. Both were conducive to the nationalization of the labor market.

This law was again revised in 1969 to adjust to the changing market situation and the clear need for more labor mobility and higher skills. Public training and intracompany training were integrated more closely by setting up the same skill standards and categories. This was one of several efforts to facilitate labor mobility. Retraining also became an important part of the policy for labor mobility. Occupational training became more market-oriented through patchwork-like policy and institutional developments, and consequently contributed to a nationalization of the labor market.

Unemployment Relief Reform   The other side of this move toward a market-oriented policy involved reform of the public job creation program. As noted above, the government developed the URPW as an important policy tool to solve unemployment problems during the 1950s. However, there was a growing awareness of unexpected problems in implementing the URPW. The first problem was how to balance the goals of job creation and public works. The URPW was often criticized for its inefficiency as a public works project in failing to develop a better economic infrastructure. This was partly because a strong leftist union organized this sector. The union resisted any government efforts to make the projects efficient, simply seeking to maximize benefits. Second, workers in this project tended to stay there rather than to return to the normal labor market. They were older workers and/or did not have enough motivation and opportunity to get jobs in the normal labor market. This was an unintended outcome of this project. Third, local governments, which implemented and partly financed the URPW, began complaining about the financial burdens and inefficiency of the project.[25] They wanted to spend their money with greater discretion and to develop their own projects more efficiently.

In 1955 MOL's Deliberation Council on the URPW, responding to these problems, proposed that the URPW should not simply create jobs but

---

[25] In 1957, the National Mayors Association formally complained about the increasing financial burden caused by the URPW. It said that 25 urban cities had to spend more than 20 per cent of their general revenue for the URPW. *Nihon rōdō nenkan*, 1958, pp. 357–8.

should be implemented efficiently as public works projects. It also advised that the government should set up an adequate project to help those employed in the project to maintain and improve their skills in order to return to the normal job market quickly. From then on, various labor ministers proclaimed the necessity of implementing the URPW efficiently. In 1957 the Deliberation Council on Employment, which succeeded the Deliberation Council on the URPW, more openly described the problem of the URPW. The council concluded that the URPW had become a program for unemployed who could not return to the normal labor market and it no longer functioned as a temporary shelter for the newly unemployed.

Recognizing these problems, MOL originally tried to solve them by forcing those employed under the URPW to return to normal jobs. For instance, MOL set up a new project called the Special URPW, which targeted relatively able workers. Its aim was to make them ready for normal jobs by letting them experience jobs similar to those in the normal job market. In implementing this program, MOL required applicants for the URPW to take a physical examination, which would tell who should go into this new category or, more preferably, into normal public works projects.

In addition, MOL, working with the Ministry of Welfare, set a clear demarcation between the social welfare programs of the Ministry of Welfare and the URPW. The idea was to screen applicants for welfare and those for the URPW, and decide who should take which. In this way MOL expected that about 20,000 mostly elderly applicants would be transferred to the welfare program.[26]

In sum, MOL tried to push the supply side of the labor market by creating ways for the unemployed to return to the labor market. However, this move had its limitations because however hard MOL pushed, many employers simply did not want to hire them. From time to time, MOL deliberately admitted that, taking the real situation in the URPW into consideration, it would be difficult to abolish or reduce it immediately.

In the 1960s, facing a shortage of skilled workers and high unemployment among the middle-aged, MOL generated an alternative solution. Focusing more on the economy itself, it began trying to train the URPW workers to promote their employment in normal jobs. It did this by subsidizing employers. In other words, MOL transformed its unemployment policy from a state-centered direct job-creation program to a market-oriented intervention program. The new idea was to facilitate the market in absorbing the unemployed, by training them and providing employers with incentives to hire them. This led to the 1963 revision of the Emergency Unemployment Relief Law.

[26] In 1959, the total number eligible for the URPW was 348,664. Of these, 15.5 per cent were over 60 years old. *Nihon rōdō nenkan*, 1960, p. 378.

One example of this new policy orientation involved the Program to Facilitate the Employment of Day Workers, established in 1962 to help those eligible for URPW to get 'permanent' jobs in the expanding national labor market. In the first year it succeeded in moving 12,000 to stable jobs.[27] Since the 1963 revision the URPW has been reduced, and no newly employed workers have become eligible since 1971. This is again the story of a shift from a state-centered to a market-oriented employment policy and toward the nationalization of the labor market.

Unemployment Insurance   Unemployment insurance was introduced for the first time in Japan in 1947. From then on, the Unemployment Insurance Law has been revised frequently to adjust to new economic situations. Here again we find a policy shift toward active intervention in the labor market, but in a market-oriented way.

The Dodge Line and the subsequent increase in unemployment required MOL to revise the law in 1949. This revision aimed at increasing insurance benefits and expanding coverage for construction workers and service sector workers, such as those in hotels and restaurants. Furthermore, MOL established unemployment insurance for day laborers, whose employment was especially vulnerable to recessions. The idea behind this revision was very similar to the establishment of the URPW in its 'passiveness.' It was largely regarded as a temporary shelter for the unemployed, one that would enable them to wait for the next economic upturn.

However, a broader economic consideration gradually become embedded in the implementation of the law. In 1954, faced with recession, MOL established a new rule to implement the Unemployment Insurance Law. This enabled employers to lay off workers for a short term (three months) using conditional unemployment insurance benefits. First, the given lay off had to be massive as a result of rationalization aimed at overcoming serious economic problems within the company. Second, the company had to have sufficient possibility for revitalization and promise to reemploy the laid-off workers. Third, the company needed recognition from the minister of labor or the prefectural governor. The coal mining and shipbuilding industries were immediate beneficiaries of this new rule.[28] This rule also indicated that MOL had begun to use unemployment insurance in a strategic way to run the economy.

This orientation became much clearer in the 1963 revision of the law. The important point of that revision was that insurance compensation

---

[27] Ministry of Labor, Shokugyō Antei Kyoku, *Shokugyō antei kōhō* (Public report on employment security) (Tokyo: Ministry of Labor, Dec. 1, 1963, public relations publication). In 1964, 15,300 of the URPW were employed in companies and 5,200 became self-employed. *Nihon rōdō nenkan*, 1966, p. 473.

[28] In 1957, this rule was applied to the synthetic fiber industry. This time, conditions were more favorable for the industry, setting no limits on the lay-off term and requiring no specific permission from the prefectural governors. *Nihon rōdō nenkan*, 1958, p. 362.

was increased significantly for individuals taking occupational training.[29] MOL obviously intended to use this insurance program as an important component of an active labor market policy rather than just as a shelter for the unemployed.

This orientation also led MOL's efforts to streamline the program. The 1963 revision introduced a clause requiring that those who changed jobs could have their subscription term counted as if they had been continuously employed. This had previously been technically impossible for MOL because it did not have a nationwide information network of the insured. The introduction of a computer network enabled the change. In 1964 MOL established the Labor Market Center as a central information center to link the local public employment security offices across the nation. On the other hand, MOL regarded compensation for seasonal workers and young females as a problem for the insurance program. The former, coming out of farming areas, routinely received unemployment compensation, while the latter, retiring for marriage, often received compensation by pretending to seek other jobs. Therefore, in 1964 MOL tried to revise the law again to restrain such practices, but the revisions failed to pass the parliament due to socialist opposition.[30] Thus, MOL tightened the screening at local offices.

These efforts at streamlining were also related to a new policy idea of using the insurance program as a part of a broader economic policy. The goal of these efforts was to shift more resources from 'abuse' to effective use by a labor force available for national economic development. This streamlining effort was finally fulfilled in the 1974 Employment Insurance Law.

The Employment Insurance Law: A Conjunction of Policy Developments
These semi-independent policy developments were eventually fused as a more systematic policy package in the 1966 Employment Measures Law described above. A subsequent development, the 1974 Employment Insurance Law, is often regarded as the completion of the innovative development of the active labor market policy. It played a considerable role in economic adjustments in Japan after the oil crisis.

The high economic growth period of the 1960s and the early 1970s enabled Japan to have a full employment economy. This was good news for MOL. The bad news was that business leaders and politicians now began talking about ending the employment policy and disbanding MOL

[29] Before this revision, beneficiaries could get additional compensation, if they were taking occupational training upon request by the Public Employment Security Office. This revision made beneficiaries taking any training based upon the laws eligible for additional compensation. *Nihon rōdō nenkan*, 1963–4, p. 413.

[30] In 1963, Prime Minister Ikeda said that the minimum employed term for compensation eligibility should be increased from six months to one year, and MOL pursued revision of the law.

as an organization. The special budget for labor insurance (including unemployment and labor accident insurance) now produced a huge surplus. MOL had to search for a new *raison d'être* and to formulate a new policy goal aimed at increasing workers' welfare and preempting unemployment.

This new policy idea appeared in the Employment Insurance Law of 1974. Using the insurance account, this law set up three programs in addition to unemployment insurance: the Employment Improvement Program, the Program to Develop Workers' Abilities, and the Employment Welfare Program. The first two are important to this chapter, because in their emphasis on training and labor mobility they involved further development of an active labor market policy beyond that of the Employment Measure Law of 1966. The important advancements were (1) creating a stable fund for policy implementation and (2) preventing unemployment.[31] These programs introduced many subsidies for employers to preempt unemployment, such as subsidies to extend the retirement age, for employment of workers from targeted declining industries, and for training employees. Since then, similar but more intensive programs, such as the Employment Stability Fund, were developed for the same purposes.[32] These policies played a positive role in helping many industries to restructure production and maintain employment levels.

Japan in Comparative Perspective: Possible Explanations

Why did Japan develop an active labor market policy? There could be a functional explanation, attributing the policy change to changes in the market or economy. Economic growth and a subsequent tight labor market allegedly required the government to facilitate labor mobility so as to control the labor cost for businesses. According to this explanation, it was natural for direct job creation to be dissolved, so as to let workers move to job openings in the private sectors. However, it took a lot of time and effort for MOL to dissolve the URPW and to introduce a new employment policy. This very fact demonstrates that the policy change was never an automatic functional adjustment to market changes. Rather, it was a highly political endeavor.

Employment policy debates in the United States, Sweden, and Japan show surprisingly similar policy ideas, such as direct job creation, public occupational training, and subsidies for the employer of the targeted jobless.[33] Intensive international learning processes have gone on, but in

[31] This is why this law is called the Employment, not Unemployment, Insurance Law.

[32] Akira Takanashi, *Aratana koyōseisaku no tenkai* (Development of new employment policy) (Tokyo: Rōmu Gyōsei Kenkyūsho, 1989).

[33] Helen Ginsburg, *Full Employment and Public Policy: The United States and Sweden* (Lexington: Lexington Books, 1983).

the United States such policy ideas were not systematically institutional-ized. In Sweden and Japan they were institutionalized with a consistent market orientation. Three possible causes have contributed to the insti-tutionalization of Japan's active labor market policy: political ideas, legitimacy building, and institution building.

Political Ideas

What differs among these three countries is a broader political idea, which supported (or did not support) the various employment policy ideas. For these policy ideas to be pursued consistently and systematically, a commitment to full employment had to be embedded within the policy community.

In the United States, although we find the emergence of a strong com-mitment to full employment during the New Deal era, the failure of the Full Employment Bill of 1945 and the passage of the Employment Act of 1946 demonstrate that such a commitment was eroded relatively quickly during the postwar economic boom. On the other hand, in Sweden there was a continuous and strong commitment to the goal of full employment across party lines. This commitment became the basis for the development of various employment policies into a broader active labor market policy.

What about Japan? As mentioned earlier, there was a prevalent fear of unemployment in postwar Japan. This was partly because of the pessi-mistic view concerning the possibilities for Japanese economic develop-ment. This forced the policy community to keep its commitment to full employment even during high economic growth and internationally low unemployment.

This commitment to full employment was, at the same time, a product of labor's strong demands for secure employment. It is well known that Japan's 'docile' labor unions tend to become very militant once manage-ment announces an intention to dismiss employees. The 'lifetime' employ-ment system in the large and usually unionized companies would present laid-off middle-aged workers with severe difficulties in finding equiva-lent jobs in the market.[34] The possibility of labor unrest due to unemploy-ment was one of the main motives within the policy community for introducing the various employment policies.[35]

In addition, at the party politics level, Japan experienced the merger of the Liberal Party and the Democratic Party into the Liberal Democratic

[34] In Japan, enterprise unions are densely organized in large companies, and not in small or medium-sized companies, partly because of the scale economy. It is mainly in the large companies where 'lifetime' employment can be found. Therefore this explanation is for large companies. However, it does not mean that workers in small and medium-sized companies are easily dismissed. In those firms, such a dismissal from time to time would result in bitter labor conflicts.

[35] In the 1950s, MOL often advocated the new employment policy as a means to prevent or relieve possible labor unrest caused by unemployment.

Party (LDP) in 1955, which since then has been continuously in power. Before 1955 the former had advocated a classical economic liberal policy, while the latter preferred a more employment-oriented policy.[36] This merger resulted in the consolidation of the market-oriented 'liberal' idea and the employment-conscious 'democratic planning' idea as the new mainstream policy idea within the governing coalition. In short, the creation of the LDP meant a market-oriented employment policy. Therefore, unlike the United States, Japan did not suffer from partisan competition designed to sell new 'innovative' employment policies, which often abolished existing policy. Japan had a relatively stable political environment for the development of employment policy. This helped MOL to pursue a consistent employment policy and to introduce a variety of employment policies, even though it has not been among the most powerful ministries in Japan.

Legitimacy Building

An active labor market policy is not the type of policy that sells itself. It requires workers in declining sectors to change jobs and, if necessary, even to relocate to other regions of the country. Therefore, the government had to sell its policy to workers in order to implement it successfully. In Sweden the active labor market policy was formulated by social democratic economists, Rehn and Meidner, and was sold enthusiastically by the central union organization LO and by the Social Democrat government. This campaign convinced workers that relocations and job transfers were necessary costs of maintaining full employment and a prosperous national economy. Social democratic hegemony was evidently conducive to the successful selling of an active labor market policy in Sweden.

In Japan it was also difficult to sell this new policy, and more so under the conservative government. As we have seen in this chapter, the idea of an active labor market policy appeared in the 1950s. However, the idea did not get massive support from workers in then declining industries. The coal mining industry provides a good example. In the 1950s coal mining was faced with a serious decline as a result of the 'energy revolution.' Many coal mining companies tried to introduce rationalization plans, but were confronted by militant opposition from labor. Originally, the unions demanded state support to maintain employment within the coal mining industries. From time to time, management also implicitly supported these demands. However, this tactic gradually became impossible, because of the increasing price differences between domestic coal and imported oil. The unions then began demanding that the government provide them with jobs in the regions where they had been working. The

---

[36] Hideo Ōtake called the former 'economic liberalism' and the latter 'social democracy.' Hideo Ōtake, *Adenaua to Yoshida Shigeru* (Adenauer and Shigeru Yoshida) (Tokyo: Chūōkōron-sha, 1985).

government responded with public works and by trying to promote alternative industries in the areas of unemployment. In a sense, the government at the beginning followed the established policy menu of direct job creation to deal with unemployment.

However, it became clear that the structural decline of the coal mining industry could not be relieved by such government-supported rationalization plans. At the same time, the problems in implementing public job creation became apparent to the policy community members as described above. On the other hand, the Miike coal miners' strike of 1960 and the subsequent coal miners' movements dramatized the necessity for the early introduction of a new employment policy. MOL, with strong support from Prime Minister Ikeda, gradually introduced various policies, including subsidies for the employers of coal miners, the occupational training of coal miners, and nationwide job placement services. In other words, an active labor market policy package was eventually introduced for the first time in Japan, although only for coal miners.

It was important to build political support for this new policy to be implemented successfully. It is well known that Prime Minister Ikeda introduced the Income-Doubling Plan in 1960, stating that the Japanese economy would be so developed that workers' incomes would double in ten years. The government could sell this policy by, for example, providing the coal miners, who had been working in dangerous and demanding conditions, with modern decent jobs in prospering industries. The government tried to change the image of relocations and job changes from necessary costs to absolute benefits. In fact, the active labor market policy for the coal miners worked fairly well and enabled MOL to fully develop that policy in the form of the 1966 Employment Measures Law. Even Sōhyō (the largest national federation of unions in Japan, representing one-third of organized workers), which had strongly criticized that policy from its leftist position, by 1968 admitted its mistake in overlooking the importance of facilitating labor mobility to increase workers' welfare.[37] Although it did not actually endorse MOL's active labor market policy, even Sōhyō came close to accepting the basics behind such a policy. Thus, the conservative government succeeded in building legitimacy for its active labor market policy in ways that allowed MOL to implement the policy rather comprehensively.

Institution Building

To establish a consistent employment policy, it is not enough to have an excellent policy idea and to sell it successfully. The employment policy development often involves a patchwork and incremental process of insti-

---

[37] Sōhyō Seisaku Iinkai, *Gijutsu kakushin to koyōhoshō*, Sōhyō 40th convention document, 1970.

tution building. This was not true for the United States but it was for Sweden. In the United States new employment policies were often formulated and implemented by newly created institutions outside the Department of Labor,[38] while in Sweden they were formulated and well managed by the National Labor Market Board (AMS). AMS was firmly embedded in the Swedish political system by extending its organization boundaries deeply into society. Consequently, stable institution building facilitated a consistent employment policy development in Sweden but not in the United States.

In Japan, MOL's institution building was a prerequisite for subsequent policy developments. For instance, MOL succeeded in gaining jurisdiction from local governments over the local labor standards offices and the public security offices. This enabled MOL to have its own nationwide network of policy implementation. In addition, unemployment and labor accident insurance programs were developed and further strengthened the national network in the 1950s, as seen in Figure 11.5 which shows increases in special account budget personnel. Furthermore, MOL introduced a computer network as early as 1963 to deal with information regarding individual job seekers as well as employers to rationalize the implementation of insurance administration. This nationwide network helped MOL to realize its idea of an active labor market policy by giving it necessary information and tools for implementation.[39] It is important that incremental policy and institutional developments in the field of employment policy have been accumulated within the institutional setting of MOL.[40]

This institutional development in Japan, however, does not explain why MOL eventually pursued its market-oriented active employment policy. For instance, the Ministry of Agriculture, Forestry, and Fisheries (MAFF) has similarly developed an integrated bureaucratic organization, but it has never initiated a market-oriented agricultural policy. The process whereby MOL was established answers the question. Before MOL's establishment, labor policy was in the jurisdiction of the Ministry of Welfare (MOW). Immediately after World War II, the discussion about establishing MOL started under the Occupation. Some argued for the establishment of an agency of social services within MOW and some argued for a ministry of labor. The former tried to learn from the European experience while the latter looked to the US Department of Labor.[41] In addition, within MOW there was some opposition to the estab-

---

[38] Weir, *Politics and Jobs*, p. 112.

[39] In Sweden, the Employment Service, administered by AMS, has a nationwide network for implementation, consisting of district and local offices as well as mobile units. Ginsburg, *Full Employment and Public Policy*, p. 136.

[40] The notorious Japanese 'horizontally compartmentalized bureaucracies' seem to be good for this institutional development.

[41] Mamoru Naka, *Rōdōshō* (Ministry of Labor) (Tokyo: Gyōsei, 1990), p. 23.

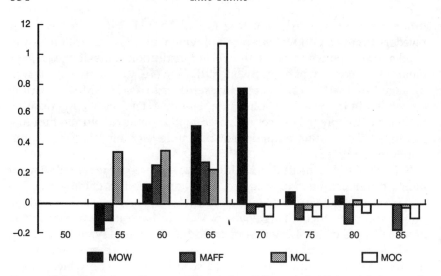

Source: Calculated from Bureau of Statistics, Office of the Prime Minister, ed., *Japan Statistical Yearbook* (Tokyo: Mainichi Shinbunsha, annual).

Fig. 11.5. Number of Personnel in Special Account Growth (per cent)

lishment of MOL, and MOW tried to retain the widest possible jurisdiction.[42] This dispute was settled under the socialist Katayama cabinet when MOL was established in roughly its present form on September 1, 1947.

This organizational development was very important in determining the nature of subsequent labor policy in that the establishment of MOL independent of MOW created a clear dividing line between welfare policy and labor policy. From the very beginning, labor policy was destined to be a part of economic policy. It should be remembered that MOL, trying to reform the URPW and to introduce a market-oriented employment policy, made clear that the older employees in the URPW should be taken care of by MOW. This clear demarcation between welfare policy and employment policy helped MOL to introduce its active labor market policy. This is similar to the Swedish case in which AMS was set up to be solely in charge of labor market policy. On the other hand, it is different from the US case where the demarcation between welfare policy and labor market policy was never clear, as can be seen from the War on Poverty program.

Moreover, various employment related policies, e.g., occupational training, unemployment insurance, and public job creation, have been formulated and implemented within this single institutional framework of MOL. This enables MOL to solve labor market problems arising in one policy arena by realigning its entire set of policies. For instance, the

---

[42] It is well known that MOW tried to keep the Labor Accident Insurance Program.

problem of public job creation was partly solved by developing an occupational training program instead. This was easily done, because these other policy repertoires are all under the jurisdiction of MOL. The various employment related policies, which later became important components of the active employment policy, were in MOL's jurisdiction. This was very conducive to the development of employment policy. If, for instance, the public job creation program had been under the jurisdiction of MOW, that policy might have evolved in a very different way, probably in line with welfare policy development.

The tripartite institutional setting of MOL also contributes to the market orientation of MOL and the logic of a market-oriented labor policy. Within MOL there are many deliberation councils, special committees, and so on, consisting of representatives of labor, management, and the public interest. This signifies that MOL is to some degree a mediatory institution that does not represent a single constituency. In other words, MOL cannot single-mindedly provide workers with pork-barrel benefits as, for example, is done by the Ministry of Construction and MAFF. Again this characteristic is attributable to the fact that MOL was not set up as a social welfare agency which prevented MOL from degenerating into the pork-barrel politics of public job creations as in the United States.[43] Moreover, with business and public interest representatives, the market consequences of labor policy are automatically part of the agenda.

Conclusions

Japan's market-oriented employment policy has had a positive impact on reducing unemployment. Furthermore, it prevented the development of an 'underclass' and kept pork-barrel politics out of the labor policy arena. In sum, market discipline was deeply embedded and made employment policy market-oriented rather than 'political.' However, somewhat paradoxically, it was necessary to have active political intervention in order for the market-oriented labor market policy to have been created. This does not mean that the government needed to have a grand design for its labor market policy from the beginning. However, several institutional characteristics contributed to its development. This story thus provides some lessons for effective market-oriented employment policy development.

---

[43] This is also because the governing LDP did not care much about political responses from the URPW employed, because they were organized by the leftist union Zen'nichijiro. However, there is a possibility that the LDP government could sell these programs to its local constituencies, as it has done in the public works project of the Ministry of Construction. Kent E. Calder, *Crisis and Compensation: Public Policy and Political Stability in Japan* (Princeton: Princeton University Press, 1988), pp. 274–311.

First, it is important for the government to set up an institution with sole responsibility for the labor market and to let that institution develop its organizational network consistently.

Second, and related to the first point, a clear line of demarcation between employment policy and social welfare policy should be drawn by setting up separate institutions in charge of these two jurisdictions.

Third, a tripartite and mediatory policy implementation, involving consultation among management, labor, and public interest representatives, can be conducive to less pork-barrel politics and less distortion of the labor market mechanism.

In addition, a strong commitment by the government to the goal of full employment combined with stable political support for employment policy are important. These, however, are conditions deeply influenced by the nature of state-society interactions rather than by simple government effort. Therefore it would be relatively difficult to transplant them in some countries. There is no one best set of state-society relations for successful employment policy development, as a comparison between Japan and Sweden shows us. In these two countries, we can find, of course, many structural differences. For instance, in Sweden, the strong centralized labor union, LO, and the hegemonic Social Democratic Party played an important role in maintaining the goal of full employment, while Japan's decentralized enterprise unions and 'lifetime' employment among other things contributed to the maintenance of the full employment goal within the society. Moreover, a conservative mix of economic liberalism and paternalistic 'welfarism' in Japan could be the functional equivalent of Swedish social democracy, and it supported an extensive employment policy development. Thus it seems that there are various pathways to the successful introduction of a market-oriented, active employment policy.

12

Institutionalizing the Local System: *The Ministry of Home Affairs and Intergovernmental Relations in Japan*

KENGO AKIZUKI

The central argument I advance in this chapter is that Japan's intergovernmental system, which has had many consequences, has most importantly provided stable institutions, the infrastructure for political and economic activities throughout the postwar period.

Institutions are important simply because they shape patterns of actors' behavior, which sometimes may seem chaotic and totally unpredictable. The world of local politics has many participants: local politicians, business, political parties, residents, central agencies, and so forth. Each has different interests to pursue and different perspectives on political events. Institutions that deal with local governments are important because they govern, shape, direct, or simply influence this complex situation. They are at the same time vulnerable as they are influenced by the environment within which they operate. Striking divergences among democratic countries on how local governmental institutions function come as no surprise.

What does Japan's experience in the postwar period tell us? It suggests that successful institutionalization of the local system (i.e., relatively stable intergovernmental relations) could promote local government activities—including policymaking in economic, welfare, and other areas—but not without significant sacrifices. Specifically, Japan's system provides local actors a financial safeguard that enables them to deal with a variety of issues. It also provides a set of stable rules for actors involved in intergovernmental processes, which enhance their willingness to participate. However, a well-institutionalized system takes some goals (such as financial independence) and functions (such as rule-making) away from local government. This double-edged effect of institutions will be found throughout this chapter.

For helpful comments, I am grateful to all the participants in this project and to Gregory Kasza.

To start, I outline basic features of Japan's intergovernmental system by focusing on one central bureaucracy, the Ministry of Home Affairs (MHA). It is a cornerstone of the entire local governmental system in Japan. First, I describe the administrative and legal framework of the system. Second, I deal with the financial dimension, especially how money is transferred from the central government to local government. Third, I consider MHA's roles in controlling local finance. Specific attention is directed to how MHA's financial control is implemented and how successful it has been in reality.

My analysis shows that Japan's intergovernmental system, financial and administrative, is not dominated by this ministry. Although its powers are extensive and its political power formidable, MHA, just like other famous Japanese ministries such as the Ministry of Finance (MOF) or the Ministry of International Trade and Industry (MITI), is by no means omnipotent. MHA faces a difficult task environment. Where I deal with MHA in relation to localities and central agencies, I offer a more nuanced image of local government and finance in Japan.

However, while it is important to stress that MHA does not control local governments, I also point out that it has been instrumental in stabilizing and institutionalizing the local system. The most important role played by MHA is its relations with local government. From this viewpoint, I will discuss the implications of the case of Japan in the concluding section.

Stability is one of the striking features of Japan's local system. Some OECD countries, such as the United Kingdom and France, have experienced revolutionary changes in their local systems. The United States has kept its basic constitutional structure of federalism intact, but it also has made drastic changes in intergovernmental financial relations. Also, the severe financial difficulties of some US localities dealt a serious blow to the credibility of the system. In Japan, changes have occurred but much more incrementally. Financial problems of local governments in Japan have been less serious. How the institutions built by and around MHA have stabilized the local financial/governmental system is the main focus of this chapter.

Conventional wisdom is that Japan's postwar local system has not matured because of its highly centralized legal and financial structure. Revisionist views, on the other hand, emphasize the politically spontaneous nature of Japanese local governments.[1] In fact, there is a mixture of what these two viewpoints represent. I argue that while MHA's control certainly has curtailed (not as much as conventional wisdom suggests) the autonomy of local governments, its involvement in institutionalizing

[1] Kurt Steiner, *Local Government in Japan* (Stanford: Stanford University Press, 1965); Kiyoaki Tsuji, *Shinban Nihon kanryōsei no kenkyū* (Bureaucracy in Japan—new edition) (Tokyo: University of Tokyo Press, 1969).

and stabilizing the local system has helped solidify the basis of local governments' activities on their initiative.

The case for Japan, as readers will see, does not provide a single, complete 'model' for other countries to follow, but merely demonstrates problems and policy implications intrinsic to a local government system in modern society. As I discuss in the last section, that is because the local system does not have a single goal to achieve; there are fundamentally different ideals people expect it to pursue. MHA's ambivalent role (which will become apparent in the following analysis) is a reflection of the complex nature of the local system itself.

Outline of the Local Government System in Japan

Japan is a unitary state in which the local government system is created by the central government. Unlike federal countries such as the United States, territorial subdivisions are determined at the national level. There have been no legal disputes over whether national law has supremacy over local ordinances.

Japan has had an organized modern local government system since the Meiji period (1868–1912). Some democratic ingredients were included in the Meiji local system: local assembly members were directly elected and the local chief executive was chosen by the assembly. But the prefectural governor was appointed by the national government, and the appointment was based not upon the national Diet but on imperial ordinances. Local governments in the Meiji period were, largely speaking, nothing but agencies for the imperial government.

Today local autonomy in Japan is protected by four articles in the Constitution of 1947:

Article 92. Regulations concerning the organization and operation of local public entities shall be fixed by law in accordance with the principle of local autonomy.

Article 93. Local public entities shall establish assemblies as their deliberative organs, in accordance with law. The chief executive officers of all local public entities, the members of their assemblies, and such other local officials as may be determined by law shall be elected by direct popular vote within their several communities.

Article 94. Local public entities shall have the right to manage their property, affairs, and administration and to enact their own regulations within law.

Article 95. A special law, applicable only to one local public entity, cannot be enacted by the Diet without the consent of a majority of the voters of the local entity concerned, obtained with law.

These provisions reveal the basic character of a unitary system. Unlike in federal countries, the central government retains final say. The one limit on what local governments do is 'law'—legislation passed by the Diet. Three major bills concerning the local system were passed after the constitution: the Local Autonomy Law in 1947, the Local Finance Law in 1948, and the Local Tax Law in 1950.

Legally speaking, the Diet can change the current local government system overnight if it chooses to. In fact, the vague term of 'local public entity' (instead of 'prefecture' or 'city') was used in the constitution to allow room for changes in the local system without constitutional amendment in the future. But there has been no drastic change in these laws and, therefore, the local system has remained largely intact since the constitution was enacted.

Local governments are organized into a basically two-tier system. The first tier is made up of the 'primary local entities'—cities (*shi*), towns (*chō*), and villages (*son*)—closest to the people and their communities. I will refer to them as 'municipalities' for brevity. There are several requirements for a municipality to be a city, such as a population of more than 50,000. There is no significant difference between a town and a village.

The chief executive of a municipality is the mayor. The municipal assembly is the legislative body for municipalities. Both the mayor and the members of the assembly are directly elected by the inhabitants. As of 1990, there were 3,245 municipalities in Japan.

Prefectures form the second tier. There are four different Japanese words to describe the 47 prefectural bodies: there is 1 *to* (metropolis; Tokyo), 1 *dō* (Hokkaido), 2 *fu* (Osaka and Kyoto), and 43 *ken*. Tokyo is somewhat different from the other three, in that it has 23 special wards in its central area along with municipalities on its periphery. These 23 wards are subdivisions of the Tokyo Metropolitan Government.[2] The differences among *dō*, *fu*, and *ken* are negligible or purely historical.

The chief executive of a prefecture is the governor, and the legislative body is the prefectural assembly. Governors and assembly members are again directly elected. The term in office for all elected local officials, prefectural and municipal, is four years. There is no limit on the number of terms an individual may serve. Twelve large cities are called 'designated cities' and retain many powers otherwise given to prefectures.[3]

The legal structure of local government is centralized. The most well-known example and perhaps a symbol of the central local system are the

---

[2] Some Tokyo residents demanded that the chief of the ward be elected instead of appointed by Tokyo's governor, but the courts denied the status of 'public entity' to these wards (Grand Bench of the Supreme Court, March 27, 1963). In 1974, the local Autonomy Law was amended to introduce direct elections in Tokyo's wards.

[3] Although the Local Autonomy Law stipulates that a minimum population of 500,000 is required to apply for the designation, in practice MHA's policy has set the standard at around a million. As of 1992, designated cities were: Osaka, Kitakyushu, Kyoto, Yokohama, Nagoya, Kobe, Kawasaki, Sapporo, Fukuoka, Hiroshima, Sendai, and Chiba.

so-called agency-assigned functions. These are functions the national government has to perform that are delegated to the chief executive of the local government. The local chief executive acts as an agent of the national government in these functions and under the relevant central ministry's supervision. If the national government finds that its agent—e.g., the prefectural governor—neglects to perform the assigned function, the minister can fire the chief executive elected by local inhabitants. Naturally, the local assembly's authority over these functions is severely limited. Although recent changes have been in the direction of more discretion for the locality—such as abolition of the provision allowing the national government to fire local chief executives—this system is a source of continuing controversy.

Another aspect of the centralized system is the financial structure of local governments. Responsible for local finance at the center is the Ministry of Home Affairs. The existence of such an agency might also symbolize the centralized nature of the system, more oriented to the authority of the national government than the local governments. But a closer look will show the much more complicated and interdependent nature of Japan's local system.

Ministry of Home Affairs: A Brief History

MHA is an unintended product of the Allied Occupation's policy to dissolve the Ministry of the Interior (MOI) after World War II. Founded in 1873, MOI was arguably the most important civilian bureaucracy in Japan until the end of the war. Its jurisdiction ranged from internal security to public works to welfare. Although the Supreme Commander of Allied Powers allowed many other central bureaucracies (i.e., MOF and MITI) to retain their prewar identities, MOI was targeted as a 'villain' and divided into four offices in 1947: the Construction Authority, Internal Bureau, Commission on Local Finance, and National Election Commission.[4] The Occupation did not recognize the need for a central office to take care of local matters, but former MOI officials tried their best to organize an independent agency.[5]

In 1949 the Commission on Local Finance was merged with the secretariat division of the Internal Bureau into the Local Autonomy Agency. In 1952 elections and local affairs, including local finance, were placed under the jurisdiction of the then-renamed Home Affairs Agency. This

---

[4] Junnosuke Masumi, *Sengo seiji* (Postwar politics) (Tokyo: University of Tokyo Press, 1983), Vol. 2, pp. 276–8; Yosoji Kobayashi, *Watashi no chihō-jichi nōto* (Local government diary) (Tokyo: Teikoku Chihōgyōsei Gakkai, 1966), pp. 208–23.
[5] Mamoru Shibata, *Jichi no nagare no naka de* (In the history of local government) (Tokyo: Gyosei, 1975), pp. 16–19.

Table 12.1 Profile of Central Ministries

Ministry	Number of		C1 Entrants in 1990[b]	Items of Permission	Public Corporations	Deliberative Councils
	Bureaus[a]	Employees				
Justice	7	50,302	33	154	—	7
Foreign Affairs	10	4,416	29	46	2	2
Finance	8 (4)	70,273	26 (28)	1,210	13	14
Education	6 (1)	137,363	26	312	8	13
Health and Welfare	9 (1)	75,406	35	1,106	7	22
Agriculture, Forestry, and Fisheries	5 (3)	39,566	177	1,315	10	14
International Trade and Industry	7 (4)	12,365	40 (77)	1,916	16	20
Transport	7 (2)	37,538	34 (15)	1,966	19	11
Posts and Telecommunications	6	2,812	36	308	6	5
Labor	5	24,878	30	565	5	14
Construction	5	24,686	71	842	11	9
Home Affairs	3 (1)	569	16 (2)	113	3	3

[a] Numbers in parentheses indicate the number of external agencies.
[b] C1 (Category One) entrants are the so-called 'career bureaucrats' who will compete for the top positions within ministries. Every year, each ministry hires graduates from top colleges who have passed the examination. Again, the number in parentheses is for those who enter external agencies.

Source: National Personnel Authority, General Affairs Agency.

became the Ministry of Home Affairs in 1960 with the addition of the fire Defense Administration.[6]

Today, MHA has a Minister's Secretariat and three bureaus (Local Administration, Local Finance, and Local Tax Bureaus) plus one external bureau (the Fire Defense Agency). Among the 12 central ministries, MHA has the fewest bureaus—others have 5–10—and employees (see Table 12.1). Despite its size, MHA is recognized as one of the most important bureaucracies. It boasts of itself as the 'direct descendant of the Ministry of the Interior.' MHA's power comes from its jurisdiction and its allies, namely, more than 3,000 entities of local government. MHA maintains close relations with local governments in various ways; by far the most important aspect is control over local finance.

The Local Finance System

The local finance system in Japan is fairly complex[7] and comprises various kinds of revenue. Local revenues come mainly from four sources: local taxes, the Local Grant Tax, subsidies, and local bonds.[8]

[6] I refer to all bureaucrats in the preceding postwar agencies as MHA officials.

[7] For a concise English reference on the local and national taxation systems, see the annually published *Outline of Japanese Taxes* (Tokyo: Printing Bureau, Ministry of Finance, annual).

[8] The Local Transfer Tax is a fifth item, which is revenue-sharing for fixed purposes, such as port management. It has consistently been around 2 per cent of total local revenue. There

Local taxes are levied at the prefectural and municipal levels. Individual inhabitants and corporations are taxed by the prefecture and municipality in which their legal address is located. The business income of corporations is also taxed at the prefectural level. Municipalities rely on property taxes as well as an inhabitant tax. The list of other taxes at the prefectural level includes taxes on automobiles, real property acquisition, tobacco, golf course utilization, mining, hunting, and light oil delivery. At the municipal level, there are taxes on light vehicles, tobacco, mineral products, public bath houses, and business offices. However, these local taxes, collected and spent by local government, are only a part of the local finance system. All together, they accounted for only 42.6 per cent of the total revenue of local governments in the 1989 fiscal year.

The Local Grant Tax is actually not a tax but a revenue-sharing system in which nationally collected taxes are transferred automatically to local governments. Thirty-two per cent of revenue from the National Income Tax, National Corporation Tax, and National Liquor Tax; 24 per cent of revenue from the National Consumption Tax; and 25 per cent of revenue from the National Tobacco Tax go to local governments. Unlike subsidies, Local Grant Tax money has no strings attached. The Local Grant Tax Act explicitly prohibits restrictions on how the money is specifically used. That, the law says, is up to local governments.

Subsidies are monies given by the national government to local governments for fixed purposes. Agency-assigned functions being a typical example, local governments take care of numerous national administrative affairs. Nationwide activities such as education and welfare are implemented through local governments. Most public works, such as roads, bridges, and ports, are paid for by subsidies, too. In each case, a certain central ministry will be responsible for specifying the project, choosing which local government will get the money—and which will not—and overseeing how the money is actually spent.

Local governments are eligible to borrow money over a long term in order to raise funds for certain purposes. As bonds could become a heavy burden for a local government's budget, they are considered only in exceptional cases by the laws regulating local finance. Bonds to pay for the construction of facilities that could yield profits later and borrowing for the emergency costs of recovery from natural disasters are examples of such exceptions.

The fact that local governments are financially dependent on the national government is undeniable. One cliché about this dependence is the phrase 'sanwari jichi,' which means that the bottle of local autonomy

are also other revenue items (donations, fees, disposition of property, etc.) and thus the total of the four main items in Table 12.2 does not add up to 100 per cent.

Table 12.2 Local Finance Revenue Structure (percentage of Total Revenue)

	Fiscal year				
	1969	*1974*	*1979*	*1984*	*1989*
Local Taxes	37.2	35.1	32.5	39.1	42.6
Local Grant Tax	17.6	17.9	17.9	15.5	18.0
Subsidies	22.0	21.4	22.8	19.4	13.9
Local Bonds	5.3	8.2	11.8	9.1	7.5

Source: Ministry of Home Affairs, *Annual Reports on Local Finance.*

in Japan is in fact only 30 per cent full. Why 30 per cent? First, in total tax revenue, local taxes have not exceeded 40 per cent throughout the postwar period. In fiscal year 1990, the national government collected 64.2 per cent of all taxes. Second, in total local government revenue, for many years only around 30 per cent came from their own taxes. That is no longer true, with more than a 40 per cent share for local taxes in the total income of local governments. As Table 12.2 shows, the revenue structure of local governments has moved toward more local autonomy, especially with subsidies (money with national strings attached) in decline. Nevertheless, critics still use the phrase 'sanwari jichi' (30 per cent self-government) mainly because of MHA's control over local finance.

Roles of MHA in Local Finance

MHA is responsible for managing and monitoring local finance. The system described above was by and large designed by MHA and its predecessors. MHA gives directions to local governments concerning local tax collection. It can also propose amendments to the laws regulating the local tax system or, if necessary, remodeling the system. The Local Tax Act in some cases specifies a ceiling on local tax rates, or just shows standard rates. But in either case, it requires MHA authorization for local governments to change rates.

The law allows each local government to create a tax in a way that does not conflict with the taxes already levied. A new tax becomes possible only after MHA approves it. These 'extralegal taxes' are rare. Some prefectures in which nuclear facilities are located levy a nuclear fuel tax. Some municipalities institute taxes on advertisements, gift certificates, and sightseeing facilities.

MHA administers the allocation of the Local Grant Tax (see Appendix). Through a very complicated formula, 94 per cent of the money is distrib-

Table 12.3   Local Grant Tax Distribution, Fiscal Year 1990

Prefecture	Local Taxes Per Capita ¥	Local Taxes Total Revenue (%)	Local Grant Tax Per Capita ¥
Tokyo	248,640	66.2	0
Osaka	154,633	65.2	0
Aichi	149,900	62.3	0
Kanagawa	121,832	66.8	2
Kyoto	110,861	45.0	38,063
Yamaguchi	89,736	25.6	97,630
Kumamoto	61,709	17.5	112,613
Kochi	59,545	11.1	198,752

Source: Ministry of Home Affairs, *Annual Report 1992*.

uted as 'normal grants' to prefectures and municipalities. The calculation is based upon the difference between a local government's projected expenditure (basic financial needs) and its projected local tax revenue (basic financial revenue). The remaining 6 per cent of the Local Grant Tax is distributed without a fixed formula. The law gives full discretion over this distribution to MHA, which justifies these 'special grants' by saying the formula for normal grants is too rigid and mechanical.[9] Special grants are used for covering unexpected emergencies such as natural disasters, or a sudden increase in personnel expenditures (e.g., when MHA pushes the early retirement of local officials).

If a local government's basic financial revenue exceeds its basic financial needs, then that government will not receive any normal Local Grant Tax money. Among the 47 prefectures, four (Tokyo, Aichi, Kanagawa, and Osaka) are such 'non-recipient bodies.' Among about 3,300 municipalities, only 170 fell into this category in the 1990 fiscal year. Alleviating regional differentials, the Local Grant Tax functions therefore as a redistributive mechanism between affluent and poor areas (see Table 12.3).

MHA assumes many other roles in local finance. Local borrowing is subject to MHA approval. The ministry sometimes serves as a 'business consultant' to public and semi-public enterprises run by local governments. MHA annually compiles a Local Finance Plan to show its view of what local finance should be like in the following year. This plan is reported to the Diet and the public. In the process of making the plan, MHA monitors the situation of local finance as a whole and uses the plan as a guideline for local financial management, so the plan is also sent to local governments.

[9] Koichiro Yano, *Chihōzei zaisei seido* (Local tax and financial system) (Tokyo: Gakuyo Shōbō, 1992), p. 133.

MHA Policy Tools

MHA monitors local governments for excessive spending and mismanagement and has a number of powers to direct and sanction local governments. The tools available to MHA range from 'hard,' ultimatum-type
legal powers to 'soft,' flexible ònes. One example of a 'hard' tool (albeit
one that has never been used) is the stipulation in the Local Grant Tax Law
that the Minister of Home Affairs is authorized to stop the flow of Local
Grant Tax money to a local government, if he recognizes that it has used
the money in a way not in accordance with principles of local autonomy.
Less coercive but more practically useful legal powers are many
permissions and approval procedures. Among them, the most important
concern local bond issues and local taxes.

Administrative guidance is a 'soft' tool. It does not have to have a legal
basis, and Japanese bureaucrats are prone to use—and sometimes abuse
—it because of its flexibility. MHA gives guidance on local administrative
matters such as personnel management and on financial matters such as
interpretations of tax-related laws.

MHA has even softer tools such as education and publishing. At the
Local Autonomy College, an auxiliary organ of MHA, MHA officials train
many mid-career local officials. MHA officials also write numerous
articles and books targeted at local officials.

MHA pressures local governments to balance their budgets, but when
they fall into deficit and have no chance of recovery on their own, they are
designated as 'reconstruction bodies.' Law requires a local government to
have an application proposal confirmed by the local assembly in order
to become a reconstruction body. Then the chief executive of the local
government submits a basic plan for regaining a balanced budget to the
Minister of Home Affairs (in a municipality's case, through the governor
to the minister).

MHA officials—usually those working in the prefectural government,
as will be described below—participate in the process of analyzing the
cause of the deficit and planning for recovery. If the plan is accepted by
MHA, the local government will receive favored treatment from MHA in
terms of bond issues and distribution of special Local Grant Tax money. In
return, the local government will get—besides the terrible image of fiscal
mismanagement—detailed advice and direction from MHA and be obligated to implement the plan until the designation is revoked. In most
cases, plans for financial reconstruction target personnel expenditures.
Pay raises are put off, and salaries for the chief executives and assembly
members are cut. Hiring stops and early retirement for senior employees
is encouraged.[10]

---

[10] For a more detailed description of the designation, see Tadamasa Hirabayashi,
'Fukuoka-ken Buzen-shi no zaiseisaiken ni tsuite' (Financial reconstruction of Buzen City,

Local governments try to avoid this humiliating designation. MHA, too, feels it is best for them to rebalance their budgets without the 'reconstruction body' designation. MHA officials in fact seem to think this undisguised intervention unwise.[11] Until 1966, the number of the designated local governments remained greater than 100, but it has steadily decreased and since the 1970s the ratio of designated governments has been less than 1 per cent. As of today, only three small municipalities in rural areas are under the designation.

As a self-appointed protector of local autonomy, MHA tends to prefer 'soft' approaches to local financial control. But whatever tools might be used, it is the people who execute the control that count. MHA officials emphasize that point repeatedly. MHA is particularly interesting in how it develops networks for securing communication with and the cooperation of local governments.

MHA's Policy Networking

To manage local matters from the center, MHA has created a pervasive system of human networks between itself and local governments. A bureaucrat in MHA undergoes a unique career path. After brief training within the ministry, he will be sent for two years to a prefectural government, where he will work in sections such as Planning, Local Affairs, and the Secretariat. He will return to the ministry for two or three years, and then go out to another—usually small—prefecture as a section chief. This shuttling between the home office in Tokyo and the prefectures will continue, with some irregular assignments to other central ministries, embassies, or big city governments.

Other central ministries also engage in this practice. But MHA officials are much more frequently sent to local governments, and usually half of their careers are spent in local governments. Another, more formalistic, difference is that MHA officials change their legal status from national public employee to local public employee, while those dispatched by other ministries remain national employees. Unlike MHA officials who tend to be assigned to a variety of prefectural (general/financial) posts, bureaucrats on external assignment from other ministries usually hold posts related to the specific functions of their home ministries (e.g., the agriculture division chief's post in a prefecture is held by officials from the Ministry of Agriculture, Forestry, and Fisheries).

Just like those in other ministries, MHA bureaucrats compete for the posts of bureau chief and, ultimately, administrative vice minister.

Fukuoka Prefecture), in Nobuo Ishihara, ed., *Gendai chihōzaisei un'eiron* (Contemporary local finance) (Tokyo: Gyōsei, 1976), pp. 647–52.

[11] Personal interview with anonymous MHA officials by the author, Tokyo, Nov. 5, 1992.

348 *Kengo Akizuki*

However, because of its size and restrictions on eligibility for these top positions, the posts available for them are more limited than in other ministries. Instead, they aim at prefectural governorships. This is considered the most successful career goal for them. As of June 1992, 14 of 47 governors were former MHA bureaucrats.[12]

As stated above, chief executives in local governments are popularly elected, not appointed. To become gubernatorial candidates, MHA bureaucrats must gain support from various sectors and municipalities within the prefecture. They are expected to have served in that prefectural government at least once, and it is customary for the candidate to serve as vice governor (an appointment subject to the approval of the prefectural assembly) right before the election.

The system that allows MHA to send its staff to local governments is often a target of criticism.[13] It is far from a personnel exchange program between the center and the local governments. There are very few examples of local government officials getting central posts. At the same time, it should be noted that this practice is not based on national law, but upon the request of local governments. Although governors tend to welcome MHA officials, they always need to pay attention, as heads of independent bureaucratic organizations, to pressure to 'promote from within.' This is especially the case in big urban prefectures, such as Tokyo and Osaka.[14]

The relationship between MHA and local governments is by and large good. MHA sees local governments as allies, sources for support and legitimacy. Local governments, on the other hand, see MHA as a useful conduit to the center and a convenient source of talent. Pressure groups of local chief executives and assembly members, called the Six Local Lobbies, have supported MHA and fought cutbacks in the money sent to local governments. Indeed, this alliance may be the most important resource MHA possesses. MHA needs local politicians' support in bureaucratic battles with other central ministries. Local politicians see MHA as a protector of the current system, from which they benefit.

[12] The 14 prefectures with former MHA officials as governor are: Akita, Gunma, Tokyo, Niigata, Toyama, Ishikawa, Fukui, Kyoto, Nara, Okayama, Yamaguchi, Nagasaki, and Kagoshima. This practice is not exclusive to MHA; other central ministries do produce governors. But currently there are only seven from other central ministries (Ministry of Agriculture, Forestry, and Fisheries, 3; Ministry of Construction, 2; MOF, 1; MITI, 1). Municipalities may be too small a pond for MHA bureaucrats, but nine cities, including two designated cities, have former MHA mayors. Data are from Chihō Gyōzaisei Chōsakai, ed., *Zenkoku chiji-shichōsoncho meibo* (Who's who in local government) (Tokyo: Jiji Tsūshinsha, 1992).

[13] Hideo Matsuoka, 'Jichi shō no ninki' (MHA's popularity), in *Hōgaku seminā zokan—kore kara no chihō-jichi* (Tokyo: Bungei Shunjū 1975), pp. 40–2.

[14] Shigeru Shiozawa, *Chihō kanryō—sono kyozō to jitsuzō* (Local officials: Their virtual and real images) (Tokyo: Sangyo Noritsu University Press, 1980), p. 130.

MHA has occasionally been in conflict with local governments. This has occurred when some prefectures were controlled by leftist (e.g., socialist or communist) or leftist-supported governors. MHA criticized in general their spending policies as being too liberal and in particular their salaries for local public employees as too high. The governors in turn accused MHA of excessive intervention.

Each local government has its own interests and political needs. MHA officials try to coordinate the different needs of municipalities within the prefecture as well as the home office of the ministry. That is a responsibility of the Local Affairs Section in the prefecture, usually headed by a dispatched MHA official. Coordination between prefectures is less institutionalized and therefore much more difficult. Even among the prefectures that have former MHA officials as governors, political conflict and animosity can develop.[15]

MHA Control: Success and Failure

MHA's record on control over local governments has been mixed. Despite its wide range of legal powers, it has been unable to keep local budgets balanced all the time. There have been two major 'hard times' for local finance, first in the late 1950s and again in the 1970s. The first shortfall happened mainly due to factors that local governments and MHA were not responsible for. Postwar reforms gave many functions to local governments but not enough money to cover them. So the deficit was caused by the absolute shortage of financial resources for local governments. Indeed, as many as 34 prefectures and 2,247 municipalities were in the red in fiscal year 1954.[16]

On the other hand, MHA attributes the second period of unbalanced budgets to local factors, such as mismanagement and excessive spending. Along with the high-speed growth of the Japanese economy, local revenue went up. Local revenue is linked to the economy (1) through the local tax base (local citizens get rich and pay more taxes to local governments), and (2) through transfers from the national budget (the national economy grows and the amount of money transferrable to local governments increases).

This means economic growth allows increases in local spending. That eventually caused some local governments to expand their activities beyond their financial limits. They adopted an easy and generous spending

---

[15] A top local (non-MHA) official told in an interview (Tokyo, Nov. 5, 1992) that his governor had very difficult relations with another MHA governor in a neighboring prefecture because the other governor was his senior, even though the other governor's prefecture was considered less important.

[16] Ishihara, *Gendai chihōzaisei*, pp. 644–5.

Table 12.4 Number of Local Governments Operating at a Deficit

	Fiscal Year							
	1969	1973	1974	1975	1976	1979	1984	1989
Prefectures	1	2	6	27	9	2	0	0
Municipalities	150	170	169	313	108	46	61	20

Note: Based on real revenue/expenditures.
Source: Ministry of Home Affairs, *Annual Reports*.

policy. According to MHA, local officials—elected and nonelected alike—are inclined to neglect tight checks on expenses. Without MHA's intervention, it would have been difficult to regain balanced local finances so quickly (see Table 12.4).

The major target for MHA has been the personnel expenditures of local governments: unlike welfare cuts, cutting personnel costs does not cause criticism that MHA is trying to lower the level of basic services. MHA has pushed local governments to reduce personnel costs by keeping their work forces leaner and limiting salary increases. As in the case of the reconstruction designation, it works well for local governments in deep trouble. Chief executives whose localities have received the reconstruction designation are cooperative and may take advantage of pressure from outside to counter local public unions.

However, many other local governments failed to heed MHA and kept paying higher salaries when MHA was pushing hard to limit local personnel expenditures. An indicator called the Laspeyres Index—the ratio of the salary of a local public employee to the salary of a national employee with the same qualifications—showed clearly that local officials have been much better paid. All 47 prefectures generate an index higher than 100. Some municipalities reach more than 115.[17]

Campaigns by MHA to cut the total number of employees of local governments have been even more unsuccessful. Table 12.5 shows that while the number of national employees actually decreased mainly because of administrative reform, the local work force has steadily grown. The gap between the actual number of local employees and the projections in each year's Local Finance Plan suggests MHA's policy goal of cutting the work force further has not been attained.

These 'failures' cause serious anxiety for MHA. The central ministries, especially MOF, would argue that local governments enjoy more financial

[17] The list of municipalities with high Laspeyres Indices shows some regional tendencies. In 1988 among the top 20, all except one were urban cities in Osaka. In 1990, 14 Osaka cities were among the top 20. See Chihō Zaimu Kyōkai, ed., *Chihō jichi binran* (Local government handbook) (Tokyo: Chihō Zaimu Kyōkai, 1989/1991), p. 41.

Table 12.5 Number of Public Employees, National and Local Government (in thousands)

	Fiscal Year								
	1974	1976	1978	1980	1982	1984	1986	1988	1990
National	1,694	1,702	1,710	1,705	1,678	1,615	1,184	1,179	1,176
Local	2,498	2,596	2,690	2,784	2,833	2,835	2,866	2,869	2,877
Local Finance Plan	2,047	2,306	2,380	2,454	2,490	2,495	2,512	2,522	2,543

Note: National employees do not include those in the defense forces. Local employees do not include those in local public enterprises.

Source: Ministry of Home Affairs, *Annual Reports*; General Affairs Agency, *Annual Reports*.

surplus while the national budget is trimmed as low as possible. Such data are cited by MOF as evidence that the money transferred to local governments can be cut during years of fiscal austerity.

Political Power of Local Governments

Behind the specific cases of failure for MHA to control local finance is the political power and legitimacy of local governments given by the constitution. If observers focus only on the centralized nature of the legal and financial structure, local governments are seen as subordinate to the central government. The orthodox interpretation of the postwar local system agrees with that conclusion.[18] However, 'a second generation of research'[19] has recently explored new aspects of Japan's local governmental system.

The most important change brought by the constitution was direct election of local chief executives and assembly members. This has generated a wide range of political input from citizens. For instance, under the seemingly oppressive system of agency-assigned functions, local governments—sometimes at their own initiative—deliver day-care and housing services demanded by inhabitants. In fact, the dramatic increase

[18] Steiner, *Local Government in Japan*; Tsuji, *Shinban Nihon kanryōsei no kenkyū*.

[19] Richard J. Samuels, *The Politics of Regional Policy in Japan: Localities Incorporated?* (Princeton: Princeton University Press, 1983), p. xx. This 'second generation' includes Michio Muramatsu, *Sengo Nihon no kanryōsei* (Bureaucracy in postwar Japan) (Tokyo: Tōyō Keizai Shinposha, 1981); Margaret McKean, *Environmental Protest and Citizen Politics in Japan* (Berkeley: University of California Press, 1981); Steven R. Reed, 'Is Japanese Government Really Centralized?' *Journal of Japanese Studies*, Vol. 8, No. 1 (Winter 1982); and Wataru Omori and Seizaburō Satō, eds., *Nihon no chihō seifu* (Japanese local government) (Tokyo: University of Tokyo Press, 1986).

of functions performed by local governments was a consequence of this functional delegation. The growth of public activities—many of them social welfare services—requires substantial manpower for implementation. The system of agency-assigned functions is a legal technique allowing the center to share functions with local governments but retain control.

Of course, the amount of activity does not necessarily guarantee local discretion. But in modern welfare states, those who actually deliver services will gain political power because they get information on the people's basic needs or what is really wrong with the current policy. In postwar Japan, that role of service delivery has been played much more by local governments than by the national ministries and their field agencies.

Political parties, especially leftist parties such as the Japan Socialist Party and the Japan Communist Party, intensified their activities at the local level starting in the early 1960s, and eventually formed a winning coalition at the prefectural level as well as municipal levels in the 1970s. These progressive local governments were born between local political movements and local administration with more expertise and knowledge on social policy.

During the heyday of progressive local governments—the late 1960s and early 1970s—a significant change occurred in the pattern of policymaking. First, local initiative for new programs influenced the center's policy; one example was the Tokyo Metropolitan Government's free medical care for senior citizens, which led the Ministry of Welfare to adopt a similar policy nationwide. Second, local governments became less hesitant to stand up to the central authority when their own policies were in conflict with the center's will. This typically occurred when environmental considerations became an important issue to local citizens and therefore to local governments; the central ministries were relatively slow to respond to these concerns.

All of these new trends have been mixed blessings to MHA. They indicate that local autonomy is growing in Japan. As an advocate of autonomous local government, MHA has largely welcomed the trends. MHA officials often have had to work in—as well as work with—these 'leftist regimes.'[20] But when it comes to local financial matters, MHA cannot be overly understanding. An extreme case of 'financial war' between the Tokyo Metropolitan Government and MHA happened in 1969. When Tokyo's progressive Governor Minobe ignored MHA's

[20] Progressive governors such as Kyoto's Ninagawa, Osaka's Kuroda, and Kanagawa's Nagasu invited MHA officials to fill top posts. Those who came to these prefectures did support the governors. Some right-wing LDP politicians described the MHA officials as 'revolutionaries paid by tax money.' See Taizō Kusayanagi, *Kanryō ōkokuron* (Bureaucratic kingdom) (Tokyo: Bungeishunjū, 1975), p. 38.

direction on salaries, MHA in turn declined approval of Tokyo's local bond issues.[21]

In short, the strategy and effectiveness of MHA cannot be determined solely by its will or the legal powers given to it, but involves many local factors such as local governments' economic bases, political leadership of the chief executive, strength of local unions, partisan composition of the local assembly, local citizens movements, and so forth. Neither can local governments' strategies be determined solely by their will, leadership, or legal powers. Certain limitations are imposed by the institutional framework in general and by MHA direct intervention in particular. The institutional arrangements also support the local governments and their political leaders. This interdependence, which is in fact the key factor of the system, affects how MHA behaves at the center.

MHA and Central Ministries

As mentioned above, the revisionist view of the Japanese local system suggests that 'centralization and local autonomy need not exist in zero-sum relation to each other.'[22] One interesting aspect of such a non-zero-sum situation is that there could be significant divisions within the central government. Needless to say, the central government is a unified entity in which final control and political responsibility fall on the prime minister, while local governments are not. A closer look, however, would often belie the image of a coherent central government. It can be seen as a group of distinct bureaucracies, each with its own perspectives, ideologies, interests, and client groups. The assumption of 'local governments versus central government' does not reflect reality. To find out how local government in an administratively centralized system can retain a certain amount of discretion, autonomy, and initiative, as the revisionist view suggests, I will explore a two-dimensional environment for MHA, its relations with line ministries and with MOF.

A line agency, as opposed to a staff agency, is a concept from military organization. Staffs work on plans, operations, and logistics, while soldiers on the front line take on the enemy. There is no such distinct boundary in civilian bureaucracies between line and staff agencies, and the distinction is blurred in Japan.[23] For example, MOF has line duties such as regulations for commercial banks and security firms. Let us here define line ministries as those more inclined to perform direct

[21] Steven R. Reed, *Japanese Prefectures and Policymaking* (Pittsburgh: University of Pittsburgh Press, 1986), p. 39.

[22] Samuels, *Politics of Regional Policy in Japan*, p. 41.

[23] Michio Muramatsu, ed., *Gyōseigaku kōgi* (Public administration) (Tokyo: Seirin Shoin, 1977), pp. 73–8.

functions, and therefore to deal with societal client groups, than staff ministries.

Relations with Line Ministries

Ministries such as Construction, Transport, and Welfare have a number of specific functions to perform. Some are done by the ministry's own officials; air traffic control, for instance, is a task directly administered by the Ministry of Transport, so all air traffic controllers are national public employees, trained by the ministry and stationed in its regional offices. Local governments have no say or interest in such matters. However, many tasks are delegated to local governments while the basic policies, such as the standards of welfare services, are determined by the central line ministries. Subsidies are useful for ministries to control specific projects assigned to local governments.

MHA has long criticized the entire subsidy system, arguing that it would make local governments financially dependent and less autonomous. In order to obtain these subsidies, local governments have to lobby either directly or through politicians (usually the ruling Liberal Democratic Party's Diet members from the local district). In December of any given year, many people from local governments come to petition the central ministries and relevant LDP organs for a larger share of subsidies.

Aside from the cost of lobbying, subsidies tend to put a heavy burden on local government officials through severe restrictions on implementation, paperwork for applications and reports, and detailed tutelage from central ministries. Nevertheless, local governments seek subsidies because their own financial resources—local tax revenue and Local Grant Tax money—cannot cover all expenditures.

MHA argues it is ministries with line duties that are the culprits; they fail to appreciate the virtues of local autonomy and damage the local government system. The most frequently mentioned example is a city government's inability to change routes, fares, or even the location of bus stops in its public bus system without authorization by the Ministry of Transport. The work of local governments is therefore divided, subdivided, and eventually immobilized by these ministries that try to defend their own bureaucratic turfs.

Unlike sporadic jurisdictional disputes between the line ministries, the battle between them and MHA is a never-ending conflict. The rivalry is so institutionalized that MHA is nicknamed 'the opposition party in Kasumigaseki.'[24] In one example, starting in 1978, MHA tried unsuccessfully to sponsor a new comprehensive program for areas hard hit by recession. This policy initiative would have put MHA into the territory of

[24] Kasumigaseki is a Tokyo neighborhood filled with offices of the central ministries. See Kusayanagi, *Kanryō ōkokuron*, p.46.

other ministries, including MITI, Construction, and Labor. Anonymous MHA officials interviewed by one journalist said that the proposed bill died because MITI blocked it by lobbying LDP politicians.[25]

Another example was recorded in the autobiography of one of the founding fathers of MHA. In 1967 when environmental protests became serious, MHA began to draft basic legislation on this issue. When the proposal was released to the media, the Ministry of Welfare interpreted it as a direct invasion of its own jurisdiction. MITI too was against such legislation, so MHA had to back the Ministry of Welfare in introducing the Basic Environmental Act in the Diet.[26]

This kind of conflict occurs due to different perspectives on policymaking. MHA officials often use the term 'comprehensive administration' when talking about their duties. Local governments and MHA, they say, deal with people, while line ministries deal with bridges, ports, farms, roads, and so on. The line ministry specialists lack the perspective of the overall interests of certain areas or communities. It becomes necessary to coordinate these ministries so that local governments are not paralyzed by 'vertical administration.' (Vertical administration refers to the administrative system organized by object or client—ports, roads, railroads—and not by policy—metropolitan transit, congestion.) MHA says that should be included in its job description.[27]

The cleavage among central agencies including MHA provides good opportunities for local governments to pursue their own goals. Line ministries are also in a sense dependent on localities, which are recipients of subsidies, providers of information, and, ultimately, an important source of support for ministries like Construction and Transport. Local political leaders enjoy the situation that allows them to have different types of allies at the center. It should be noted that they can also use LDP politicians to produce better results.

Relations with MOF

MOF is at the top of the bureaucratic world, with the powers it exerts over national taxes, monetary policy, finance, and the budget. MOF and MHA have some characteristics in common. Both are staff-oriented agencies, in charge of fiscal accountability, and they are the most prestigious among the central ministries. Communication between the two seems relatively smooth. One MHA official who had experience negotiating with MOF said, 'It is much easier for us to reach a compromise with MOF than

---

[25] Soichiro Tahara, *Nihon no kanryō 1980* (Japanese bureaucrats) (Tokyo: Bungei Shunju, 1979), pp. 52–66.

[26] Shibata, *Jichi no nagare no naka de*, pp. 400–1.

[27] MHA, *Jichishō* (Ministry of Home Affairs), recruiting pamphlet (Tokyo: MHA Secretariat, 1989), p. 4.

with line ministries, perhaps because MHA and MOF are ministries for coordination.'[28]

One important task shared by the two is authorization of local bonds. While MHA retains the chief responsibility over bond authorizations, it must decide 'in consultation with MOF.'[29] In some cases, legal jargon becomes meaningless and such consultation never takes place, but in this case MOF takes it seriously and co-screening by MOF and MHA is routine. Each fiscal year, MOF and MHA decide the total amount of money local governments can raise as funds by issuing bonds. They also determine the ceiling for each category (e.g., the total amount of bonds for financing public housing). In most cases permission on specific bond issues is granted by MHA, but if the amount is huge—like bonds for an airport project—MHA consults with MOF.

The keen interest of MOF in local bond issues is the natural consequence of the close ties between national and local budgets. MOF argues in years of fiscal austerity that local financial situations are much better than the national counterpart, so the amount of money going to local governments should be cut. Ironically, MHA sometimes finds itself in agreement with the line ministries concerning subsidies.

Subsidies in most cases do not cover 100 per cent of the cost of a proposed project and rates of subsidy vary. According to the Local Finance Act, the Minister of Home Affairs must be consulted in advance if any legislative bill requiring local governments to bear part of the cost is to be proposed. It also stipulates that each ministry's budgetary request must be sent to MHA as well as MOF. These two provisions—the former is called 'legislative bill consultation' and the latter 'budgetary consultation'—together put MHA in a crucial position in the process of national budget-making.

From the standpoint of local financial considerations, MHA might demand amendments to certain bills or budget items. MHA requires that the rate of subsidization be high enough that the remaining cost of the project will not harm the recipient local government's budget. However, MOF, which is in charge of the budget, is much more concerned with the balance of national finance and tries to lower rates of subsidization. MHA and line ministries like Construction insist on higher rates. MHA, which opposes the subsidy system in principle, has to argue for more subsidies.[30]

[28] Personal interview with MHA officials by the author, Tokyo, Nov. 5, 1992.

[29] From the Meiji era, local bond issues were regulated by both the Ministry of the Interior and the Ministry of Finance, but during World War II, the Tojo cabinet made MOI solely responsible. After the war, MOF tried to take over, but MHA officials resisted and finally retained primary responsibility for local bond authorizations. See Taizō Kusayanagi, *Naimushō tai senryōgun* (Interior vs. GHQ) (Tokyo: Asahi Shinbunsha, 1987), pp. 263–4.

[30] Personal interview by the author, Tokyo, Nov. 5, 1992. Also see MHA, *Jichishō*, pp. 15–16.

MHA and MOF have different perspectives—local finance and the national budget—but they readily agree that they do not like to see deficits in local budgets. MOF does not want local governments to fall in debt and put more pressure on the national budget for help. Nor does either ministry really like subsidies. MOF tries to lower subsidies in each year's budget; MHA wants to decrease subsidies in the long run. If MHA is able to take a long-term strategy instead of worrying about each year's local financial health, it is possible for the two strong bureaucracies to form an anti-subsidy coalition. Recent reports suggest that is happening now. In a well-known example, MOF has proposed to simplify subsidy rates (from more than 20 different levels of subsidization rates to only two levels) and to lower the rates. For some specific classifications of roads, MHA does not oppose MOF's proposal on the condition that local governments be given more powers in planning the road system. The Ministry of Construction is against the MOF proposal because of fear that simplified and lower subsidies will result in more local influence on road administration. It is now up to construction interests in the LDP to resolve the dispute.[31]

MHA has been relatively successful in managing local finance. In the 1970s, Japan's local finance did experience a difficult time as the economy fell into recession but it was able to regain its balance quickly. MHA campaigned against wasteful or excessive spending. Although not free from failure and criticism, MHA has been instrumental in keeping local governments financially accountable. It must be emphasized again that local factors account for the effectiveness of financial control, and in some cases such local factors are beyond MHA's control. If, for example, a local government is in deep financial trouble, does not have a strong economic base for recovery, and local leaders are willing to cooperate, MHA's job will be easy. If a local government has economic potential and its leadership is not happy about MHA's intervention, the effectiveness of MHA control will be severely limited. Besides these local conditions, other factors have been crucial for explaining MHA success. Let us look more closely at these factors.

Characteristics of MHA

As an institution, MHA is well positioned to oversee local finance at the macro level as well as the micro level. Unlike national finance, there is no such thing as a single 'local budget.' Local finance is an aggregate of the budgets of more than 3,000 governmental units, and laws give MHA a wide range of measures to supervise them. Perhaps more importantly, MHA is at the strategic point in the human network covering the local

---

[31] *Nihon keizai shinbun*, Nov. 24, 1992.

government system. Also, as local governments take care of a large portion of national affairs, MHA has been given significant say in the national budgetary processes too.

MHA officials are generally reputed to be administratively competent and politically tough even among the elites in Kasumigaseki. It is often explained that this is partly due to the unique career path between center and locality. They are trained and tested in an environment completely different from the experience in the central government. In the prefectural government, 'the man from MHA' will be surrounded by local assemblymen, businesses, labor unions, media, mayors, and the like. How he is judged by these locals will determine his effectiveness there and influence the home office's evaluation of his performance.[32] MHA officials seem to enjoy this environment, which they believe makes them better bureaucrats.

The small size of MHA deserves attention, too. Being small makes it easier to preserve unity within the ministry. MHA's high *esprit de corps* is well known. Except for the administration of elections and fire defense, it has very few functions concerning vertical or line operations. This enables MHA officials to concentrate on staff duties such as coordination, planning, surveys, and research. MHA is thus relatively free from direct societal pressures, and this may contribute to the depoliticization I will mention next. It may also give credibility to MHA's ideological arguments for local autonomy.

More important, such concentration on staff duties makes policy coordination within the Ministry possible. The Ministry of Welfare, for example, must pay attention to all its client groups: well-organized business interests such as the pharmaceutical industry, insurance industry, medical equipment companies, as well as medical professions including doctors, nurses, and pharmacists. Welfare-related clients such as senior citizens, caseworkers, patients, and the handicapped might be less organized but potentially powerful. In such an environment it is impossible to have cohesive policies or interests in the Ministry of Welfare. Instead, it has come to be widely described as 'not really a ministry but a bundle of bureaus, which are not really bureaus but bundles of sections.'

The situation at MHA is completely different. Local governmental lobbies are the only strong interest groups. Communication and coordination between bureaus is easy (there being only three small ones). Also, there is no difference in the backgrounds of MHA career officials, while the Ministries of Construction, Welfare, Transport, and Agriculture and MITI employ technical professionals as well as administrative officials.

---

[32] Kusayanagi, *Kanryō ōkokuron*, pp. 39–43.

Depoliticization

MHA's manner of dealing with local matters is often said to be 'depoliticized.' This does not mean MHA's behavior is nonpolitical. To the contrary, other central ministries consider MHA highly political, in the sense that it is always involved in heated bureaucratic politics.

Depoliticization in this context only means that the Local Grant Tax's distribution is done without political considerations (pressures from interest groups or political parties). This depoliticization deserves attention because it does not occur in national budgetary processes such as the granting of subsidies under line ministries' jurisdiction. Even MOF is not free from political pressures: LDP Diet members seeking favors frequently come into the offices of budget officers. In MHA, there are no such intrusions.

LDP politicians' interest in MHA and its activities is generally low. They regard the Minister of Home Affairs as one of the less attractive cabinet posts. In fact, throughout the postwar period, only two ministers have had other cabinet posts before their appointment to MHA. Related committees in the LDP's Policy Affairs Research Council (the Local Administrative Division) and in the Diet (the Local Administrative Committee) are also very unpopular, inhabited by reluctant freshmen and former MHA Diet members.[33]

The depoliticization seems rather strange, as local budgets' combined size is as big as the national budget and the Local Grant Tax's share in local budgets is significant. The most important reason for it is that MHA has institutionalized the way it transfers money to local government by limiting its own discretion. There is no room for political negotiation or special consideration as far as normal Local Grant Tax distribution is concerned. This shelters the whole process from political pressures. Therefore, lobbying activities involving LDP politicians, interest groups, central ministries, and local governments concentrate on national subsidies. In a sense, MHA has been guarded by the subsidies, which attract politicians' attention.

MHA officials seem to have been conscious of the merit of depoliticization. Before the Local Grant Tax system, a much more politicized Complementary Grant for Local Finance was established in 1950, but it lasted only four fiscal years.[34] That system was quite simple. The amount of money to be transferred from the national government to local

---

[33] PARC and the Diet committees usually foster 'clans' (*zoku*) of LDP politicians who have strong interest in and specialized knowledge of a policy area. On their activities, see Takashi Inoguchi and Tomoaki Iwai, *'Zokugiin' no kenkyū* (Study of 'clans') (Tokyo: Nihon Keizai Shinbunsha, 1987).

[34] For a detailed comparison of the two systems, see Shogo Hayashi, *Jichi gyōsei kōza, vol. 7—Chihō zaisei seido* (Local government series, vol. 7: Local financial systems) (Tokyo: Dai-ichi Hoki, 1986), pp. 507–13.

governments was based upon the difference between the basic financial needs and the basic financial revenue estimated in the Local Finance Plan. In short, the local deficit would be entirely covered by the Complementary Grant. This system, according to MHA officials, might have been 'almost perfect in theory,'[35] but in practice, the total amount of the grant was determined not by objective calculation but by fierce political disputes between MOF and the local governments and supporting politicians. MHA was caught in this controversy every year and totally incapable of mediating it. That experience taught MHA the lesson that local money transfers must be distributed without political conflict. Even if it means less discretion, it is better than being caught in this kind of mess.

The new system introduced in 1953—the Local Grant Tax—was much less politicized in that the total amount of money transferred is not decided by negotiation but by simple calculation, a fixed percentage of three national taxes.[36] MHA also limited its own discretion on how to distribute the money by instituting a fixed formula of normal Local Grant Tax distribution and by limiting the special Local Grant Tax to only 8 per cent.[37]

There has been no serious challenge to this allocation system. The LDP has supported the Local Grant Tax system for its redistributive function, which is what LDP leaders from rural areas seek. They pursue redistribution through the pork barrelling of subsidies, but they have also allowed MHA to do that job administratively. Local politicians, regardless of party affiliation, have also strongly supported the system that allows national tax revenue to come with no strings attached.

This is what institutions do to political processes. Theoretically, anything can happen in politics. But in reality, there are certain frameworks at work, limiting the course of events, if not determining them. Once institutionalized, actors usually do not even think about changing the frameworks (in the forms of laws, rules, customs, and so forth). This is especially the case when main actors share basic interests in the frameworks. Through initial mistakes MHA learned that the Local Grant Tax system works. Local governments can enjoy the Local Grant Tax money without strings attached and without worrying about tax rates and collection efforts. The Local Grant Tax system also is consistent with the LDP's inclination to redistribute money to poorer rural areas, but the LDP would never have supported the system if it had prohibited pork barrelling

---

[35] Yano, *Chihōzei zaiseiseido*, p. 121.

[36] For detailed analysis of the implications of the link between the national tax and the Local Grant Tax, Kuniaki Tanabe, '1950 nendai ni okeru chihōzaisei chōseiseido no kōzō to hen'yō' (Transformation of the local financial system in the 1950s), in *Nenpō seijigaku 1992* (Tokyo: Iwanami Shoten, 1992), pp. 115–25.

[37] The percentage of the special Local Grant Tax within total LGT has reduced from 8 to 6 in 1958.

completely. Because the system has coexisted with subsidies, the LDP as well as line ministries have accepted it.

Within localities, local politics can 'invade' the budgetary process but cannot easily make the pie bigger. As the local financial structure is heavily dependent on national transfers, in most cases MHA's pressure to keep budgets balanced is impossible to ignore. MHA might look like an entrepreneur successful in finding a niche in the bureaucratic industry. At the outset it was divided and on the verge of extinction. It was small, denied specific functions, and ignored by the LDP, but MHA turned its weakness into strength by allying with local governments. This of course is also a clear sign of the limits on MHA's power. It lacks LDP politicians' commitment, support from entrenched special interest groups such as farmers, and the resources of huge manpower and budget share.

Conclusion: Policy Implications from the Japanese Experience

Like other institutions, local government systems are created through many different motives. Some argue that they are the basis of a demo-cratic society, giving people a training field for democracy. Some see them as additional checks and balances against the abuse of political power. Some favor them because they help establish a pluralistic political system by giving citizens multiple access points. Some find local government useful for flexible policymaking. Some find it important for liberal reasons, such as creating diversity and ensuring people the right to choose meaningfully where to live. Some see that it can promote policy inno-vation by functioning as an experimentation laboratory. Some contend that local government is vital for efficient administration.

It is thus very difficult to deny the virtues of sound local government. But at the same time it is difficult to satisfy all these—and maybe more—different expectations. A local government system is the child of many hopes and mother of many disappointments. The experience of postwar Japan is no exception. Criticism from local citizens, local politicians, cen-tral and local bureaucrats, the mass media, business, and academia has been directed at the local government system. Japan does not give a definitive answer to the difficulties of designing a local government system.

What then, if anything, can be learned from the Japanese experience? Japan is an interesting case for it has come up with a unique institutional setting with MHA in a pivotal position. This central agency that repre-sents local governments and promotes their interests is in charge of controlling local governments through financial and administrative supervision.

Under such a system, policy outputs concerning local finance can be summarized as follows:

1. In postwar Japan, local governments have been dependent on financial transfers from the center.
2. Because of this dependence, local finance has sometimes deteriorated and fallen into debt, but by and large it has been balanced throughout the postwar period.
3. Through the transfer system, less affluent areas tend to get more. The system functions to remedy regional differentials.

I have shown how these policy outputs have been achieved through the institutional framework with MHA at the center.

Local governments are financially dependent on the national budget, but, as we have seen, that does not mean local governments are unable to initiate policies, pursue their own goals, and be politically autonomous. By comparison, the financial base of Japan's local governments is, generally speaking, 'stronger than most unitary states.'[38] Local Grant Tax money serves as a safeguard to local finance and its autonomy. But as impressive as it looks, there are intrinsic problems that policymakers in other countries should consider before 'importing' the system.

First, while the Local Grant Tax can be spent at the local level with little or no central intervention, it is still nationally collected and nationally administered money. Local residents never know what part of the taxes they pay go to which local government. Therefore, local governments may be given financial discretion, but among local people the American-style sense of 'local taxpayers' is much weaker and less visible in Japan.

Second, although subsidies have merits that no one can ignore, MHA, which sees them as too interventionist for central line ministries, emphasizes their demerits. Subsidies can sustain the nationally determined level of service through mandatory direction. When the central government tries to promote certain policies, subsidies will generate quick, direct results in the localities. This is especially the case when the policies are highly experimental or tend to spread the effects beyond localities' boundaries and therefore cause spillover problems.

As stated at the beginning of this chapter, there are two distinct views on Japan's local system. Conventional wisdom points out that local governments are heavily controlled from the center and therefore are severely lacking in discretion and autonomy. The revisionist views find limitations on central controls and contend that opportunities for local governments to act autonomously are wide open. This close examination of MHA's role in institutionalizing the local system suggests that it has worked both ways.

---

[38] Reed, *Japanese Prefectures and Policymaking*, p. 42.

No one can deny that local governments' autonomy is limited by MHA's direction and control. But at the same time, MHA's existence has reduced the possibility of financial trouble and has helped establish rules of the game among local governments and central ministries. Tight financial control could be a burden and/or boon for local governments. Policy areas such as tax rates and bond issues are controlled by MHA and sometimes in its hands completely. That might be good news for some local political leaders, an intolerable intervention for some, and both for others.

The double-edged effect is applicable to rules too. Well-established rules of the game limit the freedom of factions by players, but usually promote the game itself. If local and central leaders always battle on how the intergovernmental game should be played, it may be a sign of local vitality but the amount and quality of the game may also be poorer. The rules enhance predictability for the players so they can concentrate on their play. In the game of intergovernmental politics, rules lower the 'transaction cost' between governmental units.[39]

This chapter does not explicitly deal with the causal relationship between these policy outputs and much broader outcomes—such as economic growth and prosperity in postwar Japan. Here I can only make the modest statement that the postwar local government system has coexisted with the remarkable performance of the Japanese economy.

However, it is arguable, as MHA officials claim,[40] that local fiscal accountability is positively related to the growth of the Japanese economy. While there is no doubt that the Japanese economy has served as a solid basis for local finance, sound local finance based on stable local systems might have been a positive factor in national economic growth.

For example, New York City's financial trouble in the 1970s showed a different pattern. When the city almost defaulted on its bonds, the federal government first refused to help New York on the grounds that an easy bailout would lead to many other local governments following the same pattern. After a long political struggle, President Ford agreed to provide a federal loan to New York. There were no rules on how Washington should or should not act in such a situation. The less institutionalized system in this instance generated more financially turbulent local systems, less credible local governments, and a tarnished image of one country's economy.

One tangible 'policy output' at this juncture is that the local government system in postwar Japan gained legitimacy, which led to a stable political infrastructure for local governments. Within the framework of the overall system, each local government has had to cope with issues including

---

[39] For a more extensive and theoretical argument on the issue of 'transaction costs' among economic players in the market, see the chapter by Yamamura in this volume.

[40] See, for example, Ishihara, *Gendai chihōzaisei*, pp. 24–5.

economic and industrial policymaking. These specific policies and their effects are discussed and evaluated in the chapters in this volume by Miwa and Kitayama.

Stability up to the present does not guarantee stability tomorrow. Local governments have to deal with dynamic changes in society, perhaps more directly than the national government. There is talk of fundamental change in the local system today. More specifically, such concerns as the aging population, internationalization, Tokyo's hyperconcentration, and congestion all require policy innovation by local governments. Most probably, how local governments and MHA respond to these challenges will determine the viability of the local system in the future.

This chapter has illustrated some points of MHA effectiveness in controlling local governments. At the same time readers now know the limits of its control. If one is looking for efficient and well-coordinated administration in a local government system, one might be disappointed by the fact that even with the legal powers and talents of MHA, it cannot control local governments completely. The Japanese experience might also suggest some basic conditions for efficient control: a depoliticized distribution process, good communication with local governments, and coherent policymaking.

On the other hand, if one is looking for active and willful local government, one might find the very idea of a central agency in charge of controlling local governments offensive. Nevertheless, it should be encouraging that control from the center to the local governments has somehow coexisted with local initiative in postwar Japan. In other words, financial control has not been directly translated into other policy areas.

In addition to the means and extent of central control in Japan, another interesting point is justification for the control. Most central governments try to control local governments, whether they are successful or not. The reason for that tends to be assumed, rather than studied. In Japan, the central government was established earlier than local governments. Also, as a late developing country that had to catch up with the advanced nations, Japan's political leadership in the late nineteenth century shared certain national goals such as 'enrich the nation and strengthen the military,' which were given much higher priority than local preferences. These fundamental conditions have been translated into a belief shared by both elites and the masses that the central bureaucrats are morally, technically, and administratively superior to local bureaucrats.

Although these conditions have more or less diminished and the difference between central and local abilities has arguably become smaller, the political culture of the past survives and influences elites' behavior. That is why the central government still distrusts local governments and sees them as something needing direction and regulation.

This line of explanation probably has some validity, but as far as MHA is concerned, a more tangible explanation is possible. MHA is situated in central bureaucratic politics. It must negotiate with MOF over financial matters and must compete with the line ministries for policy initiatives and jurisdiction. These central rivals will jump on MHA as soon as local governments show any sign of disarray. In order to cope with pressures from these ministries, MHA must keep local governments in order.

MHA is driven to tighten control of local governments by its institutional position at the center, not necessarily by its perception of local governments. Ironically, MHA, which is perhaps the most liberal, understanding, and supportive agency for local governments, is also the most strictly institutionalized for central control over them.

As one can easily see, MHA is indeed an ambivalent entity. And it poses ambivalent questions. MHA likens itself to an advocate for local autonomy, but it is a central bureaucracy staffed with national bureaucrats. Some critics compare the MHA official to a chameleon, changing standpoints according to its surroundings.

Doubly ambivalent is the fact that MHA—the advocate for local autonomy—tries to *protect* local governments. Being autonomous and being protected, after all, contradict each other. How soon will local governments become fully grown and no longer need MHA's mothering protection? Who decides if and when that happens? If MHA acknowledges that local governments need less intervention, will it willingly forsake its powers *vis-à-vis* local governments? MHA seems to think that question is premature because local governments in Japan are still very weak, desperately seeking protection and guidance.

Throughout its history, the main concern of MHA has been to keep local governments financially accountable, and it has demonstrated the ability to do that job well. Another and much more difficult challenge is to reconcile its very existence with the principles of local autonomy. That challenge has yet to be met.

Appendix: Distribution Mechanism of the Local Grant Tax (LGT)

Part 1: Macro Calculation
LGT Total money: $LGTT = 0.32 \times$ Three National Taxes (income, corporate, liquor)
$+0.25 \times$ National Tobacco Tax
$+0.24 \times$ National Consumption Tax
$NLGT_1$: Total of Normal LGT $= 0.94 \times LGTT$
$SLGT_1$: Total of Special LGT $= 0.06 \times LGTT$

Part 2: Micro Calculation
BFN_α: Basic Financial Needs for local government α
Determined by projected costs for several categories of governmental activities such as roads, bridges, ports, police, public schools, riparian works, etc.

For each category, cost is projected by multiplying three items:

Unit expenditure $\times$ number of units $\times$ adjustment coefficient

For example:

¥216,000	30 (thousand sq. mi.)	1.01	= 6,544,800
(per 1,000 sq. mi.)	roads α has	special conditions for	
standard expenditure	to maintain	α determined by	
for road maintenance		snowfall, congestion,	
(in FY 1990)		ratio of unpaved	
		roads, etc.	

α's BFN for roads is ¥6,544,800

BFN_α: sum of all categories' BFNs

BFR_α: Basic Financial Revenue for α (prefecture) = 0.80 $\times$ standard tax revenue[1]

α (municipality) = 0.75 $\times$ standard tax revenue

$NLGT_\alpha$: α's Normal LGT money before adjustment

If $BFN_\alpha < BFR_\alpha$, then $NLGT_\alpha = 0$

If $BFN_\alpha > BFR_\alpha$, then $NLGT_\alpha = BFN_\alpha - BFR_\alpha$

Part 3: Adjustment between Macro and Micro Calculations

$NLGT_2$: The sum of all local governments' Normal LGT money[2]

If $NLGT_1 > NLGT_2$, then $SLGT = SLGT_1 + (NLGT_1 - NLGT_2)$

If $NLGT_1 < NLGT_2$, then each local government's NLGT will be cut by the same percentage.

So the amount α will get is $NLGT_\alpha \times NLGT_1 \div NLGT_2$.

Notes:

1. Standard tax revenue is projected revenue of a local government with standard rates set by the Local Tax Act.

2. If the gap between $NLGT_1$ and $NLGT_2$ is too big, MHA and MOF will negotiate for 'special treatment' to narrow the gap.

Source: *Outline of Japanese Taxes* (Tokyo: Printing Bureau, Ministry of Finance, 1990), pp. 217–19; *Chihō no jidai no zaisei* (Tokyo: Yūhikaku, 1991), pp. 64–5, and *Chihō kofuzei nyūmon* (Tokyo: Chihō Zaimu Kyoōkai, 1987).

13

Local Governments and Small and Medium-Sized Enterprises

TOSHIYA KITAYAMA

It has been decades since the 'miracle' of Japanese economic growth caught the attention of political scientists and economists. Many have focused on the role of the national bureaucracy, particularly of the Ministry of International Trade and Industry (MITI), and the role played by large companies, such as Toyota, Matsushita, and Sony. Some, most notably Chalmers Johnson, argue that MITI is the key player, indeed the economic general staff, in Japan's 'developmental state' where its industrial policy has been instrumental for Japan's rapid industrialization.[1] Others argue that the 'three sacred treasures'—the lifetime employment system, the seniority wage system, and enterprise unionism, which are found almost exclusively in large enterprises—explain the competitiveness of Japanese companies.

More recent studies have pointed out that MITI's influence has been substantially limited. Some focus on the way in which MITI and large companies have interacted to make industrial policies market-conforming and, therefore, successful.[2] Others insist that MITI's industrial policies have not been effective at all, based on their examination of the implementation process for the policies.[3] Still other studies have begun to examine

I would like to thank the editorial committee of this project, and particularly Kozo Yamamura and Martha Walsh. I would also like to thank the members of BRIE, Fumihiko Kimura, Gregory Noble, William Renner, and Toshio Sata.

[1] Chalmers Johnson, *MITI and the Japanese Miracle: The Growth of Industrial Policy, 1925–75* (Stanford: Stanford University Press, 1982).

[2] Daniel Okimoto, *Between MITI and the Market: Japanese Industrial Policy for High Technology* (Stanford: Stanford University Press, 1989). See also Richard Samuels, *The Business of the Japanese State* (Ithaca: Cornell University Press, 1987).

[3] For example, Yoshiro Miwa, *Nihon no kigyō to sangyō soshiki* (Firms and industrial organization in Japan) (Tokyo: University of Tokyo Press, 1990); David Friedman, in *Misunderstood Miracle: Industrial Development and Political Change in Japan* (Ithaca: Cornell University Press, 1988), insists that 'the record Johnson himself provides gives little support for the idea that MITI and its predecessors guided development' (p. 30).
I have argued that if one examines the implementation process of industrial policy as well as the formulation process, then one could not insist that industrial policies worked as MITI hoped they would. See Toshiya Kitayama, 'Nihon ni okeru sangyō seisaku no shikkō katei: Sen'i sangyō to tekkōgyō' (Implementing industrial policies in Japan: The textile and steel industries), in *Hōgakuronsō*, Vol. 117, No. 5 (1985), pp. 53–76, and Vol. 118,

the role of small and medium-sized enterprises (SMEs) in making it possible for the Japanese economy to respond quickly to the ever-changing world economy of the 1970s and 1980s. This reorientation is parallel to renewed attention to SMEs in Europe and the United States.

Statistics reveal that more SMEs exist and more people work for SMEs in Japan than in other major industrial democracies. Almost no attention, however, has been paid to the role of local government within the Japanese political economy. This essay deals with the missing link: the relationship between local government and SMEs. And it develops an argument to account for the ways in which SMEs are important in the Japanese economy and the ways in which policies of local government have contributed to SMEs.

This chapter is divided into three parts. The first is on the importance of SMEs in the economic system of Japan. The second is concerned with the local government policy objectives for SMEs. And the third is on the policy instruments adopted by local government.

First, SMEs play a very important role in creating competitiveness within Japanese industries, not by themselves but by forming linkages with large firms as subcontractors or parts suppliers. I argue that the coexistence of large firms and SMEs and the strategic cooperation between them are a characteristic of the Japanese economy and the key to the competitiveness of Japanese industries in world markets. This industrial governance structure has made it possible for the Japanese economy to take advantage of continual improvements in manufacturing technology, which, in turn, have made possible a constant variation of high-quality, high value-added products. Let us call this economic system 'flexible mass production.'[4]

How, then, have government policies, particularly those of local government, affected the promotion of SMEs and the relationship between large firms and SMEs? The second part of my argument is that there has been no consensus over how development was to be achieved and to what extent SMEs were to be promoted. The meaning of development changed over time, with the nature of policy objectives dependent on the political process among national and local actors who had their own political and economic interests and whose ideas about the develop-

---

No. 2 (1986), pp. 76–98; Toshiya Kitayama, 'Sangyō seisaku no seijigaku kara sangyō no seijikeizaigaku e' (From the politics of industrial policies to the political economy of industry), *Leviathan, rinji zokan* (Summer 1990), pp. 142–61. See also Gregory Noble, 'The Japanese Industrial Policy Debate,' in Stephan Haggard and Chung-in Moon, eds., *Pacific Dynamics: The International Politics of Industrial Change* (Boulder, Colo.: Westview Press, 1989), pp. 53–95.

[4] On flexible mass production, see Herbert Kitschelt, 'Industrial Governance Structures, Innovation Strategies, and the Case of Japan: Sectoral or Cross-national Comparative Analysis?', *International Organization*, Vol. 45, No. 4 (1991). I am not fully convinced by his characterization of the Japanese economy.

ment were more or less influenced by the dominant economic ideology of the day.

Two variables are critical in identifying the policy support for SMEs: the strength of political parties *vis-à-vis* the bureaucracy, and the extent of local autonomy. Where political parties are stronger and local government has more autonomy, more policies for SMEs would be expected. Local government, however, is not always a supporter of SMEs. Some are eager to promote existing SMEs in the region and some have even considered ways the local SMEs could cooperate strategically with large firms so that they could be part of a flexible mass production regime. We need to understand the conditions under which a local government becomes an important actor for SMEs in the political process. Only then can we discuss how SMEs can be promoted, if it is indeed necessary to do so.

The third element of my argument is how local governments have shaped relationships with SMEs in order to promote them and link them with large firms. I argue that low-interest loans have been one of the major policy instruments for SMEs in Japan. On the one hand, this means that SMEs have not been protected by massive subsidies from the central and local governments as in the case of the agricultural sector. On the other hand, a sense of entrepreneurship in SMEs is thus a prerequisite in order for SME policy to be successful.

The first task of this chapter is to examine SMEs in the economy and to show how subcontracting is important in the manufacturing sectors of Japan and how it has evolved from a simple dual structure to strategically cooperative relations so that large firms and SMEs can benefit from each other.

The second task is to examine what local governments have attempted to do in order to promote their regional economies. I first briefly describe the development of the postwar Japanese economy to show how the central bureaucracy and the LDP conceived regional development and the role of SMEs, how regional development occurred, and how the relations between large firms and SMEs were constructed. I then move on to analysis at the local level. I classify the policies of local government into three categories: attracting large firms from outside; promoting existing SMEs within the region; and making the relationships between large firms and SMEs reciprocal. The policies of Kumamoto Prefecture will serve as an example of a rural region and those of Osaka Prefecture as the case of an urban region. I examine when and how various local governments have selected and implemented SME policies. This analysis makes up the largest portion of this essay.

The last task is to show how local governments have shaped relations with SMEs. I examine the institutions and policy instruments of Kumamoto Prefecture and Osaka Prefecture in order to demonstrate the importance and limits of various types of low-interest loans.

SMEs in the Japanese Economy

The importance of SMEs in advanced industrial societies has attracted attention in the last decade. It has been argued that SMEs are suitable for technological innovation, able to create jobs, and instrumental for revitalization of regional economies.[5] It has also been argued that they provide opportunities for potential entrepreneurs and that they are better than larger firms at responding quickly to changing demand.

SMEs are demonstrably important in the Japanese economy. SMEs are defined in Japan as enterprises with capital of less than ¥100 million or with fewer than 300 employees in manufacturing sectors. Slightly different standards are used for service sectors.[6] In addition, 'small-scale firms' are defined as those with fewer than 20 employees in manufacturing sectors and 5 employees in the service sectors.

Table 13.1 shows the percentage of SMEs among all business establishments in the private and non-agricultural sectors. Table 13.2 shows the percentage of people employed by SMEs in the private and non-agricultural sectors. Table 13.3 shows that a larger percentage of employees work in SMEs in Japan than in other major industrial countries.

Recent attention to SMEs, however, has focused on the regional (subnational) level instead of the national. Some regions—notably Silicon Valley in the United States, Baden-Württemberg in Germany, and the northeastern and central parts of Italy, the so-called Third Italy—are said to have been very successful due to the agglomeration of SMEs there.[7] Within those regions, networks of SMEs react flexibly to the changing world economy by producing semi-customized goods on a small scale. For example, in the Third Italy, ceramic and garment industries are prospering thanks to their production flexibility. This economic order, known as 'flexible specialization,' is regulated by the cooperation of labor and management within SMEs, among SMEs, and between local government and SMEs, which in turn are supported by the principle of trust among the parties. It is suggested that local government should adopt the new doctrine of endogenous growth, according to which prosperity depends on developing under- or unused resources that range from traditional artisanal skills to petty commerce.

[5] Roy Rothwell and Walter Zegveld, *Innovation and the Small and Medium Sized Firm: Their Role in Employment and in Economic Change* (London: Frances Pinter, 1982).

[6] For wholesale sectors, SMEs are defined as enterprises with capital of less than ¥30 million or with fewer than 100 employees. For the retail and service sectors, SMEs are defined as those enterprises with capital of less than ¥10 million or fewer than 50 employees.

[7] See, for example, Charles Sable, 'Flexible Specialization and the Re-emergence of Regional Economies,' in Paul Hirst and Jonathan Zeitlin, eds., *Reversing Industrial Decline?* (Oxford: Berg, 1989), pp. 17–70; Linda Weiss, *Creating Capitalism: The State and Small Business since 1945* (Oxford: Blackwell, 1988).

Table 13.1 Number of Business Establishments by Sector, 1991 (Private and Non-Agricultural)

	Manufacturing	Construction	SMEs Wholesale	Retail	Service	Other	Total	Large Firms	Total
Number of Business Establishments	85	60	48	242	157	56	648	6	654
Percentage of SMEs in Each Sector	99.5	99.9	99.2	99.4	97.9	99.8	99.1		

Note: Numbers are in tens of thousands.

Source: Chūshō Kigyō Chō, ed., *Chūshō kigyō yōran 1992* (Handbook of small and medium-sized firms, 1992) (Tokyo: Chūshō Kigyō Sōgō Kenkyū Kaihatsu, 1992), p. 230.

Table 13.2 Number of Employees by Sector, 1991 (Private and Non-Agriculture)

	Manufacturing	Construction	SMEs Wholesale	Retail	Service	Other	Total	Large Firms	Total
Number of Employees	1,040	504	431	1,027	766	573	4,370	1,139	5,479
Percentage of SMEs in Each Sector	73.8	95.4	84.0	87.5	63.8	87.4	79.2		

Source: Chūshō Kigyō Chō, ed., *Chūshō kigyō yōran 1992* (Handbook of small and medium-sized firms, 1992) (Tokyo: Chūshō Kigyō Sōgō Kenkyū Kaihatsu, 1992), p. 230.

Table 13.3 Employment in the Manufacturing Sector, by Size of Firm

United States, 1985		Japan, 1985	
Number of Employees	Percentage of Manufacturing Work force	Number of Employees	Percentage of Manufacturing Work force
1–9	3.2	4–9	13.9
10–19	4.2	10–19	10.7
20–99	20.2	20–99	30.2
100–249	18.6	100–299	17.0
250–999	28.0	300–999	14.2
1,000+	25.8	1,000+	14.1

Great Britain, 1989		West Germany, 1986	
Number of Employees	Percentage of Manufacturing Work force	Number of Employees	Percentage of Manufacturing Work force
1–99	24.6	20–49	7.2
100–199	7.4	50–99	8.2
200–499	10.2	100–199	9.8
500–999	8.2	200–499	14.5
1,000+	49.7	500–999	10.4
		1,000+	49.9

Note: The United States and Japan are calculated on a business establishment base, Great Britain on a company base, and West Germany on a company base excluding handicrafts.

Source: Chōshō Kigyō Chō, ed., *Chūshō kigyō hakusho 1992* (White paper on small and medium-sized firms) (Tokyo: Ōkura-shō Insatsu Kyoku, 1992), attached statistics, pp. 7, 43–5.

It is debatable whether the Japanese case can be understood in these terms. On the one hand, David Friedman stresses the importance of SMEs and Japan's flexible, craft-like industrial order.[8] On the other, Stephen Cohen and John Zysman insist that Japan is competitive in high technology and high volume industries.[9] Both base their conclusions on the experience of particular sectors. I argue that both large firms and SMEs are important in Japan. Richard Florida and Martin Kenney argue that large companies are the cornerstone of the Japanese economy but that they cultivate well-organized networks of outside suppliers,[10] which are SMEs. Indeed, over half of Japanese SMEs are subcontractors: 55.9 per cent of

[8] Friedman, *Misunderstood Miracle*, Chap. 1.
[9] Stephen S. Cohen and John Zysman, *Manufacturing Matters: The Myth of the Post-Industrial Economy* (New York: Basic Books, 1987).
[10] Richard Florida and Martin Kenney, *The Breakthrough Illusion: Corporate America's Failure to Move from Innovation to Mass Production* (New York: Basic Books, 1990), Chap. 8.

SMEs were subcontractors in 1987, down from a high of 65.5 per cent in 1981.[11]

These networks centered around large companies are important because they make 'flexible mass production' possible. In other words, the political economy of Japan is not characterized by mass production of standardized goods and is not exactly like a flexible specialization regime that produces semi-customized goods on a small scale. In the Japanese economy, the largest firms are still important since only they can invest large amounts of money for research and development (R&D). But SMEs are critical in flexible mass production in supplying parts, manufacturing prototypes, and so on. They have the technological ability to respond to the increasing needs of large assembly firms for small batch production, high quality, high precision, and quick response. It is the coexistence of large firms and SMEs and strategic cooperation among them that characterize the Japanese political economy, and together they have made possible the constant variation of high-quality, high value-added products.

The relationships between large firms and SMEs—what I call strategic cooperation—are delicate. On the one hand, larger firms may be tempted to move their production to developing countries, or to sever ties with subcontractors altogether and bring this production in-house, or to keep subcontractors in a subordinate position in order to use them as a buffer. On the other hand, subcontractors seek more autonomy from parent companies by forming their own networks or having more than one parent company. This could be beneficial for larger firms because subcontractors might gain more technological ability through the SME network or transactions with other companies.[12] Large firms also gain from giving autonomy to, and becoming dependent upon, SMEs. 'Coordinated interdependence results in the creation of value that makes both parties more independent in other markets.'[13]

Therefore, the Japanese subcontracting relationship is different from a 'dualist structure' in which SMEs are used as a shock absorber. Under dualist relations, SMEs do not possess much technical capability and industries' competitiveness derives from the cheap labor of SME workers. Friedman contends that neither can be verified.[14]

---

[11] Chūshō Kigyō Chō, *Chūshō kigyō hakusho 1992* (White paper on small and medium-sized firms) (Tokyo: Ōkurashō Insatsu Kyoku, 1992), p. 85; and Chūshō Kigyō Chō, ed., *Zude miru Chūshō kigyō hakusho 1991* (White paper on small and medium-sized firms in figure, 1991) (Tokyo: Doyukan, 1991), p. 137.

[12] In fact, car assembly firms, such as Toyota and Nissan, encouraged parts suppliers to decrease their dependency on parent companies during the 1960s. Hideichirō Nakamura, *Chōsensuru chūshō kigyō* (SMEs that challenge) (Tokyo: Iwanami Shoten, 1985), p. 48.

[13] Hugh Patrick and Thomas Rohlen, 'Small-Scale Family Enterprises,' in Kozo Yamamura and Yasukichi Yasuba, eds., *The Political Economy of Japan, Volume 1: The Domestic Transformation* (Stanford: Stanford University Press, 1987), p. 347.

[14] Friedman, *Misunderstood Miracle*, Chap. 4.

Government Policy Objectives for SMEs

How has this flexible mass production regime come about? Is it the result of a grand strategy of MITI? How have local governments contributed? As I will demonstrate in the following, central and local governments have had different interests and ideologies concerning the promotion of SMEs and the process of development. Simply put, there was neither consensus nor leadership toward the economic regime that Japan has today.

SMEs and Regional Development from the National Perspective

Devastated by World War II, Japan's industries were gradually rebuilt in the early postwar years. Reconstruction was concentrated in 'three major industrial zones' that had been fully industrialized in the prewar period: the regions around Tokyo and Yokohama, Nagoya, and Osaka and Kobe. Reconstruction was followed by the location of large industrial complexes (steel furnaces, oil refineries, petrochemical plants, etc.) along the coastlines near those regions after about 1955. These complexes were located in areas east of Tokyo, south of Nagoya, south of Osaka, and west of Kobe. Together they are called the Pacific Belt region. The machinery industry, producing goods such as automobiles and home appliances, developed in inland regions. As shown in Table 13.4, the coefficient of variation of value-added, the number of plants, and the number of people employed in manufacturing in all prefectures became larger until about the mid-1960s.

Postwar Japan, like Europe, was under the influence of the dominant economic doctrine of the day, the Fordist mass production strategy. It was believed that the American way of doing business was the most rational way. Many Japanese businessmen were sent to learn the American management system. MITI attempted to promote an American-style mass production system consisting of a limited number of vertically integrated large firms. MITI thought Japanese firms were too vulnerable to compete with American multinationals, subsumed by the belief that modernization meant realizing economies of scale. In the National Income Doubling Plan of 1960, it was suggested that the Japanese economy had too many firms of too small a size and therefore could not take advantage of a mass production strategy, which would leave many small firms with cheap labor in a very unstable condition.[15] Through industrial policies for cartels, restrictions on entry, and promotion of mergers, MITI attempted to consolidate industries to establish Japanese counterparts of European

---

[15] Cited in Kōsuke Ōyama, 'Gendai Nihon ni okeru gyōsei shidō no kōzō' (The structure of administrative guidance in modern Japan), *Shakai kagaku kenkyū*, Vol. 40, No. 6 (1989), p. 54.

Table 13.4 Coefficient of Variation of Indices of Manufacturing in Prefectures (per cent)

Year	Value Added	No. of Plants	No. of Employees
1950	130.15	104.50	112.23
1955	146.09	124.88	129.56
1960	160.31	130.06	139.91
1965	149.15	128.17	128.75
1970	138.66	122.84	114.77
1975	121.47	114.09	101.47
1980	115.15	111.52	98.03
1985	111.07	109.24	94.52
1988	107.97	105.35	92.56

Note: The variables represent standard deviation divided by the mean of corresponding indices of every prefecture.

Source: Hirokazu Kajiwara and Masako Maeda, *Nihon no chiiki keizai to Ajia* (Japanese regional economies and Asia) (Tokyo: Nihon Hyōronsha, 1992), p. 50.

'national champions.'[16] MITI also hoped that SMEs would merge into larger firms in order to avoid excessive competition among them.

Recent studies, however, have argued that those industrial policies did not achieve their objectives, as I suggested at the beginning of this chapter. They could not prevent fierce competition among half a dozen large firms and they left many SMEs untouched.

On the political side, the Liberal Democratic Party has employed various policies for SMEs in order to win elections. As Kent Calder has demonstrated, national policies for SMEs grew particularly extensively during periods of political crisis. For a conservative party such as the LDP, it has been important to gain support from SMEs not just because they are voters but also because, as Suzanne Berger argues, they could block mobilization of the working class and prevent radicalization of the middle classes.[17] For leftist parties, too, it was important to devise policies for SMEs in order to broaden the political base. Leftist versions of Chambers of Commerce and Industries were organized and their memberships increased by the late 1960s. Leftist Governor Torazo Ninagawa of Kyoto Prefecture, where the communists were electorally very strong, first introduced a no-collateral loan system for small firms in 1966, and it became very popular among other prefectures. The LDP government,

[16] See Friedman, *Misunderstood Miracle*, p. 33; Toshiya Kitayama, 'Institutionalizing the Politics of Productivity in Japan,' *Kwansei Gakuin Law Review*, Vol. 12 (1991), pp. 19–32.
[17] Suzanne Berger, 'Traditional Sector in France and Italy,' in Suzanne Berger and Michael Piore, *Dualism and Discontinuity in Industrial Societies* (Cambridge: Cambridge University Press, 1980), pp. 88–131.

immediately after the election debacle of 1972, in which the LDP lost 17 seats and the Japan Communist Party gained an additional 24 seats, adopted the no-collateral loan program for 'small-scale firms' at the national level. The local Chambers of Commerce and Industries, after giving consultation and guidance to applicants from 'small-scale' firms, recommended that the Peoples' Finance Corporation lend to SMEs. Other governmental financial institutes for SMEs—the Small Business Finance Corporation, the Central Cooperative Bank for Commerce and Industry, and the Environmental Sanitation Business Finance Corporation— have been established mostly by the initiative of the Liberal Democratic Party.[18]

Regional development became an issue after the central bureaucracy drafted the National Income Doubling Plan in 1960, which attempted to relocate the industries in urban areas throughout the Pacific Belt region. Both the LDP, which included many politicians from less developed regions, and the local governments in rural areas called for more emphasis in these regions. The National Development Plan of 1962 thus included the correction of unbalanced development as one of its major objectives. To carry out this objective, several places, called New Industrial Cities, were designated for industrialization and concentration of government investment. The idea was to locate such large plants as steel furnaces and petrochemical plants in those cities. These New Industrial Cities were originally intended to be few in number, but many municipal and prefectural governments lobbied for the designation, which, in the end, was given to 15 regions. Again, the influence of LDP Diet members was instrumental in the designation process and primarily responsible for the increased number of designated regions. Most of the New Industrial Cities were not successful, however, as I will show later at the local level.

In sum, the central bureaucracy envisioned efficient economic development by concentrating investment in certain areas. The LDP, on the other hand, hoped to have more balanced development. Let us look more closely at conditions of the 1960s and 1970s to understand what followed the proclamation of the National Development Plan of 1962.

Under the favorable economic conditions of the 1960s, many firms in existing industrial zones were willing to locate new plants in peripheral areas. They were experiencing shortages of labor, land, and water, and various environmental problems began to be serious. Furthermore, in the 1970s, two laws were passed that prompted the relocation of large

[18] Kent Calder, *Crisis and Compensation: Public Policy and Political Stability in Japan, 1949–86* (Princeton: Princeton University Press, 1988), Chap. 7. Furthermore, Hugh Patrick and Thomas Rohlen infer 'an implicit political decision (within the LDP, not the Ministry of Finance) to tolerate widespread tax evasion by SFEs [small-scale family enterprises], with only modest efforts of rectification through audits and punishment of tax evaders.' Patrick and Rohlen, 'Small-Scale Family Enterprises,' p. 367.

factories from urban areas to rural areas. In addition to the expansion
of industrial activities to outlying regions, the Local Grant Tax,[19] which
started in fiscal year 1954 with the aim of redistributing resources
from rich to poor prefectures, and the rate of which was increased in
1967, and public works politically distributed to peripheral regions contributed to a more balanced development of Japan, if not more balanced
industrialization.

As a result, during the 1960s and 1970s, prefectural incomes became
more equal and the Japanese economy developed a more advanced industrial structure. Heavy and chemical industries, particularly machinery
industries, became the leading sectors of the economy. In 1955, 25 prefectures had per capita incomes below 50 per cent that of Tokyo; the number
increased to 37 in 1961, but fell to 4 in 1975.[20] The 1980s, however, brought
the 'Tokyo concentration problem,' where only Tokyo and a few surrounding prefectures seemed to flourish. Prefectures with half Tokyo's
per capita income increased to 9 in 1979 and 12 in 1980,[21] despite the
overall equalization of prefectural incomes shown in Table 13.4. This was
due to the higher rate of increase in Tokyo prefectural income. As many
metal and chemical industries lost competitiveness and were considered
structurally depressed, some localities dependent upon large plants in
those industries also had serious problems. Other localities with export-
oriented industries were in trouble because of a higher yen. Some insist
that this phenomenon reflects a recentralization of the Japanese economy
and politics.

In fact, this phenomenon developed because the region around Tokyo
responded to the changing world economy faster than the rest of Japan by
making the most of the 'flexible mass production' strategy. In the 1980s,
leading large firms in machinery industries, such as Toshiba and Canon,
were building laboratories or transforming their factories into laboratory-
factories in the western suburbs of Tokyo (around the Tamagawa district
and Kanagawa prefecture). They chose to do so because this area has
geographic proximity to the southern part of Tokyo (the Jonan district),
which has an accumulation of SMEs in machinery industries.[22] The Jonan
district is capable of responding to almost all manufacturing demands
from large firms and is therefore indispensable to large firms when they
design prototypes in R&D. The close cooperation of large firms and SMEs
is the key in flexible mass production. It was only Tokyo that had the

[19] For further explanation of the Land Grant Tax, see the chapter by Akizuki in this
volume.
[20] Tomiei Igarashi, *Chiiki kasseika no hassō* (Visions for vitalizing regional development)
(Tokyo: Gakuyo Shobo, 1991), pp. 99–100.
[21] Ibid., p. 102.
[22] Mitsuhiro Seki, 'Kōzō chōsei no naka no daitoshi kōgyō' (Urban industries in structural
adjustment), in Kiyoji Murata, ed., *Sangyō botoshi Tokyo* (Industrial 'mother city' Tokyo)
(Tokyo: Tōyō Keizai Shinpōsha, 1988), pp. 89–124.

skills and information necessary for the flexible mass production of high technology products at the time.

In response to the Tokyo concentration problem, a national project was devised to help localities develop, combining regional development with industrialization to create 'Technopolises.' There were, however, differences between this effort and the New Industrial Cities. High technology industries were the target this time rather than heavy and chemical industries, and more emphasis was placed on providing 'software' infrastructure—meaning helping R&D, information exchange, and human skill formation—rather than providing 'hardware' infrastructure—such as constructing harbors and roads. These new infrastructure projects also depended more on local initiative. Given the fiscal crisis of the late 1970s, the national government had started to reduce its financial burden by shifting the policymaking process to local governments and the private sector.[23]

As in the 1960s, many localities lobbied for the Technopolis designation, and after the law was established in 1983, 26 locations were designated. It is too early to assess whether or not Technopolis projects have been successful; the crucial question, I argue, is whether local governments have been able to take advantage of a flexible mass production strategy.

The Local Level

With these conditions for regional development under the national economy and national projects, what have local governments done? The policies of local governments can be classified into three subcategories, based on the nature of their objectives: Mark I policies are used to attract large firms from outside and therefore do not pay much attention to SMEs; Mark II policies promote existing SMEs within the territory and help potential starters; and Mark III policies are special cases of Mark II policies that make the relationships between large firms and SMEs reciprocal. I will come back to these various policies in subsequent discussion.

Let us turn our attention to the case of Kumamoto Prefecture to see what one local government has done. Kumamoto is a central prefecture in Kyushu, southernmost of the four main islands of Japan. It is 7,400 square kilometers and its population was about 1.85 million in 1992. Its per capita personal income is about ¥2 million, which ranks 30th out of the 47 prefectures of Japan. It is safe to say that Kumamoto is a typical peripheral prefecture outside the Pacific Belt region. Some of its

---

[23] See Sheridan Tatsuno, 'Building the Japanese Techno-State: The Regionalization of Japanese High Tech Industrial Policies,' in Ulrich Hilpert, ed., *Regional Innovation and Decentralization: High Tech Industry and Governmental Policy* (London: Routledge, 1991), pp. 219–35.

municipalities were designated as New Industries Cities and others as Technopolises.

Postwar Development in Kumamoto Prefecture[24]

Kumamoto after the war was, like most prefectures in Japan, basically agricultural. With a war-torn economy and an increase of population due to repatriation and a baby boom, the Kumamoto government implemented a Four-Year Plan for Industrial Promotion in 1947. Industry mainly meant agriculture, but some attempt was made to encourage production in cottage industries, such as Japanese paper, bamboo products, ceramics, and weaving.

Faced with a recession and revenue crisis, Kumamoto revised the plan in 1949. It was suggested that more emphasis should be put on export industries, that the collaboration of SMEs should be promoted, and that sales organizations for products ought to be established. More important, the prefectural government insisted as early as 1949 that heavy and chemical industries were to be promoted in order for Kumamoto to advance beyond the current industrial structure based on agriculture and SMEs.

The prefecture took several steps for industrial promotion. It reorganized the prefectural technological institute to provide more extensive technical advice. It established an organization to guarantee loans and also started a special financing program for SMEs. It established a center for industrial promotion and marketing for local products. And it provided consulting services for the managers of SMEs.

During the 1950s, more emphasis was put on promoting heavy and chemical industries in order to overcome the 'fragility and backwardness of industries in the prefecture.' The Kumamoto Prefectural Factory Promotion Ordinance of 1953 was promulgated to attract outside firms. In 1956, a 10-year general prefectural plan was announced, which identified two coastal regions as planned industrial zones. Under current economic conditions, however, the development of these zones made little progress, and the plan was revised in 1961 to emphasize the importance of agriculture. The 1961 version said that Kumamoto was still an agricultural prefecture and that it ought to promote local firms. Due to the financial constraints for investment on infrastructure, the government turned its attention from attracting large-scale industries from outside to promoting SMEs.

This turnabout was followed by the central government's New Industrial City project. Kumamoto Prefecture successfully lobbied to have

[24] The following analysis draws on Tsunatoshi Itō, *Sengo chihō kōgyō no tenkai: Kumamoto-ken kōgyō no kenkyū* (The development of postwar regional industries: The study of Kumamoto industries) (Kyoto: Minerva Shobō, 1992).

its two coastal industrial regions jointly designated in 1964 as a New Industrial City.

With its New Industrial City, Kumamoto was able to reemphasize industrialization as a main theme. The 1965 plan explicitly stated that the government would strongly promote the construction of the New Industrial City. The government also promulgated a new Prefectural Factory Promotion Ordinance, adding tax incentives. Many municipal governments also established or revised similar ordinances. Kumamoto was relatively successful in attracting outside firms. Between 1969 and 1974, 429 plants were built and 141 outside firms began business in the prefecture. Along with the national government's National Development Plan of 1969, Kumamoto prefecture devised its own Long-term Plan of 1970 to maintain a developmental strategy.

The 1970s witnessed growing environmental problems throughout Japan, and Kumamoto's Minamata Disease became a national issue.[25] Victims of the disease won a suit against the chemical company, Chisso, in Kumamoto District Court in 1973. The 1973 Kumamoto Basic Vision reflected a change in public awareness, stating that selective industrialization was to be promoted and more emphasis was to be placed on the promotion of SMEs and machinery industries, which were to be located inland, unlike the heavy and chemical industries of Kumamoto's coastal regions. The 1970s also brought the oil crises and the Japanese economy entered a period of much slower growth. The Third National Development Plan of 1977 pointed out the need to strengthen local industries. Local governments also started to promote community-based industries.

Local governments, however, did not completely abandon their efforts to attract outside firms to their territories. Rather, such efforts were strengthened as the Tokyo overconcentration problem became evident and competition among localities intensified. The Kumamoto General Plan for the 1980s was announced in 1981. It stressed the promotion of local SMEs within the prefecture and proposed specific policies for the development of technical infrastructure, information, and human capital. But at the same time, the plan mentioned 'importing' firms in electronics and various other high technology industries. For this purpose, the government established a new section in 1982 to attract outside firms, and a mission was sent to the United States to provide information about locating plants in Kumamoto. In sum, although new policy emphasis was put on the promotion of local SMEs, more effort was made for attracting new high technology firms to the region.[26]

---

[25] Minamata Disease was caused by the untreated effluent that Chisso discharged into Minamata Bay. The number of local inhabitants who consumed mercury-contaminated fish is estimated at 200,000. An accumulation of methyl mercury in the body damaged their nervous systems.

[26] Itō, *Sengo chihō kōgyō no tenkai*, p. 33.

This latter emphasis was further reinforced by the Technopolis project in which 16 municipalities in Kumamoto, mostly in the inland region, were designated as Technopolises in 1984. The Kumamoto Technopolis project had two objectives: to attract high technology firms and to upgrade the technical capabilities of local firms. For the former, a Techno Research Park was developed in the mid-1980s, including an applied electronics research center founded in 1985. Subsidies and loans were made available for municipalities. To meet the second objective, loan guarantees, low-interest loans, and subsidies were offered to SMEs. Technical advice was also available through the prefectural technological institute and the Kumamoto Technopolis Foundation. And in 1985 the prefectural technological institute was reorganized as the Kumamoto Prefecture Industrial Research Institute and expanded its services to support R&D. Various forums were established to facilitate information exchange and joint R&D. In the 1990s it has been suggested that it is important to link the large firms in the Techno Research Park with local firms.

Although it is too early to evaluate Kumamoto's Technopolis project, it has been said that the new plants have not been established as planned and that new policies for local firms have not been well implemented. Local firms have not taken advantage of the new facilities and organizations.[27] And the linkage between local SMEs and large firms from outside has not been extensive.

In sum, the experience of Kumamoto Prefecture demonstrates several characteristics that are more or less applicable to other peripheral prefectures. First, industrialization has almost always been given priority in the prefectural policy agenda. Second, during the 1950s and 1960s 'industrialization' was understood to mean attracting heavy and chemical industries from outside (Mark I policies). Third, the policies for this kind of industrialization acquired momentum when national projects, such as designating New Industrial Cities and Technopolises, provided localities with various financial and fiscal devices. Fourth, promoting existing local SMEs (Mark II policies) gathered attention during the latter half of the 1970s but has not become a major strategy. More emphasis is still put on importing manufacturing firms from outside. It is, however, recognized that policies for stronger relationships between large firms and local firms (Mark III policies) are important as the Technopolis project proceeds.

Osaka Prefecture

Osaka Prefecture is the second largest, after Tokyo. Eight and a half million people live in 1,882 square kilometers. The region between Osaka

---

[27] Itō, *Sengo chihō kōgyō no tenkai*, pp. 39–40.

Table 13.5 Percentage of Value of Shipment, by Size of Firm in Major Prefectures

	4–9	10–19	20–29	30–99	100–299	300+
Osaka	8.0	9.2	9.1	19.3	19.6	34.8
Tokyo	8.7	8.5	7.9	15.6	14.3	45.1
Kanagawa	2.5	3.2	3.4	9.9	14.4	66.7
Aiichi	4.1	4.4	4.4	12.2	13.2	61.7
Hyogo	4.2	5.4	6.2	16.3	20.7	47.2
All Japan	4.9	5.8	6.1	16.3	18.7	48.2

Source: Tsūsan-shō Chōsa Tōkei-bu Kōgyo Tōkei-ka, *Kōgyō tōkei hyō* (Census of manufacturers) (Tokyo: Tsūshō Sangyō Chōsakai, 1992).

and Kobe is one of the four major industrial zones mentioned earlier and was the largest manufacturing zone in Japan before Tokyo, Kanagawa, and Saitama Prefectures replaced it around 1940.[28] One of the most important characteristics of Osaka industries is the predominance of SMEs. Osaka Prefecture had 44,585 factories in 1990, more than any other prefecture. Tokyo was second with 42,804 factories.[29] Table 13.5 shows that the two most urbanized prefectures have higher percentages of activities of SMEs.

It is noteworthy that large Japanese cities are not completely deindustrialized, unlike, for example, New York City. This fact is important to understanding how much manufacturing matters in Japan.[30] 'The myth of the post-industrial economy' has not been so powerful in Japan, where it is recognized that mastery and control of manufacturing is the key to the competitiveness of industry.

Osaka's urban industries, however, are disadvantaged compared to those of Tokyo. Many SMEs in Osaka form community-based industries made up of geographically clustered SMEs. Most manufacture labor-intensive products, such as briefcases, pencils, eyeglasses, and flatware. Out of 392 clustering or community-based industries recognized by the government, Osaka Prefecture has the largest share, with 33; Aichi has 23; Shizuoka, 17; Tokyo, 17; and Hyogo, 16.[31] Osaka's community-based industries produce mainly low value-added products: towels, blankets, bicycles, umbrellas, glassware, etc. Furthermore, since they are oriented toward export, they are not as sophisticated as those in Tokyo which produce mostly for the domestic market.

[28] Atsuhiko Takeuchi, *Gijutsu kakushin to kōgyō chitai* (Innovation and industrial zones) (Tokyo: Taimeidō, 1988), p. 28.
[29] Tsūsan-shō Chōsa Tōkei-bu Kōgyō Tōkei-ka, *Kōgyō tōkei hyō 1990* (Census of manufacturers) (Tokyo: Tsū shō Sangyō Chōsakai, 1992). Kumamoto has 3,789 factories.
[30] Cohen and Zysman, *Manufacturing Matters*.
[31] Mitsuru Yamazaki, *Chiiki keizai kasseika no michi* (Methods to vitalize regional economies) (Tokyo: Yū hikaku, 1984), Chap. 4.

These are the products that earned foreign currency in the late 1940s and the 1950s, when Japan was still reconstructing. The postwar industrial policies of Osaka Prefecture, therefore, were oriented for the promotion of SMEs. In 1947, the governor of Osaka announced the Osaka Industry Recovery Plan which stressed the promotion of SMEs and the export/commodities industry as one of its main points. The local government particularly helped to organize cooperatives of SMEs after 1949.[32] It also established the Osaka Prefecture Small Business Credit Guarantee Corporation in 1948 to improve the financial situation of SMEs.

Osaka Prefecture is known as an innovator in policies for SMEs. As early as 1925, it established an institute to give advice and consultation for SMEs and took the lead in devising installment plans for rationalizing machinery in 1960 and in establishing the Osaka Prefecture SMEs Promotion Corporation to provide services for subcontractors in 1965. However, Osaka has also realized the weakness of its industrial structure in which light industries, such as textiles and miscellaneous goods industries, predominate. To try to remedy this weakness, a large industrial complex was built in southern Osaka. In the late 1950s tidelands were reclaimed to allow the development of a large industrial complex. Thanks to the favorable location, firms in the steel, petrochemical, oil refining, and other industries were attracted.

Although heavy and chemical industry firms were drawn to the region and the promotion of SMEs has been a consistent policy of the Osaka prefectural government, the Osaka economy has more metal and chemical industries, and SMEs in Osaka are not as technically sophisticated as those in Tokyo. It therefore has fewer high technology firms in areas such as telecommunications, electronics, and so on. Put differently, Osaka has implemented both Mark I and Mark II policies. While large firms and SMEs coexist, there is limited strategic cooperation between the two, which is crucial for flexible mass production.

Let us now consider several more examples of Mark I, II, and III policies.

Importing Large Firms from Outside (Mark I Policies)

Most local governments were preoccupied with the idea of having large firms within their territories during the late 1950s and early 1960s. Of the 15 New Industrial Cities designated in the early 1960s, all but one were coastal regions and all planned large industrial complexes. Typically, these cities passed ordinances to attract firms from outside with tax incentives and subsidies. These outside firms were usually exempted from business taxes for a few years, from the tax on the acquisition of real

[32] Osaka-fu, *Osaka hyakunen-shi* (A history of Osaka since 1868) (Osaka: Osaka Prefecture, 1968).

estate, and from fixed property taxes. New Industrial Cities also invested large amounts of money for infrastructure, such as roads, harbors, and rail lines.

Critics say that many New Industrial Cities failed to achieve their objectives. Since there were many New Industrial Cities, the ordinances passed in each region were less attractive and national resources were diluted in the process. When firms did not build plants, investment for infrastructure did not bear fruit. Even when firms did come, the number of local employees was not as many as expected since these were capital-intensive industries, and many factories were closed when they lost competitiveness after the oil crises in the 1970s. Generally speaking, it is suggested that localities did not get what they paid for.

The Toyama/Takaoka region is but one example.[33] Toyama Prefecture is located in the far north of the Pacific Belt region. The Toyama prefectural government planned to establish an industrial complex in 1961, and the government established a General Planning Bureau and appointed an ex-MITI official as the first bureau chief. He was instrumental in acquisition of the New Industrial City designation, which Toyama received in 1964. In the prefectural assembly, LDP members supported the plan, the Japan Socialist Party members supported it conditionally, and members of the Japan Communisty Party, although none held a seat in the assembly, opposed it.

According to the original plan, Toyama's industrial complex would consist of petrochemical and steel firms, and a fossil fuel power plant. But MITI, with its own vision of the most suitable industrial locations from a national standpoint, cast doubt on Toyama's plan. One local business organization was also pessimistic about the future of this large plan and claimed that the prefectural government should instead promote existing industries. In the end, the attempt to attract steel and petrochemical firms was dropped from the final plan of 1964. Opposition to the plan from residents, farmers, and fishermen followed and all that eventually came to Toyama were an aluminum smelter and businesses related to lumber processing. The aluminum plant started operation in February 1970 but lost competitiveness because of the oil shock in 1974 which brought recession and raised the cost of electricity. With much cheaper imports coming from abroad, the aluminum industry has been regarded as one of Japan's structurally depressed industries since the late 1970s.

Other New Industrial Cities have had similar experiences. Steel furnaces, chemical plants, and shipbuilding plants in particular did not materialize because too many New Industrial Cities were designated. Even

---

[33] Kitanihon Shinbun-sha Henshukyoku, ed., *Maboroshi no han'ei shinsantoshi nijū nen no kessan* (Illusory prosperity: A balance sheet of New Industrial Cities' 20 years) (Tokyo: Keisō Shobō, 1984).

when they did come, the situation ultimately brought little change because these material-related industries all lost competitiveness after the oil shocks and some of these firms have already withdrawn from the industrial complexes.

An interesting case is the Tōyo New Industrial City in Ehime Prefecture, which planned large industrial parks on reclaimed land. Part of the land was to be sold to one of the large companies in the Sumitomo group, but this land still had no factories on it in 1991. On the other hand, another part of the land was divided and purchased by local SMEs. Thirty-four out of 50 companies there are SMEs.[34] The next section deals with local governments that took the strategy of Ehime Prefecture.

Endogenous Development Strategies (Mark II Policies)

In Nagano Prefecture, different strategies were taken.[35] The Matsumoto/ Suwa region, a mountainous region north of the Pacific Belt region, was the only New Industrial City not on the coast. Partly because of its location, this region planned to establish much smaller industrial parks for firms in the precision machinery industry for the manufacture of goods such as cameras and watches. The city of Matsumoto built four industrial parks. Of the 190 firms that located there, only a few were from outside the prefecture. Suwa City's industrial park drew 31 companies, all of which moved from other parts of the city. These two cities promoted the development of existing firms.

The experience of Sakaki, also in Nagano Prefecture, is well documented. This mountain town of about 16,000 inhabitants has an accumulation of machinery firms and 1 per cent of the numerical control machine tools of Japan were in the town's limits in 1983.[36] Almost all the firms are SMEs (see Table 13.6), and most are technologically sophisticated. The town prospered and attracted attention as a model of industrialization for other small towns. The 'miracle of Sakaki' drew more than 200 observers, both domestic and foreign, in two years.

The Sakaki Township Factory Promotion Ordinance was promulgated and a Commerce and Industry Section set up in 1957. Again, development was endogenous. Friedman notes that well over 90 per cent of all companies subsequently established in Sakaki originated within the town, and 80 per cent were started by workers who left other Sakaki enterprises to start their own independent operations.[37] In 1971, the 1957 ordinance

[34] Kazuo Hoshijima *et al.*, *Shiraishi Haruki no kenkyū* (A study of Haruki Shiraishi) (Kyoto: Keibun-sha, 1993), p. 299.

[35] Kitanihon Shinbun-sha Henshukyoku, ed., *Maboroshi no han'ei*, pp. 277–83. See also Tadao Kiyonari, *80-nendai no chiiki shinko* (Promotion of regional development in the 1980s) (Tokyo: Nihon Hyōronsha, 1981), pp. 160–1.

[36] See Friedman, *Misunderstood Miracle*, p. 178.

[37] Ibid., p. 185.

Table 13.6 Size of Firms in Sakaki, 1989

No. of Employees	No. of Firms	%
1–3	161	45.2
4–9	115	32.3
10–19	30	8.4
20–29	18	5.1
30–49	11	3.1
50–99	7	2.0
100–299	9	2.5
300+	5	1.4
Total	356	100.0

Source: *Tekuno taun Sakaki* (Techno-town Sakaki) (Nagano: Sakaki Town, 1989).

was replaced by a new ordinance to promote commerce and industry, which aims simply to help existing firms and potential new firms.

Friedman, in particular, emphasizes the role of the Chamber of Commerce and Industry (CCI) in promoting the development of SMEs. He believes it was local staff rather than MITI bureaucrats in Tokyo who were instrumental in the development of the flexible production system in Sakaki. Particularly important was CCI's role as a contact point for banks and government funding sources; it acted as expert counsel on what kinds of funds were available.

From our perspective, it is interesting that the CCI in Sakaki had a kind of local autonomy *vis-à-vis* MITI in distributing resources from the central government. As shown above, MITI was aiming to realize economies of scale through cartels, entry restrictions, and consolidation. For MITI, 'industrial rationalization' meant any of those three. Sakaki's CCI, however, interpreted rationalization as 'technical advance.' It authorized funds not for the firms that had consolidated, but rather for firms eager to buy new equipment.[38] Thus, Friedman argues, local autonomy and the limited power of MITI were important in shaping the Japanese economy into a flexible production system by using networks of SMEs.

At the same time, Friedman insists that CCI activities can explain only part of Sakaki's success. 'Firms in a region had to learn to trust each other and reach an accommodation with local political authorities regarding overall industrial objectives.'[39] In sum, he finds in Sakaki regional cooperation similar to that found in Italian industrial districts where flexible specialization is the dominant industrial strategy.

Can we say, then, that the Japanese economy is a sum of flexible regional economies, such as those in the Third Italy? My hypothesis is that

---

[38] Ibid., p. 188.　　[39] Ibid., p. 178.

the political economy of Japan may not be mass production but is also not quite like the flexible specialization regime that characterizes some European regional economies or Silicon Valley in the United States. In the Japanese economy, large firms are still important actors. It is the coexistence of large firms and SMEs and strategic cooperation among them that characterizes the Japanese political economy and brings about a flexible mass production regime. And local government has been one of the factors that has contributed to it.

Coordinating Relationships between Large Firms and SMEs (Mark III Policies)

What kind of local government–SME relations best illustrate this regime? The case of Yonezawa City provides an intriguing case.[40] Yonezawa City is located in Yamagata Prefecture which is in the northeastern part of Japan. It had a population of around 93,000 in 548 square kilometers in 1992. In the electronics industry in Yonezawa, there were three factories, which were either local factories or local subsidiaries of large electronics firms. The number of employees was more than 500 as of 1985. Each of the three factories had one or two first-tier subcontractors, which in turn had second- and third-tier subcontractors.

In 1980, the municipal government and the local Chamber of Commerce and Industry conducted a survey of regional industry and found that the first-tier subcontractors in Yonezawa tended to work with only a single parent company. This meant they were vulnerable if the parent company faced economic troubles. The municipal government of Yonezawa thus sought to reshape this structure.

The municipal government proposed that the first-tier subcontractors form a network, after obtaining permission from the top companies and such an association was founded in the electronics industry in 1981. Its objective, Keiichi Kunisaki argues,[41] was to make the firms in this network able to produce not just parts but also products of their own, if not final products. In order to do this, the association collects and exchanges information, helps to train and retrain workers, and collectively performs marketing. The association also forms study groups that teach the 'just-in-time' production system, which is famous as the key to the success of the Toyota Motor Company. Each subcontractor also seeks to establish relations with new parent companies to enlarge its technological base and to gain more security.

[40] Keiichi Kunisaki, 'Nettowākuka to chiimu ka' (Networking and team spirit), in Ken'ichi Murayama and Takashi Kawakita, eds., *Chiiki sangyō no kiki to saisei* (Crisis and regeneration of regional industries) (Tokyo: Dō bunkan, 1990), pp. 147–92; and Noriyuki Hitokoto and Naomichi Yasuda, *Chiiki sangyō no saikōchiku senryaku* (Reconstruction strategy of regional industries) (Tokyo: Shinhyoron, 1993).

[41] Kunisaki, 'Nettowakuka to chiimu ka,' pp. 151–7.

The experience of Yonezawa illustrates that local government can play an important role in creating a network of SMEs and reshaping it into a flexible production system. It may look like a flexible specialization regime but the critical point is that these SMEs are in one way or another linked to the larger firms, which still produce in high volume, if not standardized products. The case of Kumamoto also showed government beginning to help local SMEs construct some links with large firms outside. It is suggested that prefectural industrial research institutes and applied electronics research centers should attempt to improve the technical ability of local SMEs so that they can engage in business relations with more technologically sophisticated parent firms.[42]

The policies of the Tokyo metropolitan government are another case of Mark III policies.[43] As suggested above, Tokyo has a very sophisticated cluster of SMEs in the machinery industry that can respond to the needs of large firms. The metropolitan government attempts to strengthen their ability to do so. In 1981, for example, the Tokyo Industrial Promotion Policy Council was established to discuss the future of Tokyo industry. The council divided Tokyo into four districts based on the specialized functions of SMEs and proposed that each district have innovation centers (for design, mechatronics [the fusion of mechanics and electronics], new science, software, and a science park). For the Jonan district, the mechatronics center is supposed to provide services for further technological sophistication in R&D.

Another interesting case is the policies of the city of Muroran in Hokkaido.[44] The government and the local Chambers of Commerce and Industry set up a foundation called Muroran Techno Center and attracted technologically sophisticated SMEs from Tokyo and Kanagawa Prefectures. That is, instead of attracting large firms in order to secure the local tax base and employment, it invited SMEs that had linkages with large firms. Technological sophistication is judged to be more important than what large firms can bring to regional economy.

At the same time, we should also bear in mind that in order for a flexible mass production regime to be realized and stabilized, some pacts between large firms and SMEs must be agreed upon. Although local governments can affect the relations, they are but one of many actors in this process. Friedman is correct when he points out that 'we would be unable to assess the policy's economic results unless we understand the resolution of political conflicts elsewhere in society.'[45] Strategic cooperation needs to be created and developed and interdependence must be coordinated.

[42] Itō, *Sengo chihō kōgyō no tenkai*, pp. 40–4.
[43] Murata, ed., *Sangyō botoshi Tōkyō*.
[44] Mitsuhiro Seki and Keiichi Yoshida, ed., *Chūshō kigyō to chiiki inkyubētā* (Small and medium-sized firms and the regional incubator) (Tokyo: Shinhyōron, 1993), pp. 207–12.
[45] Friedman, *Misunderstood Miracle*, p. 209.

Policy Instruments of Local Government

Let us turn our attention to how local government has shaped relation-ships with SMEs. To promote relations with SMEs, Kumamoto has devel-oped a Bureau in charge of Commerce, Industry, Tourism, and Labor. It has nine sections dealing with commerce and industry (mainly com-merce), industry (mainly manufacturing), SMEs, industry development, tourism, labor policies, employment security, labor training, and employ-ment insurance. The Industry Promotion Section has a subdivision, the Kumamoto Prefecture Industrial Research Institute mentioned above. This institute has sections for information and design, manufacturing engineering, biotechnology, electronics, and material science. It conducts research to promote R&D by SMEs and organizes collective projects in high technology. It also makes technical information available to SMEs and does experiments and analysis on behalf of SMEs. Every prefecture has at least one technological institute of this kind. Some large cities also have their own institutions.

There are several non-profit organizations and foundations for SMEs, most founded by the prefectural government. The Kumamoto Prefecture Small Business Credit Guarantee Corporation guarantees loans to SMEs up to ¥135 million for a single company and ¥255 million for cooperatives. The credit guarantee fee is from 0.7 to 1.0 per cent. The Kumamoto Prefecture SME Promotion Corporation provides services and guidance specifically for subcontractors. It also purchases expensive machinery and leases it to SMEs. Inside this corporation is the Kumamoto Prefectural Center of Information for SMEs which collects, processes, and provides information for SMEs. Furthermore, the Chambers of Commerce and Industry, established in most municipalities, conduct research, collect information, give related lectures, and provide consultation for small firms.

Various policies for SMEs are channeled through these institutions. Advice and guidance is available through the SME Promotion Section and the Chambers of Commerce and Industry. Any claims concerning the exercise of inappropriate power by large firms toward subcontractors are dealt with at the SME Promotion Corporation. These include claims on payment methods, terms of contracts, etc. Information on loans is avail-able at the SME Promotion section of the Commerce, Industry, Tourism, and Labor Bureau.

As mentioned above, technological advice is available to SMEs at the Kumamoto Prefecture Industrial Research Institute and Applied Elec-tronics Research Center within the Techno Research Park of the Kumamoto Technopolis. SMEs can take advantage of the facilities and machinery of the two institutes, which also train SME engineers. Subsidies are also available for R&D conducted by SMEs.

Various kinds of prefectural loans are available. For stabilization of business, modernization and rationalization, and introduction of high technology machinery, SMEs can borrow at interest rates of around 5 per cent for terms of five to seven years. For relocation of business establishments within the prefecture, loans are available at less than 5 per cent interest with a 15-year term.

For 'small-scale firms' defined at the outset of this essay, there are special loan systems requiring no collateral and no guarantors. This system is available for small firms that receive managerial guidance from local Chambers of Commerce and Industry, which basically administer this loan system. As of July 1, 1992, loans of ¥5 million were available for small firms with an annual interest rate of 5.8 per cent with no collateral or guarantors required.[46]

Another way to help SMEs is to enable them to organize and cooperate for a more modern and rational way of doing business. Several kinds of legal cooperatives are possible for various purposes and the bureau assists cooperatives by providing know-how, consultation, and loans. Particularly important is the SME Structural Upgrading Project, the loan system for SME cooperatives. When SMEs in the same sector or related sectors form cooperatives to establish factory complexes, wholesale complexes, and so on, the Japan Small Business Corporation, a public corporation, and prefectures jointly lend the cooperatives long-term and very low-interest money. As of 1993, the interest rate was 2.7 per cent and the term of redemption was up to 20 years. This corporation will provide up to 65 per cent of the money needed for the investment in land, facilities, etc. Preferential treatment on taxation is also given. From drawing up plans to actual operation, the prefectural government will give detailed advice and guidance to cooperatives.

New emphasis has been put on industrial cooperation between SMEs that belong to different industrial sectors. Under this plan, several SMEs in different sectors share technology and marketing know-how to initiate a new business. In the case of Kumamoto, the Industrial Promotion Section is in charge of the stage of bringing the SMEs together, the Commerce and Industry Policy Section oversees the development stage, and the SME Promotion Section manages the business stage.

To present an urban contrast, let us turn to Osaka Prefecture, which has a Commerce and Industry Bureau with six sections that focus on industrial policy, soft industries promotion ('soft' industries are high value-added industries desirable for Osaka and Japan to compete against NIEs), organizing cooperatives, industry (which has subsections for cottage industries, textile and chemical industries, machinery and metal

---

[46] See Calder, *Crisis and Compensation*, pp. 344–7, for the political motives of the Liberal Democratic Party in supporting the no-collateral loan system.

industries, consumer goods industries, and quarrying), commerce, and finance.

The bureau has three subdivisions. One is the Osaka Prefectural Institute for Advanced Industrial Development, which conducts surveys and research on the Osaka economy and on the management of local firms, provides consultation and guidance for SMEs, publishes periodicals based on its research, and gives seminars. Another is the Osaka Industrial Design Institute of the Osaka Prefectural Government. It provides information and consultation on industrial design, which is regarded as critical for the competitiveness of urban firms. The last is the Osaka Prefecture Industrial Technology Research Institute, which does research to promote R&D by SMEs and organizes collective projects on high technology. It also makes technical information available for SMEs. Similar non-profit organizations and foundations for SMEs exist in Osaka. The Osaka Prefecture Small Business Credit Guarantee Corporation, the Osaka Prefecture SME Promotion Corporation, the Osaka Prefectural Information Center for SMEs, and the Chambers of Commerce and Industry provide similar services for SMEs.

The policies for Osaka SMEs are similar to those in Kumamoto. Compared with the prefectures in the periphery, however, urban prefectures try harder to upgrade existing SMEs and to help the start-up of new SMEs. Osaka Prefecture has no section specifically in charge of attracting firms from outside, relying instead on the Soft Industries Promotion Section. This section and 36 companies in 1990 together established the Foundation for Osaka Research Enterprise Companies, which is engaged in 'indirect venture capital business.' To support the capital formation of R&D-oriented companies and companies providing services for them, the Foundation deposits the original capital that would otherwise have to come from venture capital.

The Osaka municipal government has already established the Osaka Shimaya Business Incubator with ¥25 million from the city and the same amount from trade associations and private companies. The foundation established through these donations in 1989 manages the incubator. It provides space for business and R&D at low rent and secretarial, technological, and managerial services are available to tenants.

There is more emphasis in Osaka on the industrial cooperation between SMEs that belong to different industrial sectors than in Kumamoto. The Soft Industries Promotion Section is in charge of this and helps SMEs from the stage of information exchange, through the development of products, and to marketing, by providing information, subsidies, tax incentives, and loans. The Center for the Industrial Cooperation of SMEs was established within the Osaka Prefectural Center of Information for SMEs to provide firms in different sectors with information, guidance, and opportunities for cooperation. There are associations of those groups that attempt fusion of activities.

It is difficult to evaluate these various local government policies for SMEs. Some services are not well utilized. Some advice, if given, is simply not implemented by SMEs. The typical dilemma is that SMEs in most need of support are firms unaware that such services exist.[47]

It seems, however, that some policies do help the more entrepreneurial SMEs. Structural Upgrading Projects in particular contribute to the promotion of SMEs. These projects are more favorable to those SMEs that, together with other SMEs, are willing to relocate or improve the business environment. According to interviews with recipients of the SME Structural Upgrading Project that established industrial parks or wholesale distribution centers,[48] this is true in a number of ways. First, the interest rate provided under these projects was 2.7 per cent when the long-term market interest rate was around 8 per cent. Second, the term of redemption was 15 years when the equivalent at private banks was around 7 years. Third, SMEs did not have to give their estate as collateral, but could use the estate acquired by the project instead. This meant more financial power for operations. Fourth, additional loans were available from the Central Cooperative Bank for Commerce and Industry, the other financial public corporation. All in all, one interviewee estimated that his firm was able to invest three times as much as it could have done without the Structural Upgrading Projects.

Another project also aims to modernize SMEs. Under the SME Modernization Promotion Law, sectors are designated and sectoral modernization plans set up for SMEs aiming for the most efficient scale of production or management. These plans have not achieved their objectives because sectors designated for modernization show little improvement compared to undesignated sectors.[49] One SME president said that cooperatives are a much better way of modernizing SMEs than mergers because the profits from collaborative projects fall into each company's hands and they could become larger companies by their own efforts.[50]

This comparison shows that the success of the policies is dependent upon the entrepreneurship of the involved SMEs. In the case of the SME Structural Upgrading Projects, SMEs have to plan a project with other SMEs for several years before the actual loan is made. From the beginning

---

[47] Yamazaki, *Chiiki keizai kasseika no michi*, Chap. 8.

[48] The SME Structural Upgrading Project Interviews, conducted by the author in Osaka, February 25 and March 3, 1993.

[49] Hisashi Yokokura, 'Chūshō kigyō' (Small and medium-sized firms), in Ryutaro Komiya, ed., *Nihon no sangyō seisaku* (Industrial policy in Japan) (Tokyo: University of Tokyo Press, 1984), pp. 461–5.

[50] The SME Structural Upgrading Project Interviews, conducted by the author in Osaka, March 3, 1993.

of the plan, the prefectural advisory institute for SMEs gives the companies necessary guidance. That is, SMEs must have a long-term perspective even before they develop relations with local government. What local government can do is to help and modernize those companies with long-term perspectives and entrepreneurship. One prefectural bureaucrat says that it is easier to give technological advice than managerial advice because it is difficult to change the attitude of many managers who choose to stop making their SMEs larger and to enjoy the success they have accomplished.[51]

Similar things, however, can be said for technical aspects. For those subcontractors that have strong relations with parent companies, guidance by large parent firms is more important and relevant. On the other hand, it would be very hard for those SMEs that need very basic technical guidance from an institute to survive in today's global market. Technological institutes work best for those SMEs that have the capability to take advantage of the advanced machinery of the institute but do not have enough funds. Here again, technical ability is a prerequisite.

Conclusion

In closing, I would like to summarize the arguments presented and offer some observations on the Japanese experience with relations between local governments and SMEs. One is concerned with the policy objectives of local governments, the other with the policy instruments.

Some Japanese localities at various times have been preoccupied with the dominant ideology of Fordist mass production. At the national level, MITI, during the period of high economic growth, attempted to promote large firms while many local governments also attempted to attract them from outside (Mark I policies). At the same time, the LDP, which has been in power since 1955, has supported various policies for SMEs, mostly for political reasons. Some localities, however, were on a different trajectory. These local governments pursued an endogenous development strategy (Mark II policies). That is, they focused on existing SMEs and tried to promote them or help the start-up of new SMEs. The resulting agglomerations of SMEs and their networks are now innovative and flexible in adjusting to economic changes.

Yet SMEs themselves are only half the total picture of the Japanese political economy. I argue that the coexistence of large firms and SMEs and strategic cooperation among them characterize the Japanese political economy and together bring about a 'flexible mass production regime,' as

---

[51] Interview conducted by the author, Kumamoto Prefecture, March 13, 1993.

opposed to both mass production and flexible specialization regimes. For this regime, local governments must pay attention to the ways in which local SMEs are linked to larger firms.

In sum, there was no consensus in Japan on how development was to be achieved and to what extent SMEs were to be promoted. The meaning of development changed over time and policies were formed through various struggles among political and economic actors whose ideas about development were more or less influenced by the dominant economic ideology of the day.

What gives one country more extensive policies for SMEs than others? Two variables seem to be critical. One is the extent of the autonomy of local governments. Some local governments tend to support local firms more than does the central government. Therefore, the more local autonomy, the more policies for SMEs, and maybe more SMEs. The other is the strength of political parties *vis-á-vis* the bureaucracy. Political parties tend to devise various policies for SMEs for electoral motivations. Hence the more powerful the political parties, the more policies for SMEs, and maybe more SMEs. Comparison with Korea, a more bureaucratic authoritarian and centralized country, and Taiwan, a more decentralized country with more power in the Kuomintang, seems to verify this proposition.[52] Korea does not enjoy the agglomeration of SMEs which Taiwan has.

The Japanese case demonstrates, however, that the coexistence of large firms and SMEs is important. In Japan, being large is indispensable because only large companies can invest heavily in R&D for high technology. Their relationships with SMEs make the flexible mass production regime possible.

Another question is why one region has more extensive policies for SMEs than others. I have no definite answer to this question. Obviously, market factors exert dominant influence. For example, Nagano Prefecture does not have a vast coastal region to reclaim even if it wanted to. But ideology may be an important factor, too. Technocratic or dirigiste leaders may favor attracting outside firms, while populist leaders may favor promoting local SMEs.[53] Another factor is that those governments where the governor or mayor has leadership *vis-à-vis* the local assembly may be oriented to attracting outside firms, while local assembly members are more embedded in society and therefore where the assembly predominates there may be more orientation for doing something for existing local firms.

---

[52] Yamazaki, *Chiiki keizai kasseika no michi*, pp. 148–9. See also Gary Gireffy and Donald L. Wyman, eds., *Manufacturing Miracles: Paths of Industrialization in Latin America and East Asia* (Princeton: Princeton University Press, 1990).

[53] See Sidney Tarrow, *Between Center and Periphery* (New Haven: Yale University Press, 1977).

The survey of policies for SMEs in Kumamoto and Osaka Prefectures demonstrated the variety of policies implemented. They include guidance, consultation, financial incentives to organize cooperatives, and other financial help. Governments also attempt to provide opportunities for SMEs in different sectors to cooperate. For managerial and technological advice, every prefecture has specific institutes. Furthermore, each local government establishes public corporations for credit guarantees and specifically for subcontracting firms. Special consideration is given to small firms with no-collateral and no-guarantor loans.

One point seems critical. It has been not so much outright subsidy as low-interest loans that the Japanese central and local governments have used to assist SMEs. This implies two related things. On the one hand, promotional rather than protective measures have been the major tone of governmental policies for SMEs. This was not a foregone conclusion for SMEs in Japan because postwar agricultural policies have used subsidies to protect farmers without giving much incentive for modernization. The question is why this has been the case. Calder argues that both small business policies and agricultural policies are parts of a compensation program with which the LDP responded to political crises,[54] but he could not explain why similarly motivated policies have different impacts on agricultural and SME sectors. Here again the important actor would be the large firms. Large firms would have found protective policies to SMEs unacceptable because subsidy-dependent SMEs are unlikely to provide the technological expertise that large firms expect.

On the other hand, the entrepreneurship of SMEs is indispensable in order for low-interest loans to bear fruit. In other words, one has to examine not just governmental policy but also the relations between firms to understand how the entrepreneurship of SMEs, or the strategic cooperation among large firms and SMEs, is possible. Although local government is the only actor that can affect strategic cooperation, it can play a critical role in ensuring the interfirm relationships are reciprocal.

[54] Calder, *Crisis and Compensation*.

PART FOUR

THE VIEW OF
A PESSIMIST

14

Policies for Small Business in Japan

YOSHIRO MIWA

One of the most striking features of recent Japanese public policy, viewed both in comparative context and against the backdrop of Japanese history, has been the fluctuating but generally pronounced bias shown toward the small, across a range of industrial, trade, and credit-policy sectors, often at the expense of the large.[1]

This statement, with which Kent Calder begins a chapter on 'Small Business Policy,' reflects the dominant academic view of Japanese small business policy. Coupled with the following three facts, this view often leads scholars to conclude that small business policies have played tremendously important roles in the economic development of Japan. First, the pace of economic development in Japan has been fast. Second, the role of the government has seemed large. Third, the many small enterprises are thought to have contributed much to Japanese economic development. Because of this academic focus on small business policy, moreover, development strategists have now also become interested in Japanese small business policies in order to learn lessons for planning strategies, particularly for small businesses in developing countries.

Like much that is said about Japanese industrial policy generally, most of what is said about Japanese small business policy is wrong. The efficacy of these policies has been extremely limited. Active small enterprises have not been created through the well organized, effective policies of government. In this chapter, I provide detailed information on what those policies have been, how they have been implemented, and why they have been ineffective. I pay special attention to the central government and its relation to local governments.

This chapter is divided into three parts. In the first, I evaluate the effectiveness of policies for small and medium-sized enterprises, focusing on financing policy which is generally regarded as the most important policy measure, and conclude that its effectiveness has been negligible. In

I received helpful comments and suggestions both from many officials in the Japanese national and local government and from the participants in this project at the preliminary Fuji meeting in October–November 1992 and the Kauai conference in January 1993. I also received insightful suggestions and advice from Mark Ramseyer of the University of Chicago Law School.

[1] Kent E. Calder, *Crisis and Compensation: Public Policy and Political Stability in Japan, 1949– 86* (Princeton: Princeton University Press, 1988), p. 312.

the second section, I provide detailed information on the actual process of policy implementation and the roles of local governments. In addition to financing policy, I address technical assistance, management guidance, and management consulting policies.[2] I focus in this part on one local government, which I call A Prefecture. The final section contains brief concluding remarks.

Central Government Policies

The main focus of this study of Japanese policies for small business is on evaluating their potential effectiveness in promoting economic development in developing countries. Before considering government policies, however, let me first comment on three points relevant to Japanese industry and economic growth.

The first point concerns the large number of, and number of employees in, small businesses and their predominance in Japan. Many readers may think of such large firms as Toyota, Nissan, and Honda in the automobile industry and NEC, Hitachi, and Sony in the electronics industry as representative of Japanese firms. Some may have the perception that large firms such as Toyota, and therefore their production systems which are famous for their 'just-in-time' delivery of parts for production, cover most of the Japanese economy. On the contrary, most Japanese firms are small, and more than half the value-added is produced in small firms. This predominance of small firms in Japan has a long history, and their share has not changed for at least 30–40 years.[3]

The total number of establishments in the whole private sector of Japan (excluding agriculture and fisheries) was 6.5 million in 1986, and 99.3 per cent were small and medium-sized enterprises (SMEs[4]). Private-sector

---

[2] In this chapter, I refer to many Japanese 'policies' and 'policy measures.' Their titles often make little sense even in Japanese and therefore are hard to translate into English. Many of these policies are simply new versions of older ones and contain new phrases with only nominal differences in meaning. This proliferation of policies with slight variations has resulted from political and administrative conditions in Japan.

[3] This was recognized by Hugh T. Patrick and Thomas P. Rohlen, in 'Small-Scale Family Enterprises,' in Kozo Yamamura and Yasukichi Yasuba, eds., *The Political Economy of Japan, Volume 1: The Domestic Transformation* (Stanford: Stanford University Press, 1987):

All too frequently big business has dominated popular perceptions of the Japanese economy. Large firms are deemed to have powered Japan's growth through their successes in generating output, raising productivity, absorbing and creating innovations through large-scale R&D, and creating and developing the 'Japanese management system' of industrial relations, internal decision making, and close intragroup affiliations. . . . small enterprise is the economic, political, and social heart and backbone of Japan. In particular, small-scale family enterprises have long been and continue to be a large and dynamic element in the political economy of Japan. (p. 331)

[4] The definition of SMEs depends on the type of industry. In manufacturing, mining, etc., SMEs include enterprises with ¥100 million or less in paid-in capital, or 300 or fewer employees.

employees total 49 million, and 80.6 per cent are in SMEs. In the manufacturing sector, we find almost the same picture: there were 874,000 manufacturing establishments in 1986, and 99.5 per cent of them were SMEs. Of the 13.3 million manufacturing employees, 74.4 per cent were in SMEs. Corresponding figures for the manufacturing sector in 1957 were 99.6 per cent and 72.3 per cent, which suggest the stable predominance of SMEs. Throughout the postwar decades, more than 55 per cent of the value-added has been produced in SMEs, and less than 45 per cent in large firms.[5]

A second important point is on the roles of government in promoting the rapid growth of the Japanese economy. I am part of the majority of economists, identified as the 'no-miracle-occurred' school by Chalmers Johnson in his *MITI and the Japanese Miracle*,[6] those of this school 'do not literally assert that nothing happened to Japan's economy, but they imply that what did happen was not miraculous but a normal outgrowth of market forces.'[7] The following statement by Hugh Patrick represents this view:

I am of the school which interprets Japanese economic performance as due primarily to the actions and efforts of private individuals and enterprises responding to the opportunities provided in quite free markets for commodities and labor. While the government has been supportive and indeed has done much to create the environment for growth, its role has often been exaggerated.[8]

Until the 1970s, at least, the predominant view on the role of government in promoting Japanese economic growth was that it had been tremendous. The government, especially the Ministry of International Trade

---

[5] For more information on these figures, see the tables in the appendix of the *Chūshō kigyō hakusho* (White paper on small and medium-sized enterprises in Japan) (Tokyo: Ministry of Finance, annual). Here I used the 1965 and 1991 editions. These figures are originally from *Jigyōsho tōkei chōsa* (Census of establishments) and *Kōgyō tōkei-hyo* (Census of manufacturing) and therefore they are establishment-based, not company-based (e.g., a company with a head office and five factories is counted as six in establishment-based statistics, but as one in company-based statistics). The total number of large firms in the manufacturing sector in 1986 was 3,739 in the establishment base and 3,263 in the company base. Also, the number of firms with more than 1,000 employees was 679 in the establishment base and 673 in the company base. Note that these small differences between the corresponding figures do not suggest the unimportance of the choice of using establishment-based data instead of company-based data.

[6] Chalmers Johnson, *MITI and the Japanese Miracle: The Growth of Industrial Policy, 1925–75* (Stanford: Stanford University Press, 1982).

[7] Ibid., p. 9.

[8] As quoted in Johnson, *MITI and the Japanese Miracle*, p. 8. This has led many, typically political scientists such as Chalmers Johnson and David Friedman, author of *The Misunderstood Miracle* (Ithaca: Cornell University Press, 1988), to ask who then led, or what made, such a miracle. These scholars will not accept the 'invisible hands' view suggested by economists as a persuasive answer. Readers who subscribe to this view are asked to consider a similar question put forward in the 1920s by non-Americans, such as Europeans or Japanese: who led, or what made, the miracle of the rapid growth of the American economy since the nineteenth century? My answer, like that of many economists, would be 'invisible hands.'

and Industry (MITI), was often regarded as the headquarters of 'Japan Inc.,' and its policies were thought to be one of the main engines of Japan's rapid economic growth.[9] Careful and systematic study of government policies, however, began in the 1980s and scholars, especially economists, have begun to ask what the government has actually done and to try to identify policy effects. The main battlefield was 'industrial policies,' and there were few remarkable effects to be found in any industrial sector,[10] forcing revision of the traditional view.

What should be pointed out is that there were so many firms in almost all Japanese industries, especially in those that exported many of their products, and competition was so severe even in the early days of industrial policies—that is, the 1950s and 1960s—that the government tried, sometimes at the request of a majority of firms in a specific industry, to intervene in order to restrict market competition. Neither deconcentration policies, such as *zaibatsu* dissolution[11] and the Law for the Elimination of Excessive Concentration of Economic Power, nor the introduction and enforcement of the Antimonopoly Law in 1947 had much effect in reducing this so-called 'excessive competition.'[12] Thus, Japanese economic performance should be interpreted as a normal outgrowth of market forces. This study is an attempt to look closely at the contents and identify the economic effects of policies for small businesses in Japan, along the lines of recent studies of industrial policy.[13]

[9] This view has been perpetuated by non-Japanese scholars and journalists and by Japanese in all fields. One reason may be the traditionally strong influence among Japanese intellectuals of the Marxian view of political economy. Chalmers Johnson's 'developmental state' seems to be along these lines.

[10] For example, see Ryutaro Komoiya *et al.*, eds., *Industrial Policy of Japan* (San Diego: Academic Press, 1988), originally published in Japanese in 1984, and Yoshiro Miwa, *Nihon no kigyō to sangyō soshiki* (Firms and industrial organization in Japan) (Tokyo: University of Tokyo Press, 1990. Revised English version with the same title is forthcoming in 1995 from Macmillan, London). In chapter 9 of the latter, I tried to identify the effects of a government policy in the steel industry called the 'investment coordination policy.' Originally published in 1977, this paper was one of the pioneering works to identify the effects of 'industrial policy.'

[11] Although there are famous examples such as Mitsui, Mitsubishi, and Sumitomo, there are various definitions of *zaibatsu*. *Zaibatsu* dissolution policy was executed by the Post-Surrender Military Government in Japan for the Democratization of Japanese Economic Institutions, which used the term *zaibatsu* 'to include any private enterprise conducted for profit, or combination of such enterprises, which, by reason of relative size in any line or the cumulative power or its position in many lines, restricts competition or impairs the opportunity for others to engage in business independently, in any important segment of business; and any individual, family, allied group, or judicial person owning or controlling such an enterprise or combination.' The total number of *zaibatsu* on the designation list was 83. See Yoshiro Miwa, 'Economic Effects of the Antimonopoly and the Deconcentration Policies in Postwar Japan,' in Juro Teranishi *et al.*, eds., *The Japanese Experience of Economic Reforms* (London: Macmillan, 1993), p. 139.

[12] See Yoshiro Miwa, 'Economic Effects of the Antimonopoly and the Deconcentration Policies in Postwar Japan,' in Juro Teranishi *et al.*, eds., *The Japanese Experience of Economic Reforms* (London: Macmillan, 1993).

[13] As is usual and common in any kind of empirical study, I do not deny the possibility of missing some important explanatory variables. In this study, as in those mentioned above,

My third point is about the meaning of 'effectiveness' in evaluating policies. Because the main focus of this study is on evaluating the potential effectiveness of policies in promoting economic development in developing countries, I will almost totally neglect their effectiveness as 'social policy' or as policies of equity and social stability. However, readers should be aware of two underlying points in the following discussion. It is usually easy to enter markets where there are many SMEs, and the keenest competition for SMEs comes from other SMEs in the same industry. Therefore, even if the subsidies for SMEs are huge, most of them should eventually be passed on via market competition to the users and consumers of the SMEs' products. Also, as I mentioned above, although the majority of firms in Japan are SMEs and the majority of workers are employed by SMEs, it is impossible to protect and subsidize everyone.

My evaluation of policy effectiveness has two steps. The first is to consider whether the policy has had any remarkable and identifiable impact on firms in the target sector. When the answer is affirmative, the second step follows: is the social gain of the policy larger than its social cost? The second step is necessary to prove the social desirability of the policy, as it tests whether the policy improves the resource allocation of the economy and promotes economic growth. Most policies for small business do not pass the first test and we seldom need to proceed to the second step. Therefore, with the first step, I reach the conclusion that the effectiveness of the policies has been negligible. Thus, the direct meaning of 'effectiveness' in this chapter is whether a policy has had significant impact on firms in the target sector.

We should keep in mind the skepticism that scholars of US policy have shown toward regulation as a whole:

> Perhaps one-fifth of United States national income originates in industries subject to some direct regulation, and yet economists know very little about how regulation affects the market performance of an industry. The preambles of regulatory statutes hardly provide a reliable guide. Neither does the intensity of the complaints of regulated businessmen.[14]

> The innumerable regulatory actions are conclusive proof, not of effective regulation, but of the desire to regulate.[15]

some policies that appear to be important are chosen from a long list of policies for small business. I reach my conclusions by studying the economic effect of each policy. Therefore, there still and always will remain, at least logically, the possibility that what has happened in Japan will not happen in some other economies, and vice versa, because of the difference of some important missing variables, for example, of some socio-political factors.

[14] Richard E. Caves, 'Direct Regulation and Market Performance in the American Economy,' *American Economic Review*, Vol. 54, No. 3 (May 1964), p. 172.

[15] George J. Stigler and Claire Friedland, 'What Can Regulators Regulate? The Case of Electricity,' *The Journal of Law and Economics*, Vol. 5 (Oct. 1962), p. 1.

These points apply also to the effectiveness of all government policy. There is of course a wide variety of opinion on the magnitude of the contribution of government policy to economic growth in Japan, at least among economists. However, the view that its contribution had been great has lost ground and the opposite view has become predominant.

There is little to gain by asking such questions as what government leaders think their policies have been, what objectives government officials have pursued, or what their evaluation has been of the effectiveness of their policies.[16] Officials in active service in responsible positions seldom tell us how effective they think government policy has been. The most we can hope for are the opinions and 'explanations' of retired officials and members of various advisory committees. Although active officials are thought sometimes to express their opinions through retired officials or through these committees, this information is unreliable. Obviously, it is also biased, and it would be simplistic and dangerous to carry out a policy study that relied too much on such information.[17]

Instead, we should ask in what sense and to what degree each policy has been effective. To answer this question, we need to clarify the standard by which we evaluate the effectiveness of each policy and estimate the cost of the policy.[18] With this information, we can then try to identify the effect of the actual policy. Again, it should be obvious that we cannot do this simply by calculating the vast amount of loans from government-affiliated financial institutions.[19]

The Image and Reality of Small Business Policies

Government policies for small business began in prewar Japan as social policies, not as economic policies. The government imposed them, in

[16] Answering these questions is not an easy task. Under the present system in Japan, precise checks and evaluations, even *ex post*, of whether each policy has attained its prescribed objectives is rarely carried out officially, except to ask whether it has been within its authorized limits, especially its budget. Detailed information on what is done and how the policy is carried out is seldom disclosed, which makes outside assessments almost impossible.

[17] See Miwa, *Nihon no kigyō to sangyō soshiki*, Chap. 11. To counter Patrick's statement quoted above in note 3, Johnson offers a view expressed by Sahashi Shigeru, former vice minister of MITI, to assert that 'many Japanese would certainly dispute Patrick's conclusion that the government provided nothing more than the environment for economic growth.' Johnson, *MITI and the Japanese Miracle*, p. 9.

[18] There is a widely held view, especially among political scientists and Japanese government officials, that since the Meiji period (1868–1912), policies in Japan have been planned and organized for rapid economic growth and have had great success. Most Japanese economists would find it impossible to agree with this view. See note 10.

[19] Ideally, identification of the policy effects can be accomplished by finding the deviations between the actual state of affairs and the hypothetical state without policy action. The difficulty lies in how to model such a state. In my view, many studies do not recognize the necessity and importance of this identifying task. The same is true for studies of postwar deconcentration policies. See Miwa, 'Economic Effects of the Antimonopoly and the Deconcentration Policies.'

other words, for reasons of 'equity' rather than 'efficiency.' At least until the beginning of the 1970s, postwar policies strongly reflected this character. The policies for small business during this period were designed to solve the 'medium and small enterprises problem.'[20]

Several important events in small business policy occurred in the early postwar period. For example, the Small and Medium-sized Enterprise Agency (SMEA) was created in 1948 as an extra-ministerial bureau of MITI, the People's Finance Corporation was founded in 1949, and the Small Business Finance Corporation was founded in 1953. Together with the Central Cooperative Bank for Commerce and Industry founded in 1936, the latter two corporations became the principal means by which the government channeled loans to small firms. However, it was not until the late 1950s that policies for small business drew public attention.

The government's *Economic White Paper* in 1956 is famous for declaring 'we are no longer in the postwar period,' and the next *White Paper* asserted the existence and emphasized the seriousness of the 'dual structure'[21] of the Japanese economy. This argument gained immediate acceptance and 'dual structure' became one of the most popular phrases of the time. This view apparently struck a responsive chord in the public, and these came to be key words in studying the Japanese economy.

In 1963, 15 years after the establishment of SMEA, the Small and Medium-sized Enterprise Basic Law was enacted with broad public support and enthusiastic political backing. It ordered the government to conduct fact-finding surveys on small and medium-sized enterprises and to submit to the Diet an annual report (the so-called *White Paper on Small and Medium-sized Enterprises in Japan,* first published for fiscal year 1963) on trends among SMEs and measures taken to assist them. From this date, policies for SMEs began to be carried out systematically.[22]

Ironically, with rapid economic growth in the 1960s, support for the dual structure view weakened rapidly. By 1970, the *White Paper on SMEs* had a subtitle: 'The Transformation of the Dual Structure and the Increasing Variety of SME Problems.' Either the situation surrounding SMEs or the public's image of SMEs had changed. In previous work, I have investigated the causes of these changes, examined the relationship between

[20] This term is closely related to 'dual structure,' which is discussed in the text below, and suggests that large firms in the modernized industrial sector subordinate, control, and exploit SMEs in the traditional sector. This view implicitly assumes that large firms have and can exercise power to exploit SMEs, whose freedom of choice is tightly restricted and likened to a 'hold-up' situation. Many Japanese have recognized this situation as a 'social problem' to be solved by government intervention. For a critical review of the debates and policies on small and medium-sized firms, see chapters 2 and 3 of Miwa, *Nihon no kigyō to sangyō soshiki.* The English translation of chapter 3 appears in *Japanese Economic Studies,* Vol. 20, No. 2 (Winter 1991–2).

[21] The words 'dual structure' suggest that there are two distinctly separate sectors in the economy and that one sector consists of small, traditional enterprises with low productivity and low wage, and the other of large enterprises with modern technology and high productivity and high wages.

[22] The standard definition of SMEs in Japan derives from Article 2 of this Law.

the 'image' and 'reality' of SMEs, and asked whether the 'dual structure' ever really existed.[23] In thus considering whether phenomena such as 'structural changes' that caused the dissolution of the 'dual structure' actually took place, I concluded that a wide gap has existed between the image and reality of SMEs and that the image of SMEs has changed more radically than the reality. My analysis was directed at the image that large corporations exploit SMEs either directly or indirectly, or use them as a cushion against market fluctuations. This image reaffirms the image of the subcontracting and subsidiary system that has also been criticized as embodying a 'dual structure.' Roughly classified, four points emerge.[24]

1. The Japanese economy grew rapidly even before the 'dual structure' was 'dissolved.' Within this environment, both SMEs (subcontractors) and large (parent) firms grew steadily. This implies that large firms provided a stable demand for the products of rapidly growing SMEs. Such a fact is not consistent with the exploitation of SMEs.
2. As shown in Table 14.1 and Figure 14.1, the profit rate for SMEs has been much higher than that for larger firms. This too is not consistent with the argument that SMEs were exploited by large firms.
3. Consistent increases have been observed in the number of SMEs. As shown in Table 14.2, between 1951 and 1984, before and after the time of the 'structural changes,' the number of establishments of every size increased constantly. This too is inconsistent with the argument that SMEs were exploited, as rational entrepreneurs would not enter markets in which they would be exploited.
4. Although it is widely argued that a 'loan-concentrating mechanism' in the financial sector targeted loans to large firms rather than SMEs—perpetuating the notion of 'dual structure'—such a mechanism in fact never existed.[25]

From these four points (or even just one or two), three propositions follow: the assertion that a large majority of SMEs were 'exploited' between the late 1950s and the early 1960s is inconsistent with reality; the assertion that they have been exploited in more recent years is likewise inconsistent with reality; and 'structural change,' in the sense of a drastic reduction in the proportion of SMEs being 'exploited,' never occurred.

[23] This question was said to have been resolved, for example, by Tadao Kiyonari, 'Nijū kōzōron no saiginmi' (A reevaluation of the dual structure thesis), *Shōkō kin'yū*, Nov. 1973.

[24] See Miwa, *Nihon no kigyō to sangyō soshiki*, chapters 2 and 4 for details.

[25] On this point, Calder on page 318 of *Crisis and Compensation* refers to a statement made by Hugh T. Patrick in 'Cyclical Instability and Fiscal-Monetary Policy in Postwar Japan,' in William W. Lockwood, ed., *The State and Economic Enterprise in Japan* (Princeton: Princeton University Press, 1965): 'As Hugh Patrick points out, credit restraint was the primary tool employed by the financial authorities in dealing with balance of payments deficits and inflationary pressures during the high-growth period; this restraint fell disproportionately on small firms lacking close ties with the commercial banks.' See also Miwa, *Nihon no kigyō to sangyō soshiki*.

Table 14.1 Rate of Profit on Equity (Paid-in Capital) of Corporate Enterprises in Japan (Before Tax, All Industries)

Firm Size by Equity (¥million)	Profit Rate (5-year running average)						Number of Years Below Average Profit Rate		
	1953–59	1960–64	1965–69	1970–74	1975–79	1980–84	1960–84	1960–74	1975–84
2–5	22.4	32.4	30.7	34.6	22.2	16.1	7	0	7
5–10	20.9	34.1	31.4	35.4	23.0	17.8	6	0	6
10–50	21.2	28.7	31.2	35.5	24.4	20.9	1	0	1
50–100	18.7	25.3	26.7	30.4	23.1	24.4	2	0	2
100–1,000	}13.1	20.5	23.3	25.6	22.0	22.3	12	10	2
1,000+		16.2	19.8	21.3	17.8	19.5	23	15	8

Note: Numbers for 1953–9 are adopted from Ryutaro Komiya, 'Nihon ni okeru dokusen to kigyō rijun' (Monopoly and corporate profit in Japan), in Tsunejiro Nakamura et al., eds., *Kigyō keizai bunseki* (Tokyo: Iwanami Shoten, 1962), Supplemental Table A.
Source: Ministry of Finance, *Hojin kigyō tōkei nenpō* (Financial statement of incorporated business) (Tokyo: Ministry of Finance, annual). Adopted from Miwa, *Nihon no kigyō to sangyō soshiki*, Table 1.1, p. 13.

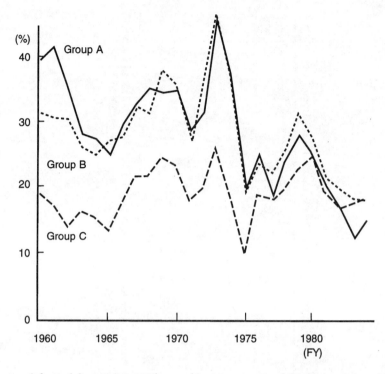

Source: Adopted from Miwa, *Nihon no kigyō to sangyō soshiki*, Figure 1.1, p. 13

Fig. 14.1. Rate of Profit on Equity (Paid-in Capital of Corporate Enterprises in Japan) (Before Tax, All Industries; in per cent)

Group A: Enterprises with ¥5–10 million in capital
Group B: Enterprises with ¥10–50 million in capital
Group C: Enterprises with more than ¥1 billion in capital.

In short, the problem that SME policies were ostensibly designed to address did not exist. If the elimination of the 'dual structure' is the standard for measuring the effectiveness of SME policies, those policies could not have been 'effective.' Let us consider, therefore, whether SME policies might still have helped promote the economic welfare of SMEs.

Overview of Policies for SMEs

Although many studies of SME policies address 'policy ideals,' 'policy targets,' and 'policy measures,' few consider 'policy effects.' Among those who do, Hajime Takaki, former chairman of the Central Cooperative Bank for Commerce and Industry, observed soon after the depression of the early 1970s:

There are so many different policy measures for SMEs that most of us would be amazed to discover how tiny the scale of each policy is. Policy efforts have been

Table 14.2 Number of Establishments by Employee Size (Private Manufacturing) (in 100s)

	1–9[a]	10–29	30–99	100–199	200–499	500+	Total[a]
1951	3,155	569	164	26	16	8	3,938
1954	3,357	698	193	30	18	9	4,304
1957	3,430	866	266	41	24	11	4,637
1960	3,456	974	335	58	31	15	4,871
1963	4,155	960	391	71	38	18	5,633
1966	4,334	1,072	406	77	40	19	5,948
1969	4,751	1,148	418	84	46	23	6,469
1972	5,229	1,200	441	88	47	22	7,026
1975	5,607	1,190	420	81	43	21	7,360
1978	5,698	1,203	405	79	40	18	7,443
1981	2,518	1,293	412	82	42	19	4,365
1984	2,432	1,293	416	88	44	19	4,290

[a] Data for 1981 and 1984 exclude establishments with 1–3 employees.

Source: Ministry of International Trade and Industry, *Kogyō tōkei hyō* (Census of manufacturing (Tokyo: MITI, annual). Adopted from Miwa, *Nihon no kigyō to sangyō soshiki*, Table 3.1, p. 56.

wide but thin. It is as though the government waters large flower pots with small sprinkling cans . . . . In the present severe depression, there is a strong demand for such policies for SMEs in order to encourage their owners and managers . . . . Each policy is well designed and sensitive; however, the scale of government's policies is too small to have any effect.[26]

A more standard view, however, would be similar to that expressed by Takashi Yokokura.[27] First, until the 1950s, policies for SMEs were but one facet of social policy and consisted of financial and cartel policies. In the 1960s, policies to assist the modernization of SME facilities were but one facet of industrial policy. In the 1970s and 1980s, modernization policies emphasized human resources (people), technology (information), and industrial adjustment policies such as assistance for firms to change their line of business. Second, policies for SMEs tended to be indiscriminate in focus and in the policy instruments they used. This was in part because of the great variety of disadvantages faced by SMEs, but was also due to the operation of political-economic mechanisms. Nonetheless, the indiscriminate use of policies for SMEs, such as in the designation of industries under the Modernization Promotion Law of 1963,[28] inevitably weakened

[26] *Nihon keizai shimbun* (Japan Economic Journal), Jan. 12, 1975, cited in Miwa, *Nihon no kigyō to sangyō soshiki*, p. 39.
[27] Takashi Yokokura, 'Small and Medium Enterprises,' in Komiya *et al.*, eds., *Industrial Policy of Japan*.
[28] This law was enacted as the embodiment of the Small and Medium-sized Enterprise Basic Law of 1963 and in order to modernize SMEs in each industry. The number of

their collective impact (effectiveness). And third, policies for SMEs relied primarily on the use of financing, operating through the market mechanism, rather than competition-restricting measures and direct subsidies. Despite the indiscriminate nature of policy, this eliminated the use of policies for SMEs as protective policy. This contrasts sharply with agricultural policies, which depended on the use of import restrictions and direct subsidies.[29]

Financing Policies for SMEs

There is wide agreement that the most important policy measures for SMEs were financial.[30] Therefore, special attention should be paid to the role of financing policies and the magnitude of their effects. The central players in carrying out government policies for SME finance are three government-affiliated financial institutions: the People's Finance Corporation (PFC), the Small Business Finance Corporation (SBFC), and the Central Cooperative Bank for Commerce and Industry (CCBCI). All were established by the government to furnish SMEs with funds for business operations (sometimes expressed as 'quantitatively to complement loans available from private banks') and to promote specific policies. Here I will concentrate on the SBFC because it is the newest and has the most clearly specified policy-oriented character.[31]

The government holds 100 per cent of SBFC stock, and all SBFC funds for loans come from the Fiscal Investment and Loan Program.[32] Until the mid-1980s more than 80 per cent of SBFC loans were provided by its

industries designated in the five years ending in fiscal year 1967 was 137. By 1975 the number had increased to 232. For a brief explanation, see Miwa, *Nihon no kigyō to sangyō soshiki*, p. 45, note 34.

[29] Yokokura has commented that:

If . . . one compares the amount and content of the budget for SME policies with that of agriculture and fisheries, the other sector that along with SMEs has been labeled 'premodern,' then the following differential can be observed. Subsidies for agriculture, forestry, and fisheries in the 1980 General Budget came to 1.9 trillion yen (including funds for land improvement and other activities to improve the infrastructure), while 1980 FILP (Fiscal Investment and Loan Program) investments came to 890 billion yen. In contrast, 1980 general budget subsidies for SME policies came to 61 billion yen, while 1980 FILP investments came to 3.4 trillion yen. In contrast to the huge subsidies expended on agriculture, those for SMEs are small, and the dependence is on FILP investments.

Yokokura, 'Small and Medium Enterprises,' p. 524.

[30] See for example, Yokokura, 'Small and Medium Enterprises,' and Calder, *Crisis and Compensation*, p. 318.

[31] There is no basic difference in the roles and character of the PFC and SBFC, except for the identity of their main customers. The PFC specializes in loans to smaller firms than does SBFC, but both provide only long-term loans. The CCBCI is not very different from a typical private bank and functions like a bank. The government, however, provides 70 per cent of its capital (¥200 billion) and allows it to issue financial bonds in the market to raise loan funds.

[32] See the essay by Noguchi in this volume for more information on the Fiscal Investment and Loan Program.

general loan system, with the remainder from a special loan system. Therefore, consideration here centers mainly on this general loan system.[33] The SBFC provides its loans directly through its approximately 60 offices and indirectly through private financial institutions appointed as its agents, which number 846 (15,131 branches). In fiscal year 1989, 75.5 per cent of SBFC loans were made directly.

The SBFC's loan rate is its designated 'base rate,' which is equal to the 'long-term prime rate' and was set at 5.5 per cent at the end of 1992. As SMEs are not always able to borrow at this rate in the regular financial market, especially when the market is tight, SBFC loans necessarily include a subsidy to SMEs. That subsidy is of course proportional to the amount of loan. However, this 'subsidy' is not large, as the discrepancy between the base rate and the market rate seldom exceeds 0.5–1.0 per cent. The SBFC and its agents check the loan applications and collateral presented by their borrowers so rigorously that it is sometimes said their requirements are more severe than those of private institutions. If a default occurs on an indirect loan, the agent bears 80 per cent of the loss. In sum, an SBFC general loan includes a 'subsidy,' although the amount is small, and loan standards are strict.

SBFC offices and their agents are open to any SME and borrowers may negotiate with them directly. They need not, in other words, acquire recommendations from third parties such as local governments, Boards of Commerce and Industry, Chambers of Commerce and Industry, or other financial institutions. At the end of the 1989 fiscal year, loans made by the SBFC and its agents to SMEs had an average value of ¥32.18 million and an average term of 6 years and 11 months. Borrowers had, on average, ¥23.49 million in paid-in capital and 48 employees.

Let us proceed to an evaluation of the effectiveness of these financing policies for SMEs and consider both the direct impact of the policies and their final consequences. The effectiveness of the financing policies for SMEs depends on the state of the capital markets and the relation between SMEs and larger firms.[34] If capital markets are competitive, below-market loans are equivalent to a direct subsidy equal to: (the difference between

---

[33] Under the special loan system, the SBFC and PFC provide special low-interest loans to be used for certain purposes, such as improving the industrial structure, preventing pollution, saving energy, etc. But readers should keep in mind that these loans constituted less than 20 per cent of all loans by these institutions and that the 'special low interest rate' is not as 'low' as might be expected, except for unusual cases. The share of special loans rose in the mid-1980s, in connection with loans to SMEs to deal with the depression caused by the yen appreciation after the 1985 Plaza Accord, and to smooth the introduction of the consumption tax. As of December 1992, there were four types of special low interest rates. The highest is 0.05 per cent lower than the base loan rate, the second highest is 0.1 per cent lower, and the third highest is 0.45 per cent lower. The lowest rate applies only in very rare cases, such as special loans to the textile industry at 4.85 per cent and to small retailers at 4.6 per cent.

[34] Actually, in some cases, the direct competitors of SMEs targeted by policies are SMEs in other countries, not 'large firms' in Japan.

the loan rate and the market rate) × (the amount of the loans). If capital
markets are not competitive and SMEs cannot obtain loans at or slightly
above the market rate (capital markets are divided into markets for large
firms and SMEs and there is a shortage of capital in the latter), the policies
may have additional policy impact.

The government-affiliated financial institutions were established in order to complement financing available from private banks. The assumption was that SMEs faced strong quantitative constraints in financing
which were thought to reflect the targeting of loans to large firms, which,
as noted above, never occurred. As a result, below-market loans could not
have had any impact beyond the direct value of the subsidy.[35]

In order to assess the policy impact of the subsidy, we should note the
ratio of policy loans to total loans for SMEs. Yokokura has shown that
during 1960–80 the three government-affiliated financial institutions provided only 10 per cent of the total amount of funds SMEs borrowed from
all financial institutions.[36] Therefore, when policy loans are provided at 1
per cent below the market rate, the average rate of funds for SMEs can be
lowered only 0.1 per cent, which cannot be considered very significant.[37]

Menu of Policies for SMEs in Japan

Following the above finding of a negligible effect of those financing policies which are considered the most important policy measures for SMEs,
let me here catalogue, for readers' convenience, the 'basic measures' of
policies for SMEs in Japan.[38]

[35] See Miwa, *Nihon no kigyō to sangyō soshiki*, chapters 2 and 5, for details.
[36] See Table II of Yokokura, 'Small and Medium Enterprises,' p. 523. Calculated on the
basis of loan balances, the figures were 8.7 per cent in 1960, 8.8 per cent in 1965, 9.3 per cent
in 1970, 12.8 per cent in 1975, and 12.6 per cent in 1980. Readers who believe there were
significant quantitative constraints on loans available for SMEs should recognize that, even
if so, this 10 per cent implies that those policies expanded the funds for SMEs by only 10 per
cent. Much of the gain, moreover, would have been passed through to other sectors via the
capital market.
[37] Even lending 2 or 3 per cent below market rate could lower the average rates only 0.2
or 0.3 per cent, which cannot be considered effective, either. There is a widely held view that
those lending policies have strong 'signaling effects' or 'cowbell effects' (that is, policy
lending has an effect of attracting private bank loans to its borrowing firms) which refutes
my evaluation. It is often asserted—and in most cases orally—that even if the ratio of the
actual loans had been less than 10 per cent, their effects have been far larger than this figure
suggests. However, I cannot agree with this view. First, as I explained above, most of the
policy loans are provided under the general loan system and the doors are open to any SME.
Therefore, there is no room for intensive screening to provide 'signals.' Second, even if
governments select firms with their own standards, why and how can they promote economic growth? An underlying, seemingly tautological, assumption or belief is that in Japan,
government always has the ability to beat the market, which is, at least, still open to careful
investigation.
[38] According to a survey by the Organization for Economic Cooperation and Development, Japan has the most extensive range of policy tools for assisting small business in the
industrialized world. Japan uses all major means of support for small business surveyed by

Finance: financial assistance by three government-affiliated institutions—the Small Business Finance Corporation, the People's Finance Corporation, and the Central Cooperative Bank of Commerce and Industry—and loans from the Japan Small Business Corporation for the promotion of joint business activities by cooperatives.

Credit supplements (financial reinforcement by means of credit supplement): to receive a loan from a financial institution, a small firm must have its loan guaranteed by a credit guarantee association (CGA); CGAs in turn apply to the Small Business Credit Corporation to insure the guarantee.

Small business taxation: reduction of the corporate income tax.

Cooperatives: aid for the joint business activities (such as joint production, joint processing, joint sales, etc.) of about 50,000 cooperatives.

Consulting and finance: provision of management consulting and guidance by specialized personnel in the prefectural government.

Personnel training (for human resource development): a variety of training programs at government institutions for small business and basic training courses at the prefectural government level.

Technological development: technical training courses at institutions for small business and technical assistance by prefectural and other public research institutions.

Promotion of small enterprises: personnel at the Board of Commerce and Industry and at the Chamber of Commerce and Industry; special loans for management improvement; special loans for equipment modernization.[39]

Although the scope of Japanese policies for SMEs is extensive, they have not effectively supported SMEs. Neither, therefore, have they stimulated overall economic growth. Any lessons to be learned from the Japanese experience are therefore negative: it is of no use to imitate Japanese policies for SMEs. To learn why so many SMEs now exist in Japan, we should search for causes and mechanisms other than government policies.

To conclude this section on SME policy, I wish to note two further points. First, the business start-up rate among SMEs (the ratio of SMEs new in a given year to all SMEs), over 7 per cent around 1970, has steadily

the OECD, a record equaled by no other nation. Cited by Calder, *Crisis and Compensation*, pp. 316–17.

[39] These are the 'basic measures' for SMEs found in SMEA, *Chūshō kigyō shisaku no aramashi* (Outline of policies for SMEs) (Tokyo: SMEA, 1992). Readers should keep in mind the comments made and sources cited in my introduction and should note that, although SMEA was established to promote SMEs, it is not the only government institution to do so. The Ministries of Labor and Construction, the Fair Trade Commission of Japan, MITI, and local governments all have policies to aid SMEs.

declined. As the business closing rate (the ratio of SMEs closed in a year to all SMEs) has stabilized at around 4 per cent, the net rate of business increase has been falling and has been below 1 per cent since 1981.[40] Because SMEs are regarded as a major factor behind Japan's rapid economic growth, the declining business start-up rate gathers wide attention. The most important point here is that this has happened even under present Japanese policies for SMEs.

Second, some observers, especially non-Japanese, have been impressed by the existence of SMEA and the wide variety of its policy measures.[41] However, this ignores the basic nature of the Japanese administration system. In Japan, almost every industry has a counterpart in government—such as the steel industry section of MITI and the Securities Bureau in MOF—which devotes all its efforts to protecting, encouraging, and supporting the firms in that industry. Therefore, almost all industries are systematically and continuously protected and supported by the government. The case of SMEs is no exception. The problem comes from the simple fact that nobody can protect and subsidize everybody.[42]

Implementation of Policies for SMEs and the Role of Local Government

The main objective of this section is to provide detailed information on the actual process of policy implementation and the role of local government. As I address several types of policies other than financing in the following sections, I shall provide information on those policies as well.

Compared with financing policies, it is more difficult to evaluate the effectiveness of other policies, such as technical assistance by prefectural and other public research institutions, management guidance by specialized personnel, provision of management consulting, and guidance by specialized personnel. The evaluations below are drawn only from what I have heard on various occasions and scattered materials. Necessarily, therefore, they are tentative. They do suggest that the overall effectiveness of these SME policies is no different than the effectiveness of the financing policies. Nevertheless, these policies are so differentiated that their effectiveness should be regarded as totally dependent on the circumstances surrounding them. Therefore, if a specific policy were judged to be effec-

[40] See SMEA, 1994 *Chūgyō kigyō hakusho*, p. 95, for example.

[41] Calder, for example, observed that: 'While the Reagan administration in the mid-1980s was attempting to disband the U.S. Small Business Administration and end its meager and declining volume of subsidized loans, the small business-oriented People's Finance Corporation in Japan disbursed nearly the volume of subsidized loans annually of the vaunted Japan Export-Import Bank.' *Crisis and Compensation*, pp. 312–13.

[42] Readers should note that, at least among economists, it is now the standard view that market competition is very keen in Japan and this keen competition has been one of the major causes of Japan's economic growth. This also applies to the field of SMEs.

tive, additional information would be necessary before we could draw useful lessons for developing countries from the Japanese experience. One of the pieces of information most necessary is on the actual process of policy implementation and in this section, I shall place greater emphasis on providing information than on evaluating the effectiveness of each policy.

Regional Economic Policies

Table 14.3 shows the policies the central government implements for the stimulation of regional economies. Again, these policies can be seen to be indiscriminate in their focus and to target regions almost evenly. The table shows those prefectures[43] receiving special treatment on fiscal measures for regional development. It also indicates (1) that in total the government tries to stimulate industries in underdeveloped regions and aims at the redistribution of income, and (2) that the government is nonetheless indiscriminate in its focus on policy targets, especially among areas at the same development level. I will not deal with 'regional policies' here, except to note that the central government has no strong powers. It generally cannot use its powers to 'control' local governments. This is particularly true where 'regional policies,' especially policies for commerce and industry, are concerned.[44]

Most of the policies of the central government are implemented through or with the assistance of local governments.[45] In most cases, however, the central government decides the general scheme of each policy. Those local governments that consider the scheme useful then develop more detailed plans and compete to have the central government adopt their specific plan.[46] The policy then implemented by the central government is a collection of policies from the local governments. This division of labor reflects the recognition that the effectiveness of such policies depends on the circumstances surrounding them, and that these circumstances greatly differ in each area. Each local government also has its own policies for SMEs.[47] As a result, there are a wide variety of objectives, the weights of which are also different, and forms among the actual policies of local governments.[48]

[43] Japan's 47 prefectures are the basic units for regional self-governance. Each prefecture has its own legislature and government apparatus.

[44] I do not intend to suggest that other types of policies discussed in other chapters are also indiscriminate or neutral.

[45] In this respect, the financing policies focused on in the first section are rather exceptional.

[46] The selection of proposals often appears to be very politicized, which may be the reason for the indeterminacy of the focus of those policies.

[47] The roles and policies of local governments have not been studied well, not even by Japanese economists and political scientists, and there is a shortage of information on them.

[48] Comparison of policies of local governments is provided in Kitayama's chapter in this volume.

Table 14.3 Summary of Special Fiscal Treatment for Regional Development by Prefecture

Prefecture	I[a]			II					III								
	1	2	3	1	2	3	4	5	1	2	3	4	5	6	7	8	9
Hokkaido				•		•	•	•	•	•	•	•	•	•	•	•	•
Aomori				•		•	•	•		•	•	•	•	•		•	•
Iwate						•	•	•		•	•	•	•	•			
Miyagi				•		•	•	•	•		•	•	•	•			
Akita				•		•	•	•		•	•	•	•	•			•
Yamagata						•	•	•	•		•	•	•	•			
Fukushima				•		•	•	•		•	•	•	•				
Ibaraki	•				•			•	•			•	•		•		
Tochigi	•					•	•	•				•	•	•	•		
Gunma	•					•		•				•	•	•	•		
Saitama	•							•					•	•	•		
Chiba	•					•							•	•		•	•
Tokyo	•									•				•	•		
Kanagawa	•																
Niigata				•		•	•	•		•		•	•	•	•		
Toyama		•	•			•	•	•				•	•	•	•		•
Ishikawa		•				•		•		•		•	•	•	•		•
Fukui	•	•				•		•				•	•	•	•		
Yamanashi	•					•	•	•				•	•	•	•		
Nagano		•	•			•	•	•				•	•	•	•		
Gifu		•				•		•				•	•	•	•		
Shizuoka		•			•		•	•	•	•		•	•	•			•
Aichi		•			•			•		•		•	•	•			
Mie	•	•				•		•		•		•	•		•		
Shiga	•	•				•		•				•	•		•		
Kyoto	•					•						•		•		•	•
Osaka	•					•											
Hyogo	•				•	•	•	•	•		•	•	•			•	
Nara	•					•							•	•	•	•	•
Wakayama	•					•				•		•	•	•	•	•	•
Tottori		•			•		•	•	•		•	•	•	•	•	•	
Shimane		•			•		•	•	•		•	•	•	•	•	•	•
Okayama		•	•	•	•	•	•	•		•	•	•		•			
Hiroshima		•	•	•	•	•	•	•		•	•	•		•		•	•
Yamaguchi		•	•	•	•	•	•	•		•		•	•	•	•		•

Outline of A Prefecture

To better understand the implementation and effect of policies, let us shift our attention to a specific prefecture, to be referred to as A Prefecture. Its population is 5.4 million, 4.4 per cent of the total Japanese population. Several indicators show that its economic power is 4–5 per cent that of the whole country. The prefecture is located in the Kinki district, which is

Table 14.3 *Continued*

Prefecture	I[a]			II					III								
	1	2	3	1	2	3	4	5	1	2	3	4	5	6	7	8	9
Tokushima		•		•			•		•				•	•	•	•	
Kagawa				•	•		•		•				•	•	•	•	
Ehime		•		•	•		•	•	•				•	•	•	•	•
Kochi				•			•	•	•				•	•	•	•	•
Fukuoka		•		•	•	•	•	•	•			•	•	•		•	
Saga				•	•	•				•			•	•	•	•	•
Nagasaki			•	•		•			•	•		•	•	•	•		
Kumamoto		•		•	•	•	•	•	•	•			•	•	•	•	•
Oita		•		•	•	•	•	•	•				•	•	•	•	•
Miyazaki		•		•	•	•	•		•	•			•	•	•	•	•
Kagoshima				•	•	•	•		•	•			•	•	•	•	•
Okinawa							•										
TOTAL	8	8	9	17	7	37	26	43	14	26	7	24	41	44	27	44	22

[a] The policies in this table are classified as follows:
- I. Policies for Improvement of the Functions of Large Cities
  1. Metropolitan district
  2. Kinki district
  3. Chubu district
- II. Policies to Promote Industry
  1. New Industrial Cities
  2. Specified Areas for Industrial Reorganization
  3. Developing Areas
  4. Technopolises
  5. Areas that Encourage Introduction of New Industry
- III. Policies to Promote Special Areas
  1. Special Soil Areas
  2. Isolated Islands
  3. Coal-mining Areas
  4. Areas of Heavy Snowfall
  5. Mountain Areas
  6. Underpopulated Areas
  7. Newly Developing Areas
  8. Isolated Areas
  9. Peninsula Areas

Source: Adapted from *Chiiki keizai tokei yoran* (Outline of statistics for regional economies (Tokyo: The Japan Regional Development Corporation, 1991), pp. 16–17.

located in the central western part of Japan and is made up of seven prefectures, and has both densely populated, highly industrialized urban areas and sparsely populated rural areas that have agricultural bases or are located in mountainous regions. The total number of establishments (excluding those in agriculture and fisheries) was 274,000 in 1986 and 99.1 per cent were SMEs. Of these establishments, 47.9 per cent were in wholesaling and retailing, 23.9 per cent in the service sector, and 12.6 per cent in manufacturing. Of total employees, 77.75 per cent are in SMEs. The manufacturing sector employed 27.5 per cent of all employees, and 69.6 per cent of those were in SMEs.[49]

The Bureau of Commerce and Industry (BCI) within the prefectural government is in charge of policies for SMEs. It has 360, or 4.2 per cent, of the approximately 8,500 prefectural employees.[50] BCI is divided into seven divisions (there were five in 1967),[51] and the Industry Policy Division, the New Industry Location Division, the Finance Division, and the Industry Division are directly involved in policies for SMEs. In addition, the General Coordination Division has indirect involvement in SME policy. Of the 360 BCI employees, 166 are in the central office, and 75 of those are in one of the SME-related divisions. In addition to the divisions in the central office, two subordinate institutions deal with policies for SMEs. The Institute for General Guidance for SMEs, subordinate to the General Coordination Division, employs 19, and the A Prefecture Institute for Industrial Research, subordinate to the Industry Division, employs 118.[52]

As shown below, most of the local government policies for SMEs are carried out in line with and as part of those of the central government. The wide array of policies means there is strong demand from both sides for coordination and cooperation. Accordingly, there is an established route for the communication between local governments and the central government. In the case of the policies for commerce and industry, Japan is divided into eight districts plus Okinawa, and in each MITI has its own Bureau of International Trade and Industry. These bureaus are positioned between the central and local governments and work as communication nodes.[53]

Financing Policy

Three groups of policy measures were at the core of 1992 BCI policies: measures for upgrading industrial structure, measures for stimulating regional economies, and measures for promoting successful SMEs. The budgets for each group reveal the predominance of the latter, which

---

[49] From *Jigyōsho tōkei chōsa*, 1986.

[50] In 1967, the corresponding numbers were 404, 8,000, and 5.0 per cent.

[51] I will refer to the corresponding numbers for 1967 hereafter to show the stability of systems for local government policies.

[52] There has been no major change in either the total scale or weight of each division during the last 25 years. A Prefecture appears to be a relatively prosperous and rich prefecture, whose government is large and whose policies are well organized.

[53] A Prefecture falls under the Kinki bureau, located in Osaka. Some may notice the existence of MITI officials in the local governments and emphasize their importance. At present, 30 MITI officials work in 29 local governments as their members, that is, no MITI officials in 18 prefectures, 1 in 28, and 2 officials in only 1 prefecture. Usually, they work there for 2–3 years.

included two significant items: ¥57.6 billion for financial assistance and ¥14.4 billion for assisting the growth of small enterprises.

Among the measures to upgrade industrial structure, the largest budget item was ¥7 billion for the 'promotion of creative scientific technology.' Of this amount, ¥3.7 billion was for developing a 'Technopolis';[54] most of this is for the construction of a Center for R&D on Frontier Technology and is not part of the policies for SMEs. Also included was ¥3.2 billion for upgrading the technological level of enterprises. The most conspicuous budget measure to stimulate regional economies is ¥4.9 billion for the 'invigoration of shopping districts.' This absorbs most of the budget for 'promoting vital retail business.' The central measure is the 'loan program for invigorating small and medium-sized retail business.' The burden of raising funds for this measure falls wholly on A Prefecture.[55] In short, the policies for SMEs are the core of local government policies for commerce and industry, and at the center of these policies are the financing policies. There is thus no significant difference between the SME policy priorities of the central and local governments.

We can observe this more clearly in the 1967 policies of A Prefecture. In the outline of BCI policies for 1967, it was declared at the outset that the most important policy was 'to promote the structural adjustment of SMEs': 'As is stated clearly in the Small and Medium-sized Enterprises Basic Law, established in 1963, the fundamental objective of the policy is, based on self-help efforts of SMEs, to improve the SME environment and to support SME efforts, and therefore, to use measures reflecting basic economic rationality.' This statement denied the traditional view that policies for SMEs were designed to rescue SMEs by eliminating the disadvantages they suffered because of their position in the 'dual structure.' Thus, already in 1967 at the local government level, at least ideally, policies for SMEs were regarded as economic policies, not social policies.[56]

The Finance Division of BCI contains four subdivisions, three (14 employees and 3 managers) of which implement policies directly related to SMEs. The Finance Subdivision (4 employees) is responsible for a wide variety of tasks such as providing information on government loan systems and assorted financial guidance. The Credit Cooperative Subdivision (7 employees) is in charge of financing through cooperatives[57] and

---

[54] 'Technopolises' were one of the regional policy schemes listed in Table 14.3 and a region of A Prefecture was designated as one of the targets. Kitayama's chapter provides more information about the Technopolis project.

[55] However, the upper limit of the amount for each policy is only ¥10 million.

[56] Of course this orientation depends on the case, and A Prefecture should be regarded as a frontrunner in the process to change the character of policies for SMEs.

[57] In Japan, it has been recognized that SMEs face various difficulties. The central government thought that it was more effective for them to form associations and carry out business operations jointly than to solve problems individually. It thus enacted the Law on the Cooperative Association of Small and Medium-sized Enterprises (1949), the Law Concerning the Organization of Small and Medium-sized Enterprise Organizations (1957), and other

tasks related to the credit guarantee system. The Equipment Modernization Subdivision (3 employees) is in charge of tasks related to loans for
modernizing equipment.

Let us consider the policies for modernizing SME equipment as an
example to illustrate the division of roles between the central and local
governments. Of these four measures, the budgetary burden for 1 and 3 is
equally divided, and that for 2 and 4 is wholly on A Prefecture:

1. Loans for modernizing equipment: ¥1.6 billion. In line with the Small
   and Medium-sized Enterprise Modernization Promotion Law.
2. Expansion of funds for loans for the promotion and modernization
   of local industries: ¥550 million.
3. Equipment-leasing system.[58] In line with the Equipment Leasing
   System established in 1966, the central and prefectural governments
   provide loans to an equipment-leasing agency (a public service corporation). The equipment-leasing company then purchases machinery and leases it to small enterprises. Total loans for leasing are ¥1.65
   billion.
4. System for leasing high technology and energy-saving equipment.
   The A Prefecture equipment-leasing agency purchases equipment
   and leases it. Total purchases for leasing are ¥700 million.

Two other financing policy measures can be found in A Prefecture's
budget for 1992. First, there is a budget to complete the Public Credit
Supplementation System by making good on losses from loans to SMEs.
The entire burden of ¥250 million is on A Prefecture. It compensates the A
Prefecture Credit Guarantee Association for its losses and financial institutions for their losses from loans for R&D in frontier technology. Second,
as a part of the policy to promote and guide credit unions, A Prefecture
provides them loans to strengthen their management bases. The entire
burden of ¥5.15 billion is on A Prefecture. This explains most of what is
done in the three principal SME subdivisions of the Finance Division.
Again, the SME financing policies of A Prefecture closely resemble the
policies of the central government.[59]

laws to establish various systems and to promote the establishment of cooperatives by
providing financial support and preferential tax treatment. Some tasks related to these laws
were delegated to local governments.

[58] Financial assistance such as 1 and 2 alone is not always sufficient for enterprises
that do not have the technical know-how and skills to select and utilize appropriate equipment. This system was established to provide assistance to small enterprises in these
cases.

[59] The following comment, however, should be added here. The earlier discussion of SBFC
focused mainly on its general loan system, which comprises more than 80 per cent. The
remaining share of less than 20 per cent, called the special loans system, sometimes requires
the assistance of local governments. The special loans system is a collection of policies for
certain purposes, with special low-interest loans. See note 33 above. Some of these loans
require a determination of whether each applicant satisfies the conditions requested, and in

Industry Division

Policies outside financing are also important. The recent rise of public interest in Japanese SMEs parallels a spreading awareness of their importance for rapid industrial development and, therefore, the spreading interest in policies for SMEs in manufacturing.

The Industry Division of BCI, with 17 employees and 6 managers, consists of two subdivisions and two offices. The Manufacturing and Mining Promotion Subdivision (4 employees) is in charge of the 'promotion of subcontracting enterprises' and 'fusion[60] of enterprises.' The Local Industry Areas Promotion Subdivision (4 employees) is for the 'promotion of local industries' and 'policies for traditional arts and crafts industries.' Its offices specialize in policies for the leather industry (3 employees) and technology promotion (7 employees). The latter office is further divided into sections for 'technology policy' (3 employees) and 'policies for technical assistance' (4 employees). The Institute of Industrial Research (118 employees), subordinate to the Industry Division, consists mainly of technically specialized personnel.

The Industry Division has a wide variety of tasks divided between nine types of policies:[61] promotion of upgrading technology, promotion of local industries and traditional arts and crafts industries, policies for the leather industry, promotion of industrial design, promotion of subcontracting SMEs, promotion of the 'fusion' of enterprises, policies for SMEs to retain their labor force, promotion of policies for upgrading management, and policies for underground resources (i.e., minerals).[62]

Let us examine more closely the policies of the Industry Division for promoting subcontracting SMEs. The budgetary burden is equally divided between the central government and A Prefecture for the seven specific policies in this category:

1. Smoothing subcontracting trade: ¥66 million.
2. Organizing meetings to promote the autonomy of subcontracting enterprises: ¥2.5 million.
3. Consultation and guidance for subcontracting SMEs: ¥9.3 million.
4. Organizing fairs to widen SME trade areas: ¥700,000.
5. Promoting an on-line computer system to broaden SME trade: ¥3.1 million.

some cases local government (mainly cities, towns, and villages, and only in rare cases prefectures) play the role, but seemingly rather automatically.

[60] 'Fusion' is a direct translation of *yūgoka*, a phrase newly created for policy slogans. Frankly, I cannot imagine what is intended by this curious and fuzzy phrase, but it is one of the policies to promote cooperative activites of SMEs.

[61] Most policy types in this list correspond closely to policies of the central government, which reflects the close relation and division of roles between the central and prefectural governments.

[62] At the top of the policies of this type is listed ¥3.7 billion for the construction of the Center for R&D on Frontier Technology mentioned above.

6. Supporting activities to develop SMEs' own distribution channels: ¥3.3 million.
7. Organizing technology fairs for subcontractors: ¥11.2 million.

This list also reveals the resemblance between local and central government SME policies. Here again the government has adopted a wide variety of policy measures but on a tiny scale. Of these policies, only the last is new, which suggests that most of such policies are repeated every year.[63]

In addition, some of the tasks of the General Coordination Division—such as promoting the establishment of SME cooperatives, promotion of guidance for small enterprises, and promotion of consulting and guidance—seem to be for SMEs, and one can find repeated similarity. For example, efforts to promote the establishment of cooperatives of SMEs include 12 policies, the budgetary burden of which is, in all cases, equally divided between the central government and A Prefecture, and none except for the twelfth policy[64] is new.

Technical Assistance, Consulting, and Guidance

Besides financing policies, the most conspicuous measures among the policies for SMEs in Japan are the various activities called consultation, diagnosis, guidance, advice, or assistance. In this subsection, I explain the scope of the 'technical assistance' granted through the A Prefecture Institute of Industrial Research, of which the Industry Division is in charge and the nature of the 'consulting' and 'guidance' services provided through the General Coordination Division.

Three technical centers (TCs), each with a special purpose, are subordinate to the Institute of Industrial Research: the TC for machinery and metals (16 employees), the TC for textiles (15 employees), and the TC for leather (13 employees). The institute has 74 employees of its own, and therefore employs 118 people in total. The origin of the institute was the establishment by the prefectural government of an Industrial Experiment Station in 1917. The newest technical center (the TC for leather) was established in 1948, just after World War II. In 1967, the allocated number of total employees was 126, and the TCs had 20, 21, and 7 employees, respectively, suggesting little change in 25 years.

These types of institutes and TCs are not peculiar to A Prefecture. Every prefecture has its own institutions, whose origins, character, and roles are quite similar. As in the case of A Prefecture, which has special interests in specific industries such as textiles and leather and has established TCs for

[63] As is true for all tasks of the Industry Division, these policies also correspond closely to those of the central government. See note 57 above.

[64] This policy supports the activities of small business cooperatives to accept jointly foreign workers as trainees.

them, each prefectural government has institutions for specific industries (usually local industries).

The total budget for the institute in 1992 was ¥1.62 billion, of which ¥1.09 billion, or 67.2 per cent, was for personnel expenses and was wholly borne by A Prefecture. The central government provided ¥20 million of the total budget of ¥290 million for 'maintenance and management' and 'experiments and research.' This occurred because the central government supports half of the budgetary burden under various 'policy expenses' such as 'expenses for the training of technical personnel' and 'expenses for meetings to study basic technology.'

According to the *1970 Chūshō kigyō shisaku no aramashi* (Outline of small business policies of the Small and Medium-sized Enterprise Agency), there were 185 public experiment stations established by prefectures[65] in Japan. Employees at these stations served as technical personnel providing consultation and guidance services to SMEs. Around 1970 the central government was eager to improve the experiment stations and the quality of their technical assistance. Thus, each year it identified specific industries that urgently needed to raise their technical levels. By providing half the funds, it supported policies to expand the scale and improve the quality of the activities for technical assistance and related experiments and research. In fiscal year 1970 the central government chose 52 experiment stations in 38 prefectures[66] and granted subsidies totaling ¥280 million.[67]

The effectiveness of the above technical assistance policies—that is, the technical assistance provided through these institutions and policies of the central government—can be evaluated in part by the ratio of the total number of technical personnel to the number of SMEs. In the case of A Prefecture, there were 188 technical personnel for 272,000 establishments (34,000 in manufacturing alone). Even if these policy measures were effective, their overall impact could not have been very great.[68]

The fourth task of the General Coordination Division, the promotion of guidance for small enterprises, is to support the activities of the Boards of Commerce and Industry, their federation, and the Chambers of

[65] To be exact, we should add *seirei shitei toshi* (cities designated by government order as cities in a special category, which have stronger autonomy than other cities). In Japan, several big cities, such as Tokyo, Osaka, and Nagoya, are designated and enjoy special privileges and responsibilities. The number of designated cities at present is 11, and at that time it was less than 10.

[66] There is not much selectivity when 38 of 47 prefectures, or 81 per cent, have such experiment stations.

[67] The central government began the subsidy in 1963, and the total amount of subsidy in 1990 was ¥620 million for 66 objectives. See MITI and SMEA, *Kigyō to josei* (Enterprises and support) (Tokyo: MITI and SMEA, 1991), pp. 471–4.

[68] As mentioned, they were originally established for specific industries and they seem to have maintained this character. On a few occasions we hear from the users of such institutions that they are quite useful, which does not contradict our overall evaluation.

Commerce and Industry. Through these groups, this division develops and improves the management and technology of small enterprises in the region through various measures, including consultation and guidance on management, financing, taxation, accounting- and labor-related problems provided by management guidance personnel stationed in the offices of these groups, and bookkeeping instruction offered by professional bookkeepers and bookkeeping instructors.

The budget of the General Coordination Division for this task lists five policies, and in each case the burden is equally divided between the central and local governments, and no policy is new:

1. Expenses for management guidance personnel: ¥2.42 billion.
2. Expenses to complete consultation and guidance: ¥840 million.
3. Expenses to strengthen the system for guidance: ¥140 million.
4. Expansion of promoting activities for local commerce and industry: ¥160 million.
5. Expenses to complete the system for guidance: ¥1 million.

Under the first policy, nearly 700 specialized personnel are employed in the offices of the Chambers of Commerce and Industry and at places of business. They include 321 management guidance personnel, 136 assistants, and 93 professional bookkeepers. In addition, a large number of specialized personnel offer consultation and guidance.

These policies of A Prefecture are part of the policies of the central government called the Management Improvement Program, and similar policies are implemented throughout Japan. The Management Improvement Program is carried out in accordance with the law Concerning the Organization, Etc. of the Commerce and Industry Association, enacted in 1960 to establish a system for guiding small enterprises.[69] The total number of specialized personnel in this program in the whole country is roughly 25 times the number in A Prefecture, that is, 17,500. More than 8,000 are management guidance personnel and more than 4,000 are assistants.[70]

To gauge the effectiveness of the policies for the promotion of guidance for small enterprises carried out in line with the Management Improvement Program, it is important to weigh several related points.

1. In 1960 the law for this program was enacted during the early stage of the rapid growth period. Therefore, the program did not help SMEs

---

[69] In the SMEA, *Chūsho kigyō shisaku no aramashi*, the program is explained as follows. 'Small-scale enterprises, which make up a large portion of the SME sector, contribute greatly to the stability of the Japanese economic structure. Many of these small enterprises, however, operate with no clear distinction between management and housekeeping. The measures universally applied to larger enterprises, therefore, are not enough to promote the healthy growth of these small concerns.' Here, 'small enterprises' stands for enterprises with fewer than 20 regular employees, or fewer than 15 regular employees in commerce and service.

[70] See SMEA, *Chūsho kigyō shisaku no aramashi* (1992), Table 7–2, p. 430, for details.

recover from the war or prepare them for rapid growth. Even if this type of policy can be effective, it takes a long time to organize the system, to prepare well trained personnel, and to be widely accepted by SMEs. By the time the effects of this policy could have appeared, people would have lost interest in the 'dual structure,' which occurred in the early 1960s.

2. There is a wide variety of views concerning the objective and character of the program. On one side is the widely held view that the program was introduced for political reasons. With this reasoning, the program can only be considered a social policy and cannot be economically rationalized.[71]

3. In order to reach an unbiased evaluation of the effectiveness of an economic policy, one should look closer at what its personnel can do for SMEs and investigate whether such a government-sponsored, centrally organized system can be efficient. At least at the first stage of the development of a market economy, I suspect that it can be effective and efficient as a basic and standardized 'education package.'[72]

4. Even if the policies in the program are effective, the program should be big enough to have effect. In the case of A Prefecture was the actual ratio of specialized personnel (700) to the number of SME establishments (200,000) big enough?[73]

5. The quality of specialized personnel and the guidance they offer should be studied closely.[74]

The ninth task of the General Coordination Division, the promotion of consulting and guidance, is to promote SMEs' self-help efforts and make their administrative management more effective. The division is to do this by carrying out research and analysis of SME management, at the request of SMEs and their cooperatives. Seven policies to accomplish this are listed here; the budgetary burden is wholly on the central government in 1, 2, and 6 and is equally divided in the others. None of the policies is new. The last four policies are carried out by the SME General Guidance Center of A Prefecture, which is subordinate to the General Coordination Division and has 19 employees.

---

[71] This view suggests that the Liberal Democratic Party strongly supported the program in order to acquire the political support of SMEs. It was chosen because just then the opposition, especially the Communist Party, was gathering the support of SMEs by providing guidance and advice services. See, for example, Izumi Yoshitani, 'Gyōsha undō to seiji no sasshin' (Movements of enterprises and their impact on politics), in Seiji Keizai Kenkyū-jo, ed., *Tenkanki no chūshō kigyō mondai* (Tokyo: Shin-Hyoron, 1975); Calder, *Crisis and Compensation*; and, for brevity, see Miwa, *Nihon no kigyō to sangyō soshiki*, p. 40, note 27.

[72] In Japan in and after the 1960s, this type of 'education' could not be as effective and I am thus skeptical about its effectiveness. Some of the supporters of the above extreme view suggest that their central role is to advise SMEs on how to save in taxes.

[73] The number of establishments with fewer than four employees was 188,000, 68.7 per cent of the total, in 1986.

[74] Many people, both inside and outside of the government, have commented that their quality, on average at least, could not be very high as the salary was too low to attract 'professionals.'

1. General consulting service: ¥24.8 million.
2. Consultation on how to modernize operations: ¥15 million.
3. Expenses to train small business consultants: ¥3.7 million.
4. Expenses for management counseling services: ¥0.3 million.
5. Expenses to support SME efforts to retain labor force: ¥0.7 million.
6. Expenses for traveling general consulting services: ¥8.4 million.
7. Expenses for linking with other consulting groups: ¥0.6 million.

These policies of A Prefecture are part of the central government's Consulting and Guidance Program. Similar policies, including the SME General Guidance Center, are carried out everywhere in Japan. *Chūsho kigyō shisaku no aramashi 1992* lists 30 consulting services and 11,391 registered small-enterprise consultants as of April 1, 1991. However, readers should note that the budget for these policies is quite small and in most cases the prefectural government must bear half their cost.[75]

Concluding Remarks

Viewed as 'economic' policies, especially policies for stimulating economic growth, Japanese policies for small and medium-sized enterprises have not been effective. This applies both to policies in total and to each policy individually. Therefore, the only lessons for developing countries are that some of the policies have proven to be ineffective and that none of the policies has proven to be effective.

Economists today generally agree that the huge number of small enterprises has contributed greatly to rapid economic growth in Japan. To promote such enterprises, the Japanese government has offered a broad array of policies. However, these policies of the central and local governments for SMEs have not played much role in promoting the development of such SMEs.

Many questions still remain: Why have SMEs been so successful in Japan? What are the necessary circumstances and conditions for such growth by SMEs? What can government policy do to encourage SMEs? One of the implications of this study is that the answers to these questions do not appear directly in the Japanese experience.[76]

Readers may wonder why the government's policy menu has been so extensive, why SMEs have been so enthusiastic about those policies, and what the basic characteristics of those policies are. Although this

[75] Comparison with *Chūsho kigyō shisaku no aramashi 1970* shows that the system and its content have not changed greatly. The total budget size of the central government for this policy was ¥170 million in 1963, ¥490 million in 1967, and ¥770 million in 1970.

[76] As was suggested at the outset, the same kind of relationship exists between Japanese economic growth and 'industrial policy.'

chapter has not considered these questions, I will close with a brief response.

1. The basic and common character of the policies for SMEs has been 'social,' and not 'economic.'[77]

2. Although the policies have not been effective in improving consumer welfare, each policy worked as a subsidy for some SMEs and had redistributional effects. The enthusiastic response from some political groups follow from this fact.[78]

3. Almost always, a new policy requires a new law and a new organization with employees. These employees will then resist any attempt later to reduce the size of government. As a result, in Japan as everywhere else, it tends to be easy to expand government organization but difficult to reorganize it and almost impossible to shrink it. The expansion trend and the extensive menu of policies is a direct reflection of this logic of government organization.

[77] In accepting this view, however, many people assert that such policies contribute finally to rapid economic growth through their policy effects, such as more equal income distribution and more stable positions of SMEs. Although this is not the place to comment on this view, I should say that social policies are not recommendable as policies for economic growth. Policies chosen should have direct effects, rather than remote and indirect results, if any. Moreover, I am on the opposite side with the majority of economists and emphasize the importance of the trade-off between efficiency and equity.

[78] Sometimes such enthusiastic movements demanding 'new' policies for SMEs appear to be for the sake of professionals in the movements, not for SMEs themselves, as is often the case for political movements.

PART FIVE

COMPARATIVE
PERSPECTIVES

15

Developmental Bureaucracy in Comparative Perspective:
The Evolution of the Korean Civil Service

MEREDITH WOO-CUMINGS

Arguments

The World Bank Project on the Japanese Civil Service seeks to understand the evolution of the Japanese bureaucracy's role in mediating the relationship between the state and the economy. This task is important not only because, as E. H. Norman observed more than 40 years ago, 'the key to understanding Japanese political life was given to whoever appreciated fully the historical role and actual position of the bureaucracy,'[1] but also because we want to know whether the Japanese case, to the extent that it exemplifies a particularly salutary relationship between the state and economic development, might be emulated elsewhere.

The transferability of a political economic paradigm remains an enormously complex issue, however, and most contributors to this volume have approached the subject gingerly, delineating historical context and social specificities in Japan in order to underscore the difficulties attendant in importing the Japanese model. Such caution is more than warranted, coming on the heels of a century and a half of determinist social science paradigms, such as Marxism and modernization theory, that saw the replication of Western capitalism on a world scale as inevitable and relatively unproblematic. All this is to suggest that the Japanese political economy, like Western capitalism, may not be the mirror of the future for the rest of the world.

In that spirit, Kozo Yamamura underscores the peculiar *Gestalt* of late industrialization, including shared ideology and norms, that is difficult, although clearly not impossible, to replicate elsewhere; Peter Hall stresses the uniquely fortuitous factors that allowed greater room for bureaucratic maneuver in postwar Japan; Masaru Mabuchi and Yukio Noguchi spell out the economic and institutional prerequisites for industrial financing

[1] E. H. Norman, *Origins of the Modern Japanese State*, edited by John W. Dower (New York: Pantheon Books, 1975).

Japanese-style; T. J. Pempel and Michio Muramatsu delimit the lessons for other countries to selected aspects of the 'bounded competition' that gives vitality to the Japanese civil bureaucracy, essentially as a matter of social-technology transfer; and Judith Thornton, in describing the Russian temptation to copy the particularly statist aspect of Japanese development, warns of the perils of incomplete and opportunistic learning from Japan.

Of course, the Japanese political economy has never stood in splendid isolation in the sea of alien systems. Already a century ago, the Japanese bureaucracy, itself a mimetic structure born of assiduous learning from the West, had begun to clone itself in neighboring countries, at first by brute force, and later by being an exemplar of developmental success (the 1894 Kabo reforms in Korea that accompanied the Sino-Japanese war might be considered an example of both); it indeed came to be the mirror of the future, at least in some areas of East Asia. In other words, the Japanese system has been replicated in the past, particularly during colonial rule, and thus the question of learning from it is far from academic.

This chapter assays how the Japanese system of political economy came to be transplanted in many essential aspects in Korea, a country that had for millenia existed near yet separate from Japan, and with a bureaucratic tradition significantly different from that of feudal Japan. The fact that Korea, too, achieved one of the world's most condensed industrialization projects should add greater urgency to exploring the Japanese experience in search of a usable developmental paradigm.

There is general consensus among scholars of the Korean political economy that the state bureaucracy has been particularly effective in negotiating economic development in Korea—up until the 1980s, anyway—and even strident advocates of economic orthodoxy observed that state interventionism might have had salutary consequences.[2] The Korean bureaucracy holds then, along with its counterparts in Japan and Taiwan, the key to what Chalmers Johnson once called the 'developmental enigma' in East Asia, by which he meant the combination of an 'absolutist state' (whether a one-party democracy in Japan or bureaucratic authoritarian structures in Korea and Taiwan for much of their history) and a capitalist economy. Or to put it in other words, the ubiquitous and highly capable civil servants in the East Asian developmental states are one step

[2] See, for instance, the studies on the economic and social modernization of Korea undertaken jointly by the Harvard Institute of International Development and the Korea Development Institute: Kim Kwang Suk and Michael Roemer, *Growth and Structural Transformation in Korea* (Cambridge, Mass.: Harvard University Press, 1979); Leroy Jones and Il Sakong, *Government, Business, and Entrepreneurship in Economic Development* (Cambridge, Mass.: Harvard University Press, 1970); and Edward Mason et al., *The Economic and Social Modernization of the Republic of Korea* (Cambridge, Mass.: Harvard University Press, 1980).

ahead of the Weberian bureaucrats on the evolutionary scale: not mere executors of a higher will, the state bureaucrats in East Asia 'set national goals and standards that are internationally oriented and based on non-ideological external referents.'[3]

The recent literature on the Korean political economy has corroborated such a view, by emphasizing the state's patronization, monitoring, and guidance of the private sector in an intensely goal-oriented economy. The salient economic policies of this 'developmental state' have been distinguished in various ways, including: first, the Korean state's mobilization and allocation of resources to selected firms and industrial sectors, especially through financial mechanisms, as I have argued elsewhere,[4] and much as described by Yukio Noguchi and Masaru Mabuchi for Japan in this volume; second, the pattern of 'getting relative prices wrong,' in Alice Amsden's words, in violation of the Holy Grail of marginal productivity theory; finally, following the logic of late industrialization (diversifying into heavy industries in order to catch up), and going against the logic of the law of comparative advantage.[5]

The civil bureaucracy is said to have implemented all of these strategies from above. Furthermore, so the argument goes, the bureaucracy has also helped mobilize the populace by inculcating certain norms and ideologies conducive for economic development, even more explicitly than in Japan. Some relate this to Korea being a divided country perched on the faultline of geopolitics, with strong demands for national security conjoining power with plenty.

Curiously enough, while the formidable power of the public bureaucracy in Korea is increasingly well analyzed, the evolution and structure of this remarkable bureaucracy itself has not received much attention outside Korea. As a consequence, we can understand conceptually what the Korean state bureaucracy does in the economy, but not what it looks like, how it is organized, or how it got to be the way it is. This is in contrast with Japan, where the bureaucracy, celebrated as the florescence of the rational-legal type of state administration, has received a great deal of academic scrutiny.

This points to the second intent of this paper: to fill that lacuna in the study of the Korean political economy. It will do so by tracing the evolution and structure of the public bureaucracy in Korea, thus to deepen our understanding of the way the relationship between the state and economy is organized and mediated in that country, and also to understand that

---

[3] Chalmers Johnson, 'Political Institutions and Economic Performance: The Government–Business Relationship in Japan, South Korea, and Taiwan,' in Frederic C. Deyo, ed., *The Political Economy of the New Asian Industrialism* (Ithaca: Cornell University Press, 1987), pp. 137, 142.

[4] Jung-en Woo, *Race to the Swift: State and Finance in Korean Industrialization* (New York: Columbia University Press, 1991).

[5] Alice Amsden, *Asia's Next Giant* (New York: Oxford University Press, 1989).

there was a bureaucratic tradition in Korea long before the advent of the Japanese.

The Thesis

Weber argued that bureaucratic organization is the most efficient form of organizing large-scale administrative activities and identified a number of critical issues such as corporate cohesion of the organization, unambiguous location of decision making and channels of authority, and internal features fostering instrumental rationality and activism.[6] We want to know about the organization of state institutions because the size and the degree of development of the bureaucratic machinery and the availability of expertise and technical personnel to plan, monitor, and implement policies are all good gauges of state capacities. But there is another sense in which the study of the structure of public bureaucracy must be an important part of the broader theory of the state: it enables us to assess the degree to which the state is insulated from, or autonomous of, the pressures of private interest.

For instance, Ben Ross Schneider has hypothesized that state administration was likely to be more autonomous if, as in Japan and France, the patterns of bureaucratic careers revealed that the base of recruitment was narrow, promotion merit-oriented, and that during normal bureaucratic careers the levels of circulation between public and private employment are relatively low. The pervasiveness of *amakudari* in Japan or *pantouflage* in France (meaning, in both cases, the parachuting of retired public officials into the private sector) might seem to undercut Schneider's conception and compromise state autonomy, as does the relative interdepartmental immobility of officials, which tends to foster proprietary relations between the bureaucracy and industry.[7] Other scholars, however, have found in this combination of bureaucratic insulation on the one hand and collaboration with the business sector on the other a highly effective interventionist combination—what Peter Evans has dubbed the case of 'embedded autonomy.'[8]

The Korean bureaucracy exhibits the same 'embedded autonomy' as its counterparts in Japan and France: it, too, is a meritocracy that recruits from an elite pool for a career that is life-long, such that a professional bureaucrat, as Weber acerbically put it, 'cannot squirm out of the appar-

[6] Max Weber, 'Bureaucracy,' in H. H. Gerth and C. Wright Mills, eds., *From Max Weber: Essays in Sociology* (New York: Oxford University Press, 1958).
[7] Ben Ross Schneider, 'The Career Connection: A Comparative Analysis of Bureaucratic Preferences and Insulation,' *Comparative Politics*, Vol. 25, No. 3 (April 1993), pp. 331–50.
[8] Peter Evans, 'Predatory, Developmental, and other Apparatuses: A Comparative Political Economy Perspective on the Third World States,' *Sociological Forum*, Vol. 4, No. 4 (Dec. 1989), pp. 561–87.

atus in which he is harnessed.'[9] It also shows sort of 'imbedded' porosity, built into the institutional structure, such that the distinction between public and private often becomes blurred.

How did the Korean bureaucracy come to bear *general* resemblance to other paragons of statist bureaucracies? Bernard Silberman has argued that highly uncertain political environments are conducive to creating an organizationally oriented administration (as in France and Japan), whereas low political uncertainty has led to the development of professionally oriented administrations in the United Kingdom and the United States.[10] The genesis and evolution of the Korean bureaucracy, however, points to the existence of another route: the situation of a post-colonial bureaucracy that inherits an 'overdeveloped' administrative structure—'overdeveloped' in that its basis lies in the metropolitan structure itself, from which it is later separated at the time of independence.[11] One might say that postcolonial Korea has inherited the 'overdeveloped' institutional structure from Japan, but combined and altered it in ways that have reflected both Korea's tradition as well as new political realities.

The thesis advanced in this chapter is that the development of the Korean civil service is explicable in historical terms: the experience of neo-Confucian statecraft and bureaucratic traditions, as well as the impact of Japan, which, through its colonial policies and postwar development, presented to Korea a kind of template of bureaucratic development. I will argue, in other words, that the rational-legal bureaucracy in Korea developed neither out of functional necessity as Weber saw it, nor out of political necessity as Silberman has argued, but as a legacy of a long tradition of effective bureaucracy, in the *ancien regime* and during colonial rule.

This chapter will also argue comparatively that there is affinity between the military regime that reigned over Korea for nearly three decades and bureaucratic-authoritarian regimes elsewhere—say, in Latin America and in prewar Japan. A comparative perspective that cuts across world regions emphasizes the general political environment for the Korean bureaucracy: namely, the situation of an unstable political system, marked by weak political parties, whereby the relationship between civil society and the state has mostly dispensed with the mediation of parties. The classic example of this is the bureaucratic-authoritarian politics that swept through much of Latin America, as well as Korea, in the 1970s.

[9] Weber, 'Bureaucracy,' p. 228.
[10] Bernard Silberman, *Cages of Reason: The Rise of the Rational State in France, Japan, the United States, and Great Britain* (Chicago: University of Chicago Press, 1993).
[11] Hamza Alavi, 'The State in Post-Colonial Societies: Pakistan and Bangladesh,' *New Left Review*, Vol. 74 (1972), pp. 59–90.

The compatibility of the meritocratic and developmentally oriented bureaucracy with an authoritarian political order is not an anomaly, of course. It happened in Korea and Taiwan, in parts of Latin America, and in pre-war Japan (to which some scholars have traced the genealogy of prominent bureaucratic careers in Japan), thus offering evidence contrary to the view, suggested by Peter Hall in this volume, that the development of an effective civil service may go hand in hand with the development of a democratic system.

Civil administration in an authoritarian polity, it is true, does tend to corrupt more easily, as the recent anticorruption campaign in Korea has revealed. Yet it may be just as true that it was the Korean bureaucracy that, in the absence of a strong party system and the recurrence of unstable regimes since 1945, provided the needed stability and direction for development. Of course it is time that will tell, because the current embryonic democratic system in Korea may last long enough to prove Peter Hall right.

The Bureaucratic State in Traditional Korea

When the literature on economic development in East Asia touches on culture and tradition, it often tends to explain everything and therefore nothing. Parroting Max Weber, scholars once saw Confucianism as a catch-all explanation for the region's *lack* of development, for the absence of a vibrant capitalism. But even Confucianism has become modernized since then, so that cultural conceptions such as 'post-Confucianism,' 'aggressive Confucianism,' and '*samurai* Confucianism'[12] claim some long-overdue credit for the recent economic dynamism in the area.

Regardless of the theoretical status of these cultural categories, the great strengths of Confucianism, or more precisely neo-Confucianism, historically lay in the institutions of the family, the school, and the bureaucracy, and to that extent it is important to pay some attention to the neo-Confucian cultural tradition.[13] In particular, Korea had a venerable bureaucratic culture that is bred in the bones of every official—even if he or she does not know it.

Yet, we do not have a clear understanding of the nature of the bureaucratic state in traditional Korea, based as it was on the most thorough adoption in East Asia of the social institutions and practices recommended by the preeminent neo-Confucian Chinese scholar Chu Hsi.

---

[12] See Kent Calder and Roy Hofheinz, *The East Asia Edge* (New York: Basic Books, 1982); Lucian Pye, *Asian Power and Politics* (Cambridge, Mass.: Belknap Press, 1985); and Michio Morishima, *Why Has Japan Succeeded?* (Cambridge: Cambridge University Press, 1982).

[13] Wm. Theodore de Bary, *East Asian Civilizations: A Dialogue in Five Stages* (Cambridge, Mass.: Harvard University Press, 1986).

Scholars in Korea often present a model of an 'organic, unitary, centralized pyramid, with the king at the apex of state institutions,'[14] and invoke this tradition to assail what are said to be the worst qualities of the Korean bureaucracy, variously denoted as 'fatalism,' 'ritualism,' 'authoritarianism,' 'factionalism,' and 'antimaterialism.'[15] Where civil service tradition is examined in detail, often the focus has been on the ideas of reformers such as Kwang-jo Cho, Yi Yi, and Yak-yong Chông, who tried (in vain) to make the old bureaucratic system more responsive.[16]

In other words, one of the oldest and most sophisticated bureaucratic traditions in the world remains anathema to the people who inherited it. This severance with the past derives in good measure from Korean nationalistic shame—that the traditional agrarian-bureaucratic system, for all its glory, failed to maintain sovereign integrity and keep Japanese imperialism at bay. (Japan colonized Korea in 1910, and foreigners have had trouble grasping that for centuries Koreans considered themselves superior to the Japanese, especially by virtue of Korea being closer to the fount of East Asian civilization, China. Thus to fall victim to Japanese militarists added insult to injury.) This dubious tradition is also said to be the source of the greatest political conundrum that besets modern Korea: bureaucratic authoritarianism and centralism. Both too feckless and too rigid then, Korea's long bureaucratic tradition has not provided a usable past, according to many Korean scholars.

Some foreign analysts have agreed. Gregory Henderson, in his book, *Korea: The Politics of Vortex*, characterized Korean politics as an unstable spiral of social mobility connected to an uninterrupted tendency toward bureaucratic centralization, such that all ambitious people engage in 'upward streaming' toward the bureaucratic apex. This, he wrote, characterized the Yi dynasty (1392–1910), the colonial state that followed on it, and South Korea since 1945: thus, 'the Korean greenhouse has had several gardeners, but its temperatures have been, on the whole, constant.'[17]

Other studies have shown, however, that the statecraft of the neo-Confucian bureaucracy was not so lamentable. Originally started in China to meet the educational needs of an expanding civil service and to reform civil service examinations to provide a relatively open channel for offical recruitment, neo-Confucian philosophy spread in the thirteenth to seventeenth centuries, and emphasized educating officials by combining

---

[14] Bun Woong Kim, 'Korean Bureaucracy in Historical Perspective,' in Bun Woong Kim and Wha Joon Rho, eds., *Korean Public Bureaucracy* (Seoul: Kyobo Publishing, Inc., 1982), p. 51.

[15] Wan Ki Paik, *Korean Administrative Culture* (Seoul: Korea University Press, 1990).

[16] Ch'un-shik Kim, 'T'oegye ûi haengjôngsasang e kwanhan yôngu' (A study of T'oegye's administrative philosophy), *Hanguk haengjông hakbo*, Vol. 26, No. 2 (Summer 1992), pp. 249–65.

[17] Gregory Henderson, *Korea: The Politics of Vortex* (Cambridge, Mass.: Harvard University Press, 1968).

classical study and learning with less esoteric subjects such as civil administration, military affairs, irrigation, and mathematics. Neo-Confucians
called this new kind of learning 'solid,' 'real' or 'practical,' in contrast to
older forms of Confucian scholarship which emphasized scholarship and
contemplation—not to mention the Buddhist and Taoist traditions. The
practice of neo-Confucian bureaucratic statecraft reached its apex in Korea. (Theodore de Bary notes that in embracing neo-Confucianism as a
complete way of life, Koreans went far beyond anything undertaken by
the Chinese themselves.)[18]

Careful scholarship on the bureaucratic state in traditional Korea has
also shown that it was not overcentralized nor was society disrupted by
'upward streaming.' Instead, the bureaucracy was dedicated to goals
quite different from the modern state. The bureaucracy often acted as a
major restraint on royal absolutism, deploying the Confucian doctrine
emphasizing the minister's right of remonstrance with his prince, and
succeeding in institutionalizing that in government agencies. James
Palais, historian of the Yi dynasty, has argued that this resulted in an
intricate network of checks and balances that was responsible for providing a solution to the problem of political stability, and that was well
adapted for governing an essentially steady-state economy. This, indeed,
is how he explains the dynasty's half-millenial longevity, which was no
mean feat.

The political stability in the Yi dynasty was made possible in part by the
quality of its bureaucracy, which recruited officials based on rational
criteria of talent and merit, even if in the context of the ascriptive system.
In order to improve the merit orientation in recruitment and procedure,
the agrarian bureaucracy required, in addition to the civil examination,
the supplementary use of personal recommendation to balance the bias of
a literary examination; stricter adherence to review procedures prior to
appointment, and through the institution of traveling secret censors; and
insistence on proper qualifications and prerequisites for certain posts.
These procedures were deemed critical to ensure ideological conformity,
seniority, and routinization of performance.[19]

In essence, the neo-Confucians believed that a desirable bureaucratic
administration reflected the values of the most basic and exemplary East
Asian social unit: the family. As in the family, bureaucratic rule had to be
based on respect for authority, not just on instrumental reason in Max
Weber's sense. Years of philosophical learning preceded the local, regional, and national exams for the bureaucracy, learning that began on a
grandfather's knee, memorizing the first and simplest classics. The exams
were then a prelude to years of practical learning and experience in the

[18] de Bary, *East Asian Civilizations*, pp. 47–8.
[19] James Palais, *Politics and Policy in Traditional Korea* (Cambridge, Mass.: Harvard University Press, 1975), pp. 43–57.

civil administration. From this discipline came an administrative culture that, like de Bary's neo-Confucian world view, permeated the lives of officials.[20] This culture also bred a deep respect for education, and especially the educated bureaucrat or 'scholar-official.' In the face of imperialism and competition with modern states, however, especially with post-Meiji Japan, the *ancien régime* could not solve the problem of creating adequate authority for the achievement of new, modernizing national goals.[21]

A long tradition of bureaucratic statecraft, drawing its legitimacy from the claim that its civil servants were 'the best and the brightest,' helps explain the alacrity with which Koreans took to Japanese bureaucratic doctrines. It survived through the colonial period to facilitate the economic transformation of Korea thereafter.

The Japanese Bureaucracy in Colonial Korea

In spite of Korea's long bureaucratic tradition, modern legal-rational bureaucracy in the Weberian sense was constructed in Korea by the same architect that had designed it for Japan: the Meiji oligarch, Hirubumi Itō. Itō as a young man had been one of the handful of leaders who had helped usher in the Meiji system. He had traveled extensively in Europe, and came away fascinated by Prussian bureaucracy, which he saw as a route to Western rationality and modernity, but which was at the same time an alternative to Anglo-American liberalism. Within Japan, Itō in 1878 had 'led the campaign to make the bureaucracy the absolute unassailable base and center of political power in the state system.'[22]

In 1907 Itō was appointed resident-general in Korea, in charge of running the protectorate. His actions as the 'uncrowned king of Korea' were swift and decisive: he dismantled the Korean army, co-opted some army officers to a Japanese-controlled gendarmerie, repressed dissenters, and forced the Korean monarch to abdicate. In place of the old system the Japanese instituted a civil service which, 'in the main, followed the lines of the Imperial Japanese services. Provision [was] made for a lower and for a high examination of candidates, for salaries and allowances, and for the appointment, resignation, and dismissal of officials.'[23]

[20] For further discussion, see Tae-hi Yi, 'Yukyosik haengjŏngmunwha e taehan saeroun haesŏk' (New interpretations on the Confucian administrative culture), *Hanguk haengjŏng hakbo*, Vol. 25, No. 2 (1991), p. 549.

[21] Palais, *Politics and Policy in Traditional Korea*, and 'Stability in Yi Dynasty Korea: Equilibrium Systems and Marginal Adjustment,' Occasional Papers on Korea No. 3, University of Washington (June 1975), pp. 1–18.

[22] Atul Kohli, 'Where Do "Developmental States" Come From: The Japanese Lineage of Korean Political Economy,' unpublished manuscript. See also T. J. Pempel, 'Bureaucracy in Japan,' *PS: Political Science and Politics*, Vol. 25, No. 1 (March 1992).

[23] Alleyne Ireland, *The New Korea* (New York: E. P. Dutton & Company, 1926), p. 104.

Japanese imperialism in Korea, like so many other aspects of Meiji development, was an act of mimesis. The 'opening' of Korea in 1876 was the Japanese version of the Anglo-American 'gun-boat diplomacy' of the 1850s and 1860s; the 'unequal treaty' that would open up trade in Korea was 'free trade imperialism' a la Japan; and the Japanese even spoke about their *mission civilatrice* in Korea.[24]

Much the same could be said about the bureaucracy; no sooner than they absorbed from Prussia the lessons of rational bureaucracy, the Japanese were practicing them in Korea. As early as 1894, the Japanese program for Korea singled out as the most urgent task the 'creation of a modern specialized bureaucracy, with functionally defined offices filled by technically competent officials, adequately paid and free from abuses of nepotism, the sale of office; a rationalized government structure, centering on a cabinet made up of functionally specialized ministries,' as well as a new judicial structure and rationalized systems of government finances and police.[25]

There was one respect, however, in which the Japanese imperialism was highly unusual: the massive presence of Japanese bureaucratic personnel. The territorial contiguity of Japanese imperialism and the security concerns that had prompted the annexation in the first place, when combined with the fact that Japan was still a developing country itself, meant that Japanese policy in its colonies would be significantly different from that of, say, Britain (which ruled its colonies with a skeleton crew, compared to Japan). Whereas the globe-trotting British imperium left open the possibility of autonomous development for its various components, Japanese control and use of its colonies was much more extensive, thorough, and sytematic.[26]

In 1910 there were some 10,000 officials in the Government-General. By 1937 this number had increased more than eight-fold to 87,552, of which 52,270 (or 60 per cent) were Japanese. This contrasted with the French in Vietnam, who ruled a similiar-sized colony with some 3,000 colonial officials. In other words, there were nearly 15 Japanese officials in Korea for every French administrator in Vietnam.[27]

The presence of Korean bureaucrats, trained and employed by the Japanese, was also sizable; nearly 40,000 Koreans qualified as government officials just before the Second World War. While they did not occupy high positions, over the four decades of colonial rule they became an integral part of a highly bureaucratic form of government. Moreover, during the Second World War, as the demand for Japanese officials grew

---

[24] Peter Duus, 'The Abacus and the Sword: The Japanese Penetration of Korea, 1895–1910,' unpublished manuscript, Chap. 10.

[25] Ibid., chapter 3.   [26] Woo, *Race to the Swift*, p. 21.

[27] Michael Robinson, 'The First Phase of Japanese Rule, 1910–19,' in Carter Eckert *et al.*, *Korea, Old and New* (Seoul: Ilchokak, 1990), pp. 256–7.

elsewhere, many Koreans moved higher up in the bureaucratic hierarchy. This sizable cadre of Japanese-trained Korean bureaucrats virtually took over the day-to-day running of a truncated South Korea, first under American military government, and eventually under the independent state formed in 1948.[28]

To understand the 'learning effect' in the Japanese economic bureaucracy, the case of the Industrial Bank of Chosen (IBC) is particularly interesting. The IBC was a major institution of industrial financing, especially toward the last two decades of the Japanese imperium. As such it was the inevitable reference point for those men who plotted economic development in postcolonial Korea: the similarities in the operation of the IBC and postwar Korean industrial financing are remarkable, as I have argued elsewhere.[29] In the early 1940s, more than half of the IBC's regular personnel were Koreans, while one-third of the employees in the Bank of Chosen (the central bank) were Koreans, with many above the clerical level. Such upward mobility for colonial subjects was undoubtedly an artifact of wartime expediency, but even in peacetime, the number was never less than a third of total bank personnel.

The bureaucracy the Japanese left behind in Korea also possessed a considerable repressive capacity. Designed on the lines of the Meiji Home Ministry and police system, the national police numbered 6,222 in 1910, grew to 20,777 in 1922, and to over 60,000 in 1941. Senior officials were normally Japanese, but over half of the police force was made up of Koreans, often from the lower classes. The Japanese also developed a 'thought police,' and a 'spy system,' to buttress the civil and police bureaucracy that was 'probably better developed in Korea than anywhere in the world.'[30]

The legacies of civil and military bureaucracy in colonial Korea facilitated the adoption of a particular pattern (or model, or template) in Korean industrial development. The first discernible pattern is one of national industrialization determined to a significant degree by an East Asian regional economic integration, led by Japan. Whether understood in terms of a regional division of labor, or dovetailing with the product cycle as Bruce Cumings has argued, the Korean industrial structure has historically exhibited a high degree of articulation with that in Japan. We find the genesis and the prototype of this articulation in the colonial experience.[31]

[28] Ibid., p. 17.   [29] See Woo, *Race to the Swift*, especially chapters 2 and 6.
[30] Andrew Grajdnazev, *Modern Korea*, p. 55, quoted in Kohli, 'Where Do "Developmental States" Come From?', p. 20.
[31] This argument on product cycles is advanced by Bruce Cumings in his 'The Origins and Development of the Northeast Asian Political Economy,' *International Organization*, Vol. 38, No. 1 (Winter 1984), pp. 1–40; on Korean inheritance of Japan's obsolete industries and new regional division of labor, see Andrew Granjdanzev, 'Korea under Changing Orders,' *Far Eastern Survey*, Vol. 8, No. 25 (1939), p. 295.

The second pattern is the bureaucracy's role in the comprehensive and semicoercive channeling of capital to target industries. We find an uncanny parallel to the 1970s in the state's manner of financing industrialization in the last decade of colonial rule (both periods of military-related heavy industrialization) and in state creation and utilization of new breeds of conglomerates (the new *zaibatsu* in the former instance, and the *chaebôl* in the latter) as the spearheads of industrial mobilization.[32]

Kazushige Ugaki, the Governor-General of Korea from 1931 to 1936, personified the leadership for the kind of industrial task ahead: an ultranationalist, he deeply believed in the need for a Japanese imperium of economic autarky and industrial self-sufficiency. Thus in the 1930s, the real growth of Korea's manufacturing production and value-added averaged over 10 per cent per annum, a much greater rate than the one achieved in Taiwan (less than 6 per cent).

Colonial Korea was, in ways that Japan proper was not, a 'capitalist paradise'; taxes on business were minimal in order to attract the *zaibatsu*, there was nothing equivalent to the Law Controlling Major Industries that regulated business in Japan proper, legislation for protecting workers was nonexistent, and wages were half what they were in Japan.

Most critical in the Japanese private sector's decision to invest in Korea, however, were the financial incentives created by the Japanese government and the latter's willingness to share the risk should the investment turn unprofitable. In a situation of excess demand for money that had prevailed since the mid-1930s, the government began intervening heavily in the bank credit allocation process, at first with respect to the Industrial Bank of Japan, and then later for the private, commercial banks as well. Through trial and error the Japanese government devised, over time, ways of channeling capital and credit into war-related heavy industries and drying up the flow into nonessential industries.[33]

Business and financial interests were not reluctant to go along with the financial policies of the state, for again, any loss suffered by the banks through the nonperforming loans would be indemnified by the state, which might pay in government securities. In this manner, even short-term credit came under the control of the state.

By the middle of 1940, private banking institutions showed signs of reaching the limit of their ability to expand credit further. Lack of funds forced a number of banks to resort to the Bank of Japan for help, and even several of the 'Big Six' banks, which had traditionally abstained from contract with the central bank, broke their custom and resorted to it. Once the financial structure became overstretched, the state turned to centralization. Given that Japan did not want and could not afford outside

[32] Woo, *Race to the Swift*, p. 20.   [33] Ibid., chapter 2, passim.

capital, and possessed insufficient capital at home, the state had either to utilize its resources or encourage the centralization of private capital in the hands of financial oligarchs for more efficient use. The effect of this was clearly visible in Korea.

In a relatively short period of time, the grip of *zaibatsu* groups on the Korean economy became tight and concentrated, and they substituted, by the 1930s, for the earlier national policy companies as the spearhead of the industrial expansion drive. Three-quarters of the total capital investment in Korea was estimated to have been made by the leading Japanese *zaibatsu* in 1940, the roster containing names such Mitsubishi, Mitsui, Nissan, Asano, Mori, Riken, Sumitomo, and Yasuda.[34]

Thus, a civil bureaucracy committed to high levels of national planning and resource mobilization, abetted by a vast network of police, characterized the political economy in Japan and Korea from the early 1930s until the end of the war. But it also characterized in some sense the political economy of the Republic of Korea from the 1960s through the 1980s.

Korea in the 1960s could not see itself finding a usable past in the wartime industrialization of the 1930s; indeed, the very idea is anathema to Korean patriots. The 1930s bequeathed a set of patterns, a model, that could be the silent companion of Korean development, the parenthetical unspoken force that brings home the truth that people make their own history, but not in circumstances of their own choosing. The Janus-faced legacy of Japanese imperialism was to make of the Korean suffering of the 1930s a usable past for the 1960s onward. If some recent work has highlighted this important legacy, it has also placed in the shade an age-old bureaucratic culture that was indigenous (as discussed above), and that an independent Korea also drew upon.

We can summarize the model or template from the colonial experience and its application to industrialization after 1965 as follows: the type of state and its role in the economy; the state's relationship to business, especially the conglomerates; the financial mechanisms peculiar to Japanese development then and Korean development now. The constant variables are a mode of industrialization connected to security needs and, more broadly, to the harsh requirements of industrialization in a world that the Western powers dominated, and a domestic social situation making the mobilization of capital difficult without heavy state intervention, and consequent state direction of funds.

Within these structural constraints, the regime type would oscillate within relatively narrow parameters. In addition to being a praiseworthy 'developmental state,' the Korean version shared the authoritarian logic of the prewar Japanese state.[35]

---

[34] Ibid.   [35] Ibid.

A Long Interlude

The American military occupation of Korea (1945–8) begat many controversial policies that had long-term consequences, but one thing it did not bring about was a lasting bureaucratic reform. Faced with the choice between the Japanese colonial government and the indigenous, decentralized 'People's Republic' which had spread like wildfire throughout Korea in the aftermath of the Japanese defeat, Americans opted for the former.[36] The Supreme Command of Allied Powers (SCAP), which sent directives from Tokyo, tended to place both Japan and Korea in the same category, and the implementation of its Korea policies was conditioned by the attitudes of the military toward the Japanese occupation, whether these policies had any connection with that operation or not.[37]

In Japan, the SCAP policy toward bureaucratic restructuring sought to increase efficiency and rationality. Beyond that, the bureaucracy was not restructured but was used to rule Japan as an integral component of politics, leaving much of the structure and character of the Japanese national bureaucracy minimally affected.[38] This cut a big contrast with SCAP policy toward politicians and big business, cameoing by default the enhanced stature of the bureaucracy.[39] Such a permissive attitude toward the Japanese bureaucracy was reflected in Korea as well, such that the military government there often retained civil servants from the Government-General, although sometimes individuals branded as collaborators had to be reassigned to other departments or localities.[40] Even reforms that seemed relatively uncontroversial, such as revision of the system of job classification in civil administration, would be jettisoned as soon as the US Military Government turned the administration over to the Koreans.[41]

Even in the First Republic of the fiercely nationalistic Syngman Rhee (1948–60), bureaucratic elites who had passed the Japanese Imperial Higher Civil Service Examination and served in the colonial civil service were instrumental in setting forth decrees on government organization, with the result that the principle and management of civil service remained essentially the same as it had been in the colonial period.[42]

[36] See Bruce Cumings, *The Origins of the Korean War*, Vol. 1 (Princeton: Princeton University Press, 1979).

[37] E. Grant Meade, *American Military Government in Korea* (New York: King's Crown Press, Columbia University, 1951), p. 76.

[38] Pempel, 'Bureaucracy in Japan,' p. 21.

[39] This argument is advanced in Chalmers Johnson, *MITI and the Japanese Miracle* (Stanford: Stanford University Press, 1982).

[40] Meade, *American Military Government in Korea*, p. 76.

[41] Sôk-hong O, 'Hanguk chongbu ûi chikwi pullyu' (The classification of positions in the Korean bureaucracy), in Un-tae Kim et al., *Hanguk chôngch'i haengjông ûi ch'egye* (The system of Korean politics and public administration) (Seoul: Pakyôngsa, 1981), p. 201.

[42] Sôk-hong O, 'Taehanminguk chôngbu ûi haengjông kaehyôk' (Administrative reforms in the government of the Republic of Korea), *Haengjôngronch'ong*, Vol. 28, No. 1 (1990), pp. 52–78.

Whereas purges of politicians ensured by default bureaucratic stability and prominence in Allied-occupied Japan, bureaucratic continuity in Korea happened in part because of the absence of the alternative administrative expertise. These bureaucratic elites were distinguishable from the nationalist leaders in having a notably legalistic bent, acquired through their Japanese education with its emphasis on a legalistic curriculum. The technical-legal expertise they possessed sometimes worked as a check against the politicians, but in general the bureaucracy was not insulated from the politicized environment of the 1950s.[43]

The literature on Korean public bureaucracy generally sees the government structure in the 1950s as an egregious case of an ineffective and tumescent bureaucracy, deeply ignorant and antipathic toward matters of economic development. Perhaps the best proof for the point is that Syngman Rhee's preferred developmental scheme, import substitution, is *ipso facto* seen as a failure. Thus this pause, the 1950s, is precisely that, a blank hiatus between the predatory developmentalism of the Japanese period and the benign miracle of export-led success; nothing remains but an olio of unflattering and contradictory images.

There was, however, method to Syngman Rhee's madness. Korea was a key 'containment' country for the United States after 1950 and thus a beneficiary of the Mutual Security Act, receiving close to $1 billion a year in economic and military assistance combined. One of the most important foreign policy objectives for Rhee, then, was to keep the American aid spigot open. Through adroit manipulation of the import substitution industrialization program and interest rate policies, he rewarded his supporters and built a political coalition.

Rhee commanded the executive and the government with many resources: a strong bureaucracy and police, plus an army that became increasingly bloated by a shower of American military aid; the 'vested' colonial enterprises, that is, firms and factories formerly owned by the Japanese; US aid money which he knew how to wheedle as well as any national leader; and ubiquitous interventionary power over economic activity in the nation. Using these assets of the state in the economy built a powerful patronage constituency, comprised of a select group of old and new entrepreneurs.[44]

The period from independence through the 1950s may be seen as a long interlude between the predatory developmentalism of the Japanese and the benign miracle of the 1960s, a breathing space in which the Korean leadership parlayed its unique geopolitical position into state-building. The civil service that emerged in the process was a politicized one that reflected Rhee's patronage, but many of the future civil servants also cut

---

[43] Hahn-been Lee, *Korea: Time, Change, and Administration* (Honoloulu: University of Hawaii Press, 1968), pp. 98–9.
[44] Woo, *Race to the Swift*, chapter 3, passim.

their bureaucratic teeth there, learning to collaborate with *and* bypass a
United States that had become deeply solicitous of its Korean charge as a
result of the Korean War, thus managing the economic reconstruction of
their country.

The Politics of Economic Development and
the Civil Bureaucracy in Korea

Much of the acrimonious debate on what the state does in the economy in
Japan is replicated in regard to Korea. Many studies of Korean economic
development through the 1970s, often under government sponsorship,
praised Korea's open economy and free trade policies, whereas the writings of the 1980s often tended to emphasize the reverse: the state's
patronization, monitoring, and guidance of the private sector in an
intensely goal-oriented economy.

These traits are not unique to Korea, and have been attributed to Japan
earlier. President Chung Hee Park (1961–79), however, probably
overdetermined the influence of the interwar legacy: he was a former
officer in the Kwantung Army, which had gained control over much of
government policy formation in Manchuria. The enormous military presence was joined by (and often counteracted by) a number of so-called
'new bureaucrats' in the civil agencies, individuals committed to high
levels of national planning and resource mobilization under their own
directly supervised lines of authority. Japan's interwar civil and military
bureaucracies, like those in Korea in the 1960s on to the 1990s, were
relatively free of major checks from the electoral or parliamentary sphere.
But as T. J. Pempel writes about the interwar Japanese bureaucracy, in
spite of nondemocratic elements, 'clarity of vision and technical efficiency
were positive counterbalances to the bureaucracy's lack of political
responsibility.'[45] The same was true in Korea.

To what extent interwar Japanese policy was consciously and assidu-
ously emulated in the years of Chung Hee Park remains difficult to assess,
since any hint of such emulation was routinely denied. In fact, much of the
literature on the reform of civil administration in the early 1960s notes the
rather large influence of the United States, citing as evidence the fact that
many of the authors of the reform were US-educated and that the reform
reflected concern with increasing efficiency, routinization, as well as
supervision.[46]

One could argue, however, that in at least two aspects the new government *organization* evoked the colonial pattern: the creation of the Econ-

[45] Pempel, 'Bureaucracy in Japan,' p. 20.
[46] Sôk-hong O, 'Taehanminguk chôngbu ûi haengjông kaehyôk,' p. 62.

omic Planning Board, a superministry responsible for budget and planning of the national economy, which signaled the beginning of high-level bureaucratic coordination and social mobilization for economic development; and the policy of bureaucratic centralization which thoroughly denied to local administration any measure of autonomy. (The short-lived Second Republic [1960–61] had sought direct election of local officials as a way to foster democracy in Korea, but the junta immediately reversed the move toward decentralization to the point where the structure of local administration in Korea remains, to this day, much the same as it was during the colonial period.[47])

There is also evidence that the Korean civil bureaucracy has often resorted to the Japanese precedent in policy formulation. One survey on policy innovation in the Korean civil administration found that 43.0 per cent of the bureaucrats surveyed listed 'foreign examples' as the source of new policy (versus 21.9 per cent for 'past precedents' and 11.4 per cent for 'original ideas'). When asked to choose two countries with the most similiar policy environment, respondents pointed to Japan (87.7 per cent), the United States (42.1 per cent), followed by Taiwan (28.1 per cent) and the former West Germany (19.3 per cent). When asked to choose two countries whose policies are most often used as referents, they again pointed to Japan (93.9 per cent), the United States (77.2 per cent), Taiwan (6.1 per cent), the former West Germany (5.2 per cent), and Singapore (2.6 per cent).[48] Thus, Korea's civil administrators believe that Korea's policy environment is most like Japan's, justifying their close scrutiny of and learning from Japan. The influence of American public policy, on the other hand, probably owes to the fact that English is the second language for most bureaucrats and that many bureaucrats have received higher education and/or training in the United States.

Although postwar Japan provides the most immediate parallel to the policies and structure of the Korean bureaucracy, there are also glaring differences in the two political systems: postwar Japan has been a stable one-party (plus some fractions) democracy, and Korea was in the grip of unstable military authoritarian regimes until very recently. Every successive republic either began or ended with civil rebellions or military coups. This difference has often led scholars to compare Korean regimes to those in Latin America, described as 'bureaucratic authoritarian.' (A closer parallel would have been with prewar Japan, but few scholars have made explicit links.)

[47] Sôk-jun Cho, 'Ilbon ûi jedo wa kyunghôm e bichuôbon urinara chibang kongmuwôn jedo ûi panghyang' (The direction for Korea's local administration in light of the Japanese system and experience), *Haengjôngronch'ong*, Vol. 26, No. 2 (1988), p. 93.
[48] Chin Min, 'Hanguk kongmuwon ûi chôngch'aek kaebaljigak e taehan t'amsaekjôk yônggu' (Analysis of policy innovations in Korean civil bureaucracy), *Hanguk haengjông hakbo*, Vol. 25, No. 3 (1991), pp. 832–3.

A bureaucratic authoritarian system is a type of authoritarianism characterized by a self-avowedly technocratic, bureaucratic, non-personalistic approach to policymaking and problem-solving. This is said to happen during certain periods of political life when the relationship between civil society and the state seems to dispense with the mediation of parties, and the powerful political and economic interests simply appropriate segments of the state apparatus to defend their interests. In a bureaucratic authoritarian polity, 'bureaucratic rings,' which are organized around high officials and articulate the immediate interests of enterprises and government bureaus, substitute for an organization that is more stable and representative, namely political parties. Particularly when regimes are centralized, these 'bureaucratic rings' end up constituting the form of political linkage that establishes connections between civil society and the state.[49]

Korea, too, had its 'bureaucratic rings,' with the military prominently placed within them. If we venture to take the presence of former military personnel as a rough index of authoritarian inclinations (as opposed to the formal route of bureaucratic recruitment based in civil education, merit, and passing the civil service exams), the evidence is strong. Retired military officers were conspicuous in important positions in government and public enterprises. During the Third Republic (1964–72), cabinet ministers with military backgrounds constituted 73 out of the total of 170, claiming a whopping 42.4 per cent of the total; the figure was 45 out of 142 (or 31.7 per cent) for the Second Republic (1973–9), and 37 out of 151 (or 24.5 per cent) for the period 1980–4 under President Doo Whan Chun. The total for 1964–84 then comes to 155 out of 465, that is, for two decades one out of every three cabinet ministers was a military man. As for the vice ministers during the same period, 73 out of 403, or 18.1 per cent, were former soldiers.[50] In certain bureaus and agencies there was even higher representation of the military: in transportation, the tobacco monoply, labor, taxation, tariffs, and patents (whose chiefs were equal to vice ministers of the core ministries), military officers claimed about 40 per cent for the same period.[51]

Even for those military officers who took civil service examinations, the favored route was not the regular competitive civil service examination, but rather a special one that allowed for lateral entry. A 1976 survey of higher civil servants showed that 14 out of 22 persons who joined the civilian bureaucracy at Grade II were military men, and at least 11 of these did so in the period after 1961. Upward mobility was also shown to be

---

[49] Fernando Henrique Cardoso and Enzo Falletto, *Dependency and Development in Latin America* (Berkeley: University of California Press, 1979), p. 215.

[50] Kwang-wung Kim, *Hanguk ûi kwallyoje yôngu* (A study of the Korean bureaucratic structure) (Seoul: Taeyôngmunhwasa, 1991), pp. 57–8.

[51] Ibid., p. 59.

higher among those who came from a military background.[52] Military officers were also sent abroad for professional education under the Military Assistance Program: in the period between the early 1950s and 1987, some 36,000 officers received short-term training and long-term education, most in the United States.[53]

Another aspect of the Korean bureaucratic structure that resembled the Latin American-style 'bureaucratic ring' was the parallel concentration of executive power and technical expertise in the Blue House (Korea's presidential residence), eventually competing with, say, the Economic Planning Board for economic policymaking. For instance, the chief architects and executers of Korea's heavy industrialization program in the 1970s were not the technocrats of the Economic Planning Board, as might be expected, but rather a nationalistic coterie headed by a political appointee at the Blue House—the first economic secretary to the president.

The *raison d'être* for this team of economic bureaucrats (called the Corps for the Planning and Management of Heavy and Chemical Industries) was the speedy formulation and execution, unfettered by bureaucracy, of policies relating to investments in heavy industrialization. The Economic Secretariat at the Presidential Palace became firmly ensconced as an important economic decision-making body in the Republic, bypassing and sometimes dictating to the Economic Planning Board and the Ministry of Finance.[54] It enjoyed the confidence of the president, which increased its power and autonomy, and it was able, by participating in various policy-coordinating forums, to mediate between economic ministries which had conflicting interests.[55] In other words, presidential protection was a critical element in the planning and execution of economic policies, and in this, the pattern of economic policymaking in Korea was not unlike that in Mexico as well as Brazil.

In the end, though, such 'bureaucratic rings' cannot be very stable, since they depend on close association with the top leader, and presidents can be removed (through assassination or popular upheavals in the case of Park and Chun), key officials can be dismissed, and the ring can thereby be broken.[56] In fact, periodic purges conducted in the name of administrative 'reform'—in the early and late 1970s, and in 1981 and 1993—have tended to disrupt this ring.

[52] Dong-Suh Bark and Chae-Jin Lee, 'The Bureaucratic Elite and Development of Orientations,' in Dae-Sook Suh and Chae-Jin Lee, eds.. *Political Leadership in Korea* (Seattle: University of Washington Press, 1976), pp. 109–11.

[53] Chong-sôp Chôn, 'Chônmungga yôkwhal kwa yunrijôk ch'aekim' (The role and ethical responsibilities of experts), *Hanguk minju haengjôngron* (Theories of democratic administration) (Seoul: Koshiwon, 1988), p. 452.

[54] Woo, *Race to the Swift*, p. 129.

[55] Byung-Sun Choi, 'Institutionalizing a Liberal Economic Order in Korea: The Strategic Management of Economic Order' (Ph.D. diss., Harvard University, 1987).

[56] Cardoso and Falletto, *Dependency and Development in Latin America*, p. 215.

The presence of the 'bureaucratic ring' at the highest level of civil administration did not mean that the professionalism of the Korean bureaucracy was significantly compromised. In fact, what is truly stunning is the persistence through regime change of a surprisingly robust civil bureaucracy—in spite of its accommodation of the military, political vicissitudes, and the occasional emergence of competing policymaking centers. It is this bureaucracy that has rendered permanence to the Korean state structure and its efficacy.

The persistence of the civil bureaucracy through the political turmoil that has prevailed in Korea for the last three decades might be likened to that noted by E. H. Norman in 1940. Observing that Japan was not swept by a complete fascist mobilization (as in Nazi Germany), Norman wondered if this insulation against totalitarian extremism had been possible to no small extent through that ubiquitous and anonymous body, the bureaucracy, acting often in conjunction with higher court circles. The Japanese bureaucracy was thus a steadying force, a 'shock absorber,' with its officials acting 'as mediators who reconcile the conflicts between the military and financial or industrial groups, shifting their weight now to one side and now to the other in order to prevent the complete domination of the military clique and to check big business from controlling politics in its exclusive interest.'[57]

This means that the Korean bureaucracy was no mere possessor of technical information, 'a fox in the position of aping the dignity of a lion,' as the old Japanese saying goes. It had to do something more than that to be as efficacious as it has been in orchestrating one of the world's most compressed economic developments. This brings us back to the original contention we started out with: as E. H. Norman, Chalmers Johnson, Bernard Silberman, and other observers of Japanese statism have noted, the efficacy of the bureaucracy ultimately rests on its ability to integrate state and society, or to mediate between the government and the private sector, and that is no less true of Korea.

The pattern of bureaucratic recruitment reflects a great effort to scout talent from society at large. The educational level of civil servants is high: whereas in 1958 only 15.3 per cent of low-ranking clerks had finished four years of college, more than 70 per cent possessed college degrees in 1988, and one third of those possessed post-graduate degrees.[58] The regular civil service examination in Korea, administered continuously since 1949, is strictly merit-oriented and highly competitive (although in recent years the ratio of competition has tended to fall). From 1963 to 1981, the rate of competition was anywhere from 50 aspirants to one successful candidate all the way to 100 to one. In the 1980s, the rate was often higher, reaching a peak of 164 contestants for every position. Table 15.1 shows

[57] Norman, *Origins of the Modern Japanese State*, p. 313.
[58] Chong-sôp Chôn, 'Chônmungga yôkwhal kwa yunrijôk ch'aekim,' p. 456.

Table 15.1 Rate of Competition for Select Government Examinations

	1985	1986	1987	1988	1989	1990	1991
Foreign Service Exam	105:1	108:1	103:1	93:1	89:1	52:1	39:1
Level 7 Civil Service Exam (Low-Ranking)	81:1	79:1	116:1	95:1	96:1	55:1	47:1

Source: Hôn-gu Kim, 'Haengjônggodûnggoshi kwamok ûi kaep'yônbangan' (Suggestions for revising civil service examination subjects), *Hanguk haengjông hakbo*, Vol. 26, No. 2 (Summer 1992), p. 754.

the trend for the foreign service and the lower-ranking civil service examinations.[59]

The decline in competitiveness in recent years reflects the increase in the attractiveness of the private sector, as well as the difficulty in preparing for state examinations; whereas examinations for entering private companies require preparation on only two to three subjects, Korea's civil service examination requires preparedness in a whopping 12 subjects.[60]

The nature of the expertise most highly valued in Korean civil bureaucracy might be gleaned from the major concentration of the successful contestants in 1982–91: economics and/or business (28.9 per cent), public administration (27.5 per cent), followed by law (13.1 per cent), sociology (5.4 per cent), and education (5.2 per cent).[61] This is in marked contrast to Japan where law graduates are preponderant in civil service: Table 15.2 shows the number and ratio of the graduates from Seoul National University Law School entering Korea's executive and judicial branches, and compares it with the number and ratio of the graduates from the University of Tokyo Law School entering their respectives services. Whereas the overwhelming majority of the University of Tokyo's law graduates had prepared themselves for civil service, the reverse was true for Korea, with less than 10 per cent of law graduates entering the bureaucracy.

This difference is due to the fact that the Korean civil service examination, which had in its early years inherited the legalistic bent of the Japanese civil service examinations, has considerably changed since the mid-1970s, gradually eliminating the excessive requirement for legal knowledge. Other reasons have to do with the relatively low pay for entry-level civil servants in comparison to that for a newly appointed prosecutor or judge, pushing law school graduates in the direction of the judiciary.

[59] Hôn-gu Kim, 'Haengjônggodûnggoshi kwamok ûi kaep'yônbangan' (Suggestions for revising civil service examination subjects), *Hanguk haengjông hakbo*, Vol. 26, No. 2 (Summer 1992), pp. 733–4.
[60] Ibid., p. 736.   [61] Ibid., p. 741.

452   *Meredith Woo-Cumings*

Table 15.2 Comparison of Graduates from Seoul National University Law School (SNULS) and University of Tokyo Law School (UTLS) Who Pass Government Examinations

	1990		*1991*	
	SNULS	*UTLS*	*SNULS*	*UTLS*
Judicial Examination	128 (92)	46 (20)	130 (89)	51 (21)
Civil Service Examination	8 (6)	172 (74)	14 (10)	174 (72)
Foreign Service Examination	9 (2)	14 (6)	2 (1)	16 (7)
Total	139 (100)	232 (100)	146 (100)	241 (100)

Note: The figures in parentheses indicate the percentage of the total from each law school.

Source: Hôn-gu Kim, 'Haengjônggodûnggoshi kwamok ûi kaep'yônbangan' (Suggestions for revising civil service examination subjects), *Hanguk haengjông hakbo*, Vol. 26, No. 2 (Summer 1992), p. 754.

Table 15.3 Number of Civil Servants per 1,000 Population

	Korea	*France*	*United States*	*United Kingdom*	*Japan*	*Singapore*
Number of Civil Servants	18	66	63	63	35	31

Source: Su-il Chôn, 'Kongmuwôn singyuimyong chedo wa ch'ungwôn chôngchaek ûi panghyang' (Directions for entry-level and supplemental hirings in civil bureaucracy), *Hanguk haengjông hakbo*, Vol. 26, No. 2 (Summer 1992), p. 722.

In spite of the relatively slow mobility in the civil service, the growth of bureaucracy has been spectacular. In the aftermath of the Korean War and the *coup d'état* in 1961, as the need to regulate the civil society increased, the number of civil servants increased rapidly—from 237,476 in 1960, to 596,431 in 1980, to 781,346 in 1989, more than tripling the figure from 1961.[62] The rate of increase for civil servants exceeds the rate for general population growth at 0.66; whereas there were 9.5 civil servants per population of 1,000 in 1960, it soon became 13.3 per 1,000 in 1970, 15.9 in 1980, and 18 in 1991.[63]

Yet, the irony of the powerful and ubiquitous bureaucracy in Korea is that its size is small relative to that of other countries. Table 15.3 shows the number of civil servants per 1,000 residents in Korea, and compares it to

---

[62] Tong-sô Pak *et al.*, 'Chakûnjôngbu ûi kaenyôm nonûi' (Discussing the 'small government' concept), *Hanguk haengjông hakbo*, Vol. 16, No. 1 (Spring 1982), p. 50.

[63] Kim, *Hanguk ûi kwallyoje yôngu*, p. 88.

Table 15.4 Government Budget as Ratio of GDP (per cent)

	1950	1970	1985
United States	20.0	30.3	36.5
United Kingdom	35.3	37.1	47.3
Sweden	23.6	37.1	68.5
India	5.8	14.1	27.9
Korea	13.4 (1955)	17.9	22.1

Source: Tong-sô Pak *et al.*, 'Chakûnjôngbu ûi kaenyôm nonûi' (Discussing the 'small government' concept), *Hanguk haengjông hakbo*, Vol. 16, No. 1 (Spring 1982), p. 50.

figures for France, the United States, the United Kingdom, Japan, and Singapore.[64]

Another gauge of the relatively small bureaucracy in Korea is the share of the government budget in GDP. Table 15.4 reveals that in advanced industrial countries government budget as a share of GDP is often one and a half to two times that in Korea.[65]

The big power of the small bureaucracy in Korea is attributable in part to the autonomy the bureaucracy enjoys, especially *vis-à-vis* the legislature. Table 15.5 shows that the majority of parliamentary statutes originated with the bureaucracy and not with the lawmakers, and that such tendencies only accelerated over time.[66] (In this there is much fruit for comparison with Japan.) Administrative policies are strictly originated and orchestrated within the bureaucracy itself. Only in a few cases entailing what is politely called 'political sensitivity' is there consultation with the ruling party—and here conflict is very rarely reported.[67]

The logic follows that the Korean bureaucracy is not accountable to the legislature, either. In parliamentary hearings since 1964, most of the substantive questions directed at the executive branch were from opposition parties (such as they were in Korea), and the responses have often been unhelpful and obfuscating, when they were not insincere. According to one study, negative responses by the administration (including categories of 'no response,' 'refusal and denial,' and 'avoidance or off-the-wall

[64] Su-il Chôn, 'Kongmuwôn singyuimyong chedo wa ch'ungwôn chôngchaek ûi panghyang' (Directions for entry-level and supplemental hirings in civil bureaucracy), *Hanguk haengjông hakbo*, Vol. 26, No. 2 (Summer 1992), p. 722.

[65] Ibid., pp. 50, 52.

[66] Shi-wôn Yi, 'Hanguk ûi tang-chông kwangge e kwanhan yôngu' (A study of the party-government relationship in Korea), *Hanguk haengjông hakbo*, Vol. 23, No. 1 (June 1989), p. 62.

[67] Yông-pyông Kim and Shin-u Shin, 'Hangukkwallyoje ûi kikwangaldûng kwa chôngchaek chojông' (Institutional conflicts and policy adjustments in the Korean bureaucracy), *Hanguk haengjông hakbo*, Vol. 25, No. 1 (May 1991), p. 310.

Table 15.5 Comparison of the Ruling Party and the Government in Initiating Statutes in the National Assembly

	Ruling Party		Government		Total	
	No. of Cases	%	No. of Cases	%	No. of Cases	%
Third Republic						
Sixth Congress (1963–67)	185	43.3	242	56.7	427	100
Seventh Congress (1967–71)	105	26.5	291	73.5	396	100
Eighth Congress (1971–72)	15	13.6	95	84.4	110	100
Fourth Republic						
Ninth Congress (1973–79)	17	3.4	479	96.6	496	100
Tenth Congress (1979–80)	2	1.6	124	98.4	126	100
Fifth Republic						
Eleventh Congress (1981–84)	41	12.5	287	87.5	328	100
Twelfth Congress (1985–88)	57	25.3	168	74.7	225	100

Source: Shi-wôn Yi, 'Hanguk ûi tang-chông kwangge e kwanhan yônggu' (A study of the party-government relationship in Korea), *Hanguk haengjông hakbo*, Vol. 23, No. 1 (June 1989), p. 62.

answers') came to 54.5 per cent, versus 45.4 per cent positive responses (including 'explanations and policy suggestions' as well as 'acceptance and accommodation').[68] This is not surprising, given the weakness, if not irrelevance, of the legislature for much of Korean political history.

The autonomy as well as insularity of the Korean bureaucracy is re-inforced by the various ways bureaucratic conflicts are resolved, in order to present a united front to carry out national policies. One scholar of Korean public administration has argued that, contrary to the common perception of the 'top-down' pattern of bureaucratic decision making in Korea, there is in fact a great deal of policy-coordinating and consensus-building within the Korean civil administration.[69] In cases of interministry conflict there are regular channels for mediation, including decrees on interagency cooperation, various rules governing ministerial meetings and economic policy meetings, committees on industrial policy, as well as a myriad of policy consultation groups set up by various ministries.

For economic bureaucracies, mechanisms for coordination and conflict mediation include the Economic Ministers' Conference, Economic Ministers' Consultative Meeting, the Industrial Policy Deliberation Council, the State Council, the Vice Ministers' Conference, as well as the Ruling Party-Government Consultation Meetings.

[68] Pyông-jun Kim, 'Haengjôngbu e taehan kukhoe ûi yônghyangryôk' (The influence of the legislature toward the executive), *Hanguk haengjông hakbo*, Vol. 23, No. 1 (June 1989), p. 10.

[69] Choi, 'Institutionalizing a Liberal Economic Order in Korea.'

The coordination and insulation of the economic bureaucracy is abetted by the fact that vice ministers of the economic superministry, the Economic Planning Board, have tended to become hoisted as ministers in other economic ministries, leading to quick dissemination of development-planning concepts and techniques and to a smoother policy coordination among economic ministers.[70] Informal channels include *hoesik* (eating-out occasions) and other socializing events based on school and hometown connections among the bureaucrats, and during which policy conflicts may be smoothed out.[71] •

Intraagency conflict tends to be muted relatively quickly. In a political culture where conflict and policy difference are seen as negative (at least within the organs of state), not to mention as proof of the lack of leadership and authority, Korean cabinet ministers are wont to resolve any conflict as quickly as possible. There is also a built-in bias against intraagency conflict; given the policy of divisional rotation, bureaucrats in general eschew offending others in different divisions and bureaus, lest they end up there at some point in their careers.[72] The upshot is that the Korean bureaucracy seems to speak uniformly and in unison, at least to outside observers.

Yet another way in which bureaucratic autonomy is preserved is through centralization. Despite much talk of decentralization and even some tepid attempts at implementing it, the central bureaucracy in Seoul (and its suburban outskirts) has managed to retain tight control over the provinces through institutional, technocratic, and financial coordination. Provincial governors as well as other important local bureaucrats down to the county level are still appointed from Seoul and are rotated rapidly by the center. When this feature of the civil bureaucracy is combined with the highly centralized character of public enterprises, decentralization of the public sector in Korea remains a distant goal.[73] The problem is compounded by the concern that decentralization might actually deepen the existing regional disparity. (Seoul, for instance, is financially self-sufficient, whereas the self-sufficiency rate for the southeastern province is only 26 per cent.[74])

Another effective policy to ensure bureaucratic autonomy and to make it remain relatively free of corruption is through adequate material compensation of civil servants. The compensation level for Korean civil servants has remained low—at some 70 per cent of that of private-sector

[70] Ibid.

[71] Kim and Shin, 'Hangukkwallyoje ûi kikwangaldûng kwa chôngchaek chojông,' p. 319.

[72] Ibid., p. 312.

[73] U-jông Yi, 'Ironjôk shigak esô pon chibangbunkwônhwa ûi munje' (The problem of decentralization: A theoretical perspective), *Hanguk Chôngch'ihakhoebo*, Vol. 24, No. 2 (1990), pp. 193–219.

[74] Ilpyong Kim and Eun Sung Chung, 'Establishing Democratic Rule in South Korea,' *In Depth*, Vol. 3, No. 1 (Winter 1993), p. 207.

employees of the comparable rank—although employees of public enterprises tended to be better compensated than those in the private sector.[75]
But the welfare of civil servants has steadily improved in recent years
to the extent that the notion of a civil servant (*kongmuwôn*) no longer
invokes the image of an immiserized and demoralized 'salaryman.' In
addition to the rationalization of official benefits, the Korean government
has been active in urging the formation of mutual aid societies for civil
servants, aimed at promoting their cooperation and welfare. Japan also
has this type of mutual aid association for bureaucrats; in fact, some
Korean associations, like that for postal workers, trace their origins to the
colonial period.[76] The work that these associations perform ranges from
the relatively simple social task of contributing money at weddings,
graduations, and funerals, to providing scholarships, health care, moving
services, housing, pensions, as well as, in some instances, providing jobs
running enterprises and other positions to retired civil servants.[77]

Democratization and Reform in the Bureaucratic Sector

Throughout its modern history, what has imparted strength to the Korean
state is its formidable power to intervene in the economy. The state has
played hard and fast with the rules of the open market, combining policies
of *laissez-faire* with stringent protection and import-substitution; it also
insulated its small financial market from the world, negotiating and
brokering the flow of foreign capital, keeping its Gorgon's eyes on capital
flight, and in doing so avoided some of the worst tribulations of dependency. The formidable achievement of the Korean state brought about a
backlash from the late 1970s on, however, as it was becoming increasingly
clear that the economy had gotten too big and too internationalized to be
pampered by an overbearing state: hence, 'economic liberalization' has
become the agenda of the 1980s and 1990s, even if its implementation has
been at a snail's pace. Since 1987, political liberalization in the direction of
democracy has filled out some major changes in the Korean model.

The meaning of economic liberalization for Korea's bureaucracy is the
substantial one of keeping its hands off the market, and not the formalistic
one of reducing the absolute size of the government (which is not likely to
happen). The concept of 'small government' actively introduced in the
fifth Republic under Doo Whan Chun (1981–88) led to a reduction in the
number of junior as well as relatively senior bureaucrats.[78] Unlike in

---

[75] Chong-hae Yu, 'Haengjôngyunri wa pup'ae' (Administrative ethics and corruption),
Sahoekwahak ronjip, Vol. 23 (1992), p. 67.

[76] Sôk-jun Cho, 'Urinara kongmuwôn sangjojojik e kwanhan yônku' (A study of mutual
aid societies for civil servants in Korea), *Haengjôngronch'ong*, Vol. 29, No. 1 (June 1991), pp.
2, 11.

[77] Ibid., pp. 13–14.   [78] Ibid., p. 50.

Japan, however, the reforms did not come from within (of course here the Korean experience is the rule and not the exception for bureaucracies generally), and were instituted from above in an effort to legitimize a highly unpopular regime. In the end the reform did not stick, and the bureaucracy grew back to its former size.

The problem with these politically charged 'reforms' has been the tendency to view corruption and other problems in civil service as a personalized or individual phenomenon, rather than as an institutional or systemic problem. Hence anticorruption drives are usually geared toward getting quick results, focusing on weeding out the rotten apples, and not on reforming the system. Therefore, the reforms have tended to be too incidental, episodic, and improvisatory.

The current spate of anticorruption measures, led since early 1993 by the first civilian government in Korea since 1961, has enjoyed greater popular support than those in the past and is aimed at both political legitimation and rooting out the legacy of the worst aspects of bureaucratic authoritarianism: the influence of the military in politics and civil bureaucracy; the monetary link between economic bureaucracies, banks, and private enterprises; as well as speculative activities of the bureaucrats. At this early date in President Young Sam Kim's tenure, much has been accomplished in this regard.

The most urgent task for the bureaucracy, however, must be the same that faces the Korean nation today: democratization. This means a decentralization of power, away from the concentration of decision making in the hands of the executive, to the relevant civil service agencies. It also means a decentralization that moves away from the center to the provinces. Finally, such reforms must also be accompanied by a significant reduction in the repressive capacity of the state, by curtailing the power of intelligence and surveillance agencies. These changes now seem possible, however, with the deepening democratic commitment in the political system.

Conclusions

This paper has argued that the modal bureaucratic form in Korea has been deeply influenced by two legacies: one, which I construe as salutary and benign, is the indigenous bureaucratic culture deriving from a deep background of neo-Confucian statecraft. The other, seen as salutary for development but malign for political freedom, derives from Korean learning at the knee of a harsh master, colonial Japan. American readers of this essay perhaps will wonder what influence the United States has had on the Korean bureaucratic milieu, since an intense Korean–American relationship began in 1945. The answer from 1945 to 1992 would seem to be, not much. But perhaps in the political liberalization now ongoing, which promises to be deeper and more lasting than the somewhat fitful economic liberalization pursued in the 1980s, the influence of American democratic pluralism may be witnessed. Whatever the democratic future of the Republic of Korea, it can safely be asserted that the civil bureaucracy will persist and accommodate itself to the necessary political realities, as it has for centuries.

16

The Japanese Bureaucracy and Economic Development:
Are There Lessons for Russia and the Reforming Socialist Economies?

JUDITH THORNTON

If there is a single important lesson for economic development in the Japanese experience, it is that institutions matter. The changes we associate with economic modernization—technological innovation, structural change, accumulation of physical capital, acquisition of new skills—all are undertaken within the framework of a set of institutions that can impede or promote underlying economic processes. Institutions influence the costs and risks of committing resources to production. They determine who makes decisions, with what information, and subject to what incentives.

Twice in Japanese history—in the 1870s and 1880s after the Meiji restoration and again at the end of World War II—the structure of Japanese political and economic institutions underwent profound and rapid changes reflecting the impact of Western influences on Japan. In both cases, a period of traumatic adjustment was followed by increased interaction with the world market, adoption of Western technology, rapid economic progress, and improved well-being for the members of society. In each of these periods, a framework of government evolved that could promote education, provide the physical and institutional infrastructure complementary to market institutions, and assist in managing the risks and costs associated with rapid change. In each of these periods, emerging markets provided opportunities and incentives for entrepreneurial activity and economic growth.

Today, Russia and the other socialist economies are undergoing a similar period of rapid institutional change. The features of their developing market institutions reflect a similar strong influence from outside. The goal of their transformation is, similarly, to modernize, to upgrade their technological base, to undertake increased trade and investment, and to enjoy the benefits of increased growth and productivity. They must also design an institutional framework for managing the risks and the costs of these changes.

In the wake of the partial collapse of the old apparatus of central planning in the former Soviet Union, Russia and the newly independent states need to create coherent governmental and non-governmental institutions to support civil society, underpin market relations, and manage a process of change that is creating big windfall gains and losses. Russia and the former socialist countries need to build large-scale organizations that can function honestly and effectively. They need to create a legal and governmental framework that will provide secure individual rights and insure that individuals can best advance their own welfare by being productive, by undertaking mutually beneficial exchange, and by investing in the future. And they need to manage the risks and the costs of change in a manner that will maintain public consensus.

There are many difficult steps in this process of economic reform. These economies must create the legal, financial, and administrative infrastructure for a private market economy; restrict government intervention in markets; and adopt trade and industrial policies that will give domestic firms access to advanced technologies, investment, and management skills. They must create social policies toward labor that will accommodate innovation and structural change and build the governmental capacity to administer a market economy and insure individual rights.

The Japanese civil service is a key part of Japan's capacity to manage what the West calls the Japanese miracle. So Russian and Western policymakers alike have much to learn from an examination of the matrix of Japanese governmental institutions and their evolution. How has Japan created the administrative capacity to deliver public services and economic infrastructure effectively, to exercise self-imposed restraint on government interference with individual rights, and to maintain political consensus in a world of rapid economic change? What is the relationship between governmental administrative guidance and dynamic industry performance? To what extent are the problems that Russia faces today similar to problems Japan faced in its history? Are there lessons to be learned from Japan's development? If so, what was the role of Japan's governmental structure in Japan's growth? Or, on the other hand, to what extent does Russia's current collapse reflect unique features of its former planned economy and its far-flung, multiethnic regions that will direct Russia's governmental institution-building on a different path from Japan's?

Complementarities and Coherent Systems

The Japanese experience shows that institutional change and economic change are complementary processes. Economic changes depend on institutional changes that remove constraints or lower the costs of achieving desired outcomes. Institutional changes, in turn, depend on the emergence of interest groups who believe they can increase the potential value of existing resources by changing the social or economic framework. Thus, there appear to be clusters of complementary political and economic institutions that create coherent social systems.[1]

Ronald Coase hypothesizes that individuals interacting in a private-property market economy with zero costs of information will attempt to choose institutional arrangements that allow them to minimize the sum of production and transaction costs of desired economic outcomes.[2] Joseph Stiglitz, looking at more general issues of institutional design, argues that a market system with private property rights may facilitate not only competition between firms, but also competition between the institutional forms that individuals adopt to coordinate their joint efforts.[3]

How does the governmental infrastructure of centrally planned and market systems differ? Can the government structures of a former planned socialist economy supply the public services demanded by market participants? In most societies, governments provide some or all of society's institutional overhead. They provide law and order, a monetary system, physical infrastructure, and, often, a mechanism of social insurance. But the institutional infrastructure of market and administrative systems differ.

Market systems require extensive legal, financial, monetary, and communications infrastructure. There must be institutions to enforce contracts, define title to assets, and facilitate transfer of title. Since private supply of goods and services is separate from the public sector, there must be a tax system to fund public expenditures. Thus, the government plays a key role in a well-functioning market system by enforcing property rights and providing the legal and financial infrastructure for private transactions.

In the classic socialist system with public ownership of capital assets, in contrast, the governmental and economic spheres are partially merged into a unified bureaucratic apparatus. The deputy minister allocating rights to oil products, the municipal official allocating rights to apartments, and the bank official allocating rights to investment funds all operate according to similar bureaucratic rules. In the administered sphere, the bureaucracy does not provide a framework for private transactions; it replaces private transactions, regulating the terms on which individuals have access to things of value.

While the institution of private ownership has desirable incentive fea-

---

[1] However, the failure of the former socialist economies reminds us that not all institutional changes succeed in improving the economic well-being of the community.

[2] Ronald Coase, 'The Nature of the Firm,' *Economica*, Vol. 4 (1937), pp. 386–405.

[3] J. E. Stiglitz, 'Incentives, Information, and Organizational Design,' *Empirica-Austrian Economic Papers*, Vol. 16, No. 1 (1989).

tures when it vests various rights of property in a single decision maker, administrative arrangements in the public sector and in some large-scale private firms segment ownership rights among stake holders. Often, in the public sector, an administrator allocates assets among uses, assigning benefits to beneficiaries, who 'own' the benefits, and assigning costs to other constituencies, possibly taxpayers, who are assigned the costs. An important element in the collapse of the centrally planned economies was the popular perception that processes of allocation in these systems were designed to assign benefits to a communist party elite and to impose costs on the remaining members of the community.

Thus, the public services that support market and administrative systems differ, so a society attempting to transform its economic institutions from central management to market will have to accomplish a transformation of governmental institutions as well. In the West, it took centuries for limited government and civil society to emerge, but the Japanese experience shows that major shifts in institutional structure can occur rapidly if changes in the external environment or in domestic trade-offs create incentives for rapid adjustment. Russia and the transforming socialist economies will have to accomplish just such rapid institutional changes in order to create the security and incentives for market-based economic growth.

The Potential for Growth in Early Industrialization

In the early nineteenth century, Japan and Russia faced a common challenge: how to apply the technologies and methods of a modernizing West to improve their own economic well-being. Both economies were traditional, feudal systems. In both, agricultural techniques were simple and labor productivity was low. In Japan, more than three-quarters and in Russia more than 90 per cent of the population were peasants. The Japanese peasantry paid a heavy annual tax that supported the samurai, a hereditary warrior class. The Russian peasantry, too, was obligated to pay heavy taxes and to supply additional labor services to the Russian lords.

Both countries lacked modern property rights in land that would allow purchase and sale of land or create incentives for investment. In Russia, moreover, the peasants shared strips in a joint field, a practice that discouraged innovation. In some Russian villages, the land was redistributed periodically in proportion to village manpower, a practice that discouraged any attempt to improve the fertility of a parcel of land.

However, there were important differences between Tokugawa Japan and Tsarist Russia in the administrative capacity of their governments and in the resulting levels of education and physical infrastructure of society. In Tokugawa Japan, some formal schooling was available to about half the male citizens; in Russia, less than 20 per cent of the new army recruits were literate a decade after emancipation. While Tokugawa Japan possessed functioning central and local governments that had preserved the peace for two centuries and a system of courts and administration that kept order, the creaky superstructure of Russian government presided over a feudal system that gave the lords complete judicial and police power over the peasantry. In Russia, there was no custom of the manor obligating the lord to provide village infrastructure. The lord's rights were not limited nor his duties defined.

The civil service of nineteenth-century Russia was still organized on principles that Peter I had adopted from Germany at the start of the eighteenth century. Positions in the civil service were classified into 14 grades, or ranks, which were the equivalents of the commissioned ranks in the army and navy. Even the church hierarchy was classified in this way. The ranks in the civil service bore titles with no relation to their duties. Each rank had its uniform and title of address. Thus, the top-ranking official of a provincial town had the rank of colonel, the commissioner of charities and the postmaster the rank of lieutenant colonel, the judge a rank of major, and the school superintendent the rank of captain. Notably, the highest ranking official was the *gorodnichy*, the chief of police, responsible for maintaining order.

All provincial officials were responsible to the central government in St Petersburg and acted as agents of the central government. The civil service was responsible for the delivery of public services to the provinces and for the collection of taxes from them. Originally, Peter the Great put in place a set of feudal institutions intended to provide the tax base for centralized economic development, but, in fact, these institutions themselves became the most important barriers impeding genuine modernization of agriculture and industry in the century that followed.

Nikolai Gogol's farce, *The Inspector General*, provides an apt portrayal of the information and incentive features of tsarist civil service. When the officials of a provincial town learn of the impending arrival of the government's inspector general, they set themselves to concealing the evidence of their corruption and slipshod administration. Mistaking an impecunious young noble for the feared inspector general, they ply him with gifts and with money in expectation of a favorable report to the center. Although fiction, Gogol's play mirrors a familiar reality of corrupt and incompetent government.

The Impetus to Growth

In the mid-nineteenth century, Japan and Russia alike underwent revolutionary changes with the Meiji Restoration in Japan and the emancipation of the serfs in Russia. In Japan, the new legal and social order created a basis for industrialization, whereas in Russia, the legal changes enacted in 1861 were implemented slowly. The peasant response to land redemption legislation resulted in a reverse flow of labor back to the rural villages. The legal institution of the Russian village, the *mir*, took over the tax-collecting function formerly belonging to the lords, continuing to restrict the rights of peasants to leave the village unless taxes were fully paid. The land redemption payments decreed by the crown were as heavy, or heavier, than earlier feudal obligations, so the amount of default on payments mounted by the year. Peasant unrest during this period bordered on spontaneous rebellion in the countryside, culminating in the Revolution of 1905. Only the Stolypin reforms of 1906 and 1910 allowed peasants to withdraw from communal institutions and claim a unitized plot of land.

At the turn of the twentieth century, the Russian government, like the Japanese government, was authoritarian. The tsar's signature was required on the charter of every joint-stock company and Russian industrialists often got their start in business through state orders, subsidies, or tariff protection. Corruption was common; bribery was a regular cost of doing business.[4]

On the other hand, both governments pursued policies that fostered investment and modernization. Both countries exported traditional agricultural products in order to generate revenues for the construction of railways, ports, and physical infrastructure. The Russian government appointed a succession of able finance ministers who maintained a stable ruble, financed development with government-guaranteed bonds, and provided the transport network for modern industries, building 81,000 kilometers of railroads.

Both countries imported modern equipment for such industries as cotton textiles, metallurgy, and machine building. While Japan was obligated by treaty to maintain open markets until 1911, Russia introduced protection once an industrial base was established. In the 1860s and 1870s, the Russian market was open to the world economy, with grain exports paying for the import of equipment. Then, in the 1890s Count Sergei Witte imposed tariffs to protect domestic metallurgy and machine-building, and industrial growth accelerated. High prices for industrial products allowed Russian industry to fund a large share of new investment from the profits of its industrial firms.

On the eve of World War I, both Japan and Russia had enjoyed 40 years of rapid growth, but their per capita standards of living were still well behind the industrializing West. The characteristics of Japan's labor force had improved together with economic well-being. In Russia, in contrast, over half of the growth of real output went to feed its expanding popu-

---

[4] Paul Gregory and Robert Stuart, *Soviet Economic Structure and Performance* (New York: Harper and Row, 1974), p. 29.

lation, while life expectancy and educational levels lagged well behind the rest of Europe and infant mortality rates were higher. In Japan, the physical and institutional infrastructure of modern industrial society was emerging, while, in Russia, government remained weak and ill prepared to supply the infrastructure of a modern, market-based economy.

Socialist Russia

In the twentieth century, Japanese growth continued, first in an environment that linked political and economic expansion and, then, within the postwar economic order of an integrated Western market. Russia, on the other hand, underwent the massive institutional upheavals that created the first communist power, the Soviet Union, and the unique bureaucratic institutions of Soviet socialism.

In *The Socialist System: The Political Economy of Communism*, Janos Kornai describes the socialist state as a bureaucratic power structure controlled by a Communist party and oriented toward the maintenance of political power. To Kornai, a key feature of both party and state is the disparity between the nominal rules of the game and real practice. Officially, says Kornai, the party is organized on the basis of democratic centralism. The party structure is a pyramid with the Central Committee at the top. Under the formal rules, all leading bodies and all party secretaries at every level are elected by the party membership, either directly or indirectly, and party resolutions can be passed only by elected bodies. This is the democratic side of democratic centralism. The other side is centralism: the decision of a higher body is binding on lower bodies, and ultimately on every member of the party. In real life, centralism prevails.[5]

Formally, the general secretary merely executes the decisions of the central leadership, but in practice, enormous power is concentrated in his hands. What ultimately emerges is a bureaucratic hierarchy that encompasses the whole of the party; instructions passed down from above must be carried out. The apparatus chooses those who will join the elected body at the next election and whom they will elect as general secretary.

Similarly, says Kornai, the reality of the socialist state contradicts its formal rules. Formally, the state has a legislature, a state administration, and a judiciary and the elected parliament nominates the government. But, in fact, the party and state are interwoven in a way that assures that the party is the dominant force. The party controls all major government appointments as well as all major decisions facing the government. There is a duplication of party apparatus and state apparatus throughout the bureaucracy, with the smaller party apparatus overseeing the functions of

---

[5] Janos Kornai, *The Socialist System: The Political Economy of Communism* (Princeton: Princeton University Press, 1992), especially Chapters 3 and 4.

the state apparatus. The government Council of Ministers controls the economy through centrally directed management of state-owned industry, agriculture, and social infrastructure. The bureaucracy, says Kornai, is united by commitment to a common ideology, by the resolve to retain power, by prestige and privileges, and by coercion. In the Stalin era, coercion meant forced collectivization of agriculture, the forcible uprooting and relocation of population groups, mass repression, and 'Stalinschina', the great terror.[6]

In the socialist system, government tax revenues are implicit rather than explicit. As the owner of land and capital, the government controls the profits of socialist enterprises. As the primary supplier of food products and consumer goods to the population, it collects implicit sales taxes on the difference between the price at which it acquires agricultural products from the rural sector and the higher price at which it sells food to the urban consumer.

In the Stalin era, the legacies of collectivization and the heavy tax burden on agriculture left the rural sector poverty-stricken and backward. For example, in *The Economic Challenge of Perestroika*, Abel Aganbegian writes:

I recall that when I married in 1953 and temporarily worked in a textile factory in a small town of Sobinka in Vladimir Region, I decided to call on my wife's relatives in the village of Zhokhovo in the same region. This village was situated 80 kilometers from the railway and there was absolutely no means of transport available to it. In actual fact there was no road in our understanding of the term either. There was a cart-track impassable in autumn and spring and covered with snow in the winter. I walked almost 20 km on foot. Zhokovo, which is situated 150 km from Moscow, did not at this time have electricity. The economy was predominantly based on exchange of goods in kind and on self-sufficient consumption, with the shop open only twice a week and in a neighboring village at that. In this shop, there was virtually nothing besides sugar and salt, so that in the village the people baked their own bread, drank their own milk and ate their own eggs.... For a 'day's work' (a unit of labour in the Kolkhoz) they received only several hundred grammes of rye or another grain.[7]

Although the regimes of Khrushchev and Brezhnev moderated the repressive features of Stalin's socialist government and brought greater security to the bureaucracy, the information and incentive features of the administrative system remained perverse. Low procurement prices for agricultural products and strict resource constraints on the production of consumer goods limited the output of consumer goods and enforced

[6] Sergo Mikoyan writes, ' "Stalinshchina" encompasses all that the system implied: brutal, cruel, and senseless mass terror; fear of repression; the almighty machine of the OGPU-NKVD-MVD-MGB; the blindness of millions who were deceived and naive.' Sergo Mikoyan, 'Stalinism as I Saw It,' Kennan Institute Occasional Paper, 1991, p. 1.

[7] Abel Aganbegian, *The Economic Challenge of Perestroika* (Bloomington: Indiana University Press, 1988), p. 51.

the transfer of resources to priority investment activities. However, in the retail market, government price controls created excess demand for most desirable products. Housing and other public services were allocated at nominal charge by industrial ministries and municipalities on the basis of administrative criteria. Individuals who did not have access to consumer services through official channels turned to the inevitable black markets. Sometimes, the privilege system became a bottomless purse for members of Russia's civil service, the *nomenklatura*, while it imposed heavy costs on other groups in the form of queuing, favor-seeking, and access activities.

With the merging of party, government, and economic apparatus, even the production sectors operated like government bureaucracies. In production sectors, too, the perception that the central government would confiscate any surpluses that it found and subsidize the weak led to pervasive adverse selection. Firms had incentives to conceal their true capacities. Low nominal prices for raw materials and energy created no demand-side incentives to conserve. Recognizing the incentive problems, the government established extensive networks for monitoring performance and imposed heavy sanctions on units that failed to meet central plans, but the central ministries themselves were often unable to deliver the requisite resources to support production. The successful factory manager became expert at influence activities to pry scarce resources out of the bureaucracy, illegal barter and purchases 'on the left' to acquire supplies informally from other firms, and payment in kind to favored employees. The government tolerated corruption and the shadow economy because, in the short run, they moved resources to higher valued activities. Without them, economic performance would have been still worse. Of course, individual bureaucrats profited from corruption.

Like the Japanese civil service, the top echelons of the branch departments in Russia's Council of Ministers were considered to be highly competent. In addition, their political credentials were considered sound. The managing elite of all Soviet hierarchies belonged to the *nomenklatura*, the list of people occupying positions requiring formal approval by the party cadres departments of the all-union central committee or the republic central committees.

In *Restructuring the Soviet Economic Bureaucracy*, Paul Gregory describes sectoral branch department officials as 'well-versed, young technocrats.'[8] He divides Soviet bureaucrats into three groups: *khoziaistvenniks* (persons who perform resource allocation and are held responsible for results), *apparatchiks* (persons who issue instructions and rules to the *khoziaistvenniks*), and *technocrats* (individuals who supply technical expertise to the other two groups).

[8] Paul Gregory, *Restructuring Soviet Economic Bureaucracy* (Cambridge: Cambridge University Press, 1990), p. 29.

Judith Thornton

Alternative Approaches to Economic Development

How should we evaluate this socialist era? At the end of World War II, Japan and Russia still shared a common economic goal to catch up with the West. Both countries had pushed saving and investment to unprecedented levels and both countries enjoyed high measured rates of economic growth and rising consumer standards of living. By 1990, the economic weight of Russia and Japan outranked that of all other countries save the United States. Russia's production accounted for more than 12 per cent of world GNP, Japan's for more than 10 per cent. And yet, as Gorbachev's *perestroika* finally allowed an informed comparison, it was clear that the Japanese experience was largely a success, the Russian experience largely a failure.

The Agenda of the Transforming Economies: Is the Japanese Experience Relevant?

Today, the primary task of the former planned economies is to build a new institutional framework with separate and complementary governmental and private institutions. But determining the relative roles of governmental and non-governmental decision makers in each area of economic policy has proved divisive. In some countries, notably in Russia and the Czech and Slovak Republics, there are difficult questions regarding the structure of various levels of government as well—the functions of the center, the regions, and localities, and, in Russia, the responsibilities of the executive, legislative, and judicial branches of government.

Many Russian policymakers turn to the Japanese model as a case in which rapid economic growth, technological dynamism, and democratic processes were consistent with a high level of state control. There are many features of the Japanese model that Russia is attempting to emulate—a large degree of state control over industrial structure and investment, explicit or implicit protection of certain sectors of the economy from foreign competition, close relationships between industrial and governmental officials, subsidization of priority sectors, and policies restricting the influence of foreign investors in the domestic arena. But there are dangers that a Russian version of the Japanese model would fail to yield the desirable dynamism that Japan enjoyed because of institutional legacies from Russia's socialist era. There are, further, dangers that Russian policymakers would turn to a distorted image of the Japanese model as an excuse to avoid dismantling state ownership and state direction, ignoring the strong role that markets play in the Japanese economy.

I will argue here that, while the origins of the Japanese civil service derive from ancient feudal traditions, the contemporary relationship between the civil service and civil society in Japan is, nevertheless, in the tradition of modern limited government. Administrative guidance not-withstanding, Japan has been building private ownership institutions and a government that was capable of supplying the infrastructure of a market economy since the middle of the nineteenth century. So, Russia cannot escape dismantling old governmental structures and erecting new limited ones, nor can it postpone the establishment of private property rights, even if its pattern is cut on the Japanese model.

It appears to me that Japan is not unique in pursuing strong govern-mental influence of industrial policy and protection of domestic pro-ducers. There are many other countries, advanced industrial nations and developing countries alike, that pursue such policies. Japan's experience is unusual in that these policies did not impede, and in some cases fostered its impressive record of economic growth.

What are the key problems that the socialist economies face in the coming five or ten years and what lessons does Japanese development hold for them? Building a healthy private economy requires both disman-tling impediments to civil society and building new social infrastructure. Redefining the sphere and role of the government requires dismantling structures whose role is ending, such as state production ministries and allocation agencies, while creating new administrative capacities to supply public goods and manage the economic policies of a market economy. These tasks include:

1. Privatizing—defining and legalizing private property rights;
2. Creating the legal, financial, and administrative infrastructure for a private market economy;
3. Liberalizing prices;
4. Managing industrial policies, including policies toward domestic and foreign firms and creating a framework for investment, inno-vation, and structural change;
5. Opening the economy to the world market;
6. Managing the macroeconomic environment, achieving fiscal balance, and managing monetary policies;
7. Coordinating central, regional, and local government activities;
8. Creating social, educational, and labor market infrastructure;
9. Creating the governmental capacity to administer a market economy including a capable and honest civil service;
10. Assuring limited government and civil society.

Looking briefly at the lessons for Russia from Japanese development, it seems to me important that Japan did supply the governmental infrastructure of a modern market economy. In the main, it did not substi-tute state ownership and management for private ownership and man-agement nor have private economic activities been immune from conventional market measures of investment performance.

An honest and efficient civil service was a necessary ingredient in

Japan's ability to accomplish its astonishing modernization. It follows that the difficulty Russia now faces in eliminating corruption and creating an effective civil service is one of the largest impediments to Russian reform.

Privatization and Creation of the Infrastructure of a Market Economy

The most important institutional change that Russia must accomplish is the legalization of private ownership of land and capital and the transfer of some substantial share of assets into private hands. Although there has been considerable progress in privatizing small-scale business and housing, the privatization of land and the establishment of institutions to document, record, and guarantee the exercise of land ownership and the right to transfer title are not yet in place.

In 1992 a reform-oriented government undertook the widespread privatization of housing and small-scale firms in consumer service sectors of the economy. In mid-1992, a majority of large firms was instructed to convert themselves into a joint-stock form of ownership. A presidential decree 'On Commercialization of State Enterprises with Simultaneous Transformation into Public Joint Stock Companies' published on July 1, 1992, established a set of procedures for conversion which allowed the employees of firms to choose among three different ownership structures providing workers, managers, outside stockholders, and the state with different percentages of the company's stock. Employees could pay for some or all of their purchases with vouchers issued under the simultaneous mass privatization program.

At the same time, the government undertook a mass privatization program through the distribution of 'privatization checks' or vouchers. During 1993 and the first half of 1994, voucher privatization transferred most small-scale firms and a majority of large-scale assets into private ownership. New private ventures in consumer sectors add an estimated 40 percent to officially-reported output.

In the rural sector, too, there is a growing population of private farmers and a growing group of former state farms that have adopted corporate forms of ownership, but changing forms do not always result in changed performance, and, in Russia, the full exercise of ownership in land is still in dispute.

Private Property Rights in Japan

If Russia were to turn to the Japanese experience with the creation of private property rights, then the basic lessons would come not from the twentieth century, but from the nineteenth century, for Japan has had clearly established private-ownership institutions, including private ownership of land, at least since the Meiji Restoration. It has long had the administrative capacity to define and enforce property rights as well as financial institutions that facilitated the creation of assets by mediating between suppliers of savings and investors. Moreover, in recent decades, Japan's conservative macroeconomic policy assured reasonable price stability, fostered long-term investment, and provided implicit insurance against some of the underlying sources of risk in financial markets. So the main thrust of Japan's experience would underscore the importance of private property rights, capital markets, and financial institutions in facilitating the process of saving and investing.

Markets and Macro-Economic Balance

Since January 1992 Russia has made considerable progress in reducing government interference in markets through price controls and rationing. Prices are liberalized in most markets except energy.

In its policy toward markets, the main thrust of the Japanese experience is, once again, to allow markets to function. There are, however, a few exceptions. The Japanese public sector does supply public housing to a minority of families—generally low-income families. Japanese trade policy does provide implicit and explicit protection to a variety of industries. The largest subsidy appears to go to the farm sector, raising the cost and diminishing the variety of the Japanese family diet. Still, Russia will find little support for a world of rationing in the Japanese example.

Russia has had less success in managing its macroeconomic policy. Many different factors underlie the emergence of hyperinflation. In the socialist era, government revenue was derived from the nominal profits of socialist enterprises, from the difference between the centrally set low prices at which the government bought agricultural produce and natural resources and the higher prices at which it sold them (called turnover taxes), and from the surplus generated by the difference between the value of exports and imports at nominal domestic prices.

With the dismantling of central administrative control over state assets and the emergence of a quasi-private sector, enterprise costs increased, reducing the government's revenue from profits and reducing the government's turnover tax. At the same time, the nominal costs of important government constituencies began to rise, increasing the size of subsidies drawn from the government budget and leading to a growing budget deficit. The weakening of central control put local and regional governments in the position to reduce their collection of taxes or to withhold the revenues from the center. As the rising government deficit was monetized, inflation created more and more excess demand at the government's price-controlled prices, while the new quasi-private sector created an alternative market in which products could be sold at true market-clearing prices. The breakup of the East European trading bloc and, later, the Soviet Union itself contributed to the precipitous fall in production.

In January 1992 Prime Minister Yegor Gaidar attempted to reduce government expenditure and to bring the budget into balance. However, the Russian central bank controverted the budget tightening with a flood of credit that saw the price level for industrial goods jump over twenty-fold. In that year, subsidies and directed credits exceeded 50 percent of GNP.

Today, the chief barrier to a reduction in government subsidies and credits in Russia is the fear of massive unemployment. As the demand for products from the military-industrial sector declines, production may virtually shut down in some medium-sized cities in the Urals and Siberia. Russia will have to undertake immense changes in industrial structure and relocate vast numbers of people. What institutions can provide the flexibility for such change?

Japanese Financial Regulation

Since 1970 the Ministry of Finance has played a crucial role, for this agency, with responsibility for macroeconomic stability, monitors the size of the fiscal deficit and enforces a hard budget constraint that, in effect, confronts the government with either-or choices. In this period, the Japanese government pursued an orthodox macroeconomic policy, a low and unchanging tax burden, and a fixed exchange rate between the yen and the dollar. Within this policy framework, the Japanese economy showed impressive vigor and flexibility in adjusting to two oil shocks, a rising value of the yen, and growing international trade barriers in some of the advanced industrial countries. These changes together with rising domestic labor costs and increased concerns about environmental costs were associated with a large and growing outflow of capital investment from Japan.

Historically, the Japanese government was a paternalistic regulator of its financial institutions, keeping banks and credit institutions tightly regulated but, also, keeping them safe from failure or even from competition. The government exercised tight control of both interest rates and the flow of credit, directing resources first to large, established firms in manufacturing. While Western observers viewed the tight regulation and the segmentation of financial markets as faults, Japan's financial sector facilitated a massive flow of savings into productive investment without experiencing the financial crises that have beset the majority of developing countries during the early development of their financial markets.

There are negative lessons for the transforming economies in the way in which property rights and financial markets interacted to direct investment in Japan as well. First, Japanese households, like Russian households, suffered from the priority given to production over consumption by government policy. Since Japanese property law left considerable uncertainty with regard to titles to the old housing stock and since government policy gave producers priority over consumers in access to finance, Japanese households had little access to the capital market for purchase of housing. At the start of the 1980s, the Japanese population viewed housing supply and housing location as their most serious social problems.

In the 1980s, a liberalization of financial markets began to allow investment to shift into housing, but as Japanese financial markets began to open up to competition, other problems emerged. Large companies began to turn to equity and bond markets for their financing, while banks began to expand their lending in the real estate market. But the combination of rapid economic growth, the government's low interest rates, and the market's perception that government policies provided protection against down-side risk generated a surge of new investment, an inflation of asset prices, and a capital market bubble.

The ultimate collapse of that bubble offers a second lesson to the transforming economies: the creation of modern capital markets and financial institutions requires a corresponding modernization of governmental institutions. The performance of financial markets may be improved by government supervision of financial institutions and by government provision of certain kinds of deposit insurance, but government intervention that shifts the distribution of risks and returns among decision makers may create adverse incentives as well.

Government financial regulation and supervision of banks can reduce some of the problems arising from imperfect information in financial markets. Banks may choose to ration credit to borrowers rather than raise interest rates if they believe that borrowers willing to pay higher interest will invest in riskier projects.[9] Bank managers may undertake excessively risky investments in the face of regulations that provide insurance against losses.

Moreover, the ability of borrowers and lenders to transact in capital markets will depend on the government's ability to maintain a stable macroeconomic policy. The lesson that Russia can learn from Japan's management of macroeconomic policy is that a balanced budget, a conservative monetary regime, and reasonable price stability are necessary components of a proinvestment policy in the market economy.

---

[9] Joseph E. Stiglitz and Adam Weiss develop this argument in, 'Credit Rationing in Markets with Imperfect Information,' *American Economic Review*, Vol. 71 (1981), pp. 393–409.

Japanese Management of Economic Balance and Change

Japan struggled with the contending pressures of macroeconomic balance and structural change immediately after the Second World War, opting for greater state control rather than greater institutional flexibility in initial attempts to manage structural change. Initially, adjustment was eased by the ability of more than half of the labor force to find employment in the agricultural sector. Still, in the period 1945 to 1949, Chalmers Johnson recounts that policy was dominated by 'two great debates and one overwhelming fact—the rise of the state as the central actor in the economy.'[10] Like Russia, Japan debated whether priority should be given to price stability or output expansion and whether future growth should focus on light industry and consumer goods or on heavy industry. In postwar Japan, too, inflation was fueled by government subsidies and war claims payments to favored industries and by the virtual collapse of production when stabilization was attempted.

Within 18 months, Japan was able to put in place budgetary and credit policies consistent with a satisfactory level of price stability—an impressive feat for an economy undergoing massive reorganization. The high degree of state control practiced in this period was conditioned on both the desire to secure macroeconomic balance through control of credit and control of foreign exchange and the desire to support the heavy industries that had produced for government demand until 1945. This latter concern was moderated when warfare erupted on the Korean peninsula in 1950 and the United States began to place extensive orders with Japanese firms for ammunition, trucks, uniforms, communications equipment, and other products.[11]

There are several lessons for Russia in the Japanese postwar adjustment. One is the hardship that a hard budget constraint imposes on an economy, but, also, the necessity of undertaking stabilization nevertheless. In the Japanese case, macroeconomic stabilization involved not only fiscal discipline and monetary control but also quantitative restrictions on foreign investment and trade. Since the capital flight from Russia is conditioned on uncertainty as to ownership as well as simple flight from a depreciating ruble, the Russian government's attempt to control export of energy and raw materials is easy to understand.

Like the Japanese government, the Russian government faces demands for assistance from its military-industrial complex. And like Japan, Russia wants to maintain tight domestic control over industry and resources. With its vast natural resources, Russia may well have long-run comparative advantage in metallurgy and a technically modernized machine-

[10] Chalmers Johnson, *MITI and the Japanese Miracle* (Stanford: Stanford University press, 1982), p. 175.
[11] Ibid., p. 201.

building sector. What kind of policies would allow existing producers in Magnitogorsk, Cheliabinsk, or Komsomolsk-na-Amur to compete on the world market? Will Russian industry, instead, have to rebuild on the basis of new, non-state entities? Can Russian management and engineering personnel gain the skills to operate competitively on the world market without direct foreign investment and active foreign participation in the Russian market? My own guess is that future Russian growth would benefit from a substantially larger participation of foreign investment and management than the Japanese government chose for Japan.

Japan is unique among the large industrial nations in the absence of a significant military establishment as a force in government policymaking. The consensus on maintaining Japan's modest military role makes it possible to focus government decision-making resources on domestic and international economic performance. Today, Russia, too, may be able to capture a peace dividend from reduction of its military burden, if it can manage regional and ethnic conflicts through negotiation.

Policies toward Industry and Trade

Russian industrial policy concerns, first, the extent of privatization of existing industry and assets; second, the way in which privatization and policy toward new firms will determine the degree of concentration of industry; and third, the role that foreign producers will have in domestic competition. The legacy of socialist production created a highly monopolized industrial structure. Further, the desire of the central planners to enforce central control of production links led to a highly uneconomic location pattern of enterprises supplying components for a single system. So the eventual emergence of either technically efficient patterns of specialization or genuine competition between firms is likely to take some time.

Russia's current trade policy is rooted in the government's need to enhance government revenue and regulate capital flight. At time of writing, the ruble is largely convertible at rapidly declining terms of exchange, but a considerable dollarization has taken place. Government regulations requiring exchange of hard currency for rubles can rarely be enforced. Export of energy products, minerals, and raw materials are licensed and subject to large export taxes and quotas, but these regulations are often evaded as well.

Japan's growth took place in an economy characterized by large, closely knit industrial groupings, *keiretsu*, and strong structural barriers to international trade. The Japanese *keiretsu* are analyzed in many recent Western studies. They are large, interlinked industrial groups, frequently centered around a major bank. They tend to be vertically integrated and involve stable cross-shareholding relationships between group members and with other institutions. Their close institutional links make it possible to insure a high degree of stable internal demand, to assure coordination of design, maintain secure supplies of critical inputs, and cross-subsidize product lines.[12] In Russia, too, large interlinked industrial-financial groups have emerged to circumvent inadequate legal and financial institutions. However, these informal relationships are a poor substitute for enforceable contracts.

The implicit protectionism of Japanese trade policy is a source of much discussion. A recent study by Robert Lawrence shows that the larger the share of industry output produced by firms that are *keiretsu* members, the smaller the import penetration.[13] Russian observers, too, interpret Japanese experience as a case of successful infant industry protection.

Assuming that Russia wishes to upgrade the technological level of its own industry as rapidly as possible, should it pursue a Japanese-style policy of promotion and protection or encourage foreign participation? In Eastern Europe, the technical and efficiency benefits of foreign involvement are already emerging, but in Russia, there seems to be a much stronger disposition to restrict foreign participation, quite possibly to the detriment of rapid recovery. This is the key political issue ahead.

Governmental Administrative Capacity and Impediments to Reform

The primary impediment to Russian economic reform is Russia's inability to put in place a government that can achieve a consensus on policy directions and implement policies. Mikhail Gorbachev's political innovations in the late 1980s were motivated by the perception that the bureaucratic system generated inefficiency and corruption and destroyed initiative. In an account in *Pravda*, he describes a walk he took in December 1984 with Eduard Shevardnadze along the beach at Pitsunda, in Georgia. The two men began to reminisce about their experiences as chief administrators of their home regions, Stavropol and the Republic of Georgia. Shevardnadze confessed that 'it had all gone rotten,' and Gorbachev agreed. They concluded, in Gorbachev's words, 'that it was impossible to live that way.'[14]

As the reforming government tried to reduce central management,

[12] Laura D'Andrea Tyson, *Who's Bashing Whom? Trade Conflict in High-Technology Industries* (Washington: Institute for International Economics, 1992), p. 56.

[13] Ibid., p. 56.

[14] This incident is recounted in Marshall Goldman, *What Went Wrong with Perestroika* (New York: Norton, 1991), p. 83.

bureaucrats in different government hierarchies found themselves in vastly different situations. Some saw their incomes and savings dwindle to nothing under the pressure of inflation. Others, who exercised control over powerful production ministries found themselves in a position to lay claim to streams of income and assets formerly belonging to the state.

Today, Russia's government is headed by its first elected president; the two branches of its parliament are genuine law-making bodies. A new constitution, enacted in December, 1993, has done much to contain the rivalry between the executive and legislative branches, although it has not eliminated wide divisions among interest groups.

The collapse of the former Soviet Union saw the demise of a portion of the apparatus of the former centralized ministries—that portion that was not taken over by the Russian government itself. The power base of the Russian parliament is less Moscow-centered than the Soviet parliament had been; it reflects the concerns of Russia's large industries and of the military-industrial complex.

The breakdown of the Union government was associated with a breakdown in the pass-through of tax revenues from the regions and territories to the central government and a breakdown, as well, in the return flow of investment financing and interregional subsidization. This shift means that territorial governments (*oblasti*) and municipalities are retaining a substantially larger share of taxes on former state enterprises in their regions, but they bear the major responsibility for regional social and welfare programs as well. Further, as former state firms privatize, the firms are shedding responsibility for the infrastructure of housing and municipal services that they managed earlier. While in the past, these services were provided on a subsidized basis by industrial ministries, today they will have to be paid for by local governments or by user fees.

At the same time, the central government retains the obligation to support a declining but still large military establishment, educational and research and development infrastructures, the unemployed, and other important constituencies from a declining revenue base. Today, the claimants for government resources vastly exceed the center's shrinking revenue base. The polycentric pressures from regional interests and the competition for control of wealth and political power that sundered the Soviet Union now pose constraints on the Russian government as well.

The President and the Parliament

In the Russian Federation, the December, 1993 Constitution concentrated authority in the hands of President Boris Yeltsin, reducing the level of conflict between the executive and legislative branches of government.

However, within both branches there was strong policy disagreement between export-oriented interests that favored an economy open to foreign trade and investment and other groups that favored an inward-oriented, nationalist development strategy. In addition, political competition to gain control rights and rights to income from Russia's vast wealth underlay many ideological arguments that divided the legislature and slowed reform. Competition for ownership of assets emerged at all levels in the privatization process.

The responsibility for privatization was shared between the executive and legislative branches under separate dual chains of authority.[15] At the top of the executive branch is the Russian Federation government with authority over the State Committee for Privatization, Goskomimushchestvo. The territorial administration is subordinate to the Russian government and controls the territorial Property Directorate with representative offices in counties and municipalities. The executive branch also supervises administrations with responsibility for managing state resources, such as the Committee on Geology and Use of Minerals.

At the top of the legislative branch is the Russian Federation Parliament which exercises authority over the Federal Property Fund. A Small Soviet, or inner parliament, in each territory supervises a territorial Property Fund with representative offices in counties and municipalities. At present, the executive-branch organization supervises the procedures for auctioning off small firms or commercializing a large firm, but the legislative-branch Property Fund carries out privatization and exercises the state's ownership rights in the company.

In the case of government exercise of ownership rights to natural resources, law and practice diverge. Under the Russian Federation Treaty, the exercise of ownership rights to resources is shared between the Russian Federation and the autonomous republics and territories. The Law on Subsoil Resources assigns control rights to the Federal Government but divides income between center region, and locality.

However, as the government and the legislature have established overlapping jurisdictions and have competed for authority over the course of economic policy, decentralized institutions have grown accustomed to disobeying the directives of one or the other competing agency and to ignoring decrees with which they do not wish to comply. With a weak and fragmented government and deficient institutional infrastructure for the exercise of private property rights, informal business groups have emerged to coordinate economic activity. Some of these groups—termed "Mafiya" by the Russian press—share similarities with the samurai of Tokugawa Japan.

---

[15] Fond Imushchestva Khabarovskogo kraia, Komitet po upravleniiu gosudarstvennym imushchestvom Khabarovskogo kraia, *Biulleten' Khabarovsk*, 1992, No. 1.

The Center and the Regions

Reform of the overcentralized Soviet system necessarily implies decentralization, but the current *de facto* balance of power between the center and the regions reflects less deliberate design than unintended collapse of central administrative functions and fiscal support. In the vacuum, local governmental, industrial, and agricultural authorities have banded together to keep local economic systems functioning. In the process, local elites have been able to acquire *de facto* control over many local assets and resources, so many of them have an interest in the continuing weakness of central government. One consequence of decentralization of political authority is that the pace of economic reform and the mechanisms of governance will show large variation from region to region.

In much of Russian Asia, Moscow's practice of centralizing income from natural resources and enforcing autarkic trade patterns stunted regional development. So many regions of Russian Asia are now pressing for the right to pursue autonomous Pacific-oriented development on the basis of local resources in spite of the fact that current laws assign ownership of natural resources to the center.

The treaty that delimits powers between the Russian Federation and the republics is the Russian Federation Treaty, initialed on March 13, 1992, by all the republics of the Russian Federation except Tatarstan and the Chechen-Ingushetia and released by the Presidium of the Russian Supreme Soviet.[16] This treaty assigns many of the powers over land and natural resources to the joint jurisdiction of federal and republic authorities.

In the treaty, the Russian Federation is given exclusive jurisdiction over the federal energy system, territorial waters, and the continental shelf. Utilization of natural resources and protection of the environment are subject to joint jurisdiction as is protection of original areas of habitation and traditional ways of life of small ethnic communities. Article III says, 'Questions of the possession, use and disposal of land, its mineral, water, and other natural resources, are settled on the basis of the legislation of the Russian Federation and the legislation of the republics in the Russian Federation. The status of federal natural resources is defined by mutual accord between the federal bodies of the Russian Federation and the bodies of state power of the republics.' This article gives the republics

---

[16] Signatories were the Russian Federation, the Soviet Socialist Republic of Adygeya, the Republic of Bashkortostan, the Buryat Soviet Socialist Republic, the Republic of Gornyy Altay, the Republic of Dagestan, the Kabardin-Balkar Republic, the Republic of Kalmykia-Khalmg Tangch, the Republic of Karachay-Cherkessia, the Republic of Karelia, the Komi Soviet Socialist Republic, the Republic of Mari El, the Mordova Soviet Socialist Republic, the North Osetian Soviet Socialist Republic, the Republic of Sakha (Yakutia), the Republic of Tuva, the Udmurt Republic, the Republic of Khakassia, and the Chuvash Republic.

complete state power on their territory, other than those powers under the jurisdiction of the federal bodies.

Today, both Russian and Japanese political institutions are in flux—in each case, in the direction of a more broadly based democracy. In both countries, the political area is the setting for hotly-debated policy choices between an internationalist and a nationalist strategy of development. However, the similarity in policy choices is not matched by similar institutional capabilities.

The Japanese Civil Service

There could hardly be a stronger contrast between the present chaos and corruption in the Russian government and the stability of role and personnel in the Japanese civil service. The Japanese bureaucracy is small by world standards and elite. It recruits broadly through the country's best universities, with (male) University of Tokyo graduates represented disproportionately at the top. Entrance and promotion are based on examination; 'victory after a trial by educational fire' is the phrase used by Pempel and Muramatsu in this volume. The economist would refer to this recruitment process as 'signaling.' Education in Japan provides a way in which high-ability workers can signal their desirability for the civil service, for, whether the material they learn at the university renders them more productive in future employment or not, the successful candidates demonstrate their willingness and ability to make heroic efforts at arduous tasks under intense pressure and to succeed at these tasks.[17]

Sometimes the match between recruitment and educational background predisposes Japanese civil servants to adopt a regulatory path. For example, Japan's Ministry of Finance recruits almost exclusively from the University of Tokyo's law school, while the US Treasury Department recruits specialists in public finance, international finance, and international economics.[18]

Winners of the educational contest enter a government agency until retirement in their fifties, receiving many opportunities for training and a broad range of experience during the course of their careers. Promotions and opportunities are seen as rewards for superior performance and dedication. So, the arrangements create incentives for the organization and the individual alike to invest in the individual's acquisition of expertise that is specific to his organization.

[17] Two classic models of job market signaling are A. Michael Spence's *Market Signaling* (Cambridge, Mass.: Harvard University Press, 1974) and M. Rothschild and J. Stiglitz, 'Equilibrium in Competitive Insurance Markets: An Essay on the Economics of Imperfect Information,' *Quarterly Journal of Economics*, Vol. 80 (Dec. 1966), pp. 629–49.

[18] Note the appointments of theorists Lawrence Summers at Treasury and Joseph Stiglitz on the Council of Economic Advisers in the current US government.

A major consequence of this system is to link individual career fortunes to hard work, approval of superiors, competition with one another, and a long-standing dedication to one's agency. All of this is conducive to the overall efficiency of each agency and in turn to the civil service as a whole.[19]

The Civil Service and Constituencies

With early retirement the rule, junior members of the bureaucracy can expect to exercise authority after a moderately long apprenticeship. After retirement, ex-bureaucrats find employment in business, in public corporations, in local government, and in the parliament.

In this volume, Takenori Inoki provides a close look at one variant of *amakudari*, the movement of retired officials of the central government to jobs in public corporations. He shows that *amakudari* not only maintains and reinforces the connection between the governmental and non-governmental sectors, but it also vitalizes the bureaucracy. His analysis is consistent with recent models of the Western corporation that argue (1) that a deferred reward may be a successful strategy to elicit effort during years of employment, and (2) a deferred reward also could provide implicit payoff to the bureaucrat who went along with political allocation of economic rents or other informal arrangements. (Since the Japanese bureaucracy might be assumed to pursue policies that create rents for important constituents, then an obligation on the constituent to employ old bureaucrats might be viewed as a deduction against the rents.)

Some of the officials retiring from the central government are sent down to local government. Japan's government is a unitary system in which local government is officially subordinate to central government, but in which considerable local autonomy and local initiative is preserved. In 'Institutionalizing the Local System: The Ministry of Home Affairs and Intergovernmental Relations in Japan,' Kengo Akizuki describes a complex network of relationships between regional and central executive, legislative, and fiscal authorities that appears to provide an effective and flexible system for supplying public infrastructure and services in the localities where they are consumed. The interests of consumers appear to be expressed more effectively at the localities than at the center, as well.

Where expenditures can be implemented more effectively at the region than in the center, the government is able to enforce reasonable criteria of efficiency on the allocation of central tax revenues to the localities. In the competition for central revenues, the process appears to generate a flow of relevant information from the localities and to minimize wasteful influence activities—both problems in the relationship between the center and

---

[19] Michio Muramatsu and T. J. Pempel, 'The Japanese Bureaucracy and Economic Development: The Structuring of a Proactive Civil Service,' at note 71.

the regions in Russia. The compact physical space of Japan and the tradition of consultation appear to provide a desirable form of monitoring in fiscal relations between the center and the regions.

In 'Japan's Postwar Civil Service: The Legal Framework,' John Haley concludes that the relative autonomy of Japan's ministries from routine political control ensures that a corps of professional civil servants is in charge of implementation of policy. He adds, 'The mechanisms of judicial redress provide an effective means for public scrutiny that, coupled with the potential of public disapproval and ultimate political accountability, promotes responsible public administration by threatening the principal prerogatives Japanese bureaucracies seek to protect: their authority and autonomy. The end result is an interdependence of discretion and accountability that underlies the balance of coherent and responsive policymaking in Japan.'

Russian Perceptions of the Japanese Experience

In Russia's current policy debates, many participants argue that Russia should pattern its institutions on Japanese institutions. But Russians, like others, observe Japan through their own prism. While Japanese development was accomplished in a framework involving both substantially more state control and more cartelization than in the US case, there is a danger that Russian policymakers will act on a biased picture. What do Russian observers think they see in the Japanese experience? They are attracted by those features of Japanese development that seem closest to their own experience with administrative management.

They cite Japanese success with public and quasipublic production as evidence that Russia can achieve efficient operation and technical modernization without privatizing. They interpret the Japanese government's close relationship with business as evidence for continued ministerial regulation of Russian industry in Moscow. They cite the industrial groupings in Japan as evidence that Soviet industrial monopolies should be left intact. They cite Japanese regulation of foreign trade in support of Russian protectionism and cite past Japanese restrictions on foreign investment as evidence favoring Russian restrictions on capital flows and Russian policies prohibiting foreign ownership of assets or enterprises. The proproducer orientation of Japanese policy is cited in support of continued Russian subsidy of state enterprises in heavy industrial sectors. So there is a danger that the Japanese example will be used as a case against reform.

Conclusions

Many policymakers, Western and Russian alike, turn to the Japanese model as a case in which rapid economic growth, technological dynamism, and democratic processes were consistent with a high level of state control. In many respects, the problems that Japan faced at the end of World War II and the strategies it adopted have their parallels in Russia's current plight. There are many features of the Japanese model that Russia is attempting to emulate: a large degree of state control over industrial structure and investment, explicit or implicit protection of certain sectors of the economy, subsidization of priority sectors including former military suppliers, and policies restricting the influence of foreign investors in the domestic arena. But there are dangers that a Russian version of the Japanese model would fail to yield the desirable dynamism that Japan enjoyed because Russian society still lacks the infrastructure of a market economy and the administrative capacity to play a prodevelopment, rather than a rent-dissipating, role. There are, further, dangers that Russian policymakers would turn to a distorted image of the Japanese model as an excuse to avoid dismantling state ownership and state direction, ignoring the strong role that markets play in the Japanese economy. And so, in my view, Russia will be better served if its policymakers look at where Japan is heading and not where it has been.

17

The Japanese Civil Service and Economic Development in Comparative Perspective

PETER A. HALL

As a result of the extraordinary success of the Japanese economy especially in the years after 1945, there is growing interest in the institutional conditions that have underpinned its development. This volume explores one dimension of those conditions, namely the character and behavior of the Japanese civil service. The purpose of this chapter is to provide an overview of the findings reported here from the perspective of one who specializes in the economic and political development of other nations.

My object is to draw the general from the particular with several questions in mind. What lessons might the Japanese civil service hold for other nations seeking rapid economic development? What features of its development and operation correspond to those of other nations? Where there are obvious points of divergence, what can we learn from them about the preconditions for economic success? The articles in this volume go a long way toward demystifying the operation of the Japanese civil service and they provide fruitful terrain for those who contemplate the role of the civil service in economic development more generally.

Beyond a Conventional Dichotomy

The most striking feature of the Japanese case, as presented in these essays, is the challenge it poses to the conventional way we think about economic management. In general, most discussions of economic management are dominated by a dichotomy that is variously described as that between 'politics' and 'markets,' between the operation of the 'public

This paper was prepared while the author was a Fellow at the Center for Advanced Study in the Behavioral Sciences with financial support provided to the Center by the National Science Foundation (SES-9022192). For critical comments on earlier versions of this essay, I am grateful to the participants in this project, as well as to T. J. Pempel, Harvey Rishikof, Rosemary Taylor, Martha Walsh, and especially Margarita Estevez.

sector' and the 'private sector,' or between management by 'markets' and management by 'hierarchies.'[1] The general assumptions behind such dichotomies are, first, that most activities in a given economy can be classified according to whether they are managed by the public authorities or by the private sector and, second, that very different principles govern decision making about the allocation of resources in the two spheres.

Around this distinction, various literatures have grown up. Many economists, for instance, have attempted to find criteria that will establish whether a particular kind of economic endeavor is likely to operate more efficiently if managed by the public or private sector.[2] Political scientists also commonly compare the decision making of public agencies to the allocation processes of markets, as if the two normally follow radically different operating principles.[3]

What the Japanese case reminds us, however, is that these are artificial dichotomies, useful for some analytical purposes, but far from exhaustive of real-world situations. In the Japanese case, we find something that goes beyond management by the public sector or management by the private sector. We find many spheres of economic activity that have been managed, more or less jointly, by public and private sector actors together.

The papers collected in this volume and the literature on Japanese economic development more generally supply many examples of instances in which public officials and firms collaborated in making the key decisions that would guide development in a given sector. These have included a wide range of decisions stretching from matters pertaining to where to concentrate long-term investment to those bearing on the most appropriate technologies to pursue, and a host of other matters.[4] Not all of

---

[1] Highly influential works include: Charles Lindblom, *Politics and Markets: The World's Political Economic Systems* (New York: Basic Books, 1977) and Oliver Williamson, *Markets and Hierarchies: Analysis and Antitrust Implications* (New York: Free Press, 1975). It should be noted that, while such a dichotomy is present in many discussions, its precise meaning often varies. Williamson, for instance, distinguishes between markets and hierarchies which are both in the private sector. However, market processes are often associated with allocation mechanisms in the private sector and distinguished from the mechanisms whereby public bodies allocated goods.

[2] For relevant reviews of the literature, see: Robert P. Inman, 'Markets, Governments, and the 'New' Political Economy,' in A. J. Auerbach and M. Feldstein, eds., *Handbook of Public Economics*, vol. 2 (Amsterdam: Elsevier, 1987), pp. 647–777, and H. Van den Doel, *Democracy and Welfare Economics* (New York: Cambridge University Press, 1979).

[3] For examples see Lindblom, *Politics and Markets*, and Gordon Tullock, *Private Wants, Public Means* (New York: Basic, 1970).

[4] In addition to the essays in this volume see: Gary D. Allinson, ed., *Japan's Negotiated Polity* (Ithaca: Cornell University Press, 1993); Richard Samuels, *The Business of the Japanese State: Energy Markets in Comparative and Historical Perspective* (Ithaca: Cornell University Press, 1987); T. J. Pempel, *Policy and Politics in Japan: Creative Conservatism* (Philadelphia: Temple University Press, 1982); Chalmers Johnson, *MITI and the Japanese Miracle: The Growth of Industrial Policy, 1925–75* (Stanford: Stanford University Press, 1982); Daniel Okimoto,

these decisions were good ones, but the crucial point is that the Japanese model of development has been based on close collaboration between public officials and private sector firms.

Several important implications follow from this observation. To begin with, it suggests that it is possible to have fruitful modes of state intervention. We need not see the participation of the state in economic development as something that is always inimical to private sector development.[5]

Second, the Japanese case suggests that we should not construe the relevant development problem entirely as one of trying to divide industrial endeavors or spheres of economic activity into those best managed by the private sector and those which are most amenable to public management. In many cases, it may be desirable for both the public and private sectors to be involved in a particular industry or endeavor. The real problem is one of finding means to improve the ways in which public and private officials can collaborate. It is the success of this collaboration that most distinguishes the Japanese case.

Third, the relationship between the public and private sector in Japan opens up ways of understanding how public and private actors might both be involved in a particular sphere of the economy that goes beyond the conventional arrangement whereby public authorities set the rules and private actors allocate resources within them. What we often see in Japan is more intense involvement and consultation between the two sides on all aspects of the relevant endeavors. Public officials there do far more than establish rules and regulations within which private actors are expected to work.

With this in mind, let us delve more deeply into the factors that permitted this kind of collaboration and defined the role and behavior of the Japanese civil service in particular.

The Character of the Civil Service

The relative success of Japanese economic policy and, in more general terms, of its style of government intervention seems related, in significant measure, to the character of the Japanese civil service itself. As Muramatsu and Pempel point out in their introduction to this volume, there are at least two ways in which a civil service can impede economic

Between MITI and the Market: Japanese Industrial Policy for High Technology (Stanford: Stanford University Press, 1989); Chalmers Johnson, Laura D'Andrea Tyson, and John Zysman, eds., *Politics and Productivity: The Real Story of Why Japan Works* (Cambridge, Mass.: Ballinger, 1989); and Frank Upham, 'Privatizing Regulation: The Implementation of the Large Scale Retail Stores Law in Contemporary Japan' (forthcoming).

[5] For another perspective on this point, see the essay by Kozo Yamamura in this volume.

growth. It can become so large as to sap resources that could otherwise be employed more efficiently elsewhere and it can become venal, namely, used for individual enrichment or partisan political patronage to such a degree that it fails to function as an effective instrument for public policy.

Several structural features of the Japanese civil service work against such deleterious tendencies. Two factors have helped to keep the Japanese bureaucracy relatively small. One is a set of legal limits on the size of the bureaucracy; the second is the presence of a powerful budget agency, with ultimate responsibility for public spending, that is relatively independent of particularistic political forces and of the agencies that it superintends.[6] As we all know, neither of these structural features absolutely guarantees the outcome. In the absence of a more general social consensus about the desirability of having a small and efficient bureaucracy, such structural barriers are often overridden. However, legal provisions of this sort can themselves underpin and contribute to the maintenance of such a consensus.

More important still is the general structure of the civil service itself. Four of its characteristics deserve special mention. First, recruitment is meritocratic and relatively independent of political considerations. Second, the general levels of status and remuneration accorded civil servants, especially in the senior grades, are relatively high. Third, promotion takes place from within a lifetime career structure and again, until the highest levels are reached, is relatively independent from politics. Fourth, and perhaps most crucially, the competition for advancement within the civil service is relatively intense.

It should be noted that many of these conditions are mutually supportive. Effective meritocracy in recruitment and reasonable remuneration tend to enhance the competition for entry and advancement, which in turn raises the status of the positions and the chances of securing high-quality candidates. In some cases, norms or procedures specific to Japan enhance the operation of the system. The *amakudari* system that Inoki discusses, for instance, enhances the income stream that individuals can expect after retirement if they achieve success in the civil service. Similarly, an informal norm prescribing that others in the same cohort should retire when one of their number assumes the top post in a ministry enhances the competitiveness that is often otherwise masked behind the deference paid to seniority in the Japanese system.[7] However, in most respects, the basic structural features of the Japanese system could be replicated elsewhere.

[6] See especially the essays by Muramatsu and Pempel and by Ito in this volume.
[7] See the essay by Takenori Inoki in this volume; Ezra Vogel, *Japan as Number One* (Cambridge, Mass.: Harvard University Press, 1979), p. 57 *et passim*; and, more generally, Susan Pharr, *Losing Face: Status Politics in Japan* (Berkeley: University of California Press, 1990).

What those features ensure is that the government will be supplied with a body of civil servants who are highly talented and hardworking—two features from which many other good results can follow. By and large, the structure of the civil service also tends to incline Japanese officials against corruption, either for personal gain or in the service of partisan politics. To reach the top, an official clearly needs some sensitivity to the factions in the Liberal Democratic Party (LDP) that dominates the Diet, but that alone will not suffice for advancement and, as Haley observes, strong legal provisions holding civil servants liable for malfeasance reinforce the norms of the system.[8]

Structural features of this sort clearly affect the operation of a civil service in important ways. And, in structural terms, the Japanese civil service is far from unique. Its general form resembles that found in many other nations with relatively meritocratic and non-political bureaucracies. However, there are several further dimensions along which civil services may vary in addition to these *structural* dimensions. In particular, we should also consider the *orientation* and *instruments* of the civil service. Civil servants may well be independent and uncorrupt but what they will do—in this case with regard to economic development—will also depend on what they think their mission is and on what instruments they have at their disposal to carry out that mission. I will take up the most general aspects of the orientation of the Japanese civil service here and then discuss those aspects of its orientation and instruments that bear directly in government–business relations in the next section.

In common with some of their counterparts elsewhere, Japanese civil servants seem especially inclined to believe that they are the guardians of the 'public interest.'[9] They see it as their duty to advance the cause of the nation as a whole rather than simply to serve the government or a special constituency. Although rather formalistic, this commitment is not of entirely negligible importance. It is a feature often found among civil services that are independent from politics, which helps to strengthen them against the demands of highly particularistic interests.

What is of capital importance, however, is how such officials come to define the public interest. Here, it is important to recognize that, especially in the decades during and after the Second World War, Japanese civil servants, in common with the governments of the day, developed a broad

[8] See the essay by John Haley in this volume.
[9] On this point compare the description of Japanese civil servants given in George C. Lodge and Ezra Vogel, *Ideology and National Competitiveness: An Analysis of Nine Countries* (Boston: Harvard Business School Press, 1987) and Ronald Dore, *Taking Japan Seriously: A Confucian Perspective on Leading Economic Issues* (Stanford: Stanford University Press, 1987) with that provided for French civil servants by Ezra Suleiman in *Elites in French Society: The Politics of Survival* (Princeton: Princeton University Press, 1974) and *Politics, Power and Bureaucracy in France* (Princeton: Princeton University Press, 1974).

orientation to a particular economic strategy.[10] This strategy placed a high value, first, on export-oriented economic growth and, second, on sacrificing consumption or leisure in favor of the investment and effort that would secure high rates of growth. Many other members of Japanese society shared this orientation. Civil servants were far from unique. But one cannot understand their actions in this era, and to some extent today, without recognizing the importance of this basic orientation.

The point becomes clear if we consider the British comparison. In structural terms, the British civil service closely resembles the postwar Japanese civil service. Both contained a large number of highly skilled and diligent officials. However, the orientation of the British civil service was entirely different, reflecting a divergence in the orientations of the two societies. By and large, well into the 1960s, the British still saw their nation as an imperial power entitled to a prominent place in the world and in need of no drastic economic reorganization. It was two decades after the Second World War before significant numbers of civil servants and politicians began to realize that Britain was falling behind its international economic competitors.[11]

As a result, although the structure of the two civil services was similar, British officials adopted a relatively 'hands-off' policy toward industry while the Japanese became deeply involved in industrial rationalization. It is often said that, in this era, the British lived in a small, open economy which they treated as if it were a large, closed economy. In these terms, Japanese officials presided over a large, closed economy but behaved as if it were a small, open economy. Today, few would dispute that superior results followed from the Japanese orientation. The general orientation of a civil service seems to matter as much as its structure to the policies that are produced.

The Relationship to Business

In the years after the Second World War, in particular, the Japanese civil service developed a relationship to business that was quite special; and it was in constructing this relationship that the structure, orientation, and instruments of the civil service all came into play and combined to produce an effect that is highly distinctive. In addition to the more general

---

[10] On the link to wartime developments, see Kent Calder, 'Linking Welfare and the Development State,' *Journal of Japanese Studies*, Vol. 16, No. 1 (Winter 1990).

[11] See Stephen Blank, 'Britain: The Politics of Foreign Economic Policy, the Domestic Economy and the Problem of Pluralistic Stagnation,' in Peter Katzenstein, ed., *Between Power and Plenty: Foreign Economic Policies of Advanced Industrial States* (Madison: University of Wisconsin Press, 1978), pp. 89–138; Andrew Shonfield, *British Economic Policy since the War* (Harmondsworth: Penguin, 1958); and Corelli Barnett, *The Audit of War* (London: Macmillan, 1986).

features and orientation described above, several other factors went into the definition of this relationship.

One such factor is what Haley describes so well as 'broad mandates with limited powers of enforcement.'[12] Many people in Britain or the United States would be shocked to read the statutory mandates given to Japanese ministries. In the economic sphere, in particular, ministries are given extremely broad responsibilities for the performance of the private sector. They are asked to ensure adequate levels of growth, efficient allocation of resources, and the like. In short, instead of circumscribing the spheres of action of officials in terms that leave large segments of the operation of the private sector beyond their purview, as would be more common in the Anglo-American tradition, civil servants are given responsibility for the success of many of the tasks that businessmen will have to execute. These responsibilities seem to have been renewed over time in a succession of legislative measures. They clearly affected the orientation of civil servants and dictated much of what they tried to do.

At the same time, however, when it comes to enforcement, the statutes generally accord Japanese civil servants formal powers that are very limited. Otherwise, we might have expected to see something closer to a command economy in Japan. This combination of broad mandates with limited powers of enforcement had a singular result: it forced Japanese civil servants to form a close partnership with business. Since the civil servants were responsible for securing economic development but had to persuade businessmen to undertake the necessary actions, Japanese officials developed very close relations with the business community. Many economic problems were managed jointly by the two sides.

One of the advantages of such a system was that it invariably brought multiple points of view to bear on any particular economic problem. Ministry officials could make their views known but ultimately they had to listen as well to the views of the businessmen active in this sphere. The strategies that would emerge often seem to have been devised jointly by the two sides via what Samuels calls 'reciprocal consent.'[13] In this case as in many others, the requirement that multiple points of view be given a hearing seems to have had a salutary effect on policy. We see something similar in the extent to which Japanese policymaking often involves interagency collaboration.[14]

---

[12] See his essay in this volume and John O. Haley, *Authority Without Power: Law and the Japanese Paradox* (New York: Oxford University Press, 1991) as well as Frank Upham, *Law and Social Change in Postwar Japan* (Cambridge, Mass.: Harvard University Press, 1987), esp. Chap. 5.

[13] Samuels, *The Business of the Japanese State*.

[14] This is to say that several Japanese agencies or ministries are often involved in the formulation of a single policy, not that some competition does not occur between these agencies. See the essays in this volume by Masaru Mabuchi and by Muramatsu and Pempel as well as Allinson, *Japan's Negotiated Policy*.

Another key feature of this system was the attitude that Japanese civil servants seem to have taken to the relationship between economic policy and market criteria. In particular, it seems that, in numerous cases, officials saw the actions of the state, not as a replacement for market mechanisms, but as a supplement to their operation.[15] That is to say, the general conception behind many Japanese industrial policies was not that they should supersede the market but that they should supplement it in such a way as ultimately to enhance market discipline. In short, the literature suggests that Japanese bureaucrats made extensive use of 'market signals' and tried to build policy around them.[16] This approach is reflected in the degree to which Japanese policy countenanced or encouraged competition in both the domestic market and export markets. Many commentators have remarked on the high levels of competition that many Japanese firms face at home and on the contribution this makes to their global strength.[17]

This aspect of the Japanese case suggests that it is possible to have a system of state intervention in the economy without forgoing market criteria and the useful signals the market can provide. The point is an important one because it belies the old view that government intervention must be inimical to market competition and because it distinguishes the Japanese case from that of many other nations, whose officials clung to the notion that the criteria whereby governments allocate resources should be very different from market criteria. They did not see, as the Japanese did, that the government could use market criteria to good effect in decision making about the allocation of its own resources.

The French case is instructive here. Although French officials worked closely with businessmen in the years after the Second World War, their general approach was to second-guess the market and to reinforce a few firms that they favored against the market. In the 1950s and early 1960s, when the primary task facing the French economy was to build industrial capacity, this strategy worked reasonably well. Once membership in the European Community began to open up the French market to foreign competition, however, the planners faced a serious dilemma. They had been reasonably good at pouring concrete and building steel mills but they did not prove very good at generating firms that would be competitive on international markets. Only in the 1970s did they fully realize how

---

[15] On this point, see especially Johnson, *MITI and the Japanese Miracle* and Samuels, *The Business of the Japanese State*.

[16] Yutaka Kosai, 'Competition and Competition Policy in Japan: Foreign Pressures and Domestic Institutions,' a paper presented at the conference on 'Domestic Institutions, Trade and the Pressures for National Convergence,' Bellagio, February 23–6, 1993, and Ira Magaziner and Thomas Hout, *Japanese Industrial Policy* (Berkeley: University of California Press, 1981).

[17] One notable example is Michael Porter, *The Competitive Advantage of Nations* (New York: Free Press, 1990).

useful market signals could be for the allocation of resources and move to a system in which firms competed for public aid. By then, however, it was largely too late, as recession and the pressures it generated from declining sectors overwhelmed the resources available to the state.[18] The Japanese learned how to use market signals and competition among candidates for public aid much earlier.

What Japanese business faced, then, was a set of public officials vitally interested in the economic performance of their sectors and prepared to give aid to their firms but generally only if the results were successful in competitive markets. Moreover, these were officials who had very limited powers to dictate strategy and were therefore, of necessity, interested in collaboration in the formation of a joint strategy. However, it should be noted that Japanese officials were far from powerless. Although they often lacked the formal authority to dictate a course of action to business, they controlled, generally in combination with other officials, substantial financial resources of the sort present in the Fiscal Investment and Loan Program and regulatory or taxing powers that could be selectively employed in favor of one firm or another.[19] Thus, it made sense for a businessperson to pay careful attention to them. But it made equal sense for the officials to pay careful heed to the assessments emanating from the business community.

How might we explain the overall posture that Japanese civil servants took to their relations with business? A full analysis is well beyond the scope of this essay, but I can offer some brief observations. Of course, the high value attached to extensive consultation with all affected interests that is reflected in their approach fits well with the cultural norms we now associate with the Japanese. But these policies were not entirely a cultural construct. To some extent, the close collaboration between state and industry that postwar Japan developed probably also reflects some learning from experience with the two extremes of more *laissez-faire* arrangements and then more state-directed approaches that proved less successful in the years before and during the Second World War.[20] It was almost certainly encouraged by the dominance that a probusiness party, the LDP, was able to secure over the legislature in the postwar years.[21] Left-wing parties are

---

[18] For more details see Peter A. Hall, *Governing the Economy: The Politics of State Intervention in Britain and France* (New York: Oxford University Press, 1986), Chapters 6 and 7; Bruce R. Scott and Audrey T. Sprout, eds., *National Industrial Planning: France and the EEC* (Boston: Harvard Business School, 1983); and Suzanne Berger, 'Lame Ducks and National Champions: Industrial Policy in the Fifth Republic,' in Stanley Hoffmann and William Andrews, eds., *The Fifth Republic at Twenty* (Brockport: State University of New York Press, 1981), pp. 292–310.

[19] See the essay in this volume by Yukio Noguchi among others as well as Johnson, *MITI and the Japanese Miracle*; Magaziner and Hout, *Japanese Industrial Policy*; and Samuels, *The Business of the Japanese State*.

[20] See especially Johnson, *MITI and the Japanese Miracle*.

[21] See T. J. Pempel, ed., *Uncommon Democracies: The One-Party Dominant Regimes* (Ithaca: Cornell University Press, 1994).

generally less willing to see the state work so closely with business. For our purposes, however, what is most striking is the way in which the organizational structure, mandate, and operating procedures of the Japanese bureaucracy, as described by Haley and others, reinforced these general orientations.

In this context, the organization of the business community was also important. Governments can only consult effectively with business if business is organized in such a way as to provide viable interlocutors with whom to consult. The French planners used to speak of an '80-20 ratio' on the premise that they could deal with a sector effectively only if 20 per cent of the firms controlled 80 per cent of the production there; to try to collaborate with more firms than that was seen as difficult.[22] In Japan, the extensive vertical and horizontal organization of business through the *zaibatsu* and their successors, the *keiretsu*, was probably crucial to the formation of such an effective business–government partnership. By the same token, it seems likely that the need for close consultation with government helped to induce businessmen to organize into associations designed both to coordinate their own activities and to provide an effective interface with government.[23]

Any account of the role of the Japanese civil service in economic development, then, should pay some attention to the role of officials in fostering the organization of Japanese business. Quite apart from the ways it facilitates collaboration with public officials, there is reason to think that the construction of effective organizational networks among businessmen can contribute to the overall strategic capacity of an economy.[24] Intercorporate linkages seem to affect the degree to which individual firms can subordinate short-term goals of the sort associated with profit maximization and shareholder return to long-term goals of the kind associated with securing market share, investment, and continuous innovation. They also seem to make it possible for firms to provide a variety of public goods, of the sort associated with industrial adjustment, wage restraint, or vocational training, with a minimum of state intervention. Thus, to the degree that the Japanese civil service helped to nurture and sustain specific forms of

[22] Andrew Shonfield, *Modern Capitalism* (New York: Oxford University Press, 1982), p. 138.

[23] This is a topic on which more research is needed. For suggestive discussions, see Michael Gerlach, *Alliance Capitalism: The Social Organizataion of Japanese Business* (Berkeley: University of California Press, 1992); Mark Fruin, *The Japanese Enterprise System* (Oxford: Oxford University Press, 1992); and Ronald Dore, *Flexible Rigidities: Industrial Policy and Structural Adjustment in the Japanese Economy* (Stanford: Stanford University Press, 1986).

[24] For a powerful elaboration of this point, see David Soskice, 'The Institutional Infrastructure for International Competitiveness: A Comparative Anayisis of the UK and Germany,' in A. B. Atkinson and R. Brunetta, eds., *The Economics of the New Europe* (London: Macmillan, 1993); David Soskice, 'Wage Determination: The Changing Role of Institutions in Advanced Industrialized Countries,' *Oxford Review of Economic Policy*, Vol. 6., No. 4 (Winter 1990), pp. 36–61; and more generally Peter Katzenstein, *Small States in World Markets* (Ithaca: Cornell University Press, 1985).

interfirm organization, it may have made an additional contribution to the Japanese economy.

In this regard, comparison with the French and German cases again helps to illuminate the distinctive features of business–government relations in Japan. Well into the 1980s and not without reason, it was customary to see the organization of Japanese economic policy as most similar to that of the French. Both nations employed a system of economic planning established shortly after the Second World War and supplemented by an activist industrial policy oriented to exports, which was superintended by a number of agencies in collaboration with their respective ministries. Presiding over these policies were professional civil servants of high quality, imbued with a sense that they were the guardians of the public interest and responsible for industrial, as well as overall economic, performance. In both cases, control over the flow of funds in the financial system and the selective application of economic regulations lent weight to the views of these officials. Both France and Japan were modernized economically from above by a state eager to secure the nation's international economic position in the postwar world.[25]

Both the French and Japanese systems of economic management changed during the 1970s and 1980s in response to the evolving challenges posed by the international system and by economies that were themselves transformed under the impetus of past policy. However, the French system for industrial policymaking collapsed far more completely than anyone expected, leaving France in the kind of difficult position that Japan seems to have avoided. How it did so is a long story which I summarize only briefly here.[26]

During the 1970s and early 1980s, membership in the European Community and the European Monetary System inspired a radical opening of the French economy to flows of foreign goods and capital while enforcing a rigid exchange rate constraint on policymakers. Once firms had ready access to international capital markets and foreign venues of production, French policymakers lost much of the leverage they once had over the private sector. At the same time, persistently high levels of unemployment and lower rates of growth led governments that had formerly been happy to claim responsibility for the economy to seek ways of shifting the responsibility for lower levels of economic performance onto the market.

[25] For a classic statement along these lines, see John Zysman, *Governments, Markets, and Growth: Financial Systems and the Politics of Industrial Change* (Ithaca: Cornell University Press, 1983) and on the role of the Allied Occupation in Japan, see Robert Ward and Yoshikazu Sakamoto, ed., *Democratizing Japan: The Allied Occupation* (Honolulu: University of Hawaii Press, 1987).
[26] The following account draws on Hall, *Governing the Economy*; Peter A. Hall, 'The State and the Market,' in Peter A. Hall, Jack Hayward, and Howard Machin, eds., *Developments in French Politics* (London: Macmillan, 1990), pp. 171–87; and Peter A. Hall, 'The Evolution of Economic Policy under Mitterrand,' in George Ross and Stanley Hoffmann, eds., *The Mitterrand Experiment* (New York: Oxford University Press, 1987), pp. 54–72.

Faced with an exchange-rate constraint, policymakers also found that it was not feasible to finance industrial investment in large measure from public funds since the resulting budget deficits put downward pressure on the French franc.

In the late 1980s and early 1990s, then, French officials remained eager to enhance the operation of the economy but faced something of a quandary as to how to do so. It was widely believed that the health of the economy demanded some major adjustments, notably in the areas of vocational training, the organization of production, and client or supplier relations, so that French industry could move toward more flexible forms of specialized and high value-added production in lieu of the Fordist techniques on which many sectors had long relied.[27]

However, industrial policymakers found that France lacked the kind of effective employer organizations and intercorporate linkages that are often essential to these sorts of adjustments. On the one hand, policymakers themselves can only effect change at the micro level of shopfloor practices, supplier–client relations, or vocational training if they can work closely with regional and sectoral associations representing the businesses that must implement them. On the other hand, quite apart from the implications for policy, the capacity of French business to adjust toward longer time horizons, more cooperative ventures, and flexible forms of higher value-added production seems to depend in some measure on having effective networks of interfirm organization of the sort that France lacks.[28]

In several respects, then, the forms of business organization contributing what we might think of as the crucial social capital or social infrastructure for industrial adjustment are relatively underdeveloped in France; and, ironically, they are underdeveloped partly because the civil servants formulating industrial policy in the 1960s and 1970s failed to encourage the growth of this kind of social infrastructure.[29] In some instances, the industrial policymakers deliberately undermined such associations and their analogues in local government in order to have a freer rein in the direction of policy. Thus, the overly *dirigiste* policies of the past gave rise to a situation in which the French political economy is not well organized to cope with the economic challenges of the 1990s.

It is in this respect that the Japanese and French cases diverge. Although Japanese policy has also been 'liberalized' in recent years, in line with the changing demands of the economy, the political economy of Japan is not

---

[27] This general problematic is discussed in Michael Piore and Charles Sabel, *The Second Industrial Divide* (New York: Basic, 1984); Robert Boyer, *The Regulation School: A Critical Introduction* (New York: Columbia University Press, 1990); and Egon Matzner and Wolfgang Streeck, eds., *Beyond Keynesianism* (London: Edward Elgar, 1992).

[28] The points in this and the following paragraph draw heavily on the pioneering doctoral dissertation on French political economy being completed for MIT by Jonah Levy.

[29] Levy, who makes this point, describes the result as 'Tocqueville's revenge.'

nearly as 'disorganized' as that of France, in large measure because policymakers nurtured the coordinating capacities and organization of Japanese business, instead of displacing them in the name of direction by the public authorities.[30] As a result, Japanese business retains a strategic capacity to coordinate a wide range of activities and to plan effectively for a long time horizon, while many sectors of French business lack such a capacity; and Japanese policymakers continue to have industrial interlocutors down to the local and sectoral level with whom they can collaborate, as necessary, on schemes of economic reorganization suited to the conditions of the 1990s.

Consequently, the European case that more closely resembles Japan today is not that of France but that of Germany, where long-standing government policy also supported the development and maintenance of business organizations capable of effectively coordinating sectoral and intersectoral activity. There have always been important differences between the German and Japanese cases. German policymakers were rarely as directive about industrial reorganization as their Japanese counterparts, preferring to let the large investment banks and industrial associations superintend such schemes, and an independent central bank limited the use that industrial policymakers could make of subsidized interest rates. Instead, the Germans tended to see their mission as one of establishing 'framework policies' in the sense of policies that provided an appropriate legal structure whereby business and labor, which is more powerful than in Japan, could administer their own affairs.

Nonetheless, the results of German policy after four decades resemble those of the Japanese in important respects. Employers' organizations coordinate an annual wage round much like the Japanese *shuntō*, an annual spring wage offensive throughout industry. Both economies are marked by semipermanent employment in the core economy bolstered by extensive subcontracting in a periphery. German financial institutions are accustomed to providing capital on a long-term basis to industry, much as the Japanese banks do, and the unions and employers collaborate in administering an effective system of vocational training. In short, quite apart from all the other similarities, Germany and Japan retain a highly organized political economy, marked by especially strong business organizations with some strategic capacity.[31] It may not be coincidental that these are now two of the most powerful economies in the world.[32]

---

[30] This is a subject on which further research is merited, but see Samuels, *The Business of the Japanese State*, and Okimoto, *Between MITI and the Market*.

[31] On Germany, see: Soskice, 'The Institutional Infrastructure for International Competitiveness'; Wolfgang Streeck, *Social Institutions and Economic Performance* (London: Sage, 1992); Herbert Giersch et al., *The Fading Miracle* (London: Cambridge University Press, 1992); and Michel Albert, *Capitalism Against Capitalism* (London: Whurr Publishers, 1993).

[32] Notwithstanding the advantages of such arrangements, it should be noted that systems that confer such authority on existing networks of firms also tend to be more closed to new entrants and susceptible to forms of collusion that may favor the interests of the participants more than the community at large. For one example, see Upham, 'Privatizing Regulation.'

The important point here is that both German and Japanese officials generally avoided the temptation of substituting their own judgment or their own organizations for the judgment and organization of business. There is no doubt that they shaped the organization of business in the interest of economic modernization; and that often entailed favoring more progressive combinations of firms over older associations with overly strong vested interests in the status quo. However, both German and Japanese civil servants collaborated with business in such a way as to enhance, rather than undermine, the strategic capacity of the latter over time.

The Relationship to Politics

Let me turn now from the relationship between civil servants and businessmen to a second relationship that is also crucial to effective policymaking. That is the relationship between civil servants and politicians.

In all cases but especially if we are thinking about lessons for the developing world, it is important to recognize that the behavior of civil servants always takes place inside a broader political framework. We need to retain an awareness of the *political* problems facing the leaders of a developing nation, as distinct from the *administrative* problems they confront, because a particular set of policies or organizational structures will work over the long term only if it resolves the relevant political problems as well as administrative ones. That is especially true in liberal democracies where the nation's leaders face the electorate at frequent intervals, but it applies to all regimes whose rulers must retain some measure of popular support.[33]

This is not to say that every economic policy must be highly popular. Most political systems embody some capacity for imposing sacrifice on their populace. The real effects of policy can often be masked in some way, and less popular policies can be balanced off against more popular ones. However, the more major or long-term the policy, the more likely it is to be susceptible to political considerations. It is not difficult to see that the best-designed administrative scheme will fail to appeal to the political leaders who must endorse it or ultimately founder in practice if it does not have a modicum of political appeal.[34]

[33] One especially insightful statement of this position can be found in Joel Migdal, 'Weak States and Strong Societies,' in Samuel P. Huntington and Myron Weiner, eds., *Understanding Development* (Boston: Little Brown, 1988). See also Merilee S. Gindle, *Politics and Policy Implementation in the Third World* (Princeton: Princeton University Press, 1988).

[34] For a more general examination of this issue in the context of Keynesian policies, see Peter A. Hall, ed., *The Political Power of Keynesian Ideas* (Princeton: Princeton University Press, 1989), pp. 361–92.

Similarly, while there are real virtues in a civil service that is independent, in important respects, from political influence, the ideal is not a civil service that is entirely independent from the politicians who are supposed to superintend it. We should avoid the temptation of seeing politics and politicians as entirely malevolent influences in putative contrast to civil servants who are expected to be more pristine or wise. To do so is to succumb to a 'technological illusion' that undervalues the contribution that political mechanisms make to governance.[35] The best-governed nation is not necessarily or even usually one managed entirely by civil servants, as a host of military regimes have discovered.[36] Politicians, especially in a democracy, provide a responsiveness to popular concerns that is ultimately crucial to good governance.

In this context, then, it is important to note that the Japanese system of governance benefits from strong political inputs. The civil service, while possessing resources that give it considerable influence over the formulation of policy, is clearly subordinate to an elected political leadership. Although each ministry usually contains only one direct political appointee (in the position of parliamentary vice minister) besides the minister, it is generally understood that advancement to the top positions in the civil service requires support from the dominant factions in the Liberal Democratic Party that has governed Japan since the 1950s. In formal terms, the legislature through the cabinet has ultimate authority over policy; and, as Haley observes, it is significant that Japan makes relatively little use of independent regulatory commissions of the sort that are more common in the United States. One result is that a larger portion of policy, in the economic sphere especially, is subject to direct control by the governing party.[37]

Ito's chapter in this volume provides a nice example of the contribution that politicians can make to the system. Although a group that he calls 'preemptive bureaucrats' contributed to the series of administrative reforms that reduced the growth of the civil service, his account suggests that politicians often provide the impetus that is crucial to periodic reform of policy. Moreover, in this case, they acted in response to the wider waves of sentiment sweeping through the political system in the classic way that politicians seeking to be responsive to the people tend to do.

Of course, the problem is to secure a system that allows for just the right *amount* and *kind* of political influence over administrative decision making. Too much political influence, especially of a venal kind, can

[35] See Jacques Ellul, *The Technological Society* (New York: Knopf, 1964).
[36] Cf. Amos Perlmutter, *The Military and Politics in Modern Times* (New Haven: Yale University Press, 1977) and Samuel P. Huntington, *The Solider and the State* (Cambridge: Harvard University Press, 1957).
[37] Cf. Okimoto, *Between MITI and the Market*.

subvert even the most promising bureaucracy. In this context, the Japanese system is especially interesting because corruption is not entirely unknown in Japanese politics. Scandals involving political corruption have toppled several recent governments, yet, by and large, the country is well administered. How do the Japanese achieve this?

That is a subject on which further research needs to be done, but a few observations can be offered here. First, it is probably important that the Japanese political system is ordered along parliamentary lines, which concentrate power in the cabinet and prime minister, rather than along congressional lines that delegate substantial power to individual legislators. When power is diffused, the opportunities for political corruption multiply and the capacity of the electorate to identify the culprits and hold them responsible is attenuated. By concentrating power in the hands of the cabinet and prime minister, responsibility for any instances of corruption can more clearly be apportioned and the threat that perpetrators will be held accountable for their actions is greater. Similarly, when political power is concentrated in the cabinet, only a few individuals are especially open to the temptation of venality, since it makes little sense for supplicants to pressure or bribe legislators who have little power, and ministers may suffer less from such temptations than ordinary legislators would because their office already provides so much power and status that they have less to gain in relative terms from petty venality and more to lose if they are caught.

Although arrangements of this sort tend to restrict corruption in Japan, their effect is offset, in some measure, by the importance of factionalism in the governing Liberal Democratic Party and by electoral laws that often force legislators to run against other candidates from the same party in multimember constituencies. To the degree that the policy committees of the LDP, which shadow each ministry, have real power, they provide a tempting entryway for those seeking to influence policy behind the scenes. And the efforts of factions to secure support for their partisans in multimember constituencies can be expensive enterprises dependent on largely unregulated donations from the private sector. In these respects, the presence of a single dominant party in which factional competition is prominent, of the sort found in both Japan and Italy, can undermine some of the safeguards against corruption that parliamentary governance might otherwise provide. It puts additional pressure on the civil service to be the bulwark that limits the penetration of partisan corruption into administrative affairs.[38]

[38] I am grateful to Margarita Estevez for drawing my attention to this point. More generally see: R. Kent Weaver and Bert A. Rockman, eds., *Do Institutions Matter? Government Capabilities in the United States and Abroad* (Washington: Brookings Institution, 1993); Thomas D. Lancaster, 'Electoral Structures and Pork Barrel Politics,' *International Political Science Review*, Vol. 7 (Jan. 1986), pp. 67–81; and Arnold Heidenheimer et al., *Political Corruption: A Handbook* (New Brunswick, NJ: Transaction, 1989).

To an outside observer, there seems to be some evidence of a division among different fields of policymaking in Japan with regard to the degree to which political patronage figures in the allocation of resources. In matters pertaining to public works and agriculture, where funds can readily be allocated to individual constituencies, the system seems to allow for a good deal of 'pork barrel' politics. In matters of economic development, however, where the effects of policy are spread more widely, political patronage is less evident. Whether this reflects an arrangement whereby some spheres of policy are used to satisfy the demands of partisan politics while others are dedicated to a more collective interest or the general difficulty we often have in perceiving the special interests served by broader development policies remains a matter for investigation.[39]

My overarching point is that we cannot expect to understand how a particular system of administration works by looking at the civil service alone. In virtually every case, the character of the political system will affect the way in which the administrative system, however designed, will function. The civil services of France and Italy, for instance, are structured along similar lines, partly because both were constructed on the Napoleonic model, but in practice they operate very differently because the character of the political system is so different in the two countries.[40] The presence in Italy of a very powerful legislature whose members rely on political patronage for electoral support helped to turn the civil service itself into a patronage machine, while the concentration of power in a president and prime minister in Fifth Republic France helped to insulate the civil service from particularistic political concerns. The explanation is ultimately more complex than this but the fundamental point remains that the character of politics in a nation will strongly influence the operation of its civil service.

This is a point of particular relevance for those seeking to redesign or reform a civil service. Since the civil service can be a vehicle for solving a variety of political problems, if it is to be redesigned, other solutions may have to be found for the political problems it once addressed. To take only the most prominent example, if a nation seeks a bureaucracy that is not corrupt or heavily used as a vehicle for political patronage, then its politi-

[39] See Kent Calder, *Crisis and Compensation* (Princeton: Princeton University Press, 1988); Ellis Krauss and Michio Muramatsu, 'Bureaucrats and Politicians in Policymaking: The Case of Japan,' *American Political Science Review*, Vol. 78, No. 1 (March 1984); Kenneth A. Shepsle and Barry R. Weingast, 'Political Preferences for the Pork Barrel: A Generalization,' *American Journal of Political Science*, Vol. 25 (Feb. 1981), pp. 96–111; and, more generalli, Robert Bates, *Markets and States in Tropical Africa* (Berkeley: University of California Press, 1981).

[40] Cf. Joseph La Palombara, *Interest Groups in Italian Politics* (Princeton: Princeton University Press, 1964); Franco Ferraresi, *Burocrazia e politica in Italia* (Bureaucracy and politics in Italy) (Bologna: Il Mulino, 1990); Jean Luc Bodiguel, *La Haute Fonction publique sous la Vième République* (The higher civil service under the Fifth Republic) (Paris: Presses Universitaires de France, 1983); and Suleiman, *Politics, Power and Bureaucracy in France*.

cal leaders must have alternative institutional vehicles available for rallying popular support. Armed with effective alternatives for building a power base, such as well-organized political parties or strong local bases of support, the politicians do not have to rely so much on the patronage that the bureaucracy can supply.

This observation implies that administrative reform may be easier to achieve when effective political mobilization has already been or can simultaneously be achieved by other means. For instance, it does not seem to be a coincidence that the rationalization of the British civil service in the late nineteenth century, commonly associated with the Northcote–Trevelyan report, occurred only when the British politicians of the day found that they could rally sufficient electoral support and adequate allegiance in the legislature by means of newly organized political parties built around constituency organizations.[41] Accordingly, they had less need to use the civil service as a vehicle for political patronage.

The more general implication, hitherto underappreciated in the literature, may be that the development of an effective civil service goes hand-in-hand with the development of a democratic political system. It is often believed, if rarely stated outright, that democratic politics brings with it a set of messy electoral pressures that can readily corrupt the administration. However, there are some respects in which a democratic political system can also counteract administrative corruption and foster efficiency. In particular, an elected legislature with the power to scrutinize policy in which the opposition has a platform can be an important watchdog over the conduct of administration. There is some reason to think, for instance, that the British were able to develop an efficient and relatively uncorrupt civil service long before many other nations precisely because the British Parliament proved to be effective at exposing and eliminating venality.[42]

For developing nations in particular, these issues go beyond electoral politics alone. Any regime that is making a transition to democracy needs to secure the support not only of the new elites it most often represents but also of the older elites whom they supplant. By and large, that entails guaranteeing those older elites some continuing access to power.[43] In some cases, local government can remain a repository of influence for

[41] See H. Parris, *Constitutional Bureaucracy* (London: Allen and Unwin, 1969); Richard Chapman and J. R. Greenaway, *The Dynamics of Administrative Reform* (London: Croom Helm, 1980), Chap. 1; and more generally, Martin Shefter, 'Party and Patronage: Germany, England and Italy,' *Politics and Society*, Vol. 7, No. 4 (1977), pp. 403–51.

[42] I owe this point to Thomas Ertman; see his dissertation, *War and Statebuilding in Early Modern Europe* (Department of Sociology, Harvard University, 1990; Ann Arbor: University Microfilms, 1991). See also John Brewer, *The Sinews of Power* (London: Unwin, Hyman, 1989); and Hilton Root, *The Fountain of Privilege* (Berkeley: University of California Press, 1984).

[43] For influential statements of this general view, see Guillermo O'Donnell, Philippe C. Schmitter, and Laurence Whitehead, eds., *Transitions From Authoritarian Rule: Prospects for Democracy* (Baltimore: Johns Hopkins University Press, 1986).

older social elites. In other cases, the presence of political parties dedicated to their interests may be an adequate substitute.[44] Electoral laws can be shaped with such an outcome in mind, but the nature of democratic elections is generally such as to confer power on the masses rather than the elites.

In these settings, although it is rarely appreciated, the bureaucracy can also be an important vehicle by which old elites retain some influence over governance. One of the classic cases can be found in nineteenth-century France when the old elites used their privileged access to positions in the bureaucracy to retain some share of power, even though a succession of regimes culminating in the Third Republic nominally transferred authority to the representatives of other groups. It is arguable that this arrangement helped to reconcile many of those elites to the new political regimes.[45] Thus, if administrative reform of the sort that tends to displace established elites is not to founder on their opposition, it may be necessary to ensure that these elites can safely be displaced or are provided with alternative access to power.

Conclusion

By way of conclusion, I turn to some broader issues related to the question of how applicable the Japanese experience and its institutions are to the problems faced by other nations in the developing world.

The premise from which I start is that we can learn a good deal that is of relevance to other nations from the Japanese case. Even when specific institutional configurations or innovations do not prove to be as 'portable' as we might like, there is much to be gained from considering the experience of other nations. History does tend to repeat itself enough that, at one level of generality or another, we can learn from contemplating it.

However, it must be noted that, from the perspective of many Third World nations today, postwar Japan enjoyed some singular political advantages, which appear especially relevant if the functioning of the civil service is seen in the context of wider political dilemmas. In particular, postwar Japan did not face some of the problems that are highest on the political agendas of many developing nations today.

By and large, the Japanese authorities had little problem securing basic political order. Notwithstanding the superficial image of Japan as a highly

---

[44] See Frances Hagopian, 'Democracy by Undemocratic Means: Elites, Political Pacts and Regime Transition in Brazil,' *Comparative Political Studies*, Vol. 23, No. 2 (July 1990).

[45] See Jean L'Homme, *La Grande Bourgeoisie au pouvoir* (The grand bourgeoisie in power) (Paris: Presses Universitaires de France, 1960); Elwitt Sanford, *The Making of the Third Republic* (Baton Rouge: Louisiana State University Press, 1975); and Judith Wishnia, *The Proletarianizing of the Fonctionnaires* (Baton Rouge: Louisiana State University Press, 1990).

consensual society, it faced some bitter conflicts, especially involving labor during the 1950s and early 1960s and involving opponents of the rapid growth model in more recent decades. However, none of these conflicts reached the magnitude of those faced by the nations fighting organized insurgencies today in Latin America, Asia, or Africa. The most fundamental problem of political order had been solved by the time Japan entered the postwar world.

Second, the military establishment in postwar Japan is unusually small in size and of minimal political importance. Quite the reverse is the case in many nations currently seeking more rapid rates of economic growth. As a result, postwar Japan enjoyed great advantages especially pertinent to the matters covered in this volume. Where a substantial element in the civil service is composed of the military or closely related to it, the dilemmas facing politicians and reformers are very different. In particular, the threat to democratic rule posed by a highly independent and powerful civil service may rise.

Third, since there are few sizable minorities in Japan, the nation has not recently suffered from open ethnic conflict to any substantial degree. The problem of ethnic conflict bedevils many contemporary nations and it has particular import for the civil service when access to positions in the latter is seen as an important privilege or when some groups resent policies that are administered by others.

Finally, in large measure, what might be described as the 'distribution problem' has not been a very serious political issue in Japan. Issues of agrarian reform were dealt with relatively early there and the power of the labor movement was crushed, for all intents and purposes, by the early 1960s. Thus, the political influence of the socialist and communist parties has remained relatively limited. Despite the concern expressed in recent decades for improvements in the quality of life, Japan escaped the bitter distributional struggles that can easily become prominent in many of the nations developing today.

Thus, during the postwar period, Japan did not face intense difficulties arising from the problem of political order, the military problem, the ethnic problem, or the distribution problem that so dominate politics in many nations seeking to industrialize more rapidly. Such a statement implicitly understates the ingenious efforts of the Japanese authorities to prevent these problems from becoming more pressing, but it draws our attention to advantages that made the operation of a particular civil service model more smooth than it might be elsewhere.

Similarly, anyone seeking to incorporate parts of the Japanese model of civil service organization into another nation should bear in mind that the most important effects it produced were almost invariably effects that followed not from the presence of a single institutional feature but from the interaction of multiple institutions. Because they are difficult to model, interaction effects are often neglected by social science. In this case, as in many others, however, they were crucial to the overall outcomes.

We see many examples of such 'interaction effects' in these papers. Most of Japan's major economic policies, for instance, were made by several agencies acting in collaboration with each other. The Ministry of Finance, in particular, as an institution with the same overall mission but slightly different institutionalized interests, acted as a check on the industrial or financial agencies proposing new economic policies. In more general terms, the operation of the Japanese civil service seems to have been affected by the nature of the political system within which it worked, and it is likely that economic policymakers were able to pursue many lines of policy only because Japanese business was organized in ways that facilitated such policymaking.

Just as we would get quite unexpected results if we transferred the British Treasury to the United States, so anyone proposing to place the Japanese civil service into the Czech Republic would want to take careful account of the ancillary institutional innovations needed if it is to perform as expected. The most radical implication of this view is that the organization of the state must be considered in the context of the organization of society, since it is interaction between the two that produces many of the results that follow from policy.[46]

Finally, any reader of these essays should bear in mind that the Japanese economy has evolved over time and that the challenges it poses to policymakers have changed in corresponding terms. The problem of building up basic industries, which was of dominant importance in the years immediately following the war, gave way to the problem of constructing industries that could compete on world markets, which in turn gave way to the problem of maintaining the health of well-established firms and of meeting rising consumer demands in an increasingly open setting.[47] The techniques that Japanese policymakers employed to steer the economy have changed in line with this shifting series of challenges. In general, economic policymaking seems more liberal and less directive today than in years past, and the private sector bears more of the burden of industrial adjustment. Anyone seeking to learn from Japanese policy

---

[46] For one argument along these lines, see Lisa Anderson, *The State and Social Transformation in Tunisia and Libya, 1830–1980* (Princeton: Princeton University Press, 1986) and, for an interesting exploration of how Japan itself borrowed from others, see D. Eleanor Westney, *Imitation and Innovation: The Transfer of Western Organizational Patterns to Meiji Japan* (Cambridge, Mass.: Harvard University Press, 1987).

[47] For cogent reviews of this problem, see: George C. Eads and Kozo Yamamura, 'The Future of Industrial Policy,' in Kozo Yamamura and Yasukichi Yasuba, eds., *The Political Economy of Japan, Volume 1: The Domestic Transformation* (Stanford: Stanford University Press, 1987); Ikuo Kume, 'Changing Relations among the Government, Labor and Business in Japan after the Oil Crisis,' *International Organization*, Vol. 42, No. 4 (1988), pp. 659–88; and Russell Hancock, 'A Farewell to Japanese Industrial Policy,' *Stanford Journal of International Affairs*, Vol. 2, No. 1 (Fall/Winter 1993), pp. 111–30.

should pay careful attention to its inefficiencies as well as to its efficiencies and to the appropriateness of policy at any one particular stage of economic development.[48]

In general, however, this evolution in policy reveals some of the residual strengths of the Japanese civil service system. This is not a case in which an organizational form proved useful only for one specific set of clearly circumscribed problems. In fact, the Japanese civil service has proved remarkably adept at handling the shifting challenges posed by multiple stages of economic development and that accomplishment suggests a robustness that may well be attractive to other nations.

A comprehensive effort to suggest which features of the Japanese civil service model could best be applied in other nations is well beyond the scope of this essay. However, I have tried to draw attention to several features of the Japanese system that seem to contain more general lessons for all concerned with such questions.

In the end, what must strike a comparativist the most about the Japanese civil service is the resemblance that it bears to other well-functioning civil services in Europe and elsewhere. Judging from these essays at least, the effectiveness with which the system operates does not seem to depend on some mysterious element of 'Japaneseness' as some would have us believe. There is no doubt that many of the cultural norms traditionally associated with Japanese society seem to enhance the functioning of the system, but none of them seems absolutely crucial to its operation.[49] On the contrary, the precepts about the importance of meritocracy, relative but circumscribed independence from politics, effective interface with the business community, and the like that might be drawn from this case seem readily applicable to other settings. They do not constitute a magic wand but they make good sense, and they suggest that there is much of value to be learned from Japan.

---

[48] For another perspective on this problem, see the essay by Kozo Yamamura in this volume.

[49] For slightly different views, see Pharr, *Losing Face*, and Dore, *Flexible Rigidities*.

18

The Japanese Civil Service and Economic Development:
Lessons for Policymakers from Other Countries

HYUNG-KI KIM

Japan's remarkable economic and political transformation to a modern economy and polity may hold some vital lessons for developing and transforming economies and for international financing institutions.[1] Some of these lessons pertain to the high savings rate and the 'catch-up' efforts that have helped spur Japan's development. Equally important, however, is the role played by Japan's bureaucracy, particularly its administrative institutions.[2] It has been argued that the skillful economic management that guided Japan through the turbulent years of modernization and brought it prosperity are due in no small measure to these institutions. It should be noted at the outset, however, that the Japanese bureaucracy, which has taken pride in its role as 'guardian of the national interest', is now having that role challenged. The Japanese bureaucracy is

[1] For a treatise on Japan's premodern social and economic institutions, especially during the Tokugawa period, and on the transition from the Tokugawa period to the Meiji period, see Chie Nakane and Shinzaburo Ōishi, eds., *Tokugawa Japan* (Tokyo: University of Tokyo Press, 1990), and Marius B. Jansen and Gilbert Rozman, eds., *Japan in Transition from Tokugawa to Meiji* (Princeton: Princeton University Press, 1988). Henry Rosovsky, *Industrialization in Two Systems* (New York: John Wiley and Sons, 1966), pp. 91–139, suggests that Japan's transition to 'modern economic growth' (the phrase was coined by Simon Kuznets in *Modern Economic Growth: Speed, Structure and Spread* [New Haven: Yale University Press, 1966]) took place between 1866 and 1885. For other informative studies on the development of Japan, see William W. Lockwood, *Economic Development of Japan: Growth and Structural Change: 1868–1938* (Princeton: Princeton University Press, 1954); Ronald P. Dore, *Land Reform in Japan* (Princeton: Princeton University Press, 1959); Thomas Smith, *Agrarian Origins of Modern Japan* (Stanford: Stanford University Press, 1959); Takafusa Nakamura, *The Postwar Japanese Economy: Its Development and Structure* (Tokyo: University of Tokyo Press 1990); and Shigeru Tsuru, *Japan's Capitalism: Creative Defeat and Beyond* (Cambridge: Cambridge University Press, 1993).

[2] In this chapter, 'government' or 'bureaucracy' is often used interchangeably with the word 'state,' although the latter obviously denotes a much broader concept. According to the Weberian perspective, the state must be considered more than the government or bureaucracy (see Alfred Stepan, *The State and Society: Peru in Comparative Perspective* (Princeton: Princeton University Press, 1978, p. xii).

currently undergoing intense scrutiny and public criticism, especially from the business community, which once maintained a close relationship with the government.[3]

This chapter attempts to amplify and reinterpret some of the points made in other chapters against the backdrop of key issues surrounding civil services in developing and transforming economies, notably those relating to the structure, size, orientation and functions of civil services, and those concerning mechanisms and instruments for policy intervention.

Some Theses Regarding the Role of Government in Japan's Economic Development

The state looms large in Japan's political economy. A number of theories have emerged concerning the kind of role the state has played in Japan's economic development, particularly during the high-growth era from the mid-1950s to the early 1970s. Perhaps the most widely known theory is the *developmental state* theory. The thesis of a dominant, proactive role for the Japanese state was developed by Chalmers Johnson, who argues that Japan became a 'developmental state'—a state that was a leader in industry, and one that set clear and substantive social and economic goals—soon after the Meiji Restoration in 1868. The Japanese state took it upon itself to devise policies and institutional mechanisms to compensate for inadequacies in the traditional economy, such as the lack of capital, technology, and infrastructure—both physical and legal—in what Gerschenkron described as 'the missing prerequisites' in 'relatively backward' economies.[4] This school of thought views the Ministry of Inter-

---

[3] The *Nihon Keizai Shimbun* (Japanese Economic Daily), a widely subscribed newspaper, recently (July 27, 1993) carried an editorial on the advent of the new government, calling for significant qualitative reform of the administration, with an emphasis on fairness and transparency, on dismantling *all* regulations inhibiting competition (such as the barriers to new entrants), and on adopting the principle of *laissez-faire* by discarding the principle of regulation. See also the *Hiraiwa Report* (December 11, 1993), named after Gaishi Hiraiwa, Chairman of the Economic Reform Study Group (a private advisory group for then Prime Minister Morihiro Hosokawa), who was at that time the chairman of the influential *Keidanren*, the Japan Federation of Economic Organizations. This report called for a major deregulation, if not outright elimination, of economic regulations in Japan. In addition, debates on the appropriate role of bureaucrats and the reforms that the executive branch of the government should undergo have been constant features of newspaper articles and columns, especially in the last couple of years. Notable among these is the featured articles on *Kanryo* (bureaucrats) in *Nihon Keizai Shimbun* (*Japanese Economic Daily*), which appeared one hundred times from November 1993 to July 1994. The collection of this column has now come out as a monograph, *Kanryo* (Tokyo: Nihon Keizai Shimbun, 1994).

[4] Alexander Gerschenkron, *Economic Backwardness in Historical Perspective* (Cambridge, Mass.: Belknap Press of Harvard University, 1962).

national Trade and Industry (MITI) as the leading state actor in the economy.[5]

The developmental state theory suggests that the Japanese bureaucracy, rather than its legislature, was primarily responsible for making most of the decisions concerning development. Early in the country's history of industrialization, the bureaucracy began to take advantage of the information asymmetry that existed (created to a large extent) between it and the legislature, and started drafting virtually all legislation known as cabinet bills (see Figure 2.1 in Haley's chapter). These cabinet bills emerged from a widely practiced system known as *ringisei* (which circulates *ringisho* [policy or legislative proposals] drafted by officials of lower ranks for approval by officials in upper echelons, thereby engaging a broad spectrum of the bureaucracy in policy initiatives). This system in Japan is similar to systems in France and Korea.[6]

Some critics of the state or bureaucratic-dominance thesis argue that in practice the bureaucracy finds it difficult to exercise power over several policy areas simultaneously, since each requires specialized information and knowledge.[7] Okimoto contends that MITI was never a dominant or autonomous entity.[8] Others point to the policymaking role of the Diet, especially of ruling party politicians,[9] or to the fact that economic development in Japan was promoted in surprisingly 'close accordance with the games rules of classical capitalism.'[10] Still others advance a notion of

---

[5] Chalmers Johnson, *MITI and the Japanese Miracle: The Growth of Industrial Policy 1925–75* (Stanford: Stanford University Press, 1982).

[6] The bills introduced by the government in France are known as *projets de loi* (as against *propositions de loi* introduced by individual parliamentarians) and must be debated in the Council of Ministers after consultation with the *Conseil d'État* (Council of the State) before tabling them before one of the two houses. Article 39 of the French Constitution of October 4, 1958 (with revisions in November 1983), stipulates the concurrent rights to initiate legislation by the government (through the prime minister) and members of parliament.

[7] Hideo Otake, *Gendai Nihon no Seiji Kenryoku Keizai Kenryoku* (Political and economic power in modern Japan) (Tokyo: Sanichi Shobo, 1979).

[8] Daniel I. Okimoto, *Between MITI and the Market: Japanese Industrial Policy for High Technology* (Stanford: Stanford University Press, 1989).

[9] Michio Muramatsu, *Sengo Nihon no Kanryōsei* (The postwar Japanese bureaucratic system) (Tokyo: Toyo Keizai Shinposha, 1981); Yung H. Park, in his book, *Bureaucrats and Ministers in Contemporary Japanese Government* (Berkeley: University of California Press, 1986), documented the shift in policymaking supremacy during the 1980s as ruling party politicians became increasingly assertive. While there certainly must have been an increased involvement of the Diet in initiating legislation, the widely held perception of the predominance of the bureaucrats in policymaking still persists. According to the survey undertaken in April 1994 by the Political Reform Promotion Consultative Group, a private initiative, 94 per cent of the Diet members acknowledged that policymaking is bureaucrat-led (Reported in *Nihon Keizai Shimbun*, May 3, 1994). It is in contrast to some earlier surveys that portrayed an opposite view (see Takashi Inoguchi, 'Bureaucrats and Politicians: Shifting Influence,' in Daniel I. Okimoto and Thomas P. Rohlen, eds., *Inside the Japanese System: Readings on Contemporary Society and Political Economy* (Stanford: Stanford University Press, 1988, pp. 185–6).

[10] Yutaka Kosai, *The Era of High-Speed Growth: Notes on the Postwar Japanese Economy* (Tokyo: University of Tokyo Press, 1986). Eisuke Sakakibara, a senior official in the Ministry

'indicative intervention' or 'promotional intervention', which relies on informal, sufficiently impartial, rule based, long-term relationships between all parties concerned, as the principal characteristic of state-private sector relationships.[11]

The *market-dominance* theory, espoused mainly by economists,[12] is that the Japanese state functions in a complementary and subordinate role to the market mechanism. Its task, according to this view, is to create a progrowth environment which will facilitate private business activities, including decentralized decision making concerning business investment and innovative activities. That is, the primary impetus to growth comes from the private sector, while the role of government is to respond effectively to the requests and wishes of the business community by (a) creating a stable macroeconomic framework to facilitate savings and investment, (b) promoting R&D, education and training; and (c) building infrastructure and institutions, all of which aim at achieving transaction-cost economizing.

The *state-market bargaining* theory suggests that circumstances in Japan fostered a symbiotic relationship between the state and business, along the lines of a 'reciprocal consent' model of interaction (mainly in the form of negotiations through a kind of bargaining as well as advocacy) between the various constituents of the state and various actors in the private sector.[13]

Rejecting the notion of the Japanese bureaucracy as a 'monolithic, rational social engineer and a passive black-box processor of pluralist interest,' Aoki, in elaborating on what he calls 'bureaupluralism,' observes:

It [the Japanese bureaucracy] is a multitude of entities (ministries, agencies, and their bureaus, divisions, etc.), each of which has its own jurisdiction, acquires its political resources through interactions with other bureaucratic and private entities and is staffed with career civil servants whose motivations are conditioned by a unique structure of rewards and tenure. Each bureaucratic entity seems to have two faces in its operation: one is that of a delineator of public interests in its jurisdiction, and the other is that of an agent representing the interests of its

---

of Finance, offers a slightly different observation by characterizing the working of the Japanese economy as a 'non-capitalist market economy' that has manifested itself in the form of labor sovereignty within the corporation, and the emphasis on the independent and land-owning farmers in agriculture. See his recent book, *Beyond Capitalism: The Japanese Mode of Market Economies* (Lanham, Md.: University Press of America, 1993).

[11] Yasuke Murakami, 'The Japanese Model of Political Economy,' in Kozo Yamamura and Yasukichi Yasuba, eds., *The Political Economy of Japan, Volume 1: The Domestic Transformation* (Stanford: Stanford University Press, 1987), pp. 33–90.

[12] See, for example, Hugh Patrick and Henry Rosovsky, eds., *Asia's New Giant: How the Japanese Economy Works* (Washington: The Brookings Institution, 1976).

[13] Richard J. Samuels, *The Business of the Japanese State: Energy Markets in Comparative and Historical Perspective* (Ithaca: Cornell University Press, 1987).

constituents vis-à-vis the other interests in the bureaucractic coordinating processes: budgetary, administrative, and planning.[14]

In this view, the Japanese state is less autonomous than is often thought, and is often weaker than the private sector in coordinating economic activities and private interests.

When the Mitsubishi Heavy Industries tried to establish a new automobile company in 1969, for example, the move was in direct defiance of the prevailing administrative guidance (*gyosei shido*) of MITI, which prohibited the creation of a fourth major automobile company in Japan. Masayoshi Ohira, minister of international trade and industry at the time, adjusted to this new reality of an assertive private sector by publicly embracing a 'private-sector industrial guidance model' that was distinct from the conventional 'government industrial guidance model.'

These theories indicate that no one disputes the active involvement of the state in promoting economic development in Japan, or the contribution of competitive market forces to its economic success. What has not yet been established is the precise nature of the mix of state intervention and market activity over time, and whether this mix was the result of conscious design or the fortuitous events of the postwar period. If, as some suggest, the Japanese experience reflects a historically unique configuration of fortuitous external circumstances and internal institutions, it may offer few lessons of value to other economies. If, however, paradigms can be obtained for the nature of the state's involvement in the economy and why it proved growth-enhancing, then Japan can indeed serve as a model of state involvement in economic growth.

Is the Japanese Experience Relevant?

The attention Japan has been attracting in recent years is due not only to the meteoric rise of its industrial competitiveness relative to the United States and Europe, but also owing to a growing desire on the part of policymakers to find an 'intermediate and functional' model of state involvement in the economy that relies on state intervention to enhance a nation's ability to save, invest, innovate, and take risks, while making maximum use of the market. This search has been motivated by the fact that all the states now on the path to a market economy simply do not have the constellation of institutions needed to support a *laissez-faire* economic system. For some of these states, as for the developing economies, Japan's 'late development' and transformation from 'relative backwardness' by means of the 'catch-up' strategies it followed during the late

[14] Masahiko Aoki, *Information, Incentives, and Bargaining in the Japanese Economy* (Cambridge: Cambridge University Press, 1988), p. 263.

nineteenth century, are of considerable interest. Policymakers in developing economies would doubtless be interested in learning how the state and financial institutions can create conditions favorable to growth in countries that are latecomers to the industrialization process.

Many policymakers from developing countries tend to look upon Japan's economic development as *unique*, largely because many Japanese and foreign scholars alike, particularly cultural anthropologists, have emphasized the uniqueness of Japanese culture and institutions.[15] The phrase 'Confucian capitalism'·embodies one such perspective; it seeks to convey the spirit of Japan's high-saving economy, in which the profit motive alone is seldom the central concern of economic entities.

But does Japan's particular pattern of development necessarily mean that its experience has been unique? Or does it share some features with the pattern of development of all relatively backward economies? Certainly, like other relatively backward developers in the late nineteenth century, such as Germany and Czarist Russia, Japan has emphasized industrialization, dynamic technological efficiency (closely related to investment behavior), industrial exports, and an enhanced role for the state in the period of modern economic growth, characterized by some as a kind of 'national Schumpeterianism.'[16] A number of other factors might also be considered in assessing the relevance of the Japanese experience to other countries.

The Legal Framework

First, as pointed out by Haley, there is certainly nothing unique about the fundamental premise of Japanese governance, which is to 'rule by law.' However, some laws were written in a deliberately ambiguous way and thus left scope for working out details through administrative guidance; this of course enlarged the range of discretion on the part of the concerned government ministries. The Banking Act of 1927, which laid the foundation for bank regulation both before and after World War II, is a prime example.[17] It is in this sense that Okuno-Fujiwara characterizes the

---

[15] See Michio Morishima, *Why Has Japan 'Succeeded'?* (Cambridge: Cambridge University Press, 1982) on the spiritual ethos behind Japanese economic development; I. Muaka, 'The Distinctive Features of Japanese Development: Basic Cultural Patterns and Political-Economic Processes,' in P. L. Berger and H. H. M. Hsiao, eds., *In Search of an East Asian Development Model* (Oxford: Oxford University Press, 1988) on the transferability of traditional values; and Byron K. Marshall, *Capitalism and Nationalism in Prewar Japan* (Stanford: Stanford University Press, 1967) on the cultural environment of growth. Among more recent writings, see Karl van Wolferen, *The Enigma of Japanese Power* (New York: Alfred A. Knopf, 1990).

[16] See Richard J. Samuels, *'Rich Nations, Strong Army': National Security and Technological Transformation of Japan* (Ithaca: Cornell University Press, 1994), p. 14.

[17] See Kazuo Ueda, 'Industrial and Regulatory Frameworks for the Main Bank System,' in Masahiko Aoki and Hugh Patrick, eds., *Japanese Main Bank System: Its Relevance for Developing and Transforming Economies* (Oxford: Oxford University Press, 1995).

Japanese administration style as deriving from a discretion model, and taking the form of long, sustained, and interdependent relationships working on 'implicit agreement.'[18]

Creative Adaptation of Foreign Institutions: Japan itself Borrowed

There is other evidence to suggest that the unique culture thesis is shallow. In its modernization drive, Japan emulated various foreign (mostly Western) institutions and practices, particularly with regard to savings and financing institutions, the judicial system, central and development banking, the educational system, and the military, not to mention some outright copying of selected organizational structures. For example, the Bank of Japan, established in 1882, was modeled after the Belgian National Bank, the postal system after the British General Post Office, the Tokyo Police Headquarters after the Paris Prefecture of Police, and the modern forestry service after the German forestry service.[19] Japan also borrowed, as Haley suggests in his chapter, most of its legal and governance mechanisms from Western countries—particularly the French concept of the separation of powers, and German notions about justiciable intervention. In creating new institutions, as well as in transforming old ones, Japan not only borrowed extensively, but also employed numerous foreigners. During the Meiji period, it drew more than 2,300 foreign experts from 23 countries and thereby acquired the image of a 'rational shopper.'[20]

Fortunate Accidents

As in other countries, but perhaps more significantly, external events also played a considerable role in Japanese development. 'Fortunate accidents'[21] included the military defeat which turned into a blessing, as it quickened the pace of institutional change and civil service reform, and: (a) windfall gains from the colonization of Korea, Taiwan, and Manchuria, which became important sources of raw materials for Japanese firms and provided markets for their industrial goods; (b) the winning of the Sino-Japanese War (1894–5), as a result of which Japan received substantial war reparations for the next five years (amounting to 6 per cent of Japan's

---

[18] See Magahiro Okuno-Fujiwara, Nihon no Gyosei Sisutemu (Administrative Systems in Japan). Unpublished manuscript, February 7, 1994.

[19] See, for example, D. Eleanor Westney, *Imitation and Innovation: The Transfer of Western Organizational Patterns to Meiji Japan* (Cambridge, Mass.: Harvard University Press, 1987).

[20] Hazel J. Jones, *Live Machines: Hired Foreigners and Meiji Japan* (Vancouver: University of British Columbia Press, 1980).

[21] John Hicks, *A Theory of Economic History* (Oxford: Clarendon Press, 1969).

GNP in 1899, the final year of reparation);[22] (*c*) the export boom of World War I during 1915–19, and the 'special procurement boom' associated with the Korean War (1950–53), each provided a massive Keynesian-type stimulus, along with sizeable foreign exchange earnings for Japan during those periods;[23] (*d*) the uninhibited access to American technology; and (*e*) perhaps more important, the institutional realignments, including the changes in the constitution during the Allied Occupation that precluded the build-up of Japan's armed forces and that reinstated a nonpoliticized civil service. Akizuki, in his chapter in this volume, records the remarkable transformation of the then powerful and invasive Ministry of the Interior after World War II into what eventually turned out to be the Ministry of Home Affairs—a small, but highly effective central agency looking after the interest of the local governments: 'at the same time, it also assumed the function of a monitoring and disciplining (where necessary) agent to ensure sound, fiscally-responsible management of the local governments.' (For transforming economies, this experience should be of interest in transforming such security-related machinery into a benign monitoring or coordinating agency.)

Allied Plan for Reconstruction: Another External Factor

The character of Japan's civil service was also shaped by other provisions of the Allied plan for reconstruction during the preindependence period up to 1952. Under that plan, the pay of civil servants was not to rise beyond their productivity gains (meaning not more than the rates of economic growth); civil servants were not allowed to strike; private damage actions could be brought against the civil service under the National Compensation Law (1947), thereby ensuring the legal accountability of the civil service and safeguarding against administrative malfeasance; and tight fiscal management was introduced under the Dodge Line (named after the American who in 1949 formulated and implemented the plan on behalf of the Allied Occupation forces).[24] All these factors gave rise to a responsible and respected civil service.

[22] Juro Teranishi and Yutaka Kosai, 'Introduction: Economic Reform and Stabilization in Postwar Japan,' in Teranishi and Kosai, eds., *The Japanese Experience of Economic Reforms* (New York: St Martin's Press, 1993), p. 7.

[23] Johnson (*MITI and the Japanese Miracle*, p. 191) attributes the war profits of the Korean War beginning in 1950 to overcoming Dodge's deflation. The Korean War had the same effect on economies, such as those in Taiwan and West Germany. See, for example, Herbert Giersch, Karle-Heinz Paqué, and Holger Schmieding, 'Openness, Wage Restraint, and Macroeconomic Stability: West Germany's Road to Prosperity 1948–59,' in Rudiger Dornbush, Wilhelm Nölling, and Richard Layard, eds., *Postwar Economic Reconstruction and Lessons for the East Today* (Cambridge, Mass.: The MIT Press, 1993), pp. 9–10.

[24] See Haley's chapter for a discussion of civil service accountability.

From Command to Market Economy: Strategies and Policies of Relevance to Transforming Economies

Japan's experience in moving away from 'state corporatism'[25] by trans-forming its wartime command economy to a vibrant market economy is particularly instructive, for it shows how a developing economy coped with hyperinflation, and realigned and established market-friendly econ-omic institutions for growth and institutionalized indicative economic planning with the participation of major stakeholders.[26]

Some of the institutional arrangements introduced in the war years (such as the foreign exchange control laws established in 1942 and the control associations, the predecessors of industry associations) survived the war and continued to exist in one form or another.[27] The wartime central economic planning agency was replaced in 1946 by an equally powerful economic control agency, the Economic Stabilization Board, which helped move Japan toward a market economy by stabilizing the production and distribution of commodities, labor, prices, finance, and trade, and by coordinating and supervising the policies of other ministries and agencies.[28] To put it differently, the Economic Stabilization Board pursued micro and supply-side policies in earnest, and set into motion the rehabilitation of enterprises and financial institutions. In 1952, with the achievement of economic stabilization, the Economic Stabilization Board was replaced by the Economic Deliberation Agency, which in turn was replaced by the Economic Planning Agency in 1955, which made econ-omic projections and formulated economic plans in tandem with the Economic Council, an advisory body to the prime minister.

Further lessons can be gleaned from other aspects of Japan's experience with reconstruction and transformation after World War II, including the plight of its bank for financing industrial reconstruction, which eventually had to be scrapped for its inflation-prone practice of resorting to central bank debentures as the chief source of capital.[29] This was the period in which the Japan Development Bank was created (in 1951) to assume the development banking function. One of its main tasks was to rigorously screen loan applications and to manage directed credits coming from the Fiscal Investment and Loan Program, as explained by Noguchi's chapter

[25] Japan practiced 'state corporatism' from 1938 to 1945 by replacing all autonomous interest associations with a state-controlled organ of control, known then as *Toseikai*, literally meaning control associations. See Tetsuji Okazaki, 'The Japanese Firm under the Wartime-Planned Economy,' *Journal of Japanese and International Economies*, Vol. 7, No. 2 (June 1993), pp. 175–203.
[26] See Takeo Komine, 'The Role of Economic Planning in Japan,' in Teranishi and Kosai, eds., *The Japanese Experience of Economic Reform*.
[27] The first legislation authorizing trade associations (*dōgyō kumiai*) was promulgated in 1884 to encourage cooperation among small-scale manufacturers. By 1925, the interfirm cooperation formula expanded to industry associations (*kōgyō kumiai*).
[28] Komine, 'The Role of Economic Planning,' p. 307.
[29] See Teranishi and Kosai, eds., *The Japanese Experience of Economic Reform*.

in this volume. As the principal actor in arranging for major loan syndication immediately after the war, the central bank had to contend with many problems that are not unlike the predicaments in which many transforming economies find themselves today.[30] The bureaucracy too faced many problems similar to those experienced elsewhere, particularly with regard to politicization. Not surprisingly, it took several decades for Japan's Western-style civil service to function as a nonpoliticized entity. Muramatsu and Pempel's chapter offers a brief historical account of how notions of a politically neutral, but proactive corps, dedicated to the national interest, while harmonizing the career aspirations of individual civil servants, were institutionalized.

The State and Economic Development: The Japanese Experience

Let us now look more closely at the strategic role the government played in Japan's development and at the institutional mechanisms through which it operated. The logical place to begin with is the developmental ideology adopted by the state.

The Ideology of 'Catching Up' and 'Shared Growth'

The idea of catching up with and surpassing the West (*oitsuki, oikose*) was particularly significant in Japan's development. It was generally accepted throughout the population, including by the elite in the ruling party and in the bureaucracy, which were thus able to forge a critical alliance that was mutually reinforcing. Catching up entailed mobilization of resources and industrialization. According to Samuels,[31] it was the pervasive anxiety arising from what the Japanese refer to as *fuan* (insecurity) that helped mobilize the people. The establishment of the Industrial Bank of Japan as the principal public institution for financing industrial and infrastructural development was a direct instance of mobilizing resources for catching up purposes.

At the same time, the state adopted the principle of shared growth, a point too often overlooked, which brought many benefits to Japan's citizens, particularly to its farmers.[32] The state vigorously promoted

[30] The Bank of Japan organized as many as 5,964 syndicated loans from January 1947 to April 1950. See Juro Teranishi, 'Financial Sector Reform after the War,' in Teranishi and Kosai, eds., *The Japanese Experience of Economic Reforms*, p. 170.

[31] Richard J. Samuels, *Rich Nation, Strong Army: National Security and the Technological Transformation of Japan*, p. ix.

[32] *The East Asian Miracle: Economic Growth and Public Policy*, published for the World Bank by Oxford University Press in 1993, underscores the importance of *a principle of shared growth* in Chapter 4, pp. 157–90.

agricultural research and extension services to improve agricultural productivity, and carried out land reform. In addition, it protected farmers from foreign competition by introducing import controls and guaranteed their relative incomes through rice subsidies. In short, the government's ideological commitment to fulfilling the social expectations of its people was an important part of ensuring economic success. This was also true in Taiwan.[33]

The Strategy of Development

The government's catch-up ideology is far from a new phenomenon. It dates back to at least 1867, the year of the Meiji Restoration. The Proposal for Industrial Promotion, issued in 1874 by Toshimichi Okubo (the found-ing minister of the Ministry of Home Affairs, and a noted champion of the Industrial policy during the Meiji period) was largely influenced by mercantilist ideas à la Frederich List. The proposal is thus regarded as Japan's 'first formal rejection of laissez-faire principles.'[34] Indeed, as early as 1884, Japan had formulated what in current jargon would be called an indicative plan. Since then, the ideology has had a profound influence on state strategy. The objectives given top priority are summarized in this section. These pertain primarily to the high-growth period from the mid-1950s to the early 1970s, but many of them, to a varying degree, appear throughout the longer sweep of the Japanese development process. The state's strong commitment to economic development underlies all its strategic objectives, of which the following have been given top priority:[35]

- Emphasize rapid accumulation of physical and human capital.
- Direct resources towards industries with increasing returns to scale and income-elastic demand.
- Promote autonomy of local authorities.
- Foster entrepreneurial impulses and talents in the private sector.
- Create a competitive environment within a cooperative framework.

The state has put considerable emphasis on the rapid accumulation of physical and human capital through a well-articulated 'active' labor policy as described in Kume's chapter, and an education policy that emphasizes science and mathematics, and compulsory primary education (which was instituted in Japan in the 1880s, much earlier than in the United Kingdom). During the 1880s alone (the Ministry of Education, Science and Culture was created in 1871), some 24,000 elementary schools

[33] K. T. Li, *The Evolution of Policy Behind Taiwan's Development Success* (New Haven: Yale University Press, 1988), p. 54.
[34] Thomas B. McCraw, 'Schumpeter Ascending,' *American Scholar*, Summer 1991, p. 390.
[35] Obviously, the relative emphasis on these points varied over the development process since the 19th century.

were built in Japan. This is close to the present number of primary schools. (According to the Education White Paper of 1991, there were 24,827 elementary schools in 1991.) The educational system showed no bias toward either gender.

The state has consciously attempted to direct resources towards industries with increasing returns to scale and income-elastic demand for their products. The Japanese government has been the key actor in creating a favourable investment climate, as well as in alleviating a coordination failure through a range of strategic interventions, including the extensive use of indicative plans. The mobilization of postal savings and pension funds into the Fiscal Investment and Loan Program (FILP), managed by the Trust Fund Bureau of the Ministry of Finance like the 'second budget', is an important example of strategic intervention. FILP has financed infrastructural and other priority investment programs, at an interest rate marginally lower than the rates charged by the commercial banks, at the same time providing a 'cowbell effect,' signalling the commitment of government to desired areas of investment. FILP resources were channelled mainly through public institutions, in particular the Japan Development Bank, to ensure the proper selection of investments, thereby sustaining public confidence in the use of the funds originating in private savings.[36] In contrast, many developing countries fail to make sound investment choices because their banks lack the appropriate appraisal and monitoring capabilities, or because of political interference in the selection of projects to be supported with 'directed credit.'

In selecting industries to promote and support, the state has focused primarily on adopting, adapting, improving, and disseminating modern technology.[37] MITI was the institution created to oversee these activities.[38] Further, it emphasized strengthening the export performance of industries in this area. The export-promotion strategy included an emphasis on monitoring export performance, which provided an unequivocal and transparent yardstick for formulating incentives, and in addition helped the state move ahead with its program of transformation. The strategy's

---

[36] For descriptions on the way FILP was managed, see Kozo Kato *et al.*, *Policy-Based Finance: The Experience of Postwar Japan*, World Bank Discussion Papers, No. 221, 1994. For a succinct treatment of the Fiscal Investment and Loan Program, see Noguchi's chapter in this volume. For a more extensive treatment on the political economy of the FILP, see Kent E. Calder, *Strategic Capitalism: Private Business and Public Purpose in Japanese Industrial Finance* (Princeton: Princeton University Press, 1993).

[37] Even the governments of the Tokugawa era (1600–1868), which imposed isolation from 1639 on, created a channel for importing technology from the Dutch. For a comprehensive discussion of Japan's postwar experience in importing technology, see Akira Goto, 'Technology Importation: Japan's Postwar Experience,' in Teranishi and Kosai, eds., *The Japanese Experience of Postwar Reform*, and Richard J. Samuels, *Rich Nation, Strong Army*.

[38] See Terumoto Ozawa, 'Government Control over Technology Acquisition and Firms' Entry into New Sectors: The Experience of Japan's Synthetic Fiber Industry,' *Cambridge Journal of Economics* (June, 1980), and Leonard Lynn, *How Japan Innovates: A Comparison with U.S. in the Case of Oxygen Steelmaking* (Boulder, Colo.: Westview Press, 1982)

externalities were widely approved of and thus also helped control rent-seeking behavior and corruption. This export-push strategy disciplined the behavior of government, firms, banks, and all other participants in the growth process more effectively than any other mechanism.

Emphasis has also been placed on increasing the autonomy of local authorities by allowing them to exercise their discretion in using the revenues transferred from the central government under the local grant tax (which is not really a tax, but a transfer) without any strings attached. In fact, the Local Grant Tax Law specifically prohibits any restrictions by the central government on how the money is to be spent. The details of local finance and intergovernmental relations—especially between local governments and the Ministry of Home Affairs, and between the latter ministry and the Ministry of Finance—are provided in the chapter by Akizuki.

Another important step has been to foster, rather than to suppress, entrepreneurial impulses and talents in the private sector. This move was a direct response to Schumpeter's theory of economic development and to the notion of 'creative destruction,' both of which had a great impact on Japanese thinking. In this entrepreneur-friendly environment, commercial banks were made autonomous, in contrast to the financially disastrous government-designated banks for the munitions industry of the war period, and were allowed to engage in relationship banking. They came to be known as 'main banks,' since their function was to serve their client firms; they were also permitted to have a modest equity (not more than 10 per cent) in the firms; they effectively performed the corporate governance function through their monitoring of firms.[39]

The government has been deliberately attempting to create a competitive environment within a cooperative framework, using among others, the following coordinating mechanisms: *indicative planning*, which plays both educational and information-sharing roles, signals long-term policy commitment, and makes possible interaction and consultation with the private sector,[40] and *deliberation councils*,[41] made up of representatives of

[39] It would be unthinkable, for example, to evaluate the performance of NEC, a giant electronics firm, without considering its relationship with the Sumitomo Bank, which has been NEC's main bank. For a comprehensive analysis of the Japanese main bank system, see Masahiko Aoki and Hugh Patrick, eds., *Japanese Main Bank System and Its Relevance for Developing and Transforming Economies*.

[40] See Japan's Economic Council, *Keizai Keikaku Kihon-Mondai Kenkyukai Hokoku* (Report of the Basic Problems of Economic Plan Committee) (Tokyo: Economic Council of Japan, 1969). For a discussion on the role of indicative plans in Korea, see Il Sakong, 'Indicative Planning in Korea: Discussion,' *Journal of Comparative Economics*, Vol. 14 (1990), pp. 677–80.

[41] Some characterize deliberation councils (collectively referring to such forums as *shingikai* [commonly known as policy council], *chōsakai* [investigation council], and *iinkai* [committee]), as an 'institutionalized form of wealth sharing aimed primarily at winning the support and cooperation of business elites.' See World Bank, *The East Asian Miracle*, p. 181). The deliberation councils originated before World War II. Their prominence is, however, a postwar phenomenon. According to a survey undertaken by *Nikkei Business* (September 12,

various stakeholders (in industry, labor, the mass media, consumer groups, and the government), which help shape government thinking on major policy issues and provide a forum for the articulation of private sector interests.

Such coordination mechanisms have not only generated trust and confidence, but have also helped disseminate information, and have reduced the transaction costs and risks each participant faces. Perhaps the best example from the early stages of postwar development is the coordination of additions to capacity in industries with increasing returns to scale, which left overall supply in line with rising demand. Because of the increasing returns to scale arising from cooperative behavior (the diffusion of information, and the resulting reduction of risks arising from adverse selection and moral hazard), industrial development has been able to proceed at a fairly rapid rate. Similar observations have been made about Korea and Taiwan. Rodrick identifies as a key explanatory variable underlying rapid growth to be government interventions that effectively addressed the issue of coordination failures in investment:

> [I]n the early 1960s and thereafter the Korean and Taiwanese governments managed to engineer a significant increase in the private return to capital. They did so not only by removing a number of impediments to investment and establishing a sound investment climate, but more importantly by alleviating a coordination failure which had blocked economic take-off. The latter required a range of strategic interventions—including investment subsidies, administrative guidance, and the use of public enterprise—which went considerably beyond those discussed in the standard account.[42]

The distinctive feature of the decision-making process in Japan is that it has a much greater input of information than other systems, and thereby constitutes a collective assessment of what Keynes called the possibilities of things. The decisions made by MITI, the MOF, or firms, are not based simply on individual information bases, but on a base of collective information. For instance, the export performance of firms provides information that MITI or MOF or the Bank of Japan can use to prevent rent seeking by government ministries or firms. The strategies, institutional

1994), there are 215 deliberation councils, involving some 4,700 persons serving on those councils. Some of the important ones are the Economic Reconstruction Planning Council (consisting of 377 members), the Industrial Rationalization Deliberation Council, the Economic Council—an advisory council to the prime minister—the Industrial Structure Deliberation Council, and the Administrative Reform Councils (as described in the chapter by Ito). Largely because of the publicity associated with the Industrial Structure Deliberation Council, an advisory council to the minister of international trade and industry, analysts often fail to recognize that other ministries also maintain considerable numbers of significant deliberation councils of various kinds and significance, for example, about twenty affiliated with Ministry of Agriculture, Forestry, and Fisheries.

[42] Dani Rodrick, 'Getting Interventions Right: How South Korea and Taiwan Grew Rich,' a paper dated June 1994, prepared for the 20th Panel Meeting of Economic Policy, October 13–14, 1994.

mechanisms, and policies that have contributed to Japan's economic performance are rooted in this cooperative behavior.

· At the same time, Japan encourages individuals to compete within the bureaucracy, firms, or banks for promotions, with a view to serving the collective interest of the institution concerned. These collectivities then compete with each other, so as to further the national interest. Such collective competition also promotes group loyalty. Several institutional arrangements—notably associations of various kinds—were created to stimulate competition in a cooperative framework. Some of these associations were created by law to promote a specific industrial subsector, say the electronics industry, and some for broader purposes, for example to promote engineering services or the export of plants.

Other associations have their roots in wartime industry groups known as *toseikai* (literally 'control associations'), which were essentially cartels of the *zaibatsu* and were subsequently transformed into quasi-public institutions as intermediaries between the government and the business community, that allowed firms to voice the views of the concerned industry, while also acting as a conduit for the wishes of government, or providing forums for the exchange of information and ideas.[43] These groups also performed some designated statutory functions such as rationing raw materials and intermediate products during and following the war, and testing product quality. In addition, the state encouraged interfirm cooperative undertakings by promoting horizontal *keiretsu*—networks of firms belonging to the same business group—and by neutralizing the opposition of the Fair Trade Commission to cooperative ventures in R&D, while refraining from 'picking winners,' in contrast to what American industrial policy debates often allege Japan does. It also tried to devise imaginative ways of funding public institutions or priority programs. The Japan External Trade Research Organization, for example, was created not through support from the government budget but with proceeds from the importation of bananas, while automation R&D activities of the Machinery Industry Promotion Association were initially funded by revenues generated from professional cycling.[44] A more recent trend is to seek the coop-

[43] Japan made extensive use of industry associations during the war to act as *de facto* agents of the government for such tasks as formulating plans to expand production capacity, allocating resources (especially foreign exchange), and managing distribution of the materials, and the allocation of production quotas; hence the name control associations. There were more than twenty such associations linked with the industrial sector during the war. These associations underwent a postwar transformation, reemerging as the key intermediary institutions between the government and the business sector. For example, the Steel Industry Control Association, established in 1941, was transformed into the Steel Industry Association of Japan in December 1945. For the wartime roles of control associations, see Okazaki, 'The Japanese Firm under the Wartime-Planned Economy.'

[44] The Ministry of Finance's reluctance to provide funding for the creation of new institutions or programs may have been a factor in the proliferation of such 'idiosyncratic' funding ideas.

eration of *Keidanren* (Japan Federation of Economic Organizations) in the establishment of industry-sponsored public foundations, the Foundation for the Future of Children being one such example.

Policy Instruments

Japan has used various policy instruments to achieve its economic objectives within the framework of competitive cooperation. These range from protection and discriminatory subsidies to the promotion of cartel arrangements for the restructuring of firms in financial distress. Restructuring aid is channeled through the Japan Development Bank, the Industrial Bank of Japan, or even the main banks, and is seen to preserve the physical and human resources accumulated in firms which might otherwise be lost. The government also endeavors to procure the products of enterprising firms, and encourages the exchange of information between the government and firms, particularly regarding technologies and indigenous research results.

In addition, tax policies and industry-specific laws are extensively used to achieve economic goals. The overall aim is to reduce the risks entrepreneurs face, provided their behavior is consistent with the government's overall strategy. Despite the huge size of the nation's R&D efforts, the government's share of R&D funding is lowest among the Organization for Economic Cooperation and Development member countries, largely because of the heavy outlays by firms, which are bolstered in part by favorable tax policies for R&D.[45] These are selective and nonneutral interventions designed to promote export competitiveness, take advantage of increasing returns to scale, and avoid wastage of accumulated human and physical resources.

There has been some debate as to whether these instruments have been used primarily to improve dynamic technological efficiency (DTE), an efficiency which achieves the highest long-term productivity growth rate, as Yamamura suggests, or to promote exports. The fact is that the push for DTE could not have taken place without promoting exports. Exports provided the resources needed to import equipment and technology, and served as a means of acquiring information about multinational firms, international markets, and marketing technologies, all of which created extremely important externalities. In addition, export performance provided a transparent and unequivocal yardstick for measuring the performance of industries and firms—a yardstick that was much more reliable than any sophisticated cost–benefit analysis, since it yielded

---

[45] According to the *Science and Technology White Paper*, published by the Japanese Agency for Science and Technology in 1993, the government share of Japan's R&D expenditure in 1991 was 16.8 per cent whereas the shares for US, France, and Germany were 43.2 per cent, 47.5 per cent, and 36.6 per cent respectively.

information the government needed to formulate its incentives and subsidies, as well as its penalties. Finally, the export push imposed rigid discipline on both the government and on firms in formulating their plans and policies; no other disciplinary factor was as effective as export performance.

How the Industrialization Ideology Gained Popular Support

Several factors have made it possible for Japan's various social classes and groups to accept the industrialization ideology and development strategy: single-party rule and a critical alliance between the LDP and the civil service; various mechanisms for coordinating decision making between the civil service and the private sector; the role of the Ministry of Education in propagating this ideology through the school and university systems; public education through the public broadcasting system (NHK); and suppression of the labor movement and the weakening of the country's leftist parties.

Several other factors also account for popular acceptance. First, the government instituted a full employment policy, implemented through various devices: an active national labor market, and placement services and training programs sponsored by the government as well as the development of large firms (see chapter by Kume). This indirect protection of labor, along with MITI policies supporting cartel arrangements for declining industries, and general support for the system of lifetime employment in large firms, has made labor a significant stakeholder in the growth of firms and of the economy. It is in this line of logic that some disagree with the notion of 'corporatism without labor.'[46]

Second, the government encouraged the formation of vertical keiretsu—which have become the vital link between large manufacturers and small and medium-sized suppliers and distributors. This sparked the rise of small entrepreneurs and gave them a stake in the growth of large firms, as well as in the economy as a whole. Here it should be noted that the move towards vertical integration began out of necessity, in an effort to enable large manufacturers to contain the competition from small and medium-sized enterprises, as well as to modernize them. This development has been aptly described as a 'double encapsulization "from above," both by the state bureaucracy and large firms, all in the interest of national economic success.'[47]

Third, Japan's farmers readily accepted the state's ideology, as already

[46] See Masahiko Aoki, *Information, Incentives, and Bargaining in the Japanese Economy*, p. 262.
[47] T.J. Pempel and Keichi Tsunekawa, 'Corporatism without Labor? The Japanese Anomaly' in Phillipe C. Schmitter and Gerhard Lehmbruch, eds., *Trends Toward Corporatist Intermediation* (Beverly Hills: Sage Publications, 1979), p. 261.

mentioned, because their relative incomes were protected by subsidies (rice subsidies) and other instruments. The government ignored market signals in formulating its agricultural policies but heeded them in its industrial policies. Thus, labor, small enterprises, and farmers—all important socioeconomic groups—accepted the industrialization ideology and its underlying principle of shared growth.

The Political Factor

Single-party rule has undoubtedly played an important role in Japan's economic development. But how has it been possible for a single party to remain in power for more than 38 years in a parliamentary democracy? One reason for the tenacity of the LDP may have been its broadly based constituencies, as well as the population's acceptance of its industrialization ideology. Or it may have been due to the critical alliance between the LDP and the civil service, or possibly due to the peculiar design of the election system, under which it is possible to elect multiple candidates from any electoral district, an element which is to be abolished under the newly introduced system during the Hosokawa government.

Of these three, the most likely explanation is that in Japan there has been no basic fundamental disagreement with regard to what Schumpeter calls 'the structural or tectonic principle of the social fabric.'[48] The acceptance of the industrialization ideology by all socioeconomic classes, and hence the weakening of the leftist parties in Japan, made it possible for such a principle to be adopted. Muramatsu and Krause emphasize the contributing role of political leadership, political strategy, and political coalitions and competition in maintaining social and political stability based on *hoshu honryū* (conservative policy line), and in fostering the socio-political context for economic growth. This was especially true during the early years of the LDP rule.[49] They write:

If Japan is a 'developmental state,' then that development has been as much a *means* toward political goals as an end in itself. And as the postwar evolution of *hoshu honryū* has shown, development has been variously adapted, modified, and changed toward that goal. Politics has not just been a safety valve allowing for rational economic development; development, variously defined in different periods, has been one of the key strategies to accomplish political goals.[50]

[48] Joseph A. Schumpeter, *Capitalism, Socialism, and Democracy* (New York: Harper and Row, 1975).

[49] See Michio Muramatsu and Ellis S. Krauss, 'The Conservative Policy Line and the Development of Patterned Plurarism,' in Kozo Yamamura and Yasukichi Yasuba, eds., *The Political Economy of Japan, Volume 1: The Domestic Transformation*, pp. 516–54.

[50] Ibid., p. 554.

The Civil Service and its Contributions to Economic Development

Historically, Japan's civil service has provided the country with unusual flexibility in adapting to changing circumstances through the creation of new institutions, the modification of old ones, and through the continuous rethinking of the role of government in the economy. Driven by the overriding political imperative of catching up with and surpassing the West economically, there has been little inertia in devising roles for government in implementing strategies that will achieve these ends.

The roles of government in all countries are substantially performed by their civil servants. Japan's civil service has proven indispensable to the strategic vision that all elements of Japanese society subscribe to and which has been described above. The country has developed a small, elite, efficient cadre of civil servants that is relatively insulated from the pressures of short term political considerations, and has considerable scope for action. The remainder of this chapter is concerned with an analysis of the major features of the Japanese civil service, and the evolution of its role in the economy and polity.

A senior civil servant in the government of Japan characterizes the Japanese bureaucracy as follows:[51]

- In Japan, the doors are kept open to anyone with proven ability to become a civil servant.
- Within the civil service, there are many measures to help executive-position candidates acquire expertise and experience. These include job assignment leeway, interministry personnel exchanges, systematic training under the National Personnel Authority.
- There is a high degree of integrity throughout the civil service. Japanese officials seem to be content with 'honest' poverty.
- Merit ratings of personnel are very strict. Civil servants are continuously evaluated from the day they are recruited. Evaluations take into account appraisals by both subordinates and colleagues.
- There is a clear division of responsibility in the government as a whole and in individual organizations.
- Mechanisms of overall coordination are firmly in place.
- Within the government as a whole, as well as within individual

[51] Toshiyuki Masujima, 'Civil Service in Time of Change: The Salient Features of Japanese Bureaucracy and Its Reform,' a keynote address at the International Colloquium on the Civil Service and Its Role in Economic Development: The Experience of Japan, Tokyo, Japan, March 22–5, 1994. For a more comprehensive description of the management of the Japanese bureaucracy, see Toshiyuki Masujima and Minoru Ouchi, eds., *The Management and Reform of Japanese Government* (Tokyo: The Institute of Administrative Management, 1993).

organizations, there is a high regard placed on decision making by consensus in the planning stages of programs, which in turn ensures coherence, speediness, and uniformity in program implementation.

- Adjustment mechanisms to complement the market mechanism have been devised and introduced to prevent proliferation of public administration. Such mechanisms force continual reexamination of policies, programs, and the means available for their implementation.

- There are high-level organs specialized in overall coordination which exercise control through management rather than via the budget. The Management and Coordination Agency and the Cabinet Legislation Bureau are examples. They coordinate policies and programs through their authority over organizational structure, manpower, administrative process, and legislative review.

- There are established procedures for administrative reform. In the 1980s, there was a dramatic reform (usually called the *rincho* administrative reform) against the backdrop of the government's tight fiscal position. One of the most notable reform items was the privatization of giant public corporations including Japanese National Railways and Nippon Telegraph and Telephone. A drastic reexamination of existing policies and programs also took place, which led to amendments of relevant laws.

The Evolution of Japan's Modern Civil Service

From the outset of its modernization, during the Meiji period (1868–1912), Japan's bureaucracy was a lean, merit-based extension of the ruling elite (see Silberman's chapter). Japan was merely transformed from a 'feudal police state' into a 'centralized bureaucratic state.'[52] Although a spoils system was in wide use during the first two decades of the Meiji period, once the modern civil service was introduced, Japan quickly saw the need to institutionalize a modern meritocracy if it was to receive 'equal' treatment in its treaties with Western powers.[53]

The first step was to make the necessary changes in the judicial system, and then to enact a constitution, as well as administrative, civil, and criminal laws along Western lines. In conjunction with this effort, government officials were instructed to modernize the economy and thereby strengthen the military. In the case of Meiji Japan, the state itself recognized what needed to be done in this regard and took the necessary measures, often under the tutelage of foreign advisers. Of course, the civil

---

[52] Masamichi Royama, 'Kindai kanri seido no hattatsu' (Development of a modern bureaucratic system), in Royama, *Gyoseigaku Kenkyūron Bunshu* (Collection of research papers on public administration) (Tokyo: Keiso Shobo, 1965), p. 229.

[53] See B. C. Koh, *Japan's Administrative Elite* (Berkeley: University of California Press, 1989).

service reforms undertaken immediately after World War II were by and large imposed, although indigenous elements did shape the final outcome.[54]

Another noteworthy feature of the evolution of Japan's modern civil service is that Japanese leaders searched for modern 'models' in Western countries, notably France, Germany, Austria, and to a lesser extent, Great Britain and the United States. As pointed out by Silberman, Japan's primary concern was to construct a bureaucratic system that could integrate state and society in an 'organizationally oriented mode,' along the lines of the French bureaucracy, instead of a 'professionally oriented mode,' as typified by the English and US civil service systems.

Specifically, Japan took the career system in building its civil service (like the French and most other European civil services) rather than the job system. Indeed, it is often said that much of the success of the Japanese bureaucracy rests on its capacity to take individuals trained for careers, and to assign them many different jobs so that they gain a wide variety of experiences and a wide range of skills. A problem with the career system is that individuals are appointed in a 'grade' which does not imply any specific function. They carry amorphous titles such as 'administrator.' What exactly does that mean? Administrators do many different things, and people with the same salary and the same place in the hierarchy may carry out varying responsibilities. It is usually desirable to know exactly what kind of function must be accomplished in each job; so it seems that the career system could be improved if there were more precise job descriptions. Operationally, the career system made good sense, for if a country does not have a large pool of trained professionals, nor the capacity to produce large numbers of well-trained professionals to fill the civil service on a position by position basis, then it should focus on strengthening the organizational aspects of the system.

To fill the initial needs for staffing the modern civil service, Japan created Tokyo Imperial University (also known as Todai), which became the primary institution for training future high-level government officials. Many of these officials received their training in the university's Faculty of Law (which is made up of several departments that specialize in public law, private or corporate law, and public administration). This training was patterned after the Prussian civil service and was based on its concept of Rechtstaat.[55] Until 1893, Todai graduates were not even required to take

---

[54] For an excellent account of the evolution of the economic bureaucracy in Japan, see C. Johnson, *MITI and the Japanese Miracle*, Part Two, pp. 35–82.

[55] Milton Esman, who worked on the public administration staff at the Supreme Command for the Allied Forces in Tokyo after World War II, suggests that the Prussian *Rechtstaat* was adopted 'primarily to convince the western world that because all acts of Japanese officials were regulated by a strict rule of law, extraterritoriality could safely be withdrawn.' See Milton Esman, 'Japanese Administration: A Comparative View,' *Public Administration Review*, Vol. 7, No. 2 (1947), p. 111.

the higher civil service examination. As in the case of Japan, countries whose administrative institutions are to be run by rules of law and subordinate ordinances formulated by civil servants in accordance with a system of administrative laws, are bound to recruit persons with legal training in the broad sense of the word.

Japan's choice of an organizationally oriented system may also have been influenced by the political uncertainty in the early years of the Meiji period. Countries coping with major political change but devoid of well-trained professionals are more likely to find the organizational approach less risky. As already stated, most of the legal and other institutional mechanisms Japan finally adopted were borrowed from Western countries: 'Hence neither the institutions nor the patterns of governance that emerged in the course of time as a result of the constitutional and other legal reforms of the late nineteenth century or as modified and restructured by an occupying military conqueror in the mid-twentieth century were produced by either internal historical evolution or a coherent agenda or structural change. Rather they reflect a complex and often elusive mixture of selective borrowing and cultural adaptation' (see Haley's chapter), guided closely by the Meiji oligarchs, notably Aritomo Yamagata who believed local government and bureaucracy to be the most effective foundation of governance and Hirobumi Itō, who saw the importance of the political party and the parliamentary system in maintaining political stability.

The oligarchs established a degree of bureaucratic authority by explicitly linking such authority to imperial prerogatives. That is to say, they treated the new civil servants as the emperor's officials. Article 10 of the Meiji constitution of 1889 stipulated that 'the Emperor determines the organization of the different branches of the administration and salaries of all civil and military officers, and appoints and dismisses the same.'[56]

The most drastic of Japan's civil service reforms were those carried out after World War II under the rubric of 'political democratization', and under the direction of the General Headquarters of the Supreme Commander for the Allied Powers (SCAP). The National Public Service Law of October 21, 1947, among others, stipulated that Japan was to establish a nonpolitical central personnel agency, the National Personnel Authority which was to be a part of the cabinet, but not of the prime minister's office.[57] In addition, the law prohibited strikes by government officials and

---

[56] Koh, *Japan's Administrative Elite*, p. 14.

[57] A frequent corruption scandal in the political world in contrast to the virtual lack of such scandals within the Japanese bureaucracy deserves particular attention. To safeguard the integrity of the National Personnel Authority, the following provisions are made: (i) the appointment of the three commissioners, *jinjikan*, is made by the cabinet for a tenure of four years with the approval of both houses of the Diet; (ii) the commissioners, once appointed, cannot be removed until their term expires other than through impeachment; (iii) the commissioners can be reappointed for a maximum of three terms, allowing for some conti-

divided national public service jobs into regular government service positions and special government service positions, which included prime
ministers, ministers, and vice ministers. To ensure that the civil service
would remain accountable, the new constitution provided for judicial
redress in cases where actions of the civil service caused damage to any
class or group (see Haley's chapter, which discusses the 1962 Administrative Case Litigation Law and the National Compensation Law of 1947,
among others).

On the advice of its Prussian and Austrian mentors, Japan decided to
work on the framework of the bureaucratic system before establishing the
Diet. In this way, it was able to give an upper hand, so to speak, to the
executive branch of the government. The power of the early bureaucracy
is clear from the fact that only two of the thirty prewar prime ministers did
not have any bureaucratic service, either civil or military.[58]

Recruitment, Promotion, and Performance-Related Incentives

In general the civil service in Japan attracts 'the best and brightest'. Candidates are screened through three levels of competitive examination and
evaluation, although there has never been a formal educational requirement. Competitive examinations consist of a general test and a specialized
test (in areas such as public administration law, civil engineering, forestry). These tests are administered by the National Personnel Authority.
This agency subsequently compiles rosters of successful candidates by
field of specialization and ranks them in the order of the scores earned.
The ministries and agencies select people from these lists for interviews,
but the openings available are usually far fewer than the number of
successful candidates.[59]

Those who pass the competitive examinations are recruited individually by each agency, which serves to inspire loyalty to the agency and to
its objectives. Although the emphasis on allegiance to one agency, or to
be more precise, allegiance to one bureau, makes it easier to develop
substantial expertise in the administrative elite, this tradition has bred
so-called sectionalism, both at interagency and intraagency levels. Phrases
in common usage such as 'there are bureaus, but no ministry' aptly

---

nuity; and (iv) no two commissioners can belong to the same political party or come from the
same university to minimize the possibility of collusion among the commissioners.

[58] Masamichi Inoki, 'The Civil Bureaucracy,' in Robert E. Ward and Dankakwart A.
Rustow, eds., *Political Modernization in Japan and Turkey* (Princeton: Princeton University
Press, 1964), p. 293.

[59] For a detailed description of the recruitment and promotion systems of the Japanese
civil service, see Koh, *Japan's Administrative Elite*, chap. 4 on recruitment and chap. 5 on
promotion; and *Handbook on Japan's Civil Service: Statistical Overview 1993–4*, published by
the National Personnel Authority.

convey the intense preoccupation with bureaus in each agency of Japan's government.[60]

Up to a certain limit, promotion depends on length of service, although functional promotion depends on merit. Thus the system generates fierce competition for functional promotion, which is extremely important for later promotion to selective merit-based positions as well as for postretirement (*amakudari*) assignments. Interestingly, this incentive structure not only fosters individual competition, but it also furthers the *collective* interest of the agency, in that the task of *amakudari* is to strengthen the relationship between government and business firms, between the Bank of Japan and the banks, and between the central and local governments and public corporations. Inoki, in his chapter observes: '[A]makudari vitalizes human resources in the bureaucracy by its built-in mechanism of a deferred payment element and early retirement, both of which seem to provide strong incentives to actualize the potentially rich resources in the Japanese bureaucracy.' Inoki, of course, elaborates on the costs associated with such a system. In a survey conducted in July, 1994 by *Nihon Keizai Shimbun*, 62 per cent of the respondents stated their opposition to the practice of *amakudari* for fear of collusion between the government agencies and the private sector, whereas only 24 per cent of the bureaucrats surveyed thought likewise, showing a wide perception gap on this matter. Furthermore, salary scales have been attractive, although not quite as high as they are in Japan's large private sector. These scales, as well as changes in them, are monitored by the NPA which makes recommendations for appropriate annual adjustments.[61]

The Japanese system is typical of one of two models of promotion.[62] It is known as the closed multitrack model of promotion, since the entry track (lower, intermediate, or elite) is what governs how far civil servants can rise in the system. Also, this model does not permit lateral entry from outside. The promotion systems in Korea and Taiwan are in principle also of the closed multitrack variety. Although the closed model leaves little room for abuse, the system is rigid and thus it is extremely difficult, if not impossible, to introduce 'new blood' into the civil service. To get around this problem, Korea has left a small window for nonregular civil servants to enter into higher levels of the civil service via transparent eligibility requirements and selection procedures.[63] This device may have some

---

[60] Organizational loyalty can effectively reduce selfish behavior among the organizational participants. See Albert Hirschman, *Exit, Voice, and Loyalty* (Cambridge, Mass.: Harvard University Press, 1970).

[61] For a description on the NPA's pay recommendation system, see *National Personnel Authority and Civil Service System*, chapter 5 on Remuneration, published by the National Personnel Authority in 1993.

[62] Ibid., pp. 125–6.

[63] To become eligible to take special higher-level civil service examinations in Korea (meaning the examination is not competitive but qualifying), one must have served a

advantages for governments seeking to beef up their administrative core without inordinately compromising the merit-based bureaucracy.

The other model of promotion is the open competitive type, of which the American system is a prime example. Here, all personnel have an equal chance of promotion, regardless of their entry level, and lateral entry is permitted at all levels. While the open competitive type can ensure a steady flow of fresh talent, it can be easily abused.

As already mentioned, competition among agencies for the right to undertake crucial tasks promotes intense loyalty within each agency. (This phenomenon is described in greater detail in Mabuchi's chapter.) Since each agency has to compete for additional tasks and functions, agencies compile a great deal of information and conduct numerous analyses, all of which the government—the ruling party—uses to arrive at its policy decisions. This process, though prolonged, ensures that decisions are well-informed and thus that their implementation is rapid. The overriding test is whether the decision will enable an agency to promote growth in terms of the strategic objectives of the government.

In this system, the bureaucracy is tightly controlled by the imperative of fiscal balance. Hence it is not subject to Parkinson's law, as in other countries; it has to prove its effectiveness and efficiency through its performance. MOF, through its budgeting processes and procedures, plays a critical role in operationalizing such control over bureaucratic action. Further, administrative reforms can be instigated by the prime minister, the ruling party, and lately by the business community; these reforms and their implementation are a check on bureaucratic expansion. For example, the privatization of Japanese National Railways and Nippon Telephone and Telegraph, and pension plan reforms, were initiated at this level, (but had to be executed by the bureaucrats) because of the prestige of the prime minister and the LDP. The coordinating ministries—MOF and the Management and Coordination Agency (MCA)—shoulder the responsibility for formulating and implementing reforms for other ministries. Ito in his chapter observes that a system that would strengthen the office of the prime minister so as to exert stronger leadership may be in order to deal effectively with the issues calling for administrative reforms.

Reconciling Autonomy with Accountability

Since the civil service in Japan is insulated from partisan politics, has operational autonomy, and a very broad mandate to promote economic development (in terms of constitutional and legal provisions), why then does it not behave in an autocratic manner, issuing directives and commands to the private sector? This question is discussed in depth in this

minimum of three years in nonregular civil service (for example, as a special assistant to a minister) at the grade level at which entrance is being sought.

book. The fundamental answer is that the emphasis in the Japanese constitution and legal framework falls on the *rule of law* rather than on the whims and caprices of the political and bureaucratic authorities.

Some observers strongly disagree on this point. Those from the business community in particular complain about the intrusive measures taken by the state bureaucracy, often under the guise of administrative guidance.

Under the constitution (which although imposed by the occupation is favored by Japanese politicians), Japan has a democratic form of government; this means the political leaders have to be elected by the people. It has a parliamentary democracy, an independent civil service (recruited by a nonpolitical independent agency—the National Personnel Authority), and an independent judiciary. Even so, until recently Japan has had one-party rule by the LDP. However, this party sought popular approval for its aims and objectives by formulating and implementing the principle of shared growth, which makes all socioeconomic classes stakeholders in the fruits of Japanese growth.

Second, the constitution's unique provision for judicial redress in the event of damage caused to any interest or class as a result of an action of the civil service prevents the civil service from indulging in coercive acts or in the arbitrary pursuit of power. The Japanese civil service is extremely proud of its image as 'guardian of the public interest,' and any judicial action or even threat of such action is regarded as causing 'shame' or 'disgrace' and thus undermining its popular image. This again is a deterrent to the arbitrary pursuit of power.

Third, since the civil service is legally accountable to the public, it does not use commands or directives to achieve its overriding objective of development. Instead, it seeks the cooperation of industries and other interests in this endeavor. Hence, it has established several coordination mechanisms, such as deliberation councils, to ensure such cooperative behavior. The decisions taken by the civil service therefore generally represent a consensus arrived at through various coordination mechanisms.

Controlling the Size of the Civil Service

Japan's bureaucracy has been described as 'one of the smallest and least expensive systems in the world.'[64] Of the methods used to limit the expansion of the civil service, the actions of the Ministry of Finance are noteworthy, comparable to the budgetary authority in Korea. These budgetary authorities put great stress on maintaining macroeconomic stability through fiscal balance, and on avoiding any misdirection of resources

[64] Paul S. Kim, *Japan's Civil Service System: Its Structure, Personnel, and Politics* (New York: Greenwood Press, 1988), p. 1.

away from productive investment by the private sector to potentially 'unproductive' government consumption. For example in Japan the budget must be balanced. This means that in the event of a budget deficit, a special law must be enacted to approve issue of deficit-financing bonds. In other words, the government cannot issue bonds simply for the sake of consumption, although construction bonds for public investment are permitted. In addition, the Government Tax Council as early as 1960 advised that a limit of 20 per cent should be placed on the ratio of tax revenue to national income so as to maintain the vitality of the private sector. In addition, in the 1980s a long-run limit of 50 per cent was set on the national burden ratio (which is the sum of tax revenue and social security contributions divided by national income). Together, such measures provide an upper limit on government expenditures. The across-the-board downsizing of the ministries undertaken in Japan by the Sato government in the late 1960s is a crude, but at times effective, approach to reducing the size of the civil service. The Japanese government may also deliberate such matters through a blue-ribbon commission, namely the Administrative Reform Commission (see the chapter by Ito).

Other measures to limit the size of the civil service are incorporated in the National Government Organization Law and Total Staff Number Law, and derive from the implementation of a 'scrap and build' principle.

In Japan, the Government Organization Law has imposed a strict limit on the number of bureaus and secretariats in the government (128 in total) at twelve ministries and eight agencies (equivalent to a ministry), and the Total Staff Number Law of 1967 sets ceilings on the number of civil servants in each agency of government. The Japanese Government Organizational manual, published annually for public dissemination, contains a list of the ceilings, which can only be changed with the approval of the Cabinet and the legislative branch. Ceilings are seldom increased, although in a few instances new agencies (such as the Environmental Protection Agency) have been created.

The functions of the secretariats and bureaus are provided by Cabinet order. A secretariat or a bureau may sometimes have a deputy director (*jicho*) or a department (*bu*) within it, but the basic functional units are divisions (*ka*). The number of divisions in the whole government is less than 1500. Their names and functions are also specified by Cabinet orders. A Cabinet order is necessary to finalize allocation of new functions to cope with a demand for new services.

The enforcement of the 'scrap and build' principle is another method by which the size of the Japanese bureaucracy is kept in check, in this case by preventing the unnecessary proliferation of government organizations. The Management and Coordination Agency is authorized to examine and decide whether or not to grant the request for the creation of organizations of any size within the executive branch. Permission for the creation of a new unit is granted only if an organization of equivalent level is abolished from within the ranks of the executive organ requesting it. This principle has been rigorously upheld. The philosophy is that a new organization is an additional decision-making unit within the government, and thus represents an increase in the range of government operations. Scrap and build curbs the proliferation of the sphere of government activities. In addition, there has been an active, coordinated, personnel reduction plan under the initiative of the Management and Coordination Agency, which has operated with some success.

'Hidden' Aspects of the Japanese Civil Service

According to Kosai,[65] hidden aspects of Japanese government make it appear smaller than it actually is.

One such institution, unique to Japan, is the Fiscal Investment and Loan Program (FILP or *zaito*), directed by the Ministry of Finance's Trust Fund Bureau. This off-budget program makes use of funds collected in the form of postal savings and social security payments to finance government-affiliated banking institutions such as the Overseas Economic Cooperation Fund (OECF), the Japan Development Bank (JDB), and others. The FILP in recent years has amounted to 50–70 per cent of the central government's general account. These funds have served as an important source of government influence on the private sector.

Also, in some instances, regulation can be a substitute for government expenditure, thereby attenuating the fiscal burden and making government appear smaller than it actually is. For instance, agricultural protection can be carried out in two ways. One is the provision of subsidies. However, subsidies involve direct government expenditure. Instead, the imposition of an import quota or a complete prohibition of imports, although transferring the burden onto consumers in terms of higher prices for agricultural goods, requires minimal government expenditure.

The use of administrative guidance by Japanese civil servants is well known. It is by no means legally binding, but it can be an effective instrument for pursuing public policy. Although certain prerequisites for the effectiveness of such moral suasion must be met, such as the creation of an intimate relationship of trust between the private sector and government, and the respectability of civil servants, guidance provides a way for government to influence the private sector without direct expenditure. However, the passage of the Administrative Procedure Law on November 12, 1993 sets limits on the use of this procedure.[66]

Strict management of the ceilings on the civil service has prompted

[65] Yutaka Kosai, 'The Role of Bureaucracy in the Japanese Economic Development,' a keynote speech at the International Colloquium on the Civil Service System and Economic Development: The Japanese Experience, Tokyo, Japan, March 23–5, 1994.

[66] The Administrative Procedure Law, which took almost three decades in making since the first Administrative Reform Commission report, attempts, among others, to enhance transparency and justice in administrative measures taken by the government agencies.

government agencies to resort to creating *tokushu hōjin* (special legal person), which is a *de facto* and *de jure* public corporation affiliated with the agencies concerned, but which is also under strict controls. The *tokushu hōjin* is analogous to Canada's departmental or agency crown corporation, whose mandates include public and some business domains. The Japan Development Bank is one of 92 such corporations (as of February 1992) that carry out various public functions for either central or local agencies. These entities often provide former civil servants an opportunity to assume a managerial position, a phenomenon known as *amakudari* (described by Inoki). In 1992, the percentage of *amakudari* among the legal entities associated with MITI stood at 78.9 per cent, while 17.1 per cent were those promoted from within. In the Ministries of Labor and Transportation, the ratios of *amakudari* were 90 per cent and 96.2 per cent, respectively. Science and Technology had the lowest share (50 per cent), largely because of the technical requirements of the position.

How Government Agencies and Public Corporations Are Monitored, Inspected, and Audited

As in many other countries, two nodal agencies are largely responsible in Japan for monitoring, inspection, and auditing of government agencies and public corporations. The Board of Audit, established under the authority of the constitution, is external to the cabinet and is responsible for statutory and independent auditing, as is the case with *Cour des Comptes* in France.

The Board is subject to auditing by its own finance bureau's auditing division, which also audits the House of Representatives and the House of Councillors. The accounting division personnel are afraid of this auditing, which is usually quite strict, since they are reviewing their own organization and want to demonstrate impartiality. The Diet is the final monitoring organ. The MCA and other internal auditing systems are audited by the Board of Audit.

Another key agency is the Management and Coordination Agency within the Office of the Prime Minister which (with a status equivalent to that of a ministry) is responsible for making improvements in administration systems and operations across the government. In other words, the MCA is a kind of outside party monitoring the operations of ministries and agencies, although it is in fact a ministerial agency within the Executive Branch. A couple of areas where MCA is involved deserve special attention as they are of relevance to many other systems. One is the way MCA goes about with administrative inspection and the other is providing administrative counselling.

Administrative inspection provides a venue for 'self-criticism' for the government as a whole, in that information concerning the actual performance and results of administrative systems and policies is fed back to be used for better planning. The scope of administrative inspection is very broad. There are virtually no limits on the matters that can be taken up or on the criteria to be employed in carrying out inspections. Common criteria include efficiency, effectiveness, fairness, and transparency. Since resources are limited, inspections are carried out both at central and local levels on three-year plans. The reports and recommendations of investigations are made available to the public after being issued to the relevant ministry or agency, and the more important ones are reported to the Cabinet as well.

There has been a gradual shift in the focus of operations of the MCA and its predecessors. Soon after the war, the discipline of officials was a major problem. Government officials, like the rest of the population, had to live under conditions of very low wages, hyperinflation, and the like, making it very difficult to create high morale and to maintain the integrity of public administration. With the return of stability, the focus moved to the improvement of public administration in general.

In the 1970s and 1980s the focus again shifted, this time to providing assistance in administrative reform. Previously investigations were mostly ex post and involvement in implementation of particular programs was very rare. However, by the late 1980s and into the 1990s, the MCA's reputation has allowed it to be used as the arm of the Prime Minister for monitoring programs under his initiative.

Japan also has a process for redress of citizen's grievances against public administration similar to the Swedish ombudsmen or French *médiateur*, and the parliamentary commissioner systems in other countries. Operated by the Administrative Inspection Bureau (AIB), within the MCA, it receives grievances and uses its good offices to settle the matter with the ministries and agencies concerned. The over 5,000 'administrative counselors' are locally respected private citizens such as doctors, teachers, and businesspeople, as well as housewives and former civil servants, who volunteer their services without pay. They assist in receiving and communicating the public's grievances to the AIB, the agency involved, or other concerned parties. The status and function of administrative counselors are stipulated in the Administrative Law.

Administrative counselling is an offshoot of administrative inspection. It was initiated in 1955 because the large number of grievances received during inspections were deemed to warrant separate treatment. A link has remained between inspection and counselling. Indeed, it can be said that they are inseparable components of monitoring and evaluating the activities of government ministries, agencies, and in some cases, local governments. They provide an important source of feedback to the central government, the Cabinet, and the Prime Minister as to what is happening at the point where services are actually provided to the people. Sometimes grievances are the visible tip of a huge problem hidden within the bureaucracy. Thus, several administrative inspections often stem from a single grievance. The connection between administrative inspection and counselling provides an incentive to officials to respond to complaints seriously and swiftly.

Administrative counselling is a service provided free to all the people of Japan. When someone has a complaint, they can either go to the administrative inspection offices (eight in total, some open even during the weekend), or they can visit their local administrative counselors. If the complaint is made to a counselor, it is reported to the regional AIB. Bureau personnel then contact the agency involved and ask for an explanation. Although there is no legal power for it to implement or even recommend a solution, the majority of the complaints filed with the AIB have been resolved in favor of complainants, with less than 15 per cent found to be the complainants' own faults, according to the MCA Annual Report of 1993.

There is also a system of litigation against public administration, but there is no separate administrative court. People can file suits in the ordinary courts, but it is very time-consuming and costly, a problem common in other countries as well. Administrative counselling in effect complements the formal system of redress against public administration. It is simple and inexpensive, yet perhaps more effective.

Congruence of the Ruling Party and the Civil Service

As discussed by Pempel and Muramatsu, there is 'a generally high level of congruence between "political" and "bureaucratic" goals in Japan', and this helps to promote stability in economic policymaking. This congruence is due to several factors. First, the civil service, at least from the 1930s up to the Allied Occupation, was well established and had gained enormous experience and competence in managing the development process, whereas the LDP lacked such experience and was forced to rely on the civil service to formulate and implement its development objectives and strategy. Second, about 25 per cent of LDP membership was constituted by former bureaucrats. Third, the Allied Occupation strengthened the power of the civil service by making it the instrument for carrying out political and economic reform. Fourth, single-party rule since 1955 has cemented the bond between the LDP and the civil service. Fifth, hardly any minister has been in office for more than a year; hence, it was up to the civil service, perhaps *amakudari, to* provide continuity and coherence to development policies. And sixth, perhaps the *amakudari* system helped the civil service to broaden its area of influence, a phenomenon which can be observed in France and Korea, among others.

Lessons From the Japanese Experience

Alexander Gerschenkron powerfully demonstrates that the 'relative backwardness' of a country will determine the role to be played by government in its industrialization effort, and the nature of the institutional instruments employed to promote catch-up.[67] Given rapid technological change, the catch-up effort in the context of late development, as is evident from the Japanese experience, is made viable in an important sense through the agency of the state. The Japanese government quickly moved away from serving as a direct producer to function as a socializer of the risks associated with industrialization, and as a critical coordinator of private sector activity. However, the Japanese state, or for that matter other states in East Asia, do not therefore conform to a rigid developmental state model. State–private sector relations have obviously changed over time with the quickening tempo of industrialization to accommodate progressively higher levels of consensus-building. However, it is also clear that throughout their industrialization efforts, governments in Japan and in other East Asian countries have actively promoted the 'crowding in' of private sector participation in national development efforts, and towards this end have developed flexible and innovative channels of communication and collaboration with key private sector participants.

A hallmark of late capitalist development in Japan is then the collaborative nature of state-private sector relations. While the government in Japan has adopted broad mandates to promote structural change, it has been able to initiate change more often than not through sustained collaboration with private sector participants.

Provided they are committed to economic development, developing countries should be able to reshape many of the institutional mechanisms and instruments used in Japan to suit their own contexts and needs. Despite Japan's unique culture and history, and the homogeneity of its population, there is no reason why some of its policies cannot be adopted by other countries, notably its emphasis on technological transformation, the diffusion of up-to-date information, and export promotion through various institutional and policy instruments. Institutional arrangements for reducing transaction costs and risk, or addressing coordination failures include: a *main bank system* for allocating credit as well as for monitoring the performance of bank clients; a strong Ministry of Finance and Ministry of International Trade and Industry; and effective civil service recruitment, promotion, and performance incentives. In fact, some of these arrangements have already been creatively adapted by several

---

[67] Alexander Gerschenkron, *Economic Backwardness in Historical Perspective* (1962).

economies of East Asia, such as Korea, Taiwan, Singapore, Thailand, Malaysia, and Indonesia.[68]

While it is clear that successful institutional arrangements evolve over time and come about importantly owing to factors beyond individual and collective agencies, an innovative reconsideration of the modes of public policymaking in the light of Japanese success may serve as a critical first step towards reform. In doing so, it is important to bear in mind that public policymaking in Japan has not been without its flaws. The system or culture that emphasizes participatory decisionmaking processes, group interaction, loyalty, and harmony can itself severely impede the flourishing of individual initiatives and creativity, interagency or interoffice coordination, and grass-roots participation in policy debates.[69] However, the Japanese experience has been marked by a willingness to learn from mistakes, and most importantly, by a capacity for adapting the institutions governing individual and collective action to emerging situations.

Perhaps the most important lesson of the Japanese experience is that development cannot proceed without a strong commitment to this goal in every corner of the government and its civil service. Such a commitment can only be effective on certain conditions like the following: if attempts are made to ensure the diffusion of modern technological knowledge; if government incentives are guided by reliable information on economic performance, as judged by export competitiveness, for example; if there are coordination mechanisms, often through the formulation of indicative medium- to long-term economic plans, to establish a cooperative framework for making policy decisions and for promoting competitive behavior; if the state has an autonomous financial intermediation system; and if civil servants are recruited through competitive examination and have a strong incentive to maintain an effective and efficient bureaucracy.

Concluding Remarks

This volume provides an integrated view of the role, structure, and functions of the civil service in Japan, and its contribution to that nation's economic development. It also sheds new light on historical processes of development and the relative role and functions of the state, and thus contributes substantially to the literature on development management.[70]

[68] Even China is in the process of trying to emulate MITI in its recent restructuring of the central government agencies. The Economic Planning Agency model is also being considered for possible use in China.

[69] See Jong S. Jun and Hiromi Muto, 'The Hidden Dimensions of Japanese Administration,' to be published in *Public Administration Review*, 1994.

[70] On the strategic determinants in the historical development process, I benefited from V. V. Bhatt, 'Economic Development: An Analytic-Historical Approach,' *World Development*, Vol. 4, No. 7 (1976).

The central point that has emerged from the discussion is that Japan has managed to keep its public sector fairly small—indeed, it is much smaller than its counterparts in the industrialized countries—with little or no direct public ownership of the means of production. Yet the Japanese government has remained a pervasive market player. It has succeeded in this endeavor by emphasizing fiscal balance and macroeconomic stability and by avoiding misdirecting resources away from productive investment by the private sector to 'unproductive government consumption.' To this end, it has devised various institutional mechanisms and policies that provide nonneutral incentives and penalties (nonneutral among industrial sectors and firms alike).

According to neoclassical theory or the emerging consensus on development theory, such discriminatory intervention is dysfunctional. On the contrary, the Japanese experience has shown that intervention can be not only functional but also very effective in achieving economic growth, which in Japan has been unsurpassed by any other country over the long period between 1950 and 1973, or even between 1950 and 1990. However, the government could not have formulated and implemented such interventions without a competent, motivated, and effective bureaucracy—a vital organ of society, particularly in a democratic state.[71] In particular, a high degree of competence in helping ruling party ministers formulate their strategies and policies and an inspiring *esprit de corps* have helped the bureaucracy maintain its integrity and independence, as this book amply demonstrates. Just how the Japanese civil service addresses some of the issues that stem from this success—such as sectionalism at the level of agencies, the relationship of the civil service to the legislatures and to the public at large, and the civil service's omnipresence (in spite of its relatively small 'size')—remains a challenging puzzle to unravel.

[71] See Joseph Schumpeter, *Capitalism, Socialism and Democracy* (New York: Harper and Row, 1975), pp. 289–96.

INDEX